LITERATURE OF THE AMERICAN WEST

A Cultural Approach

Greg Lyons

Central Oregon Community College

Longman

New York   San Francisco   Boston
London   Toronto   Sydney   Tokyo   Singapore   Madrid
Mexico City   Munich   Paris   Cape Town   Hong Kong   Montreal

Vice President and Editor-in-Chief: Joseph Terry
Acquisitions Editor: Erika Berg
Associate Editor: Barbara Santoro
Marketing Manager: Melanie Craig
Senior Supplements Editor: Donna Campion
Project Manager/Electronic Page Makeup: Dianne Hall
Production Coordinator: Shafiena Ghani
Cover Design Manager: John Callahan
Cover Designer: Joe DePinho
Cover Image: The Oregon Trail (oil on canvas) by Albert Bierstadt (1830–1902).
  Private Collection/Bridgeman Art Library
Senior Manufacturing Buyer: Dennis Para
Printer and Binder: Courier Corporation, Westford
Cover Printer: Phoenix Color Corp.

For permission to use copyrighted material, grateful acknowledgment is made to the
copyright holders on pp. 480–481, which are hereby made part of this copyright page.

Library of Congress Cataloging-in-Publication Data

Literature of the American West: a cultural approach / [compiled by] Greg Lyons.
    p. cm.
  Includes index.
  ISBN 0-205-32461-4
    1. American literature—West (U.S.) 2. American literature—West (U.S.)—History
and criticism. 3. Western stories—History and criticism. 4. West (U.S.)—Literary
collections. 5. West (U.S.)—In literature. 6. West (U.S.)—Biography. 7. Western
stories. I. Lyons, Greg, 1950–

PS561.L59 2002
810.8'03278—dc21   2002028672

Please visit our Website at http://www.ablongman.com

ISBN 0-205-32461-4

CONTENTS

CHAPTER 8   The New West   419

APPENDIX: How to Watch a Film   471

PREFACE

⊷

In North American history, "the West" begins with its indigenous peoples—a foundation which this text attempts to incorporate. In European history, the West begins with the colonial exploitation of the Spanish, who shaped their initial settlements in often fierce cultural conflicts with Native Americans. From the viewpoint of seventeenth-century British-American colonies, the first "western" lands lay just across the Allegheny Mountains. However, in the development of a national mythology of self-invention through individual opportunity, the West is more often understood as the region between the Mississippi River and the Pacific Ocean, especially during the nineteenth century. Thus, most of the writings included here are set within this space and time.

Nonetheless, the West and the notion of "frontier" continue to reverberate in American culture. Historians argue reasonably that the West extends geographically to Alaska, Hawaii, the Philippines, even to the moon; and chronologically not only into the twentieth century, but to post–World War II America, the present century, and into the future. This text attempts to acknowledge the continuing relevance of American belief in this region, even though it may not be a geopolitical reality. In any case, a number of writers continue to produce a "literature" of the West—in both historical and contemporary settings—that succeeds in quality and popularity.

Besides considering the New West, alongside the Old, this text assumes an inclusive definition of "literature" so that selections range from traditional "literary" prose to personal narrative, history, pulp fiction, and essays. In addition, suggested learning materials include not only instructional videos and Hollywood films, but also print advertising and honky-tonk music.

FEATURES OF THIS TEXT

Literature of the American West offers a unique approach to the study of both a place and a time. Historical backgrounds for the selections provide students opportunities for thoughtful reflection and synthesis. Throughout, the anthology advocates a student-centered reading strategy in order to contest the meanings of the American West and to expand the possibilities for interpretation and sympathy. Thus, readers are invited to question the differences between older texts and contemporary cultural expectations by exploring multiple perspectives, rather than seeking a simplistic continuity. Likewise, the integration of Western films and other visual materials into the anthology allows students to view these cultural artifacts within a web of meanings about the West. A comprehensive "cultural studies" approach is emphasized through the following text features:

- Selections from both "literary" and "popular" authors in fiction, autobiography, history, critical essay, and poetry
- Representative sampling of ethnic perspectives and historical periods
- "Fine art" and popular images showing American cultural trends and providing opportunities to develop students' visual literacy
- Eight thematic chapter introductions providing students historical contexts for the development of Western myths and stereotypes, as well as subversive viewpoints
- Bio-critical author introductions providing students cultural contexts for the development of generic conventions, experimentation, and satire
- Discussion questions for each reading and for a film integrated to each chapter
- Topics for research and writing for each chapter, juxtaposing a variety of media, including art, advertising, film, and music
- Appendix: How to Watch a Film, introducing the analysis of movies

ORGANIZATION

The text is divided into two parts. Part One, Foundations for a Western Mythology, takes a roughly historical approach in presenting representative readings and images that have established a tradition of understandings about the American West from the limited perspective of "Manifest Destiny." Chapter 1, Mapping the Terrain, presents a historical foundation and samples of Western stereotypes. Chapter 2, Crossing Frontiers, presents stories of initial contact between Euro-Americans and Native Americans. Chapter 3, Working the Land, presents stories of the cowboy, the land speculator, and the lawman—figures who shaped naïve Euro-American meanings about the "taming" of the West. Chapter 4, Spiritual Landscapes, presents nineteenth-century models for depicting the values of untamed Nature. Part Two, Challenges to a Western Mythology, takes a recursive approach, re-examining the tradition represented in Part One in order to reveal the subversive voices and neglected perspectives of women, Native Americans, and other ethnic minorities. In effect, Part Two critiques the limitations of heroic Western narratives and, moreover, celebrates various stories of adaptation, endurance, and cross-cultural sharing. Thus, Chapter 5, Satires and Entertainments, presents early works that either mocked the Western myths that so many Americans accepted at face value or nostalgically perpetuated those myths in a mass-marketable product. Chapters 6 and 7 present viewpoints of Western women and Native Americans, respectively, to provide critical insights into the Euro-American, male-dominated tradition. Finally, Chapter 8, The New West, includes contemporary writers in order to enlarge our perspectives on the West, to complicate our understandings of that heritage, and to offer tentative guidelines for the future of this space that is criss-crossed by opposing cultures, values, and priorities of use.

This organization attempts to reproduce a historical process of examining naïve cultural understandings through more complex, yet finally contested, conditional and multiple interpretations of Western narratives.

For ancillary materials supporting this text, please visit the Website at *www.cocc.edu/glyons/pop/western.*

ADDITIONAL RESOURCES FOR STUDENTS AND INSTRUCTORS

For Instructors
Teaching Literature On-line, 2e (0-321-10618-0). *Teaching Literature On-line* provides instructors with practical strategies and advice for incorporating elements of computer technology into the literature classroom. Available FREE to adopters of *Literature of the American West.*

Resources for Students
Responding to Literature: A Writer's Journal (0-321-09542-1). This journal provides students with their own personal space for writing. Prompts for responding to fiction, poetry, and drama are integrated throughout. Available FREE when value-packed with *Literature of the American West.*

Researching Online 6e (0-321-11733-6). This guide shows students how to do research on the Internet in an easy-to-follow, step-by-step format. Available FREE when value-packed with *Literature of the American West.*

*For a complete list of supplements available with this text,
please contact your Longman representative.*

ACKNOWLEDGMENTS

———<◆>———

First, my gratitude goes to Central Oregon Community College (COCC) and our Faculty Professional Improvement Review Committee for granting me a sabbatical leave during winter and spring quarters of 2001, which allowed me to begin researching and writing the anthology manuscript. I wish to thank JoAnne Cordis and Janet Obert for their constant vigilance, which assured a swift flow of interlibrary-loan materials. I also appreciate the gracious assistance of the staff at the following libraries: The Harry Ransom Humanities Research Center and The Earl and Vada Vandale Collection of Western Americana, both at the University of Texas at Austin; and the Manuscript and Special Collections of the Pacific Northwest at the University of Washington. For her detailed and helpful suggestions for revising the historical chapter introductions, I appreciate the work of my colleague Nancy Zens, an American History specialist in the COCC Social Sciences Department. For her timely help with text processing, I wish to thank Elaine Bridwell. I have relied repeatedly on the good graces and Yankee efficiency of the Humanities Secretary, Kathy Williams. I would also like to thank my colleagues in American Western studies who have reviewed the text-in-process: Kerry Ahearn, Oregon State University; Susan Kollin, Montana State University; Alex Kuo, Washington State University; Alison Russell, Xavier University; Gary Scharnhorst, University of New Mexico; Phillip Snyder, Brigham Young University; Jennifer Sorensen, Western Wyoming Community College; Eleanor Sumpter-Latham, Central Oregon Community College; and Howard Waltersdorf, Indiana State University.

Most of all, I am indebted to Micaela Hayden for her patience, emotional support, and affection.

INTRODUCTION

◆

Since the 1970s the widespread embrace of multicultural and interdisciplinary perspectives has strongly affected the study of literature in the United States. Spurred by civil rights activism, the production, dissemination, and popularity of ethnic literatures has been phenomenal. The "canon" of American literature has expanded to include contemporary ethnic authors, while neglected works by racial "minority" and women authors have been recovered from past obscurity and have been newly popularized in college courses and textbook anthologies. Even the notion of a literary canon—a widely accepted list of "great works" worthy of study—has been challenged or eliminated in some college curricula. At the same time, critics, teachers, and students of American writing have adopted historical and anthropological approaches to interpretation in an attempt to account for "lived experience," the ethnographic details of everyday life. American Studies, for instance, has certainly tried to embed the humanistic study of literature within a groundwork of geography, history, economics, and social relations.

In the last two decades, "cultural studies" approaches to teaching the analysis of both literature and "media" (film, music, advertising, broadcast news, Internet communication) have become even more overtly political through practicing critical readings of the myths behind messages. For example, students are taught to expose and to challenge the sexist representation of women in cosmetics advertising or the macho image in Army National Guard commercials. Likewise, college classes are becoming more sophisticated in discussing the middle-class bias in news reports about the homeless. These kinds of insights into the American ideology of "individual success through hard work" have also been applied within a historical context, for example, in comparing the sympathetic portraits of family farmers and industrial workers in Hamlin Garland's *Well-Travelled Roads* (1891) and Rebecca Harding Davis's "Life in the Iron Mills" (1861); students can extend this analysis by examining the contemporary reception of these works in the nineteenth century.

Literature of the American West: A Cultural Approach embraces these trends in the study of American literatures by including not only a variety of women and ethnic authors from within and outside the mainstream of "Western" writing, but also a variety of genres. In addition, the "cultural studies" approach of the anthology encourages a critical perspective to the artificial distinction between "literary" and "popular" stories by juxtaposing works by Mary Austin, Willa Cather, and Owen Wister to selections from dime-novelist Edward Ellis, mountain-man chronicler Lewis Garrard, and frontier school teacher Angeline Mitchell Brown, along with a contemporary essay on cross-dressing women in the nineteenth-century West. Indeed, this text strives to recover unduly neglected "pulp" authors, like Ellis, who was just as popular in his time as Wister and Twain were in theirs, although the latter have "stood the test of time" and been studied in college for decades as "literature." Such "mass-market" dime-fiction, along with the "minority" viewpoint of Sui Sin Far's story of Chinese immigrants, should be read alongside so-called canonical works because both "high" and "low" (literary and popular) art reflect the values of American culture and evaluate similar myths of heroic individualism in a classless society. Thus, this anthology encourages you to read against the grain of the American tradition and to challenge the mythic components of historical, autobiographical, and imaginative writings about the West.

Also adopting the multimedia approach of "cultural studies," the text includes images from popular culture, such as a poster for Buffalo Bill's Wild West Show, and from museum art, such as a "classic" Western canvas of Albert Bierstadt, as well as the "revisionist" contemporary Chippewa/Lakota painting of David Bradley. This mix encourages you to extend the analysis of Western icons to another manifestation of American traditions. Complementing the multimedia emphasis, at the end of each chapter a related film is suggested, with questions for analysis. It is helpful to consider these "Focus on Film" questions, which encourage comparisons of Western characters and themes, just before viewing the film. In several chapters, the multimedia approach is further expressed in writing topics that analyze themes in country music and Western imagery in art. Likewise, the Appendix features a brief guide to viewing and analyzing films, especially for students who have never studied the technical aspects of movies.

Throughout the eight thematic chapters, the readings and related images of the West are designed to stimulate fruitful comparative analyses of perspectives, historical periods, genres, and media of expression. Welcome to the rendezvous, the round-up, and the rodeo!

PART
ONE

·——◄◆►——·

FOUNDATIONS FOR A
WESTERN MYTHOLOGY

Detail from Fig. 3.3, Frederic Remington, *A Dash for the Timber* (1889), oil on canvas. Amon Carter Museum, Ft. Worth, TX; 1961.381.

CHAPTER

1

◄◆►

MAPPING THE TERRAIN

INTRODUCTION

One story of the West is the colonization of lands supporting multitudes of Indian nations. The exploration of the North American continent was but the beginning of an imperial conquest that devastated the native population. Beginning with Columbus, such infections as smallpox, measles, and typhus decimated as much as 90 percent of some native groups (Milner, "Heritage" 9), while frontier battles, Spanish practices of slavery, and U.S. policies of relocation accounted for thousands of Native American deaths.

Another story of the West is its initiation as an "international borderland," characterized by violent conflicts among native tribes, among Europeans, and between Europeans and Native Americans, although there were also instances of cooperation. The explorations of the French and the Russians were initially directed toward trading and hunting. Gradually, French commercial communities developed along the Great Lakes, along Midwestern rivers, and down the Mississippi all the way to New Orleans. Likewise, the Russians built ports in present-day British Columbia and Alaska. The explorations of the Spanish were initially concerned with gold and silver, as royally licensed entrepreneurs sought plunder, taking their model from Cortez in Mexico. While Coronado never found the Seven Cities of Gold, Franciscan missionaries remained, and by the 1600s a colonial society of farmers and artisans evolved in scattered settlements in the Southwest desert. Between about 1700 and 1800, a significant Spanish ranching industry in sheep, cattle, and horses contributed to a colonial population of nearly 20,000 in New Mexico alone (White 36). And the adoption of a horse culture dramatically altered the Plains Indians across the Southwest, stimulating rivalries and warfare among different tribes and against encroaching Europeans. Beginning in the seventeenth century, the British were initially concerned with colonization of the Eastern seaboard, but as cities grew and farmers sought new land, explorers like Daniel Boone crossed the Appalachians to break new trails into the wilderness.

Westering Europeans and official U.S. policies supplanted native populations while breaking over four hundred treaties with them and exploiting the natural resources of their lands in a fierce, often lawless, and ruinous desecration. After the Revolutionary War, when national boundaries were extended to the Mississippi River, the new Congress passed an ordinance to adopt a standard survey grid for the United States in 1785. This act was significant in technologizing nature—that is, in delineating territory in terms of lines, numbers, and legal codes rather than natural landmarks—as well as advancing the European values of individualism and personal property, in contrast to native values of community and ecological interdependence. In 1787, the Northwest Ordinance established the procedure by which U.S. "territories" could be spatially delineated and ultimately organized for legal association with the federation of states. Of course, this act presumed that U.S. sovereignty superceded that of the multiple Indian communities and nations that recognized no ownership over their environment.

The Lewis and Clark expedition of 1804–1806, a military mission under direct instructions from the President, served to extend U.S. territorial claims from the Mississippi to the Pacific, thus reinforcing the presumption behind the doctrine of Manifest Destiny. This doctrine was secured by treaty after the Mexican-American war of 1846–1848, in which the nation gained Texas, California, and much of Arizona, New Mexico, Nevada, Utah, and Colorado. Many other surveys of the early nineteenth century were sponsored by the military, which represented a national power "with the expectation of commercial, diplomatic, or political benefits" (Milner, "National" 159). In 1806–1807, Lieutenant Zebulon Pike actually invaded Mexican territory to explore the Southwest, opening the upper Arkansas River to fur trappers. Major Stephen H. Long also trespassed while mapping the Great Plains in 1819–1820. Of course, some trappers explored on their own; for example, in the 1820s Jedediah Smith crossed the Great Basin, the Sierra Nevada, and the Wyoming Rockies, establishing a major pass there for the Oregon Trail. And some mountain men worked together with the military. For instance, Kit Carson scouted for John Charles Fremont (1813–1890), who led scientific explorations for the U.S. Army Corps of Topographical Engineers through the Rockies, the Great Basin, Oregon, and California in 1843–1844. The Topographical Engineers also contributed to incursion into Indian lands, expansion by settlers, and exploitation by miners in very practical ways through their 1853–1855 transcontinental railroad surveys.

In the selections from Lewis and Clark's *Journals*, this chapter directly considers the exploration and geography of the American West. However, the other selections consider "mapping the terrain" in a metaphorical sense, providing historical background for the concerns and themes of Western literature and culture. De Crèvecoeur and Turner describe the influence of the frontier on the American character and thus present a heroic role model for Western literature that has been appropriated, but also resisted, since the eighteenth and nineteenth centuries. Harte presents some Western characters that have become stereotypes of the genre, as well as foils to more realistic representations. Even John Ford's film, *Stagecoach*, affirms the value of these stereotypes in defining Western myths about the outlaw, natural justice, and the virtues of antisocial individualism. This film, and the earlier works, also portray a negligence toward Native Americans as humans, treating them as foes for Western heroes to conquer or as representatives of uncivilized savagery. More often, the traditional West seems an unpeopled space that beckoned immigrant settlers forward. All the works of this chapter suggest an initial charting of the ambiguous region of American Western literature, its lines and contours, its dimensions and features. The map itself is here to be questioned, challenged, altered, but not completed.

Milner, Clyde A., II. "Heritage: Introduction and Chronology." *The Oxford History of the American West*. Eds. Clyde A. Milner II, Carol A. O'Connor, and Martha A. Sandweiss. New York: Oxford University, 1994. 9–11.

Milner, Clyde A., II. "National Initiatives." *The Oxford History of the American West*. Eds. Clyde A. Milner II, Carol A. O'Connor, and Martha A. Sandweiss. New York: Oxford University, 1994. 155–93.

White, Richard. *"It's Your Misfortune and None of My Own": A History of the American West*. Norman, OK: University of Oklahoma, 1991.

Fig. 1.1 Emmanuel Leutze, *Westward the Course of Empire Takes Its Way* (1861), mural study, U.S. Capitol. Smithsonian American Art Museum; Bequest of Sarah Carr Upton; 1931.6.1.

HECTOR ST. JOHN DE CRÈVECOEUR
(1735–1813)

Christened Michel Guillaume Jean de Crèvecoeur in Caen, France, the author was born to an ancient Norman family. At a Jesuit boarding school, he received a comprehensive education in Latin, rhetoric, theology, mathematics, and cartography. In 1754 he lived in Salisbury, England, where he began a love for British culture that developed throughout his life. Serving in the French colonial army in Canada, during the French and Indian Wars, he resigned in 1759 after being honorably wounded at the battle of Quebec, which ended French claims to Canadian lands. Emigrating to New York, he changed his name to James Hector St. John to disguise his French origins and began working as a surveyor and traveling salesman. In 1767, he joined an exploring party, mapping their route over the Appalachians, down the Ohio River, and up the Mississippi to the Great Lakes. Two years later, he married, bought 120 acres in Orange County, New York, and began a flourishing homestead he called Pine Hill (Stone ix–xi).

His idyllic agrarian existence, which he began to write about during the long winters, continued for seven years until the outbreak of the Revolutionary War, which brought conflict with patriot neighbors who objected to his Anglophile sentiments. His position became increasingly tense, so he sought to return to France—in part to ensure his children's inheritance of family property there. But what he expected to be a short business trip became, due to the war, an absence of five years. Departing his farm and family in 1778, he took his elder son Alexandre and obtained safe passage through the patriot lines only to be captured by the British in New York City as a suspected spy. Imprisoned for three months, he suffered permanent damage to his health, and his book manuscript was impounded. Although friends in the city obtained his release, in 1779 he had a nervous breakdown due to anxiety over Alexandre, who was critically ill with a fever, and over the safety of his family at Pine Hill, who were subject to potential harm from Tory supporters and the Indians they sponsored. The next year, he finally left for London, where he sold his manuscript of *Letters from an American Farmer*, published in 1782 (Stone xi–xiv).

Returning finally to France, de Crèvecoeur became something of a celebrity as the rising reputation of his book permitted entry into the fashionable intellectual salons of Paris. At the same time, for the French government he wrote an extensive report on American society, for which he was rewarded with the position of consul to New York in 1783. However, leaving Alexandre with relatives in Normandy and returning to Pine Hill, he found his home had been burned to the ground by Indians, his wife was dead, and his younger children had been removed to Boston. Oddly enough, a prominent citizen there, Gustave Fellowes, was merely repaying the aid de Crèvecoeur had given one of his relatives, an American seaman who had escaped from a British prison to Normandy. Due to his work in New York and the extremely severe winter of 1784, it was several months before de Crèvecoeur could be reunited with his children. That summer, after two months together, he left Fanny with the Fellowes family and sent Louis to join Alexandre in France. Then de Crèvecoeur settled conscientiously to his role as consul, achieving some success in promoting Franco-American commerce: establishing a boat line between Brittany and New York; encouraging French imports (wine, silk, pianos); and exchanging agricultural knowledge and practices. When his health deteriorated in 1790, he returned to France (Stone xii–xiv).

Though excerpts of *Letters from an American Farmer* appeared widely in American periodicals, the full volume was not published in the United States until 1793; only moderately popular here, it was not even reprinted until 1904. But the book proved a continued success in Europe for fifty years after its initial publication. Through multiple editions and translations, "it provided two generations of European intellectuals with their chief impressions of America" (Stone viii), about which they were intensely curious.

The book is clearly a work of fiction, rather than autobiography. Indeed, the work is a deliberately structured narrative balanced by both dramatic and reflective episodes. The first three of the twelve letters praise both the American landowner's freedom from tyranny and injustice, and the resulting development of personal virtues (self-respect, civic responsibility, and social mobility through hard work). The middle five letters praise the human happiness possible through Quaker ideology as practiced in the seafaring communities of Nantucket and Martha's Vineyard. Finally, the last four letters admit the inherent evil in human nature, as evidenced by American slavery and the violent atrocities of the Revolutionary War (McElroy 104–5).

Thus, a strong appeal of de Crèvecoeur's work—similar to Ben Franklin's *Autobiography* (1791) in this way—was the theme of moral education, a major concern of eighteenth-century Enlightenment culture. European readers could also recognize in *Letters* traces of the romanticism of Jean-Jacques Rousseau (1712–1778), who idealized the beneficence of nature and the noble savage. However, as literature, the distinctive American character of de Crèvecoeur's work is emphasized by the naïve, self-mocking persona of the narrator, who seems somewhat satirical toward the more sophisticated European reader, the imaginary London addressee of these letters. And the author is balanced in his treatment of the effects of living on the frontier, exposed to both savage and civilizing influences (Stone xviii). As a man of both cosmopolitan and exotic experience, European heritage and American practicalities, de Crèvecoeur was engaged in exploring the character of the "new man" shaped by these opposing influences and by the intense physical challenges of a wild environment.

The excerpts from his chapter "What Is an American?" are from the reprint edition of *Letters from an American Farmer* (New York: Fox and Duffield, 1904), pages 56–60 and 66–68.

McElroy, John H. "Michel Guillaume Jean de Crèvecoeur." *Dictionary of Literary Biography, Volume 37: American Writers of the Early Republic.* Ed. Emory Elliott. Detroit: Gale, 1985. 103–7.

Stone, Albert E., Jr. "Foreword." *Letters from an American Farmer [1782] and Sketches of Eighteenth Century America [1925].* By Hector St. John de Crèvecoeur. New York: Signet, 1963. vii–xxvi.

FROM *LETTERS FROM AN AMERICAN FARMER*

FROM "WHAT IS AN AMERICAN?"

Men are like plants; the goodness and flavour of the fruit proceeds from the peculiar soil and exposition in which they grow. We are nothing but what we derive from the air we breathe, the climate we inhabit, the government we obey, the system of religion we profess, and the nature of our employment. Here you will find but few crimes; these have acquired as yet no root among us. I wish I were able to trace all my ideas; if my ignorance prevents me from describing them properly, I hope I shall be able to delineate a few of the outlines, which are all I propose.

Those who live near the sea, feed more on fish than on flesh, and often encounter that boisterous element. This renders them more bold and enterprising; this leads them to neglect the confined occupations of the land. They see and converse with a variety of people; their intercourse with mankind becomes extensive. The sea inspires them with a love of traffic, a desire of transporting produce from one place to another; and leads them to a variety of resources which supply the place of labour. Those who inhabit the middle settlements, by far the most numerous, must be very different; the simple cultivation of the earth purifies them, but the indulgences of the government, the soft remonstrances of religion, the rank of independent freeholders, must necessarily inspire them with sentiments, very little known in Europe among people of the same class. What do I say? Europe has no such class of men; the early knowledge they acquire, the early bargains they make, give them a great degree of sagacity. As freemen they will be litigious; pride and obstinacy are often the cause of law suits; the nature of our laws and governments may be another. As citizens it is easy to imagine, that they will carefully read the newspapers, enter into every political disquisition, freely blame or censure governors and others. As farmers they will be carful and anxious to get as much as they can, because what they get is their own. As northern men they will love the chearful cup. As Christians, religion curbs them not in their opinions; the general indulgence leaves every one to think for themselves in spiritual matters; the laws inspect our actions, our thoughts are left to God. Industry, good living, selfishness, litigiousness, country politics, the pride of free-men, religious indifference, are their characteristics. If you recede still farther from the sea, you will come into more modern settlements; they exhibit the same strong lineaments, in a ruder appearance. Religion seems to have still less influence, and their manners are less improved.

Now we arrive near the great woods, near the last inhabited districts; there men seem to be placed still farther beyond the reach of government, which in some measure leaves them to themselves. How can it pervade every corner; as they were driven there by misfortunes, necessity of beginnings, desire of acquiring large tracks of land, idleness, frequent want of œconomy, ancient debts; the re-union of such people does not afford a very pleasing spectacle. When discord, want of unity and friendship; when either drunkenness or idleness prevail in such remote districts; contention, inactivity, and wretchedness must ensue. There are not the same remedies to these evils as in a long established community. The few magistrates they have, are in general little better than the rest; they are often in a perfect state of war; that of man against man, sometimes decided by blows, sometimes by means of the law; that of man against every wild inhabitant of these venerable woods, of which they are come to dispossess them. There men appear to be no beter than carnivorous animals of a superior rank, living on the flesh of wild animals when they can catch them, and when they are not able, they subsist on grain. He who would wish to see America in its proper light, and have a true idea of its feeble beginnings and barbarous rudiments, must visit our extended line of frontiers where the last settlers dwell, and where he may see the first labours of settlement, the mode of clearing the earth, in all their different appearances; where men are wholly left dependent on their native tempers, and on the spur of uncertain industry, which often fails when not sanctified by the efficacy of a few moral rules. There, remote from the power of example, and check of shame, many families exhibit the most hideous parts of our society. They are a kind of forlorn hope, preceding by ten or twelve years the most respectable army of veterans which come after them. In that space, prosperity will polish some, vice and the law will drive off the rest, who uniting again with others like themselves will recede still farther; making room for more industrious people, who will finish their improvements, convert the loghouse into a convenient habitation, and rejoicing that the first heavy labours are finished, will change in a few years that hitherto barbarous country into a fine fertile, well regulated district. Such is our progress, such is the march of the Europeans toward the interior parts of this continent. In all societies there are off-casts; this impure part serves as our precursors or pioneers; my father himself was one of that class, but he came upon honest principles, and was therefore one of the few who held fast; by good conduct and temperance, he transmitted to me his fair inheritance, when not above one in fourteen of his contemporaries had the same good fortune.

* * *

But to return to our back settlers. I must tell you, that there is something in the proximity of the woods, which is very singular. It is with men as it is with the plants and animals that grow and live in the forests; they are entirely different from those that live in the plains. I will candidly tell you all my thoughts but you are not to expect that I shall advance any reasons. By living in or near the woods, their actions are regulated by the wildness of the neighbourhood. The deer often come to eat their grain, the wolves to destroy their sheep, the bears to kill their hogs, the foxes to catch their poultry. This surrounding hostility, immediately puts the gun into their hands; they watch these animals, they kill some; and thus by defending their property, they soon become professed hunters; this is the progress; once hunters, farewell to the plough. The chase renders them ferocious, gloomy, and unsociable; a hunter wants no neighbour, he rather hates them, because he dreads the competition. In a little time their success in the woods makes them neglect their tillage. They trust to the natural fecundity of the earth, and therefore do little; carelessness in fencing, often exposes what little they sow to destruction; they are not at home to watch; in order therefore to make up the deficiency, they go oftener to the woods. That new mode of life brings along with it a new set of manners, which I cannot easily describe. These new manners being grafted on the old stock, produce a strange sort of lawless profligacy, the impressions of which are indelible. The manners of the Indian natives are respectable, compared with this European medley. Their wives and children live in sloth and inactivity; and having no proper pursuits, you may judge what education the latter receive. Their tender minds have nothing else to contemplate but the example of their parents; like them they grow up a mongrel breed, half civilized, half savage, except nature stamps on them some constitutional propensities. That rich, that voluptuous sentiment is gone that struck them so forcibly; the possession of their freeholds no longer conveys to their minds the same pleasure and pride. To all these reasons you must add, their lonely situation, and you cannot imagine what an effect on manners the great distances they live from each other has. . . !

Discussion Questions

1. Describe how de Crèvecoeur characterizes the pioneer at the very edge of the frontier. Contrast this description to his brief portrait of the second wave of settlers.
2. Compare de Crèvecoeur's description of the American pioneer to the portrait of Ringo in *Stagecoach*.

FREDERICK JACKSON TURNER
(1861–1932)

Born in Portage, Wisconsin, Turner spent his boyhood observing the vestiges of a frontier environment—"virgin forests, Indian villages, lawless raftsmen, fur trade" (Becker 302). However, the growing town was no longer in the backwoods. His father ran the local weekly paper and served four terms as mayor. As a youth, Turner learned firsthand a great deal about local politics, studied enthusiastically at school, and excelled in public speaking (Wrobel 366).

In 1878, he enrolled at the University of Wisconsin and turned to history when he discovered an encouraging mentor in William Francis Allen. Graduating in 1884 with prizes for oratory, he worked briefly as a reporter, but he returned the following year to teach history and rhetoric, and to pursue his Master's degree. Completing his thesis on "The Influence of the Fur Trade in the Development of Wisconsin" in 1888, he then pursued a Ph.D. at Johns Hopkins University, then the top graduate school in the country. In 1889, he married and began a fulfilling lifelong relationship. In the same year, when Professor Allen died, the University of Wisconsin offered Turner the open position, so he returned and completed his doctorate while teaching (Wrobel 366–67).

In 1891, he published his first groundbreaking essay, "The Significance of History," which laid out general principles for his discipline that other historians had neglected. He acknowledged the principle of historical relativism: "Each age writes the history of the past anew with reference to the conditions uppermost in its own time" (qtd. in Wrobel 367). He also expressed the need for historians to study the working and middle classes, not merely the upper class. Finally, he recommended examining both negative and positive changes, so history would not merely praise the strengths of U.S. society, but point out its weaknesses. In an 1892 essay, "Problems in American History," Turner advanced the popular Darwinian notion of society as a "developing organism." Moreover, he criticized the insular bias of East Coast historians, whose perspective was limited to the original colonies and their ties to Europe. Instead, he recommended looking to Westward expansion, to the "migration and interaction of various races and cultures" for an understanding of U.S. history (Wrobel 368).

In 1893, when he delivered a speech on "The Significance of the Frontier in American History" at the meeting of the American Historical Association in Chicago, the impact was negligible. However, his theory was to dominate his field for fifty years. There were at least three reasons for its acceptance. First, Turner was a constant self-promoter; after the speech was printed in a longer essay form in 1894, he bought and distributed hundreds of copies to fellow historians and other intellectuals across the country. He also lectured regularly and successfully to college alumni, teachers, and civic groups; and then published these talks in such leading national periodicals as *Atlantic Monthly*. Second, Turner's ideas were integrated into widely held beliefs about the century's end; they helped to explain contemporary events, such as the stock-market crash of 1893, the depression and high unemployment in the 1890s, and the Populist revolt that supported William Jennings Bryan (1860–1925) as presidential candidate in 1896. Turner's theory implied that, if the "frontier" had functioned as a "safety valve" on the pressures of urban population growth and the frustrations of industrial labor, then the "closing" of that same frontier would presumably eliminate opportunities for the restless masses to seek their fortunes—or at least the land for a family farm— out West (Faragher 3–4). A third reason for the success of Turner's frontier thesis was his personal accomplishment in training a new generation of historians, in stimulating them with his independence and freshness of thought. To his students, Turner was an admirable role model for what a historian should do: ask questions dispassionately, question the authority of previous interpretations, and examine primary sources minutely (Becker 277–95).

Though later work helpfully suggested that education might compensate for the lost opportunities of the West (Faragher 8), Turner's frontier thesis has been largely discredited today. In fact, beginning during the Depression, other historians began to criticize various aspects of the theory, especially its relevance to an "urban industrial society in the midst of economic catastrophe and in desperate need of cooperation in order to survive" (Wrobel 376). In the 1960s, scholars especially attacked its ethnocentric bias, which made heroes of Euro-American men and represented Native Americans as obstacles to the inevitable advance of a supposedly superior white culture. In the 1980s, such critics as Patricia Nelson Limerick have argued that Turner's thesis hides "the darker realities of the settlement of the West—the exploitation of labor, women, peoples of color, and the environment" (Wrobel 377).

The text is from *Annual Report of the American Historical Association for 1893* (Washington, DC: GPO, 1894), pages 199–201, 213–15, and 226–27.

Becker, Carl. "Frederick Jackson Turner." *American Masters of Social Science.* Ed. Howard W. Odum. New York: Holt, 1927. 271–318.

Faragher, John M., ed. "Introduction." *Rereading Frederick Jackson Turner.* New York: Holt, 1994. 1–10.

Wrobel, David M. "Frederick Jackson Turner." *Dictionary of Literary Biography, Volume 186: Nineteenth-Century American Western Writers.* Ed. Robert L. Gale. Detroit: Gale, 1997. 365–78.

THE SIGNIFICANCE OF THE FRONTIER IN AMERICAN HISTORY

In a recent bulletin of the Superintendent of the Census for 1890 appear these significant words: "Up to and including 1880 the country had a frontier of settlement, but at present the unsettled area has been so broken into by isolated bodies of settlement that there can hardly be said to be a frontier line. In the discussion of its extent, its westward movement, etc., it can not therefore, any longer have a place in the census reports." This brief official statement marks the closing of a great historic movement. Up to our own day American history has been in a large degree the history of the colonization of the Great West. The existence of an area of free land, its continuous recession, and the advance of American settlement westward, explain American development.

Behind institutions, behind constitutional forms and modifications, lie the vital forces that call these organs into life and shape them to meet changing conditions. The peculiarity of American institutions is, the fact that they have been compelled to adapt themselves to the changes of an expanding people—to the changes involved in crossing a continent, in winning a wilderness, and in developing at each area of this progress out of the primitive economic and political conditions of the frontier into the complexity of city life. Said Calhoun in 1817, "We are great, and rapidly—I was about to say fearfully—growing!" So saying, he touched the distinguishing feature of American life. All peoples show development. . . . In the case of most nations, however, the development has occurred in a limited area; and if the nation has expanded, it has met other growing peoples whom it has conquered. But in the case of the United States we have a different phenomenon. Limiting our attention to the Atlantic coast, we have the familiar phenomenon of the evolution of institutions in a limited area, such as the rise of representative government; the differentiation of simple colonial governments into complex organs; the progress from primitive industrial society, without division of labor, up to manufacturing civilization. But we have in addition to this a recurrence of the process of evolution in each western area reached in the process of expansion. Thus American development has exhibited not merely advance along a single line, but a return to primitive conditions on a continually advancing frontier line, and a new development for that area. American social development has been continually beginning over again on the frontier. This perennial rebirth, this fluidity of American life, this expansion westward with its new opportunities, its continuous touch with the simplicity of primitive society, furnish the forces dominating American character. The true point of view in the history of this nation is not the Atlantic coast, it is the great West. Even the slavery struggle, which is made so exclusive an object of attention by writers like Prof. von Holst, occupies its important place in American history because of its relation to westward expansion.

In this advance, the frontier is the outer edge of the wave—the meeting point between savagery and civilization. Much has been written about the frontier from the point of view of border warfare and the chase, but as a field for the serious study of the economist and the historian it has been neglected.

The American frontier is sharply distinguished from the European frontier—a fortified boundary line running through dense populations. The most significant thing about the American frontier is, that it lies at the hither edge of free land. In the census reports it is treated as the margin of that settlement which has a density of two or more to the square mile. The term is an elastic one, and for our purposes does not need sharp definition. We shall consider the whole frontier belt, including the Indian country and the outer margin of the "settled area" of the census reports. This paper will make no attempt to treat the subject exhaustively; its aim is simply to call attention to the frontier as a fertile field for investigation, and to suggest some of the problems which arise in connection with it.

In the settlement of America we have to observe how European life entered the continent, and how America modified and developed that life and reacted on Europe. Our early history is the study of European germs developing in an American environment. Too exclusive attention has been paid by institutional students to the Germanic origins, too little to the American factors. The frontier is the line of most rapid and effective Americanization. The wilderness masters the colonist. It finds him a European in dress, industries, tools, modes of travel, and thought. It takes him from the railroad car and puts him in the birch canoe. It strips off the garments of civilization and arrays him in the hunting shirt and the moccasin. It puts him in the log cabin of the Cherokee and Iroquois and runs an Indian palisade around him. Before long he has gone to planting Indian corn and plowing with a sharp stick; he shouts the war cry and takes the scalp in orthodox Indian fashion. In short, at the frontier the environment is at first too strong for the man. He must accept the conditions which it furnishes, or perish, and so he fits himself into the Indian clearings and follows the Indian trails. Little by little he transforms the wilderness, but the outcome is not the old Europe, not simply the development of Germanic germs, any more than the first phenomenon was a case of reversion to the Germanic mark. The fact is, that here is a new product that is American. At first, the frontier was the Atlantic coast. It was the frontier of Europe in a very real sense. Moving westward, the frontier became more and more American. As successive terminal moraines result from successive glaciations, so each frontier leaves its traces behind it, and when it becomes a settled area the region still partakes of the frontier characteristics. Thus the advance of the frontier has meant a steady movement away from the influence of Europe, a steady growth of independence on American lines. And to study this advance, the men who grew up under these conditions, and the political, economic, and social results of it, is to study the really American part of our history.

COMPOSITE NATIONALITY

First, we note that the frontier promoted the formation of a composite nationality for the American people. The coast was preponderantly English, but the later tides of continental immigration flowed across to the free lands. This was the case from the early colonial days. The Scotch-Irish and the Palatine Germans, or "Pennsylvania Dutch," furnished the dominant element in the stock of the colonial frontier. With these peoples were also the freed indented servants, or redemptioners, who at the expiration of their time of service passed to the frontier. Governor Spottswood of Virginia writes in 1717, "The inhabitants of our frontiers are composed generally of such as have been transported hither as servants, and, being out of their time, settle themselves where land is to be taken up and that will produce the necessarys of life with little labour." Very generally these redemptioners were of non-English stock. In the crucible of the frontier the immigrants were Americanized, liberated, and fused into a mixed race, English in neither nationality nor characteristics. The process has gone on from the early days to our own. Burke and other writers in the middle of the eighteenth century believed that Pennsylvania was "threatened with the danger of being wholly foreign in language, manners, and perhaps even inclinations." The German and Scotch-Irish elements in the frontier of the South were only less great. In the middle of the present century the German element in Wisconsin was already so considerable that leading publicists looked to the creation of a German state out of the commonwealth by concentrating their colonization. Such examples teach us to beware of misinterpreting the fact that there is a common English speech in America into a belief that the stock is also English.

INTELLECTUAL TRAITS

From the conditions of frontier life came intellectual traits of profound importance. The works of travelers along each frontier from colonial days onward describe certain common traits, and these traits have, while softening down, still persisted as survivals in the place of their origin, even when a higher social organization succeeded. The result is that to the frontier the American intellect owes its striking characteristics. That coarseness and strength combined with acuteness and inquisitiveness; that practical, inventive turn of mind, quick to find expedients; that masterful grasp of material things, lacking in the artistic but powerful to effect great ends; that restless, nervous energy; that dominant individualism, working for good and for evil, and withal that buoyancy and exuberance which comes with freedom—these are traits of the frontier, or traits called out elsewhere because of the existence of the frontier. Since the days when the fleet of Columbus sailed into the waters of the New World, America has been another name for opportunity, and the people of the United States have taken their tone from the incessant expansion which has not only been open but has even been forced upon them. He would be a rash prophet who should assert that the expansive character of American life has now entirely ceased. Movement has been its dominant fact, and, unless this training has no effect upon a people, the American energy will continually demand a wider field for its exercise. But never again will such gifts of free land offer themselves. For a moment, at the frontier, the bonds of custom are broken and unrestraint is triumphant. There is not tabula rasa. The stubborn American environment is there with its imperious summons to accept its conditions; the inherited ways of doing things are also there; and yet, in spite of environment, and in spite of custom, each frontier did indeed furnish a new field of opportunity, a gate of escape from the bondage of the past; and freshness, and confidence, and scorn of older society, impatience of its restraints and its ideas, and indifference to its lessons, have accompanied the frontier. What the Mediterranean Sea was to the Greeks, breaking the bond of custom, offering new experiences, calling out new institutions and activities, that, and more, the ever retreating frontier has been to the United States directly, and to the nations of Europe more remotely. And now, four centuries from the discovery of America, at the end of a hundred years of life under the Constitution, the frontier has gone, and with its going has closed the first period of American history.

Discussion Questions

1. Compare Turner's view of the frontier pioneer to de Crèvecoeur's portrait.
2. Analyze the comparisons or metaphors that Turner uses to describe westward expansion. Explain their effect on developing his ideas.
3. Consider Turner's traits of the American character. To what extent do these apply today? Are they relevant to all Americans or are they more applicable to the Westerner? Why?

MERIWETHER LEWIS (1774–1809)
AND
WILLIAM CLARK (1770–1838)

The exploration of Lewis and Clark up the Missouri River, over the Continental Divide, and down the Columbia Gorge to the Pacific Ocean was a stupendous achievement, and their record of it is a literary epic. In 28 months, traveling an average of ten miles daily, the thirty men of the permanent party covered 7,689 miles, many in a region of North America no white man or woman had ever seen (*Brief Account* 5; Bergon ix). And besides thousands of specimens of plants and animals, they brought back detailed observations of the region's climate, geography, geology, botany, and zoology, as well as field notes on Indian cultures they encountered. Of course, gaining this knowledge was part of their mission, as instructed by President Thomas Jefferson (1743–1826), although a central purpose was to search for the long-anticipated Northwest Passage that would link the Mississippi River by a commercially navigable course to the Pacific.

Less publicized at the time was the political aim to secure some territorial claim to Oregon Territory—comprising the present states of Oregon, Washington, Idaho, and parts of Montana and Wyoming—in contention with Spain to the south and Britain to the north. Actually, this imperial expansion was foremost in Jefferson's mind when he planned the expedition some months before he arranged for the United States to purchase Louisiana from France for $15 million, more than doubling the nation's area. The Lewis and Clark expedition was also designed to establish American trapping and shipping routes that would challenge the control the Canadian North West Company and the British Hudson Bay Company had over the fur trade from the upper Missouri River through present-day British Columbia, not to mention potential trade with China. Lewis and Clark were aware of this grand design when they undertook the expedition, just as they were confident in their abilities to fulfill Jefferson's instructions (*Brief Account*; DeVoto).

Born in Virginia, both men grew up in slave-holding families that possessed land, but not wealth. When Lewis was nine he moved with his stepfather and mother to the wilderness of northeast Georgia to create a new settlement. There, Lewis learned hunting and other frontier skills. At thirteen, he returned to Virginia to be educated by tutors, mostly in math and science, but at eighteen he quit his studies to assume responsibility for the family plantation. In 1794, he joined the

Virginia militia and a year later was commissioned as a lieutenant in the regular army. Clark did not receive as much education as Lewis, but he had similar wilderness training as a boy. When he was fourteen, his family moved to a homestead in Kentucky, where he joined the militia as a teenager and fought the Native Americans north of the Ohio River. He, too, joined the U.S. infantry as a lieutenant, in 1792, and fought in several frontier battles. While Lewis did not see combat, he and Clark became friends in the infantry and gained valuable experience in wilderness travel and with the native peoples (Dunlay).

When asked to join the expedition in 1803, "both men were courageous, tactful, fertile in expedient and persistent" (*Brief Account* 4), but each brought somewhat different skills to the enterprise. "Lewis served as the expedition's botanist and zoologist; Clark was the cartographer and geographer" (Bergon xv). "Lewis was the diplomatic and commercial thinker, Clark the negotiator" with the Indians and the principal boat-handler (DeVoto xliii–xliv). Perhaps because of these complementary divisions of labor, the two men worked together with amazing cooperation. In this way, they represent a contradiction to the mythic frontier hero: "They are not the self-sufficient, independent, gunslinging western loners so popular in American fiction and film. They are dependent on each other, on the other members of the expedition, on the native peoples of the West, and especially on the natural world through which they pass" (Bergon xix).

Despite this contradiction, Lewis and Clark contributed to the westering yearn of thousands by securing the Oregon territory for future American pioneers, at least in the frontier myth of popular imagination. An immediate effect of the expedition, which reported a wealth of beaver in the intermountain West, was to stimulate the fur trade. In 1807, Manuel Lisa hired three men from the Lewis-and-Clark party and organized the Missouri Fur Company, backed by St. Louis money. This venture began the era of the mountain men, who also advanced the exploration of the West (DeVoto).

The first published version of *Journals* was actually a condensed paraphrase in two volumes edited by Nicholas Biddle in 1814, eight years after the expedition returned. The excerpts below (from volume 2, pages 33–37, 369–74; and volume 5, pages 223–27) are from *Original Journals of the Lewis and Clark Expedition, 1804–1806* (Dodd, Mead and Company, 1904–1905) published in eight volumes and edited by Rueben Gold Thwaites, who inserted omitted words and letters (within brackets) to clarify some sentences. However, more accessible to the general reading public is Bernard DeVoto's edition (Houghton Mifflin,

1953), which includes about a third of the Thwaites text. In the original daily entries, the explorers recorded the courses of rivers and trails, the mileage traveled, and notes about the weather; these details have been omitted here.

All of the excerpts below were written by Lewis, the more colorful and psychological of the two authors. The first passage, occurring after the party wintered in North Dakota with the Mandan Indians, is set along the Missouri River in northern Montana. It shows some of the dangers the expedition met and survived on a daily basis.

Bergon, Frank. "Introduction." *The Journals of Lewis and Clark*. New York: Viking Penguin, 1989. ix–xix.

Brief Account of the Lewis and Clark Expedition from St. Louis, Missouri, to the Mouth of the Columbia River, Oregon, and Return, 1804–1806. [Exhibit for the Lewis and Clark Centennial Exposition, Portland]. Washington, DC: Department of the Interior, 1905.

DeVoto, Bernard. "Introduction." *The Journals of Lewis and Clark*. Boston: Houghton Mifflin, 1953. xv–lii.

Dunlay, Thomas W. "Meriwether Lewis and William Clark." *Dictionary of Literary Biography, Volume 186: Nineteenth-Century American Western Writers*. Ed. Robert L. Gale. Detroit: Gale, 1997. 208–18.

FROM *ORIGINAL JOURNALS OF THE LEWIS AND CLARK EXPEDITION, 1804–1806*

<>

TUESDAY MAY 14th. 1805

Some fog on the river this morning, which is a very rare occurrence; the country much as it was yesterday with this difference that the bottoms are somewhat wider; passed some high black bluffs. saw immence herds of buffaloe today also Elk deer wolves and Antelopes. passed three large creeks one on the Star^d. and two others on the Lar^d. side, neither of which had any runing water. Capt Clark walked on shore and killed a very fine buffaloe cow. I felt an inclination to eat some veal and walked on shore and killed a very fine buffaloe calf and a large woolf, much the whitest I had seen, it was quite as white as the wool of the common sheep. one of the party wounded a brown bear very badly, but being alone did not think proper to pursue him. In the evening the men in two of the rear canoes discovered a large brown bear lying in the open grounds about 300 paces from the river, and six of them went out to attack him, all good hunters; they took the advantage of a small eminence which concealed them and got within 40 paces of him unperceived, two of them reserved their fires as had been previously conscerted, the four others fired nearly at the same time and put each his bullet through him, two of the balls passed through the bulk of both lobes of his lungs, in an instant this monster ran at them with open mouth, the two who had reserved their fir[e]s discharged their pieces at him as he came towards them, boath of them struck him, one only slightly and the other fortunately broke his shoulder, this how-ever only retarded his motion for a moment only, the men unable to reload their guns took to flight, the bear pursued and had very nearly overtaken them before they reached the river; two of the party betook themselves to a canoe and the others seperated an[d] concealed themselves among the willows, reloaded their pieces, each discharged his piece at him as they had an oppor-tunity, they struck him several times again but the guns served only to direct the bear to them, in this manner he pursued two of them seperately so close that they were obliged to throw aside their guns and pouches and throw them-selves into the river altho' the bank was nearly twenty feet perpendicular; so enraged was this anamal that he plunged into the river only a few feet behind the second man he had compelled [to] take refuge in the water, when one of those who still remained on shore shot him through the head and finally killed him; they then took him on shore and butch[er]ed him when they found eight balls had passed through him in different directions; the bear being old the flesh was indifferent, they therefore only took the skin and fleece, the latter made us several gallons of oil; it was after the sun had set before these men come up with us, where we had been halted by an occurrence, which I have now to recappitulate, and which altho' happily passed without ruinous injury, I cannot recollect but with the utmost trepidation and horror; this is the upseting and narrow escape of the white perogue. It happened unfortu-nately for us this evening that Charbono was at the helm of this Perogue, in stead of Drewyer, who had previously steered her; Charbono cannot swim and is perhaps the most timid waterman in the world; perhaps it was equally unluckey that Capt. C. and myself were both on shore at that moment, a cir-cumstance which rarely happened; and tho' we were on the shore opposite to the perogue, were too far distant to be heard or to do more than remain spec-tators of her fate; in this perogue were embarked, our papers, Instruments, books medicine, a great part of our merchandize and in short almost every article indispensibly necessary to further the views, or insure the success of the enterprize in which we are now launched to the distance of 2200 miles.

surfice it to say, that the Perogue was under sail when a sudon squawl of wind struck her obliquely, and turned her considerably, the steersman allarmed, in stead of puting, her before the wind, lufted her up into it, the wind was so violent that it drew the brace of the squarsail out of the hand of the man who was attending it, and instantly upset the perogue and would have turned her completely topsaturva, had it not have been from the resistance mad[e] by the oarning [awning] against the water; in this situation Capt. C. and myself both fired our guns to attract the attention if possible of the crew and ordered the halyards to be cut and the sail hawled in, but they did not hear us; such was their confusion and consternation at this moment, that they suffered the perogue to lye on her side for half a minute before they took the sail in, the perogue then wrighted but had filled within an inch of the gunwals; Charbono still crying to his god for mercy, had not yet recollected the rudder, nor could the repeated orders of the Bowsman, Cruzat, bring him to his recollection untill he threatend to shoot him instantly if he did not take hold of the rudder and do his duty, the waves by this time were runing very high, but the fortitude, resolution and good conduct of Cruzat saved her; he ordered 2 of the men to throw out the water with some kettles that fortunately were convenient, while himself and two others rowed her as[h]ore, where she arrived scarcely above the water; we now took every article out of her and lay them to drane as well as we could for the evening, baled out the canoe and secured her. there were two other men beside Charbono on board who could not swim, and who of course must also have perished had the perogue gone to the bottom. while the perogue lay on her side, finding I could not be heard, I for a moment forgot my own situation, and involluntarily droped my gun, threw aside my shot pouch and was in the act of unbuttoning my coat, before I recollected the folly of the attempt I was about to make; which was to throw myself into the river and inde[a]vour to swim to the perogue; the perogue was three hundred yards distant the waves so high that a perogue could scarcely live in any situation, the water excessively could, and the stream rappid; had I undertaken this project therefore, there was a hundred to one but what I should have paid the forfit of my life for the madness of my project, but this had the perogue been lost, I should have valued but little. After having all matters arranged for the evening as well as the nature of circumstances would permit, we thought it a proper occasion to console ourselves and cheer the sperits of our men and accordingly took a drink of grog and gave each man a gill of sperits.

*   *   *

[The second passage is set near Lemhi Pass at the headwaters of the Missouri, where the party crossed the Bitterroot Range, whose peaks form the Continental

Divide. It was fortuitous that Sacajawea met her own tribe of Shoshones here and facilitated hospitality and trade with her people. It was critical that Lewis and Clark negotiate to purchase horses and arrange for a guide in order to continue their journey north and west along the Nez Perce trail since the Salmon River, flowing south and west, was impassable by canoe. This passage demonstrates some of the "anthropological" sorts of observations Lewis made of Native Americans.]

MONDAY AUGUST 19th. 1805

This morning I arrose at d[a]ylight and sent out three hunters. some of the men who were much in want of legings and mockersons I suffered to dress some skins. the others I employed in repacking the baggage, making pack saddles &c. we took up the net this morning but caught no fish. one beaver was caught in a trap. the frost which perfectly whitened the grass this morning had a singular appearance to me at this season. this evening I made a few of the men construct a sein of willow brush which we hawled and caught a large number of fine trout and a kind of mullet about 16 Inches long which I had not seen before. the scales are small, the nose is long and obtusely pointed and exceeds the under jaw. the mouth is not large but opens with foalds at the sides, the colour of it's back and sides is of a bluish brown and belley white; it has the faggot bones, from which I have supposed it to be of the mullet kind. the tongue and pallate are smooth and it has no teeth. it is by no means as good as the trout. the trout are the same which I first met with at the falls of the Missouri, they are larger than the speckled trout of our mountains and equally as well flavored. The hunters returned this evening with two deer. from what has been said of the Shoshones it will be readily perceived that they live in a wretched stait of poverty. yet notwithstanding their extreem poverty they are not only cheerfull but even gay, fond of gaudy dress and amusements; like most other Indians they are great egotists and frequently boast of heroic acts which they never performed. they are also fond of games of wrisk. they are frank, communicative, fair in dealing, generous with the little they possess, extreemly honest, and by no means beggarly. each individual is his own sovereign master, and acts from the dictates of his own mind; the authority of the Cheif being nothing more than mere admonition supported by the influence which the prop[r]iety of his own examplary conduct may have acquired him in the minds of the individuals who compose the band. the title of cheif is not hereditary, nor can I learn that there is any cerimony of instalment, or other epo[c]h in the life of a Cheif from which his title as such can be dated. in fact every man is a chief, but all have not an equal influence on the minds of the other members of the community, and he who happens to enjoy the greatest share of confidence is the principal Chief. The Shoshonees may be estimated at about 100 warriors, and about three times that number of woomen and children. they have more children among them than I expected to have seen among a people who procure subsistence with such difficulty. there are but few very old persons, nor did they appear to treat those with much tenderness or rispect. The man is the sole propryetor of his wives and daughters, and can barter or dispose of either as he thinks proper. a plurality of wives is common among them, but these are not generally sisters as with the Minnitares & Mandans but are purchased of different fathers. The father frequently disposes of his infant daughters in marriage to men who are grown or to men who have sons for whom they think proper to provide wives. the compensation given in such cases usually consists of horses or mules which the father receives at the time of contract and converts to his own uce. the girl remains with her parents untill she is conceived to have obtained the age of puberty which with them is considered to be about the age of 13 or 14 years. the female at this age is surrendered to her soveriegn lord and husband agree-ably to contract, and with her is frequently restored by the father quite as much as he received in the first instance in payment for his daughter; but this is discretionary with the father. Sah-car-gar-we-ah had been thus disposed of before she was taken by the Minnetares, or had arrived to the years of puberty. the husband was yet living with this band. he was more than double her age and had two other wives. he claimed her as his wife but said that as she had had a child by another man, who was Charbono, that he did not want her. They seldom correct their children particularly the boys who soon become masters of their own acts. they give as a reason that it cows and breaks the sperit of the boy to whip him, and that he never recovers his independence of mind after he is grown. They treat their women but with little rispect, and compel them to perform every species of drudgery. they collect the wild fruits and roots, attend to the horses or assist in that duty, cook, dress the skins and make all their apparel, collect wood and make their fires, arrange and form their lodges, and when they travel pack the horses and take charge of all the baggage; in short the man dose little else except attend his horses hunt and fish. the man considers himself degraded if he is compelled to walk any dis-tance; and if he is so unfortunately poor as only to possess two horses he rides the best himself and leavs the woman or women if he has more than one, to transport their baggage and children on the other, and to walk if the horse is unable to carry the additional weight of their persons. the chastity of their women is not held in high estimation, and the husband will for a trifle barter the companion of his bead for a night or longer if he conceives the reward adiquate; tho' they are not so importunate that we should caress their women as the siouxs were. and some of their women appear to be held more sacred than in any nation we have seen. I have requested the men to give them no cause of jealousy by having connection with their women without their knowledge, which with them, strange as it may seem is considered as disgracefull to the husband, as clandestine connections of a similar kind are among civilized nations. to prevent this mutual exchange of good officies altogether I know it impossible to effect, particularly on the part of our young men whom some months abstanence have made very polite to those tawney damsels. no evil has yet resulted and I hope will not from these connections. notwithstanding the late loss of horses which this people sustained by the Minnetares the stock of the band may be very safely estimated at seven hundred of which they are perhaps about 40 coalts and half that number of mules. these people are deminutive in stature, thick ankles, crooked legs, thick flat feet and in short but illy formed, at least much more so in general than any nation of Indians I ever saw. their complexion is much that of the Siouxs or darker than the Minnetares Mandands or Shawnees. generally both men and women wear their hair in a loos lank flow over the sholders and face; tho' I observed some few men who confined their hair in two equal cues hanging over each ear and drawnn in front of the body. the cue is formed with throngs of dressed leather or Otterskin a[l]ternately crossing each other. at present most of them have their hair cut short in the neck in consequence of the loss of their relations by the Minnetares. Cameahwait has his cut close all over his head. this constitutes their cerimony of morning for their deceased relations. the dress of the men consists of a robe long legings, shirt, tippet and Mockersons, that of the women is also a robe, chemise, and Mockersons; sometimes they make use of short legings. the ornements of both men and women are very similar, and consist of several species of sea shells, blue and white beads, bras and Iron arm bands, plaited cords of the sweet grass, and collars of leather ornamented with the quills of the porcupine dyed of various colours among which I observed the red, yellow, blue, and black. the ear is purforated in the lower part to receive various ornaments but the nose is not, nor is the ear lasserated or disvigored for this purpose as among many nations. the men never mark their skins by birning, cuting, nor puncturing and introducing a colouring matter as many nations do. there women sometimes puncture a small circle on their forehead nose or cheeks and thus introduce a black matter usually soot and grease which leaves an indelible stane. tho' this even is by no means common. their arms offensive and defensive consist in the bow and arrows shield, some, lances, and a weapon called by the Cippeways who formerly used it, the pog-gar´-mag-gon´. in fishing they employ wairs, gigs, and fishing hooks. the salmon is the principal object of their pursuit. they snair wolves and foxes. I was anxious to learn whether these people had the venerial, and made the enquiry through the intrepreter and his wife; the information was that they sometimes had it but I could not learn their remedy; they most usually die with it's effects. this seems a strong proof that these disorders bothe ganaraehah [gonorrhea] and Louis Venerae are native disorders of America. tho' these people have suffered much by the small pox which is known to be imported and perhaps those other disorders might have been contracted from other indian tribes who by a round of communications might have obtained from the Europeans since it was introduced into that quarter of the globe. but so much detatched on the other ha[n]d from all communication with the whites that I think it most probable that those disorders are original with them. from the middle of May to the first of September these people reside on the waters of the Columbia where they consider themselves in perfect security from their enimies as they have not as yet ever found their way to this retreat; during this season the salmon furnish the principal part of their subsistence and as this fish either perishes or returns about the 1st. of September they are compelled at this season in surch of subsistence to resort to the Missouri, in the vallies of which, there is more game even within the mountains. here they move slowly down the river in order to collect and join other bands either of their own nation or the Flatheads, and having become sufficiently strong as they conceive venture on the Eastern side of the Rockey mountains into the plains, where the buffaloe abound. but they never leave the interior of the mountains while they can obtain a scanty subsistence, and always return as soon as they have acquired a good stock of dryed meat in the plains; when this stock is consumed they venture again into the plains; thus alternately obtaining their food at the risk of their lives and retiring to the mountains, while they consume it. These people are now on the eve of their departure for the Missouri, and inform us that they expect to be joined at or about the three forks by several bands of their own nation, and a band of the Flatheads. as I am now two busily engaged to enter at once into a minute discription of the several articles which compose their dress, impliments of war hunting fishing &c I shall pursue them at my leasure in the order they have here occurred to my mind, and have been mentioned. This morning cap^t. Clark continued his rout with his party, the Indians accompanying him as yesterday; he was obliged to feed them. nothing remarkable happened during the day. he was met by an Indian with two mules on this side of the dividing ridge at the foot of the mountain, the Indian had the politeness to offer Capt. C. one of his mules to ride as he was on foot, which he accepted and gave the fellow a waistcoat as a reward for his politeness. in the evening he reached the creek on this side of the Indian camp and halted for the night. his hunters killed nothing today. The Indians value their mules very highly. a good mule can not be obtained for less than three and sometimes four horses, and the most indifferent are rated at two horses. their mules generally are the finest I ever saw without any comparison.

* * *

[The third passage is set north of the Great Falls of the Missouri when Lewis, on the return journey in 1806, explored Maria's River with a detachment of six men to see if its route flowed northerly enough to allow a portage to the Saskatchewan River and thus a means to ship Canadian furs to American ports. He was disappointed in this hope. At the same time, Clark sent a middle party to transport the boats around the Great Falls and down the river, while he traveled with a southern party along the Yellowstone River to their common rendezvous at its junction with the Missouri. The passage describes the only violence between the expedition and Native Americans—in part due to Lewis's lack of vigilance and caution when traveling with a band of Blackfeet, who had a reputation for aggressiveness, at least according to the friendly Nez Perce and Flathead tribes that Lewis had encountered.]

JULY 27th. 1806. SUNDAY

This morning at daylight the indians got up and crouded around the fire, J. Fields who was on post had carelessly laid his gun down behi[n]d him near where his brother was sleeping, one of the indians the fellow to whom I had given the medal last evening sliped behind him and took his gun and that of his brother unperceived by him, at the same instant two others advanced and seized the guns of Drewyer and myself, J. Fields seeing this turned about to look for his gun and saw the fellow just runing off with her and his brother's he called to his brother who instantly jumped up and pursued the indian with him whom they overtook at the distance of 50 or 60 paces from the camp s[e]ized their guns and rested them from him and R. Fields as he seized his gun stabed the indian to the heart with his knife the fellow ran about 15 steps and fell dead; of this I did not know untill afterwards, having recovered their guns they ran back instantly to the camp; Drewyer who was awake saw the indian take hold of his gun and instantly jumped up and s[e]ized her and rested her from him but the indian still retained his pouch, his jumping up and crying damn you let go my gun awakened me I jumped up and asked what was the matter which I quickly learned when I saw drewyer in a scuffle with the indian for his gun I reached to seize my gun but found her gone, I then drew a pistol from my holster and terning myself about saw the indian making off with my gun. I ran at him with my pistol and bid him lay down my gun which he was in the act of doing when the

Fieldses returned and drew up their guns to shoot him which I forbid as he did not appear to be about to make any resistance or commit any offensive act, he droped the gun and walked slowly off, I picked her up instantly, Drewyer having about this time recovered his gun and pouch asked me if he might not kill the fellow which I also forbid as the indian did not appear to wish to kill us, as soon as they found us all in possession of our arms they ran and indeavored to drive off all the horses. I now hollowed to the men and told them to fire on them if they attempted to drive off our horses, they accordingly pursued the main party who were dr[i]ving the horses up the river and I pursued the man who had taken my gun who with another was driving off a part of the horses which were to the left of the camp. I pursued them so closely that they could not take twelve of their own horses but continued to drive one of mine with some others; at the distance of three hundred paces they entered one of those steep nitches in the bluff with the horses before them being nearly out of breath I could pursue no further, I called to them as I had done several times before that I would shoot them if they did not give me my horse and raised my gun, one of them jumped behind a rock and spoke to the other who turned arround and stoped at the distance of 30 steps from me and I shot him through the belly, he fell to his knees and on his wright elbow from which position partly raised himself up and fired at me, and turning himself about crawled in behind a rock which was a few feet from him. he overshot me, being bearheaded I felt the wind of his bullet very distinctly. not having my shotpouch I could not reload my peice and as there were two of them behind good shelters from me I did not think it prudent to rush on them with my pistol which had I discharged I had not the means of reloading untill I reached camp; I therefore returned leasurely towards camp, on my way I met with Drewyer who having heared the report of the guns had returned in surch of me and left the Fieldes to pursue the indians, I desired him to haisten to the camp with me and assist in catching as many of the indian horses as were necessary and to call to the Fieldes if he could make them hear to come back that we still had a sufficient number of horses, this he did but they were too far to hear him. we reached the camp and began to catch the horses and saddle them and put on the packs. the reason I had not my pouch with me was that I had not time to return about 50 yards to camp after geting my gun before I was obliged to pursue the indians or suffer them to collect and drive off all the horses. we had caught and saddled the horses and began to arrange the packs when the Fieldses returned with four of our horses; we left one of our horses and took four of the best of those of the indian's; while the men were preparing the horses I put four sheilds and two bows and quivers of arrows which had been left on the fire, with sundry other articles; they left all their baggage at our mercy. they had but 2 guns and one of them they left the others were armed with bows and arrows and eyedaggs. the gun we took with us. I also retook the flagg but left the medal about the neck of the dead man that they might be informed who we were. we took some of their buffaloe meat and set out ascending the bluffs by the same rout we had decended last evening leaving the ballance of nine of their horses which we did not want. the Fieldses told me that three of the indians whom they pursued swam the river one of them on my horse. and that two others ascended the hill and escaped from them with a part of their horses, two I had pursued into the nitch one lay dead near the camp and the eighth we could not account for but suppose that he ran off early in the contest. having ascended the hill we took our course through a beatifull level plain a little to the S. of East. my design was to hasten to the entrance of Maria's river as quick as possible in the hope of meeting with the canoes and party at that place having no doubt but that they [the Indians] would pursue us with a large party and as there was a band near the broken mountains or probably between them and the mouth of that river we might expect them to receive inteligence from us and arrive at that place nearly as soon as we could, no time was therefore to be lost and we pushed our horses as hard as they would bear. at 8 miles we passed a large branch 40 y^{ds}. wide which I called battle river. at 3 P. M. we arrived at rose river about 5 miles above where we had passed it as we went out, having traveled by my estimate compared with our former distances and cou[r]ses about 63 m^s. here we halted an hour and a half took some refreshment and suffered our horses to graize; the day proved warm but the late rains had supplyed the little reservors in the plains with water and had put them in fine order for traveling, our whole rout so far was as level as a bowling green with but little stone and few prickly pears. after dinner we pursued the bottoms of rose river but finding [it] inconvenient to pass the river so often we again ascended the hills on the S. W. side and took the open plains; by dark we had traveled about 17 miles further, we now halted to rest ourselves and horses about 2 hours, we killed a buffaloe cow and took a small quantity of the meat. after refreshing ourselves we again set out by moonlight and traveled leasurely, heavy thunderclouds lowered arround us on every quarter but that from which the moon gave us light. we continued to pass immence herds of buffaloe all night as we had done in the latter part of the day. we traveled untill 2 OCk in the morning having come by my estimate after dark about 20 m^s. we now turned out our horses and laid ourselves down to rest in the plain very much fatiegued as may be readily conceived. my indian horse carried me very well in short much better than my own would have done and leaves me with but little reason to complain of the robery. . . .

Discussion Questions

1. How does Lewis create drama and portray emotion in the first passage? Do you feel these effects are realistically achieved? Explain.
2. In the first passage, to what extent are the men's actions portrayed as heroic? To what extent are "heroic" explanations avoided or deemphasized?
3. In the second passage, describe the characteristics of the Shoshone people as Lewis depicts them. Which of these seem to be objective observations? Which of these seem to be subjective judgments about an alien culture? How can you tell the difference?
4. In the third passage, does Lewis seem to make an error in judgment? Explain. To what extent does his error seem to depend on a difference between the Blackfeet culture and his own? Explain this difference.

BRET HARTE
(1836–1902)

Francis Brett Harte was born in Albany, New York, from mostly English and Dutch heritage. His father was a teacher who moved from school to school almost yearly, never able to find or keep a good position. The family followed, fully aware of their own financial desperation. When his father died in 1845, his mother and the four children moved to New York City, supported by the charity of relatives. Frank, as he was called by his family, was sickly as a boy and sought pleasure in novels, which he read passionately. This home reading proved more beneficial to him than public school, which he left at age thirteen to work in a lawyer's office. His health improved as a young man, active in various office work about town. In 1850, his elder brother was drawn to California by the gold rush. His mother followed in 1853 to marry "Colonel" Andrew Williams, a college friend of his father, while Frank and his younger sister suffered a difficult sea passage early the next year to join the new couple in the dull, stagnant village of Oakland (Stewart).

Before settling in San Francisco in 1860, Harte worked in the Sierra foothills as a teacher and, briefly, as a gold-miner; and in Uniontown (now Arcata) he was a tutor, apothecary clerk, typesetter, editorial assistant, and finally reporter for the weekly newspaper *The Northern Californian*. This last year-long experience helped the young author to prune his pretentious literary style and develop more concise and accurate prose. However, he resigned this position under death threats after writing an editorial condemning the slaughter of over 60 Digger Indians, mostly women and children, by white vigilantes near Eureka (Stewart). This response suggested the attitude he would later develop through his fiction and poetry—sympathy for social outcasts and ironic criticism toward hypocrites who profited by frontier corruption or lawlessness (Golemba).

In the city by the bay, he first began using the pen name Bret Harte, but he languished for a year as a typesetter and minor contributor to the *Golden Era* newspaper. Through the intercession of Jessie Fremont, wife of the explorer John Charles Fremont and patron to the young author, he received lucrative appointments to federal government jobs. These positions allowed him the financial stability to quit his typesetting job and to marry New Yorker Anna Griswold in 1862, and eventually they provided him a steady income and free time to work on his writing. He was fairly prolific during this period, publishing poems and fiction in both the *Golden Era* and *The Californian*, a respectable literary newspaper that also attracted the talents of Mark Twain (Golemba).

By 1867, Harte was a central figure in the "local color" movement, which sought to capture the lore, folkways, and dialects of picturesque Western characters who told tall tales about con games, horse swapping, and hunting. Initially, the local color writers were journalists outside the literary mainstream who humorously criticized the values and customs of the West. But Harte tried to temper this debunking tendency when he became editor of the *Overland Monthly* in 1868. Anton Roman, the publisher, was a capitalistic booster of California's natural beauty, seeking to encourage wealthy Eastern and Midwestern families to relocate. Therefore, in Harte's Gold Rush tales, most of which he wrote while editing the magazine for three years, he balanced the satire and vernacular style of Western humor with a sentimental perspective so that these parables could both romanticize character types (such as the charitable gambler or the whore with a heart of gold) and advance a socially critical view (Morrow 346–48).

Unfortunately, these characteristic works, collected in *The Luck of Roaring Camp, and Other Sketches* (1870), which brought Harte national fame, marked his literary peak, after which he merely parodied himself. There is some evidence, too, that celebrity spoiled him when he put the West behind him and returned to the East, which remained for him the locus of civilization. In New York through the 1870s, he had trouble writing, lavishly outspent his income, became estranged from his wife, and spent time away from his family on ill-prepared lecture tours, desperately trying to raise funds to pay off hounding creditors. When in 1878 President Rutherford Hayes offered Harte a position as commercial agent for the United States in Germany, he jumped at the opportunity, leaving his family behind. He subsequently served for five years as U.S. consul to Glasgow, but spent more time in London hobnobbing with British writers than at his post, which he lost in 1895 for "inattention to duty." It is doubly ironic that he was able to attain his lifelong goal of becoming a gentleman only through writing about the unrefined West, but that his cultured life was impoverished as literary material (Golemba 139–41).

"The Outcasts of Poker Flat" first appeared in the January 1869 issue of the *Overland Monthly*, though the setting is 1850, just after the California gold rush began. The text is from the collection *The Luck of Roaring Camp, and Other Sketches* (New York: Regent, 1871), pages 19–36.

Golemba, Henry L. "Bret Harte." *Dictionary of Literary Biography, Volume 74: American Short Story Writers before 1880.* Ed. Bobby Ellen Kimbel and William E. Grant. Detroit: Gale, 1988. 134–42.

Morrow, Patrick D. "Harte, Twain, and the San Francisco Circle." *A Literary History of the American West.* Ed. Thomas J. Lyon, et al. Fort Worth, TX: Texas Christian University Press and The Western Literature Association, 1987. 339–58.

Stewart, George R., Jr. *Bret Harte: Argonaut and Exile.* Boston: Houghton Mifflin, 1931.

THE OUTCASTS OF POKER FLAT

A s Mr. John Oakhurst, gambler, stepped into the main street of Poker Flat on the morning of the twenty-third of November, 1850, he was conscious of a change in its moral atmosphere from the preceding night. Two or three men, conversing earnestly together, ceased as he approached, and exchanged significant glances. There was a Sabbath lull in the air, which, in a settlement unused to Sabbath influences, looked ominous.

Mr. Oakhurst's calm, handsome face betrayed small concern of these indications. Whether he was conscious of any predisposing cause, was another question. "I reckon they're after somebody," he reflected; "likely it's me." He returned to his pocket the handkerchief with which he had been whipping away the red dust of Poker Flat from his neat boots, and quietly discharged his mind of any further conjecture.

In point of fact, Poker Flat was "after somebody." It had lately suffered the loss of several thousand dollars, two valuable horses, and a prominent citizen. It was experiencing a spasm of virtuous reaction, quite as lawless and ungovernable as any of the acts that had provoked it. A secret committee had determined to rid the town of all improper persons. This was done permanently in regard of two men who were then hanging from the boughs of a sycamore in the gulch, and temporarily in the banishment of certain other objectionable characters. I regret to say that some of these were ladies. It is but due to the sex, however, to state that their impropriety was professional, and it was only in such easily established standards of evil that Poker Flat ventured to sit in judgment.

Mr. Oakhurst was right in supposing that he was included in this category. A few of the committee had urged hanging him as a possible example, and a sure method of reimbursing themselves from his pockets of the sums he had won from them. "It's agin justice," said Jim Wheeler, "to let this yet young man from Roaring Camp—an entire stranger—carry away our money." But a crude sentiment of equity residing in the breasts of those who had been fortunate enough to win from Mr. Oakhurst, overruled this narrower local prejudice.

Mr. Oakhurst received his sentence with philosophic calmness, none the less coolly, that he was aware of the hesitation of his judges. He was too much of a gambler not to accept Fate. With him life was at best an uncertain game, and he recognized the usual percentage in favor of the dealer.

A body of armed men accompanied the deported wickedness of Poker Flat to the outskirts of the settlement. Besides Mr. Oakhurst, who was known to be a coolly desperate man, and for whose intimidation the armed escort was intended, the expatriated party consisted of a young woman familiarly known as "The Duchess;" another, who had gained the infelicitous title of "Mother Shipton," and "Uncle Billy," a suspected sluice-robber and confirmed drunkard. The cavalcade provoked no comments from the spectators, nor was any word uttered by the escort. Only when the gulch which marked the uttermost limit of Poker Flat was reached, the leader spoke briefly and to the point. The exiles were forbidden to return at the peril of their lives.

As the escort disappeared, their pent-up feelings found vent in a few hysterical tears from "The Duchess," some bad language from Mother Shipton, and a Partheian volley of expletives from Uncle Billy. The philosophic Oakhurst alone remained silent. He listened calmly to Mother Shipton's desire to cut somebody's heart out, to the repeated statements of "The Duchess" that she would die in the road, and to the alarming oaths that seemed to be bumped out of Uncle Billy as he rode forward. With the easy good-humor characteristic of his class, he insisted upon exchanging his own riding-horse, "Five Spot," for the sorry mule which the Duchess rode. But even this act did not draw the party into any closer sympathy. The young woman readjusted her somewhat draggled plumes with a feeble, faded coquetry; Mother Shipton eyed the possessor of "Five Spot" with malevolence, and Uncle Billy included the whole party in one sweeping anathema.

The road to Sandy Bar—a camp that not having as yet experienced the regenerating influences of Poker Flat, consequently seemed to offer some invitation to the emigrants—lay over a steep mountain range. It was distant a day's severe journey. In that advanced season, the party soon passed out of the moist, temperate regions of the foot-hills, into the dry, cold, bracing air of the Sierras. The trail was narrow and difficult. At noon the Duchess, rolling out of her saddle upon the ground, declared her intention of going no further, and the party halted.

The spot was singularly wild and impressive. A wooded amphitheatre, surrounded on three sides by precipitous cliffs of naked granite, sloped gently toward the crest of another precipice that overlooked the valley. It was undoubtedly the most suitable spot for a camp, had camping been advisable. But Mr. Oakhurst knew that scarcely half the journey to Sandy Bar was accomplished, and the party were not equipped or provisioned for delay. This fact he pointed out to his companions curtly, with a philosophic commentary on the folly of "throwing up their hand before the game was played out." But they were furnished with liquor, which in this emergency stood then in place of food, fuel, rest and prescience. In spite of his remonstrances, it was not long before they were more or less under its influence. Uncle Billy passed rapidly from a bellicose state into one of stupor, the Duchess became maudlin, and Mother Shipton snored. Mr. Oakhurst alone remained erect, leaning against a rock, calmly surveying them.

Mr. Oakhurst did not drink. It interfered with a profession which required coolness, impassiveness and presence of mind, and, in his own language, he "couldn't afford it." As he gazed at his recumbent fellow-exiles, the loneliness begotten of his pariah-trade, his habits of life, his very vices, for the first time seriously oppressed him. He bestirred himself in dusting his black clothes, washing his hands and face, and other acts characteristic of his studiously neat habits, and for a moment forgot his annoyance. The thought of deserting his weaker and more pitiable companions never perhaps occurred to him. Yet he could not help feeling the want of that excitement, which singularly enough was most conducive to that calm equanimity for which he was notorious. He looked at the gloomy walls that rose a thousand feet sheer above the circling pines around him; at the sky, ominously clouded; at the valley below, already deepening into shadow. And doing so, suddenly he heard his own name called.

A horseman slowly ascended the trail. In the fresh, open face of the new-comer, Mr. Oakhurst recognized Tom Simson, otherwise known as "The Innocent" of Sandy Bar. He had met him some months before over a "little game," and had, with perfect equanimity, won the entire fortune—amounting to some forty dollars—of that guileless youth. After the game was finished. Mr. Oakhurst drew the youthful speculator behind the door and thus addressed him: "Tommy, you're a good little man, but you can't gamble worth a cent. Don't try it over again." He then handed him his money back, pushed him gently from the room, and so made a devoted slave of Tom Simson.

There was a remembrance of this in his boyish and enthusiastic greet-ing of Mr. Oakhurst. He had started, he said, to go to Poker Flat to seek his fortune. "Alone?" No, not exactly alone; in fact—a giggle—he had run away with Piney Woods. Didn't Mr. Oakhurst remember Piney? She that used to wait on the table at the Temperance House? They had been engaged a long time, but old Jake Woods had objected, and so they had run away, and were going to Poker Flat to be married, and here they were. And they were tired out, and how lucky it was they had found a place to camp and company. All this The Innocent delivered rapidly, while Piney—a stout, comely damsel of fifteen—emerged from behind the pine tree, where she had been blushing unseen, and rode to the side of her lover.

Mr. Oakhurst seldom troubled himself with sentiment. Still less with propriety. But he had a vague idea that the situation was not felicitous. He retained, however, his presence of mind sufficiently to kick Uncle Billy, who was about to say something, and Uncle Billy was sober enough to recognize in Mr. Oakhurst's kick a superior power that would not bear trifling. He then endeavored to dissuade Tom Simson from delaying further, but in vain. He even pointed out the fact that there was no provision, nor means of mak-ing a camp. But, unluckily, "The Innocent" met this objection by assuring the party that he was provided with an extra mule loaded with provisions, and by the discovery of a rude attempt at a log-house near the trail. "Piney can stay with Mrs. Oakhurst," said The Innocent, pointing to the Duchess, "and I can shift for myself."

Nothing but Mr. Oakhurst's admonishing foot saved Uncle Billy from bursting into a roar of laughter. As it was, he felt compelled to retire up the cañon until he could recover his gravity. There he confided the joke to the tall pine trees, with many slaps of his leg, contortions of his face, and the usual profanity. But when he returned to the party, he found them seated by a fire—for the air had grown strangely chill and the sky overcast—in apparently ami-cable conversation. Piney was actually talking in an impulsive, girlish fashion to the Duchess, who was listening with an interest and animation she had not shown for many days. The Innocent was holding forth, apparently with equal effect, to Mr. Oakhurst and Mother Shipton, who was actually relaxing into amiability. "Is this yer a d——d picnic?" said Uncle Billy, with inward scorn, as he surveyed the sylvan group, the glancing fire-light and the tethered animals in the foreground. Suddenly an idea mingled with the alcoholic fumes that disturbed his brain. It was apparently of a jocular nature, for he felt impelled to slap his leg again and cram his fist into his mouth.

As the shadows crept slowly up the mountain, a slight breeze rocked the tops of the pine trees, and moaned through their long and gloomy aisles. The ruined cabin, patched and covered with pine boughs, was set apart for the ladies. As the lovers parted, they unaffectedly exchanged a parting kiss, so honest and sincere that it might have been heard above the swaying pines. The frail Duchess and the malevolent Mother Shipton were probably too stunned to remark upon this last evidence of simplicity, and so turned without a word to the hut. The fire was replenished, the men lay down before the door, and in a few minutes were asleep.

Mr. Oakhurst was a light sleeper. Toward morning he awoke benumbed and cold. As he stirred the dying fire, the wind, which was now blowing strongly, brought to his cheek that which caused the blood to leave it—snow!

He started to his feet with the intention of awakening the sleepers, for there was no time to lose. But turning to where Uncle Billy had been lying he found him gone. A suspicion leaped to his brain and a curse to his lips. He ran to the spot where the mules had been tethered; they were no longer there. The tracks were already rapidly disappearing in the snow.

The momentary excitement brought Mr. Oakhurst back to the fire with his usual calm. He did not waken the sleepers. The Innocent slumbered peacefully, with a smile on his good-humored, freckled face; the virgin Piney slept beside her frailer sisters as sweetly as though attended by celestial guardians, and Mr. Oakhurst, drawing his blanket over his shoulders, stroked his mustachios and waited for the dawn. It came slowly in a whirling mist of snow–flakes, that dazzled and confused the eye. What could be seen of the landscape appeared magically changed. He looked over the valley, and summed up the present and future in two words—"Snowed in!"

A careful inventory of the provisions, which, fortunately for the party, had been stored within the hut, and so escaped the felonious fingers of Uncle Billy, disclosed the fact that with care and prudence they might last ten days longer. "That is," said Mr. Oakhurst, *sotto voce* to The Innocent, "if you're willing to board us. If you aint—and perhaps you'd better not—you can wait till Uncle Billy gets back with provisions." For some occult reason, Mr.

Oakhurst could not bring himself to disclose Uncle Billy's rascality, and so offered the hypothesis that he had wandered from the camp and had accidentally stampeded the animals. He dropped a warning to the Duchess and Mother Shipton, who of course knew the facts of their associate's defection. "They'll find out the truth about us all, when they find out anything," he added, significantly, "and there's no good frightening them now."

Tom Simson not only put all his worldly store at the disposal of Mr. Oakhurst, but seemed to enjoy the prospect of their enforced seclusion. "We'll have a good camp for a week, and then the snow'll melt, and we'll all go back together." The cheerful gayety of the young man and Mr. Oakhurst's calm infected the others. The Innocent, with the aid of pine boughs, extemporized a thatch for the roofless cabin, and the Duchess directed Piney in the rearrangement of the interior with a taste and tact that opened the blue eyes of that provincial maiden to their fullest extent. "I reckon now you're used to fine things at Poker Flat," said Piney. The Duchess turned away sharply to conceal something that reddened her cheeks through its professional tint, and Mother Shipton requested Piney not to "chatter." But when Mr. Oakhurst returned from a weary search for the trail, he heard the sound of happy laughter echoed from the rocks. He stopped in some alarm, and his thoughts first naturally reverted to the whiskey—which he had prudently *cachéd*. "And yet it don't somehow sound like whiskey," said the gambler. It was not until he caught sight of the blazing fire through the still blinding storm, and the group around it, that he settled to the conviction that it was "square fun."

Whether Mr. Oakhurst had *cachéd* his cards with the whiskey as something debarred the free access of the community, I cannot say. It was certain that, in Mother Shipton's words, he "didn't say cards once" during that evening. Haply the time was beguiled by an accordeon, produced somewhat ostentatiously by Tom Simson, from his pack. Notwithstanding some difficulties attending the manipulation of this instrument, Piney Woods managed to pluck several reluctant melodies from its keys, to an accompaniment by The Innocent on a pair of bone castinets. But the crowning festivity of the evening was reached in a rude camp-meeting hymn, which the lovers, joining hands, sang with great earnestness and vociferation. I fear that a certain defiant tone and Covenanter's swing to its chorus, rather than any devotional quality, caused it to speedily infect the others, who at last joined in the refrain:

"I'm proud to live in the service of the Lord,
And I'm bound to die in His army."

The pines rocked, the storm eddied and whirled above the miserable group, and the flames of their altar leaped heavenward, as if in token of the vow.

At midnight the storm abated, the rolling clouds parted, and the stars glittered keenly above the sleeping camp. Mr. Oakhurst, whose professional habits had enabled him to live on the smallest possible amount of sleep, in dividing the watch with Tom Simson, somehow managed to take upon himself the greater part of that duty. He excused himself to The Innocent, by saying that he had "often been a week without sleep." "Doing what?" asked Tom. "Poker!" replied Oakhurst, sententiously; "when a man gets a streak of luck—nigger-luck—he don't get tired. The luck gives in first. Luck," continued the gambler, reflectively, "is a mighty queer thing. All you know about it for certain is that it's bound to change. And it's finding out when it's going to change that makes you. We've had a streak of bad luck since we left Poker Flat—you come along and slap you get into it, too. If you can hold your cards right along you're all right. For," added the gambler, with cheerful irrelevance,

"I'm proud to live in the service of the Lord,
And I'm bound to die in His army."

The third day came, and the sun, looking through the white-curtained valley, saw the outcasts divide their slowly decreasing store of provisions for the morning meal. It was one of the peculiarities of that mountain climate that its rays diffused a kindly warmth over the wintry landscape, as if in regretful commiseration of the past. But it revealed drift on drift of snow piled high around the hut; a hopeless, uncharted, trackless sea of white lying below the rocky shores to which the castaways still clung. Through the marvellously clear air, the smoke of the pastoral village of Poker Flat rose miles away. Mother Shipton saw it, and from a remote pinnacle of her rocky fastness, hurled in that direction a final malediction. It was her last vituperative attempt, and perhaps for that reason was invested with a certain degree of sublimity. It did her good, she privately informed the Duchess. "Just you go out there and cuss, and see." She then set herself to the task of amusing "the child," as she and the Duchess were pleased to call Piney. Piney was no chicken, but it was a soothing and ingenious theory of the pair to thus account for the fact that she didn't swear and wasn't improper.

When night crept up again through the gorges, the reedy notes of the accordeon rose and fell in fitful spasms and long-drawn gasps by the flickering camp-fire. But music failed to fill entirely the aching void left by insufficient food, and a new diversion was proposed by Piney—story-telling. Neither Mr. Oakhurst nor his female companions caring to relate their personal experiences, this plan would have failed, too, but for The Innocent. Some months before he had chanced upon a stray copy of Mr. Pope's ingenious translation of the Iliad. He now proposed to narrate the principal incidents of that poem having thoroughly mastered the argument and fairly forgotten the words—in the current vernacular of Sandy Bar. And so for the rest of that night the Homeric demi-gods again walked the earth. Trojan bully and wily Greek wrestled in the winds, and the great pines in the cañon seemed to bow to the wrath of the son of Peleus. Mr. Oakhurst listened with quiet satisfaction. Most especially was he interested in the fate of "Ash-heels," as The Innocent persisted in denominating the "swift-footed Achilles."

So with small food and much of Homer and the accordeon, a week passed over the heads of the outcasts. The sun again forsook them, and again from leaden skies the snow-flakes were sifted over the land. Day by day closer around them drew the snowy circle, until at last they looked from their prison over drifted walls of dazzling white, that towered twenty feet above their heads. It became more and more difficult to replenish their fires, even from the fallen trees beside them, now half-hidden in the drifts. And yet no one complained. The lovers turned from the dreary prospect and looked into each other's eyes, and were happy. Mr. Oakhurst settled himself coolly to the losing game before him. The Duchess, more cheerful than she had been, assumed the care of Piney. Only Mother Shipton—once the strongest of the party—seemed to sicken and fade. At midnight on the tenth day she called Oakhurst to her side. "I'm going," she said, in a voice of querulous weakness, "but don't say anything about it. Don't waken the kids. Take the bundle from under my head and open it." Mr. Oakhurst did so. It contained Mother Shipton's rations for the last week, untouched. "Give 'em to the child," she said, pointing to the sleeping Piney. "You've starved yourself," said the gambler. "That's what they call it," said the woman querulously, as she lay down again, and turning her face to the wall, passed quietly away.

The accordeon and the bones were put aside that day, and Homer was forgotten. When the body of Mother Shipton had been committed to the snow, Mr. Oakhurst took The Innocent aside, and showed him a pair of snow-shoes, which he had fashioned from the old pack-saddle. "There's one chance in a hundred to save her yet," he said, pointing to Piney; "but it's there," he added, pointing toward Poker Flat. "If you can reach there in two days she's safe." "And you?" asked Tom Simson. "I'll stay here," was the curt reply.

The lovers parted with a long embrace. "You are not going, too," said the Duchess, as she saw Mr. Oakhurst apparently waiting to accompany him. "As far as the cañon," he replied. He turned suddenly, and kissed the Duchess, leaving her pallid face aflame, and her trembling limbs rigid with amazement.

Night came, but not Mr. Oakhurst. It brought the storm again and the whirling snow. Then the Duchess, feeding the fire, found that some one had quietly piled beside the hut enough fuel to last a few days longer. The tears rose to her eyes, but she hid them from Piney.

The women slept but little. In the morning, looking into each other's faces, they read their fate. Neither spoke; but Piney, accepting the position of the stronger, drew near and placed her arm around the Duchess's waist. They kept this attitude for the rest of the day. That night the storm reached its greatest fury, and rending asunder the protecting pines, invaded the very hut.

Toward morning they found themselves unable to feed the fire, which gradually died away. As the embers slowly blackened, the Duchess crept closer to Piney, and broke the silence of many hours: "Piney, can you pray?" "No, dear," said Piney, simply. The Duchess, without knowing exactly why, felt relieved, and putting her head upon Piney's shoulder, spoke no more. And so reclining, the younger and purer pillowing the head of her soiled sister upon her virgin breast, they fell asleep.

The wind lulled as if it feared to waken them. Feathery drifts of snow, shaken from the long pine boughs, flew like white-winged birds, and settled about them as they slept. The moon through the rifted clouds looked down upon what had been the camp. But all human stain, all trace of earthly travail, was hidden beneath the spotless mantle mercifully flung from above.

They slept all that day and the next, nor did they waken when voices and footsteps broke the silence of the camp. And when pitying fingers brushed the snow from their wan faces, you could scarcely have told from the equal peace that dwelt upon them, which was she that had sinned. Even the Law of Poker Flat recognized this, and turned away, leaving them still locked in each other's arms.

But at the head of the gulch, on one of the largest pine trees, they found the deuce of clubs pinned to the bark with a bowie knife. It bore the following, written in pencil, in a firm hand:

BENEATH THIS TREE
LIES THE BODY
OF
JOHN OAKHURST,
WHO STRUCK A STREAK OF BAD LUCK
ON THE 23D OF NOVEMBER, 1850,
AND
HANDED IN HIS CHECKS
ON THE 7TH DECEMBER, 1850

And pulseless and cold, with a Derringer by his side and a bullet in his heart, though still calm as in life, beneath the snow, lay he who was at once the strongest and yet the weakest of the outcasts of Poker Flat.

Discussion Questions

1. Explain how human nature is depicted in the story.
2. Explain how Harte uses stereotypes to characterize his "outcasts."
3. Considering each type, to what extent does each character remain a stereo-type, and to what extent does he or she behave outside of expectations?
4. Analyze Oakhurst's possible motives in staying with the group and in ending his own life.
5. Compare and contrast Harte's characters with those stereotypes developed in *Stagecoach*.

◆ ◆ ◆

FOCUS ON FILM: JOHN FORD'S *STAGECOACH* (1939)

Before viewing the film, consider question 1 and take notes about character stereotypes while viewing. The subsequent questions may be answered to prepare for class discussion or a subsequent essay assignment and to build a critical groundwork for later readings and film viewings.

1. Describe the stereotypes that are conventional to the Western film, based on this example.
2. How important is the romantic subplot to the main story line?
3. Describe the Western hero/heroine's relationship to the law.
4. Does the narrative usually present a "man's story"? How so?
5. Is character development usually very sketchy or unrealistic for the supporting characters? Is character development lacking in any of the major characters?
6. To what extent is morality portrayed in black-and-white extremes? Give examples.
7. Considering the opening and closing scenes of the film, does a cyclical structure or narrative pattern connect these scenes? If so, describe a thematic purpose for this structure.

TOPICS FOR RESEARCH AND WRITING

1. Compare and contrast the major characterizations in *Stagecoach* with those in "The Outcasts of Poker Flat." Especially, contrast the portraits of the two gamblers, the two drunkards, The Duchess vs. Dallas, and Piney vs. Mrs. Mallory. In your conclusion, reach some generalization about these contrasts.

2. Compare and contrast the theme of social criticism in "The Outcasts of Poker Flat" and *Stagecoach*. Which narrative seems more earnest in its criticism? Is the satire on "civilized" morality mitigated or softened by sentimentality, humor, or the outcome of the story? Consider the difference in the times the stories were produced (1869 vs. 1939). Does that difference in the social context have an impact on the severity of the satire?

3. Define the character of Meriwether Lewis as he represents himself in the three passages from the *Journals*. Consider physical and psychological traits, but also speculate on his moral character insofar as you find suggestions from the evidence presented and the concerns he expresses.

4. To prepare for writing critically about a film, first read the Appendix, "How to Watch a Film" (pages 471–79). Then read Ernest Haycox's "The Stage to Lordsburg" in *By Rope and Lead* (Boston: Little, Brown, 1951), pages 3–21. Compare and contrast the story with its film adaptation in *Stagecoach*, considering both what the film version *leaves out* in comparison to the story and what the film version *adds* that the story does not even mention. Try to explain *why* these changes were made and evaluate their effect on the film. Avoid obvious contrasts of the reading versus the viewing experience.

5. Read pages 274–75 and 284–86 from Thomas Schatz's "The Western" in Chapter 5. First, *summarize* his interpretation of *Stagecoach* and then *evaluate* his interpretation, agreeing or disagreeing with his main points and arguing what he explains well or fails to explain well.

6. Read pages 20–22 from Michael Coyne's "Mirror for Prewar America: *Stagecoach* and the Western, 1939–1941," in *The Crowded Prairie: American National Identity in the Hollywood Western* (London: Tauris, 1997). First, *summarize* his interpretation of the film and then *evaluate* his interpretation, agreeing or disagreeing with his main points and arguing what he explains well or fails to explain well.

7. If you have read Louis L'Amour's *The Daybreakers*, compare Turner's and de Crèvecouer's views of the frontier with Tye's remarks about the potential of the West and the role of the Indians.

8. If you have read Owen Wister's *The Virginian*, compare and contrast the theme of justice as depicted in the characters of the Virginian in this novel and of Ringo in *Stagecoach*. Consider Ringo's "outlaw" status, his revenge motive, and the role of the sheriff. Likewise, consider the Virginian's role in vigilante justice.

9. Read Frank Popper's "The Strange Case of the Contemporary American Frontier" (*The Yale Review* 27 [Autumn 1986]:103–21). Then, compare and contrast his viewpoint to Turner's original thesis. Explain how Popper helps students of the American Western to understand the continued impact of setting on the Western character.

10. If you have read Jack Schaefer's *Shane*, analyze the struggle between the land baron cattleman and the family farmers as a "survival of the fittest" or the success of the strong. Compare this analysis of struggle between people in frontier society to your analysis of this struggle as portrayed in one selection from this chapter.

CHAPTER

2

———— ‹◆› ————

CROSSING FRONTIERS

INTRODUCTION

Contrary to European perceptions, the Native Americans of the West represented many different cultures with different goals, levels of organization, and modes of living. Most groups did share the ideals of community cooperation and did believe themselves to be intimately connected to the land, rather than competing individually to possess or control property. Beyond this basic similarity, different Indian groups followed their own traditional practices, but adapted to their environments as they changed through drought, declining resources, or contact with other native groups or newly arrived Europeans (Iverson). A brief survey of representative tribes in three geographical regions reveals Native American diversity and strategies of adaptation.

The Tlingit people are representative of the Pacific Northwest coastal Indians, even though they have lived in lands that now form parts of Alaska and Western Canada. Indeed, we can consider Alaska in the story of the West since its history repeated the same exploitation of natural resources and native peoples that characterized the lower forty-eight states (Wyatt). In their original villages, the Tlingits followed a seasonal cycle of hunting and fishing informed by religious rites, gratitude toward their prey, thorough knowledge of animal behavior, and strategic cooperation in the hunt. Until the mid-nineteenth century, their contact with whites was largely beneficial in expanding their economy, through trading fish and pelts, and in improving their already refined carving skills and designs through the introduction of metal tools. Even the destructive effects of European diseases—wiping out as many as half the members of a village—were mitigated by large tribal populations, which could recover from an epidemic within a few years (Iverson).

Among the northern Plains Indians, the Cheyennes, for example, migrated from the upper Midwest, where they were hunters and farmers. In the eighteenth century they followed the buffalo west. By the early nineteenth century they began to transform their culture as they acquired horses and guns, which made hunting more effective, enlarged the range of hunting lands, increased their mobility, and stimulated greater competition with other tribes for natural resources, leading not only to conflict but to compromise (Iverson). Moreover, "a new horse and hide trade dramatically intensified the work of the Plains Indian women, who spent more and more time processing the hides," resulting in a narrowing of roles which they could perform within the tribe (Jameson and Armitage 83). However, the greatest challenge to their culture, due to more aggressive hunting practices made possible by the new technologies, was the potential increase in individual efforts and family acquisitiveness, as opposed to group cooperation. But the Cheyennes have sustained their traditions, due in part to their ideals of generosity and reciprocity (Iverson).

The Native American presence in the Southwest was more complex and can be best represented by three different native groups. The Acoma Pueblos had been most affected by Spanish colonization, noted for bloody cruelty beginning with Coronado in 1540. However, many Pueblo communities assisted the Spanish in repelling Navajo and Apache raiding parties. Nonetheless, the great Acoma revolt of 1680 was overturned twelve years later by brutal Spanish suppression, so by the end of the seventeenth century the Pueblo populations were reduced by warfare and disease from an estimated 50,000 to 16,000 (Jameson and Armitage 83). But by the early eighteenth century an uneasy tolerance developed. Many Pueblos converted to Catholicism, but continued to practice traditional native ceremonies as well. By contrast, the Hopi peoples repelled the overtures of Spanish priests and the attacks of soldiers throughout the eighteenth century and gained a greater sense of community by uniting against the outsiders. The Navajos, hunters who migrated to the Southwest in about the fourteenth century, gradually learned from neighboring tribes to farm and eventually adopted Spanish livestock—horses, sheep, cattle, and goats. The Navajos also incorporated their new agrarian lifestyle into their elaborate religious ceremonies by adopting corn as a primary image of fertility. Having settled in an area remote from Spanish outposts, the Navajos did not initially come into conflict with these Europeans; in fact, they benefited from the revolt of 1680, after which many Pueblos fled the Spanish oppression and joined Navajo communities. Their culture was invigorated not only by expanding clans and trade, but also by the Pueblos' contributions to the art of weaving. During the eighteenth century, the Navajos increased their wealth and independence through trade, war, and raiding parties. Both the Navajos and the Hopis represent native groups who persisted and found continuity amid change (Iverson).

However, the change in Euro-American migration became an onslaught in early to mid-nineteenth-century America. The "opening" of the trans-Mississippi West occurred at an unprecedented rate, and the mountain men, responsible for much of the white exploration of the wilderness, witnessed, within their lifetimes, the destruction of the wildness they loved. Trapper Jim Bridger was the first to penetrate the intermountain West and "discover" the Great Salt Lake in 1825. Two years later, Jedediah Smith was the first Anglo-American to cross the Sierra Mountains into California. John Jacob Astor extended the trapping territory for his American Fur Company by agreements with the Blackfeet in 1830, but in 1837 the trappers held the last great rendezvous on Wyoming's Green River. The stimulus for the trade—the demand for as many as 100,000 beaver pelts a year to be made into fine headwear—ended when fashion turned to silk hats (Lewis).

The "Oregon Trail" was popularized in 1842, though it was really a crude, confusing maze of routes that could easily dead-end in a box canyon or at a mountain cliff. Still, lucky and persistent emigrants stumbled for six months over their two-thousand-mile paths from Independence, Missouri, toward the lush valleys of the Pacific Northwest and California. In the Southwest, Mexico revolted from Spain in 1820, opening up the lucrative Santa Fe trade with Missouri, and then Texans revolted from Mexico, becoming independent in 1836 and gaining statehood in 1845. The Mexican-American War (1846–1848) assured the gain of even greater territory for U.S. development, and the gold rush brought thousands of fevered miners and ruthless entrepreneurs to California, which gained statehood in 1850. All over the West, it was a time of seemingly infinite possibilities, heartless disappointments, treacherous journeys, and back-breaking labors.

Those journeys were often achieved only through beneficent contact with Native American peoples. In the tradition of the Mandan and Shoshone tribes, who aided Lewis and Clark, Indians along the Overland

Trail often helped migrants by bartering for food or assistance with river crossings. Despite white paranoia over Indian massacres, by 1860 only 362 Euro-Americans had been killed by natives out of more than 250,000 migrants on the Trail. By contrast, Indian killings numbered 426 by 1860 (Unruh). More significantly, under the guise of humanitarian concerns for the preservation and assimilation of Native Americans, federal policies served to starve and drive them from ancestral homes. By the second half of the nineteenth century, the Indian Removal Act (1830) and the Dawes Act (1887) had effectively appropriated, for white settlement, fully two-thirds of the lands granted by treaties to the Indians (Limerick). Such policies reinforced a popular pattern of illegal expropriation: settlers first broke treaties and massacred unarmed Indian elders, women, and children in their camps; Indian warriors retaliated; and then whites claimed victimization by Indians as the excuse for stealing Native American lands.

The stories told about the period of initial contact have been based in historical events, no doubt. But in the West facts have always been commingled with myths. Even before American independence, the frontier experience was dramatized by Daniel Boone, whose 1775 crossing through the Cumberland Gap in the Alleghenies and settling of the bluegrass country of Kentucky sparked the imaginations of other pioneers and urban readers alike. Not always representing a promise of real frontier achievements, the Boone stories became a metaphor for the boundless possibilities in the American character. Likewise, the first great literature of the West—the five *Leatherstocking Tales* by James Fenimore Cooper—created a heroic type in the backwoodsman Natty Bumppo, who was at once a rugged individualist, a humane sympathizer with Indian values, and an inevitable tool for "progress." In the order of the narrative, *The Deerslayer* (1841), *The Last of the Mohicans* (1826), *The Pathfinder* (1840), *The Pioneers* (1823), and *The Prairie* (1827) developed the complex conflict between frontier freedoms and civilized constraints while evoking a romantic portrait of the Native American as a "noble savage" fated for extinction. For later authors who exploited the frontier as a scene of narrative and symbolic conflict, Cooper's work—though biased by racial and class prejudice—was the implicit foundation for their characterizations and thematic concerns.

Their stories have most often been told from the perspectives of male American settlers, assuming a movement into empty space, ignoring the multiple viewpoints of different Native American tribes, the French and the Spanish who preceded the Americans, the Africans who came as slaves, the Asians who came as coolies, and the ethnic minorities and women among the settlers. Moreover, these stories reflect a belief that "the dominant motive for moving West was improvement and opportunity, not injury to others" (Limerick 36), so Western migrants, in forging ahead for empire, always assumed a cloak of virtue and innocence. Whether the quest was for land, gold, or Indian souls to be Christianized, Americans entered their journeys with optimistic expectations and realistic acceptance of struggle. Thus, "episodes of frustration and defeat seemed inexplicable, undeserved, and arbitrary. . . . When nature or natives interrupted the progression from risk to reward, the Westerner felt aggrieved" (Limerick 42). This attitude led to blaming the government for any setbacks in their ambitions, so a tradition of relying on federal intervention and relief actually began in the nineteenth century—belying the pioneers' faith in self-reliance and individual enterprise. For the reader of Western stories, whether in history or fiction, it is helpful to keep these attitudes and realities in mind as we assess the mythic portraits of the early pioneers, especially in their encounters with Native Americans.

Iverson, Peter. "Native Peoples and Native Histories." *The Oxford History of the American West.* Ed. Clyde A. Milner II, Carol A. O'Connor, and Martha A. Sandweiss. New York: Oxford University, 1994. 12–43.

Jameson, Elizabeth, and Susan Armitage, ed. *Writing the Range: Race, Class, and Culture in the Women's West.* Norman, OK: University of Oklahoma, 1997.

Lewis, Jon E. *The Mammoth Book of the West.* New York: Carroll & Graf, 1996.

Limerick, Patricia Nelson. *The Legacy of Conquest: The Unbroken Past of the American West.* New York: Norton, 1987.

Unruh, John D., Jr. *The Plains Across: The Overland Emigrants and the Trans-Mississippi West, 1840–1860.* Urbana, IL: University of Illinois, 1979.

Wyatt, Victoria. "Alaska and Hawaii." *The Oxford History of the American West.* Ed. Clyde A. Milner II, Carol A. O'Connor, and Martha A. Sandweiss. New York: Oxford University, 1994. 562–601.

Fig. 2.1 George Catlin, *Buffalo Bull's Backfat, Head Chief, Blood Tribe* (1832). Smithsonian American Art Museum; gift of Mrs. Joseph Harrison, Jr.; 1985.66.149.

LEWIS HECTOR GARRARD
(1829–1887)

Garrard's significant literary output was the single volume *Wah-to-Yah and the Taos Trail* (1850). At seventeen, he had the adventure of his life. At twenty-one, he published his Western book. At twenty-four, he became a doctor, eventually settling in Minnesota territory in relative obscurity (Bieber). Nonetheless, he was briefly something of a frontiersman.

Born in Cincinnati, Garrard was a wanderer from the age of seventeen, when he took an extended vacation in Texas and Louisiana, riding horses on the plains and shooting alligators and ducks in the swamps. Upon his return, after reading the Rocky Mountain expeditions of John Charles Fremont (1813–1890), he persuaded his parents to fund a mountain adventure—in part as therapy for his sickly constitution.

In July 1846, he took a steamer down the Ohio and up the Mississippi to St. Louis, where he arranged to join a trade caravan led by Ceran St. Vrain of Bent, St. Vrain and Company, which extracted beaver and other pelts from Rocky Mountain streams and traded extensively with Native American tribes (Cheyenne, Comanche, Ute, Arapaho, Arikara, Kiowa, Pawnee, and Sioux) for buffalo robes and horses. The trading company also brought city merchandise to Western settlements as far as Santa Fe. In September, at the western Missouri border, Garrard joined the wagons, which crawled along the Santa Fe Trail at an average daily rate of ten or eleven miles. Three weeks later he reached Bent's Fort on the Arkansas River in what is now western Kansas, and he stayed in this region until the end of January 1847. But he was not idle, traveling with William Bent on his trading missions, living in the Cheyenne villages, and adopting the Western frontier costume of choice—the fringed buckskin suit and moccasins. He took to the prairie life enthusiastically and enjoyed sleeping in tepees, smoking with the Indian chiefs, eating dog stew, learning some of the Cheyenne lingo, and singing in the scalp dance (Bieber 19–25).

One dramatic event of the Mexican-American War shook Garrard from this idyllic existence. On January 19, 1847, Pueblo Indians and Mexicans in Taos revolted against American rule and killed twenty U.S. citizens, including William's brother, Charles Bent, the appointed governor of New Mexico Territory. This act so enraged the Bent's Fort population that they instantly formed a volunteer militia to seek vengeance. Garrard joined the volunteers, but they could not arrive in Taos until April, just in time to witness the frontier court and the hanging of the rebels. Back at Bent's Fort in May, he resolved to return home. However, upon reaching Fort Mann, a new government wagon repair depot at the Arkansas River crossing of the Santa Fe Trail, Garrard arranged to stay on for about a month, hoping for the "excitement" of "an Indian fight." He didn't see any action, though perhaps the real threat and fear of attack was thrilling enough for his imagination. When he finally headed back east to Ohio in June 1847, he had spent about ten months on the Western frontier. This, then, was the basis for his account in *Wah-to-Yah*, which he labored over for two years between intermittent bouts of intense chills and fevers (Bieber 25–37).

Because he wrote only one book about the West, Garrard's reputation has never matched that of Francis Parkman, whose *The California and Oregon Trail* (1849) was followed by several substantial volumes of history. Nonetheless, according to A. B. Guthrie, Garrard's work is superior in some ways: it is more vigorous and fresh, less literary and labored. Of course, Parkman's style became less engaging and personal as he revised his notebooks for publication in book form (Taylor 96). The greatest contrast is seen in Garrard's warm tone and concrete realism, which makes his book more accessible to readers. He seems to genuinely like his companions, though the traders, mountain men, and Cheyennes may have been rude, uncouth, and ignorant of European education. He enjoyed their fireside yarns and colorful backwoods lingo, and his reproach of Indian savagery and lack of civilization springs more from convention than earnest censure. On the other hand, Parkman's tone is critical; he seems to like few of the people he observed and judged them by Boston standards (Guthrie).

The text of "The Village," Chapter 3 from Garrard's *Wah-to-Yah and the Taos Trail*, is from the reprint (Norman, OK: University of Oklahoma Press, 1955), pages 45–57.

Bieber, Ralph. "Editor's Introduction." *Wah-to-Yah and the Taos Trail* by Lewis H. Garrard. Philadelphia: Porcupine Press, 1974 [1938]. 19–43.

Guthrie, A. B. "Introduction." *Wah-to-Yah and the Taos Trail: Or, Prairie Travel and Scalp Dances, with a Look at Los Rancheros from Muleback and the Rocky Mountain Campfire.* Norman, OK: University of Oklahoma Press, 1955 [1850]. ix–xvi.

Taylor, J. Golden. "Across the Wide Missouri: The Adventure Narrative from Lewis and Clark to Powell." *A Literary History of the American West.* Ed. Thomas J. Lyon, et al. Fort Worth, TX: Texas Christian University Press and The Western Literature Association, 1987. 71–103.

THE VILLAGE

FROM *WAH-TO-YAH AND THE TAOS TRAIL*

<(◆)>

I t is Indian rule that the first lodge a stranger enters on visiting a village is his home during his stay—whether invited or not, it is all the same—and, as we wished to be at the "Lean Chief's," we inquired for him. Without saying a word or going in the lodge first, we unsaddled in front of it, putting our "possibles" in the back part, the most honored and pleasant place, for there is no passing by or other annoyance.

The owner occupies the back of the lodge, which is given up for a guest; and the Lean Chief's squaw and daughters removed his robes, etc., to one side. The women and children crowded around us while unsaddling; the strange dress and appearance of the boys attracted my attention; which latter, from their infancy to the age of six and seven, go without a particle of clothing, *dans costume à l'Adam*—a string of beads around the neck. The girls are clothed from the earliest hour.

The white man is always welcome with the Cheyenne, as he generally has *mok-ta-bo-mah-pe*—coffee. We went in the lodge; the grave-looking head, *Vip-po-nah*, or the Lean Chief, and his two solemn coadjutors shook hands with us, with the salutation of, "*Hook-ah-hay! num-whit!*"—equivalent to "*Welcome, how do you do*"; and then they relapsed into silence. Water was handed us to drink, as they suppose a traveler must be thirsty after riding; then meat was set before us, as they think a tired man needs refreshment. When we had finished, the pipe was passed around, during which soothing pastime the news were asked.

There is much to admire in this praiseworthy forbearance; and, although the Indians are as curious as any people, yet, through their consideration, the cravings of hunger and thirst are first satisfied; then, under the communicative influence of the long pipe, the topics of the season are discussed.

A lodge, generally, is composed of seventeen or more slender poles of pine, three inches in diameter at the butts, finely tapering to the small ends, and eighteen to twenty-three or four feet in length. These poles are tied together a few inches from the small ends, with the butts resting on the ground, so that the frame resembles a cone, over which a covering of buffalo skin is neatly fitted, divested of hair and rendered pliant by means of the *dubber*—an adze-shaped piece of iron fitted to an angular section of elk's horn—which chips off pieces of the hard skin until it is reduced to the requisite thinness. Brains are then rubbed on it, making it still softer. The skins are then cut and sewed together with awl and sinew, so that they fit neatly the pole frame. By rolling up the lower edge of this covering, it makes a commodious, airy habitation in summer, and, by closing all the apertures, a warm shelter in winter. At the apex an opening is left, through which the ends of the poles protrude and by which the smoke finds its way out. The fire is built in the center; and, to prevent the smoke being driven back by the wind, there are two flaps or continuations of the upper skins, with poles attached on the outside. These flaps they shut, shift, or extend, as occasion requires.

We made known our business, and immediately a "crier" was sent out. Throwing back the skin-door of the lodge, he protruded his head and then his whole body, and uttered in a stentorian voice something similar to the following, "*Hibbolo, hibbolo! Po-ome, ho-o-o, nah wah-he, se-ne-mone, hah tah-ti-ve woh-pshe-o-nun, nah mod-ta-bo woh-pshe-o-nun, nah who-pi woh-pshe-o-nun, nah mo-tah-ke, nah o-ne-ah-wokst*"; meaning, in regular succession, that "Blackfoot [Smith] had come for mules; and all who wished, to come and trade; that we had tobacco, blue blankets, black [deep blue] blankets, white blankets, knives, and beads."

It is contrary to Indian medicine or religion, to pass between the landlord (owner of the lodge) and the fire, for, they say, it dissolves friendship, and any infringement of this custom is looked upon with displeasure.

We were very comfortably situated; the lodge was large enough to admit our lying with feet to the fire—made true Indian fashion in a small space, and heaped continually in a rounding, compact form. As the night waned apace, we were visited by the prominent men; who, in a dignified manner, shook hands with us, and sat with crossed legs, propounding questions: *ad interim*, passing the pipe. As each Indian appeared at the lodge entrance, "*Hook-ah-hay*" or "*hum-whit*" (the mode of congratulation) escaped his lips; to which a like response was given by the land-lord or us.

We sat in our places at the back part, and the Indians, according to rank, took seats to our left, on mother earth or their own robes. To the right was our host; and, if a man entitled to notice by right of seniority or daring deeds of valor entered, those inferior in honors gave place next the white man (us). Sometimes Indians of equal rank were in the lodge at the same time, and then a *sotto voce* dispute as to the "upper seat" would be carried on with much gesticulatory motion.

Their dusky faces, viewed by the yellow blaze, together with the unintelligible jargon, filled me with new and strange thoughts; and, when the old crones swung the seething black pot of meat from the fire of dried sticks, I could not but think of the gipsy tribes, who possess many traits resembling theirs, and who, in common with them, have an unconquerable love for roaming. . . .

Early in the morning we sat around the fire, waiting for the host's meat to cook, to which we contributed the coffee—the most important and rare addition.

The Indians talked of moving to the "Big Timber," a few miles above, and soon the village was in commotion, the young men driving up their different bands of horses, the squaws catching them. Some took down the lodges, and tying the poles in two bundles, fastened them on either side of a mule or horse, like the shafts of a dray—the lower ends dragging the ground; and, behind the horse, a tray-shaped basket or hoop, latticed with hide thongs, was tied on these poles, in which were put the children too young to ride alone, and other things not easily carried on a horse. Some of the mules were saddled, and on each side were slung square bags, of thick buffalo hide divested of hair, in which stone hammers, dubbers, wooden bowls, horn spoons, etc., were thrown.

The skin of which these convenient hampers are made is called *par fleche*—a French term Anglicised, as are many other foreign words in the mountains, by general usage. Its literal meaning is, "*arrow fender*," or "*warder*"; for, from it, the prairie Indians construct their almost impenetrable shields. Moccasin soles is the principal use, for which purpose it is admirably suited, it being pliant to the foot, while it serves as a protection from the cactus growing so prolifically in this country. Without care, one in walking will stumble over these, and the long, slender thorns, penetrating with ease, cause an acute, stinging pain, worse even than nettles. Being without socks most of the time (and none to be had), often, while hunting, a hole would wear in the toe of my moccasin, and unavoidably, the thorns would stick most painfully. My "big toe" looked like a lady's finger punctured in sewing.

The village was, ere long, in motion. Looking back to the old site, we saw nothing but eighteen thin pillars of smoke finding their way to the upper air, marking where had been the lodges; pieces of old, cast-off robes, and the usual *debris* of a deserted Indian camp; which, with a few snarling coyotes and large gray wolves, were all the signs of life remaining of the noisy, bustling town. . . .

The animals with the lodgepole *travéés* jogged along, no care being taken of them, while the fat little inmates laughed, or, with "wond'ring eyes," stared at us silently.

The young squaws take much care of their dress and horse equipments; they dashed furiously past on wild steeds, astride of the high-pommeled saddles. A fancifully colored cover, worked with beads or porcupine quills, making a flashy, striking appearance, extended from wethers to rump of the horse, while the riders evinced an admirable daring, worthy of Amazons. Their dresses were made of buckskin, high at the neck, short sleeves, or rather none at all, fitting loosely, and reaching obliquely to the knee, giving a relieved, Diana look to the costume; the edges scalloped, worked with beads, and fringed. From the knee downward, the limb was encased in a tightly fitting leggin, terminating in a neat moccasin—both handsomely worked with beads. On the arms were bracelets of brass, which glittered and reflected in the radiant morning sun, adding much to their attractions. In their pierced ears, shells from the Pacific shore were pendant; and, to complete the picture of *savage* taste and profusion, their fine complexions were eclipsed by a coat of flaming vermillion.

Altogether it was a pleasing and desirable change from the sight of the pinched waists and constrained motions of the women of the States, to see these daughters of the prairie dressed loosely—free to act, unconfined by the ligatures of fashion; but I do not wish to be understood that I prefer seeing our women dressed *à la Cheyenne*, as it is a costume forbidden by modesty, the ornaments gaudy and common and altogether unfit for a civilized woman to wear; but here, where novelty constitutes the charm, 'twas indeed a relief to the eye.

Many of the largest dogs were packed with a small quantity of meat, or something not easily injured. They looked queerly, trotting industriously under their burdens; and, judging from a small stock of canine physiological information, not a little of the wolf was in their composition. These dogs are extremely muscular, and are compactly built.

We crossed the river on our way to the new camp; the alarm manifested by the *ki-kun*—children—in the lodgepole drays, as they dipped in the water, was amusing; the little fellows, holding their breaths, not daring to cry, looked imploringly at their inexorable mothers, and were encouraged by words of aprobation from their stern fathers. Regaining the grassy bottom, we once more went in a fast walk.

The different-colored horses, the young Indian beaux, the bold, bewildering belles, and the newness of the scene was gratifying in the extreme, to my unaccustomed senses. After a ride of two hours, we stopped, and the chiefs, fastening their horses, collected in circles, to smoke the pipe and talk, letting their squaws unpack the animals, pitch the lodges, build fires, arrange the robes, and, when all was ready, these "lords of creation" dispersed to their several homes, to wait until their patient and enduring spouses prepared some food. I was provoked, nay, angry, to see the lazy, overgrown men do nothing to help their wives; and, when the young women pulled off their bracelets and finery to *chop wood*, the cup of my wrath was full to overflowing, and, in a fit of honest indignation, I pronounced them ungallant and savage in the true sense of the word. A wife here is, indeed, a helpmeet.

Once more ensconced in the back part of Vip-po-nah's lodge, we felt at home. A large wooden bowl of meat was set before us, to which, with coffee, we did ample justice.

The horses belonging to an Indian community are numerous; with us, there were nearly or quite two hundred, of different colors and sizes, scattered over the gentle hillsides in picturesque groups.

After two days' entertaining sojourn at the village, we left, with four fine mules, for the fort, which place we reached at the close of the second evening, where we found the employees reloading the wagons for a start to Santa Fé. I learned that Colonel Doniphan's regiment, with which I wished to travel, had left Santa Fé; and, being pleased with Indian life, I returned with Smith and William Bent, with full complements of goods for robe trading. We encamped the first night on an island in the river, with plenty of wood and grass near and sheltered by a patch of high weeds from the winds.

Crossing the clear stream on the firm sandy bottom, we regained the trace early in the morning, and, at night, after a continuous day's jog, we were at the village. William Bent stayed in his own lodge; Smith and I, in Vip-po-nah's, by whom we were welcomed.

The air was much cooler than before; quantities of thin ice floated down the gliding river current. It was right pleasant to get back and be surrounded by Indians.

In Vip-po-nah's lodge was his grandson, a boy of six or seven months old. Every morning, his mother washed him in cold water and sent him out to the air to make him hardy; he would come in, perfectly nude, from his airing, about half-frozen. How he would laugh and brighten up as he felt the warmth of the fire! Being a boy, the parents have great hopes of him as a brave and chief (the acme of Indian greatness); his father dotes upon him, holding him in his arms, singing in a low tone, and in various ways showing his extreme affection.

The girls do not receive much attention from the father; they are reared to implicit obedience, and with a feeling of inferiority to the males. What a happy contrast does the state of society show in enlightened countries, where woman is in her proper sphere, loved and looked up to as an adviser and friend—here, a mere "hewer of wood and drawer of water"—a nonenity, a mere cypher—treated as a slave and unnoticed. It is, indeed, an almost inappreciable blessing that we live in an age of progressive civilization—an age in which true worth is rewarded, irrespective of sex; though there yet is room for improvement.

Discussion Questions

1. Using four or five categories, classify the different kinds of details that seem to interest Garrard in his narrative.
2. Describe the tone or emotional attitude of Garrard's narrative.

Fig. 2.2 Karl Bodmer, *Bison Dance of the Mandan Indians in Front of Their Medicine Lodge* (1836), engraving with aquatint. Joslyn Art Museum; gift of the Enron Foundation (Tableau 18), Omaha, NE.

3. Relate several examples of positive traits he appreciates about the Cheyenne people he encounters. Relate several examples of criticisms he makes against these people. Describe his overall attitude about the Native Americans and their lifestyle.

4. Evaluate his consideration of gender issues among both whites and Cheyennes.

5. Compare Garrard's description of the Cheyenne Indians with Lewis's description of the Shoshone Indians in the second passage from the *Journals* excerpted in Chapter 1. Which viewpoint seems more unbiased and non-judgmental to you?

EDWARD ELLIS
(1840–1916)
AND THE DIME WESTERN

Something of a unique literary phenomenon, yet representative of the pulp fiction industry in the nineteenth century, Ellis became a prolific author beginning at the age of nineteen. Though he also worked as a New Jersey teacher, vice principal, textbook author, and newspaper columnist, he actually wrote fiction under 24 pseudonyms, completing 53 novels for Beadle's Dime Novel series and another 38 books for Beadle's Half Dime Library, as well as over 90 novels for Munro's Ten Cent Novels. *Seth Jones; or, the Captives of the Frontier* (1860), which sold over 450,000 copies in the first year of publication and earned him a mere $75, was the first in a long string of successfully mass-marketed and cheaply produced works (Brown 41–42, 165–66).

Actually, this success was due not merely to talent and the publisher's relentless advertising campaign, but also to widespread social and economic changes. In a time when the average working-class wage was only six dollars a week and standard cloth-covered books cost a dollar or more, the Beadle brothers offered their pulp novels for only a dime. Such a bargain was made possible by several technological improvements: new, inexpensive processes for producing paper from wood pulp, steam-powered presses, reusable printing plates, and more efficient methods of transportation. Likewise, the cultural sensibility about reading began to change from its tradition as family entertainment and moral improvement to a private amusement with sensational appeals. Books became something to consume while commuting to work, not always to be studied and pondered. Beadle Publishing was central to this shift—partly a cause and partly a response, in a complex relationship common to many striking changes in popular culture (Brown).

Even though *Seth Jones* is set in eighteenth-century New York, it tells a frontier story relevant to contemporary popular sentiment about the West. Certainly, Ellis drew from Cooper's *Leatherstocking Tales* and from the legendary figure of Daniel Boone to create his own Yankee woodsman character, Seth Jones. Nonetheless, the relevance of his captivity narrative had some historical immediacy that ensured a national interest in pioneer-Indian conflicts. After the Mexican-American War, the entire southwest was opened to exploitation and settlement. Spurred on by the gold rush of 1849, the California and Oregon Trails were becoming teeming pathways of pioneers (Brown 166–67). Contacts with Native Americans, initially peaceful and helpful, turned violent when thousands of settlers encroached on traditional hunting grounds and river campsites. Thus, satanizing the "Redskin" enemy led to the stereotypical characterizations of savages adopted from the seventeenth-century Puritan captivity narrative tradition. However, by 1860, the newer adventure story had lost much of its model's spiritual concern for personal salvation. Of course, Ellis wrote occasional passages to remind readers of that moral discourse, as at the beginning of Chapter XI: "I trust Heaven is aiding us"; but the practical pioneer response to that imploring tone is "Heaven will, if we help ourselves." Rather than describing the captive's spiritual conflict in a metaphorical landscape, Ellis employs evil heathens as villains to be vanquished, just as he repeats scenarios of capture-pursuit-rescue merely to sustain suspense and to produce drama. This novel established the narrative structure of "a regularized rhythm of crisis and resolution, event and explanation" (Brown 27) that became the dime Western formula.

In the following excerpts, the setting is about 1785 in the wilds of western New York, where pioneer Alfred Haverland has homesteaded. A band of Mohawks has kidnapped his beautiful sixteen-year-old daughter, Ina, and torched the family cabin. Hot in pursuit are Seth Jones, a Yankee dressed in frontier garb; Everard Graham, a handsome hunter and suitor to Ina; and Ned Haldidge, a family friend in the nearby white settlement who has provided shelter to the Haverlands. In the scene opening Chapter VII, Seth, who was spying on the Mohawks, has accidentally tumbled down a small hill from his hiding place.

The text of the three chapters from *Seth Jones* is from the Bill Brown edition of the novel cited just below, pages 198–202 and 206–15.

Brown, Bill. *Reading the West: An Anthology of Dime Westerns.* Boston: Bedford, 1997.

FROM *SETH JONES; OR, THE CAPTIVES OF THE FRONTIER*

CHAPTER VII. THE EXPERIENCE OF SETH

"By gracious! Stars and garters! &c.! &c.! This is a new way of introducing one's self!" exclaimed Seth, as he sprawled out among the savages around the council-fire.

The consternation of the Indians at his sudden apparition among them may well be imagined. The crackling of the undergrowth above had aroused them, yet the advent of Seth was so sudden and almost instantaneous that ere they could form a suspicion of the true nature of things, he was among them. Their habitual quickness of thought came to them at once. Graham was seen as he wheeled and fled, and as has been shown, a number sprung at once in pursuit, while a dozen leaped upon Seth, and as many tomahawks were raised.

"Now jest hold on," commanded Seth; "there ain't any need of being in a hurry. Plenty time to take my hair. Fact, by gracious."

His serio-comical manner arrested and amused his captors. They all paused and looked at him, as if expecting another outburst, while he contented himself with gazing at them with a look of scornful contempt. Seeing this, one sprung forward, and clenching his hair in a twist, hissed:

"Oh! cuss Yankee! we burn him!"

"If you know what's best, ole chap, you'll take yer paw off my head in a hurry. Ef you don't you mought find it rather convenient to."

The savage, as if to humor him, removed his hand and Seth's rifle, too. Seth gazed inquiringly at him a moment, and then, with an air of conscious superiority, said:

"I'll lend that to you awhile, provided you return it all right. Mind, you be keerful now, 'cause that ar' gun cost something down in New Hampshire."

From what has just been written, it will doubtless be suspected that Seth's conduct was a part which he was playing. When thrown into peril by the impatience of his companion, he saw at once that an attempt at flight was useless. Nothing was left but to submit to his misfortune with the best grace possible; and yet there was a way in which this submission could be effected which would result better for himself than otherwise. Had he offered resistance, or submitted despairingly, as many a man would have done, he would doubtless have been tomahawked instantly. So, with a readiness of thought which was astonishing, he assumed an air of reckless bravado. This, as we have shown, had the desired result thus far. How it succeeded after, will be seen in the remaining portion of this history.

Seth Jones was a man whose character could not be read in an hour, or day. It required a long companionship with him to discover the nicely-shaded points, and the characteristics which seemed in many cases so opposite. United with a genial, sportive humor and apparent frankness, he was yet far-seeing and cautious, and could read the motives of a man almost at a glance. With a countenance which seemed made expressly to vail his soul, his very looks were deceptive; and, when he chose to play a certain *role*, he could do it to perfection. Had any one seen him when the conversation above recorded took place, he would have unhesitatingly set him down as a natural-born idiot.

"How you like to burn, eh, Yankee?" asked a savage, stooping and grinning horribly in his face.

"I don't know; I never tried it," replied Seth, with as much *nonchalance* as though it was a dinner to which he was referring.

"E-e-e-e! you will try it, Yankee."

"Don't know yet; there are various opinions about that, p'raps. When the thing is did I mought believe it."

"You *sizzle* nice—nice meat—good for burn!" added another savage, grasping and feeling his arm.

"Just please do not pinch, my friend."

The savage closed his fingers like iron rods, and clenched the member till Seth thought it would be crushed. But, though the pain was excruciating, he manifested not the least feeling. The Indian tried again, and again, till he gave up and remarked, expressive of his admiration of the man's pluck:

"Good Yankee! stand pinch well."

"Oh! you wa'n't pinching me, was you? Sorry, I didn't know it. Try again, you mought p'raps do better."

The savage, however, retired, and another stepped forward and grasped the captive's hand.

"Soft, like squaw's hand—let me feel it," he remarked, shutting his own over it like a vise. Seth winced not in the least; but as the Indian in turn was about to relinquish his attempt at making sport for his comrades, Seth said:

"Your paws don't appear very horny," and closed over it with a terrific gripe. The savage stood like a martyr, till Seth felt the bones of his hand actually displacing, and yielding like an apple. He determined, as he had in reality suffered himself, to be revenged, and closed his fingers tighter and more rigid till the poor wretch sprung to his feet, and howled with pain!

"Oh! did I hurt you?" he asked, with apparent solicitude, as the savage's hand slid from his own with much the appearance of a wet glove. The discomfited Indian made no reply but retired amid the jeers of his comrades. Seth, without moving a muscle, seated himself deliberately upon the ground, and coolly asked a savage to lend him a pipe. It is known, that when an Indian sees such hardihood and power, as their captive had just evinced, he does not endeavor to conceal his admiration. Thus it was not strange that Seth's impudent request was complied with. One handed him a well-filled pipe, with a grin in which could be distinctly seen admiration, exultation, and anticipated revenge. From the looks of the others, it was plain they anticipated an immense deal of sport. Our present hero continued smoking, lazily watching the volumes of vapor, as they slowly rolled before and around him. His captors sat about him a moment, conversing in their own tongue (every word of which, we may remark, was perfectly understood by Seth), when one arose and stepped forward before him.

"White man strong; him pinch well, but me make him cry."

So saying he stooped, and removing the captive's cap, seized a long tuft of yellow hair which had its roots at the temple. A stab in the eye would not have caused an acuter twinge of pain; but, as he jerked it forth by the roots, Seth gave not the slightest indication save a stronger whiff at the pipe. The savages around did not suppress a murmur of admiration. Seeing no effect from this torture, the tormentor again stooped and caught another tuft that grew low upon the neck. Each single hair felt like the point of a needle thrust into the skin, and as it came forth, the Indians seated around noticed a livid paleness, like the track of a cloud, quickly flash over their captive's countenance. He looked up in his tormentor's eyes with an indescribable look. For a moment he fixed a gaze upon him, that, savage as he was, caused a strange shiver of dread to run through him.

To say that Seth cared nothing for these inflicted agonies would be absurd. Had the savage dreamed what a whirlwind of hate and revenge he had awakened by them he would not have attempted what he did. It was only by an almost unaccountable power that Seth controlled the horrible pains of both body and mind he suffered. He felt as though it was impossible to prevent himself from writhing on the ground in torment, and springing at his persecutor and tearing him limb from limb. But he had been schooled to Indian indignities, and bore them unflinchingly.

His temple had the appearance of white parchment, with innumerable bloody points in it, as the blood commenced oozing from the wound, and his neck seemed as though the skin had been scraped off! His momentary paleness had been caused by the sickening pain and the intensest passion. His look at the savage was *to remember him.* After the events which have just transpired they remained seated a moment in silence. At last one who appeared to be the leader, addressed, in an undertone, the Indian whom we have just seen retire from the post of tormentor. Seth, however, caught the words, and had he not, it is not probable he would have successfully undergone the last trying ordeal.

The same savage again stepped forward in the circle before the helpless captive, and removing the cap which had been replaced, clinched the long yellow locks in his left hand and threw the head backward. Then whipping out his scalping-knife, he flashed it around his head with the rapidity of lightning. The skin was not pierced, and it was only an artifice. Seth never took his eyes from the Indian during this awful minute.

The tormentor again retired. The savages were satisfied, but Seth was not. He handed his pipe back, replaced his cap, and rising to his feet, surveyed for a few seconds the group around. He then addressed the leader.

"Can the white man now try the red-man's courage?"

The voice sounded like another person's. Yet the chief noticed it not, and nodded assent to the request, while the looks of the others showed the eagerness and interest they felt in these dreadful proceedings.

The savage who had inflicted all this agony seated himself directly beside the chief. Seth stepped to him, and grasping his arm pressed moderately. The Indian gave a scornful grunt. Seth then stooped and gently took the tomahawk from his belt. He raised it slowly on high, bent down till his form was like the crouching panther ready to spring. The glittering blade was seen to flash as it circled through the air, and the next instant it crashed clean through the head of the unsuspecting savage!

* * *

CHAPTER IX. THE CHASE

The night was even closer at hand than our friends suspected. In the forest, where the withdrawal of the sun was almost simultaneous with darkness, it came without much warning. The gloom was already settling over the water, and Haverland instantly shot the canoe from under the shrubbery out into the stream. There were rowlocks and oars for a second person, and Graham took up a couple of them and joined his labors with his friend, while Haldidge took the steering-oar. As they passed boldly into the channel, the canoe ahead was just disappearing around a bend below.

"Come, this won't do; we mustn't let them keep out of our sight," said Haverland, dipping his oars deep into the water.

A heavy darkness was fast settling over the river, and our friends noted another thing. A thick, peculiar fog, or mist, such as is often seen of summer nights, upon a sheet of water, was already beginning to envelop the bank and river. This, as will be evident, while it would allow the pursuers to approach the Indian canoe much closer than otherwise, still gave the latter a much greater chance of eluding them. Haldidge hardly knew whether to be pleased with this or not.

"It may help us in the beginning, boys, but we've got to hold on till it's fairly down on us. If the rascals catch a glimpse of us before, they'll give us the slip as sure as fate. Just lay on your oars a few minutes. We can float down with the current."

"I allow it's the best plan, although I am much in favor of dashing ahead, and ending the matter at once," remarked Graham, nervously handling his oars.

"And while I think of it," pursued Haldidge, "I don't see as it would do any hurt to muffle the oars."

Before starting they had abundantly provided themselves with means for this, and in a few moments a quantity of cloth was forced into the rowlocks, so as to be able to give full sweep to the oars without making enough noise to attract suspicion from the shore, unless an ear was listening more intently than usual.

By this time, too, the thick mist mentioned had enveloped the river in an impenetrable cloud, and they shot boldly into it. The light vessel flew as swiftly and noiselessly as a bird over the water. Haldidge understood every turn and eddy in the stream, and guided the canoe with unerring certainty around the sharp bends, and by the rocks whose black heads now and then shot backward within a few feet of their side.

In this way a mile was passed, when he raised his hand as a signal for them to cease efforts for a moment.

"Listen!" he uttered.

All did so, and faintly, yet distinctly and distantly, they heard the almost inaudible dip of oars, and the click of the rowlocks.

"Is that above or below?" asked Haverland, bending his head and intently listening.

"I think we have *passed* them, sure enough," replied Graham.

The sound certainly appeared to come from above them, and all were constrained to believe that, rowing as swiftly and powerfully as they did, they must have swept by them in the darkness without suspecting their proximity.

"Can it be possible?" questioned Haldidge, wonderingly and doubtingly.

But such was the character of the river-banks at this point, that all had been deceived in listening to the sounds, and the Indians were all the time leaving them far behind. It was not until they heard unmistakably the sounds receding in the distance that they became conscious of the true state of matters. At that moment, as they were dying out, they all heard them plainly enough far below.

"We might have known it," said Haldidge, in vexation. "You've got to lay to it, to catch them now."

"But is there not danger of running afoul of them?"

"Not if we are careful. I think they will run in to shore, soon, and if so, it will be the eastern bank. I will hug that closely, and keep my ears open."

The two now bent to their oars and redoubled powers. They dipped the ashen blades deeply, and pulled until they bent dangerously, while the water parted in foam at the rushing prow, and spread away in a foamy pyramid behind.

The effect of this was soon apparent. The rattle of the oars ahead grew plainer and plainer at each stroke, and it was evident they were gaining finely. Haverland's arm was thrilled with tenfold power, as he felt that he was rushing to the rescue of his only darling child, and he only wished he might have the chance to spring upon her abductors and rend them limb from limb. Graham's heart beat faster as he reflected that, perhaps, in a few moments, he should be face to face with her who had hovered about his pillow, in visions, for many a night.

Haldidge sat perfectly cool and possessed. He had formed his plan and imparted it to the others; it was to pursue the canoe noiselessly until they were almost upon it, when the instant they were near enough to distinguish forms, they would fire upon the Indians, and dash ahead and rescue Ina at all hazards.

This Haldidge, who has been introduced to notice in this chapter, was a middle-aged man, who ten years before had emigrated from the settlements along the Hudson, with a company which had formed the settlement from which he started, and where we saw Haverland and his wife and sister safely domiciled. He was a married man, and his cabin happened to be on the outskirts of the village. He joined and led the whites in several forays against the savages, when the latter became too troublesome; and in this way became a prominent object for the Indians' hatred. His residence became known to them, and one dark, stormy night a half-dozen made a descent upon it. By the merest chance, Haldidge was in the village at that time, and thus escaped their malignant revenge. Being disappointed of their principal prey, they cowardly vented their hatred upon his defenseless wife and child. When the father returned, he found them both tomahawked, side by side, and weltering in each other's blood. So silently had this onslaught been made that not a neighbor suspected anything wrong, and were horror-struck to find that such deadly peril had been so near their own doors. Haldidge took a fearful revenge upon the destroyers of his happiness. He succeeded, a couple of years afterward, in discovering them, and, before six months were over, shot them all. As may be supposed, his natural aversion to the race was intensified by this tragic occurrence, and had become so distinguished, that his name was a terror to the savages in that section. This will account for his readiness in accompanying Haverland upon his perilous expedition.

As was said, our friends were rapidly gaining upon the Indian canoe. At the rate at which they were going, they would be up to them in the course of half an hour. They were so close to the shore, as to see the dark line of the shrubbery along the bank, and several times an overhanging limb brushed over their heads. Suddenly Haldidge raised his hand again. All ceased rowing and listened. To their consternation not the slightest sound was heard. Graham leaned over, and placed his ear almost to the water, but detected nothing but the soft ripple of the stream against the roots and dipping branches along the shore.

"Can it be?" he asked, with a painful whisper, as he raised his head, "that we have been heard?"

"I do not think so," replied Haldidge, apparently in as much doubt as the rest.

"Then they have run in to shore, and departed."

"I fear that has been done."

"But we have kept so close to the shore, would we not have seen or heard the boat?"

"Provided they landed alone. They may have run in this very minute, and may not be more than a few yards off."

"If so, we must hear them yet, and it won't do to slide down upon them in the manner we are now going or we shall find ourselves in the same fix we expected to get them in."

"Very true, and a good suggestion," remarked Haldidge, and as he did so, he reached up and caught an overhanging limb, and held the canoe still.

"Now, boys, if you've got ears—"

"Sh! Look there!" interrupted Haverland, in an excited whisper.

Each turned his head and saw what appeared to be a common lighted candle floating upon the surface of the stream. It was a small point of light, which at intervals glowed with a fuller redness, and which for the time completely confounded our friends. On it came as noiselessly as death, gliding forward with such a smooth, regular motion as to show that it was certainly borne by the current.

"What in the name of—"

"Stop!" cried Haldidge; "that's the canoe we're after! It's the light of one of their pipes we see. Are your guns ready?"

"Yes," replied the two, just loud enough for him to hear.

"Make right toward it, then, and fire the instant you see your mark. Now!"

At the same instant he released his hold upon the limb, and they threw all their force upon their oars. The canoe bounded like a ball directly ahead, and seemed about to cut the other in twain. A minute after, the shadowy outlines of three forms could be dimly seen, and the avenging rifles were already raised, when the beacon-light was suddenly extinguished and the Indian canoe vanished as if by magic.

"It's one of their tricks!" excitedly exclaimed Haldidge. "Dash ahead! Curse them; they can't be far off."

The two dropped their rifles, and again seized the oars, and Haldidge sheered it abruptly up-stream, for he fancied they had turned in that direction. He bent his head forward, expecting each moment to see the forms of their enemies loom up to view in the mist, but he was mistaken; no savages greeted his anxious vision. He guided his boat in every direction—across the stream, up and down—but all to no purpose. They had surely lost their prey this time. The Indians had undoubtedly heard the pursuers—had muffled their own oars, and so proceeded as silently as they.

"Hold a minute!" commanded Haldidge.

As they rested, they listened deeply and intently.

"Do you hear anything?" he asked, leaning breathlessly forward. "There! Listen again."

They could distinguish the ripple of water, growing fainter and fainter each minute.

"They are below us again, and now for a trial of speed."

The two needed no more incentives, and for a time the canoe skimmed over the water with astonishing speed. The moon was now up, and there were patches in the stream, where the wind had blown away the fog, and being exposed to the light, were as clear as midday. Now and then they crossed such spots, sometimes but a few feet wide, and at others several rods. At these times the shore on either hand was perfectly outlined, and they glided over with a sort of instinctive terror, as they felt how easily a enemy might be concealed.

In crossing one of these, broader than usual, a glimpse of the Indian canoe showed itself, just disappearing upon the opposite shore. They were not more than a hundred yards apart, and they bounded toward it with great rapidity. The patches of light became more frequent, and the fog was evidently disappearing. Quite a breeze had arisen, which was fast sweeping it away. Haldidge kept close in to the eastern shore, feeling sure that their enemies would land upon this side!

Suddenly the whole mist lifted from the surface of the water in a volume, and rolled off toward the woods. The bright moon was reflected a long distance, and the pursuers gazed searchingly about, fully expecting to see their enemies not a dozen rods away. But they were again doomed to disappointment. Not a ripple disturbed the waters, except their own canoe. The moon was directly overhead, so that there was not a shadow cast along the banks, sufficient to conceal the slightest object. The Indians had evidently landed, and were far distant in the forest. "It is no use," remarked Haverland, gloomily, "they are gone, and we might as well be too."

"It is a sore disappointment," said Graham.

"And as much so to me as to either of you," said Haldidge. "I have an old score against the infernal wretches that will take many years to wipe out. I hoped to do something toward it to-night, but have been prevented. There is no use of hoping more at this time; they have eluded us, that is self-evident, and we must try some other means. No doubt you are wearied of body as well as of mind, and don't fancy particularly this remaining out in the river here, a shot for any one who might possess the will; so let us go into shore, have a rest, and talk over things." Dispiritedly and gloomily the trio ran the canoe to the bank and landed.

CHAPTER X. A COUPLE OF INDIAN CAPTIVES

So sudden, so unexpected, so astonishing was the crash of Seth's tomahawk through the head of the doomed savage, that, for a moment after, not an Indian moved or spoke. The head was nearly cleft in twain (for an arm fired by consuming passion had driven it), and the brains were spattered over numbers of those seated around. Seth himself stood a second to satisfy himself the work was complete, when he turned, walked to his seat, sat down, coolly folded his arms and *commenced whistling.*

A second after, nearly every savage drew a deep breath, as if a load had been removed from his heart; then each looked at his neighbor, and in the scowling, ridged brows, the glittering eyes, the distorted visages, the strained breathing through the set teeth, could be read the fearful intention. Every face but that of the chieftain's was livid with fury. He alone sat perfectly unagitated. Three Indians arose, and, grasping their knives, stood before him waiting for the expected words.

"Touch him not," said he, with a shake of the head; "him no right here."

As the chief spoke, he tapped his forehead significantly with his finger, meaning that the prisoner was demented. The others believed the same, still it was hard to quell the pent-up fire which was scorching their breasts. But his word was law inviolate, and without a murmur, they seated themselves on the ground again.

Seth, although his eye appeared vacant and unmeaning, had noted all these movements with the keenness of the eagle. He knew that a word or sign from the chief would be sufficient to hack him to a thousand pieces. When he stood before his inhuman tormentor, with the keen tomahawk in his hand, the certainty of instant death or prolonged torture would not have prevented him from taking the savage vengeance he did. Now that it was over, he was himself again. His natural feelings came back, and with it the natural desire for life. The words of the chief convinced him that he was regarded as either insane or idiotic, and consequently as not deserving death. Still, although saved for the present, he ever stood in imminent peril. The fallen savage had living friends, who would seize the first opportunity to avenge his death. At any rate, let matters stand as they might, Seth felt that he was in hot quarters, and the safest course was to get out of them as soon as possible.

It was perhaps ten minutes after the horrid deed, that the savages commenced bestirring themselves. Several arose and carried their comrade to one side, while the others commenced preparations for taking up the day's march. At this moment the runners who had pursued Graham to the water's edge, returned, and the tragical occurrence was soon made known to them. A perfect battery of deadly, gleaming eyes were opened upon Seth, but he stood it unflinchingly. The Indians would have relished well the idea of venting their baffled vengeance upon the helpless captive in their hands; but the commanding presence of their chief restrained the slightest demonstration, and they contented themselves with meaning looks.

One thing did not escape Seth's notice from the first, and it was an occasion of wonder and speculation to him. Nothing could be seen of Ina. In fact, the appearance of things was such as to lead one to believe that the savages knew nothing of her. Could it be that he and Graham had been mistaken in the party? Could some other tribe have made off with her? Or, had they separated, and taken her in another direction? As he ruminated upon these questions, he became convinced that the last suggested the certain answer. They could not have mistaken the party, as they had never lost sight of the trail since taking it; and, moreover, he had noticed several slight occurrences, since his advent among them, that satisfied him, beyond a doubt, of the identity of the party with the one which had descended upon the home of the woodman. From the caution which the aggressors evinced in their flight, together with the haste with which it had been conducted, it was plain they had some fears of pursuit; and to guard their treasure, a number had left them at a favorable point, intending to join the main body where pursuit was not to be expected, or where the pursuers had been sufficiently misled to warrant it. As he reflected, Seth was satisfied that this was the only and true explanation of her non-appearance.

The preparations were soon completed, and the Indians commenced moving forward. If Seth had entertained any doubts of their intention relating to him, they were soon dispelled by his experience. It was not at all likely that he would be reserved as a prisoner, unless they intended to put him to some use. Accordingly he found himself loaded down with an enormous burden, consisting mostly of food, in the shape of deer's meat, which the savages had brought with them. They buried their fallen comrade, without the ceremony and mourning which might be expected. The North American Indian rarely gives way to his emotions, except upon such occasions as the burial of one of their number, a "war-dance," or something similar, when the whole nest of devilish passions is allowed free vent. They indulged in no such ceremonies—if ceremonies they may be called—at this time. A comparatively shallow grave was dug, and into this the fallen one was placed in an upright position, his face turned toward the east. His rifle, knives, and all his clothing were buried with him.

The day was a suffocating one in August, and Seth's sufferings were truly great. He was naturally lithe, wiry, and capable of enduring prolonged exertion, but, unfortunately for him, the savages had become aware of this and loaded him accordingly. Most of the journey was through the forest where the arching tree-tops shut out the withering rays of the sun. Had they encountered any such open plains as the one passed over near their encampment, Seth would have never lived through it. As it was, his load nearly made him insensible to pain. A consuming thirst was ever tormenting him, although he found abundant means to slake it in the numberless rills which gurgled through the wilderness.

"How Yankee like it?" grinned a savage by his side, stooping and peering fiendishly into his face.

"First rate; goes nice. Say, you, s'posen you try it?"

"Ugh! walk faster," and a whack accompanied the word.

"Now I cac'late, I'm going to walk just about as fast as I durned please, and if you ain't a mind to wait, you can heave ahead. Fact, by gracious."

And Seth did not hasten his steps in the least. Toward noon he found he should be obliged to have a short rest or give out entirely. He knew it would be useless to ask, and consequently he determined to take it without asking. So, unloosing the cords which bound the pack to his back, he let it fall to the ground, and, seating himself upon it, again went to whistling.

"Go faster, Yankee—you no keep up!" exclaimed one, giving him a stunning blow.

"See here, you, p'raps you don't know who it mought be you insulted in that way. I'm Seth Jones, from New Hampshire, and consequently you'll be keerful of tetching me."

The savage addressed was upon the point of striking him insolently to the earth, when the chieftain interfered.

"No touch pale-face—him tired—rest a little."

Some unaccountable whim had possessed the savage, as this mercy was entirely unexpected by Seth, and he knew not how to account for it, unless it might be he was reserving him for some horrible torture.

The resting-spell was but a moment, however, and just as Seth had begun to really enjoy it, the chieftain gave orders for the replacement of the load. Seth felt disposed to tamper awhile, for the sake of prolonging his enjoyment, but, on second thought, concluded it the better plan not to cross the chief who had been so lenient to him thus far. So, with a considerable number of original remarks, and much disputation about the placing of the burden, he shouldered it at last and trudged forward.

Seth was right in his conjectures about Ina. Toward the latter part of the day, the three Indians who had been pursued by our other friends, rejoined the main party, bearing her with them. She noticed her companion in captivity at once, but no communication passed between them. A look of melancholy relief escaped her as she became assured that her parents were still safe, and that only she and her new friend were left to the sufferings and horrors of captivity. But there was enough in that to damp even such a young and hopeful spirit as was hers. Not death alone, but a fate from the sensuous captors far worse than death itself, was to be apprehended. In the future, there was but one Hand that could sustain and safely deliver them, and to that One she looked for deliverance.

Discussion Questions

1. Describe the likeable traits you find in the character of Seth.
2. How did you respond as a reader to the tests of courage that Seth endures? Do you believe these are realistic? Why or why not?
3. In what ways does the writing style of these chapters differ from the style of Garrard? In what ways is it more entertaining? In what ways is it less developed?

Fig. 2.3 George Caleb Bingham, *The Concealed Enemy* (1845). Stark Museum of Art, Orange, TX; 31.221/1.

A. B. GUTHRIE, JR.
(1901–1991)

Though born in Indiana, Guthrie soon moved to Choteau, Montana, because his father, wanting freedom and adventure, took a job as principal and teacher at Teton County's first high school (Ford 23). As a boy, "Buddy" spent his youth fishing, hunting, swimming in frigid creeks, and playing baseball for fun. He also did his share of country chores: chopping firewood; tending cows, horses, and chickens; and pumping water by hand for the house tank. He was shaped by "space and distance and the outdoors" (Backes 62), with the Rocky Mountains twenty miles to the west beyond the Teton River. It was rich training for a balanced relationship with nature and an appreciation for solitude. Also, from his father he learned a deep love for and curiosity about Western history. Together, they read pioneer journals and visited old Indian camps and buffalo graveyards (Ford 24). In the early twentieth century, the cowtown of Choteau—with a population of 1,200—was still very much Western frontier, characterized by spurs and boardwalks, cattle drives through the main street, a stagecoach, a freight wagon, several saloons, and a whorehouse (Backes 61).

After high school, Guthrie attended the Universities of Washington and Montana, graduating from the latter with a degree in journalism—an ambition held since he had worked on his hometown paper. Then he left his home state for the great world, wandering through a series of temporary jobs in Mexico, California, and New York. Finally, he joined the staff of the Lexington Leader, advancing quickly from cub reporter, to newsman, to feature writer, to editor. This two-decade apprenticeship in Kentucky taught him to hone his craft, to gradually develop a style of compression, which is evident in each consecutive work's skill in packing more action and meaning into shorter sentences, shorter paragraphs, and shorter chapters (Chatterton 928).

His first novel, *Murder at Moon Dance* (1943), was a cross-genre Western mystery, which he later regretted writing and considered a failure. Undiscouraged, he sat down at age forty-four to write his mountain-man novel, *The Big Sky* (1947). Through perseverance, he won a year fellowship at Harvard, where the writing program director gently guided him away from his journalistic style toward more original expression. With several chapters of the novel finished, Guthrie spent the summer of 1945 at the Bread Loaf Writers' Conference, where he was offered a $5,000 advance from publisher William Sloane to complete the novel. After publication, he quit his newspaper job and devoted himself to fiction (Ford).

His second book in the Western settlement series, *The Way West* (1949), was even more popular than the first, earning selection as Book-of-the-Month for October, as well as the Pulitzer Prize for 1950. This story traces the movement of settlers along the Oregon Trail in 1845. His notoriety led to other creative opportunities; in 1951, he earned $1,500 a week to write the screenplay for Jack Schaefer's novel *Shane*, to be directed by George Stevens. The film, released in 1953, was a great critical and popular success. Guthrie returned to his historical saga with *These Thousand Hills* (1956), focusing on Montana cattle ranching in the 1880s. The final two novels to be written in sequence were *Arfive* (1971) and *The Last Valley* (1975), which relate the founding and growth of a small Montana town, based on Choteau, from the turn of the century to the 1940s. Most critics have found these last three volumes not as rich in the epic and imaginative power of the earlier two works; in fact, they are much more novels of manners than of action or adventure (Ford).

Although Guthrie's major achievement is his novel series, he wrote thirteen Western stories collected in *The Big It* (1960). One of the best is

"Mountain Medicine," which fictionalizes a historical incident, John Colter's dramatic escape from the Blackfeet. Having been honorably discharged by Lewis and Clark in 1806, Colter was outfitted from the expedition supplies for a trapping enterprise. In the course of his travels, he became the first white man to "discover" the Yellowstone geysers in 1807. A year later, as he was trapping with his expedition buddy, John Potts, they were attacked by a band of Blackfeet, who killed Potts. However, Colter so demonstrated his courage that the Indians were impressed and, stripping him of clothes and weapons, gave him the chance to run for his life. The short story indicates Guthrie's skill in expanding a brief anecdote into an engaging, fully developed narrative (Taylor 79). A major change from the historical incident is his characterization of the companion, Bill Potter in the story, as a greenhorn whose inexperience leads to his death. Another change amounts to a narrative trick: the hero, John Clell, is clever enough to impress the Blackfeet by his skill with a unique two-barreled gun.

"Mountain Medicine" first appeared in *The Saturday Evening Post* (16 August 1947), pages 10 and 27. The text below is from the reprint in *The Big It and Other Stories* (Boston: Houghton Mifflin, 1960), pages 132–50.

Backes, Clarus, ed. "A. B. Guthrie, Jr." *Growing Up Western: Recollections*. New York: Knopf, 1990. 37–62.

Chatterton, Wayne. "A. B. Guthrie, Jr." *A Literary History of the American West*. Ed. Thomas J. Lyon, et al. Fort Worth, TX: Texas Christian University Press and The Western Literature Association, 1987. 912–34.

Ford, Thomas W. *A. B. Guthrie, Jr.* Boston: Twayne, 1981.

Taylor, J. Golden. "Across the Wide Missouri: The Adventure Narrative from Lewis and Clark to Powell." *A Literary History of the American West*. Ed. Thomas J. Lyon, et al. Fort Worth, TX: Texas Christian University Press and The Western Literature Association, 1987. 71–103.

MOUNTAIN MEDICINE

The mist along the creek shone in the morning sun, which was coming up lazy and half-hearted, as if of a mind to turn back and let the spring season wait. The cottonwoods and quaking aspens were still bare and the needles of the pines old and dark with winter, but beaver were prime and beaver were plenty. John Clell made a lift and took the drowned animal quietly from the trap and stretched it in the dugout with three others.

Bill Potter said, "If 'tweren't for the Injuns! Or if 'tweren't for you and your notions!" For all his bluster, he still spoke soft, as if on the chance that there were other ears to hear.

Clell didn't answer. He reset the trap and pulled from the mud the twig that slanted over it and unstoppered his goat-horn medicine bottle, dipped the twig in it and poked it back into the mud.

"Damn if I don't think sometimes you're scary," Potter went on, studying Clell out of eyes that were small and set close. "What kind of medicine is it makes you smell Injuns with nary one about?"

"Time you see as many of them as I have, you'll be scary too," Clell answered, slipping his paddle into the stream. He had a notion to get this greenhorn told off, but he let it slide. What was the use? You couldn't put into a greenhorn's head what it was you felt. You couldn't give him the feel of distances and sky-high mountains and lonely winds and ideas spoken out of nowhere, ideas spoken into the head by medicines a man couldn't put a name to. Like now. Like here. Like this idea that there was brown skin about, and Blackfoot skin at that.

"I seen Blackfeet enough for both of us," he added. His mind ran back to Lewis and Clark and a time that seemed long ago because so much had come between; to days and nights and seasons of watching out, with just himself and the long silence for company; to last year and a hole that lay across the mountains to the south, where the Blackfeet and the Crows had fought, and he had sided with the Crows and got a wound in the leg that hurt sometimes yet. He could still see some of the Blackfeet faces. He would know them, and they would know him, being long-remembering.

He knew Blackfeet all right, but he couldn't tell Bill Potter why he thought some of them were close by. There wasn't any sign he could point to; the creek sang along and the breeze played in the trees, and overhead a big eagle was gliding low, and nowhere was there a footprint or a movement or a whiff of smoke. It was just a feeling he had, and Potter wouldn't understand it, but would only look at him and maybe smile with one side of his mouth.

"Ain't anybody I knows of carries a two-shoot gun but you," Potter said, still talking as if Clell was scared over nothing.

Clell looked down at it, where he had it angled to his hand. It had two barrels, fixed on a swivel. When the top one was fired, you slipped a catch and turned the other up. One barrel was rifled, the other bigger and smooth-bored, and sometimes he loaded the big one with shot, for birds, and sometimes with a heavy ball, for bear or buffalo, or maybe with ball and buck both, just for what-the-hell. There was shot in it this morning, for he had thought maybe to take ducks or geese, and so refresh his taste for buffalo meat. The rifle shone in the morning sun. It was a nice piece, with a patch box a man wouldn't know to open until someone showed him the place to press his thumb. For no reason at all, Clell called his rifle Mule Ear.

He said, "You're a fool, Potter, more ways than one. Injuns'll raise your hair for sure, if it don't so happen I do it myself. As for this here two-shooter, I like it, and that's that."

Bill Potter always took low when a man dared him like that. Now all he said was "It's heavy as all hell."

Slipping along the stream, with the banks rising steep on both sides, Clell thought about beaver and Indians and all the country he had seen— high country, pretty as paint, wild as any animal and lonesome as time, and rivers unseen but by him, and holes and creeks without a name, and one place where water spouted hot and steaming and sometimes stinking from the earth, and another where a big spring flowed with pure tar; and no one believed him when he told of them, but called him the biggest liar yet. It was all right, though. He knew what he knew, and kept it to himself now, being tired of queer looks and smiles and words that made out he was half crazy.

Sometimes, remembering things, he didn't see what people did or hear what they said or think to speak when spoken to. It was all right. It didn't matter what was said about his sayings or his doings or his ways of thinking. A man long alone where no other white foot ever had stepped got different. He came to know what the Indians meant by medicine. He got to feeling like one with the mountains and the great sky and the lonesome winds and the animals and Indians, too, and it was a little as if he knew what they knew, a little as if there couldn't be a secret but was whispered to him, like the secret he kept hearing now.

"Let's cache," he said to Potter. The mist was gone from the river and the sun well up and decided on its course. It was time, and past time, to slide back to their hidden camp.

"Just got one more trap to lift," Potter argued.

"All right, then."

Overhead the eagle still soared close. Clell heard its long, high cry.

He heard something else, too, a muffled pounding of feet on the banks above. "Injuns!" he said, and bent the canoe into the cover of an overhanging bush. "I told you."

Potter listened. "Buffalo is all. Buffalo trampin' around."

Clell couldn't be sure, except for the feeling in him. Down in this little canyon a man couldn't see to the banks above. It could be buffalo, all right, but something kept warning, "Injuns! Injuns!"

Potter said, "Let's git on. Can't be cachin' from every little noise. Even sparrers make noise."

"Wait a spell."

"Scary." Potter said just the one word, and he said it under his breath, but it was enough. Clell dipped his paddle. One day he would whip Potter, but right now he reckoned he had to go on.

It wasn't fear that came on him a shake later, but just the quick knowing he had been right all along, just the holding still, the waiting, the watching what to do, for the banks had broken out with Indians—Indians with feathers in their hair, and bows and war clubs and spears in their hands; Indians yelling and motioning and scrambling down to the shores on both sides and fitting arrows to their bow strings.

Potter's face had gone white and tight like rawhide drying. He grabbed at his rifle.

Clell said, "Steady!" and got the pipe that hung from around his neck and held it up, meaning he meant peace.

These were the Blackfeet sure enough. These were the meanest Indians living. He would know them from the Rees and Crows and Pierced Noses and any other. He would know them by their round heads and bent noses and their red-and-green leather shields and the moccasins mismatched in color, and their bows and robes not fancy, and no man naked in the bunch.

The Indians waved them in. Clell let go his pipe and stroked with his paddle. Potter's voice was shrill. "You fool! You gonna let 'em torment us to death?"

That was the way with a mouthy greenhorn—full of himself at first, and then wild and shaken. "Steady!" Clell said again. "I aim to pull to shore. Don't point that there rifle 'less you want a skinful of arrows."

There wasn't a gun among the Indians, not a decent gun, but only a few rusty trade muskets. They had battle axes, and bows taken from their cases, ready for business, and some had spears, and all looked itching for a white man's hair. They waited, their eyes bright as buttons, their faces and bare forearms and right shoulders shining brown in the sun. Only men were at the shore line, but Clell could see the faces of squaws and young ones looking down from the bank above.

An Indian splashed out and got hold of the prow of the canoe and pulled it in. Clell stepped ashore, holding up his pipe. He had to watch Potter. Potter stumbled out, his little eyes wide and his face white, and fear showing even for an Indian to see. When he stepped on the bank, one of the Indians grabbed his rifle and wrenched it from him, and Potter just stood like a scared rabbit, looking as if he might jump back in the dugout any minute.

Clell reached out and took a quick hold on the rifle and jerked it away and handed it back to Potter. There was a way to treat Indians. Act like a squaw and they treated you bad; act like a brave man and you might have a chance.

Potter snatched the gun and spun around and leaped. The force of the jump carried the canoe out. He made a splash with the paddle. An arrow whispered in the air and made a little thump when it hit. Clell saw the end of it, shaking from high in Potter's back.

Potter cried out, "I'm hit! I'm hit, Clell!"

"Come back! Easy! Can't get away!"

Instead, Potter swung around with the rifle. There were two sounds, the crack of the powder and the gunshot plunk of a ball. Clell caught a glimpse of an Indian going down, and then the air was full of the twang of bowstrings and the whispered flight of arrows, and Potter slumped slowly back in the canoe, his body stuck like a pincushion. An Indian splashed out to take the scalp. Two others carried the shot warrior up the bank. Already a squaw was beginning to keen.

Clell stood quiet as a stump, letting only his eyes move. It was so close now that his life was as good as gone. He could see it in the eyes around him, in the hungry faces, in the hands moving and the spears and the bows being raised. He stood straight, looking their eyes down, thinking the first arrow would come any time now, from anyplace, and then he heard the eagle scream. Its shadow lazed along the ground. His thumb slipped the barrel catch, his wrist twisted under side up. He shot without knowing he aimed. Two feathers pulled out of the bird. It went into a steep climb and faltered and turned head down and spun to the ground, making a thump when it hit.

The Indians' eyes switched back to him. Their mouths fell open, and slowly their hands came over the mouth holes in the sign of surprise. It was as he figured in that flash between life and death. They thought all guns fired a single ball. They thought he was big medicine as a marksman. One of them stepped out and laid his hand on Mule Ear, as if to draw some of its greatness into himself. A murmur started up, growing into an argument. They ordered Clell up the bank. When he got there, he saw one Indian high-tailing it for the eagle, and others following, so's to have plumes for their war bonnets, maybe, or to eat the raw flesh for the medicine it would give them.

There was a passel of Indians on the bank, three or four hundred, and more coming across from the other side. The man Clell took for the chief had mixed red earth with spit and dabbed it on his face. He carried a bird-wing fan in one hand and wore a half-sleeved hunting shirt made of bighorn skin and decorated with colored porcupine quills. His hair was a wild bush over his eyes and ears. At the back of it he had a tuft of owl feathers hanging. He yelled something and motioned with his hands, and the others began drifting back from the bank, except for a couple of dozen that Clell figured were head men. Mostly, they wore leggings and moccasins, and leather shirts or robes slung over the left shoulder. A few had scarlet trade blankets, which had come from God knew where. One didn't wear anything under his robe.

The squaws and the little squaws in their leather sacks of dresses, the naked boys with their potbellies and swollen navels, and the untried and middling warriors were all back now. The chief and the rest squatted down in a half circle, with Clell standing in front of them. They passed a pipe around. After a while they began to talk. He had some of the hang of Blackfoot, and he knew, even without their words, they were arguing what to do with him. One of them got up and came over and brought his face close to Clell's. His eyes picked at Clell's head and eyes and nose and mouth. Clell could smell grease on him and wood smoke and old sweat, but what came to his mind above all was that here was a man he had fought last season while siding with the Crows. He looked steadily into the black eyes and saw the knowing come into them, too, and watched the man turn back and take his place in the half circle and heard him telling what he knew.

They grunted like hogs, the Blackfeet did, like hogs about to be fed, while the one talked and pointed, arguing that here was a friend of their old enemies, the Crows. The man rubbed one palm over the other, saying in sign that Clell had to be rubbed out. Let them stand him up and use him for a target, the man said. The others said yes to that, not nodding their heads as white men would, but bowing forward and back from the waist.

Clell had just one trick left. He stepped over and showed his gun and pointed to the patch box and, waving one hand to catch their eyes, he sprang the cover with the other thumb. He closed the cover and handed the gun to the chief.

The chief's hands were red with the paint he had smeared on his face. Clell watched the long thumbnail, hooked like a bird claw, digging at the cover, watched the red fingers feeling for a latch or spring. While the others stretched their necks to see, the chief turned Mule Ear over, prying at it with his eyes. It wasn't any use. Unless he knew the hidden spot to press, he couldn't spring the lid. Clell took the piece back, opened the patch box again, closed it and sat down.

He couldn't make more medicine. He didn't have a glass to bring the sun down, and so to light a pipe, or even a trader's paper-backed mirror for the chief to see how pretty he was. All he had was the shot at the eagle and the patch box on Mule Ear, and he had used them both and had to take what came.

Maybe it was the eagle that did it, or the hidden cover, or maybe it was just the crazy way of Indians. The chief got up, and with his hands and with his tongue asked if the white hunter was a good runner.

Clell took his time answering, as a man did when making high palaver. He lighted his pipe. He said, "The white hunter is a bad runner. The other Long Knives think he runs fast. Their legs are round from sitting on a horse. They cannot run."

The chief grunted, letting the sign talk and the slow words sink into him. "The Long Knife will run." He pointed to the south, away from the creek. "He will run for the trading house that the whiteface keeps among the Crows. He will go as far as three arrows will shoot, and then he will run. My brothers will run. If my brothers run faster—" The chief brought his hand to his scalp lock.

The other Indians had gathered around, even the squaws and the young ones. They were grunting with excitement. The chief took Mule Ear. Other hands stripped off Clell's hunting shirt, the red-checked woolen shirt underneath, his leggings, his moccasins, his small-clothes, until he stood white and naked in the sun, and the squaws and young ones came up close to see what white flesh looked like. The squaws made little noises in their throats. They poked at his bare hide. One of them grabbed the red-checked shirt from the hands of a man and ran off with it. The chief made the sign for "Go!"

Clell walked straight, quartering into the sun. He walked slow and solemn, like going to church. If he hurried, they would start the chase right off. If he lazed along, making out they could be damned for all he cared, they might give him more of a start.

He was two hundred yards away when the first whoop sounded, the first single whoop, and then all the voices yelling and making one great whoop. From the corner of his eye he saw their legs driving, saw the uncovered brown skins, the feathered hair, the bows and spears, and then he was running himself, seeing ahead of him the far tumble and roll of high plains and hills, with buffalo dotting the distances and a herd of prairie goats sliding like summer mist, and everywhere, so that not always could his feet miss them, the angry knobs of cactus. South and east, many a long camp away where the Bighorn joined the Roche Jaune, lay Lisa's Fort, the trading house among the Crows.

He ran so as to save himself for running, striding long and loose through the new-sprouting buffalo grass, around the cactus, around the pieces of sandstone where snakes were likely to lie. He made himself breathe easy, breathe deep, breathe full in his belly. Far off in his feelings he felt the cactus sting him and the spines pull off to sting again. The sun looked him in the face. It lay long and warm on the world. At the sky line the heat sent up a little shimmer. There wasn't a noise anywhere except the thump of his feet and his heart working in his chest and his breath sucking in and out and, behind him, a cry now and then from the Indians, seeming not closer or farther away than at first. He couldn't slow himself with a look. He began to sweat.

A man could run a mile, or two or three, and then his breath wheezed in him. It grew into a hard snore in the throat. The air came in, weak and dry, and burned his pipes and went out in one spent rush while his lungs sucked for more. He felt as if he had been running on forever. He felt strange and out of the world, a man running in a dream, except that the ache in his throat was real and the fire of cactus in his feet. The earth spread away forever, and he was lost in it and friendless, and not a proper part of it any more; and it served him right. When a man didn't pay any mind to his medicine, but went ahead regardless, as he had done, his medicine played out on him.

Clell looked back. He had gained, fifty yards, seventy-five, half a musket shot; he had gained on all the Indians except one, and that one ran as swift and high-headed as a prairie goat. He was close and coming closer.

Clell had a quick notion to stop and fight. He had an idea he might dodge the spear the Indian carried and come to grips with him. But the rest would be on him before he finished. It took time to kill a man just with the hands alone. Now was the time for the running he had saved himself for. There was strength in his legs yet. He made them reach out, farther, faster, faster, farther. The pound of them came to be a sick jolting inside his skull. His whole chest fought for air through the hot, closed tunnel of his throat. His legs weren't a part of him; they were something to think about, but not to feel, something to watch and to wonder at. He saw them come out and go under him and come out again. He saw them weakening, the knees bending in a little as the weight came on them. He felt wetness on his face, and reached up and found his nose was streaming blood.

He looked over his shoulder again. The main body of Indians had fallen farther back, but the prairie goat had gained. Through a fog he saw the man's face, the chin set high and hard, the black eyes gleaming. He heard the moccasins slapping in the grass.

Of a sudden, Clell made up his mind. Keep on running and he'd get a spear in the back. Let it come from the front. Let it come though the chest. Let him face up to death like a natural man and to hell with it. His feet jolted him to a halt. He swung around and threw up his hands as if to stop a brute.

The Indian wasn't ready for that. He tried to pull up quick. He made to lift his spear. And then he stumbled and fell ahead. The spear handle broke as the point dug in the ground. Clell grabbed at the shaft, wrenched the point from the earth and drove it through the man. The Indian bucked to his hands and knees and strained and sank back. It was as easy as that.

Bending over him, Clell let his chest drink, let his numb legs rest, until he heard the yells of the Indians and, looking up, saw them strung out in a long file, with the closest of them so close he could see the set of their faces. He turned and ran again, hearing a sudden, louder howling as the Indians came on the dead one, and then the howling dying again to single cries as they picked up the chase. They were too many for him, and too close. He didn't have a chance. He couldn't fort up and try to stand them off, not with his hands bare. There wasn't any place to hide. He should have listened to his medicine when it was talking to him back there on the creek.

Down the slope ahead of him a river ran—the Jefferson Fork of the Missouri, he thought, while he made his legs drive him through a screen of brush. A beaver swam in the river, its moving head making a quiet V in the still water above a dam. As he pounded closer, its flat tail slapped the water like a pistol shot, the point of the V sank from sight, and the ripples spread out and lost themselves. He could still see the beaver, though, swimming under water, its legs moving and the black tail plain, like something to follow. It was a big beaver, and it was making for a beaver lodge at Clell's right.

Clell dived, came up gasping from the chill of mountain water, and started stroking for the other shore. Beaver lodge! Beaver lodge! It was as if something spoke to him, as if someone nudged him, as if the black tail pulled him around. It was a fool thing, swimming under water and feeling for the tunnel that led up into the lodge. A fool thing. A man got so winded and weak that he didn't know medicine from craziness. A fool thing. A man couldn't force his shoulders through a beaver hole. The point of his shoulder pushed into mud. A snag ripped his side. He clawed ahead, his lungs bursting. And then his head was out of water, in the dark, and his lungs pumped air.

He heard movement in the lodge and a soft churring, but his eyes couldn't see anything. He pulled himself up, still hearing the churring, expecting the quick slice of teeth in his flesh. There was a scramble. Something slid along his leg and made a splash in the water of the tunnel, and slid again and made another splash.

His hands felt sticks and smooth, dry mud and the softness of shed hair. He sat up. The roof of the lodge just cleared his head if he sat slouched. It was a big lodge, farther across than the span of his arms. And it was as dark, almost, as the inside of a plugged barrel. His hand crossing before his eyes was just a shapeless movement.

He sat still and listened. The voices of the Indians sounded far off. He heard their feet in the stream, heard the moccasins walking softly around the lodge, heard the crunch of dried grass under their steps. It was like something dreamed, this hiding and being able to listen and to move. It was like being a breath of air, and no one able to put a hand on it.

After a while the footsteps trailed off and the voices faded. Now Clell's eyes were used to blackness, the lodge was a dark dapple. From the shades he would know it was day, but that was all. He felt for the cactus spines in his feet. He had been cold and wet at first, but the wetness dried and the lodge warmed a little to his body. Shivering, he lay down, feeling the dried mud under his skin, and the soft fur. When he closed his eyes he could see the sweep of distances and the high climb of mountains, and himself all alone in all the world, and, closer up, he could see the beaver swimming under water and its flat tail beckoning. He could hear voices, the silent voices speaking to a lonesome man out of nowhere and out of everywhere, and the beaver speaking, too, the smack of its tail speaking.

He woke up later, quick with alarm, digging at his dream and the noise that had got mixed with it. It was night outside. Not even the dark dapple showed inside the lodge, but only such a blackness as made a man feel himself to make sure he was real. Then he heard a snuffling of the air, and the sound of little waves lapping in the tunnel, and he knew that a beaver had nosed up and smelled him and drawn back into the water.

When he figured it was day, he sat up slowly, easing his muscles into action. He knew, without seeing, that his feet were puffed with the poison of the cactus. He crawled to the tunnel and filled his lungs and squirmed into it. He came up easy, just letting his eyes and nose rise above the water. The sun had cleared the eastern sky line. Not a breath of air stirred; the earth lay still, flowing into spring. He could see where the Indians had flattened the grass and trampled an edging of rushes, but there were no Indians about, not on one side or the other, not from shore line to sky line. He struck out for the far shore.

Seven days later a hunter at Fort Lisa spotted a figure far off. He watched it for a long spell, until a mist came over his eyes, and then he called to the men inside the stockade. A half dozen came through the big gate, their rifles in the crooks of their arms, and stood outside and studied the figure too.

"Man, all right. Somep'n ails him. Look how he goes."

"Injun, I say. A Crow, maybe, with a Blackfoot arrer in him."

"Git the glass."

One of them went inside and came back and put the glass to his eye. "Naked as a damn jay bird."

"Injun, ain't it?"

"Got a crop of whiskers. Never seed a Injun with whiskers yet."

"Skin's black."

"Ain't a Injun, though."

They waited.

"It ain't! Yes, I do believe it's John Clell! It's John Clell or I'm a Blackfoot!"

They brought him in and put his great, raw swellings of feet in hot water and gave him brandy and doled out roast liver, and bit by bit, that day and the next, he told them what had happened.

They knew why he wouldn't eat prairie turnips afterward, seeing as he lived on raw ones all that time, but what they didn't understand, because he didn't try to tell them, was why he never would hunt beaver again.

Discussion Questions

1. Explain the nature of John Clell's "medicine." Provide some synonyms for its meaning.
2. Select a quotation from the story that helps to explain it.
3. Contrast the characters of Potter and Clell. Then compare Potter to another greenhorn in Western fiction or film.

Fig. 2.4 William Tylee Ranney, *Advice on the Prairie* (1853). Buffalo Bill Historical Center, Cody, WY; gift of Mrs. J. Maxwell Moran; 10.91.

◆ ◆ ◆

FOCUS ON FILM:
ELLIOT SILVERSTEIN'S
A MAN CALLED HORSE (1970)

1. Assess some of the effects of the sound track in the film.
2. Describe the extensive ritual of the "Sun Ceremony" that Horse performs in order to prove his manhood and earn his bride. These scenes were not in the original story by Dorothy Johnson, so explain what you believe to be the purpose in expanding on this process. What do these scenes add to the film narrative?
3. Are there any characters you find unrealistically portrayed? Explain.
4. Analyze the conclusion of the film, which seems open-ended in the outcome to Horse. Explain the advantages of ambiguity.

TOPICS FOR RESEARCH AND WRITING

1. Based on the selection from Ellis, analyze the character of Seth Jones. What traits do you find realistic and what traits or behaviors do you find unbelievable in this hero? Then compare his character to that of John Clell in Guthrie's "Mountain Medicine." Determine which portrayal is more realistic and explain why you think so.
2. The film *A Man Called Horse* is told from a perspective favorable to the Indians, but has still been popular in our predominantly white culture. Explain how the story assures its popularity by appealing to specific "American" values among its readers.
3. Compare and contrast Seth Jones's and Garrard's attitudes toward Native Americans. Consider the traits they criticize, as well as the traits they appreciate. You might also consider the genre in which their portraits of Native Americans appear: dime novel versus personal travel narrative.
4. Compare and contrast Guthrie's portrait of the mountain man John Clell with de Crèvecoeur's or Turner's characterizations of the frontier pioneer in Chapter 1.
5. Read Dorothy Johnson's "A Man Called Horse" in *Indian Country* (New York: Ballantine Books, 1953), pages 180–97. Compare and contrast the short story with the film, considering both what the film *leaves out* in

comparison to the story and what the film *adds* that the story does not even mention. Try to explain *why* these changes were made and evaluate their effect on the film. Avoid obvious contrasts of the reading versus the viewing experiences.

6. Read Chapters 6 and 14 of Ann Stephen's *Malaeska; The Indian Wife of the White Hunter,* in Bill Brown's *Reading the West: An Anthology of Dime Westerns* (Boston: Bedford, 1997), pages 107–12 and 156–64. Compare and contrast this excerpt with the anthology reading from *Seth Jones.* Consider the similarities and differences in characterization, content, and theme. Also, determine to what extent you believe that the gender of the hero/heroine explains some of the differences. Quote specific passages to provide evidence for your interpretations.

7. Read about a specific historical mountain man (Jim Beckwourth, Daniel Boone, Jim Bridger, Kit Carson, or Jedediah Smith) in a library reference work, such as *Wild and Woolly: An Encyclopedia of the Old West* (McLoughlin, 1975); *The Reader's Encyclopedia of the American West* (Lamar, 1977); *The Encyclopedia of the American West* (Phillips and Axelrod, 1996); or *The New Encyclopedia of the American West* (Lamar, 1998). Instead of using a reference work, you could search for an Internet site from a reliable source. In either case, determine to what extent the source is interested in the "myths" about the mountain man you select and to what extent the source reports only the "facts." Compare and contrast the ways the historical figure is portrayed in the source with the ways the mountain man is portrayed in Guthrie's "Mountain Medicine."

CHAPTER

3

◆

WORKING THE LAND

INTRODUCTION

By the second half of the nineteenth century, pioneers streamed toward land "opened" to settlement; frontier villages developed not only saloons and stores, but also schools and churches; territories became states and towns elected sheriffs; Native Americans were consistently pushed from their land, relocated, lied to, cheated in unfair treaties, confined to reservations, and slaughtered. At the same time, two powerful factors contributed to this "civilizing" of the West: (1) a federal presence in the shape of an occupying army, the cavalry; and (2) the growth of technology to speed transportation and communication, especially in the transcontinental railroad and telegraph, and to exploit resources, especially in corporate mining and logging. These historical realities eventually helped to shape Western stories written toward the end of the century, but the early efforts contributed more to myth-making than reality and celebrated "progress" in spite of predictable conflicts with "evil" forces that could be defeated only by morally robust heroes. The Natty Bumppo-style characters of the mountain man and the pioneer evolved, with modest changes, into a more idealized hero, the cowboy, while also assuming a wider set of roles required by changing circumstances in the West—the small rancher or farmer, the miner or other outdoors entrepreneur (of railroad, telegraph, or stagecoach line), the cavalryman, the lawman, the vigilante, and the outlaw. This chapter includes works that help to define the quintessentially Western character of the cowboy and that introduce some of these other heroic roles.

Historically, the working cowboy was a widespread phenomenon in the West for only two decades—from 1867 until the disastrous blizzard of 1887. Of course, in the sixteenth century, the Spanish had brought organized ranching to California and the Southwest. The Spanish also brought horses to North America and provided the terms adopted in cattle-work: *lariat, lasso, corral,* chaps (*chaparejos*), *bronco* (Spanish for "unruly"), stampede (*estampida* or "uproar"), and even buckaroo (derived from *vaquero*). Americans began herding cattle in Texas from the 1820s, but when the Eastern cities' demands for beef soared after the Civil War, there was no efficient way to transport the product. However, when entrepreneur Joe McCoy promised to buy Texas beef if cowboys could drive them to the railhead, he encouraged the railroad to lay a spur to Abilene, Kansas. This action, in 1867, helped establish the thousand-mile Chisholm Trail (Flexner). The year before, two Texas cattlemen had opened the Goodnight-Loving Trail from central Texas through the territories of New Mexico and Colorado all the way to Cheyenne, Wyoming, in order to exploit new markets—mature beef cattle to supply soldiers at Fort Sumner, New Mexico, the Apache-Navaho reservations nearby, and miners in Colorado; as well as immature stock to supply new ranches in the northern grasslands of Wyoming, Nebraska, and Montana. "Somewhere between six and nine million cattle were driven out of Texas to the railheads and the plains between 1867 and 1886, with around 25,000 cowboys making the trip north" (Lewis 160–61).

During this period, the cattle business was becoming consolidated with huge Eastern- and British-owned companies controlling millions of acres, trying to squeeze out small-herd ranchers and homesteaders. But everyone suffered in the winter of 1886–1887, when snow drifts of 20 feet and temperatures of 60 degrees below 0 wiped out as much as 90 percent of some herds and 30 percent of stock overall—in part, due to cattle and horses becoming trapped against barbed-wire fencing. This blizzard devastated the cattle market and most of the owners. Likewise, thousands of cowboys were fired and never recovered their livelihood on the range. Some drifted ever west to change their luck and occupations; some took jobs digging irrigation ditches, stringing barbed wire, and haying for the corporate ranches; some took to rustling. Butch Cassidy gathered the roughest of these ex-cowboys into the Wild Bunch (Reisner 106), continuing the popularly supported "social bandit" tradition that began with Robin Hood. The heyday of the cowboy—an emblem of the nature-taming, free-roving, rugged individual—was at an end.

The late nineteenth century proved no better for farmers in the West. For decades, federal land policy inconsistencies and private speculation had stimulated settlement. Likewise, promotional schemes by the railroads, territorial and town boosters, and "paper-town" swindlers promised fertile lands and bountiful harvests. In response, immigrants flooded onto the high plains. It is fair to say that the settlers' story was "a chronicle of hope, new homes, adaptation, family success, and sometimes, tragedy or failure" (Bogue 311). The Homestead Act of 1862 promised 160 acres of public land to settlers who lived on their quarter section and made improvements for five years, but the Act also led to profits for "capitalists and developers." Moreover, the original act did not recognize that most Western lands, with porous soil and scant rainfall, required at least 320 acres for cultivation or 640 acres for grazing, but amendments to the act adjusting the acreage were not made until 1909 and 1916, respectively. It is true that between 1850 and 1910 the number of Euro-American farmers increased from 1.5 to 6.4 million. However, most of the growth west of the Mississippi was in states adjacent to the river from Iowa to the gulf, or in the eastern halves of states from North Dakota to Texas (Bogue).

In fact, Western homesteaders were victims of bad science and wishful thinking. Most migrants and even agricultural experts believed in the dubious theory that "rain follows the plow," that increased population contributes to increased moisture, even in those regions beyond the hundredth meridian that historically have gotten an average of fewer than twenty inches of rain annually. And there was a misleading cycle of very wet years after the Civil War that seemed to shrink the Great American Desert, apparently proving once again that Providence was smiling down on a chosen people—as Americans have thought themselves from the first. But in 1888 a severe drought began in the West, ruining crops, killing the land, and sending thousands of homesteaders back East or to Oklahoma territory, recently stolen back from five Indian tribes by the same federal government that had resettled them there. By 1890, between a quarter and a half of the population in Kansas and Nebraska had left. In the West, "only 400,000 homesteading families had managed to persevere on the plains, of more than a million who tried" (Reisner 106–7).

Nature was not the only enemy of both cowboys and family farmers. Against these "common people" in the livestock and agrarian trades, the cattle barons conducted a kind of class warfare. Consolidation of ranchlands and herds led to territory- and state-wide consolidation of power by railroad and ranching interests, which controlled grazing and water rights, citizens' votes, law enforcement, and even the courts. Working cowboys realized that the often absentee owners were getting fabulously wealthy on their hard labor, which was so physically demanding that their average career lasted only seven years, while the typical cause of death was pneumonia or a riding accident (Flexner). Since they were poorly paid—traditionally earning only $30 a month, besides their bunkhouse and grub—cowboys sometimes tried to organize and strike for better wages, but without success. They also tried to start their own small, independent herds to avoid continued exploitation.

In Wyoming, the cattlemen's efforts at even greater control over workers and new homesteaders—their major competitors for land—became violent in the so-called Johnson County War. A complex dispute concerned the ownership of mavericks, motherless unbranded calves that could be claimed off the open range by any hand. However, to ensure their power and wealth, the barons of the Wyoming Stock Growers' Association pushed through state legislation that gave them ownership over all unbranded calves, which was essentially a legal form of rustling from unaffiliated cattle breeders. The conflict erupted into vigilante executions and, in 1892, an all-out invasion of Johnson County by regulators, range detectives, and hired gunslingers. The Association was successful in murdering several small-time ranchers and farmers, but in response a citizen's posse of 300 men lay siege to the regulators, who were saved only by the U.S. Cavalry. However, witnesses were bribed, the Johnson County treasury was depleted by imprisonment costs, and the guilty parties were never prosecuted (Lewis 236–44). This episode not only shows how big business extended its repressive labor practices from the East to the West, but also serves as another example of how the real West was always contested. Despite the myth of "humanizing" an "empty" wilderness, land was never exactly free for the taking. Nature could well be the enemy for the ill-informed homesteader, as well as for the skilled horseman and outdoorsman. But other Americans, competing for limited resources or striving for untold wealth, were likely to prove the more insidious foe.

Thus, for both the farmer and the cowboy, the dream of rugged self-sufficiency and individual achievement in a noble struggle often proved unattainable for the majority. More often, success demanded some coordinated collective effort. This was no less true of mining, which promised immediate payoff for individual enterprise. Although in the California gold rush one independent prospector collected $26,000 worth of gold dust in a single summer (Lewis 115), this sort of bonanza was typical only of the initial, short-lived "egalitarian" phase of mining, when the resource was plentiful and easily accessible (Limerick 105). For instance, in the Comstock Lode of Nevada, that initial phase lasted from 1859 only until the mid-1860s, when absentee-owned, monopolistic corporations had taken control. Wherever a big strike occurred—in California, Colorado, Nevada, Montana, or South Dakota—the inevitable second phase of hydraulic or underground mining "required capital, technology, and coordinated effort" (105–7).

Another dramatic feature of mining was its aggressive push of frontier expansion; from 1848 to 1852, the California non-Indian population exploded from 14,000 to 250,000 (Lewis 115). At the same time, slaughter and disease reduced the Native American populace by disastrous proportions. Although historians disagree on the precise numbers, which are based on flawed census data, one report is suggestive: the California Indian population declined from about 150,000 in 1849 to about 30,000 by the 1850s (Hurtado 1). Even though mining encouraged an extractive mentality of "get in, get rich, get out" and a boom-and-bust pattern of development, the non-native population growth also included the merchants and farmers that followed the adventurers. Other negative effects of mining strikes included the rapid industrialization and environmental degradation of a previously "unsettled" region. Wage-slave miners, initially lured West by promises of easy wealth or at least independent self-employment, soon realized their lot was no better than working in Eastern urban factories. Their lives were not the material for Western myths, legends, or popular culture. Their only illusion was the perpetual American "reverence for individual responsibility," which actually prevented miners and their families from receiving compensation for work-related injuries or death (Limerick 99–109).

Yet most Western stories written or set between the Civil War and the century's end feature conquering heroes and hide the historical realities of failure or tragedy. Of course, proletarian and middle-class readers, who cherish the myths of American innocence and Providential good fortune, want to read only of triumph over nature, Indians, or patrician greed and evil. Therefore, most classic Western tales reinforce frontier mythology. Only a few writers critical of the mythic West served to disclose more complex realities; representatives of these minority voices will be considered in Chapter 5.

Bogue, Allan G. "An Agricultural Empire." *The Oxford History of the American West.* Ed. Clyde A. Milner II, Carol A. O'Connor, and Martha A. Sandweiss. New York: Oxford University, 1994. 274–313.

Flexner, Stuart B. "Cowboys." *I Hear America Talking: An Illustrated Treasury of American Words and Phrases.* New York: Van Nostrand Reinhold, 1976. 109–12.

Hurtado, Albert. *Indian Survival on the California Frontier.* New Haven, CN: Yale University, 1988.

Lewis, Jon E. *The Mammoth Book of the West.* New York: Carroll & Graf, 1996.

Limerick, Patricia Nelson. *The Legacy of Conquest: The Unbroken Past of the American West.* New York: Norton, 1987.

Reisner, Marc. *Cadillac Desert: The American West and Its Disappearing Water.* Revised ed. New York: Penguin, 1993.

Fig. 3.1 N. C. Wyeth, *Rounding Up* (1904). Buffalo Bill Historical Center, Cody, WY; gift of John M. Schiff; 1.77.

OWEN WISTER
(1860–1938)

The only son of a prosperous country physician and a cultured mother, the author had the advantage of an upper-crust education, studying briefly at private schools in Switzerland and England and then at St. Paul's preparatory school in New Hampshire. In 1878, he enrolled at Harvard (with Teddy Roosevelt as a classmate for two years), graduated summa cum laude with a music degree, and then studied composing for a year in Paris (Butler 325).

His father, frowning on so frivolous a career as music, recalled him from Europe and advised him to go into business. For two years, Wister worked as a teller at Union Safe Deposit Vaults in Boston. Suffering from painful neuralgia and mental depression during the winter of 1885, he took his doctor's advice that summer to take a "rest cure" in Wyoming (Vorpahl 289). Wister was physically and mentally restored by the climate and landscape. Similarly, the West got in his blood, and he visited regularly during vacations. Years later he described his typical Wyoming activities in *Roosevelt: The Story of a Friendship, 1880–1919* (1930): "camps in the mountains, camps in the sage-brush, nights in town, cards with cavalry officers, meals with cow-punchers, round-ups, scenery, the Yellowstone Park, trout fishing, hunting with Indians, shooting antelope, white tail deer, black tail deer, elk, bear, mountain sheep—and missing these same animals" (qtd. in Lambert 521–22). Returning to Boston in the fall of 1885, he enrolled in Harvard Law School, graduated in 1888, and began a Philadelphia practice in 1890. Unexcited by his profession, he was enthralled by the prospect of writing fiction about the West, capturing "that epic which was being lived at a gallop out in the sage-brush" (qtd. in Butler 326).

His first attempt at the genre was "Hank's Woman," published in *Harper's Weekly* in 1892. This was the first of over 60 stories, many of which were later developed into chapters for the novels *Lin McLean* (1898) and *The Virginian: A Horseman of the Plains* (1902). It was the short-story format, however, that was Wister's metier, as he found a steady market in the "slicks"—quality periodicals such as *Harper's New Monthly Magazine*, *The Saturday Evening Post*, *Collier's Weekly*, and *Cosmopolitan*. Compared to his contemporaries, his fiction was often "more realistic in setting, situation, and characters," except for the narrowness of women's roles (Butler 325–27). Typically, his stories involve some conflict between East and West. While he admired the "possibilities for freedom, simplicity, and spontaneity" in the West, he also acknowledged its tendencies toward "a certain cruelty, violence, and social chaos that were antithetical to the tradition, refinement, and culture" that he valued in the East, the home of his patrician roots (Lambert 524). Oddly enough, though Western values come out ahead in his stories, the viewpoint is often controlled by an Eastern narrator, "a cultured personality superior to his subject in civilized qualities" (Butler 326).

When, in 1893, *Harper's* invited Wister to submit a string of Western stories, he quit his law practice to devote himself to fiction and began a decade of productive success. The periodical publications were subsequently collected in *Red Men and White* (1896) and *The Jimmyjohn Boss and Other Stories* (1900). In 1898, at the age of 38, he married his cousin Mary Channing Wister, who kept his working routines free of distraction. Besides pulling together five previous stories and writing much original material for *The Virginian*, Wister wrote eight new Western tales later collected, in 1911, as *Members of the Family* (Butler 327–33).

In his most productive story-writing decade, he also published a revealing essay, "The Evolution of the Cow-Puncher" (*Harper's New Monthly Magazine*, September 1895), which delineated his own racist sociology of the Western type and reinforced the popular conviction that the country was at the end of an era. Disagreeing with Turner's thesis that the frontier created a new man, Wister argued, along with Roosevelt, that the cowboy was an expression of Anglo-Saxon racial superiority, naturally rising to the challenge of the rugged Western environment. As he wrote of the United States,

> No rood of modern ground is more debased and mongrel with its hordes of encroaching alien vermin, that turn our cities to Babels and our citizenship to a hybrid farce. . . . But to survive in the clean cattle country requires spirit of adventure, courage, and self-sufficiency; you will not find many Poles or Huns or Russian Jews in that district; but the Anglo-Saxon is still forever homesick for out-of-doors. (qtd. in Butler 327)

He celebrated the West nostalgically, seeing its end as fated and nothing to replace its glory. A political and social conservative, he distrusted populism and even democracy; he even failed to perceive "the people" in his beloved Western spaces (Butler 333). Nonetheless, his stories still entertain, even if their vision is somewhat fixed in time by his idealism.

Actually, if Wister had written only *The Virginian*, he would still be read and remembered today since this novel has had lasting impact on the Western genre. Its achievement was to elevate the frontier story from the sensationalism of the dime Westerns to its full realization—in setting, style, character, and theme—as mainstream literature. The novel brought him an international reputation and sold more than 50,000 copies in a period of two months. To some extent, its success was a matter of timing. First, the popularity of Buffalo Bill's Wild West Show in Europe peaked at the turn of the century and left audiences yearning to read tales of frontier adventure. Second, in 1902, the year of publication, Teddy Roosevelt was in the White House, so the U.S. market was generally supportive of literature promoting the "strenuous life." Third, in the following year, Thomas Edison's new film production company released its first feature, a Western adventure called *The Great Train Robbery*. In 1903, Wister also adapted *The Virginian* into a Broadway play, which was a popular success. A deluxe edition of the novel, with illustrations by both Charley Russell and Frederic Remington, followed. In 1914, D. W. Griffith filmed the first of four cinematic adaptations. By 1952, *The Virginian* had sold 18 million copies, an impressive number even over five decades (Estleman 389–96).

The text of "The Jimmyjohn Boss" is from *The Jimmyjohn Boss and Other Stories* (New York: Harper, 1900), pages 3–63.

Butler, Michael. "Owen Wister." *Dictionary of Literary Biography, Volume 78: American Short-Story Writers, 1880–1910*. Ed. Bobby Ellen Kimbel and William E. Grant. Detroit: Gale, 1989. 324–34.

Estleman, Loren D. "Owen Wister." *Dictionary of Literary Biography, Volume 186: Nineteenth-Century American Western Writers*. Ed. Robert L. Gale. Detroit: Gale, 1997. 388–96.

Lambert, Neal. "Owen Wister." *Fifty Western Writers: A Bio-Bibliographical Sourcebook*. Ed. Fred Erisman and Richard W. Etulain. Westport, CN: Greenwood, 1982. 519–31.

Vorpahl, Ben M. "Roosevelt, Wister, Turner, and Remington." *A Literary History of the American West*. Ed. Thomas J. Lyon, et al. Fort Worth, TX: Texas Christian University Press and The Western Literature Association, 1987. 276–302.

THE JIMMYJOHN BOSS

I

One day at Nampa, which is in Idaho, a ruddy old massive jovial man stood by the Silver City stage, patting his beard with his left hand, and with his right the shoulder of a boy who stood beside him. He had come with the boy on the branch train from Boise, because he was a careful German and liked to say everything twice—twice at least when it was a matter of business. This was a matter of very particular business, and the German had repeated himself for nineteen miles. Presently the east-bound on the main line would arrive from Portland; then the Silver City stage would take the boy south on his new mission, and the man would journey by the branch train back to Boise. From Boise no one could say where he might not go, west or east. He was a great and pervasive cattle man in Oregon, California, and other places. Vogel and Lex—even to-day you may hear the two ranch partners spoken of. So the veteran Vogel was now once more going over his notions and commands to his youthful deputy during the last precious minutes until the east-bound should arrive.

"Und if only you haf someding like dis," said the old man, as he tapped his beard and patted the boy, "it would be five hoondert more dollars salary in your liddle pants."

The boy winked up at his employer. He had a gray, humorous eye; he was slim and alert, like a sparrow-hawk—the sort of boy his father openly rejoices in and his mother is secretly in prayer over. Only, this boy had neither father nor mother. Since the age of twelve he had looked out for himself, never quite without bread, sometimes attaining champagne, getting along in his American way variously, on horse or afoot, across regions of wide plains and mountains, through towns where not a soul knew his name. He closed one of his gray eyes at his employer, and beyond this made no remark.

"Vat you mean by dat vink, anyhow?" demanded the elder.

"Say," said the boy, confidentially—"honest now. How about you and me? Five hundred dollars if I had your beard. You've got a record and I've got a future. And my bloom's on me rich, without a scratch. How many dollars you gif me for dat bloom?" The sparrow-hawk sailed into a freakish imitation of his master.

"You are a liddle rascal!" cried the master, shaking with entertainment. "Und if der peoples vas to hear you sass old Max Vogel in dis style they would say, 'Poor old Max, he lose his gr-rip.' But I don't lose it." His great hand closed suddenly on the boy's shoulder, his voice cut clean and heavy as an axe, and then no more joking about him. "Haf you understand that?" he said.

"Yes, sir."

"How old are you, son?"

"Nineteen, sir."

"Oh my, that is offle young for the job I gif you. Some of dose man you go to boss might be your father. Und how much do you weigh?"

"About a hundred and thirty."

"Too light, too light. Und I haf keep my eye on you in Boise. You are not so goot a boy as you might be."

"Well, sir, I guess not."

"But you was not so bad a boy as you might be, neider. You don't lie about it. Now it must be farewell to all that foolishness. Haf you understand? You go to set an example where one is needed very bad. If those men see you drink a liddle, they drink a big lot. You forbid them, they laugh at you. You must not allow one drop of whiskey at the whole place. Haf you well understand?"

"Yes, sir. Me and whiskey are not necessary to each other's happiness."

"It is not you, it is them. How are you mit your gun?"

Vogel took the boy's pistol from its holster and aimed at an empty bottle which was sticking in the thin December snow. "Can you do this?" he said, carelessly, and fired. The snow struck the bottle, but the unharming bullet was buried half an inch to the left.

The boy took his pistol with solemnity. "No," he said. "Guess I can't do that." He fired, and the glass splintered into shapelessness. "Told you I couldn't miss as close as you did," said he.

"You are a darling," said Mr. Vogel. "Gif me dat lofely weapon."

A fortunate store of bottles lay, leaned, or stood about in the white snow of Nampa, and Mr. Vogel began at them.

"May I ask if anything is the matter?" inquired a mild voice from the stage.

"Stick that lily head in-doors," shouted Vogel; and the face and eye-glasses withdrew again into the stage. "The school-teacher he will be beautifool virtuous company for you at Malheur Agency," continued Vogel, shooting again; and presently the large old German destroyed a bottle with a crashing smack. "Ah!" said he, in unison with the smack. "Ah-ha! No von shall say der old Max lose his gr-rip. I shoot it efry time now, but the train she whistle. I hear her."

The boy affected to listen earnestly.

"Bah! I tell you I hear de whistle coming."

"Did you say there was a whistle?" ventured the occupant of the stage. The snow shone white on his glasses as he peered out.

"Nobody whistle for you," returned the robust Vogel. "You listen to me," he continued to the boy. "You are offle yoong. But I watch you plenty this long time. I see you work mit my stock on the Owyhee and the Malheur; I see you mit my oder men. My men they say always more and more, 'Yoong Drake he is a goot one,' und I think you are a goot one mine own self. I am the biggest cattle man on the Pacific slope, und I am also an old devil. I have think a lot, und I like you."

"I'm obliged to you, sir."

"Shut oop. I like you, und therefore I make you my new sooperinten-dent at my Malheur Agency r-ranch, mit a bigger salary as you don't get before. If you are a sookcess, I r-raise you some more."

"I am satisfied now, sir."

"Bah! Never do you tell any goot business man you are satisfied mit vat he gif you, for eider he don't believe you or else he think you are a fool. Und eider ways you go down in his estimation. You make those men at Malheur Agency behave themselves und I r-raise you. Only I do vish, I do certainly vish you had some beard on that yoong chin."

The boy glanced at his pistol.

"No, no, no, my son," said the sharp old German. "I don't want gun-powder in dis affair. You must act kviet und decisif und keep your liddle shirt on. What you accomplish shootin'? You kill somebody, und then, pop! somebody kills you. What goot is all that nonsense to me?"

"It would annoy me some, too," retorted the boy, eying the capitalist. "Don't leave me out of the proposition."

"Broposition! Broposition! Now you get hot mit old Max for nothing."

"If you didn't contemplate trouble," pursued the boy, "what was your point just now in sampling my marksmanship?" He kicked some snow in the direction of the shattered bottle. "It's understood no whiskey comes on that ranch. But if no gunpowder goes along with me, either, let's call the deal off. Buy some other fool."

"You haf not understand, my boy. Und you get very hot because I hap-pen to make that liddle joke about somebody killing you. Was you thinking maybe old Max not care what happen to you?"

A moment of silence passed before the answer came: "Suppose we talk business?"

"Very well, very well. Only notice this thing. When oder peoples talk oop to me like you haf done many times, it is not they who does the getting hot. It is me—old Max. Und when old Max gets hot he slings them out of his road anywheres. Some haf been very sorry they get so slung. You invite me to buy some oder fool? Oh, my boy, I will buy no oder fool except you, for that was just like me when I was yoong Max!" Again the ruddy and grizzled magnate put his hand on the shoulder of the boy, who stood looking away at the bottles, at the railroad track, at anything save his employer.

The employer proceeded: "I was afraid of nobody und noding in those days. You are afraid of nobody and noding. But those days was different. No Pullman sleepers, no railroad at all. We come oop the Columbia in the steamboat, we travel hoonderts of miles by team, we sleep, we eat nowheres in particular mit many unexpected interooptions. There was Indians, there was offle bad white men, und if you was not offle yourself you vanished quickly. Therefore in those days was Max Vogel hell und repeat."

The magnate smiled a broad fond smile over the past which he had kicked, driven, shot, bled, and battled through to present power; and the boy winked up at him again now.

"I don't propose to vanish, myself," said he.

"Ah-ha! you was no longer mad mit der old Max! Of coorse I care what happens to you. I was alone in the world myself in those lofely wicked days."

Reserve again made flinty the boy's face.

"Neider did I talk about my feelings," continued Max Vogel, "but I nefer show them too quick. If I was injured I wait, and I strike to kill. We all paddles our own dug-out, eh? We ask no favors from nobody; we must win our spurs! Not so? Now I talk business with you where you interroopt me. If cow-boys was not so offle scarce in the country, I would long ago haf bounce the lot of those drunken fellows. But they cannot be spared; we must get along so. I cannot send Brock, he is needed at Harper's. The dumb fellow at Alvord Lake is too dumb; he is not quickly coorageous. They would play high jinks mit him. Therefore I send you. Brock he say to me you haf joodgement. I watch, und I say to myself also, this boy haf goot joodgement. Und when you look at your pistol so quick, I tell you quick I don't send you to kill men when they are so scarce already! My boy, it is ever the moral, the say-noding strength what gets there—mit always the liddle pistol behind, in case—joost in case. Haf you understand? I ask you to shoot. I see you know how, as Brock told me. I recommend you to let them see that aggomplishment in a friendly way. Maybe a shooting-match mit prizes—I pay for them—pretty soon after you come. Und joodgement—und joodgement. Here comes that train. Haf you well understand?"

Upon this the two shook hands, looking square friendship in each other's eyes. The east-bound, long quiet and dark beneath its flowing clots of smoke, slowed to a halt. A few valises and legs descended, ascended, herding and hurrying; a few trunks were thrown resoundingly in and out of the train; a woolly, crooked old man came with a box and a bandanna bundle from the second-class car; the travellers of a thousand miles looked torpidly at him through the dim, dusty windows of their Pullman, and settled again for a thousand miles more. Then the east-bound, shooting heavier clots of smoke laboriously into the air, drew its slow length out of Nampa, and away.

"Where's that stage?" shrilled the woolly old man. "That's what I'm after."

"Why, hello!" shouted Vogel. "Hello, Uncle Pasco! I heard you was dead."

Uncle Pasco blinked his small eyes to see who hailed him. "Oh!" said he, in his light, crusty voice. "Dutchy Vogel. No, I ain't dead. You guessed wrong. Not dead. Help me up, Dutchy."

A tolerant smile broadened Vogel's face. "It was ten years since I see you," said he, carrying the old man's box.

"Shouldn't wonder. Maybe it'll be another ten till you see me next." He stopped by the stage step, and wheeling nimbly, surveyed his old-time acquaintance, noting the good hat, the prosperous watch-chain, the big, well-blacked boots. "Not seen me for ten years. Hee-hee! No. Usen't to have a cent more than me. Twins in poverty. That's how Dutchy and me started. If we was buried to-morrow they'd mark him 'Pecunious' and me 'Impecunious.' That's what. Twins in poverty."

"I stick to von business at a time, Uncle," said good-natured, successful Max.

A flicker of aberration lighted in the old man's eye. "H'm, yes," said he, pondering. "Stuck to one business. So you did. H'm." Then, suddenly sly, he chirped: "But I've struck it rich now." He tapped his box. "Jewelry," he half-whispered. "Miners and cow-boys."

"Yes," said Vogel. "Those poor, deluded fellows, they buy such stuff." And he laughed at the seedy visionary who had begun frontier life with him on the bottom rung and would end it there. "Do you play that concertina yet, Uncle?" he inquired.

"Yes, yes. I always play. It's in here with my tooth-brush and socks." Uncle Pasco held up the bandanna. "Well, he's getting ready to start. I guess I'll be climbing inside. Holy Gertrude!"

This shrill comment was at sight of the school-master, patient within the stage. "What business are you in?" demanded Uncle Pasco.

"I am in the spelling business," replied the teacher, and smiled, faintly.

"Hell!" piped Uncle Pasco. "Take this."

He handed in his bandanna to the traveller, who received it politely. Max Vogel lifted the box of cheap jewelry; and both he and the boy came behind to boost the old man up on the stage step. But with a nettled look he leaped up to evade them, tottered half-way, and then, light as a husk of grain, got himself to his seat and scowled at the school-master.

After a brief inspection of that pale, spectacled face, "Dutchy," he called out of the door, "this country is not what it was."

But old Max Vogel was inattentive. He was speaking to the boy, Dean Drake, and held a flask in his hand. He reached the flask to his new superintendent. "Drink hearty," said he. "There, son! Don't be shy. Haf you forgot it is forbidden fruit after now?"

"Kid sworn off?" inquired Uncle Pasco of the school-master.

"I understand," replied this person, "that Mr. Vogel will not allow his cowboys at the Malheur Agency to have any whiskey brought there. Personally, I feel gratified." And Mr. Bolles, the new school-master, gave his faint smile.

"Oh," muttered Uncle Pasco. "Forbidden to bring whiskey on the ranch? "H'm." His eyes wandered to the jewelry-box. "H'm," said he again; and becoming thoughtful, he laid back his moth-eaten sly head, and spoke no further with Mr. Bolles.

Dean Drake climbed into the stage and the vehicle started.

"Goot luck, goot luck, my son!" shouted the hearty Max, and opened and waved both his big arms at the departing boy. He stood looking after the stage. "I hope he come back," said he. "I think he come back. If he come I r-raise him fifty dollars without any beard."

II

The stage had not trundled so far on its Silver City road but that a whistle from Nampa station reached its three occupants. This was the branch train starting back to Boise with Max Vogel aboard; and the boy looked out at the locomotive with a sigh.

"Only five days of town," he murmured. "Six months more wilderness now."

"My life has been too much town," said the new school-master. "I am looking forward to a little wilderness for a change."

Old Uncle Pasco, leaning back, said nothing; he kept his eyes shut and his ears open.

"Change is what I don't get," sighed Dean Drake. In a few miles, however, before they had come to the ferry over Snake River, the recent leave-taking and his employer's kind but dominating repression lifted from the boy's spirit. His gray eye wakened keen again, and he began to whistle light opera tunes, looking about him alertly, like the sparrow-hawk that he was. "Ever see Jeannie Winston in 'Fatinitza'?" he inquired of Mr. Bolles.

The school-master, with a startled, thankful countenance, stated that he had never.

"Ought to," said Drake.

"'You a man? that can't be true!
Men have never eyes like you.'

That's what the girls in the harem sing in the second act. Golly whiz!" The boy gleamed over the memory of that evening.

"You have a hard job before you," said the school-master, changing the subject.

"Yep. Hard." The wary Drake shook his head warningly at Mr. Bolles to keep off that subject, and he glanced in the direction of slumbering Uncle Pasco. Uncle Pasco was quite aware of all this. "I wouldn't take another lonesome job so soon," pursued Drake, "but I want the money. I've been working eleven months along the Owyhee as a sort of junior boss, and I'd earned my vacation. Just got it started hot in Portland, when biff! old Vogel telegraphs me. Well, I'll be saving instead of squandering. But it feels so good to squander!"

"I have never had anything to squander," said Bolles, rather sadly.

"You don't say! Well, old man, I hope you will. It gives a man a lot he'll never get out of spelling-books. Are you cold? Here." And despite the school-master's protest, Dean Drake tucked his buffalo coat round and over him. "Some day, when I'm old," he went on, "I mean to live respectable under my own cabin and vine. Wife and everything. But not, anyway, till I'm thirty-five."

He dropped into his opera tunes for a while; but evidently it was not "Fatinitza" and his vanished holiday over which he was chiefly meditating, for presently he exclaimed: "I'll give them a shooting-match in the morning. You shoot?"

Bolles hoped he was going to learn in this country, and exhibited a .22 Smith & Wesson revolver.

Drake grieved over it. "Wrap it up warm," said he. "I'll lend you a real one when we get to the Malheur Agency. But you can eat, anyhow. Christmas being next week, you see, my programme is, shoot all A.M. and eat all P.M. I wish you could light on a notion what prizes to give my buccaroos."

"Buccaroos?" said Bolles.

"Yep. Cow-punchers. Vaqueros. Buccaroos in Oregon. Bastard Spanish word, you see, drifted up from Mexico. Vogel would not care to have me give 'em money as prizes."

At this Uncle Pasco opened an eye.

"How many buccaroos will there be?" Bolles inquired.

"At the Malheur Agency? It's the headquarters of five of our ranches. There ought to be quite a crowd. A dozen, probably, at this time of year."

Uncle Pasco opened his other eye. "Here, you!" he said, dragging at his box under the seat. "Pull it, can't you? There. Just what you're after. There's your prizes." Querulous and watchful, like some aged, rickety ape, the old man drew out his trinkets in shallow shelves.

"Sooner give 'em nothing," said Dean Drake.

"What's that? What's the matter with them?"

"Guess the boys have had all the brass rings and glass diamonds they want."

"That's all you know, then. I sold that box clean empty through the Palouse country last week, 'cept the bottom drawer, and an outfit on Meacham's hill took that. Shows all you know. I'm going clean through your country after I've quit Silver City. I'll start in by Baker City again, and I'll strike Harney, and maybe I'll go to Linkville. I know what buccaroos want. I'll go to Fort Rinehart, and I'll go to the Island Ranch, and first thing you'll be seeing your boys wearing my stuff all over their fingers and Sunday shirts, and giving their girls my stuff right in Harney City. That's what."

"All right, Uncle. It's a free country."

"Shaw! Guess it is. I was in it before you was, too. You were wet behind the ears when I was jammin' all around here. How many are they up at your place, did you say?"

"I said about twelve. If you're coming our way, stop and eat with us."

"Maybe I will and maybe I won't." Uncle Pasco crossly shoved his box back.

"All right, Uncle. It's a free country," repeated Drake.

Not much was said after this. Uncle Pasco unwrapped his concertina from the red handkerchief and played nimbly for his own benefit. At Silver City he disappeared, and, finding he had stolen nothing from them, they did not regret him. Dean Drake had some affairs to see to here before starting for Harper's ranch, and it was pleasant to Bolles to find how Drake was esteemed through this country. The school-master was to board at the Malheur Agency, and had come this way round because the new superintendent must so travel. They were scarcely birds of a feather, Drake and Bolles, yet since one remote roof was to cover them, the in-door man was glad this boy-host had won so much good-will from high and low. That the shrewd old Vogel should trust so much in a nineteen-year-old was proof enough at least of his character; but when Brock, the foreman from Harper's, came for them at Silver City, Bolles witnessed the affection that the rougher man held for Drake. Brock shook the boy's hand with that serious quietness and absence of words which shows the Western heart is speaking. After a look at Bolles and a silent bestowing of the baggage aboard the team, he cracked his long whip and the three rattled happily away through the dips of an open country where clear streams ran blue beneath the winter air. They followed the Jordan (that Idaho Jordan) west towards Oregon and the Owyhee, Brock often turning in his driver's seat so as to speak with Drake. He had a long, gradual chapter of confidences and events; through miles he unburdened these to his favorite.

The California mare was doing well in harness. The eagle over at White-horse ranch had fought the cat most terrible. Gilbert had got a mule-kick in the stomach, but was eating his three meals. They had a new boy who played the guitar. He used maple-syrup on his meat, and claimed he was from Alabama. Brock guessed things were about as usual in most ways. The new well had caved in again. Then, in the midst of his gossip, the thing he had wanted to say all along came out: "We're pleased about your promotion," said he; and, blushing, shook Drake's hand again.

Warmth kindled the boy's face, and next, with a sudden severity, he said: "You're keeping back something."

The honest Brock looked blank, then labored in his memory.

"Has the sorrel girl in Harney married you yet?" said Drake.

Brock slapped his leg, and the horses jumped at his mirth. He was mostly grave-mannered, but when his boy superintendent joked, he rejoiced with the same pride that he took in all of Drake's excellences.

"The boys in this country will back you up," said he, next day; and Drake inquired: "What news from the Malheur Agency?"

"Since the new Chinaman has been cooking for them," said Brock, "they have been peaceful as a man could wish."

"They'll approve of me, then," Drake answered. "I'm feeding 'em hyas Christmas muck-a-muck."

"And what may that be?" asked the school-master.

"You no kumtux Chinook?" inquired Drake. "Travel with me and you'll learn all sorts of languages. It means just a big feed. All whiskey is barred," he added to Brock.

"It's the only way," said the foreman. "They've got those Pennsylvania men up there."

Drake had not encountered these.

"The three brothers Drinker," said Brock. "Full, Half-past Full, and Drunk are what they call them. There's the names; they've brought them from Klamath and Rogue River."

"I should not think a Chinaman would enjoy such comrades," ventured Mr. Bolles.

"Chinamen don't have comrades in this country," said Brock, briefly. "They like his cooking. It's a lonesome section up there, and a Chinaman could hardly quit it, not if he was expected to stay. Suppose they kick about the whiskey rule?" he suggested to Drake.

"Can't help what they do. Oh, I'll give each boy his turn in Harney City when he gets anxious. It's the whole united lot I don't propose to have cut up on me."

A look of concern for the boy came over the face of foreman Brock. Several times again before their parting did he thus look at his favorite. They paused at Harper's for a day to attend to some matters, and when Drake was leaving this place one of the men said to him: "We'll stand by you." But from his blithe appearance and talk as the slim boy journeyed to the Malheur River and Headquarter ranch, nothing seemed to be on his mind. Oregon twinkled with sun and fine white snow. They crossed through a world of pines and creviced streams and exhilarating silence. The little waters fell tinkling through icicles in the loneliness of the woods, and snowshoe rabbits dived into the brush. East Oregon, the Owyhee and the Malheur country, the old trails of General Crook, the willows by the streams, the open swales, the high woods where once Buffalo Horn and Chief E-egante and O-its the medicine-man prospered, through this domain of war and memories went Bolles the school-master with Dean Drake and Brock. The third noon from Harper's they came leisurely down to the old Malheur Agency, where once the hostile Indians had drawn pictures on the door, and where Castle Rock frowned down unchanged.

"I wish I was going to stay here with you," said Brock to Drake. "By Indian Creek you can send word to me quicker than we've come."

"Why, you're an old bat!" said the boy to his foreman, and clapped him farewell on the shoulder.

Brock drove away, thoughtful. He was not a large man. His face was clean-cut, almost delicate. He had a well-trimmed, yellow mustache, and it was chiefly in his blue eye and lean cheek-bone that the frontiersman showed. He loved Dean Drake more than he would ever tell, even to himself.

The young superintendent set at work to ranch-work this afternoon of Brock's leaving, and the buccaroos made his acquaintance one by one and stared at him. Villany did not sit outwardly upon their faces; they were not villains; but they stared at the boy sent to control them, and they spoke together, laughing. Drake took the head of the table at supper, with Bolles on his right. Down the table some silence, some staring, much laughing went on—the rich brute laugh of the belly untroubled by the brain. Sam, the Chinaman, rapid and noiseless, served the dishes.

"What is it?" said a buccaroo.

"Can it bite?" said another.

"If you guess what it is, you can have it," said a third.

"It's meat," remarked Drake, incisively, helping himself; "and tougher than it looks." The brute laugh rose from the crowd and fell into surprised silence; but no rejoinder came, and they ate their supper somewhat thoughtfully. The Chinaman's quick, soft eye had glanced at Dean Drake when they laughed. He served his dinner solicitously. In his kitchen that evening he and Bolles unpacked the good things—the olives, the dried fruits, the cigars—brought by the new superintendent for Christmas; and finding Bolles harmless, like his gentle Asiatic self, Sam looked cautiously about and spoke:

"You not know why they laugh," said he. "They not talk about my meat then. They mean new boss, Misser Dlake. He velly young boss."

"I think," said Bolles, "Mr. Drake understood their meaning, Sam. I have noticed that at times he expresses himself peculiarly. I also think they understood his meaning."

The Oriental pondered. "Me like Misser Dlake," said he. And drawing quite close, he observed, "They not nice man velly much."

Next day and every day "Misser Dlake" went gayly about his business, at his desk or on his horse, vigilant, near and far, with no sign save a steadier keenness in his eye. For the Christmas dinner he provided still further, sending to the Grande Ronde country for turkeys and other things. He won the heart of Bolles by lending him a good horse; but the buccaroos, though they were boisterous over the coming Christmas joy, did not seem especially grateful. Drake, however, kept his worries to himself.

"This thing happens anywhere," he said one night in the office to Bolles, puffing a cigar. "I've seen a troop of cavalry demoralize itself by a sort of contagion from two or three men."

"I think it was wicked to send you here by yourself," blurted Bolles.

"Poppycock! It's the chance of my life, and I'll jam her through or bust."

"I think they have decided you are getting turkeys because you are afraid of them," said Bolles.

"Why, of course! But d' you figure I'm the man to abandon my Christmas turkey because my motives for eating it are misconstrued?"

Dean Drake smoked for a while; then a knock came at the door. Five buccaroos entered and stood close, as is the way with the guilty who feel uncertain.

"We were thinking as maybe you'd let us go over to town," said Half-past Full, the spokesman.

"When?"

"Oh, any day along this week."

"Can't spare you till after Christmas."

"Maybe you'll not object to one of us goin'?"

"You'll each have your turn after this week."

A slight pause followed. Then Half-past Full said: "What would you do if I went, anyway?"

"Can't imagine," Drake answered, easily. "Go, and I'll be in a position to inform you."

The buccaroo dropped his stolid bull eyes, but raised them again and grinned. "Well, I'm not particular about goin' this week, boss."

"That's not my name," said Drake, "but it's what I am."

They stood a moment. Then they shuffled out. It was an orderly retreat—almost.

Drake winked over to Bolles. "That was a graze," said he, and smoked for a while. "They'll not go this time. Question is, will they go next?"

III

Drake took a fresh cigar, and threw his legs over the chair arm.

"I think you smoke too much," said Bolles, whom three days had made familiar and friendly.

"Yep. Have to just now. That's what! as Uncle Pasco would say. They are a half-breed lot, though," the boy continued, returning to the buccaroos and their recent visit. "Weaken in the face of a straight bluff, you see, unless they get whiskey-courageous. And I've called 'em down on that."

"Oh!" said Bolles, comprehending.

"Didn't you see that was their game? But he will not go after it."

"The flesh is all they seem to understand," murmured Bolles.

Half-past Full did not go to Harney City for the tabooed whiskey, nor did any one. Drake read his buccaroos like the children that they were. After the late encounter of grit, the atmosphere was relieved of storm. The children, the primitive, pagan, dangerous children, forgot all about whiskey, and lusted joyously for Christmas. Christmas was coming! No work! A shooting-match! A big feed! Cheerfulness bubbled at the Malheur Agency. The weather itself was in tune. Castle Rock seemed no longer to frown, but rose into the shining air, a mass of friendly strength. Except when a rare sledge or horseman passed, Mr. Bolles's journeys to the school were all to show it was not some pioneer colony in a new, white, silent world that heard only the playful shouts and songs of the buccaroos. The sun overhead and the hard-crushing snow underfoot filled every one with a crisp, tingling hilarity.

Before the sun first touched Castle Rock on the morning of the feast they were up and in high feather over at the bunk-house. They raced across to see what Sam was cooking; they begged and joyfully swallowed lumps of his raw plum-pudding. "Merry Christmas!" they wished him, and "Melly Clismas!" said he to them. They played leap-frog over by the Stable, they put snow down each other's backs. Their shouts rang round corners; it was like boys let out of school. When Drake gathered them for the shooting-match, they cheered him; when he told them there were no prizes, what did they care for prizes? When he beat them all the first round, they cheered him again. Pity he hadn't offered prizes! He wasn't a good business man, after all!

The rounds at the target proceeded through the forenoon, Drake the acclaimed leader; and the Christmas sun drew to mid-sky. But as its splendor in the heavens increased, the happy shoutings on earth began to wane.

The body was all that the buccaroos knew; well, the flesh comes pretty natural to all of us—and who had ever taught these men about the spirit? The further they were from breakfast the nearer they were to dinner; yet the happy shoutings waned! The spirit is a strange thing. Often it dwells dumb in human clay, then unexpectedly speaks out of the clay's darkness.

It was no longer a crowd Drake had at the target. He became aware that quietness had been gradually coming over the buccaroos. He looked, and saw a man wandering by himself in the lane. Another leaned by the stable corner, with a vacant face. Through the windows of the bunk-house he could see two or three on their beds. The children were tired of shouting. Drake went in-doors and threw a great log on the fire. It blazed up high with sparks, and he watched it, although the sun shown bright on the window-sill. Presently he noticed that a man had come in and taken a chair. It was Half-past Full, and with his boots stretched to the warmth, he sat gazing into the fire. The door opened and another buccaroo entered and sat off in a corner. He had a bundle of old letters, smeared sheets tied with a twisted old ribbon. While his large, rope-toughened fingers softly loosened the ribbon, he sat with his back to the room and presently began to read the letters over, one by one. Most of the men came in before long, and silently joined the watchers round the great fireplace. Drake threw another log on, and in a short time this, too, broke into ample flame. The silence was long; a slice of shadow had fallen across the window-sill, when a young man spoke, addressing the logs:

"I skinned a coon in San Saba, Texas, this day a year."

At the sound of a voice, some of their eyes turned on the speaker, but turned back to the fire again. The spirit had spoken from the clay, aloud; and the clay was uncomfortable at hearing it.

After some more minutes a neighbor whispered to a neighbor, "Play you a game of crib."

The man nodded, stole over to where the board was, and brought it across the floor on creaking tip-toe. They set it between them, and now and then the cards made a light sound in the room.

"I treed that coon on Honey," said the young man, after a while—"Honey Creek, San Saba. Kind o' dry creek. Used to flow into Big Brady when it rained."

The flames crackled on, the neighbors still played their cribbage. Still was the day bright, but the shrinking wedge of sun had gone entirely from the window-sill. Half-past Full had drawn from his pocket a mouth-organ, breathing half-tunes upon it; in the middle of "Suwanee River" the man who sat in the corner laid the letter he was beginning upon the heap on his knees and read no more. The great genial logs lay glowing, burning; from the fresher one the flames flowed and forked; along the embered surface of the others ran red and blue shivers of iridescence. With legs and arms crooked and sprawled, the buccaroos brooded, staring into the glow with seldom-winking eyes, while deep inside the clay the spirit spoke quietly. Christmas Day was passing, but the sun shone still two good hours high. Outside, over the snow and pines, it was only in the deeper folds of the hills that the blue shadows had come; the rest of the world was gold and silver; and from far across that silence into this silence by the fire came a tinkling stir of sound. Sleighbells it was, steadily coming, too early for Bolles to be back from his school festival. The toy-thrill of the jingling grew clear and sweet, a spirit of enchantment that did not wake the stillness, but cast it into a deeper dream. The bells came near the door and stopped, and then Drake opened it.

"Hello, Uncle Pasco!" said he. "Thought you were Santa Claus."

"Santa Claus! H'm. Yes. That's what. Told you maybe I'd come."

"So you did. Turkey is due in—let's see—ninety minutes. Here, boys! some of you take Uncle Pasco's horse."

"No, no, I won't. You leave me alone. I ain't stoppin' here. I ain't hungry. I just grubbed at the school. Sleepin' at Missouri Pete's to-night. Got to make the railroad tomorrow." The old man stopped his precipitate statements. He sat in his sledge deeply muffled, blinking at Drake and the buccaroos, who had strolled out to look at him. "Done a big business this trip," said he. "Told you I would. Now if you was only givin' your children a Christmas-tree like that I seen that feller yer school-marm doin' just now—hee-hee!" From his blankets he revealed the well-known case. "Them things would shine on a tree," concluded Uncle Pasco.

"Hang 'em in the woods, then," said Drake.

"Jewelry, is it?" inquired the young Texas man.

Uncle Pasco whipped open his case. "There you are," said he. "All what's left. That ring'll cost you a dollar."

"I've a dollar somewheres," said the young man, fumbling.

Half-past Full, on the other side of the sleigh, stood visibly fascinated by the wares he was given a skilful glimpse of down among the blankets. He peered and he pondered while Uncle Pasco glibly spoke to him.

"Scatter your truck out plain!" the buccaroo exclaimed, suddenly. "I'm not buying in the dark. Come over to the bunk-house and scatter."

"Brass will look just the same anywhere," said Drake.

"Brass!" screamed Uncle. "Brass your eye!"

But the buccaroos, plainly glad for distraction, took the woolly old scolding man with them. Drake shouted that if getting cheated cheered them, by all means to invest heavily, and he returned alone to his fire, where

Bolles soon joined him. They waited, accordingly, and by-and-by the sleigh-bells jingled again. As they had come out of the silence, so did they go into it, their little silvery tinkle dancing away in the distance, faint and fainter, then, like a breath, gone.

Uncle Pasco's trinkets had audibly raised the men's spirits. They remained in the bunkhouse, their laughter reaching Drake and Bolles more and more. Sometimes they would scuffle and laugh loudly.

"Do you imagine it's more leap-frog?" inquired the school-master.

"Gambling," said Drake. "They'll keep at it now till one of them wins everything the rest have bought."

"Have they been lively ever since morning?"

"Had a reaction about noon," said Drake. "Regular home-sick spell. I felt sorry for 'em."

"They seem full of reaction," said Bolles. "Listen to that!"

It was now near four o'clock, and Sam came in, announcing dinner.

"All leady," said the smiling Chinaman.

"Pass the good word to the bunk-house," said Drake, "if they can hear you."

Sam went across, and the shouting stopped. Then arose a thick volley of screams and cheers.

"That don't sound right," said Drake, leaping to his feet. In the next instant the Chinaman, terrified, returned through the open door. Behind him lurched Half-past Full, and stumbled into the room. His boot caught, and he pitched, but saved himself and stood swaying, heavily looking at Drake. The hair curled dense over his bull head, his mustache was spread with his grin, the light of cloddish humor and destruction burned in his big eye. The clay had buried the spirit like a caving pit.

"'Twas false jewelry all right!" he roared, at the top of his voice. "A good old jimmyjohn full, boss. Say, boss, goin' to run our jimmyjohn off the ranch? Try it on, kid. Come over and try it on!" The bull beat on the table.

Dean Drake had sat quickly down in his chair, his gray eye upon the hulking buccaroo. Small and dauntless he sat, a sparrow-hawk caught in a trap, and game to the end—whatever end.

"It's a trifle tardy to outline any policy about your demijohn," said he, seriously. "You folks had better come in and eat before you're beyond appreciating."

"Ho, we'll eat your grub, boss. Sam's cooking goes." The buccaroo lurched out and away to the bunk-house, where new bellowing was set up.

"I've got to carve this turkey, friend," said the boy to Bolles.

"I'll do my best to help eat it," returned the school-master, smiling.

"Misser Dlake," said poor Sam, "I solly you. I velly solly you."

IV

"Reserve your sorrow, Sam," said Dean Drake. "Give us your soup for a starter. Come," he said to Bolles. "Quick."

He went into the dining-room, prompt in his seat at the head of the table, with the school-master next to him.

"Nice man, Uncle Pasco," he continued. "But his time is not now. We have nothing to do for the present but sit like every day and act perfectly natural."

"I have known simpler tasks," said Mr. Bolles, "but I'll begin by spreading this excellently clean napkin."

"You're no school-marm!" exclaimed Drake; "you please me."

"The worst of a bad thing," said the mild Bolles, "is having time to think about it, and we have been spared that."

"Here they come," said Drake.

They did come. But Drake's alert strategy served the end he had tried for. The drunken buccaroos swarmed disorderly to the door and halted. Once more the new superintendent's ways took them aback. Here was the decent table with lights serenely burning, with unwonted good things arranged upon it—the olives, the oranges, the preserves. Neat as parade drill were the men's places, all the cups and forks symmetrical along the white cloth. There, waiting his guests at the far end, sat the slim young boss talking with his boarder, Mr. Bolles, the parts in their smooth hair going with all the rest of this propriety. Even the daily tin dishes were banished in favor of crockery.

"Bashful of Sam's napkins, boys?" said the boss. "Or is it the bald-headed china?"

At this bidding they came in uncertainly. Their whiskey was ashamed inside. They took their seats, glancing across at each other in a transient silence, drawing their chairs gingerly beneath them. Thus ceremony fell unexpected upon the gathering, and for a while they swallowed in awkwardness what the swift, noiseless Sam brought them. He in a long white apron passed and repassed with his things from his kitchen, doubly efficient and civil under stress of anxiety for his young master. In the pauses of his serving he watched from the background, with a face that presently caught the notice of one of them.

"Smile, you almond-eyed highbinder," said the buccaroo. And the Chinaman smiled his best.

"I've forgot something," said Half-past Full, rising. "Don't let 'em skip a course on me." Half-past left the room.

"That's what I have been hoping for," said Drake to Bolles.

Half-past returned presently and caught Drake's look of expectancy. "Oh no, boss," said the buccaroo, instantly, from the door. "You're on to me, but I'm on to you." He slammed the door with ostentation and dropped with a loud laugh into his seat.

"First smart thing I've known him do," said Drake to Bolles. "I am disappointed."

Two buccaroos next left the room together.

"They may get lost in the snow," said the humorous Half-past. "I'll just show 'em the trail." Once more he rose from the dinner and went out.

"Yes, he knelt too much to bring it in here," said Drake to Bolles. "He knew none but two or three would dare drink, with me looking on."

"Don't you think he is afraid to bring it in the same room with you at all?" Bolles suggested.

"And me temperance this season? Now, Bolles, that's unkind."

"Oh, dear, that is not at all what—"

"I know what you meant, Bolles. I was only just making a little merry over this casualty. No, he don't mind me to that extent, except when he's sober. Look at him!"

Half-past was returning with his friends. Quite evidently they had all found the trail.

"Uncle Pasco is a nice old man!" pursued Drake. "I haven't got my gun on. Have you?"

"Yes," said Bolles, but with a sheepish swerve of the eye.

Drake guessed at once. "Not Baby Bunting? Oh, Lord! and I promised to give you an adult weapon!—the kind they're wearing now by way of full-dress."

"Talkin' secrets, boss?" said Half-past Full.

The well-meaning Sam filled his cup, and this proceeding shifted the buccaroo's truculent attention.

"What's that mud?" he demanded.

"Coffee," said Sam, politely.

The buccaroo swept his cup to the ground, and the next man howled dismay.

"Burn your poor legs?" said Half-past. He poured his glass over the victim. They wrestled, the company pounded the table, betting hoarsely, until Half-past went to the floor, and his plate with him.

"Go easy," said Drake. "You're smashing the company's property."

"Bald-headed china for sure, boss!" said a second of the brothers Drinker, and dropped a dish.

"I'll merely tell you," said Drake, "that the company don't pay for this china twice."

"Not twice?" said Half-past Full, smashing some more. "How about thrice?"

"Want your money now?" another inquired.

A riot of banter seized upon all of them, and they began to laugh and destroy.

"How much did this cost?" said one, prying askew his three-tined fork.

"How much did you cost yourself?" said another to Drake.

"What, our kid boss? Two bits, I guess."

"Hyas markook. Too dear!"

They bawled at their own jokes, loud and ominous; threat sounded beneath their lightest word, the new crashes of china that they threw on the floor struck sharply through the foreboding din of their mirth. The spirit that Drake since his arrival had kept under in them day by day, but not quelled, rose visibly each few succeeding minutes, swelling upward as the tide does. Buoyed up on the whiskey, it glittered in their eyes and yelled mutinously in their voices.

"I'm waiting all orders," said Bolles to Drake.

"I haven't any," said Drake. "New ones, that is. We've sat down to see this meal out. Got to keep sitting."

He leaned back, eating deliberately, saying no more to the buccaroos; thus they saw he would never leave the room till they did. As he had taken his chair the first, so was the boy bound to quit it the last. The game of prying fork-tines staled on them one by one, and they took to songs, mostly of love and parting. With the red whiskey in their eyes they shouted plaintively of sweethearts, and vows, and lips, and meeting in the wild wood. From these they went to ballads of the cattle-trail and the Yuba River, and so inevitably worked to the old coast song, made of three languages, with its verses rhymed on each year since the first beginning. Tradition laid it heavy upon each singer in his turn to keep the pot a-boiling by memory or by new invention, and the chant went forward with hypnotic cadence to a tune of larkish, ripping gayety. He who had read over his old stained letters in the homesick afternoon had waked from such dreaming and now sang:

"Once, jes' onced in the year o' '49,
I met a fancy thing by the name o' Keroline;
I never could persuade her for to leave me be;
She went and she took and she married me."

His neighbor was ready with an original contribution:

"Once, once again in the year o' '64,
By the city of Whatcom down along the shore—

I never could persuade them for to leave me be—
A Siwash squaw went and took and married me."

"What was you doin' between all them years?" called Half-past Full.
"Shut yer mouth," said the next singer:

"Once, once again in the year o' '71
('Twas the suddenest deed that I ever done)—
I never could persuade them for to leave me be—
A rich banker's daughter she took and married me."

"This is looking better," said Bolles to Drake.
"Don't you believe it," said the boy.
Ten or a dozen years were thus sung.
"I never could persuade them for to leave me be" tempestuously brought down the chorus and the fists, until the drunkards could sit no more, but stood up to sing, tramping the tune heavily together. Then, just as the turn came round to Drake himself, they dashed their chairs down and herded out of the room behind Half-past Full, slamming the door.

Drake sat a moment at the head of his Christmas dinner, the fallen chairs, the lumpy wreck. Blood charged his face from his hair to his collar. "Let's smoke," said he. They went from the dinner through the room of the great fireplace to his office beyond.

"Have a mild one?" he said to the school-master.
"No, a strong one to-night, if you please." And Bolles gave his mild smile.
"You do me good now and then," said Drake.
"Dear me," said the teacher, "I have found it the other way."

All the rooms fronted on the road with doors—the old-time agency doors, where the hostiles had drawn their pictures in the days before peace had come to reign over this country. Drake looked out, because the singing had stopped and they were very quiet in the bunk-house. He saw the Chinaman steal from his kitchen.

"Sam is tired of us," he said to Bolles.
"Tired?"
"Running away, I guess. I'd prefer a new situation myself. That's where you're deficient, Bolles. Only got sense enough to stay where you happen to be. Hello. What is he up to?"

Sam had gone beside a window of the bunk-house and was listening there, flat like a shadow. Suddenly he crouched, and was gone among the sheds. Out of the bunk-house immediately came a procession, the buccaroos still quiet, a careful, gradual body.

Drake closed his door and sat in the chair again. "They're escorting that jug over here," said he. "A new move, and a big one."

He and Bolles heard them enter the next room, always without much noise or talk—the loudest sound was the jug when they set it on the floor. Then they seemed to sit, talking little.

"Bolles," said Drake, "the sun has set. If you want to take after Sam—"

But the door of the sitting-room opened and the Chinaman himself came in. He left the door a-swing and spoke clearly. "Misser Dlake," said he, "slove bloke" (stove broke).

The superintendent came out of his office, following Sam to the kitchen. He gave no look or word to the buccaroos with their demijohn; he merely held his cigar sidewise in his teeth and walked with no hurry through the sitting-room. Sam took him through to the kitchen and round to a hind corner of the stove, pointing.

"Misser Dlake," said he, "slove no bloke. I hear them inside. They going kill you."

"That's about the way I was figuring it," mused Dean Drake.

"Misser Dlake," said the Chinaman, with appealing eyes, "I velly solly you. They no hurtee me. Me cook."

"Sam, there is much meat in your words. Condensed beef don't class with you. But reserve your sorrows yet a while. Now what's my policy?" he debated, tapping the stove here and there for appearances; somebody might look in. "Shall I go back to my office and get my guns?"

"You not goin' run now?" said the Chinaman, anxiously.

"Oh yes, Sam. But I like my gun travelling. Keeps me kind of warm. Now if they should get a sight of me arming—no, she's got to stay here till I come back for her. So long, Sam! See you later. And I'll have time to thank you then."

Drake went to the corral in a strolling manner. There he roped the strongest of the horses, and also the school-master's. In the midst of his saddling, Bolles came down.

"Can I help you in any way?" said Bolles.

"You've done it. Saved me a bothering touch-and-go play to get you out here and seem innocent. I'm going to drift."

"Drift?"

"There are times to stay and times to leave, Bolles; and this is a case of the latter. Have you a real gun on now?"

Poor Bolles brought out guiltily his .22 Smith & Wesson. "I don't seem to think of things," said he.

"Cheer up," said Drake. "How could you thought-read me? Hide Baby Bunting, though. Now we're off. Quietly, at the start. As if we were merely jogging to pasture."

Sam stood at his kitchen door, mutely wishing them well. The horses were walking without noise, but Half-past Full looked out of the window.

"We're by, anyhow," said Drake. "Quick now. Burn the earth." The horse sprang at his spurs. "Dust, you son of a gun! Rattle your hocks! Brindle! Vamoose!" Each shouted word was a lash with his quirt. "Duck!" he called to Bolles.

Bolles ducked, and bullets grooved the spraying snow. They rounded a corner and saw the crowd jumping into the corral, and Sam's door empty of that prudent Celestial.

"He's a very wise Chinaman!" shouted Drake, as they rushed.

"What?" screamed Bolles.

"Very wise Chinaman. He'll break that stove now to prove his innocence."

"Who did you say was innocent?" screamed Bolles.

"Oh, I said you were," yelled Drake, disgusted; and he gave over this effort at conversation as their horses rushed along.

V

It was a dim, wide stretch of winter into which Drake and Bolles galloped from the howling pursuit. Twilight already veiled the base of Castle Rock, and as they forged heavily up a ridge through the caking snow, and the yells came after them, Bolles looked seriously at Dean Drake; but that youth wore an expression of rising merriment. Bolles looked back at the dusk from which the yells were sounding, then forward to the spreading skein of night where the trail was taking him and the boy, and in neither direction could he discern cause for gayety.

"May I ask where we are going?" said he.

"Away," Drake answered. "Just away, Bolles. It's a healthy resort."

Ten miles were travelled before either spoke again. The drunken bucca-roos yelled hot on their heels at first, holding more obstinately to this chase than sober ruffians would have attempted. Ten cold, dark miles across the hills it took to cure them; but when their shoutings, that had followed over heights where the pines grew and down through the open swales between, dropped off, and died finally away among the willows along the south fork of the Malheur, Drake reined in his horse with a jerk.

"Now isn't that too bad!" he exclaimed.

"It is all very bad," said Bolles, sorry to hear the boy's tone of disappointment.

"I didn't think they'd fool me again," continued Drake, jumping down.

"Again?" inquired the interested Bolles.

"Why, they've gone home!" said the boy, in disgust.

"I was hoping so," said the school-master.

"Hoping? Why, it's sad, Bolles. Four miles farther and I'd have had them lost."

"Oh!" said Bolles.

"I wanted them to keep after us," complained Drake. "Soon as we had a good lead I coaxed them. Coaxed them along on purpose by a trail they knew, and four miles from here I'd have swung south into the mountains they don't know. There they'd have been good and far from home in the snow without supper, like you and me, Bolles. But after all my trouble they've gone back snug to that fireside. Well, let us be as cosey as we can."

He built a bright fire, and he whistled as he kicked the snow from his boots, busying over the horses and the blankets. "Take a rest," he said to Bolles. "One man's enough to do the work. Be with you soon to share our little cottage." Presently Bolles heard him reciting confidentially to his horse, "'Twas the night after Christmas, and all in the house—only we are not all in the house!" He slapped the belly of his horse Tyee, who gambolled away to the limit of his picket-rope. "Appreciating the moon, Bolles?" said he, returning at length to the fire. "What are you so gazeful about, father?"

"This is all my own doing," lamented the school-master.

"What, the moon is?"

"It has just come over me," Bolles continued. "It was before you got in the stage at Nampa. I was talking. I told Uncle Pasco that I was glad no whiskey was to be allowed on the ranch. It all comes from my folly!"

"Why, you hungry old New England conscience!" cried the boy, clapping him on the shoulder. "How in the world could you foresee the crookedness of that hoary Beelzebub?"

"That's all very well," said Bolles, miserably. "You would never have mentioned it yourself to him."

"You and I, Bolles, are different. I was raised on miscellaneous wickedness. A look at my insides would be liable to make you say your prayers."

The school-master smiled. "If I said any prayers," he replied, "you would be in them."

Drake looked moodily at the fire. "The Lord helps those who help themselves," said he. "I've prospered. For a nineteen-year-old I've hooked my claw fairly deep here and there. As for to-day—why, that's in the game too. It was their deal. Could they have won it on their own play? A joker dropped into their hand. It's my deal now, and I have some jokers myself. Go to sleep, Bolles. We've a ride ahead of us."

The boy rolled himself in his blanket skilfully. Bolles heard him say once or twice in a sort of judicial conversation with the blanket—"and all in the house—but we were not all in the house. Not all. Not a full house—" His tones drowsed comfortably into murmur, and then to quiet breathing. Bolles fed the fire, thatched the unneeded wind-break (for the calm, dry night was breathless), and for a long while watched the moon and a tuft of the sleeping boy's hair.

"If he is blamed," said the school-master, "I'll never forgive myself. I'll never forgive myself anyhow."

A paternal, or rather maternal, expression came over Bolles's face, and he removed his large, serious glasses. He did not sleep very well.

The boy did. "I'm feeling like a bird," said he, as they crossed through the mountains next morning on a short cut to the Owyhee. "Breakfast will brace you up, Bolles. There'll be a cabin pretty soon after we strike the other road. Keep thinking hard about coffee."

"I wish I could," said poor Bolles. He was forgiving himself less and less.

Their start had been very early; as Drake bid the school-master observe, to have nothing to detain you, nothing to eat and nothing to pack, is a great help in journeys of haste. The warming day, and Indian Creek well behind them, brought Drake to whistling again, but depression sat upon the self-accusing Bolles. Even when they sighted the Owyhee road below them, no cheerfulness waked in him; not at the nearing coffee, nor yet at the companionable tinkle of sleigh-bells dancing faintly upward through the bright, silent air.

"Why, if it ain't Uncle Pasco!" said Drake, peering down through a gap in the foot-hill.

"We'll get breakfast sooner than I expected. Quick! Give me Baby Bunting!"

"Are you going to kill him?" whispered the school-master, with a beaming countenance. And he scuffled with his pocket to hand over his hitherto belittled weapon.

Drake considered him. "Bolles, Bolles," said he, "you have got the New England conscience rank. Plymouth Rock is a pudding to your heart. Remind me to pray for you first spare minute I get. Now follow me close. He'll be much more useful to us alive."

They slipped from their horses, stole swiftly down a shoulder of the hill, and waited among some brush. The bells jingled unsuspectingly onward to this ambush.

"Only hear 'em!" said Drake. "All full of silver and Merry Christmas. Don't gaze at me like that, Bolles, or I'll laugh and give the whole snap away. See him come! The old man's breath streams out so calm. He's not worried with New England conscience. One, two, three—" Just before the sleigh came opposite, Dean Drake stepped out. "Morning, Uncle!" said he. "Throw up your hands!"

Uncle Pasco stopped dead, his eyes blinking. Then he stood up in the sleigh among his blankets. "H'm," said he. "The Kid."

"Throw up your hands! Quit fooling with that blanket!" Drake spoke dangerously now. "Bolles," he continued, "pitch everything out of the sleigh while I cover him. He's got a shot-gun under that blanket. Sling it out."

It was slung. The wraps followed. Uncle Pasco stepped obediently down, and soon the chattels of the emptied sleigh littered the snow. The old gentleman was invited to undress until they reached the six-shooter that Drake suspected. Then they eat his lunch, drank some whiskey that he had not sold to the buccaroos, told him to repack the sleigh, allowed him to wrap up again, bade him take the reins, and they would use his six-shooter and shot-gun to point out the road to him.

He had said very little, had Uncle Pasco, but stood blinking, obedient and malignant. "H'm," said he now, "goin' to ride with me, are you?"

He was told yes, that for the present he was their coachman. Their horses were tired and would follow, tied behind. "We're weary, too," said Drake, getting in. "Take your legs out of my way or I'll kick off your shins. Bolles, are you fixed warm and comfortable? Now start her up for Harper ranch, Uncle."

"What are you proposing to do with me?" inquired Uncle Pasco.

"Not going to wring your neck, and that's enough for the present. Faster, Uncle. Get a gait on. Bolles, here's Baby Bunting. Much obliged to you for the loan of it, old man."

Uncle Pasco's eye fell on the .22-caliber pistol. "Did you hold me up with that lemonade straw?" he asked, huskily.

"Yep," said Drake. "That's what."

"Oh, hell!" murmured Uncle Pasco. And for the first time he seemed dispirited.

"Uncle, you're not making time," said Drake after a few miles. "I'll thank you for the reins. Open your bandanna and get your concertina. Jerk the bellows for us."

"That I'll not!" screamed Uncle Pasco.

"It's music or walk home," said the boy. "Take your choice."

Uncle Pasco took his choice, opening with the melody of "The Last Rose of Summer." The sleigh whirled up the Owyhee by the winter willows, and the levels, and the meadow pools, bright frozen under the blue sky. Late in this day the amazed Brock by his corrals at Harper's beheld arrive his favorite, his boy superintendent, driving in with the school-master staring through his glasses, and Uncle Pasco throwing out active strains upon his concertina. The old man had been bidden to bellows away for his neck.

Drake was not long in explaining his need to the men. "This thing must be worked quick," said he. "Who'll stand by me?"

All of them would, and he took ten, with the faithful Brock. Brock would not allow Gilbert to go, because he had received another mule-kick in the stomach. Nor was Bolles permitted to be of the expedition. To all his protests, Drake had but the single word: "This is not our fight, old man. You've done your share with Baby Bunting."

Thus was the school-master in sorrow compelled to see them start back to Indian Creek and the Malheur without him. With him Uncle Pasco would have joyfully exchanged. He was taken along with the avengers. They would not wring his neck, but they would play cat and mouse with him and his concertina; and they did. But the conscience of Bolles still toiled. When Drake and the men were safe away, he got on the wagon going for the mail, thus making his way next morning to the railroad and Boise, where Max Vogel listened to him; and together this couple hastily took train and team for the Malheur Agency.

The avengers reached Indian Creek duly, and the fourth day after his Christmas dinner Drake came once more in sight of Castle Rock.

"I am doing this thing myself, understand," he said to Brock. "I am responsible."

"We're here to take your orders," returned the foreman. But as the agency buildings grew plain and the time for action was coming, Brock's anxious heart spoke out of its fulness. "If they start in to—to—they might—I wish you'd let me get in front," he begged, all at once.

"I thought you thought better of me," said Drake.

"Excuse me," said the man. Then presently: "I don't see how anybody could 'a' told he'd smuggle whiskey that way. If the old man [Brock meant Max Vogel] goes to blame you, I'll give him my opinion straight."

"The old man's got no use for opinions," said Drake. "He goes on results. He trusted me with this job, and we're going to have results now."

The drunkards were sitting round outside the ranch house. It was evening. They cast a sullen inspection on the new-comers, who returned them no inspection whatever. Drake had his men together and took them to the stable first, a shed with mangers. Here he had them unsaddle. "Because," he mentioned to Brock, "in case of trouble we'll be sure of their all staying. I'm taking no chances now."

Soon the drunkards strolled over, saying good-day, hazarding a few comments on the weather and like topics, and meeting sufficient answers.

"Goin' to stay?"

"Don't know."

"That's a good horse you've got."

"Fair."

But Sam was the blithest spirit at the Malheur Agency. "Hiyah!" he exclaimed. "Misser Dlake! How fashion you come quick so?" And the excellent Chinaman took pride in the meal of welcome that he prepared.

"Supper's now," said Drake to his men. "Sit anywhere you feel like. Don't mind whose chair you're taking—and we'll keep our guns on."

Thus they followed him, and sat. The boy took his customary perch at the head of the table, with Brock at his right. "I miss old Bolles," he told his foreman. "You don't appreciate Bolles."

"From what you tell of him," said Brock, "I'll examine him more careful."

Seeing their boss, the sparrow-hawk, back in his place, flanked with supporters, and his gray eye indifferently upon them, the buccaroos grew polite to oppressiveness. While Sam handed his dishes to Drake and the new-comers, and the new-comers eat what was good before the old inhabitants got a taste, these latter grew more and more solicitous. They offered sugar to the strangers, they offered their beds; Half-past Full urged them to sit companionably in the room where the fire was burning. But when the meal was over, the visitors went to another room with their arms, and lighted their own fire. They brought blankets from their saddles, and after a little concertina they permitted the nearly perished Uncle Pasco to slumber. Soon they slumbered themselves, with the door left open, and Drake watching. He would not even share vigil with Brock, and all night he heard the voices of the buccaroos, holding grand, unending council.

When the relentless morning came, and breakfast with the visitors again in their seats unapproachable, the drunkards felt the crisis to be a strain upon their sobered nerves. They glanced up from their plates, and down; along to Dean Drake eating his hearty porridge, and back at one another, and at the hungry, well-occupied strangers.

"Say, we don't want trouble," they began to the strangers.

"Course you don't. Breakfast's what you're after."

"Oh, well, you'd have got gay. A man gets gay."

"Sure."

"Mr. Drake," said Half-past Full, sweating with his effort, "we were sorry while we was a-fogging you up."

"Yes," said Drake. "You must have been just overcome by contrition."

A large laugh went up from the visitors, and the meal was finished without further diplomacy.

"One matter, Mr. Drake," stammered Half-past Full, as the party rose. "Our jobs. We're glad to pay for any things what got sort of broke."

"Sort of broke," repeated the boy, eying him. "So you want to hold your jobs?"

"If—" began the buccaroo, and halted.

"Fact is, you're a set of cowards," said Drake, briefly. "I notice you've forgot to remove that whiskey jug."

The demijohn still stood by the great fireplace. Drake entered and laid hold of it, the crowd standing back and watching. He took it out, with what remained in its capacious bottom, set it on a stump, stepped back, levelled his gun, and shattered the vessel to pieces. The whiskey drained down, wetting the stump, creeping to the ground.

Much potency lies in the object-lesson, and a grin was on the faces of all present, save Uncle Pasco's. It had been his demijohn, and when the shot struck it he blinked nervously.

"You ornery old mink!" said Drake, looking at him. "You keep to the jewelry business here-after."

The buccaroos grinned again. It was reassuring to witness wrath turn upon another.

"You want to hold your jobs?" Drake resumed to them. "You can trust yourselves?"

"Yes, sir," said Half-past Full.

"But I don't trust you," stated Drake, genially; and the buccaroos' hopeful eyes dropped. "I'm going to divide you," pursued the new superintendent. "Split you far and wide among the company's ranches. Stir you in with decenter blood. You'll go to White-horse ranch, just across the line of Nevada," he said to Half-past Full. "I'm tired of the brothers Drinker. You'll go—let's see—"

Drake paused in his apportionment, and a sleigh came swiftly round the turn, the horse loping and lathery.

"What vas dat shooting I hear joost now?" shouted Max Vogel, before he could arrive. He did not wait for any answer. "Thank the good God!" he exclaimed, at seeing the boy Dean Drake unharmed, standing with a gun. And to their amazement he sped past them, never slacking his horse's lope until he reached the corral. There he tossed the reins to the placid Bolles, and springing out like a sure-footed elephant, counted his saddle-horses; for he was a general. Satisfied, he strode back to the crowd by the demijohn. "When dem men get restless," he explained to Drake once, "always look out. Somebody might steal a horse."

The boy closed one gray, confidential eye at his employer. "Just my idea," said he, "when I counted 'em before breakfast."

"You liddle r-rascal," said Max, fondly. "What you shoot at?"

Drake pointed at the demijohn. "It was bigger than those bottles at Nampa," said he. "Guess you could have hit it yourself."

Max's great belly shook. He took in the situation. It had a flavor that he liked. He paused to relish it a little more in silence.

"Und you have killed noding else?" said he, looking at Uncle Pasco, who blinked copiously. "Mine old friend, you never get rich if you change your business so frequent. I tell you that thirty years now." Max's hand found Drake's shoulder, but he addressed Brock. "He is all what you tell me," said he to the foreman. "He have joodgement."

Thus the huge, jovial Teuton took command, but found Drake had left little for him to do. The buccaroos were dispersed at Harper's, at Port Rinehart, at Alvord Lake, towards Stein's peak, and at the Island Ranch by Harney Lake. And if you know east Oregon, or the land where Chief E-egante helped out Specimen Jones, his white soldier friend, when the hostile Bannocks were planning his immediate death as a spy, you will know what wide regions separated the buccaroos. Bolles was taken into Max Vogel's esteem; also was Chinese Sam. But Max sat smoking in the office with his boy superintendent, in particular satisfaction.

"You are a liddle r-rascal," said he. "Und I r-raise you fifty dollars."

Discussion Questions

1. Describe the character of Mr. Bolles, the schoolmaster. To what extent does he characterize the greenhorn or Easterner?
2. Using at least three examples and/or quotations, analyze the relationship between Drake and Bolles. Explain Bolles's role in giving some perspective or viewpoint on the story's conflict and on Drake's character.

Fig. 3.2 Charles Schreyvogel, *The Summit Springs Rescue—1869* (1908). Buffalo Bill Historical Center, Cody, WY; bequest in memory of Houx and Newell families; 11.64.

Fig. 3.3 Frederic Remington, *A Dash for the Timber* (1889), oil on canvas. Amon Carter Museum, Ft. Worth, TX; 1961.381.

Fig. 3.4 Charles Nahl, *Sunday Morning at the Mines* (1872). Crocker Art Museum, Sacramento, CA; E. B. Crocker Collection; 1872.381.

Fig. 3.5 Cassily Adams and Otto Becker, *Custer's Last Fight* (1896), chromolithograph. Amon Carter Museum, Ft. Worth, TX; 1964.194.

WILLA CATHER
(1873–1947)

The author was born in Back Creek Valley, Virginia, among the Blue Ridge Mountains. Her parents exposed her to the vigor of pioneer life when the family moved to the virgin prairie of Nebraska in 1883 (Hewitt 55). When the family first witnessed the bare and open land, she recalled, "I felt a good deal as if we had come to the end of everything—it was a kind of erasure of personality" (qtd. in Van Antwerp 71). Once settled in, she came to appreciate "the simplicity of a stoic people rooted to a harsh existence" (Hewitt 55). However, her father was ill-suited to sod-busting, so within two years the family moved to Red Cloud, a growing town of 2,500 (Woodress 38–39).

After graduating from the public high school there, she moved to Lincoln to take a preparatory year of studies. Then she attended the University of Nebraska, where she expressed her unconventionality by dressing in a masculine attire of tailored suit coat, starched shirt, and necktie. In the Panic of 1893, when banks failed, depression hit the United States, and the high plains drought led to crop failure and unpaid taxes, she began supporting herself at college by writing sketches and reviews of touring theatrical productions for the *Nebraska State Journal*. After receiving her degree in 1895, she returned to Red Cloud, but continued to write for that newspaper and for the weekly Lincoln *Courier*. In 1896, she published "On the Divide," her first story in a national literary magazine, *Overland Monthly* (Gerber 27–36). However, her literary career was to be much frustrated by the necessity of earning a living and by poor job choices that postponed her true calling.

Moving to Pittsburgh in 1896, she worked for a year editing the *Home Monthly*, a women's magazine, where at least she was able to publish her own short fiction. Then she worked on the Pittsburgh *Leader* for four years, editing news stories and writing theater criticism and book reviews. She tried teaching high school for five years, but could devote only her summers to writing fiction (Gerber 37–42). Anxious for work more involved with writing, Cather returned to editing in 1906, with a job at *McClure's*, a New York muckraking magazine. On a research trip to Boston, she met author Sarah Orne Jewett, who helped her gain perspective on her Nebraska experience. Jewett advised her, "You must find your own quiet centre of life, and write from that to the world" (qtd. in Gerber 55). But it was not until 1912 that Cather could escape her commitments to the magazine and turn exclusively to fiction.

By that time, she had just completed her first novel and, more significantly, a story called "The Bohemian Girl" that was to become the opening episode for her first Nebraska novel, *O Pioneers!* (1913). When she began to explore her Nebraska experiences through the medium of fiction, she had achieved an emotional maturity and integrative distance on those memories that allowed her to transform them into art. In her most famous Nebraska novel, *My Antonia* (1918), this distancing achieved through memory allowed her to balance her affirmation of "the positive values of the Midwestern experience" in the pioneer days (Woodress 40) against her "harshest criticism of the post-pioneer period. The society that developed lost feeling for the land, became absorbed in business and . . . small-minded, materialistic values" (Murphy 56).

Besides exploiting the high plains of Nebraska in her mature fiction, the other Western landscape that proved profoundly productive for Cather's work was the desert Southwest. Beginning in 1912, on various trips she became familiar with the cliff dwellings, adobe villages, and missionary chapels of Arizona and New Mexico. She incorporated her experiences with the landscape and its people in the novels *The Song of the Lark* (1915), *The Professor's House* (1925), and *Death Comes for the Archbishop* (1927) (Gerber 57–64). In the last work, she expressed her feeling for the significance of the Catholic Church in shaping the Southwest. But also, in the character of Archbishop Latour, Cather created her "most successful western hero, an atypical pistol-carrying horseman, rescuing those in need, righting wrongs, bringing law to lawless regions" (Murphy 55). For its epic and elegiac evocation of the past, *Death Comes for the Archbishop* received the William Dean Howells Medal of the American Academy of Arts and Letters in 1930.

"El Dorado: A Kansas Recessional" was first published in *New England Magazine*, June 1901, pages 357–69. The text is from the reprint in *Willa Cather's Collected Short Fiction, 1892–1912*, ed. Mildred R. Bennett (Lincoln, NE: University of Nebraska, 1965), pages 293–310.

Gerber, Philip L. *Willa Cather*. Boston: Twayne, 1975.

Hewitt, Rosalie. "Willa Cather." *Dictionary of Literary Biography, Volume 78: American Short-Story Writers, 1880–1910*. Ed. Bobby Ellen Kimbel and William E. Grant. Detroit: Gale, 1989. 54–63.

Murphy, John J. "Willa Cather." *Fifty Western Writers: A Bio-Bibliographical Sourcebook*. Ed. Fred Erisman and Richard W. Etulain. Westport, CN: Greenwood, 1982. 51–62.

Van Antwerp, Margaret A., ed. "Willa Cather." *Dictionary of Literary Biography: Documentary Series, an Illustrated Chronicle, Volume 1*. Detroit: Gale, 1982. 57–104.

Woodress, James. "Willa Cather." *Concise Dictionary of American Literary Biography: Realism, Naturalism, and Local Color, 1865–1917.* Detroit: Gale, 1988. 36–51.

EL DORADO: A KANSAS RECESSIONAL

—————⟨✦⟩—————

I

P eople who have been so unfortunate as to have traveled in western Kansas will remember the Solomon Valley for its unique and peculiar desolation. The river is a turbid, muddy little stream, that crawls along between naked bluffs, choked and split by sand bars, and with nothing whatever of that fabled haste to reach the sea. Though there can be little doubt that the Solomon is heartily disgusted with the country through which it flows, it makes no haste to quit it. Indeed, it is one of the most futile little streams under the sun, and never gets anywhere. Its sluggish current splits among the sand bars and buries itself in the mud until it literally dries up from weariness and ennui, without ever reaching anything. The hot winds and the river have been contending for the empire of the valley for years, and the river has had decidedly the worst of it. Never having been a notably ambitious stream, in time it grew tired of giving its strength to moisten barren fields and corn that never matured. Beyond the river with its belt of amber woodland rose the bluffs, ragged, broken, covered with shaggy red grass and bare of trees, save for the few stunted oaks that grew upon their steep sides. They were pathetic little trees, that sent their roots down through thirty feet of hard clay bluff to the river level. They were as old as the first settler could remember, and yet no one could assert that they had ever grown an inch. They seldom, if ever, bore acorns; it took all the nourishment that soil could give just to exist. There was a sort of mysterious kinship between those trees and the men who lived, or tried to live, there. They were alike in more ways than one.

Across the river stretched the level land like the top of an oven. It was a country flat and featureless, without tones or shadows, without accent or emphasis of any kind to break its vast monotony. It was a scene done entirely in high lights, without relief, without a single commanding eminence to rest the eye upon. The flat plains rolled to the unbroken horizon vacant and void, forever reaching in empty yearning toward something they never attained. The tilled fields were even more discouraging to look upon than the unbroken land. Although it was late in the autumn, the corn was not three feet high. The leaves were seared and yellow, and as for tassels, there were none. Nature always dispenses with superfluous appendages; and what use had Solomon Valley corn for tassels? Ears were only a tradition there, fabulous fruits like the golden apples of the Hesperides; and many a brawny Hercules had died in his own sweat trying to obtain them. Sometimes, in the dusk of night, when the winds were not quite so hot as usual and only the stars could hear, the dry little corn leaves whispered to each other that once, long ago, real yellow ears grew in the Solomon Valley.

Near the river was a solitary frame building, low and wide, with a high sham front, like most stores in Kansas villages. Over the door was painted in faded letters, "Josiah Bywaters, Dry Goods, Groceries and Notions." In front of the store ran a straight strip of ground, grass grown and weedy, which looked as if it might once have been a road. Here and there, on either side of this deserted way of traffic, were half demolished buildings and excavations where the weeds grew high, which might once have been the sites of houses. For this was once El Dorado, the Queen City of the Plains, the Metropolis of Western Kansas, the coming Commercial Center of the West.

Whatever may have been there once, now there were only those empty, windowless buildings, that one little store, and the lonely old man whose name was painted over the door. Inside the store, on a chair tilted back against the counter, with his pipe in his mouth and a big gray cat on his knee, sat the proprietor. His appearance was not that of the average citizen of western Kansas, and a very little of his conversation told you that he had come from civilization somewhere. He was tall and straight, with an almost military bearing, and an iron jaw. He was thin, but perhaps that was due to his diet. His cat was thin, too, and that was surely owing to its diet, which consisted solely of crackers and water, except when now and then it could catch a gopher; and Solomon Valley gophers are so thin that they never tempt the ambition of any discerning cat. If Colonel Bywaters's manner of living had anything to do with his attenuation, it was the solitude rather than any other hardship that was responsible. He was a sort of "Last Man." The tide of emigration had gone out and had left him high and dry, stranded on a Kansas bluff. He was living where the rattlesnakes and sunflowers found it difficult to exist.

The Colonel was a man of determination; he had sunk his money in this wilderness and he had determined to wait until he had got it out. His capital had represented the industry of a lifetime. He had made it all down in Virginia, where fortunes are not made in a day. He had often told himself that he had been a fool to quit a country of honest men for a desert like this. But he had come West, worse than that, he had come to western Kansas, even to the Solomon Valley, and he must abide the consequences. Even after the whole delusion was dispelled, and the fraud exposed, when the other buildings had been torn down or moved away, when the Eastern brokers had foreclosed their mortgages and held the land empty for miles around, Colonel Bywaters had stubbornly refused to realize that the game was up. Every one had told him that the best thing he could do was to get out of the country; but he refused to listen to advice. Perhaps he had an unreasoning conviction that money could not absolutely vanish, and that, if he stayed there long enough, his must some time come back to him. Perhaps, even had he wished to go, he actually lacked the means wherewith to get away. At any rate, there he remained, becoming almost a part of that vast solitude, trying to live the life of an upright Christian gentleman in this desert, with a heart heavy and homesick for his kind, always living over again in memory the details of that old, peaceful life in the valley of Virginia. He rose at six, as he had always done, ate his meagre breakfast and swept out his store, arranged his faded calicoes and flyspecked fruit cans in the window, and then sat down to wait. Generally he waited until bedtime. In three years he had not sold fifty dollars' worth. Men were almost unknown beings in that region, and men with money were utterly so. When the town broke up, a few of the inhabitants had tried to farm a little—tried until they had no grain to sow and no horses to plough and no money to get away with. They were dead, most of them. The only human faces the Colonel ever saw were the starved, bronzed countenances of the poor fellows who sometimes passed in wagons, plodding along with their wives and children and cookstoves and feather beds, trying to get back to "God's country." They never bought anything; they only stopped to water their horses and swear a little, and then drove slowly eastward. Once a little girl had cried so bitterly for the red stick candy in the window that her father had taken the last nickel out of his worn, flat pocketbook. But the Colonel was too kind a man to take his money, so he gave the child the money and the candy, too; and he also gave her a little pair of red mittens that the moths had got into, which last she accepted gratefully, though it was August.

The first day of the week brought the exceptions in the monotonous routine of the Colonel's life. He never rose till nine o'clock on Sunday. Then, in honor of the day, he shaved his chin and brushed out his mustache, and dressed himself in his black suit that had been made for him down in Winchester four years ago. This suit of clothes was an object of great care with the Colonel, and every Sunday night he brushed it out and folded it away in camphor gum. Generally he fished on Sunday. Not that there are any fish in the Solomon; indeed, the mud turtles, having exhausted all the nutriment in the mud, have pretty much died out. But the Colonel was fond of fishing, and fish he would. So in season, every Sunday morning, he would catch a bottle of flies for bait and take his pole and, after locking his store against impossible intruders, he would go gravely down the street. He really went through the weed patch, but to himself and his cat he always spoke of it as the street.

II

On this particular afternoon, as the Colonel sat watching the autumn sunlight play upon the floor, he was feeling more bitterly discouraged than usual. It was exactly four years ago that day that Major Penelton had brought into his store on Water Street a tall, broad-shouldered young man, with the frankest blue eyes and a good-natured smile, whom he introduced as Mr. Apollo Gump of Kansas. After a little general conversation, the young man had asked him if he wished to invest in Western lands. No, the Colonel did not want to put out any money in the West. He had no faith in any of the new states. Very well; Apollo did not wish to persuade him. But some way he saw a good deal of the young man, who was a clever, openhanded sort of a chap, who drank good whiskey and told a good story so that it lost nothing in the telling. So many were the hints he threw out of the fortunes made every day in Western real estate, that in spite of himself the Colonel began to think about it. Soon letters began pouring in upon him, letters from doctors, merchants, bankers, all with a large map on the envelope, representing a town with all the railroads of the West running into it. Above this spidery object was printed the name, El Dorado. These communications all assured him of the beauty of the location, the marvellous fertility of the surrounding country, the commercial and educational advantages of the town. Apollo seemed to take a wonderful liking to him; he often had him to dine with him at the little hotel, and took him down to Washington to hear Patti, assuring him all the time that the theatres of Kansas City were much better than anything in the East, and that one heard much better music there. The end of the matter was that when Apollo went back to Kansas the Colonel sold out his business and went with him. They were accompanied by half a dozen men from Baltimore, Washington and the smaller towns about, whom Apollo had induced to invest in the fertile tracts of land about El Dorado and in stock in the Gump banking house.

The Colonel was not a little surprised to find that El Dorado, the metropolis of western Kansas, was a mere cluster of frame houses beside a muddy stream, that there was not a railroad within twenty-five miles, and that the much boasted waterworks consisted of a number of lead pipes running from the big windmill tank on the hill; but Apollo assured him that high buildings were dangerous in that windy country, that the railroads were anxious and eager to come as soon as the town voted bonds, and that the waterworks—pipes, pumps, filters and all, a complete "Holly" system—were ordered and would be put in in the spring. The Colonel did not quite understand how an academy of arts and science could be conducted in the three-room sod shack on the hill; but Aristotle Gump showed him the plan of a stately building with an imposing bell tower that hung over the desk in his office, assuring him that it would go up in May, and that the workmen from Topeka were already engaged for the job. He was surprised, too, to find so few people in a town of two thousand inhabitants; but he was told that most of the business men had gone East to settle up their affairs, and would be back in the spring with their new goods. Indeed, in Ezekiel Gump's office, the Colonel saw hundreds of letters, long glowing letters, from these absent citizens, telling of their great business schemes and their unshaken faith in the golden future of El Dorado. There were few houses, indeed, but there were acres and acres of foundations; there were few businesses in operation, but there were hundreds of promises; and Apollo laughingly said that Western towns were built on promises.

But what most puzzled the Colonel was the vast number and importance of the Gumps. The Gumps seemed to be at the head of everything. The eldest brother was Isaiah Gump, the minister, a red-faced, clean-shaven man, with a bald pate and dark, wrinkled little hands. Then there were De Witt Gump, the physician and druggist; Chesterfield Gump, the general dry goods merchant; Aristotle Gump, architect and builder, and professor of mathematics in the Gump Academy; Hezekiah Gump, the hardware merchant and president of the El Dorado Board of Trade; Ezekiel Gump, real estate agent, superintendent of waterworks, professor of natural sciences, etc. These were the Gumps. But stay—were there not also Almira Gump, who taught history and Italian in the academy, and Venus Gump, who conducted a dressmaking and millinery establishment? The Colonel learned from Apollo that the Gump brothers had bought the land and founded the town, that it was, in short, a monument of Gump enterprise, it having been their long cherished ambition to become municipal promoters.

The Sunday after the Colonel's arrival, Isaiah preached a sermon on the rebuilding of Jerusalem, and told how the Jews built each man before his own door, with a trowel in one hand and a sword in the other. This was preliminary to urging the citizens of El Dorado to build sidewalks before their respective residences. He gave a long and eloquent discourse upon the builders of great cities from Menes, Nimrod and Romulus down, and among these celebrated personages, the Gumps were by no means forgotten.

After the sermon, the Colonel went to dine with Apollo at the little hotel. As they sat over their claret and cigars, Apollo said, "Colonel, if you can work any kind of a deal with Zeke, I would advise you to buy up your land before the railroad comes, for land is sure to go up then. It's a good plan out here to buy before a road comes and sell as soon as possible afterwards."

"About how much would you advise me to invest in land, Mr. Gump?" inquired the Colonel.

"Well, if I were you, I would about halve my pile. Half I would put into real estate and half into bank stock. Then you've got both realty and personal security and you are pretty safe."

"I think I will get back into business. I may as well open a little shop and give your brother Chesterfield a little competition. I find I have been in the harness so long that I scarcely know what to do with myself out of it. I am too old to learn to be a gentleman of leisure."

"That's a good idea; but whatever you do, do it before the road comes. That's where the mistake is made in Western towns; men buy at high tide of the boom instead of having foresight enough to buy before. A boom makes the man it finds; but woe to the man it leaves in its track." A year later the Colonel found that Apollo had spoken a great truth.

"I think I rather like that land your brother showed me yesterday. Right next to the 'eighty' Mr. Thompson just bought. I would a little rather get tilled land, though."

"Now, Colonel, you are buying this land to sell; and wild land will sell just as well as any. You don't want to bother with crops; that's for the fellows that come in later. Let them do the digging. As soon as you have made up your mind, I want to spring a little scheme on you. I want to run you for city mayor next spring; and as soon as you have invested, we can begin to talk it up."

That suggestion pleased the Colonel and it rather soothed his conscience. He had his own scruples about land speculation; it seemed to him a good deal like gambling. But if he could really make an effort to further the interests of the town, he felt he would have a better right to make his fortune there.

After dinner they went out to look at Apollo's blooded horses, and then to Apollo's rooms over the bank to smoke. Apollo's rooms were very interesting apartments. They were decorated with boxing gloves, ball bats, fishing rods, an old pair of foils and pictures of innumerable theatrical people, mostly vaudeville celebrities and ladies of the ballet. As the Colonel showed some interest in these, Apollo began rattling off their names and various accomplishments, professional and otherwise, with a familiarity that astonished the old gentleman. One, he declared, could do the best double dislocation act on the horizontal bars to be seen in Europe or America, and his talents had been highly applauded by the Prince of Wales. Another was the best burnt cork artist of his time; and another a languishing blond lady, whose generous outlines were accentuated by the nature of her attire, he declared was "the nearest thing in tights that ever struck Kansas City." From Apollo that was a sweeping statement; for Kansas City was the unit of measure which he applied to the universe. At one end of his sleeping room there was a large, full length painting of a handsome, smiling woman, in short skirts and spangles. She stood on the toe of her left foot, her right foot raised, her arms lifted, her body thrown back in a pose of easy abandon. She was just beginning to dance, and there was something of lassitude in the movement of the picture. Behind her hung a dark red curtain, creating a daring effect of color through the sheer whiteness of her skirts, and the footlights threw a strong glare up into her triumphant face. It was broadly and boldly painted, something after the manner of Degas, but handled less cruelly than his subjects. The name at the bottom of the picture was that of a young American painter, then better known in Paris than in his own country. There were several photographs of the same person ranged about on Apollo's dressing case, and, as he thought her extremely beautiful, and as Apollo had not mentioned her, the Colonel politely inquired who she was.

"She was called Therese Barittini," replied Apollo, not looking at the picture.

"I never heard of her," remarked the Colonel, wondering at Apollo's strange manner.

"Probably not; she is dead," said Apollo shortly; and as the Colonel saw that he did not wish to discuss the subject, he let it drop. But he could never refrain from looking at that picture when he was in Apollo's room; and he had conjectures of his own. Incidentally he learned that Apollo had grown up about the theatres of Kansas City, ushering as a boy, and later working up to the box office. Had he known more of the theatres of that river metropolis, the Colonel would have realized that they are bad places for a boy. As it was, he attributed Apollo's exaggerated manner and many of his bad habits to his early environment.

It chanced that the next day was the day for voting on railroad bonds, and of course bonds were voted. There was great rejoicing among the builders of the city. The Gump band was out, and Apollo fired a fine display of fireworks which he had ordered from Kansas City in anticipation of the happy event. Those fireworks must have cost Apollo a nice little sum, for there were a great many of them. Why, there were actually some of the blackened rocket sticks lying around the streets next spring when every one knew that the railroad companies had never heard of such a place as El Dorado.

None of the Gumps had their families with them; they were to come out in the spring. They spoke often and affectionately of their families—all but Apollo, who never mentioned having any. The Colonel had supposed that he had never been married, until one day when he and Apollo were dining with Isaiah. Isaiah, after droning away in his prosy fashion about his wife and little ones and commenting upon the beauty of family ties, began moralizing upon Apollo's unfortunate marriage. Apollo, who had been growing whiter and whiter, rose, set down his glass and, reaching across the table, struck the

Reverend Isaiah in the mouth. This was the first that the Colonel saw of the bitter altercations which sometimes arose among the Gump brothers.

By the close of the winter the Colonel had put out his money and opened his store. Everything went on at a lively enough pace in El Dorado. Men took large risks because their neighbors did, as blind to the chances against them as the frequenters of the bucket shops on Wall Street. Hope was in the atmosphere, and each man was immersed in his own particular dream of fortune. One thinking man might have saved the community; but many communities have gone to ruin through the lack of that rare man. Afterwards, when the news of the great Gump swindle spread abroad over the land, and its unique details commanded a column's space in one of the New York papers, financiers laughed and said that a child could have grasped the situation. The inhabitants of El Dorado were chiefly men who had made a little capital working for corporations in large cities, and were incompetent to manage an independent business. They had been mere machines in a great system, consulted by no one, subject to complete control. Here they were "prominent citizens," men of affairs, and their vanity and self-confidence expanded unduly. The rest were farming people who came to make homes and paid little attention to what went on in the town. And the farmer is always swindled, no matter by whom offences come. The crash may start in Wall Street, but it ends in the hillside farms and on the prairie. No matter where the lightning strikes, it blackens the soil at last.

As the winter wore away, Apollo Gump drank harder than ever, drank alone in his rooms now, indulging in the solitary form of the vice, which is its worse form. No one saw much of him after business hours. He was gloomy and abstracted and seemed to dread even the necessary intercourse with men which his position in the bank entailed. The Gump brothers commissioned the Colonel to remonstrate with him upon the error of his ways, which he did without much effect. Still, there were many likable things about Apollo. He was different from the rest; his face was finer and franker, in spite of its heavy marks of dissipation, and his heart was kinder. His dogs were better treated than many men's children. His brothers were very clever fellows, some of them, all of them freehanded enough, except old Isaiah, who was the greatest bore and the sorriest rascal of them all. But the Colonel liked Apollo best. The great end of his life was to serve Mammon, but on the side he served other and better gods. Dante's lowest hell was a frozen one; and wherever Apollo's tortured soul writhes, it is not there; that is reserved for colder and perhaps cleaner men than he.

At last spring came, that fabled spring, when all the business men were to return to El Dorado, when the Gump Academy was to be built, when the waterworks were to be put in, when the Gumps were to welcome their wives and children. Chesterfield, Hezekiah and Aristotle had gone East to see to bringing out their families, and the Colonel was impatiently awaiting their return, as the real estate business seemed to be at a standstill and he could get no satisfaction from Apollo about the condition of affairs. One night there came a telegram from New York, brought post-haste across the country from the nearest station, announcing that the father of the Gumps was dying, and summoning the other brothers to his bedside. There was great excitement in El Dorado at these tidings, and the sympathy of its inhabitants was so genuine that they scarcely stopped to think what the departure of the Gumps might mean.

De Witt and Ezekiel left the next day accompanied by Miss Venus and Miss Almira. Apollo and Isaiah remained to look after the bank. The Colonel began to feel anxious, realizing that the Gumps had things pretty much in their own hands and that if the death of their father should make any material difference in their projects and they should decide to leave Kansas for good, the town and his interests would be wofully undone. Still, he said very little, not thinking it a time to bring up business considerations; for even Apollo looked worried and harassed and was entirely sober for days together.

The Gumps left on Monday. On the following Sunday Isaiah delivered a particularly powerful discourse on the mutability of riches. He compared temporal wealth to stock in the great bank of God, which paid such rich dividends of grace daily, hourly. He earnestly exhorted his hearers to choose the good part and lay up for themselves treasures in heaven, where moths cannot corrupt nor thieves break through and steal. Apollo was not at church that morning. The next morning the man who took care of Apollo's blooded horses found that two of them were missing. When he went to report this to Apollo he got no response to his knock, and, not succeeding in finding Isaiah, he went to consult the Colonel. Together they went back to Apollo's room and broke in the door. They found the room in wretched disorder, with clothing strewn about over the furniture; but nothing was missing save Apollo's grip and revolver, the picture of the theatrical-looking person that had hung in his sleeping room, and Apollo himself. Then the truth dawned upon the Colonel. The Gumps had gone, taking with them the Gump banking funds, land funds, city improvement funds, academy funds, and all funds, both public and private.

As soon as the news of the hegira of the Gumps got abroad, carriages and horses came from all the towns in the country, bringing to the citizens of El Dorado their attentive creditors. All the townsmen had paid fabulous prices for their land, borrowed money on it, put the money into the Gump bank, and done their business principally on credit obtained on the Gump indorsement. Now that their money was gone, they discovered that the land was worth nothing, was a desert which the fertile imagination of the Gumps had made to blossom as the rose. The loan companies also discovered the worthlessness of the land, and used every possible means to induce the tenants to remain on it; but the entire country was panic-stricken and would hear no argument. Their one desire was to get away from this desolate spot, where they had been duped. The infuriated creditors tore down the houses and carried even the foundation stones away. Scarcely a house in the town had been paid for; the money had been paid to Aristotle Gump, contractor and builder, who had done his business in the East almost entirely on credit. The loan agents and various other creditors literally put the town into wagons and carried it off. Meanwhile, the popular indignation was turned against the Colonel as having been immediately associated with the Gumps and implicated in their dishonesty. In vain did he protest his innocence. When men are hurt they must have something to turn upon, like children who kick the door that pinches their fingers. So the poor old Colonel, who was utterly ruined and one of the heaviest losers, was accused of having untold wealth hidden away somewhere in the bluffs; and all the tempest of wrath and hatred which the Gumps had raised broke over his head. He was glad, indeed, when the town was utterly deserted, and he could live without the continual fear of those reproachful and suspicious glances. Often as he sat watching those barren bluffs, he wondered whether some day the whole grand delusion would not pass away, and this great West, with its cities built on borrowed capital, its business done on credit, its temporary homes, its drifting, restless population, become panic-stricken and disappear, vanish utterly and completely, as a bubble that bursts, as a dream that is done. He hated western Kansas; and yet in a way he pitied this poor brown country, which seemed as lonely as himself and as unhappy. No one cared for it, for its soil or its rivers. Every one wanted to speculate in it. It seemed as if God himself had only made it for purposes of speculation and was tired of the deal and doing his best to get it off his hands and deed it over to the Other Party.

III

On this particular morning, the fourth anniversary of the fatal advent of Apollo Gump into his store at Winchester, as the Colonel sat smoking in his chair, a covered wagon came toiling slowly up from the south. The horses were thin and fagged, and it was all that they could do to drag the creaking wagon. The harness was old and patched with rope. Over the hames and along the back strap hung pieces of sunflower brush to serve as fly nets. The wagon stopped at the well and two little boys clambered out and came trotting up the path toward the store. As they came the Colonel heard them chattering together in a broad Southern dialect; and the sound of his own tongue was sweet to his ears.

"What is it, boys?" he asked, coming to the door.

"Say, boss, kin we git some watah at yo' well?"

"Of course you can, boys. Git all you want."

"Thank yo', sir"; and the lads trotted back to the wagon.

The Colonel took up his stick and followed them. He had not seen such good natured, towheaded little chaps for a long while; and he was fond of children. A little girl, dressed in that particularly ugly shade of red in which farming people seem to delight, clambered out of the wagon and went up to the well with a tin cup, picking her way carefully with her bare feet to avoid the sand burrs. A fretful voice called from the wagon.

"Law me, boys, haint you most got that watah yit?"

A wan woman's face appeared at the front of the wagon, and she sat down and coughed heavily, holding her hand over her chest as if it hurt her. The little girl filled the tin cup and ran toward the wagon.

"Howdy do, sir?" said the woman, turning to the Colonel as soon as she had finished drinking.

"Right smart, ma'am, thank 'ee."

"Mercy, air yo' from the South? Virginy? Laws! I am from Mizzoura myself an' I wisht I was back there. I 'low we'd be well enough off if we could git back to Pap."

She looked wistfully off toward the southwest and put her hand to her side again. There was something in the look of her big, hollow eyes that touched the Colonel. He told her she had better stay there a few days and rest the horses—she did not look well enough to go on.

"No, thank yo', sir, we must git on. I'll be better in the mornin', maybe. I was feelin' right smart yesterday. It's my lungs, the slow consumption. I think I'll last till I git back to Pap. There has been a good deal of the consumption in our family, an' they most all last." She talked nervously on, breathing heavily between her words. "Haint there a town Eldorader somewheres about here?"

The Colonel flushed painfully. "Yes, this is El Dorado."

"Law me, purty lookin' town!" said the woman, laughing dismally. "Superb's better'n this." She pronounced Superb as though it had but one syllable. "They got a black-smith shop an' a hardware store there, anyways. I am from nigh Superb, yo' see. We moved there ten years ago, when the country was lookin' mighty green and purty. It's all done burnt up long ago. It's that dry we couldn't raise any garden stuff there these three years. Everything's gone now, exceptin' these horses Pap give me when I was married. No, my man haint with me; he died just afore we come away. A bull gored him through an' through, an' he crawled outsiden the bob-wire fence and died. It was mighty hard. He didn't want to die there; he craved to die in Mizzoura. We shot the bull and brought t'other cattle with us; but they all died on the way."

She closed her eyes and leaned back against the side of the wagon. Suddenly she roused herself and said:

"Law me, boys, this must be the sto' that man told us on. Yo' see our meat and stuff give out most a week ago, an' we been a livin' on pancakes ever since. We was all gittin' sick, fur we turned agin' 'em, when we met a feller on horseback down the valley, a mighty nice lookin' feller, an' he give us five dollars an' told us we'd find a store someers up here an' could git some groceries."

"It must have been one of them loan company fellows," said the Colonel meditatively. "They still come sneakin' about once in a while, though I don't know what they're after. They haven't left us much but the dirt, an' I reckon that wouldn't do 'em much good if they could carry it off."

"That I can't tell yo'. I never seen him befo'—but he was a mighty kind sort of a feller. He give us the money, and he give me some brandy."

The Colonel helped her out of the wagon, and they went up to the store, while the boys watered the horses. Their purchases were soon made; but the Colonel refused to take their money.

"No, ma'am, I can't do that. You'll need your money before you get to Missouri. It's all in the family, between blood kin like. We're both from the South; and I reckon it would have been enough better for us if we'd never left it."

"Thank yo' mighty kindly, sir. Yo' sholey can't be doin' much business heah; better git in an' go with us. Good day to yo', an' thank you kindly, sir."

The Colonel stood wistfully watching the wagon until it rolled slowly out of sight, and then went back to his store, and with a sigh sat down—sat down to wait until water came from the rock and verdure from the desert, a sort of Sphinx of the Solomon who sat waiting for the end of time. This was a day when his mind dwelt even more than usual upon his misfortunes, and homesickness was heavy upon him, and he yearned for his own people and the faces of his kindred; for the long Virginia twilights in which he and Major Denney used to sit under the great trees in the courthouse yard, living the siege of Richmond over again; for the old comrades who took a drink with him at the Taylor House bar; for the little children who rolled their hoops before his door every morning, and went nutting with him in the fall; for the Great North Mountains, where the frosts would soon be kindling the maples and hickories into flame; for the soft purple of the Blue Ridge lying off to the eastward; and for that sound which every Virginian hears forever and forever in his dreams, that rhythmic song of deathless devotion, deep and solemn as the cadence of epic verse, which the Potomac and Shenandoah sing to the Virginia shore as they meet at Harper's Ferry. To every exile from the Valley of Virginia that sound is as the voice of his mother, bidding him keep his honor clean, and forever calling him to come home. The Colonel had stopped his horse there on the moonlight night in '62 when he rode away to the wars, and listened long to that sound; and looking up at the towering grandeur of Maryland heights above him, he had lifted his hand

and sworn the oath that every young Virginian swore and that every young Virginian kept. For if the blood shed for those noble rivers could have been poured into their flood, they would have run crimson to the sea; and it is of that that they sing always as they meet, chanting the story over and over in the moonlight and the sunlight, through time and change unable to forget all that wasted glory of youth, all that heroic love. Before now, when the old man had heard them calling to him in the lonely winter nights, he had bowed his head in his hands and wept in an almost physical passion of homesickness.

Toward evening the clouds banked up in the western sky, and with the night a violent storm set in, one of those drenching rains that always come too late in that country, after a barren summer has waned into a fruitless autumn. For some reason he felt indisposed to go to bed. He sat watching the lightning from the window and listening to the swollen Solomon, that tore between its muddy banks with a sullen roar, as though it resented this intrusion upon its accustomed calm and indolence. Once he thought he saw a light flash from one of the bluffs across the river, but on going to the door all was dark. At last he regretfully put out his lamp and went to bed.

IV

That night, a few hours before, when the storm was at its worst, a horseman had come galloping along the bank of the Solomon. He drew rein at the foot of a steep, naked bluff and sat in his saddle looking about him. It was a sorry night for a man to be out. The blackness of the sky seemed to bear down upon him, save when now and then it was ripped from end to end by a jagged thrust of lightning, which rent it like the veil of the temple. At each flash he could see the muddy water of the swollen river whirling along wraiths of white foam over the little shivering willows. Save for that one lonely light across the river, there was no sign of man. He dismounted from his horse and, tying it to a sapling, he took a spade, strapped to the saddle, and began to climb the bluff. The water from the uplands was running down the hill wearing channels in the soft stone and made the grass so slippery that he could scarcely stand. When he reached the top he took a dark lantern from his pocket and lit it, sheltering it under the cape of his mackintosh; then he set it behind a clump of bunch grass. Starting from a lone oak, he carefully paced a distance and began to dig. His clothing was wet through, and even his mackintosh was wet enough to impede his arms. He impatiently threw off everything but his shirt and trousers and fell to work again. His shirt was wet and his necktie hung like a rag under his collar. His black hair hung wet over his white forehead, his brows were drawn together and his teeth were set. His eyes were fixed on the ground, and he worked with the desperation of a man who works to forget. He drove the spade in to the top at every thrust and threw the soggy earth far down the hillside, blistering his white hands with the rigor of his toil. The rain beat ceaselessly in his face and dripped from his hair and mustache; but he never paused save when now and then he heard some strange sound from the river. Then he started, shut off the light from his dark lantern and waited until all was quiet.

When he had been digging for some time, he knelt down and thrust his arm into the hole to feel its depth. Close beside him he heard a shrill, whirring, metallic sound which a man who hears it once remembers to his dying day. He felt a sharp pain in the big vein of his right arm and sprang to his feet with an oath; and then the rattlesnake, having been the avenger of many, slid quietly off through the wet grass.

V

Next morning the sun rose radiantly over the valley of the Solomon. The sky was blue and warm as the skies of the South, the hard, straight line of the horizon was softened by a little smokelike haze, and the yellow leaves of the cottonwoods, still wet from the drenching rain, gleamed in the sunshine, and through the scant foliage the white bark glittered like polished silver. All the land was washed fresh and clean from the dust of the desert summer. It was a day of opal lights, a day set in a heaven of gold and turquoise and bathed in sapphirine airs; one of those rare and perfect days that happen only in desert countries, where Nature seems sometimes to repent of her own pitilessness and by the glory of her skies seems trying to compensate for the desolation of the lands that stretch beneath them. But when the Colonel came out to view the ravages of the storm the exultant beauty of the morning moved him little. He knew how false it was and how fleeting. He knew how soon Nature forgets. Across the river he heard a horse whinnying in the bushes. Surprised and curious, he went over to see what it might mean. The horse stood, saddled and bridled, among the sumac bushes, and at the back of the saddle carried a long waterproof roll. He seemed uneasy and stood pawing the wet ground and chewing at the withered leaves. Looking about the Colonel could see no rider and he went up the bluff to look for him. And there he found him. About five paces from the oak tree was a newly dug hole, with the spade still sticking upright in the earth. The grass around it was cut and crushed as though it had been beaten by a strong man in his rage. Beside the hole was the body of a man. His shirt was torn open to the waist and was wet and spattered with mud; his left hand was wound in the long grass beside him; his right, swollen and black, was thrown over his head; the eyes were wide open, and the teeth were set hard upon the lower lip. The face was the handsome, dissolute face of Apollo Gump.

The Colonel lifted him up and laid him under the little tree. A glance at his arm told how he died. There was a brandy flask beside him, and the wound had been enlarged with his knife, but the snake had struck a vein and the poison had been too swift. Taking up the spade, the Colonel set to work to finish what the dead man had begun. At a depth of about four feet he found a wooden box, cased in tin. He whistled softly to himself as he loosened the earth about it. So the Gumps had not been so clever, after all; they had brought down more game than they could bag, and at the last moment they had been compelled to bury part of their spoil. For what else on earth or in heaven would Apollo Gump have risked his rascally neck in the Solomon Valley?

But no, there was no money, only the picture of the handsome, theatrical looking woman he had seen in Apollo's room, a few spangled stage dresses, a lot of woman's clothing, dainty garments that looked like a trousseau and some tiny gowns made for a little, little baby, that had never been worn. That was all. The Colonel drew a long breath of astonishment, and stood looking at the picture. There, at the back of the saddle, was the waterproof roll which was to have carried it away. This then was Apollo Gump's weakness, and this was the supreme irony that life had held in store for him, that when he had done evil without penalty and all his sins had left him scathless, his one poor virtue should bring him to his death! As the Colonel glanced at that poor distorted body, lying there in the sunlight amid the glistening grasses, he felt for a moment a throb of that old affection he had once known for him. Already the spiders had woven a rainbow web over that set, white face, a gossamer film of protection against man's vengeance; and it seemed as though Nature had already begun her magnificent and complete work of pardon, as though the ground cried out for him, to take him into her forgiving breast and make him again a part of the clean and fruitful earth.

When he searched the dead man's body he found a leather belt and pouch strapped about his waist next his skin. In this were ten thousand dollars in bank notes and a ticket to San Francisco. The Colonel quietly counted the money and put it into his own pocket.

"There, sir, I've waited a long time to square my account with you. You owe me six thousand still, but they say a dead man's debts are cancelled and I'll take your horse and call it square. If there is a recording angel that keeps the run of these things, you can tell him you are square with me and take that much off your poor soul; you'll have enough to answer for without that, God knows."

That afternoon the Colonel dragged up the bluff a long rough box made from weather boards torn from his store. He brought over his best suit of clothes from its odorous camphor chest and with much difficulty succeeded in forcing it on to the stiffened limbs of the dead man.

"Apollo, I liked you mighty well. It cut me to the heart when you turned rascal—and you were a damned rascal. But I'll give you a decent burial, because you loved somebody once. I always knew you were too good a fellow for your trade and that you'd trip up in it somewhere. This would never have happened to those precious brothers of yours. I guess I won't say any prayers over you. The Lord knows you better than I do; there have been worse men who have lived and died Christians. If I thought any words of mine could help you out, I'd say 'em free. But the Lord has been forgiving sin from the beginning of the world, till it must have kept him pretty busy before now. He knows his business by this time. But I hope it will go a bit easy with you, Apollo, that I do."

He sunk the box in the hole and made a pillow of the light spangled dresses and laid the dead man in upon them. Over him he laid the picture of the handsome, smiling woman, who was smiling still. And so he buried them.

Next day, having got his money out of the place, the Colonel set fire to his old store and urged his horse eastward, never once casting back a look at the last smoking ruin of El Dorado.

In the spring the sunflowers grew tall and fair over every street and house site; and they grew just as fair over the mound beside the oak tree on the bluff. For if Nature forgets, she also forgives. She at least holds no grudge, up in her high place, where she watches the poles of the heavens. The tree itself has stopped growing altogether. It has concluded that it is not worth the effort. The river creeps lazily through the mud; it knows that the sea would be only a great, dirty, salty pond if it should reach it. Year by year it buries itself deeper in the black mud, and burrows among the rotting roots of the dead willows, wondering why a river should ever have been put there at all.

Discussion Questions

1. Define "recessional" from a dictionary. Then, explain the word's meaning in the story's subtitle. Do you find it appropriate with the rest of the story's meaning?
2. Describe the impression you receive from the first three paragraphs of setting description. Explain Cather's purpose in giving the setting before the main character is introduced.
3. Describe the character of Colonel Bywaters, as developed in parts I and II of the story. Especially contrast his strengths and weaknesses.
4. Explain the purpose of part III in the story.
5. Define the "justice" done in the conclusion. Also, describe the role of nature in contributing to this justice. The narrator comments extensively about nature in part V. Select a brief quotation about nature that suggests a theme for the story and explain how this theme works in the story.

Fig. 3.6 Charley Russell, *Smoke of a .45* (1908), oil on canvas. Amon Carter Museum, Ft. Worth, TX; 1961.205.

ZANE GREY
(1872–1939)

Born in Zanesville, Ohio, Grey grew up hearing family legends about his pioneer ancestors. During the Revolutionary War, Betty Zane—the subject of his first historical novel—braved British gunfire and Indian arrows to deliver a gunpowder-filled tablecloth to the troops defending Fort Henry, at the present site of Wheeling, West Virginia. Her brother, Colonel Ebenezer Zane, not only commanded the garrison, but in 1796 scouted a trail from Wheeling into the Ohio frontier and founded Grey's hometown. In contrast to this romantic past, his upbringing in an upper-middle-class family was comfortably mundane and unchallenging (Topping 152–53). In 1890, the family moved to Columbus, Ohio, where he played semi-pro baseball and was discovered by a scout who offered him an athletic scholarship to the University of Pennsylvania (Ronald 7). At Penn, Ivy League society did not lure him into the Eastern old-boy network, and he remained something of a loner, escaping into the adventure romances of Alfred Lord Tennyson and Robert Louis Stevenson. These books provided him models of virtuous, muscular heroism in contrast to what he viewed as sheepish social conformity.

Completing his schooling in 1896, he moved to New York to set up an unfulfilling dental practice, which he escaped through fishing trips and through writing about these trips, as well as about his pioneer ancestors. Beginning in 1903, he published three historical novels that failed to attract a readership (Topping 153).

His career took off only after he had experienced the West first-hand and after he had given up dentistry to write full-time. He convinced Colonel C. J. "Buffalo" Jones, on an eastern lecture tour describing his "Wild West" adventures, to let him observe and record the Colonel's hunting trips in the Grand Canyon. Once in Arizona, Grey admired the ruggedness of the frontier conditions and people. His first Western novel, *The Heritage of the Desert* (1910), gained some success, but he had to appeal to the vice president at Harper's publishing house to accept *Riders of the Purple Sage* (1912), which became one of the most popular Western stories of all. In this work and through the mid-1920s, he achieved his greatest story-telling triumphs, inventing vivid descriptions, original plot lines, and various character types. During this period, in such novels as *The Man of the Forest* (1920), *The Call of the Canyon* (1924), and *Under the Tonto Rim* (1926), Grey also advanced his most developed social criticism. Through consistent productivity, averaging two novels a year with Harper's, and through magazine serialization and movie rights, Grey achieved fantastic wealth and settled in the ritzy Los Angeles suburb of Altadena with movie-star neighbors (Topping 153–55).

Any fair assessment of Grey's work must acknowledge his contribution to popular meanings of the West. Like Owen Wister, Grey "turned to the West as a refreshing, indeed redemptive, alternative to the perceived amorality, banality, effeminacy, and artificial social standards" of the East (Topping 152). The typical formula of his novels portrays an innocent greenhorn who faces harsh nature and evil men, but learns to conquer the elements, to fight the evil, and to appreciate the land (Ronald 13). Thus, Grey depicts a moral initiation, with nearly Calvinistic characterization of "the elect and the damned." Linked to this moral determinism was his belief in social Darwinism, whereby the primitive Western environment challenges and affirms the natural virtues, strengths, and emotions; the good prove to be the strong, and only the strong survive (Topping 155). Like both Wister and Roosevelt, Grey contrasted the freedom, innocence, and nobility of the stoic hunter or cowboy with the constraint, corruption, and superficiality of civilization. However, in this ethical contrast, he failed to acknowledge the potential destructiveness of the Western antisocial element—the violent outlaws, renegades, and misfits who are products of the frontier, but not of its supposedly purifying influence. In this naiveté, Grey is clearly writing in the tradition not of social realism but of romance, exemplified by "the larger-than-life hero, the innocent heroine, the chase, the disguise, the colorful costume, the mistaken identity, the duel" (Topping 156).

Within a somewhat limited artistic range, his novels were still enormously popular. Between 1915 and 1924, they were on the best-seller list nine times. In 1975, an estimate of the number of copies sold stood at 40 million. His popularity may be explained, in part, by his complex appeals to romantic fantasy, idealism, escapism, and optimism in the face of shocking social changes in the United States from World War I through the Roaring Twenties and the Great Depression. Idealizing the frontier West, he gave his middle-class audience comforting, stabilizing, conservative solutions to problems of law and order, justice, and morality (Ronald 5–6).

"The Ranger" was first serialized in the October, November, and December issues of *Ladies Home Journal* in 1929. The text is from the reprint in *The Ranger and Other Stories* (New York: Harper, 1960), pages 3–49.

Ronald, Ann. *Zane Grey*. Boise, ID: Boise State University, 1975.

Topping, Gary. "Zane Grey." *Fifty Western Writers: A Bio-Bibliographical Source-book*. Ed. Fred Erisman and Richard W. Etulain. Westport, CN: Greenwood, 1982. 152–61.

THE RANGER

1

Periodically of late, especially after some bloody affray or other, Vaughn Medill, ranger of Texas, suffered from spells of depression and longing for a ranch and wife and children. The fact that few rangers ever attained these cherished possessions did not detract from their appeal. At such times the long service to his great state, which owed so much to the rangers, was apt to lose its importance.

Vaughn sat in the shade of the adobe house, on the bank of the slow-eddying, muddy Rio Grande, outside the town of Brownsville. He was alone at this ranger headquarters for the very good reason that his chief, Captain Aller-ton, and two comrades were laid up in the hospital. Vaughn, with his usual notorious luck, had come out of the Cutter rustling fight without a scratch.

He had needed a few days off, to go alone into the mountains and there get rid of the sickness killing always engendered in him. No wonder he got red in the face and swore when some admiring tourist asked him how many men he had killed. Vaughn had been long in the service. Like other Texas youths he had enlisted in this famous and unique state constabulary before he was twenty, and he refused to count the years he had served. He had the stature of the born Texan. And the lined, weathered face, the resolute lips, grim except when he smiled, and the narrowed eyes of cool gray, and the tinge of white over his temples did not begin to tell the truth about his age.

Vaughn watched the yellow river that separated his state from Mexico. He had reason to hate that strip of dirty water and the hot mosquito and cactus land beyond. Like as not, this very day or tomorrow he would have to go across and arrest some renegade native or fetch back a stolen calf or shoot it out with Quinola and his band, who were known to be on American soil again. Vaughn shared in common with all Texans a supreme contempt for people who were so unfortunate as to live south of the border. His father had been a soldier in both Texas wars, and Vaughn had inherited his conviction that all Mexicans were his natural enemies. He knew this was not really true. Villa was an old acquaintance, and he had listed among men to whom he owed his life, Martiniano, one of the greatest of the Texas *vaqueros.*

Brooding never got Vaughn anywhere, except into deeper melancholy. This drowsy summer day he got in very deep indeed, so deep that he began to mourn over the several girls he might—at least he believed he might— have married. It all seemed so long ago, when he was on fire with the ranger spirit and would not have sacrificed any girl to the agony of waiting for her ranger to come home—knowing that some day he would never come again. Since then sentimental affairs of the heart had been few and far between; and the very latest, dating to this very hour, concerned Roseta, daughter of Uvaldo, foreman for the big Glover ranch just down the river.

Uvaldo was a Mexican of quality, claiming descent from the Spanish sol- dier of that name. He had an American wife, owned many head of stock, and in fact was partner with Glover in several cattle deals. The black-eyed Roseta, his daughter, had been born on the American side of the river, and had shared advantages of school and contact, seldom the lot of most señoritas.

Vaughn ruminated over these few facts as the excuse for his infatuation. For a Texas ranger to fall in love with an ordinary Mexican girl was unthink- able. To be sure, it had happened, but it was something not to think about. Roseta, however, was extraordinary. She was pretty, and slight of stature— so slight that Vaughn felt ludicrous, despite his bliss, while dancing with her. If he had stretched out his long arm and she had walked under it, he would have had to lower his hand considerably to touch her glossy black head. She was roguish and coquettish, yet had the pride of her Spanish forebears. Lastly she was young, rich, the belle of Las Animas, and the despair of cow- boy and *vaquero* alike.

When Vaughn had descended to the depths of his brooding he discov- ered, as he had many times before, that there were but slight grounds for any hopes which he may have had of winning the beautiful Roseta. The sweet- ness of a haunting dream was all that could be his. Only this time it seemed to hurt more. He should not have let himself in for such a catastrophe. But as he groaned in spirit and bewailed his lonely state, he could not help recalling Roseta's smiles, her favors of dances when scores of admirers were thronging after her, and the way she would single him out on those occa- sions. "*Un señor grande,*" she had called him, and likewise "handsome gringo," and once, with mystery and fire in her sloe-black eyes, "You Texas ranger—you bloody gunman—killer of Mexicans!"

Flirt Roseta was, of course, and doubly dangerous by reason of her mixed blood, her Spanish lineage, and her American upbringing. Uvaldo had been quoted as saying he would never let his daughter marry across the

Rio Grande. Some rich rancher's son would have her hand bestowed upon him; maybe young Glover would be the lucky one. It was madness for Vaughn even to have dreamed of winning her. Yet there still abided that much youth in him.

Sounds of wheels and hoofs interrupted the ranger's reverie. He listened. A buggy had stopped out in front. Vaughn got up and looked round the corner of the house. It was significant that he instinctively stepped out sideways, his right hand low where the heavy gun sheath hung. A ranger never presented his full front to possible bullets; it was a trick of old hands in the service.

Someone was helping a man out of the buggy. Presently Vaughn recognized Colville, a ranger comrade, who came in assisted, limping, and with his arm in a sling.

"How are you, Bill?" asked Vaughn solicitously, as he helped the driver lead Colville into the large whitewashed room.

"All right—fine, in fact, only a—little light-headed," panted the other. "Lost a sight of blood."

"You look it. Reckon you'd have done better to stay at the hospital."

"Medill, there ain't half enough rangers to go-round," replied Colville. "Cap Allerton is hurt bad—but he'll recover. An' he thought so long as I could wag I'd better come back to headquarters."

"Ahuh. What's up, Bill?" asked the ranger quietly. He really did not need to ask.

"Shore I don't know. Somethin' to do with Quinela," replied Colville. "Help me out of my coat. It's hot an' dusty. . . . Fetch me a cold drink."

"Bill, you should have stayed in town if it's ice you want," said Vaughn as he filled a dipper from the water bucket. "Haven't I run this shebang many a time?"

"Medill, you're slated for a run across the Rio—if I don't miss my guess."

"Hell you say! Alone?"

"How else, unless the rest of our outfit rides in from the Brazos. . . . Anyway, don't they call you the 'lone star ranger'? Haw! Haw!"

"Shore you don't have a hunch what's up?" inquired Vaughn again.

"Honest I don't. Allerton had to wait for more information. Then he'll send instructions. But we know Quinela was hangin' round, with some deviltry afoot."

"Bill, that bandit outfit is plumb bold these days," said Vaughn reflectively. "I wonder now."

"We're all guessin'. But Allerton swears Quinela is daid set on revenge. Lopez was some relation, we heah from Mexicans on this side. An' when we busted up Lopez' gang, we riled Quinela. He's laid that to you, Vaughn."

"Nonsense," blurted out Vaughn. "Quinela has another raid on hand, or some other thievery job of his own."

"But didn't you kill Lopez?" asked Colville.

"I shore didn't," declared Vaughn testily. "Reckon I was there when it happened, but Lord! I wasn't the only ranger."

"Wal, you've got the name of it an' that's jist as bad. Not that it makes much difference. You're used to bein' laid for. But I reckon Cap wanted to tip you off."

"Ahuh. . . . Say, Bill," continued Vaughn, dropping his head. "I'm shore tired of this ranger game."

"My Gawd, who ain't! But, Vaughn, *you* couldn't lay down on Captain Allerton right now."

"No. But I've a notion to resign when he gets well an' the boys come back from the Brazos."

"An' that'd be all right, Vaughn, although we'd hate to lose you," returned Colville earnestly. "We all know—in fact everybody who has followed the ranger service knows you should have been a captain long ago. But them pig-headed officials at Houston! Vaughn, your gun record—the very name an' skill that make you a great ranger—have operated against you there."

"Reckon so. But I never wanted particularly to be a captain—leastways of late years," replied Vaughn moodily. "I'm just tired of bein' eternally on my guard. Lookin' to be shot at from every corner or bush! Think what an awful thing it was—when I near killed one of my good friends—all because he came suddenlike out of a door, pullin' at his handkerchief!"

"It's the price we pay. Texas could never have been settled at all but for the buffalo hunters first, an' then us rangers. We don't get much credit, Vaughn. But we know someday our service will be appreciated. . . . In your case everythin' is magnified. Suppose you did quit the service? Wouldn't you still stand most the same risk? Wouldn't you need to be on your guard, sleepin' an' wakin'?"

"Wal, I suppose so, for a time. But somehow I'd be relieved."

"Vaughn, the men who are lookin' for you now will always be lookin', until they're daid."

"Shore. But, Bill, that class of men don't live long on the Texas border."

"Hell! Look at Wes Hardin', Kingfisher, Poggin—gunmen that took a long time to kill. An' look at Cortina, at Quinela—an' Villa. . . . Nope, I reckon it's the obscure relations an' friends of men you've shot that you have most to fear. An' you never know who an' where they are. It's my belief you'd be shore of longer life by stickin' to the rangers."

"Couldn't I get married an' go way off somewhere?" asked Vaughn belligerently.

Colville whistled in surprise, and then laughed. "Ahuh? So that's the lay of the land? A gal!—Wal, if the Texas ranger service is to suffer, let it be for that one cause."

Toward evening a messenger brought a letter from Captain Allerton, with the information that a drove of horses had been driven across the river west of Brownsville, at Rock Ford. They were in charge of Mexicans and presumably had been stolen from some ranch inland. The raid could be laid to Quinela, though there was no proof of it. It bore his brand. Medill's instructions were to take the rangers and recover the horses.

"Reckon Cap thinks the boys have got back from the Brazos or he's had word they're comin'," commented Colville. "Wish I was able to ride. We wouldn't wait."

Vaughn scanned the short letter again and then filed it away among a stack of others.

"Strange business this ranger service," he said ponderingly. "Horses stolen— fetch them back! Cattle raid—recover stock! Drunken cowboy shootin' up the town—arrest him! Bandits looted the San Tone stage—fetch them in! Little Tom, Dick, or Harry lost—find him! Farmer murdered—string up the murderer!"

"Wal, come to think about it, you're right," replied Colville. "But the rangers have been doin' it for thirty or forty years. You cain't help havin' pride in the service, Medill. Half the job's done when these hombres find a ranger's on the trail. That's reputation. But I'm bound to admit the thing is strange an' shore couldn't happen nowhere else but in Texas."

"Reckon I'd better ride up to Rock Ford an' have a look at that trail."

"Wal, I'd wait till mawnin'. Mebbe the boys will come in. An' there's no sense in ridin' it twice."

The following morning after breakfast Vaughn went out to the alfalfa pasture to fetch in his horse. Next to his gun a ranger's horse was his most valuable asset. Indeed a horse often saved a ranger's life when a gun could not. Star was a big-boned chestnut, not handsome except in regard to his size, but for speed and endurance Vaughn had never owned his like. They had been on some hard jaunts together. Vaughn fetched Star into the shed and saddled him.

Presently Vaughn heard Colville shout, and upon hurrying out he saw a horseman ride furiously away from the house. Colville stood in the door waving.

Vaughn soon reached him. "Who was that feller?"

"Glover's man, Uvaldo. You know him."

"Uvaldo!" exclaimed Vaughn, startled. "He shore was in a hurry. What'd he want?"

"Captain Allerton, an' in fact all the rangers in Texas. I told Uvaldo I'd send you down pronto. He wouldn't wait. Shore was mighty excited."

"What's wrong with him?"

"His gal is gone."

"Gone?"

"Shore. He cain't say whether she eloped or was kidnaped. But it's a job for you, old man. Haw! Haw!"

"Yes, it would be—if she eloped," replied Vaughn constrainedly. "An' I reckon not a bit funny, Bill."

"Wal, hop to it," replied Colville, turning to go into the house.

Vaughn mounted his horse and spurred him into the road.

2

Vaughn's personal opinion, before he arrived at Glover's ranch, was that Roseta Uvaldo had eloped, and probably with a cowboy or some *vaquero* with whom her father had forbidden her to associate. In some aspects Roseta resembled the vain daughter of a proud don; in the main, she was American bred and educated. But she had that strain of blood which might well have burned secretly to break the bonds of conventionality. Uvaldo, himself, had been a *vaquero* in his youth. Any Texan could have guessed this seeing Uvaldo ride a horse.

There was much excitement in the Uvaldo household. Vaughn could not get any clue out of the weeping kin folks, except that Roseta had slept in her bed, and had risen early to take her morning horseback ride. All Mexicans were of a highly excitable temperament, and Uvaldo was no exception. Vaughn could not get much out of him. Roseta had not been permitted to ride off the ranch, which was something that surprised Vaughn. She was not allowed to go anywhere unaccompanied. This certainly was a departure from the freedom accorded Texan girls; nevertheless any girl of good sense would give the river a wide berth.

"Did she ride out alone?" asked Vaughn, in his slow Spanish, thinking he could get at Uvaldo better in his own tongue.

"Yes, señor. Pedro saddled her horse. No one else saw her."

"What time this morning?"

"Before sunrise."

Vaughn questioned the lean, dark *vaquero* about what clothes the girl was wearing and how she had looked and acted. The answer was that Roseta had dressed in *vaquero* garb, looked very pretty and full of the devil. Vaughn reflected that this was quite easy to believe. Next he questioned the stable boys and other *vaqueros* about the place. Then he rode out to the Glover ranch house and got hold of some of the cowboys, and lastly young Glover himself. Nothing further was elicited from them, except that this same thing had happened before. Vaughn hurried back to Uvaldo's house.

He had been a ranger for fifteen years and that meant a vast experience in Texas border life. It had become a part of his business to look through people. Not often was Vaughn deceived when he put a query and bent his gaze upon a man. Women, of course, were different. Uvaldo himself was the only one here who roused a doubt in Vaughn's mind. This Americanized Mexican had a terrible fear which he did not realize that he was betraying. Vaughn conceived the impression that Uvaldo had an enemy and he had only to ask him if he knew Quinela to get on the track of something. Uvaldo was probably lying when he professed fear that Roseta had eloped.

"You think she ran off with a cowboy or some young feller from town?" inquired Vaughn.

"No, señor. With a *vaquero* or a peon" came the amazing reply.

Vaughn gave up here, seeing he was losing time.

"Pedro, show me Roseta's horse tracks," he requested.

"Señor, I will give you ten thousand dollars if you bring my daughter back—alive," said Uvaldo.

"Rangers don't accept money for their services," replied Vaughn briefly, further mystified by the Mexican's intimation that Roseta might be in danger of foul play. "I'll fetch her back—one way or another—unless she has eloped. If she's gotten married I can do nothin'."

Pedro showed the ranger the small hoof tracks made by Roseta's horse. He studied them a few moments, and then, motioning those following him to stay back, he led his own horse and walked out of the courtyard, down the lane, through the open gate, and into the field.

Every boy born on the open range of vast Texas had been a horse tracker from the time he could walk. Vaughn was a past master at this cowboy art, long before he joined the rangers, and years of man-hunting had perfected it. He could read a fugitive's mind by the tracks he left in dust or sand.

He rode across Glover's broad acres, through the pecans, to where the ranch bordered on the desert. Roseta had not been bent on an aimless morning ride.

Under a clump of trees someone had waited for her. Here Vaughn dismounted to study tracks. A mettlesome horse had been tethered to one tree. In the dust were imprints of a riding boot, not the kind left by cowboy or *vaquero*. Heel and toe were broad. He found the butt of a cigarette smoked that morning. Roseta's clandestine friend was not a Mexican, much less a peon or *vaquero*. There were signs that he probably had waited there on other mornings.

Vaughn got back on his horse, strengthened in the elopement theory, though not yet wholly convinced. Maybe Roseta was just having a lark. Maybe she had a lover Uvaldo would have none of. This idea grew as Vaughn saw where the horses had walked close together, so their riders could hold hands. Perhaps more! Vaughn's silly hope oozed out and died. And he swore at his own ridiculous, vain dreams. It was all right for him to be young enough to have an infatuation for Roseta Uvaldo, but to have entertained a dream of winning her was laughable. He laughed, though mirthlessly. And jealous pangs consumed him. What an adorable, fiery creature she was! Some lucky dog from Brownsville had won her. Mingled with Vaughn's romantic feelings was one of relief.

"Reckon I'd better get back to rangerin' instead of moonin'," he thought grimly.

The tracks led in a roundabout way through the mesquite to the river trail. This was two miles or more from the line of the Glover ranch. The trail was broad and lined by trees. It was a lonely and unfrequented place for lovers to ride. Roseta and her companion still were walking their horses. On this beautiful trail, which invited a gallop or at least a canter, only lovemaking could account for the leisurely gait. Also the risk! Whoever Roseta's lover might be, he was either a fool or plain fearless. Vaughn swore lustily as the tracks led on and on, deeper into the timber that bordered the Rio Grande.

Suddenly Vaughn drew up sharply, with an exclamation. Then he slid out of his saddle, to bend over a marked change in the tracks he was trailing. Both horses had reared, to come down hard on forehoofs, and then jump sideways.

"By God! A holdup!" grunted Vaughn in sudden concern.

Sandal tracks in the dust! A native bandit had been hiding behind a thicket in ambush. Vaughn swiftly tracked the horses off the trail, to an open glade on the bank, where hoof tracks of other horses joined them and likewise boot tracks. Vaughn did not need to see that these new marks had been made by Mexican boots.

Roseta had either been led into a trap by the man she had met or they had both been ambushed by three Mexicans. It was a common thing along the border for Mexican marauders to kidnap Mexican girls. The instances of abduction of American girls had been few and far between, though Vaughn remembered several over the years whom he had helped to rescue. They had been pretty sorry creatures, and one was even demented. Roseta being the daughter of the rich Uvaldo, would be held for ransom and therefore she might escape the usual horrible treatment. Vaughn's sincere and honest love for Roseta made him at once annoyed with her heedless act, jealous of the unknown who had kept tryst with her, and fearful of her possible fate.

"Three hours start on me," he muttered, consulting his watch. "Reckon I can come up on them before dark."

The ranger followed the broad, fresh trail that wound down through timber and brush to the river bottom. A border of arrow weed stretched out across a sand bar. All at once he halted stock-still, then moved as if to dismount. But it was not necessary. He could read from the saddle another story in the sand and this one was one of tragedy. A round depression in the sand and one spot of reddish color, obviously blood, on the slender white stalk of arrow weed, a heavy furrow, and then a path as though made by a dragged body through the green to the river—these easily-read signs added a sinister note to the abduction of Roseta Uvaldo. In Vaughn's estimation it cleared Roseta's comrade of all complicity, except that of heedless risk. And the affair began to savor somewhat of Quinela's work. The ranger wondered whether Quinela, the mere mention of whose name had brought a look of terror into Uvaldo's eyes when Vaughn had spoken to him, might not be a greater menace than the Americans believed. If so, then God help Roseta!

Vaughn took time enough to dismount and trail the path through the weeds where the murderers had dragged the body. They had been bold and careless. Vaughn picked up a cigarette case, a glove, and a watch, and he made sure that by the latter he could identify Roseta's companion on this fatal ride. A point of gravel led out to a deep current in the river, to which the body had been consigned. It might be several days and many miles below where the Rio Grande would give up its dead.

The exigencies of the case prevented Vaughn from going back after food and canteen. Many a time had he been caught in the same predicament. He had only his horse, a gun, and a belt full of cartridges. But they were sufficient for the job that lay ahead of him.

Hurrying back to Star he led him along the trail to the point where the Mexicans had gone into the river. The Rio was treacherous with quicksand, but it was always safe to follow Mexicans, provided one could imitate them. Vaughn spurred his horse across the oozy sand, and made deep water just in the nick of time. The swift current, however, was nothing for the powerful Star to breast. Vaughn emerged at precisely the point where the Mexicans had climbed out, but to help Star he threw himself forward, and catching some arrow weeds, hauled himself up the steep bank. Star floundered out and plunged up to solid ground.

The ranger mounted again and took the trail without any concern of being ambushed. Three Mexicans bent on a desperate deal of this sort would not hang back on the trail to wait for pursuers. Once up on the level mesquite land it was plain that they had traveled at a brisk trot. Vaughn loped Star along the well-defined tracks of five horses. At this gait he felt sure that he was covering two miles while they were traveling one. He calculated that they should be about fifteen miles ahead of him, unless rough country had slowed them, and that by early afternoon he ought to be close on their heels. If their trail had worked down the river toward Rock Ford he might have connected these three riders with the marauders mentioned in Captain Allerton's letter. But it led straight south of the Rio Grande and showed that the kidnapers had a definite destination in mind.

Vaughn rode for two hours before he began to climb out of the level river valley. Then he struck rocky hills covered with cactus and separated by dry gorges. There was no difficulty in following the trail, but he had to proceed more slowly. He did not intend that Roseta Uvaldo should be forced to spend a night in the clutches of these desperadoes. Toward noon the sun grew hot and Vaughn began to suffer from thirst. Star was soaked with sweat, but showed no sign of distress.

He came presently to a shady spot where it was evident that the abductors had halted, probably to eat and rest. The remains of a small fire showed in a circle of stones. Vaughn got off to put his hand on the mesquite ashes. They were still hot. This meant something, though not a great deal. Mesquite wood burned slowly and the ashes retained heat for a long while. Vaughn also examined horse tracks so fresh that no particle of dust had yet blown into them. Two hours behind, perhaps a little more or less!

He resumed the pursuit, making good time everywhere, at a swift lope on all possible stretches.

There was a sameness to the brushy growth and barren hills and rocky dry ravines, though the country was growing rougher. He had not been through this section before. He crossed no trails. And he noted that the tracks of the Mexicans gradually were heading from south to west. Sooner or later they were bound to join the well-known Rock Ford trail. Vaughn was concerned about this. Should he push Star to the limit until he knew he was close behind the abducters? It would not do to let them see or hear him. If he could surprise them the thing would be easy. While he revolved these details of the problem in his mind he kept traveling full speed along the trail.

He passed an Indian corn field, and then a hut of adobe and brush. The tracks he was hounding kept straight on, and led off the desert into a road, not, however, the Rock Ford road. Vaughn here urged Star to his best speed, and a half hour later he was turning into a well-defined trail. He did not need to get off to see that no horses but the five he was tracking had passed this point since morning. Moreover, it was plain that they were not many miles ahead.

Vaughn rode on awhile at a full gallop, then turning off the trail, he kept Star to that same ground-eating gait in a long detour. Once he crossed a stream bed, up which there would be water somewhere. Then he met the trail again, finding to his disappointment and chagrin that the tracks indicated that the riders had passed. He had hoped to head off the desperadoes and lie in wait for them here.

Mid-afternoon was on him. He decided not to force the issue at once. There was no ranch or village within half a night's ride of this spot. About sunset the Mexicans would halt to rest and eat. They would build a fire.

Vaughn rode down into a rocky defile where he found a much-needed drink for himself and Star. He did not relish the winding trail ahead. It kept to the gorge. It was shady and cool, but afforded too many places where he might be ambushed. Still, there was no choice; he had to go on. He had no concern for himself that the three hombres would ambush him. But if they fell in with another band of cutthroats! It was Roseta of whom he was thinking.

Vaughn approached a rocky wall. He was inured to danger. And his ranger luck was proverbial. As he turned the corner of the rock wall he found himself facing a line of men with leveled rifles.

"Hands up, gringo ranger!"

3

Vaughn was as much surprised by the command given in English as by this totally unexpected encounter with a dozen or more Mexicans. He knew the type all too well. These were Quinela's bandits.

Vaughn raised his hands. Why this gang leader was holding him up instead of shooting on sight was beyond Vaughn's ken. The Mexicans began to jabber like a lot of angry monkeys. If ever Vaughn expected death it was at that moment. He had about decided to pull his gun and shoot it out with them, and finish as many a ranger had before him. But a shrill authoritative voice deterred him. Then a swarthy little man, lean-faced, and beady-eyed, stepped out between the threatening rifles and Vaughn. He silenced the shrill chatter of his men.

"It's the gringo ranger, Texas Medill," he shouted in Spanish. "It's the man who killed Lopez. Don't shoot. Quinela will pay much gold for him alive. Quinela will strip off the soles of his feet and drive him with hot irons to walk on the choya."

"But it's the dreaded gun ranger, señor," protested a one-eyed bandit. "The only safe way is to shoot his cursed heart out here."

"We've had our orders to draw this ranger across the river," returned the leader harshly. "Quinela knew his man and the hour. The Uvaldo girl brought him. And here we have him—alive! . . . Garcia, it'd cost your life to shoot this ranger."

"But I warn you, Juan, he is not alone," returned Garcia. "He is but a leader of many rangers. Best kill him quick and hurry on. I have told you already that plenty gringo *vaqueros* are on the trail. We have many horses. We cannot travel fast. Night is coming. Best kill Texas Medill."

"No, Garcia. We obey orders," returned Juan harshly. "We take him alive to Quinela."

Vaughn surveyed the motley group with speculative eyes. He could kill six of them at least, and with Star charging and the poor marksmanship of native bandits, he might break through. Coldly Vaughn weighed the chances. They were a hundred to one that he would not escape. Yet he had taken such chances before. But these men had Roseta, and while there was life there was always some hope. With a tremendous effort of will he forced aside the deadly impulse and applied his wits to the situation.

The swarthy Juan turned to cover Vaughn with a cocked gun. Vaughn read doubt and fear in the beady eyes. He knew Mexicans. If they did not kill him at once there was hope. At a significant motion Vaughn carefully shifted a long leg and stepped face front, hands high, out of the saddle.

Juan addressed him in Spanish.

"No savvy, señor," replied the ranger.

"You speak Spanish?" repeated the questioner in English.

"Very little. I understand some of your Mexican lingo."

"You trailed Manuel alone?"

"Who's Manuel?"

"My *vaquero*. He brought Señorita Uvaldo across the river."

"After murdering her companion. Yes, I trailed him and two other men, I reckon. Five horses. The Uvaldo girl rode one. The fifth horse belonged to her companion."

"Ha! Did Manuel kill?" exclaimed the Mexican, and it was quite certain that this was news to him.

"Yes. You have murder as well as kidnaping to answer for."

The Mexican cursed under his breath.

"Where are your rangers?" he went on.

"They got back from the Brazos last night with news of your raid," said Vaughn glibly. "And this morning they joined the cowboys who were trailing the horses you stole."

Vaughn realized then that somewhere there had been a mix-up in Quinela's plans. The one concerning the kidnaping of Roseta Uvaldo and Vaughn's taking the trail had worked out well. But Juan's dark, corded face, his volley of unintelligible maledictions directed at his men betrayed a hitch somewhere. Again Vaughn felt the urge to draw and fight it out. What crazy fiery-headed fools these tattered marauders were! Juan had lowered his gun to heap abuse on Garcia. That luckless individual turned green of face. Some of the others still held leveled rifles on Vaughn but they were looking at their leader and his lieutenant. Vaughn saw a fair chance to get away, and his gun hand itched. A heavy-booming Colt—Juan and Garcia dead—a couple of shots at those other outlaws—that would have stampeded them. But Vaughn as yet had caught no glimpse of Roseta. He put the grim, cold impulse behind him.

The harangue went on, ending only when Garcia had been cursed into sullen agreement.

"I'll take them to Quinela," cried Juan shrilly, and began shouting orders.

Vaughn's gun belt was removed. His hands were tied behind his back. He was forced upon one of the Mexicans' horses and his feet were roped to the stirrups. Juan appropriated his gun belt, which he put on with the Mexican's love of vainglory, and then mounted Star. The horse did not like the exchange of riders, and there followed immediate evidence of the cruel iron hand of the outlaw. Vaughn's blood leaped, and he veiled his eyes lest someone see his savage urge to kill. When he raised his head, two of the squat, motley-garbed, and wide-sombreroed Mexicans were riding by, and the second led a horse upon which sat Roseta Uvaldo.

She was bound to the saddle, but her hands were free. She turned her face to Vaughn. With what concern and longing did he gaze at it! Vaughn needed only to see it flash white toward him, to meet the look of gratitude in her dark eyes, to realize that Roseta was still unharmed. She held her small proud head high. Her spirit was unbroken. For the rest, what mattered the dusty disheveled hair, the mud-spattered and dust-covered *vaquero* riding garb she wore? Vaughn flashed her a look that brought the blood to her pale cheeks.

Juan prodded Vaughn in the back. "Ride, gringo." Then he gave Garcia a last harsh command. As Vaughn's horse followed that of Roseta and her two guards into the brook, there rose a clattering, jabbering melee among the Mexicans left behind. It ended in a receding roar of pounding hoofs.

The brook was shallow and ran swiftly over gravel and rocks. Vaughn saw at once that Juan meant to hide his trail. An hour after the cavalcade would have passed a given point here, no obvious trace would show. The swift water would have cleared as well as have filled the hoof tracks with sand.

"Juan, you were wise to desert your gang of horse thieves," said Vaughn coolly. "There's a hard-ridin' outfit on their trail. And some, if not all of them, will be dead before sundown."

"*Quien sabe?* But it's sure Texas Medill will be walking choya on bare-skinned feet *mañana*," replied the Mexican bandit chief.

Vaughn pondered. Quinela's rendezvous, then, was not many hours distant. Travel such as this, up a rocky gorge, was necessarily slow. Probably this brook would not afford more than a few miles of going. Then Juan would head out on to the desert and try in other ways to hide his tracks. As far as Vaughn was concerned, whether he hid them or not made no difference. The cowboys and rangers in pursuit were but fabrications of Vaughn's to deceive the Mexicans. He knew how to work on their primitive feelings. But Vaughn poignantly realized the peril of the situation and the brevity of the time left him.

"Juan, you've got my gun," said Vaughn, his keen mind working. "You say I'll be dead in less than twenty-four hours. What's it worth to untie my hands so I can ride in comfort?"

"Señor, if you have money on you it will be mine anyway," replied the Mexican.

"I haven't any money with me. But I've got my checkbook that shows a balance of some thousands of dollars in an El Paso bank," replied Vaughn, and he turned round.

The bandit showed his gleaming white teeth in derision. "What's that to me?"

"Some thousands in gold, Juan. You can get it easily. News of my death will not get across the border very soon. I'll give you a check and a letter, which you can take to El Paso, or send by messenger."

"How much gold, señor?" Juan asked.

"Over three thousand."

"Señor, you would bribe me into a trap. No. Juan loves the glitter and clink of your American gold, but he is no fool."

"Nothing of the sort. I'm trying to buy a little comfort in my last hours. And possibly a little kindness to the señorita there. It's worth a chance. You can send a messenger. What do you care if he shouldn't come back? You don't lose anythin'."

"No gringo can be trusted, much less Texas Medill of the rangers," replied the Mexican.

"Sure. But take a look at my checkbook. You know figures when you see them."

Juan rode abreast of Vaughn, impelled by curiosity. His beady eyes glittered.

"Inside vest pocket," directed Vaughn. "Don't drop the pencil."

The Mexican procured the checkbook and opened it. "Señor, I know your bank," he said, vain of his ability to read, which to judge by his laborious task was limited.

"Ahuh. Well, how much balance have I left?" asked Vaughn.

"Three thousand, four hundred."

"Good. Now, Juan, you may as well get that money. I've nobody to leave it to. I'll buy a little comfort for myself—and kindness to the señorita."

"How much kindness, señor?" asked the Mexican craftily.

"That you keep your men from handlin' her rough—and soon as the ransom is paid send her back safe."

"Señor, the first I have seen to. The second is not mine to grant. Quinela will demand ransom—yes—but never will he send the señorita back."

"But I—thought—"

"Quinela was wronged by Uvaldo."

Vaughn whistled at this astounding revelation. He had divined correctly the fear Uvaldo had revealed. The situation then for Roseta was vastly more critical. Death would be merciful compared to the fate the half-breed peon Quinela would deal her. Vaughn cudgled his brains in desperation. Why had he not shot it out with these yellow desperadoes? But rage could not further Roseta's cause.

Meanwhile the horses splashed and clattered over the rocks in single file up the narrowing gorge. The steep walls were giving way to brushy slopes that let the hot sun down. Roseta looked back at Vaughn with appeal and trust—and something more in her dark eyes that tortured him.

Vaughn did not have the courage to meet her gaze, except for that fleeting moment. It was only natural that his spirits should be at a low ebb. Never in his long ranger service had he encountered such a desperate situation. More than once he had faced what seemed inevitable death, where there had seemed to be not the slightest chance to escape. Vaughn was not of a temper to give up completely. He would watch for a break till the very last second. For Roseta, however, he endured agonies. He had looked at the mutilated bodies of more than one girl victim of these bandits.

When at length the gully narrowed to a mere crack in the hill, and the water failed, Juan ordered his guards to climb a steep brush slope. There was no sign of any trail. If this brook, which they had waded to its source, led away from the road to Rock Ford, it would take days before rangers or cowboys could possibly run across it. Juan was a fox.

The slope was not easy to climb. Both Mexicans got off their horses to lead Roseta's. If Vaughn had not been tied on his saddle he would have fallen off. Eventually they reached the top, to enter a thick growth of mesquite and cactus. And before long they broke out into a trail, running, as near as Vaughn could make out, at right angles to the road and river trail. Probably it did not cross either one. Certainly the Mexicans trotted east along it as if they had little to fear from anyone traveling it.

Presently a peon came in sight astride a mustang, and leading a burro. He got by the two guards, though they crowded him into the brush. But Juan halted him, and got off Star to see what was in the pack on the burro. With an exclamation of great satisfaction he pulled out what appeared to Vaughn to be a jug or demijohn covered with wickerwork. Juan pulled out the stopper and smelled the contents.

"*Canyu!*" he said, and his white teeth gleamed. He took a drink, then smacked his lips. When the guards, who had stopped to watch, made a move to dismount he cursed them vociferously. Sullenly they slid back into their saddles. Juan stuffed the demijohn into the right saddlebag of Vaughn's saddle. Here the peon protested in a mixed dialect that Vaughn could not translate. But the meaning was obvious. Juan kicked the ragged peon's sandaled foot, and ordered him on, with a significant touch of Vaughn's big gun, which he wore so pompously. The peon lost no time riding off. Juan remounted, and directed the cavalcade to move forward.

Vaughn turned as his horse started, and again he encountered Roseta's dark intent eyes. They seemed telepathic this time, as well as filled with unutterable promise. She had read Vaughn's thought. If there were anything that had dominance in the Mexican's nature it was the cactus liquor, *canyu*. Ordinarily he was volatile, unstable as water, flint one moment and wax the next. But with the burn of *canyu* in his throat he had the substance of mist.

Vaughn felt the lift and pound of his heavy heart. He had prayed for the luck of the ranger, and lo! a peon had ridden up, packing *canyu*.

4

Canyu was a distillation made from the maguey cactus, a plant similar to the century plant. The peon brewed it. But in lieu of the brew, natives often cut into the heart of a plant and sucked the juice. Vaughn had once seen a Mexican sprawled in the middle of a huge maguey, his head buried deep in the heart of it and his legs hanging limp. Upon examination he appeared to be drunk, but it developed that he was dead.

This liquor was potential fire. The lack of it made the peons surly: the possession of it made them gay. One drink changed their mental and physical world. Juan whistled after the first drink: after the second he began to sing "La Paloma." His two guards cast greedy, mean looks backward.

Almost at once the fairly brisk pace of travel that had been maintained slowed perceptibly. Vaughn began to feel more sanguine. He believed that he might be able to break the thongs that bound his wrists. As he had prayed for his ranger luck so he now prayed for anything to delay these Mexicans on the trail.

The leader Juan either wanted the *canyu* for himself or was too crafty to share it with his two men; probably both. With all three of them, the center of attention had ceased to be in Uvaldo's girl and the hated gringo ranger. It lay in that demijohn in Star's saddlebag. If a devil lurked in this white liquor for them, there was likewise for the prisoners a watching angel.

The afternoon was not far enough advanced for the sun to begin losing its heat. Shade along the trail was most inviting and welcome, but it was scarce. Huge pipelike masses of organ cactus began to vary the monotonous scenery. Vaughn saw deer, rabbits, road runners, and butcherbirds. The country was uninhabited and this trail an unfrequented one which certainly must branch into one of the several main traveled trails. Vaughn hoped the end of it still lay many miles off.

The way led into a shady rocky glen. As of one accord the horses halted, without, so far as Vaughn could see, any move or word from their riders. This was proof that the two guards in the lead had ceased to ride with the sole idea in mind of keeping to a steady gait. Vaughn drew a deep breath, as if to control his nervous feeling of suspense. No man could foretell the variety of effects of *canyu* on another, but certain it must be that something would happen soon.

Juan had mellowed considerably. A subtle change had occurred in his disposition, though he was still the watchful leader. Vaughn felt that he was now in even more peril from this Mexican than before the advent of the *canyu*. This, however, would not last long. He could only bide his time, watch and think. His luck had begun to take over. He divined it, trusted it with mounting hope.

The two guards turned their horses across the trail, blocking Roseta's horse, while Vaughn's came up alongside. If he could have stretched out his hand he could have touched Roseta. Many a time he had been thrilled and bewildered in her presence, not to say stricken speechless, but he had never felt as he did now. Roseta contrived to touch his bound foot with her stirrup, and the deliberate move made Vaughn tremble. Still he did not yet look directly down at her.

The actions of the three Mexicans were as clear to Vaughn as crystal. If he had seen one fight among Mexicans over *canyu*, he had seen a hundred. First the older of the two guards leisurely got off his horse. His wide straw sombrero hid his face, except for a peaked, yellow chin, scantily covered with black whiskers. His clothes hung in rags, and a cartridge belt was slung loosely over his left shoulder. He had left his rifle in its saddle sheath, and his only weapon was a bone-handled machete stuck in a scabbard attached to his belt.

"Juan, we are thirsty and have no water," he said. And his comrade, sitting sideways in his saddle, nodded in agreement.

"Gonzalez, one drink and no more," returned Juan, and lifted out the demijohn.

With eager cry the man tipped it to his lips. And he gulped steadily until Juan jerked it away. Then the other Mexican tumbled off his horse and eagerly besought Juan for a drink, if only one precious drop. Juan complied, but this time he did not let go of the demijohn.

Vaughn felt a touch—a gentle pressure on his knee. Roseta had laid her gloved hand there. Then he had to avert his gaze from the Mexicans.

"Oh, Vaughn, I *knew* you would come to save me," she whispered. "But they have caught you. . . . For God's sake, do something."

"Roseta, I reckon I can't do much, at this sitting," replied Vaughn, smiling down at her. "Are you—all right?"

"Yes, except I'm tired and my legs ache. I was frightened badly before you happened along. But now—it's terrible. . . . Vaughn, they are taking us to Quinela. He is a monster. My father told me so. . . . If you can't save me you must kill me."

"I shall save you, Roseta," he whispered low, committing himself on the altar of the luck that had never failed him. The glance she gave him then made his blood run throbbing through his veins. And he thanked the fates, since he loved her and had been given this incredible opportunity, that it had fallen to his lot to become a ranger.

Her eyes held his and there was no doubt about the warm pressure of her hand on his knee. But even during this sweet stolen moment, Vaughn had tried to attend to the argument between the three Mexicans. He heard their mingled voices, all high-pitched and angry. In another moment they would be leaping at each others' throats like dogs. Vaughn was endeavoring to think of some encouraging word for Roseta, but the ranger was replaced for the moment by the man who was revealing his heart in a long look into the small pale face, with its red, quivering lips and great dark eyes uplifted, filled with blind faith.

The sound of struggling, the trample of hoofs, a shrill cry of "Santa Maria!" and a sodden blow preceded the startling crash of a gun.

As Vaughn's horse plunged he saw Roseta's mount rear into the brush with its rider screaming, and Star lunged out of a cloud of blue smoke. A moment later Vaughn found himself tearing down the trail. He was helpless, but he squeezed the scared horse with his knees and kept calling, "Whoa there—whoa boy!"

Not for a hundred rods or more did the animal slow up. It relieved Vaughn to hear a clatter of hoofs behind him, and he turned to see Juan tearing after him in pursuit. Presently he turned out into the brush, and getting ahead of Vaughn, turned into the trail again to stop the ranger's horse. Juan proceeded to beat the horse over the head until it almost unseated Vaughn.

"Hold on, man," shouted Vaughn. "It wasn't his fault or mine. Why don't you untie my hands—if you want your nag held in?"

Juan jerked the heaving horse out of the brush and onto the trail, finally leading him back toward the scene of the shooting. But before they reached it Vaughn saw one of the guards coming with Roseta and a riderless horse. Juan grunted his satisfaction, and let them pass without a word.

Roseta seemed less disturbed and shaken than Vaughn had feared she would be. Her dilated eyes, as she passed, said as plainly as any words could have done that they now had one less enemy to contend with.

The journey was resumed. Vaughn drew a deep breath and endeavored to arrange his thoughts. The sun was still only half-way down toward the western horizon. There were hours of daylight yet! And he had an ally more deadly than bullets, more subtle than any man's wit, sharper than the tooth of a serpent.

Perhaps a quarter of an hour later, Vaughn, turning his head ever so slightly, saw, out of the corner of his eye, Juan take another drink of *canyu*. And it was a good stiff one. Vaughn thrilled as he contained himself. Presently Juan's latest act would be as if it had never been. *Canyu* was an annihilation of the past.

"Juan, I'll fall off this horse pronto," began Vaughn.

"Very good, señor. Fall off," replied Juan amiably.

"But my feet are tied to the stirrups. This horse of yours is skittish. He'll bolt and drag my brains out. If you want to take me alive to Quinela, so that he may have a fiesta while I walk choya, you'd better not let me fall off."

"S. Ranger, if you fall you fall. How can I prevent it?"

"I am damned uncomfortable with my hands tied back this way. I cain't sit straight. I'm cramped. Be a good fellow, Juan, and untie my hands."

"S. Texas Medill, if you are uncomfortable now, what will you be when you tread the fiery cactus on your naked feet?"

"But that will be short. No man lives such torture long, does he, Juan?"

"The choya kills quickly, señor."

"Juan, have you thought about the gold lying in the El Paso bank? Gold that can be yours for the ride. It will be long before my death is reported across the river. You have plenty of time to get to El Paso with my check and a letter. I can write it on a sheet of paper out of my notebook. Surely you have a friend or acquaintance in El Paso or Juarez who can identify you at the bank as Juan—whatever your name is."

"Yes, señor, I have. And my name is Juan Mendoz."

"Have you thought about what you could do with three thousand dollars? Not Mexican pesos, but real gringo gold!"

"I have not thought, señor, because I do not like to give in to dreams."

"Juan, listen. You are a fool. I know I am as good as daid. What have I been a ranger all these years for? And it's worth this gold to me to be free of this miserable cramp—and to feel that I have tried to buy some little kindness for the señorita there. She is part Mexican, Juan. She has Mexican blood in her don't forget that. . . . Well, you are not betraying Quinela. And you will be rich. You will have my horse and saddle, if you are wise enough to keep Quinela from seeing them. You will buy silver spurs—with the long Spanish rowels. You will have jingling gold in your pocket. You will buy a *vaquero's* sombrero. And then think of your *chata*—your sweetheart, Juan. . . . Ah, I knew it. You have a *chata*. Think of what you can buy her. A Spanish mantilla, and a golden cross, and silver-buckled shoes for her little feet. Think how she will love you for that! . . . Then, Juan, best of all, you can go far south of the border—buy a hacienda, horses, and cattle, and live there happily with your *chata*. You will only get killed in Quinela's service—for a few dirty pesos. . . . You will raise mescal on your hacienda, and brew your own *canyu*. . . . All for so little, Juan!"

"Señor not only has gold in a bank but gold on his tongue. . . . It is indeed little you ask and little I risk."

Juan rode abreast of Vaughn and felt in his pockets for the checkbook and pencil, which he had neglected to return. Vaughn made of his face a grateful mask. This Mexican had become approachable, as Vaughn had known *canyu* would make him, but he was not yet under its influence to an extent which justified undue risk. Still, Vaughn decided, if the bandit freed his hands and gave him the slightest chance, he would jerk Juan out of that saddle. Vaughn did not lose sight of the fact that his feet would still be tied. He calculated exactly what he would do in case Juan's craftiness no longer possessed him. As the Mexican stopped his horse and reined in Vaughn's, the girl happened to turn round, as she often did, and she saw them. Vaughn caught a flash of big eyes and a white little face as Roseta vanished round a turn in the trail. Vaughn was glad for two things, that she had seen him stop and that she and her guard would be unable to see what was taking place.

All through these anxious moments of suspense Juan appeared to be studying the checkbook. If he could read English, it surely was only a few familiar words. The thought leaped to Vaughn's mind to write a note to the banker quite different from what he had intended. Most assuredly, if the El Paso banker ever saw that note Vaughn would be dead; and it was quite within the realm of possibility that it might fall into his hands.

"Señor, you may sign me the gold in your El Paso bank," said Juan, at length.

"Fine. You're a sensible man, Juan. But I cain't hold a pencil with my teeth."

The Mexican laughed. He was more amiable. Another hour and another few drinks of *canyu* would make him maudlin, devoid of quick wit or keen sight. A more favorable chance might befall Vaughn, and it might be wiser to wait. Surely on the ride ahead there would come a moment when he could act with lightning and deadly swiftness. But it would take iron will to hold his burning intent within bounds.

Juan kicked the horse Vaughn bestrode and moved him across the trail so that Vaughn's back was turned.

"There, señor," said the Mexican, and his lean dark hand slipped book and pencil into Vaughn's vest pocket.

The cunning beggar, thought Vaughn, in sickening disappointment. He had hoped Juan would free his bonds and then hand over the book. But Vaughn's ranger luck had not caught up with him yet.

He felt the Mexican tugging at the thongs around his wrists. They were tight—a fact to which Vaughn surely could attest. He heard him mutter a curse. Also he heard the short expulsion of breath—almost a pant—that betrayed the influence of the *canyu*.

"Juan, do you blame me for wanting those rawhides off my wrists?" asked Vaughn.

"Señor Medill is strong. It is nothing," returned the Mexican.

Suddenly the painful tension on Vaughn's wrists relaxed. He felt the thongs fall.

"*Muchas gracias*, señor!" he exclaimed. "Ahhh! . . . That feels good."

Vaughn brought his hands round in front to rub each swollen and discolored wrist. But all the time he was gathering his forces, like a tiger about to leap. Had the critical moment arrived?

"Juan, that was a little job to make a man rich—now wasn't it?" went on Vaughn pleasantly. And leisurely, but with every muscle taut, he turned to face the Mexican.

5

The bandit was out of reach of Vaughn's eager hands. He sat back in the saddle with an expression of interest on his swarthy face. The ranger could not be sure, but he would have gambled that Juan did not suspect his deadly intentions. Star was a mettlesome animal, but Vaughn did not like the Mexican's horse, to which he sat bound, and there were several feet between them. If Vaughn had been free to leap he might have, probably would have, done so.

He swallowed his eagerness and began to rub his wrists again. Presently he removed the pencil and book from his pocket. It was not mere pretense that made it something of an effort to write out a check for Juan Mendoz for the three thousand and odd dollars that represented his balance in the El Paso bank.

"There, Juan. May some gringo treat your *chata* someday as you treat Señorita Uvaldo," said Vaughn, handing the check over to the Mexican.

"*Gracias*, señor," replied Juan, his black eyes upon the bit of colored paper. "Uvaldo's daughter then is your *chata*?"

"Yes. And I'll leave a curse upon you if she is mistreated."

"Ranger, I had my orders from Quinela. You would not have asked more."

"What has Quinela against Uvaldo?" asked Vaughn.

"They were *vaqueros* together years ago. But I don't know the reason for Quinela's hate. It is great and just. . . . Now, señor, the letter to your banker."

Vaughn tore a leaf out of his bankbook. On second thought he decided to write the letter in the bankbook, which would serve in itself to identify him. In case this letter ever was presented at the bank in El Paso he wanted it to mean something. Then it occurred to Vaughn to try out the Mexican. So he wrote a few lines.

"Read that, Juan," he said, handing over the book.

The man scanned the lines, which might as well have been written in Greek.

"Texas Medill does not write as well as he shoots," said Juan.

"Let me have the book. I can do better. I forgot something."

Receiving it back Vaughn tore out the page and wrote another.

Dear Mr. Jarvis:

    If you ever see these lines you will know that I have been murdered by Quinela. Have the bearer arrested and wire to Captain Allerton, of the Rangers, at Brownsville. At this moment I am a prisoner of Juan Mendoz, lieutenant of Quinela. Miss Roseta Uvaldo is also a prisoner. She will be held for ransom and revenge. The place is in the hills somewhere east and south of Rock Ford trail.

                                              Medill

Vaughn reading aloud to the Mexican improvised a letter which identified him, and cunningly made mention of the gold.

"Juan, isn't that better?" he said, as he handed the book back. "You'll do well not to show this to Quinela or anyone else. Go yourself *at once* to El Paso."

As Vaughn had expected the Mexican did not scan the letter. Placing the check in the bankbook he deposited it in an inside pocket of his tattered coat. Then without a word he drove Vaughn's horse forward on the trail, and following close behind soon came up with Roseta and her guard.

The girl looked back. Vaughn contrived, without making it obvious, to show her that his hands were free. A look of radiance crossed her wan face. The exertion and suspense had begun to tell markedly. Her form sagged in the saddle.

Juan appeared bent on making up for lost time, as he drove the horses forward at a trot. But this did not last long. Vaughn, looking at the ground, saw the black shadow of the Mexican as he raised the demijohn to his mouth to drink. What a sinister shadow! It forced Vaughn to think of what now should be his method of procedure. Sooner or later he was going to get his hand on his gun, which stuck out back of Juan's hip and hung down in its holster. The moment, when it came, would see the end of his captor. But Vaughn remembered how the horse he bestrode had bolted at the previous gunshot. He would risk more, shooting from the back of this horse than at the hands of the other Mexican. Vaughn's feet were tied in the stirrups with the rope passing underneath the horse. If he were thrown sideways out of the saddle it would be a perilous and very probably a fatal accident. He decided that at the critical time he would grip the horse with his legs so tightly that he could not be dislodged, and at that moment decide what to do about the other Mexican.

After Juan had a second drink, Vaughn slowly slackened the gait of his horse until Juan's mount came up to his horse's flank. Vaughn was careful to keep to the right of the trail. One glance at the Mexican's eyes sent a gush of hot blood over Vaughn. The effect of the *canyu* had been slow on this tough little man, but at last it was working.

"Juan, I'm powerful thirsty," said Vaughn.

"Señor, we come to water hole bime-by," replied the Mexican thickly.

"But won't you spare me a nip of *canyu*?"

"Our mescal drink is bad for gringos."

"I'll risk it, Juan. Just a nip. You're a good fellow and I like you. I'll tell Quinela how you had to fight your men back there, when they wanted to kill me. I'll tell him Garcia provoked you. . . . Juan, you can see I may do you a turn."

Juan came up alongside Vaughn and halted. Vaughn reined his horse head and head with Juan's. The Mexican was sweating; his under lip hung a little; he sat loosely in his saddle. His eyes had lost their beady light and appeared to have filmed over.

Juan waited till the man ahead had turned another twist in the trail with Roseta. Then he lifted the obviously lightened demijohn from the saddlebag and extended it to Vaughn.

"A drop—señor," he said.

Vaughn pretended to drink. The hot stuff was like vitriol on his lips. He returned the jug, making a great show of the effect of the *canyu*, when as a matter of cold fact he was calculating distances. Almost he yielded to the temptation to lean and sweep a long arm forward. But a ranger could not afford to make mistakes. If Juan's horse had been a little closer! Vaughn expelled deeply his bated breath.

"Ah-h! Great stuff, Juan!" he exclaimed, and relaxed again.

They rode on, and Juan either forgot to drop behind or did not think it needful. The trail was wide enough for two horses. Soon Roseta's bright red scarf burned against the gray-green brush again. She was looking back. So was her Mexican escort. And their horses were walking. Juan did not appear to take note of their slower progress. He long had passed the faculty for making minute observations. Presently he would take another swallow of *canyu*.

Vaughn began to talk, to express more gratitude to Juan, to dwell with flowery language on the effect of good drink—of which *canyu* was the sweetest and most potent in the world—of its power to make fatigue as if it were not, to alleviate pain and grief, to render the dreary desert of mesquite and stone a region of color and beauty and melody—even to resign a doomed ranger to his fate.

"Aye, señor—*canyu* is the blessed Virgin's gift to the peon," said Juan, and emphasized this tribute by having another generous drink.

They rode on. Vaughn asked only for another mile or two of lonely trail, free of interruption.

"How far, Juan?" asked Vaughn. "I cannot ride much farther with my feet tied under this horse."

"Till sunset—señor—which will be your last," replied the Mexican.

The sun was still high above the pipes of organ cactus. Two hours and more above the horizon! Juan could still speak intelligibly. It was in his lax figure and his sweating face, especially in the protruding eyeballs, that he betrayed the effect of the contents of the demijohn. After the physical letdown would come the mental slackening. That had already begun, for Juan was no longer alert.

They rode on, and Vaughn made a motion to Roseta that she must not turn to look back. Perhaps she interpreted it to mean more than it did, for she immediately began to engage her guard in conversation—something Vaughn had observed she had not done before. Soon the Mexican dropped back until his horse was walking beside Roseta's. He was a peon, and a heavy drink of *canyu* had addled the craft in his wits. Vaughn saw him bend down and loosen the rope that bound Roseta's left foot to the stirrup. Juan did not see this significant action. His gaze was fixed to the trail. He was singing:

"*Ay, mía querida chata.*"

Roseta's guard took a long look back. Evidently Juan's posture struck him apprehensively, yet did not wholly overcome the interest that Roseta had suddenly taken in him. When he gave her a playful pat she returned it. He caught her hand. Roseta did not pull very hard to release it, and she gave him another saucy little slap. He was reaching for her when they passed out of Vaughn's sight round a turn in the green-bordered trail.

Vaughn gradually and almost imperceptibly guided his horse closer to Juan. At that moment a dog could be heard barking in the distance. It did not make any difference to Vaughn, except to accentuate what had always been true—he had no time to lose.

"Juan, the curse of *canyu* is that once you taste it you must have more—or die," said Vaughn.

"It is—so—señor," replied the Mexican.

"You have plenty left. Will you let me have one more little drink. . . . My last drink of *canyu*, Juan! . . . I didn't tell you, but it has been my ruin. My father was a rich rancher. He disowned me because of my evil habits. That's how I became a ranger."

"Take it, señor. Your last drink," said Juan.

Vaughn braced every nerve and fiber of his being. He leaned a little. His left hand went out—leisurely. But his eyes flashed like cold steel over the unsuspecting Mexican. Then, with the speed of a striking snake, his hand snatched the bone-handled gun from its sheath. Vaughn pulled the trigger. The hammer fell upon an empty chamber.

Juan turned. The gun crashed. "*Dios!*" he screamed in a strangled death cry.

The leaps of the horses were not quicker than Vaughn. He lunged to catch the Mexican—to keep him upright in the saddle. "Hold, Star!" he called sternly. "Hold!"

Star came down. But the other horse plunged and dragged him up the trail. Vaughn had his gun hand fast on the cantle and his other holding Juan upright. But for this grasp the frantic horse would have unseated him.

It was the ranger's job to manage both horses and look out for the other Mexican. He appeared on the trail riding fast, his carbine held high.

Vaughn let go of Juan and got the gun in his right hand. With the other then he grasped the Mexican's coat and held him straight on the saddle. He drooped himself over his pommel, to make it appear he had been the one shot. Meanwhile, he increased his iron leg grip on the horse he straddled. Star had halted and was being dragged.

The other Mexican came at a gallop, yelling. When he got within twenty paces Vaughn straightened up and shot him through the heart. He threw the carbine from him and pitching out of his saddle, went thudding to the ground. His horse bumped hard into the one Vaughn rode, and that was fortunate, for it checked the animal's first mad leap. In the melee that followed Juan fell off Star to be trampled under frantic hoofs. Vaughn hauled with all his might on the bridle. But he could not hold the horse and he feared that he would break the bridle. Bursting through the brush the horse ran wildly. What with his erratic flight and the low branches of mesquite, Vaughn had a hard job sticking on his back. Presently he got the horse under control and back onto the trail.

Some few rods down he saw Roseta, safe in her saddle, her head bowed with her hands covering her face. At sight of her Vaughn snapped out of the cold horror that had enveloped him.

"Roseta, it's all right. We're safe," he called eagerly as he reached her side.

"Oh, Vaughn!" she cried, lifting her convulsed and blanched face. "I knew you'd—kill them. . . . But, my God—how awful!"

"Brace up," he said sharply.

Then he got out his clasp knife and in a few slashes freed his feet from the stirrups. He leaped off the horse. His feet felt numb, as they had felt once when frozen.

Then he cut the ropes which bound Roseta's right foot to her stirrup. She swayed out of the saddle into his arms. Her eyes closed.

"It's no time to faint," he said sternly, carrying her off the trail, to set her on her feet.

"I—I won't," she whispered, her eyes opening, strained and dilated. "But hold me—just a moment."

Vaughn folded her in his arms, and the moment she asked was so sweet and precious that it almost overcame the will of a ranger in a desperate plight.

"Roseta—we're free, but not yet safe," he replied. "We're close to a hacienda—perhaps where Quinela is waiting. . . . Come now. We must get out of here."

Half carrying her, Vaughn hurried through the brush along the trail. The moment she could stand alone he whispered, "Wait here." And he ran onto the trail. He still held his gun. Star stood waiting, his head up. Both other horses had disappeared. Vaughn looked up and down the trail. Star whinnied. Vaughn hurried to bend over Juan. The Mexican lay on his face. Vaughn unbuckled the gun belt Juan had appropriated from him, and put it on. Next he secured his bankbook. Then he sheathed his gun. He grasped the bridle of Star and led him off the trail into the mesquite, back to where Roseta stood. She seemed all right now, only pale. But Vaughn avoided her eyes. The thing to do was to get away and not let sentiment deter him one instant. He mounted Star.

"Come, Roseta," he said. "Up behind me."

He swung her up and settled her in the saddle.

"There. Put your arms round me. Hold tight, for we're going to ride."

When she had complied, he grasped her left arm. At the same moment he heard voices up the trail and the rapid clipclop of hoofs. Roseta heard them, too. Vaughn felt her tremble.

"Don't fear, Roseta. Just you hang on. Here's where Star shines," whispered Vaughn, and guiding the nervous horse into the trail, he let him have a loose rein. Star did not need the shrill cries of the peons to spur him into action.

6

As the fleeing ranger sighted the peons, a babel of shrill voices arose. But no shots! In half a dozen jumps Star was going swift as the wind and in a moment a bend of the trail hid him from any possible marksman. Vaughn's concern for the girl behind him gradually eased.

At the end of a long straight stretch he looked back again. If *vaqueros* were riding in pursuit the situation would be serious. Not even Star could run away from a well-mounted cowboy of the Mexican haciendas. To his intense relief there was not one in sight. Nevertheless, he did not check Star.

"False alarm, Roseta," he said, craning his neck so he could see her face, pressed cheek against his shoulder. He was most marvelously aware of her close presence, but the realization did not impede him or Star in the least. She could ride. She had no stirrups, yet she kept her seat in the saddle.

"Let 'em come," she said, smiling up at him. Her face was pale, but it was not fear that he read in her eyes. It was fight.

Vaughn laughed in sheer surprise. He had not expected that, and it gave him such a thrill as he had never felt in his life before. He let go of Roseta's arm and took her hand where it clung to his coat. And he squeezed it with far more than reassurance. The answering pressure was unmistakable. A singular elation mounted in Vaughn's heart.

It did not, however, quite render him heedless. As Star turned a corner in the trail, Vaughn's keen glance saw that it was completely blocked by the same motley crew of big-sombreroed Mexicans and horses from which he had been separated not so long before that day.

"Hold tight!" he cried warningly to Roseta, as he swerved Star to the left. He drew his gun and fired two quick shots. He did not need to see that they took effect, for a wild cry arose, followed by angry yells.

Star beat the answering rifle shots into the brush. Vaughn heard the sing and twang of the bullets. Crashings through the mesquites behind, added to the gunshots and lent wings to Star. This was a familiar situation to the great horse. Then for Vaughn it became a strenuous job to ride him, and a doubly fearful one, owing to Roseta. She clung like a broom to the speeding horse. Vaughn, after sheathing his gun, had to let go of her, for he needed one hand for the bridle and the other to ward off the whipping brush. Star made no allowance for that precious part of his burden at Vaughn's back, and he crashed through every opening between mesquites that presented itself. Vaughn dodged and ducked, but he never bent low enough for a branch to strike Roseta.

At every open spot in the mesquite, or long aisle between the cacti, Vaughn looked back to see if any of his pursuers were in sight. There was none, but he heard a horse pounding not far behind and to the right. And again he heard another on the other side. Holding the reins in his teeth

Vaughn reloaded the gun. To be ready for snap shots he took advantage of every opportunity to peer on each side and behind him. But Star appeared gradually to be outdistancing his pursuers. The desert grew more open with a level gravel floor. Here Vaughn urged Star to his limit.

It became a dead run then, with the horse choosing the way. Vaughn risked less now from the stinging mesquite branches. The green wall flashed by on each side. He did not look back. While Star was at his best Vaughn wanted to get far enough ahead to slow down and save the horse. In an hour it would be dusk—too late for even a *vaquero* to track him until daylight had come again.

Roseta stuck like a leech, and the ranger had to add admiration to his other feelings toward her. Vaughn put his hand back to grasp and steady her. It did not take much time for the powerful strides of the horse to cover the miles. Finally Vaughn pulled him into a gallop and then into a lope.

"*Chata*, are you all right?" he asked, afraid to look back, after using that romantic epithet.

"Yes. But I can't—hold on—much longer," she panted. "If they catch us—shoot me first."

"Roseta, they will never catch us now," he promised.

"But—if they do—promise me," she entreated.

"I promise they'll never take us alive. But, child, keep up your nerve. It'll be sunset soon—and then dark. We'll get away sure."

"Vaughn, I'm not frightened. Only—I hate those people and I mustn't fall—into their hands again. It means worse—than death."

"Hush! Save your breath," he replied, and wrapping a long arm backward round her slender waist he held her tight. "Come, Star, cut loose," he called, and dug the horse's flank with a heel.

Again they raced across the desert, this time in less of a straight line, though still to the north. The dry wind made tears dim Vaughn's eyes. He kept to open lanes and patches to avoid being struck by branches. And he spared Star only when he heard the animal's heaves of distress. Star was not easy to break from that headlong flight, but at length Vaughn got him down to a nervous walk. Then he let Roseta slip back into the saddle. His arm was numb from the long strain.

"We're—far ahead," he panted. "They'll trail—us till dark." He peered back across the yellow and green desert, slowly darkening in the sunset. "But we're safe—thank Gawd."

"Oh, what a glorious ride!" cried Roseta between breaths. "I felt that—even with death so close. . . . Vaughn, I'm such a little—fool. I longed—for excitement. Oh, I'm well punished. . . . But for you—"

"Save your breath, honey. We may need to run again. After dark you can rest and talk."

She said no more. Vaughn walked Star until the horse had regained his wind, and then urged him into a lope, which was his easiest gait.

The sun sank red in the west; twilight stole under the mesquite and the *pale verde*; dusk came upon its heels; the heat tempered and there was a slight breeze. When the stars came out Vaughn took his direction from them, and pushed on for several miles. A crescent moon, silver and slender, came up over the desert.

Young as it was, it helped brighten the open patches and the swales. Vaughn halted the tireless horse in a spot where a patch of grass caught the moonlight.

"We'll rest a bit," he said, sliding off, but still holding on to the girl. "Come."

She just fell off into his arms, and when he let her feet down she leaned against him. "Oh, Vaughn!" He held her a moment, sorely tempted. But he might take her weakness for something else.

"Can you stand? . . . You'd better walk around a little," he said.

"My legs are dead."

"I want to go back a few steps and listen. The night is still. I could hear horses at a long distance."

"Don't go far," she entreated him.

Vaughn went back where he could not hear the heaving, blowing horse, and turned his keen ear to the breeze. It blew gently from the south. Only a very faint rustle of leaves disturbed the desert silence. He held his breath and listened intensely. There was no sound! Even if he were trailed by a hound of a *vaquero* he was still far ahead. All he required now was a little rest for Star. He could carry the girl. On the way back across the open he tried to find the tracks Star had left. A man could trail them, but only on foot. Vaughn's last stern doubt took wing and vanished. He returned to Roseta.

"No sound. It is as I expected. Night has saved us," he said.

"Night and *canyu*. Oh, I watched you, ranger man."

"You helped, Roseta. That Mexican who led your horse was suspicious. But when you looked at him—he forgot. Small wonder. . . . Have you stretched your legs?"

"I tried. I walked some, then flopped here. . . . Oh, I want to rest and sleep."

"I don't know about your sleeping, but you can rest riding," he replied, and removing his coat folded it around the pommel of his saddle, making a flat seat there. Star was munching the grass. He was already fit for another race. Vaughn saw to the cinches, and then mounted again, and folded the sleeves of his coat up over the pommel. "Give me your hand. . . . Put your foot in the stirrup. Now." He caught her and lifted her in front of him, and settling her comfortably upon the improvised seat, he put his left arm around her. Many a wounded comrade had he packed this way. "How is—that?" he asked unsteadily.

"It's very nice," she replied, her dark eyes looking inscrutable in the moonlight. And she relaxed against his arm and shoulder.

Vaughn headed Star north at a brisk walk. He could not be more than six hours from the river in a straight line. Canyons and rough going might deter him. But even so he could make the Rio Grande before dawn. Then and then only did he surrender to the astonishing presence of Roseta Uvaldo, to the indubitable fact that he had saved her, and then to thoughts wild and whirling of the future. He gazed down upon the oval face so blanched in the moonlight, into the staring black eyes whose look might mean anything.

"Vaughn, was it that guard or you—who called me *chata*?" she asked, dreamily.

"It was I—who dared," he replied huskily.

"Dared! Then you were not just carried away—for the moment?"

"No, Roseta. . . . I confess I was as—as bold as that poor devil."

"Vaughn, do you know what *chata* means?" she asked gravely.

"It is the name a *vaquero* has for his sweetheart."

"You mean it, señor?" she asked, imperiously.

"Lord help me, Roseta, I did, and I do. . . . I've loved you long."

"But you never told me!" she exclaimed, with wonder and reproach. "Why?"

"What hope had I? A poor ranger. Texas Medill. . . . Didn't you call me 'killer of Mexicans'?"

"I reckon I did. And it is because you *are* that I'm alive to thank God for it. . . . Vaughn, I always liked you, respected you as one of Texas' great rangers—feared you, too. I never knew my real feelings. . . . But I—I love you *now*."

The night wore on, with the moon going down, weird and coldly bright against the dark vaulted sky. Roseta lay asleep in Vaughn's arm. For hours he had gazed, after peering ahead and behind, always vigilant, always the ranger, on that wan face against his shoulder. The silent moonlit night, the lonely ride, the ghastly forms of cactus were real, though Vaughn never trusted his senses there. This was only the dream of the ranger. Yet the sweet fire of Roseta's kisses still lingered on his lips.

At length he changed her again from his right arm back to his left. And she awakened, but not fully. In all the years of his ranger service, so much of which he lived over on this ride, there had been nothing to compare with this. For his reward had been exalting. His longings had received magnificent fulfillment. His duty had not been to selfish and unappreciative officials, but to a great state—to its people—to the native soil upon which he had been born. And that hard duty, so poorly recompensed, so bloody and harrowing at times, had by some enchantment bestowed upon one ranger at least a beautiful girl of the border, frankly and honestly Texan, yet part Spanish, retaining something of the fire and spirit of the Dons who had once called Texas their domain.

In the gray of dawn, Vaughn lifted Roseta down from the weary horse upon the south bank of the Rio Grande.

"We are here, Roseta," he said gladly. "It will soon be light enough to ford the river. Star came out just below Brownsville. There's a horse, Roseta! He shall never be risked again. . . . In an hour you will be home."

"Home? Oh, how good! . . . But what shall I say, Vaughn?" she replied, evidently awakening to the facts of her predicament.

"Dear, who was the feller you ran—rode off with yesterday mawnin'?" he asked.

"Didn't I tell you?" And she laughed. "It happened to be Elmer Wade— *that* morning. . . . Oh, he was the unlucky one. The bandits beat him with quirts, dragged him off his horse. Then they led me away and I didn't see him again."

Vaughn had no desire to acquaint her then with the tragic fate that had overtaken that young man.

"You were not—elopin'?"

"*Vaughn!* It was only fun."

"Uvaldo thinks you eloped. He was wild. He raved."

"The devil he did!" exclaimed Roseta rebelliously. "Vaughn, what did *you* think?"

"Dearest, I—I was only concerned with trackin' you," he replied, and even in the gray gloom of the dawn those big dark eyes made his heart beat faster.

"Vaughn, I have peon blood in me," she said, and she might have been a princess for the pride with which she confessed it. "My father always feared I'd run true to the Indian. Are you afraid of your *chata*?"

"No, darlin'."

"Then I shall punish Uvaldo. . . . I shall elope."

"Roseta!" cried Vaughn.

"Listen." She put her arms around his neck, and that was a long reach for her. "Will you give up the ranger service? I—I couldn't bear it, Vaughn. You have earned release from the service all Texans are so proud of."

"Yes, Roseta. I'll resign," he replied with boyish, eager shyness. "I've some money—enough to buy a ranch."

"Far from the border?" she entreated.

"Yes, far. I know just the valley—way north, under the *Llano Estacado*. . . . But, Roseta, I shall have to pack a gun—till I'm forgotten."

"Very well, I'll not be afraid—way north," she replied. Then her sweet gravity changed to mischief. "We will punish Father. Vaughn, we'll elope right now! We'll cross the river—get married—and drive out home to breakfast. . . . How Dad will rave! But he would have me elope, though he'd never guess I'd choose a ranger."

Vaughn swung her up on Star, and leaned close to peer up at her, to find one more assurance of the joy that had befallen him. He was not conscious of asking, when she bent her head to bestow kisses upon his lips.

Discussion Questions

1. Describe the mood and character of Vaughn Medill in part 1 of the story.
2. Describe Roseta Uvaldo's character as revealed in parts 1 and 2. To what extent does the narrator rely on racial stereotyping?
3. In the portrayal of Quinela's bandits in parts 3 and 4, to what extent are their characters realistically and fully delineated, and to what extent do their descriptions indicate the narrator's racial prejudice? Provide a few brief quotations as examples.
4. Analyze the conclusion in part 6. Explain each conflict in the story and how each is resolved. Read the introduction to Chapter 6 on the concept of gender and apply it to this story.
5. Based on "The Ranger," list five or six elements of melodrama.
6. Based on this Zane Grey story, list five or six features that characterize a "popular" Western story. Then compare your criteria to the excerpt from Edward Ellis's *Seth Jones* in Chapter 2.

◆ ◆ ◆

FOCUS ON FILM:
HOWARD HAWKS'S *RED RIVER* (1948)

1. List several themes you noticed in the film. Explain one of these themes and then compare its development in one of the readings of this chapter.
2. Define the characters of Tom Dunson and Matthew Garth and then analyze the conflict between them.
3. Contrast their differing approaches to management-labor relations.
4. Explain the significance of Nadine Groot in the film and comment on the change in his loyalty toward Dunson.

5. Describe Tess Millay's role in the film. To what extent is her role dramatically significant to the film? To what extent is her role and the romantic subplot a mere convention or expectation of the Hollywood Western?

6. Describe several scenes representing the trail drive itself, considering both visual and sound elements. What effects do the trail scenes achieve in themselves? What enjoyment do these scenes offer to film spectators? Notice where they come in the sequence of scenes showing dramatic action among the characters. Besides their importance in the narrative or plot line, speculate about their cinematic purpose in contrasting the character-based scenes in the film.

TOPICS FOR RESEARCH AND WRITING

1. Compare the character of Ringo in John Ford's *Stagecoach* with the John Wayne character of Dunson in Howard Hawks's *Red River*. Explain the major differences.

2. By comparing the two protagonists in *Red River*, analyze the psychology of Dunson's quest for power and control. Why is he so driven on the trail drive? How does Garth's character emphasize a weakness in Dunson? Finally, how are the dynamics of their relationship dramatized by the psychological role of women in the film? To help with this analysis, you could read David Lusted, "Social Class and the Western as Male Melodrama" in *The Book of Westerns*, ed. Ian Cameron and Douglas Pye (New York: Continuum, 1996), pages 63–74.

3. Comparing and contrasting Grey's "The Ranger" to Cather's "El Dorado," analyze the features that—in your judgment—might lead some readers to consider the first story "popular" fiction and the second story "literary" fiction. (You might actually begin your thinking about this problem by discussing these features with other students.) Likewise, what features do both stories share as "Western" fiction? Finally, argue whether the similarities as "Westerns" or the differences between "popular" and "literary" fiction are more significant.

4. Explain how Zane Grey presents the mix of cultures in "The Ranger." Consider how Vaughn, Roseta, and Quinela's bandits—with Anglo, Spanish, and Mexican heritage—represent features supposedly typical of their cultures. Comment on the realism and possible racism of these stereotypes in terms of the narrator that Grey created to tell the story.

5. If you have read Jack Schaefer's *Shane*, view the film version and compare it to the novel. If you like, you might read and refer to Charles Albright's movie review on page 363 of James C. Work, ed., *Shane: The Critical Edition* (Lincoln, NE: University of Nebraska, 1984).

6. If you have read Owen Wister's *The Virginian*, explain a major theme in the novel. For instance, you might analyze: (A) the conflicts in courtship; (B) East vs. West; (C) the transformation of the tenderfoot; *or* (D) the morality of vigilantes vs. outlaws.

7. If you have read *Shane*, first consider a few central ideas or themes in the novel. Which of these themes relates to a central idea or theme in "The Jimmyjohn Boss"? Explain in detail how this theme works and becomes important to the meaning of *Shane*. Then compare and contrast how this same idea works and becomes important to the meaning of the Wister short story.

8. If you have read *The Virginian*, compare and contrast the relationship between the narrator and the title character and the relationship between Dean Drake and Mr. Bolles in "The Jimmyjohn Boss."

9. Read Mary Austin's "The Pocket Hunter" from *The Land of Little Rain* (New York: Houghton Mifflin, 1903), pages 61–89; *or* Stewart Edward White's "The Prospector" in John Seelye's *Stories of the Old West* (New York: Penguin, 1994), pages 330–40. Consider first how the conclusion relates to the beginning of the story. Then analyze the character of the miner, considering the significance of the Western environment that shapes his struggles and choices.

10. Read Charles Siringo's chapter, "A True Sketch of 'Billy the Kid's' Life," from *A Texas Cowboy* (New York: Penguin, 2000), pages 146–54. Note the kinds of details Siringo provides and the conclusions he draws about Billy's character. Then read Jon Lewis's chapter, "Billy the Kid" from *The Mammoth Book of the West* (New York: Carroll & Graf, 1996), pages 206–21. Compare and contrast the two versions of Billy's life, remarking both on the details selected by the authors and their interpretations of Billy's character, including his positive traits.

11. Read Jon Lewis's chapter on "Little Big Horn" from *The Mammoth Book of the West* (New York: Carroll & Graf, 1996), pages 415–30. Note the kinds of details he selects to represent this historical episode. Then read either the Last Stand section of Brian Dippie's "The Visual West " from *The Oxford History of the American West* (New York: Oxford University, 1994), pages 677–80; *or* William H. Goetzmann and William N. Goetzmann's "Views of Tragedy" from *The West of the Imagination* (New York: Norton, 1986), pages 217–27. Compare and contrast the two selections, noting the features of the episode that the historical narrative describes well and those it neglects vs. the features that the art analysis describes well and those it neglects. Which description do you find more forceful in shaping your understanding of the cultural significance of Custer's Last Stand?

CHAPTER

SPIRITUAL LANDSCAPES

INTRODUCTION

As explained in Chapter 7, the Native Americans' traditional relations to the land were integral to their livelihood and consciousness. In a way, the land was never outside them because they were fully a part of it, both physically and spiritually. In the Euro-American consciousness, however, landscape was forever something apart, and at best something to be reunited with by a romantic recovery of mutuality. Christianity's belief in banishment from Eden devalued the physical world as a "fallen" and corrupted nature. Thus, to colonial Americans the meaning of wilderness was associated with not only "heathen" Indians, but also Satan. However, the Protestant Reformation reinvigorated the language of the Old Testament, especially in the notion of a "chosen people" seeking a New Jerusalem, a quest consistent with "dreams of empire and a higher civilization" (Sanford 300). In westering to the New World, the early militant English Protestants were disposed to see themselves on a moral and spiritual quest—certainly to establish colonies where religious freedom would prevail. But in the doctrine of "election" by God to his Heavenly Kingdom, the church members who felt confident of being among the "saved" were also inclined to believe in "a direct causal relationship between moral effort and material reward" (302) in their colonial communities.

Eighteenth-century American intellectuals, including Benjamin Franklin, espoused an agrarian social theory in which "industrious frugal farmers" formed the core of our citizenry (qtd. in Smith 141). The popular "freehold concept" consisted of several related beliefs: that America provided a unique opportunity to fulfill "a natural right to land"; that land ownership grants "independence" and thus "dignity"; and that working in "constant contact with nature" makes farmers "virtuous and happy" (Smith 141). De Crèvecoeur, in his *Letters from an American Farmer* (1782), spoke for many American frontier colonialists in extolling the moral and political virtues of an agrarian lifestyle:

> We are a people of cultivators. . . , united by the silken bands of mild government, all respecting the laws, without dreading their power, because they are equitable. We are all animated with the spirit of an industry which is unfettered and unrestrained, because each works for himself. . . . We have no princes, for whom we toil, starve, and bleed; we are the most perfect society now existing in the world. (49–50)

In sum, both religious and social beliefs contributed to Euro-American ambitions to cultivate a "garden in the desert." This tradition is illustrated no more definitively than in the Mormon settlement of Utah, where in a valley surrounded by fierce desert on three sides, Brigham Young declared "This is the place!" and subsequently instituted a vast system of irrigation.

In the literature of the American West, an almost mystical relation between a farmer and his land is expressed by Willa Cather in "Neighbor Rosicky" (1932), as the old man reflects on his imminent death after learning of his bad heart:

> It was a nice graveyard, Rosicky reflected, sort of snug and homelike, not cramped or mournful,—a big sweep all round it. A man could lie down in the long grass and see the complete arch of the sky over him, hear the wagons go by; in summer the mowing-machine rattled right up to the wire fence. And it was so near home. Over there across the cornstalks his own roof and windmill looked so good to him that he promised himself to mind the Doctor and take care of himself. He was awful fond of his place, he admitted. He wasn't anxious to leave it. And it was a comfort to think than he would never have to go farther than the edge of his own hayfield. (18–19)

Here, Rosicky seems to confuse lying down in the grass with dying because living in nature and returning to the earth are both of a piece. He imagines that, in death, he will still sense the sky—which becomes an emblem for Heaven—and the familiar sounds of working and harvest. Though he is loathe to "leave" his farm, he realizes that in dying he will still be a part of the land, just on the edge of the patch he has labored over all his life. This vision is a kind of agrarian ideal, and by the end of the story, Rosicky also has the assurance that the cycles of nature will continue without him, as his daughter-in-law will bear his grandchild and guarantee that family will continue to work his land.

In a very different relation of self to landscape, John Muir also expressed a religious connection that was immediate, powerful, and reassuring. However, not an agrarian, he envisioned a spiritual relationship between his soul and the wildness of nature in the Sierra Nevada Mountains. Rather than seeking a garden in the desert, he explored the meaning of meeting nature head-on, without attempting to cultivate or manage, but instead to appreciate and to somehow assimilate the wildness. Similar in some ways to transcendentalists Henry Thoreau and Ralph Waldo Emerson, Muir embraced a romantic manifestation of the sublime in the fierce storms, forbidding chasms, and lofty peaks of Yosemite. For him, as for the English Romantic poets, the sublime in nature signified terrible power, wonderful beauty, and divine mysteries. Other nineteenth-century Western mountain writers, such as explorer John Charles Fremont (1813–1890), could also wax poetic: "a stillness the most profound and terrible solitude forced themselves constantly on the mind as the great features of the place" (qtd. in Lyon 229). However, in his survey reports Fremont made no sustained argument about the spiritual significance of wilderness. Also, in his classic work *Mountaineering in the Sierra Nevada* (1872), Clarence King (1842–1901) certainly matched Muir as an expert geologist and descriptive writer:

> The summer haze had been banished from the region by autumnal frosts and wind. We looked into the gulf below through air as clear as a vacuum, discerning small objects upon the valley floor and cliff-front. . . . All stern sublimity, all geological terribleness, are veiled away behind magic curtains of cloud shadow and broken light. (qtd. in Goetzmann and Goetzmann 145)

However, King "did not venture into a philosophy of nature" (Lyon 232). On the other hand, Muir combined both disciplined observer and poet-philosopher: "Muir's great contribution to western writing was to bring the holistic or participant experience alive, but at the same time not to relegate the intellect and science to vagueness" (234).

Extending the Muir tradition into the twentieth century, Aldo Leopold (1886–1948) and Joseph Wood Krutch (1893–1970) have reiterated the importance of sustaining wilderness. In *A Sand County Almanac* (1949), Leopold argued that "the extension of system into ethical behavior and indeed into the whole of the man-nature relationship was the next necessary step in human evolution" (qtd. in Lyon 244). In a 1970 essay published in *The American Scholar*, Krutch went a bit farther: "Faith in wildness, or in nature as a creative force, has the deeper, possibly the deepest, significance for our future. It is a philosophy, a faith; it is even, if you like, a religion" (qtd. in Lyon 254). Contemporary restatements and revisions of this notion of wilderness will be presented in Chapter 8, The New West.

Like the history and nature writing of the West, the landscape painting of nineteenth-century America in some ways reflected the poles of civilization and wildness. One popular trend for painting landscapes of the Eastern states was to locate habitations, humans, cultivated fields, and domesticated animals in a harmonious relationship to nature. In particular, "the formula of the middle landscape [depicted] a rural Arcadia gently shaped by the hand of the farmer and aesthetically balanced between the extremes of wilderness and city" (Miller 13). Contributing to a sense of "national unity, pride of place, and a unique identity distinct from that of Europe," the middle landscape "implied stability in a period of rapid change; its modulated topography was the expression of a yearning for uncomplicated social relations" (12–13). Even when mountain precipices were foreboding, as in the Catskills, the painter's focus drew the viewer into observation of the human figures. For example, Asher Durand (1796–1886) portrayed nature as a source of spiritual delight and moral education, but his landscapes were balanced and serene, designed for contemplation rather than stimulation (Taylor 111). In *Kindred Spirits* (1849), he also represented the Sister Arts ideal, which associated painting and poetry as similar modes of humanistic expression: painter Thomas Cole is pictured strolling in the hills with his longtime friend, poet William Cullen Bryant. This choice of literary companion is significant since Bryant had earlier expressed a moral view of nature that matched Durand's own beliefs, as these opening lines from "Thanatopsis" (1817) suggest:

> To him who in the love of Nature holds
> Communion with her visible forms, she speaks
> A various language, for his gayer hours
> She has a voice of gladness, and a smile
> And eloquence of beauty, and she glides

Into his darker musings, with a mild
And healing sympathy, that steals away
Their sharpness, ere he is aware. . . . (qtd. in Taylor 104)

This mildness of nature is altogether opposed to Muir's celebration of death-defying mountain ascents or to the rocky precipices popularized by Western painters.

In the West, since landscapes proved more spectacular and over-whelming than in the East, artists more often found manifestations of the sublime, "surpassing the control or rational comprehension of man" (Taylor 98). As members of exploration parties in the Rockies and the Yellowstone, the first painters exposed to "a wild American majesty of mountains, light, and primal air" expressed "a highly emotional response to nature" in images that also "symbolized the expansive aspirations of the American public" (Taylor 118–19, 124). In 1859, Albert Bierstadt joined an expedition, led by Colonel Frederick West Lander, to survey an overland wagon trail to California. Likewise, Thomas Moran journeyed to the Yellowstone in 1871 on a scientific expedition led by Ferdinand Hayden, head of the U.S. Geological and Geographical Survey of the Ter-ritories; one consequence of the trip was that Congress later preserved the pristine wilderness of the area as the first National Park (Goetzmann and Goetzmann 150–51, 171–9). Both artists returned to their studios with marvelous sketches and studies, prepared to capture the stupendous landscapes they had seen. In their works, they often eliminated human figures or used them as minute indicators of the massive scale of the landscape. They pictured "a West of swirling atmospheric forces, of pri-mordial geological drama, of natural—almost supernatural wonder" (148). Bierstadt also represented the sublime in ferocious Sierra Moun-tain storms and in light flooding the upper elevations with a spiritual glow. From his experiences of rambling in the Alps and studying painting in Germany, Bierstadt learned to delineate the "romantic trajectory of eye and spirit into the elevated mountain vistas through a graceful arrange-ment of receding planes and the alternation of brilliant light with dark shadow" (Goetzmann and Goetzmann 150). Moran, in his brilliant watercolors of Yellowstone, the Grand Canyon, and the Southwestern mesas, often captured other-worldly colors that suggest the ethereal, rather than the earthly. These images complemented Muir's evocation of the sublime. For gallery viewers in the nineteenth century, these images also worked on the imagination and created Western landscapes as larger-than-life spectacles of wonder. Moreover, paintings of the Far West "avoided the divisive political realities" of more familiar terrain bloodied by the Civil War and implied "a renewal of national hopes with land-scapes of heroic and unfamiliar dimensions" (Miller 205).

Cather, Willa. "Neighbor Rosicky." *Obscure Destinies.* New York: Knopf, 1932. 3–37.

De Crèvecoeur, Hector St. John. *Letters from an American Farmer* [1782]. New York: Fox and Duffield, 1904.

Goetzmann, William H., and William N. Goetzmann. *West of the Imagination.* New York: Norton, 1986.

Lyon, Thomas J. "The Nature Essay in the West." *A Literary History of the American West.* Ed. Thomas J. Lyon, et al. Fort Worth, TX: Texas Christian University Press and The Western Literature Association, 1987. 221–65.

Miller, Angelina. *Empire of the Eye: Landscape Representation and American Cultural Politics, 1825–1875.* Ithaca, NY: Cornell University, 1993.

Sanford, Charles L. "An American *Pilgrim's Progress.*" *American Quarterly* 6 (1954): 297–310.

Smith, Henry Nash. *Virgin Land: The American West as Symbol and Myth.* New York: Vintage, 1950.

Taylor, Joshua C. "The Virtue of American Nature." *America as Art.* New York: Harper and Row, 1976. 96–131.

Fig. 4.1 Asher Durand, *Kindred Spirits* (1849). Collection of the New York Public Library; Astor, Lenox and Tilden Foundation.

Fig. 4.2 Albert Bierstadt, *Among the Sierra Mountains, California* (1868). Smithsonian American Art Musuem; bequest of Helen Huntington Hull, granddaughter of William Brown Dinsmore, who acquired the painting in 1873 for "The Locusts," the family estate in Dutchess County, New York; 1977.107.1.

JOHN MUIR
(1838–1914)

Much has been made of Muir's Calvinist upbringing and the harsh discipline of his father that he rejected in favor of the wild. In actuality, living in Scotland until age eleven had two positive effects: introducing him to nature in his free roaming of the fields near home, and setting him against a formally rigid education system that depended on rote learning, rather than on a search for knowledge. Even after moving to Wisconsin, young John and his brothers worked long, physically exhausting hours to further his father's ambitions for expanding the family farm. Later, he came to see the materialistic, acquisitive aspects of this struggle, along with his religion's focus on the cataclysmic moral drama of humanity, as mistakes of "civilized" thinking. Instead, he embraced a belief in the flow of natural processes and a philosophy that included the earth and other creatures, rather than considering humans as the center of creation. However, he never escaped the ascetic self-denial of his religious tradition, which actually allowed him to abandon himself to the wilderness, to revel in the ravages of a storm, to hike miles for days with only bread and tea as nourishment and only his jacket as a bed (Lyon 13–17).

It must also be acknowledged that Muir's education at the University of Wisconsin (1861–1863) contributed to his natural philosophy. In effect, his enthusiasm for observing nature was channeled by his training in the scientific method of gathering empirical data. Likewise, Muir was exposed to innovations in geological evolutionary theory, which proposed another type of natural flow; to the popular transcendentalism of Emerson, whose writing also influenced him to keep a journal of observations; and to the formal study of botany, which suggested another type of divine order within nature. With these intellectual tools, Muir was later able to argue convincingly against the reigning theory that the Sierra Mountains were formed by catastrophic upheavals. Instead, by painstaking observations over months around Yosemite Valley, Muir showed that the glacial polish on the valley walls, the heaping up of loose deposits or moraines, the fracturing of huge masses of granite, and the active glaciers in the upper ranges all pointed to a slow erosion of the mountains over millennia. Moreover, these discoveries stimulated his own writing for a public audience in San Francisco's *Overland Monthly*, which published five of his articles on Yosemite in 1872 and 1873 (Lyon 18–24).

But before he began his California explorations, he left Wisconsin to wander, first "botanizing" in Canada for two years. In 1867, working in a factory in Indianapolis, Muir successfully created automatic gadgets to improve production, but an accident dramatically forced him to rethink his occupation. When he was blinded by a sharp file stabbing his right eye, his left eye went blind in sympathetic response. Flat on his back for four weeks in recovery, he thought about the work that might fulfill his life. Finally, when his sight returned, he felt a conversion experience and determined to devote himself to study in what he called "the University of the Wilderness." He tramped from Kentucky to Florida, keeping a journal from which the posthumous travel narrative *A Thousand-Mile Walk to the Gulf* (1916) was later edited (Lyon 28–29). Having suffered a debilitating attack of malaria in Florida, Muir set his sights on California, where the cool, dry air would be conducive to his recovery. For the following thirteen years he wandered over much of that state, earning a meager living as a day laborer, an odd jobber around James Hutchings's Yosemite Valley hotel, a shepherd, or a casual sawmill worker (Holmes). In the 1870s Muir also explored parts of Nevada, Oregon, Utah, and Washington (Smith).

Over this period, until he married and settled down on a fruit farm in 1880, Muir developed his natural philosophy, influenced greatly by a meticulous reading of Henry David Thoreau (Holmes). From 1878 to 1881, he published seven nature essays in *Scribner's* (O'Grady). However, through the 1880s he focused his activity on his very successful orchard in Martinez, which earned him $10,000 yearly. When he turned his attention to a practical application of his philosophy, he began to publicly criticize his culture's abuse of natural resources. His social criticism was based clearly on the reasoning of scientific ecology, not merely on Muir's belief in humans' ethical relationship to nature. For instance, his observations led him to support saving the giant sequoias because their ecosystems absorb the massive California winter precipitation, releasing the water slowly during the dry half of the year. Likewise, his observations in the Sierra high country sparked his protests against the damage by the "hoofed locust," or domestic sheep (Smith).

Muir found a public voice to address his arguments on natural preservation in the influential national magazine the *Century*, where he published "The Treasures of the Yosemite" in August and "Features of the Proposed Yosemite National Park" in September 1890. Largely due to these efforts, the Yosemite National Park Act passed Congress later that same year. In order to help establish a forest protection policy—a plan and practice entirely new to the nation—Muir founded the Sierra

Club in 1892. However, he found an opponent in Gifford Pinchot, the first director of the Forest Service, whose notion of conservation meant only a utilitarian delay in the human exploitation of timber. By contrast, Muir was intent on preservation of wildlands, and he was successful in raising the country's awareness of environmental logic—in part, due to his immensely popular 1894 volume, *The Mountains of California* (O'Grady).

Today's environmental movement owes much to Muir's nature writings and practical political activism, especially for its goal to preserve wilderness in its various meanings: "spontaneity, naturalness, the possibility of renewal, diversity" (Lyon 8). However, he was unsuccessful in his biggest battle against development in national parks. In spite of his national campaign of letter-writing, articles, and even a book, *The Yosemite* (1912), he could not save the Tuolumne Valley from being flooded by the Hetch-Hetchy Dam, designed to create a reservoir which San Francisco claimed was essential for drinking water and power generation. Arguing against politicians and engineers, Muir exclaimed, "These temple destroyers, devotees of a ravaging commercialism, seem to have a perfect contempt for Nature, and, instead of lifting their eyes to the god of the mountains, lift them to the Almighty Dollar" (qtd. in O'Grady 248).

The text for the selections from *My First Summer in the Sierra* is from its initial publication (New York: Houghton Mifflin, 1911), pages 13–16 and 131–48. However, the experiences recounted in the book actually occurred in 1869, and there is evidence that, in writing up his early adventures, Muir drew largely from three notebooks composed in 1887, probably based on original journals, now lost. One effect of this revising process is to create a "conversion" experience, in which the young persona suddenly realizes the psychological and spiritual meanings of wilderness. It is likely that Muir's insights as recorded in the book are the result of his mature thinking about the human relationship to nature, arrived at over years of observation, reflection, and writing (Holmes 253–59).

Holmes, Steven J. *The Young John Muir: An Environmental Biography*. Madison, WI: University of Wisconsin, 1999.

Lyon, Thomas J. *John Muir*. Boise, ID: Boise State College, 1972.

O'Grady, John P. "John Muir." *Dictionary of Literary Biography, Volume 186: Nineteenth-Century American Western Writers*. Ed. Robert L. Gale. Detroit: Gale, 1997. 247–59.

Smith, Herbert F. *John Muir*. New York: Twayne, 1965.

FROM *MY FIRST SUMMER IN THE SIERRA*

———⟨✦⟩———

JUNE 5

The sculpture of the landscape is as striking in its main lines as in its lavish richness of detail; a grand congregation of massive heights with the river shining between, each carved into smooth, graceful folds without leaving a single rocky angle exposed, as if the delicate fluting and ridging fashioned out of metamorphic slates had been carefully sand-papered. The whole landscape showed design, like man's noblest sculptures. How wonderful the power of its beauty! Gazing awe-stricken, I might have left everything for it. Glad, endless work would then be mine tracing the forces that have brought forth its features, its rocks and plants and animals and glorious weather. Beauty beyond thought everywhere, beneath, above, made and being made forever. I gazed and gazed and longed and admired until the dusty sheep and packs were far out of sight, made hurried notes and a sketch, though there was no need of either, for the colors and lines and expression of this divine landscape-countenance are so burned into mind and heart they surely can never grow dim.

The evening of this charmed day is cool, calm, cloudless, and full of a kind of lightning I have never seen before—white glowing cloud-shaped masses down among the trees and bushes, like quick-throbbing fire-flies in the Wisconsin meadows rather than the so-called "wild fire." The spreading hairs of the horses' tails and sparks from our blankets show how highly charged the air is.

JUNE 6

. . . .We are now in the mountains and they are in us, kindling enthusiasm, making every nerve quiver, filling every pore and cell of us. Our flesh-and-bone tabernacle seems transparent as glass to the beauty about us, as if truly an inseparable part of it, thrilling with the air and trees, streams and rocks, in the waves of the sun,—a part of all nature, neither old nor young, sick nor well, but immortal. Just now I can hardly conceive of any bodily condition dependent on food or breath any more than the ground or the sky. How glorious a conversion, so complete and wholesome it is, scarce memory enough of old bondage days left as a standpoint to view it from! In this newness of life we seem to have been so always.

Through a meadow opening in the pine woods I see snowy peaks about the headwaters of the Merced above Yosemite. How near they seem and how clear their outlines on the blue air, or rather in the blue air; for they seem to be saturated with it. How consuming strong the invitation they extend! Shall I be allowed to go to them? Night and day I'll pray that I may, but it seems too good to be true. Some one worthy will go, able for the Godful work, yet as far as I can I must drift about these love-monument mountains, glad to be a servant of servants in so holy a wilderness.

* * *

JULY 20

. . . . Sketching on the North Dome. It commands views of nearly all the valley besides a few of the high mountains. I would fain draw everything in sight—rock, tree, and leaf. But little can I do beyond mere outlines,—marks with meanings like words, readable only to myself,—yet I sharpen my pencils and work on as if others might possibly be benefited. Whether these picture-sheets are to vanish like fallen leaves or go to friends like letters, matters not much; for little can they tell to those who have not themselves seen similar wildness, and like a language have learned it. No pain here, no dull empty hours, no fear of the past, no fear of the future. These blessed mountains are so compactly filled with God's beauty, no petty personal hope or experience has room to be. Drinking this champagne water is pure pleasure, so is breathing the living air, and every movement of limbs is pleasure, while the whole body seems to feel beauty when exposed to it as it feels the campfire or sunshine, entering not by the eyes alone, but equally through all one's flesh like radiant heat, making a passionate ecstatic pleasure-glow not explainable. One's body then seems homogeneous throughout, sound as a crystal.

Perched like a fly on this Yosemite dome, I gaze and sketch and bask, oftentimes settling down into dumb admiration without definite hope of ever learning much, yet with the longing, unresting effort that lies at the door of hope, humbly prostrate before the vast display of God's power, and eager to offer self-denial and renunciation with eternal toil to learn any lesson in the divine manuscript.

It is easier to feel than to realize, or in any way explain, Yosemite grandeur. The magnitudes of the rocks and trees and streams are so delicately harmonized they are mostly hidden. Sheer precipices three thousand feet high are fringed with tall trees growing close like grass on the brow of a lowland hill, and extending along the feet of these precipices a ribbon of meadow a mile wide and seven or eight long, that seems like a strip a farmer might mow in less than a day. Waterfalls, five hundred to one or two thousand feet high, are so subordinated to the mighty cliffs over which they pour that they seem like wisps of smoke, gentle as floating clouds, though their voices fill the valley and make the rocks tremble. The mountains, too, along the eastern sky, and the domes in front of them, and the succession of smooth rounded waves between, swelling higher, higher, with dark woods in their hollows, serene in massive exuberant bulk and beauty, tend yet more to hide the grandeur of the Yosemite temple and make it appear as a subdued subordinate feature of the vast harmonious landscape. Thus every attempt to appreciate any one feature is beaten down by the overwhelming influence of all the others. And, as if this were not enough, lo! in the sky arises another mountain range with topography as rugged and substantial-looking as the one beneath it—snowy peaks and domes and shadowy Yosemite valleys—another version of the snowy Sierra, a new creation heralded by a thunder-storm. How fiercely, devoutly wild is Nature in the midst of her beauty-loving tenderness!—painting lilies, watering them, caressing them with gentle hand, going from flower to flower like a gardener while building rock mountains and cloud mountains full of lightning and rain. Gladly we run for shelter beneath an over-hanging cliff and examine the reassuring ferns and mosses, gentle love tokens growing in cracks and chinks. Daisies, too, and ivesias, confiding wild children of light, too small to fear. To these one's heart goes home, and the voices of the storm become gentle. Now the sun breaks forth and fragrant steam arises. The birds are out singing on the edges of the groves. The west is flaming in gold and purple, ready for the ceremony of the sunset, and back I go to camp with my notes and pictures, the best of them printed in my mind as dreams. A fruitful day, without measured beginning or ending. A terrestrial eternity. A gift of good God.

Wrote to my mother and a few friends, mountain hints to each. They seem as near as if within voice-reach or touch. The deeper the solitude the less the sense of loneliness, and the nearer—our friends. Now bread and tea, fir bed and good-night to Carlo, a look at the sky lilies, and death sleep until the dawn of another Sierra to-morrow.

JULY 21

Sketching on the Dome—no rain; clouds at noon about quarter filled the sky, casting shadows with fine effect on the white mountains at the heads of the streams, and a soothing cover over the gardens during the warm hours.

Saw a common house-fly and a grasshopper and a brown bear. The fly and grasshopper paid me a merry visit on the top of the Dome, and I paid a visit to the bear in the middle of a small garden meadow between the Dome and the camp where he was standing alert among the flowers as if willing to be seen to advantage. I had not gone more than half a mile from camp this morning, when Carlo, who was trotting on a few yards ahead of me, came to a sudden, cautious standstill. Down went tail and ears, and forward went his knowing nose, while he seemed to be saying, "Ha, what's this? A bear, I guess." Then a cautious advance of a few steps, setting his feet down softly like a hunting cat, and questioning the air as to the scent he had caught until all doubt vanished. Then he came back to me, looked me in the face, and with his speaking eyes reported a bear near by; then led on softly, careful, like an experienced hunter, not to make the slightest noise, and frequently looking back as if whispering, "Yes, it's a bear; come and I'll show you." Presently we came to where the sunbeams were streaming through between the purple shafts of the firs, which showed that we were nearing an open spot, and here Carlo came behind me, evidently sure that the bear was very near. So I crept to a low ridge of moraine boulders on the edge of a narrow garden meadow, and in this meadow I felt pretty sure the bear must be. I was anxious to get a good look at the sturdy mountaineer without alarming him; so drawing myself up noiselessly back of one of the largest of the trees I peered past its bulging buttresses, exposing only a part of my head, and there stood neighbor Bruin within a stone's throw, his hips covered by tall grass and flowers, and his front feet on the trunk of a fir that had fallen out into the meadow, which raised his head so high that he seemed to be standing erect. He had not yet seen me, but was looking and listening attentively, showing that in some way he was aware of our approach. I watched his gestures and tried to make the most of my opportunity to learn what I could about him, fearing he would catch sight of me and run away. For I had been told that this sort of bear, the cinnamon, always ran from his bad brother man, never showing fight unless wounded or in defense of young. He made a telling picture standing alert in the sunny forest garden. How well he played his part, harmonizing in bulk and color and shaggy hair with the trunks of the trees and lush vegetation, as natural a feature as any other in the landscape. After examining at leisure, noting the sharp muzzle thrust inquiringly forward, the long shaggy hair on his broad chest, the stiff, erect ears nearly buried in hair, and the slow, heavy way he moved his head, I thought I should like to see his gait in running, so I made a sudden rush at him, shouting and swinging my hat to frighten him, expecting to see him make haste to get away. But to my dismay he did not run or show any sign of running. On the contrary, he stood his ground ready to fight and defend himself, lowered his head, thrust it forward, and looked sharply and fiercely at me. Then I suddenly began to fear that upon me would fall the work of running; but I was afraid to run, and therefore, like the bear, held my ground. We stood staring at each other in solemn silence within a dozen yards or thereabouts, while I fervently hoped that the power of the human eye over wild beasts would prove as great as it is said to be. How long our awfully strenuous interview lasted, I don't know; but at length in the slow fullness of time he pulled his huge paws down off the log, and with magnificent deliberation turned and walked leisurely up the meadow, stopping frequently to look back over his shoulder to see whether I was pursuing him, then moving on again, evidently neither fearing me very much nor trusting me. He was probably about five hundred pounds in weight, a broad, rusty bundle of ungovernable wildness, a happy fellow whose lines have fallen in pleasant places. The flowery glade in which I saw him so well, framed like a picture, is one of the best of all I have yet discovered, a conservatory of Nature's precious plant people. Tall lilies were swinging their bells over that bear's back, with geraniums, larkspurs, columbines, and daisies brushing against his sides. A place for angels, one would say, instead of bears. . . .

The house-fly also seemed at home and buzzed about me as I sat sketching, and enjoying my bear interview now it was over. I wonder what draws house-flies so far up the mountains, heavy gross feeders as they are, sensitive to cold, and fond of domestic ease. How have they been distributed from continent to continent, across seas and deserts and mountain chains, usually so influential in determining boundaries of species both of plants and animals. Beetles and butterflies are sometimes restricted to small areas. Each mountain in a range, and even the different zones of a mountain, may have its own peculiar species. But the house-fly seems to be everywhere. I wonder if any island in mid-ocean is flyless. The bluebottle is abundant in these Yosemite woods, ever ready with his marvelous store of eggs to make all dead flesh fly. Bumblebees are here, and are well fed on boundless stores of nectar and pollen. The honeybee, though abundant in the foothills, has not yet got so high. It is only a few years since the first swarm was brought to California.

A queer fellow and a jolly fellow is the grasshopper. Up the mountains he comes on excursions, how high I don't know, but at least as far and high as Yosemite tourists. I was much interested with the hearty enjoyment of the one that danced and sang for me on the Dome this afternoon. He seemed brimful of glad, hilarious energy, manifested by springing into the air to a height of twenty or thirty feet, then diving and springing up again and making a sharp musical rattle just as the lowest point in the descent was reached. Up and down a dozen times or so he danced and sang, then alighted to rest, then up and at it again. The curves he described in the air in diving and rattling resembled those made by cords hanging loosely and attached at the same height at the ends, the loops nearly covering each other. Braver, heartier, keener, carefree enjoyment of life I have never seen or heard in any creature, great or small. The life of this comic red-legs, the mountain's merriest child, seems to be made up of pure, condensed gayety. The Douglas squirrel is the only living creature I can compare him with in exuberant, rollicking, irrepressible jollity. Wonderful that these sublime mountains are so loudly cheered and brightened by a creature so queer. Nature in him seems to be snapping her fingers in the face of all earthly dejection and melancholy with a boyish hip-hip-hurrah. How the sound is made I do not understand. When he was on the ground he made not the slightest noise, nor when he was simply flying from place to place, but only when diving in curves, the motion seeming to be required for the sound; for the more vigorous the diving the more energetic the corresponding outbursts of jolly rattling. I tried to observe him closely while he was resting in the intervals of his performances; but he would not allow a near approach, always getting his jumping legs ready to spring for immediate flight, and keeping his eyes on me. A fine sermon the little fellow danced for me on the Dome, a likely place to look for sermons in stones, but not for grasshopper sermons. A large and imposing pulpit for so small a preacher. No danger of weakness in the knees of the world while Nature can spring such a rattle as this. Even the bear did not express for me the mountain's wild health and strength and happiness so tellingly as did this comical little hopper. No cloud of care in his day, no winter of discontent in sight. To him every day is a holiday; and when at length his sun sets, I fancy he will cuddle down on the forest floor and die like the leaves and flowers, and like them leave no unsightly remains calling for burial.

Sundown, and I must to camp. Good-night, friends three,—brown bear, rugged boulder of energy, in groves and gardens fair as Eden; restless, fussy fly with gauzy wings stirring the air around all the world; and grasshopper, crisp, electric spark of joy enlivening the massy sublimity of the mountains like the laugh of a child. Thank you, thank you all three for your quickening company. Heaven guide every wing and leg. Good-night friends three, goodnight.

JULY 22

A fine specimen of the black-tailed deer went bounding past camp this morning. A buck with wide spread of antlers, showing admirable vigor and grace. Wonderful the beauty, strength, and graceful movements of animals in wildernesses, cared for by Nature only, when our experience with domestic animals would lead us to fear that all the so-called neglected wild beasts would degenerate. Yet the upshot of Nature's method of breeding and teaching seems to lead to excellence of every sort. Deer, like all wild animals, are as clean as plants. The beauties of their gestures and attitudes, alert or in repose, surprise yet more than their bounding exuberant strength. Every movement and posture is graceful, the very poetry of manners and motion. Mother Nature is too often spoken of as in reality no mother at all. Yet how wisely, sternly, tenderly she loves and looks after her children in all sorts of weather and wildernesses. The more I see of deer the more I admire them as mountaineers. They make their way into the heart of the roughest solitudes with smooth reserve of strength, through dense belts of brush and forest encumbered with fallen trees and boulder piles, across cañons, roaring streams, and snowfields, ever showing forth beauty and courage. Over nearly all the continent the deer find homes. In the Florida savannas and hummocks, in the Canada woods, in the far north, roaming over mossy tundras, swimming, lakes and rivers and arms of the sea from island to island washed with waves, or climbing rocky mountains, everywhere healthy and able, adding beauty to every landscape,—a truly admirable creature and great credit to Nature. . . .

JULY 24

Clouds at noon occupying about half the sky gave half an hour of heavy rain to wash one of the cleanest landscapes in the world. How well it is washed! The sea is hardly less dusty than the ice-burnished pavements and ridges, domes and cañons, and summit peaks plashed with snow like waves with foam. How fresh the woods are and calm after the last films of clouds have been wiped from the sky! A few minutes ago every tree was excited, bowing to the roaring storm, waving, swirling, tossing their branches in glorious enthusiasm like worship. But though to the outer ear these trees are now silent, their songs never cease. Every hidden cell is throbbing with music and life, every fibre thrilling like harp strings, while incense is ever flowing from the balsam bells and leaves. No wonder the hills and groves were God's first temples, and the more they are cut down and hewn into cathedrals and churches, the farther off and dimmer seems the Lord himself. The same may be said of stone temples. Yonder, to the eastward of our camp grove, stands one of Nature's cathedrals, hewn from the living rock, almost conventional in form, about two thousand feet high, nobly adorned with spires and pinnacles, thrilling under floods of sunshine as if alive like a grove-temple, and well named "Cathedral Peak." Even Shepherd Billy turns at times to this wonderful mountain building, though apparently deaf to all stone sermons. Snow that refused to melt in fire would hardly be more wonderful than unchanging dullness in the rays of God's beauty. I have been trying to get him to walk to the brink of Yosemite for a view, offering to watch the sheep for a day, while he should enjoy what tourists come from all over the world to see. But though within a mile of the famous valley, he will not go to it even out of mere curiosity. "What," says he, "is Yosemite but a cañon—a lot of rocks—a hole in the ground—a place dangerous about falling into—a d——d good place to keep away from." "But think of the waterfalls, Billy—just think of that big stream we crossed the other day, falling half a mile through the air— think of that, and the sound it makes. You can hear it now like the roar of the sea." Thus I pressed Yosemite upon him like a missionary offering the gospel, but he would have none of it. "I should be afraid to look over so high a wall," he said. "It would make my head swim. There is nothing worth seeing anywhere, only rocks, and I see plenty of them here. Tourists that spend their money to see rocks and falls are fools, that's all. You can't humbug me. I've been in this country too long for that." Such souls, I suppose, are asleep, or smothered and befogged beneath mean pleasures and cares.

JULY 25

Another cloudland. Some clouds have an over-ripe decaying look, watery and bedraggled and drawn out into wind-torn shreds and patches, giving the sky a littered appearance; not so these Sierra summer mid-day clouds. All are beautiful with smooth definite outlines and curves like those of glacier-polished domes. They begin to grow about eleven o'clock, and seem so wonderfully near and clear from this high camp one is tempted to try to climb them and trace the streams that pour like cataracts from their shadowy fountains. The rain to which they give birth is often very heavy, a sort of waterfall as imposing as if pouring from rock mountains. Never in all my travels have I found anything more truly novel and interesting than these midday mountains of the sky, their fine tones of color, majestic visible growth, and ever-changing scenery and general effects, though mostly as well let alone as far as description goes. I oftentimes think of Shelley's cloud poem, "I sift the snow on the mountains below." . . .

Discussion Questions

1. Describe the style of Muir's description in the first passage (June 5 and 6).
2. Analyze the passage from the phrase "We are now in the mountains and they are in us . . ." to the end of the paragraph. Define the experience Muir is describing here. Explain the imagery and any metaphors you find.
3. In the second passage (July 20–25), why does he think his sketches are so inadequate in description? Judging from his word descriptions from July 20 only, do you feel they match your own personal experience of being in the wilderness? Why or why not?
4. Explain your opinion of his encounter with the bear, when Muir charges the animal, wishing "to see his gait in running." Compare Muir's attitude and description of the grasshopper to his attitude and description of the bear.
5. Analyze the entry for July 24. Explain the religious imagery he uses to describe the landscape. To what extent is Muir describing a "religious" experience? To what extent do you sympathize with Billy, who sees only "rocks and falls"? In your opinion, which character has the more reasonable viewpoint?

Fig. 4.3 Thomas Moran, *The Grand Canyon of the Yellowstone* (1872). Smithsonian American Art Musuem; lent by the Department of the Interior Museum; L1968.84.1.

Fig. 4.4 Gilbert Munger, *Eocene Bluffs, Green River, Wyoming*, chromolithograph, from Clarence King, *Systematic Geology* (1878). DeGolyer Library, Southern Methodist University, Dallas, TX.

Fig. 4.5 Edward S. Curtis, *Cañon de Chelly—Navaho* (1904). Yale Collection of Western Americana, Beinecke Rare Book Room and Manuscript Library, Yale University, New Haven, CN.

Fig. 4.6 Georgia O'Keeffe, *Mule's Skull with Pink Poinsettias* (1936). Georgia O'Keeffe Museum, Santa Fe, NM; gift of the Burnett Foundation.

◆ ◆ ◆

FOCUS ON FILM:
LAWRENCE HOTT AND DIANE GAREY'S
THE WILDERNESS IDEA: JOHN MUIR,
GIFFORD PINCHOT AND THE FIRST GREAT
BATTLE FOR WILDERNESS (1990)

1. Before the title runs, what tone is set by the opening words and images?
2. Do you believe that there is a bias in the video's selection of expert interviews? Describe that bias.
3. What is the effect of the background music in the video?
4. What is the effect of the selection of details from the biographies of Muir and Pinchot?
5. Describe how science and technology are represented in the biographies of Muir and Pinchot. Which representation do you find more conducive to your own beliefs?
6. Describe the injustices in the notion of wilderness. What is the effect of placing this criticism in the middle of the video? Does the video's presentation of this irony undercut the positive idea of wilderness?
7. What is the video's "lesson" about the Hetch-Hetchy Dam controversy?
8. In its conclusion, what position does the video seem to take? Do you believe its overall goal is "education" or "persuasion"? Explain.
9. To what extent does the video effectively dramatize the conflict between "preservation" and "conservation" of the environment?

TOPICS FOR RESEARCH AND WRITING

1. Based on the selections from John Muir, analyze his philosophy of nature. Explain the social and spiritual meanings wildness has for him. Referring to the biographical note, explain his viewpoints in the reading in terms of the historical context of the period in which he lived.
2. Read the introduction to Chapter 7, Native American Images and Voices. Then compare and contrast Muir's relationship to nature, as revealed in the reading, to the Indian relationship to nature, as described in the later chapter. Try to account for the differences in viewpoints.
3. If you wish to interpret a visual image of nature, such as a painting or photograph, employ the following process in order to observe closely, describe concretely, and analyze carefully. First, examine the artwork,

taking notes on the colors, the texture (or brush strokes), the use of light, the composition, the technique and style, the mood. Ask yourself: What feeling does the picture give me? Why? What is the effect of certain colors or lines or textures? How has the artist achieved that effect? How are the parts of the picture organized or composed? If human or animal figures are involved, how are they arranged and what is their impact? How are certain parts of the picture "framed," surrounded or set off by other parts or lines or by the edge of the picture itself? What statement does the artist seem to be making? What is his or her point in representing the scene in this way? Do I like or dislike the picture? Why? Does my attitude toward it change as I examine it?

After taking notes about your initial impressions, organize your essay responses to the picture. Begin with a brief, concrete description of what every viewer would see in the picture, assuming your reader has never seen it. Then explain your reaction or analysis. Argue for your own interpretation of the visual impact and meaning of the picture. Support your viewpoint with descriptive details.

Referring to three or more paintings, first describe the artist's style (realistic or idealized, dynamic or serene, smooth or textured, high or low in contrast), color emphasis, and subject matter. Then, explain your interpretation of the style and the artist's involvement with the subject matter. What objects seem to be important, and in what way are they important? What qualities in the paintings seem to be emphasized? What feeling, attitude, or message about the West is suggested by the paintings? In your essay, you can refer to written comments by art historians in the books or Internet sites, but give credit to the author after each use of this commentary. Choose works from the following sources:

A. Barbara Novak, *Nature and Culture: American Landscape and Painting, 1825–1875*, rev. ed. (New York: Oxford, 1995), color plates between pages 100 and 101.

B. Miller, *Empire of the Eye* (see Chapter 4 introduction), after page 146: plates 5, 6, 7, and 8.

C. Paul Fees and Sarah Boehme, *Frontier America: Art and Treasures of the Old West from the Buffalo Bill Historical Center* (Cody, WY, and New York: The Buffalo Bill Historical Center and Abrams, 1988).

D. *Treasures from the National Museum of American Art*, 2nd ed. (Washington, DC: Smithsonian Institution, 1986).

E. Sarah E. Boehme, *Whitney Gallery of Western Art* (Cody, WY: Buffalo Bill Historical Center, 1997).

F. At the Smithsonian Institute site, *www.americanart.si.edu*, click on the "search" button at the top of the screen and then click on "search for

objects in our collection." Search for paintings by either Albert Bierstadt or Thomas Moran. Two other images by these artists are available at *www.butlerart.com/collection.htm.*

To help you interpret landscapes, you can also read and refer to Clive
Bush, "Landscape" in *The BFI Companion to the Western,* ed. Edward
Buscombe (New York: Atheneum, 1988), pages 167–70; or Chapter III
in Novak, pages 34–44. If you choose to focus on Bierstadt, you might
read and incorporate some ideas from Lee Mitchell, "Bierstadt's Settings, Harte's Plots" in *Reading the West: New Essays on the Literature of
the American West,* ed. Michael Kowalewski (New York: Cambridge University, 1996), pages 99–124.

4. Use the same strategy outlined in Topic 3 to analyze three or four Georgia O'Keeffe paintings depicting nature in Peter Hassrick, ed., *The
Georgia O'Keeffe Museum* (New York: Abrams, in association with The
Georgia O'Keeffe Museum, 1997). To focus your essay, choose one of
the following strategies:

    A. If you are interested in focusing on the paintings of bones, consider
        O'Keeffe's statement in her 1939 exhibition catalog: "The bones
        seem to cut sharply to the center of something that is keenly alive on
        the desert even tho' it is vast and empty and untouchable—and
        knows no kindness with all its beauty" (qtd. in Laurie Lisle, *Portrait
        of an Artist: A Biography of Georgia O'Keeffe,* rev. ed. [New York:
        Simon & Schuster, 1986], page 241). You might also read O'Keeffe's
        commentary "About Painting Desert Bones" in her catalog *Georgia
        O'Keeffe: Paintings—1943* (New York: An American Place, 1944)
        and/or the article "Georgia O'Keeffe Turns Dead Bones to Live Art,"
        Life, 14 February 1938, pages 28–30.

    B. To assist with your analysis and interpretation, you might read and
        incorporate some ideas from Barbara Novak, "Georgia O'Keeffe and
        American Intellectual and Visual Traditions" in the museum catalog
        cited above, pages 73–98.

    C. To assist with your analysis and interpretation, you might read and
        incorporate some ideas from Elizabeth Duvert, "With Stone, Star
        and Earth: The Presence of the Archaic in the Landscape Visions of
        Georgia O'Keeffe, Nancy Holt, and Michelle Stuart" in *The Desert Is
        No Lady: Southwestern Landscapes in Women's Writing and Art* (Tuc-
        son, AZ: University of Arizona, 1997), pages 197–221—especially
        pages 199–210 on O'Keeffe.

PART

TWO

—◆—

CHALLENGES TO A
WESTERN MYTHOLOGY

Detail from Fig. 1.1, Emmanuel Leutze, *Westward the Course of Empire Takes Its Way* (1861), mural study, U.S. Capitol. Smithsonian American Art Museum; Bequest of Sarah Carr Upton; 1931.6.1.

CHAPTER

5

————<•>————

SATIRES AND
ENTERTAINMENTS

INTRODUCTION

The final years of the nineteenth century were marked by an American nostalgia for the country's lost "greatness." Frederick Jackson Turner equated that greatness with the continued availability of land on the frontier. He announced this view at the 1893 Chicago World Columbian Exposition, which was designed to celebrate this greatness by commemorating the "discovery" of the Americas, the beginning of their conquest, and the peculiar success of this nation in exploiting their resources. But juxtaposed with exhibits of the automobile, the telephone, and the electric dynamo—the new source of power for factories and city lights—was Sitting Bull's cabin. And near the exposition, "Buffalo Bill" Cody set up his circus tent, holding 20,000 spectators, for his Wild West Show. This extravaganza enlisted, at different times, such Native American luminaries as Sitting Bull, Geronimo, and Black Elk to perform pantomimes of cavalry–Indian battles that had only lately been concluded. Actually, Cody's show-biz success is emblematic of America's transition to the twentieth century. He initially gained his famous nickname after killing 4,280 buffalo over eight months in 1867–1868, supplying meat to the Union Pacific Railroad construction crews (Lewis), which a year later joined tracks with the Central Pacific at Promontory, Utah, to complete the first transcontinental railroad.

In *Roughing It* (1872) Mark Twain suggested the fierce pace of change in the nineteenth century in his comparison between stage and rail travel.

Delighting in the swiftness of the stagecoach in 1861, he was amazed by his trip to the North Platte River crossing, "*fifty-six hours out from St. Joe—* THREE HUNDRED MILES" (45). But then he observed that about a decade later the railroad achieved the same distance in under sixteen hours, exclaiming, "I can scarcely comprehend the new state of things" (45). Of course, if we recall the pace of the Overland Trail pioneers—10 to 12 miles a day even as Twain was racing West—the improvement from 130 miles a day by stage to 460 miles a day by rail is just part of a continuum of change. Rail development also contributed to the pace of growth in Western port cities, such as Los Angeles, San Francisco, Portland, and Seattle, whose steamship companies connected to markets in South America and Asia—thus fulfilling one goal of the Lewis and Clark expedition, to find a passage to the Orient.

Other prominent changes in the West toward the turn of the century included the admission of seven new states between 1889 and 1896: Washington, Montana, North and South Dakota, Idaho, Wyoming, and Utah. And most Western farming, mining, and labor interests supported William Jennings Bryan and his populist proposals for resuming federal silver coin production and establishing an inflated currency to ease farmers' debts (Malone and Peterson). These interests had suffered in the Panic of 1893, a four-year national economic depression that resulted in widespread unemployment; the bankruptcy of 600 banks, 1,500 major businesses, and a third of the nation's railways; and violent strikes among Carnegie steelworkers, coal miners in Pennsylvania, silver miners in the West, garment workers in New York, and railroad workers at Pullman Palace Company (Flexner). Though the "Gay Nineties" may have been a period of prosperity among middle- and upper-class Americans, it was rough times for farmers and working-class laborers until the economy began to recover in 1896.

Another measure that the days of the Wild West were past was the end of the "Indian Wars" after a forty-year cavalry campaign. In 1875, after thirty years of fighting the U.S. army on the southern plains, Comanche Quanah Parker put down his arms and assimilated to white culture, leasing pasture lands to Texas stockmen, lobbying governments for his people's benefit, investing in railroads, and serving as judge and even sheriff in Oklahoma. After the defeat of Custer at Little Big Horn in 1876, the military assumed control over the northern plains reservations. Subsequently, Crazy Horse surrendered and was killed trying to escape imprisonment. After evading the cavalry for 1,300 miles, Chief Joseph surrendered when falsely promised that his Nez Perce tribe would be returned to Idaho. After over ten years of raiding Mexico and southern Arizona for horses and cattle, Geronimo was forced to surrender in 1886. When his band of Apaches was exiled to Florida, many, unaccustomed to that humid climate, died of tuberculosis and pneumonia, and he remained a captive for twenty-three years. In 1890, the cavalry attempted to suppress the Ghost Dance, a northern plains religious ritual that promised to restore the buffalo, whose numbers had been reduced from about 25 million to only 12 animals. The ritual was also supposed to eliminate white people and renew the Native American world. In an attempt to arrest Sitting Bull, Sioux policemen from the Indian Agency met resistance from his people and ended up killing him, and the cavalry eliminated further opposition by slaughtering between 150 and 300 unarmed Indians, mostly women and children, at Wounded Knee (Lewis 413–56). This was the final military "battle" between whites and Native Americans.

Another kind of peace in the West came about by eliminating the notorious outlaw gangs of rustlers and bandits. The Hole-in-the-Wall Gang, also called the Wild Bunch, was formed in 1897 by Robert LeRoy Parker, a.k.a. "Butch Cassidy"; Harry Longbaugh, a.k.a. "Sundance Kid"; and the Logan and Ketchum brothers, among others. They began their exploits by robbing a mining camp paymaster in Utah, followed by a bank heist in Nevada, but their favorite target was the express car safe on the Union Pacific Railroad in Wyoming. After a $40,000 score from the Great Northern Railroad in Montana in 1901, Butch and Sundance disappeared to South America, where they may have been killed after other robberies, or they may have returned to the United States under aliases and lived peaceable lives. Other members of the Wild Bunch continued their railroad holdups, and most were killed by posses by 1904 (Lewis 472–79). However, throughout their exploits, the outlaws appealed to public sympathy for a kind of desperate heroism of individuals against powerful organizations, such as banks and railroads. In effect, popular opinion felt a kinship toward the underdogs as "social bandits," even though the outlaws did not really steal from the rich to give to the poor.

One response to this end-of-an-era nostalgia was an attempt to capture some essence of the West by packaging its values in a marketable product. Of course, since 1860 dime-novelists had been providing hundreds of adventure fantasies that resolved conflicts in simplistic moral resolutions, and beginning in 1869 Ned Buntline turned Buffalo Bill into a fictional hero in dozens of action stories. It seemed a natural transition to move from pulp fiction to live theater in Buntline's *The Scouts of the Plains* and on to Buffalo Bill's first "Wild West, Rocky Mountain, and Prairie Exhibition" in 1883. Of course, among the working class—frustrated by industrial wage labor and diminishing economic opportunities—such displays of "rugged individualism" and its promise of self-determination held a powerful appeal. These public performances were just one of many manifestations of America's longing for what expansionist success and "progress" seemed to have destroyed. Beginning in the late nineteenth century and continuing into the twentieth were several cultural trends that reveal a nostalgic attempt to capture and package some semblance of "wildness" and an immediate experience with "nature": professional rodeo; Mexican circuses operating along the U.S. border; country-western music; "Indian Detour" tourist trips organized by Fred Harvey in the Southwest; and the commercial development of the national parks and dude ranches, which combined outdoor experiences and creature comforts (Butler).

Mature literary responses to the declining years of the wild West included spoofs and satires, works that questioned or mocked the myths that so many Americans accepted at face value. In rewriting Western mythology, these authors exploited the potential in the tradition for melodramatic extremes of danger, courage, and nobility of motive. Twain found humor in criticizing naivete in the myths of get-rich-quick opportunity and the unhindered freedom of self-reliance on the frontier. Crane, whose metaphor for human existence was war, may have had a more tragic view of the dangers of believing in romantic Western models for human behavior. Later twentieth-century authors, such as Dorothy Johnson, as well as filmmakers beginning in the fifties, have exploited the trappings of the Western genre to critique its most deeply held tenets about heroism and frontier success. But such authors and directors, even in questioning Western values, cannot avoid evoking the particular appeal of a time that is forever lost. According to Marilynne Robinson, "In the myth, every concession is made to the way of life being suppressed. Romantic lawlessness is honorably met and defeated on its own ground. Westerns are always elegiac. Their world is always bringing itself to an end" (148). To recapture the past, even if that past is false and even if the work's intent is to tell the truth, will always be a draw of the Western.

Butler, Anne. "Selling the Popular Myth." *The Oxford History of the American West.* Ed. Clyde A. Milner II, Carol A. O'Connor, and Martha A. Sandweiss. New York: Oxford University, 1994. 770–801.

Flexner, Stuart B. "The Gay 90s." *I Hear America Talking: An Illustrated Treasury of American Words and Phrases.* New York: Van Nostrand Reinhold, 1976. 162–63.

Lewis, Jon E. *The Mammoth Book of the West.* New York: Carroll & Graf, 1996.

Malone, Michael P., and F. Ross Peterson. "Politics and Protests." *The Oxford History of the American West.* Ed. Clyde A. Milner II, Carol A. O'Connor, and Martha A. Sandweiss. New York: Oxford University, 1994. 501–33.

Robinson, Marilynne. "Hearing Silence: Western Myth Reconsidered." *The True Subject: Writers on Life and Craft.* Ed. Kurt Brown. Saint Paul, MN: Graywolf Press, 1993. 135–51.

Twain, Mark. *The Writings of Mark Twain, Author's National Edition, Volume VII: Roughing It.* New York: Harper, 1899. Volume I.

Fig. 5.1 Beadle's New York Dime Library, *Kit Carson* (1878), pulp book cover. Judson Collection at the Magic Lantern Castle Museum, San Antonio, TX.

MARK TWAIN
(1835–1910)

Born in Florida, Missouri, Samuel Langhorne Clemens moved with his family to the larger burg of Hannibal on the Mississippi River. There, the writer collected the memories that he later developed into his portraits of riverboat gamblers and con men, slavetraders and slaves, adventurous boys and rough-living backwoodsmen, frontier violence and irregular justice. At age twelve, he began his journalism career at the Hannibal *Gazette*. By 1851, he was helping his brother Orion at two other local papers. In the following years, working as a typesetter and assistant editor, he began including some of his own writing—mostly humorous sketches and travel-letter parodies, experimenting with comic techniques later perfected in his short fiction (Hill 57).

In 1859, Clemens earned his license as a riverboat pilot on the Mississippi River, working the Saint Louis–New Orleans run until the Union blockade shut down river traffic at the beginning of the Civil War. In the summer of 1861, he accompanied Orion on the Overland stage to Carson City, Nevada Territory. After an unsuccessful stint at silver prospecting and mining stock speculation, Clemens resumed his newspaper work, contributing comic pieces to the *Virginia City Territorial Enterprise*. From 1862 to 1864, he worked full-time for the paper, writing both news and humorous sketches and adopting Mark Twain as his pen name (Hill 57–58). One literary hoax typical of his *Enterprise* output was the satire "A Bloody Massacre near Carson," which pretended to report a father's grisly murder of his family. Several Nevada and California papers ran the story as straight news, and their editors were outraged when they learned of the farce. In fact, Twain was careful to drop hints to reveal the joke, but his satire did effectively parody the sensationalism of newspaper writing in his time while also criticizing "crooked practices in various mining and water companies" (Gribben 63). His comic writing gained such an audience that he was able to move to San Francisco in 1864 and to work for a number of periodicals. During this period, he continued to dabble in gold prospecting in the Sierra Nevada Mountains. After the national success of his story "Jim Smiley and His Jumping Frog," published in 1865 by the New York *Saturday Press* (Rasmussen), the *Sacramento Union* commissioned Twain to travel to Hawaii and compose a series of letters describing his trip and observations. After his return, he traveled around California and Nevada performing a lecture series about Hawaii, but by 1866 his Western residence was over (Hill 58).

His comic literary style was by then well established. In fact, he adapted a "frame technique" in order to encourage reader sympathy for the country-bumpkin Western character and scorn for the urban Eastern character. In effect, as the narrative was taken over by the "common man," American readers of the mid-nineteenth century identified with his unlearned wisdom while laughing at the empty sentimentality and false refinement of the educated narrative voice. A second comic technique is Twain's use of the tall tale, a duel of wits in which the storyteller tries to draw in and fool the audience through presenting realistic details and then shifting gradually toward absurdity. A third characteristic of Twain's comic style is his celebration of "colloquial language: slang, vernacular, regionalism, and argot" whose effect, in contrast to the "rigid formality" of traditional East-Coast literature, was honesty and energy (Hill 59).

This was the style he employed in his first best-seller, *The Innocents Abroad, or The New Pilgrims' Progress* (1869), an embellished record of his five-month tourist cruise through the Mediterranean to the Holy Land in 1867. Sales from this first book enabled him to marry Olivia Landon in 1870 and settle down as newspaper editor of the Buffalo, New York, *Express*.

His principal Western work, *Roughing It* (1872), is much less a travel narrative than *The Innocents Abroad* because it considers Twain's five-year tenure out West, rather than a single voyage, and was composed from memory many years after the events recounted (Rasmussen). Like his first travelogue, this book is not strictly autobiographical, and the narrator is "deliberately made more naïve, more romantic, less world-wise than the author had been in 1861" (Hill 63). The Twain persona assumes the attitude of the tenderfoot Eastern outsider who gradually becomes more Westernized, only to lose his romantic illusions and dreams of wealth and success; and to see the West as a place of violence, injustice, rampant speculation, and disappointment. Many critics have read the book as Twain's renunciation of his footloose, drinking, gambling Western past and his accommodation to the Eastern cultural establishment that his wife's family epitomized. According to Hamlin Hill, "*Roughing It* is, in fact, the announcement of the end of the antebellum myth of the Garden of Eden regained on the American Frontier. . . . The illusion of freedom, independence, democracy, and self-reliance is splintered over and over by harsh reality" (63).

Nonetheless, from another viewpoint, we can see that Twain did achieve the American Dream to a great extent. He eventually earned fame and sufficient wealth from his writing to finance an elaborate nineteen-room mansion in the chic Hartford, Connecticut, suburb of Nook

Farm (Gribben 58). Firmly established as a book author by 1874, Twain went on to write his masterpiece, *Huckleberry Finn* (1884); light satires, such as *A Connecticut Yankee in King Arthur's Court* (1889); and the brooding, cynical meditations of his later years, such as *The Mysterious Stranger* (1916). But the American conflict between civilization and individual fulfillment—an insight that he realized in his Western work—informed much of his creative expression for decades. The ideals of the West—a slapdash sense of freedom, a rough-and-ready pragmatism, a youthful earnestness—permeate his finest works, despite his realization that his own attempt to "light out for the Territory" was futile.

The text for the following selections from *Roughing It* is *The Writings of Mark Twain, Author's National Edition, Volume VII* (New York: Harper, 1899), published in two volumes. The excerpts are from Volume I, pages 35–39, 80–86, and 89–91. The first passage (Chapter IV) describes Overland stagecoach travel and the social hierarchy of its employees. The second passage (Chapters IX and X) describes a notorious outlaw, Jack Slade.

Gribben, Alan. "Samuel Langhorne Clemens (Mark Twain)." *Dictionary of Literary Biography, Volume 74: American Short-Story Writers Before 1880.* Ed. Bobby Ellen Kimbel and William E. Grant. Detroit: Gale, 1988. 54–83.

Hill, Hamlin. "Samuel Langhorne Clemens (Mark Twain)." *Dictionary of Literary Biography, Volume 186: Nineteenth-Century American Western Writers.* Ed. Robert L. Gale. Detroit: Gale, 1997. 55–70.

Rasmussen, R. Kent. *Mark Twain A-Z: The Essential Reference to His Life and Writings.* New York: Oxford University Press, 1995.

FROM *ROUGHING IT*

CHAPTER IV

As the sun went down and the evening chill came on, we made preparation for bed. We stirred up the hard leather letter-sacks, and the knotty canvas bags of printed matter (knotty and uneven because of projecting ends and corners of magazines, boxes and books). We stirred them up and redisposed them in such a way as to make our bed as level as possible. And we *did* improve it, too, though after all our work it had an upheaved and

billowy look about it, like a little piece of a stormy sea. Next we hunted up
our boots from odd nooks among the mailbags where they had settled, and
put them on. Then we got down our coats, vests, pantaloons and heavy
woolen shirts, from the arm-loops where they had been swinging all day, and
clothed ourselves in them—for, there being no ladies either at the stations or
in the coach, and the weather being hot, we had looked to our comfort by
stripping to our underclothing, at nine o'clock in the morning. All things
being now ready, we stowed the uneasy Dictionary where it would lie as quiet
as possible, and placed the water-canteen and pistols where we could find
them in the dark. Then we smoked a final pipe, and swapped a final yarn;
after which, we put the pipes, tobacco, and bag of coin in snug holes and
caves among the mailbags, and then fastened down the coach curtains all
around and made the place as "dark as the inside of a cow," as the conductor
phrased it in his picturesque way. It was certainly as dark as any place could
be—nothing was even dimly visible in it. And finally, we rolled ourselves up
like silk-worms, each person in his own blanket, and sank peacefully to sleep.

Whenever the stage stopped to change horses, we would wake up, and
try to recollect where we were—and succeed—and in a minute or two the
stage would be off again, and we likewise. We began to get into country, now,
threaded here and there with little streams. These had high, steep banks on
each side, and every time we flew down one bank and scrambled up the
other, our party inside got mixed somewhat. First we would all be down in
a pile at the forward end of the stage, nearly in a sitting posture, and in a second we would shoot to the other end, and stand on our heads. And we
would sprawl and kick, too, and ward off ends and corners of mailbags that
came lumbering over us and about us; and as the dust rose from the tumult,
we would all sneeze in chorus, and the majority of us would grumble, and
probably say some hasty thing, like: "Take your elbow out of my ribs!—can't
you quit crowding?"

Every time we avalanched from one end of the stage to the other, the
Unabridged Dictionary would come too; and every time it came it damaged
somebody. One trip it "barked" the Secretary's elbow; the next trip it hurt
me in the stomach, and the third it tilted Bemis's nose up till he could look
down his nostrils—he said. The pistols and coin soon settled to the bottom,
but the pipes, pipestems, tobacco, and canteens clattered and floundered
after the Dictionary every time it made an assault on us, and aided and abet-
ted the book by spilling tobacco in our eyes, and water down our backs.

Still, all things considered, it was a very comfortable night. It wore gradually away, and when at last a cold gray light was visible through the puck-
ers and chinks in the curtains, we yawned and stretched with satisfaction,
shed our cocoons, and felt that we had slept as much as was necessary. By

and by, as the sun rose up and warmed the world, we pulled off our clothes and got ready for breakfast. We were just pleasantly in time, for five minutes afterward the driver sent the weird music of his bugle winding over the grassy solitudes, and presently we detected a low hut or two in the distance. Then the rattling of the coach, the clatter of our six horses' hoofs, and the driver's crisp commands, awoke to a louder and stronger emphasis, and we went sweeping down on the station at our smartest speed. It was fascinating—that old Overland stage-coaching.

We jumped out in undress uniform. The driver tossed his gathered reins out on the ground, gaped and stretched complacently, drew off his heavy buckskin gloves with great deliberation and insufferable dignity—taking not the slightest notice of a dozen solicitous inquiries after his health, and humbly facetious and flattering accostings, and obsequious tenders of service, from five or six hairy and half-civilized station-keepers and hostlers who were nimbly unhitching our steeds and bringing the fresh team out of the stables—for, in the eyes of the stage-driver of that day, station-keepers and hostlers were a sort of good enough low creatures, useful in their place, and helping to make up a world, but not the kind of beings which a person of distinction could afford to concern himself with; while, on the contrary, in the eyes of the station-keeper and the hostler, the stage-driver was a hero—a great and shining dignitary, the world's favorite son, the envy of the people, the observed of the nations. When they spoke to him they received his insolent silence meekly, and as being the natural and proper conduct of so great a man; when he opened his lips they all hung on his words with admiration (he never honored a particular individual with a remark, but addressed it with a broad generality to the horses, the stables, the surrounding country *and* the human underlings); when he discharged a facetious insulting personality at a hostler, that hostler was happy for the day; when he uttered his one jest—old as the hills, coarse, profane, witless, and inflicted on the same audience, in the same language, every time his coach drove up there—the varlets roared, and slapped their thighs, and swore it was the best thing they'd ever heard in all their lives. And how they would fly around when he wanted a basin of water, a gourd of the same, or a light for his pipe!—but they would instantly insult a passenger if he so far forgot himself as to crave a favor at their hands. They could do that sort of insolence as well as the driver they copied it from—for, let it be borne in mind, the Overland driver had but little less contempt for his passengers than he had for his hostlers.

The hostlers and station-keepers treated the really powerful *conductor* of the coach merely with the best of what was their idea of civility, but the *driver* was the only being they bowed down to and worshiped. How admiringly they would gaze up at him in his high seat as he gloved himself with lingering deliberation, while some happy hostler held the bunch of reins aloft, and waited patiently for him to take it! And how they would bombard him with glorifying ejaculations as he cracked his long whip and went careering away.

* * *

CHAPTER IX

. . . . There was much magic in that name, SLADE! Day or night, now, I stood always ready to drop any subject in hand, to listen to something new about Slade and his ghastly exploits. Even before we got to Overland City, we had begun to hear about Slade and his "division" (for he was a "division-agent") on the Overland; and from the hour we had left Overland City we had heard drivers and conductors talk about only three things—"Californy," the Nevada silver mines, and this desperado Slade. And a deal the most of the talk was about Slade. We had gradually come to have a realizing sense of the fact that Slade was a man whose heart and hands and soul were steeped in the blood of offenders against his dignity; a man who awfully avenged all injuries, affronts, insults or slights, of whatever kind—on the spot if he could, years afterward if lack of earlier opportunity compelled it; a man whose hate tortured him day and night till vengeance appeased it—and not an ordinary vengeance either, but his enemy's absolute death—nothing less; a man whose face would light up with a terrible joy when he surprised a foe and had him at a disadvantage. A high and efficient servant of the Overland, an outlaw among outlaws and yet their relentless scourge, Slade was at once the most bloody, the most dangerous, and the most valuable citizen that inhabited the savage fastnesses of the mountains.

CHAPTER X

Really and truly, two-thirds of the talk of drivers and conductors had been about this man Slade, ever since the day before we reached Julesburg. In order that the Eastern reader may have a clear conception of what a Rocky Mountain desperado is, in his highest state of development, I will reduce all this mass of overland gossip to one straightforward narrative, and present it in the following shape:

Slade was born in Illinois, of good parentage. At about twenty-six years of age he killed a man in a quarrel and fled the country. At St. Joseph, Missouri, he joined one of the early California-bound emigrant trains, and was given the post of trainmaster. One day on the plains he had an angry dispute with one of his wagon-drivers, and both drew their revolvers. But the driver was the quicker artist, and had his weapon cocked first. So Slade said it was a pity to waste life on so small a matter, and proposed that the pistols be thrown on the ground and the quarrel settled by a fist-fight. The unsuspecting driver agreed, and threw down his pistol—whereupon Slade laughed at his simplicity, and shot him dead!

He made his escape, and lived a wild life for awhile, dividing his time between fighting Indians and avoiding an Illinois sheriff, who had been sent to arrest him for his first murder. It is said that in one Indian battle he killed three savages with his own hand, and afterward cut their ears off and sent them, with his compliments, to the chief of the tribe.

Slade soon gained a name for fearless resolution, and this was sufficient merit to procure for him the important post of overland division-agent at Julesburg, in place of Mr. Jules, removed. For some time previously, the company's horses had been frequently stolen, and the coaches delayed, by gangs of outlaws, who were wont to laugh at the idea of any man's having the temerity to resent such outrages. Slade resented them promptly. The outlaws soon found that the new agent was a man who did not fear anything that breathed the breath of life. He made short work of all offenders. The result was that delays ceased, the company's property was let alone, and, no matter what happened or who suffered, Slade's coaches went through, every time! True, in order to bring about this wholesome change, Slade had to kill several men—some say three, others say four, and others six—but the world was the richer for their loss. The first prominent difficulty he had was with the ex-agent Jules, who bore the reputation of being a reckless and desperate man himself. Jules hated Slade for supplanting him, and a good fair occasion for a fight was all he was waiting for. By and by Slade dared to employ a man whom Jules had once discharged. Next, Slade seized a team of stage-horses which he accused Jules of having driven off and hidden somewhere for his own use. War was declared, and for a day or two the two men walked warily about the streets, seeking each other, Jules armed with a double-barreled shotgun, and Slade with his history-creating revolver. Finally, as Slade stepped into a store, Jules poured the contents of his gun into him from behind the door. Slade was pluck, and Jules got several bad pistol wounds in return. Then both men fell, and were carried to their respective lodgings, both swearing that better aim should do deadlier work next time. Both were bed-ridden a long time, but Jules got on his feet first, and gathering his possessions together, packed them on a couple of mules, and fled to the Rocky Mountains to gather strength in safety against the day of reckoning. For many months he was not seen or heard of, and was gradually dropped out of the remembrance of all save Slade himself. But Slade was not the man to forget him. On the contrary, common report said that Slade kept a reward standing for his capture, dead or alive!

After awhile, seeing that Slade's energetic administration had restored peace and order to one of the worst divisions of the road, the Overland Stage Company transferred him to the Rocky Ridge division in the Rocky Mountains, to see if he could perform a like miracle there. It was the very paradise of outlaws and desperadoes. There was absolutely no semblance of law there. Violence was the rule. Force was the only recognized authority. The commonest misunderstandings were settled on the spot with the revolver or the knife. Murders were done in open day, and with sparkling frequency, and nobody thought of inquiring into them. It was considered that the parties who did the killing had their private reasons for it; for other people to meddle would have been looked upon as indelicate. After a murder, all that Rocky Mountain etiquette required of a spectator was, that he should help the gentlemen bury his game—otherwise his churlishness would surely be remembered against him the first time he killed a man himself and needed a neighborly turn in interring him.

Slade took up his residence sweetly and peacefully in the midst of this hive of horse-thieves and assassins, and the very first time one of them aired his insolent swaggerings in his presence he shot him dead! He began a raid on the outlaws, and in a singularly short space of time he had completely stopped their depredations on the stage stock, recovered a large number of stolen horses, killed several of the worst desperadoes of the district, and gained such a dread ascendancy over the rest that they respected him, admired him, feared him, obeyed him! He wrought the same marvelous change in the ways of the community that had marked his administration at Overland City. He captured two men who had stolen Overland stock, and with his own hands he hanged them. He was supreme judge in his district, and he was jury and executioner likewise—and not only in the case of offenses against his employers, but against passing emigrants as well. On one occasion some emigrants had their stock lost or stolen, and told Slade, who chanced to visit their camp. With a single companion he rode to a ranch, the owners of which he suspected, and, opening the door, commenced firing, killing three, and wounding the fourth.

* * *

In due time we rattled up to a stage-station, and sat down to breakfast with a half-savage, half-civilized company of armed and bearded mountaineers, ranchmen and station employés. The most gentle-manly-appearing, quiet, and affable officer we had yet found along the road in the Overland Company's service was the person who sat at the head of the table, at my elbow. Never youth stared and shivered as I did when I heard them call him SLADE!

Here was romance, and I sitting face to face with it!—looking upon it— touching it—hobnobbing with it, as it were! Here, right by my side, was the actual ogre who, in fights and brawls and various ways, *had taken the lives of twenty-six human beings,* or all men lied about him! I suppose I was the proudest stripling that ever traveled to see strange lands and wonderful people.

He was so friendly and so gentle-spoken that I warmed to him in spite of his awful history. It was hardly possible to realize that this pleasant person was the pitiless scourge of the outlaws, the raw-head-and-bloody-bones the nursing mothers of the mountains terrified their children with. And to this day I can remember nothing remarkable about Slade except that his face was rather broad across the cheekbones, and that the cheekbones were low and the lips peculiarly thin and straight. But that was enough to leave something of an effect upon me, for since then I seldom see a face possessing those characteristics without fancying that the owner of it is a dangerous man.

The coffee ran out. At least it was reduced to one tin-cupful, and Slade was about to take it when he saw that my cup was empty. He politely offered to fill it, but although I wanted it, I politely declined. I was afraid he had not killed anybody that morning, and might be needing diversion. But still with firm politeness he insisted on filling my cup, and said I had traveled all night and better deserved it than he—and while he talked he placidly poured the fluid, to the last drop. I thanked him and drank it, but it gave me no comfort, for I could not feel sure that he would not be sorry, presently, that he had given it away, and proceed to kill me to distract his thoughts from the loss. But nothing of the kind occurred. We left him with only twenty-six dead people to account for, and I felt a tranquil satisfaction in the thought that in so judiciously taking care of No. 1 at that breakfast-table I had pleasantly escaped being No. 27. Slade came out to the coach and saw us off, first ordering certain rearrangements of the mailbags for our comfort, and then we took leave of him, satisfied that we should hear of him again, some day, and wondering in what connection.

Discussion Questions

1. Explain what you find funny about the description of stagecoach travel in Chapter IV. Likewise, explain what you find funny in Twain's description of the stage-driver.

2. Describe how Twain's commentary on the stagecoach superintendent Slade, in Chapters IX and X, serves to reinforce reader expectations about the myths of the "bad man" or outlaw. Describe each of the myths that Twain evokes. To what extent does this passage undercut or question those myths?

Fig. 5.2 *Great Wild West Exhibition* (1883), poster. Hertzberg Circus Collection and Museum, San Antonio Public Library, San Antonio, TX.

STEPHEN CRANE
(1871–1900)

Born last among nine children to Reverend Jonathan Townley Crane and Mary Helen Peck Crane, the author was a preacher's kid and spent some energy living down that label. Due to his assignments as a Methodist minister, the Reverend moved the family repeatedly, so young Stephen was always the new student among his schoolhouse peers and grew up a frail and lonely child. In 1883, the family moved to Asbury Park, a seaside resort where he observed "plural standards of morality" in the ostentatious displays of the wealthy, the shabby boardwalk hustlers, the sensuality of leisured vacationers, and the vices of liquor and gambling. Becoming something of a rebel to his parents' morality, he fashioned a tough exterior and expressed his freedom by smoking and swearing like a sailor. Beginning in 1885, he spent time at a series of prep schools and colleges, but he failed to reform, studied little, and succeeded only at baseball. In the summers, beginning when he was sixteen, he began writing for his brother Townley's *New York Tribune* office in Asbury Park. In the fall of 1891, he moved to New York and began to associate with Bowery bums and bohemians (Cady 27–38).

This informal education proved more valuable than the classroom. Crane continued to write for the *Tribune* as a stringer until one of his articles offended labor interests, capitalists, and the Republican publisher, who fired him. But he did occasionally publish entertaining sketches about Asbury Park and kept busy writing creative portraits of New York street life. Finally, he did not succeed as a journalist because the simple facts interested him less than the reasons and feelings associated with events. Payments for stories were irregular. He depended on friends for meals, a temporary place to sleep, or a quiet corner to write. He was desperately poor. Between 1892 and 1894 he spent the winters ill-clothed, cold, and undernourished—deprived of the most basic comforts. Still, he managed to complete his first novel, *Maggie: A Girl of the Streets*. In this work, he developed a realist viewpoint which worked to discredit romanticism's encouragement of extravagant expectations about life. Thus, he represented the New York tenements of Rum Alley in all their pathetic horror—the hopeless poverty; the alcoholic mother's murder of her husband; brother Jimmy's street-hoodlum vice; Maggie's whoredom, degeneration, and death. Crane also emphasized the environmental origins of these evils and condemned the "hypocritical sentimentality" of American culture that ignored them. Because of the realism and the authentic use of profanity (mostly "hell," "damn," and "Gawd"), his first novel did not sell. But he used the work to renew his acquaintance with Hamlin Garland (1860–1940) and to gain introductions to influential men of letters, such as William Dean Howells (1837–1920), who could write favorable reviews to promote his work (Cady 40–43, 107–12). The privations Crane stoically suffered as he developed his craft ruined his health. Nonetheless, he seemed undaunted and began writing his master work, *The Red Badge of Courage* (1895), which was to bring him international fame.

After the Bacheller newspaper syndicate had accepted this novel in abridged form for serial publication in 1893, Crane proposed that the syndicate fund a journey to the West and Mexico so that he could write a series of newspaper articles about conditions of life in those relatively remote and colorful locations. This trip proved fruitful to his artistic development, for when he left he was essentially an Easterner, whose cultural hub was New York City. And although he had experienced the gritty reality of life in the Bowery slums, he was still only twenty-three years old and somewhat inexperienced in the world. However, on the journey, "the unfamiliar forced him to confront himself and his understandings" (Katz x). While the trip did result in a string of journalistic pieces, more importantly, his three months out West stimulated his fiction writing over the next five years (Wolford 27). In fact, Crane was much impressed by his Western travels. In an 1895 letter, Crane wrote: "We in the east are overcome a great deal by a detestable superficial culture. . . . Damn the east! I fell in love with the straight out-and-out, sometimes hideous, often braggart westerners because I thought them to be the truer men" (qtd. in Wolford 95)

On his journey west and south, he visited Nebraska and reported on the horrific drought of 1894. In his article titled "Nebraska's Bitter Fight for Life," Crane reveals his sympathy and admiration for the struggling but courageous landholders, and his naturalistic imagery anticipates his later masterpiece, "The Open Boat" (1897):

> The farmers helpless, with no weapon against this terrible and inscrutable wrath of nature, were spectators at the strangling of their hopes, their ambitions, all that they could look to from their labor. It was as if upon the massive altar of the earth, their homes and their families were being offered in sacrifice to the wrath of some blind and pitiless deity. ("Nebraska's Bitter Fight" in Katz 4)

An experience in Lincoln, Nebraska, also suggests his understanding of the Western character, as contrasted with Easterners like himself. It seems that he broke up a barroom fight between two men who fought each other nightly and thus, according to Crane, "offended a local custom. . . . I was a darned nuisance with my Eastern scruples and all that. So first everybody cursed me fully and then they took me off to a judge who told me I was an imbecile and let me go; it was very saddening" (qtd. in Katz xiv). This awareness of a contrast between Western social behaviors and "Eastern scruples" certainly features in his later story "The Blue Hotel" (1898).

Though most of his newspaper pieces are mundane, "Nebraska's Bitter Fight" is exceptional, as are two short travel sketches about Mexico. "The Viga Canal" suggests Crane's mature theme of Nature's indifference toward human activity—a theme fully realized in "The Open Boat." Likewise, the travel sketch "Above All Things" seems to rehearse Crane's ironic perspective in "The Blue Hotel." Reflecting on the near impossibility of one culture understanding another, Crane judges the typically superior attitude of the tourist:

> The visitor feels scorn. He swells with a knowledge of his geographical experience. "How futile are the lives of these people," he remarks, "and what incredible ignorance that they should not be aware of their futility." This is the arrogance of the man who has not yet solved himself and discovered his own actual futility. ("Above All Things" citation of "Nebraska's Bitter Fight" in Katz 74)

Observing the apparently "meek and submissive" attitude of the Mexican Indians, Crane concludes "Above All Things" by refusing to judge or pity the impoverished natives, realizing—as Katz points out—that "morality is not at all based on traditions of behavior. . . . Morality is a complex notion based on economy, freedom, and self-denial. The way in which Crane establishes these principles demonstrates an irony that is at once self-reflexive and anti-bourgeois" (xxiii). These early reflections on the problem of morality inform Crane's later notion of interpersonal complicity in his critique of social responsibility in "The Blue Hotel."

After he returned to New York from Mexico, in 1896 he met Cora Stewart, a Jacksonville brothel madam who became his mistress and eventually his common-law wife. Soon after, he left again to report on the Cuban rebellion against Spain. When the gun-running ship *Commodore* sank accidentally, he and three other men spent 27 hours in a ten-foot dinghy before washing ashore near Jacksonville, Florida (Johnson 119–21). This life-threatening experience became the basis for a newspaper article, as well as his fictional treatment in "The Open Boat." The rest of his brief life followed a pattern of restlessness, as Crane traveled as war correspondent to Greece and Cuba, where he suffered from tuberculosis and malaria. In 1899 he settled in a stylish

Sussex manor in England, but the next year he went to take a rest cure in Germany, where he died of pulmonary hemorrhage. His final four years were the most productive of his life. Writing desperately to pay off debts, Crane published two fine but uneven short-story collections, *The Open Boat and Other Stories* (1898) and *The Monster and Other Stories* (1899). These contain all his Western stories and represent many of his experiments as "realist, naturalist, symbolist, impressionist, and expressionist" (Johnson 121).

Crane's own restlessness was expressed as a theme in many of his stories, whose discontented characters often seek either adventures or explanations for experience—such as the romanticized justifications of popular fiction—that are unavailable in their familiar environments. Crane's realism, then, consists of denying the assurances of Christianity, which sustained his parents, and admitting the losses, frustrations, and disappointments that experience can bring. What is particularly modern about Crane's irony is his skilled manipulation of point of view. Typically, he asks the reader to shift perspective three times: from enjoying the satire of a hysterical, exaggerated, misguided character; to sympathizing with this naivete that brings the character into real danger; to finally realizing an alternative perspective that reveals the confused character's viewpoint as either comic or tragic and the supposedly reasonable viewpoint as defective for its lack of human sympathy or understanding. This pattern is repeated in such stories as "Horses—One Dash," "The Bride Comes to Yellow Sky," and "The Blue Hotel." In these tales, Crane shifts viewpoints in order to parody the "shoot-'em-up Westerns" of the dime novel tradition and to create realistic narratives about authentic characters' confrontations with actual or potential violence (Johnson 123–31).

"The Blue Hotel" was first published in two installments in the November 26 and December 3, 1898, issues of *Collier's Weekly*. The text is from *The Monster and Other Stories* (New York: Harper & Row, 1899), pages 109–61.

Cady, Edwin H. *Stephen Crane*. Rev. ed. Boston: Twayne, 1980.

Johnson, Glen M. "Stephen Crane." *American Short-Story Writers, 1880–1910*. Ed. Bobby Ellen Kimball and William E. Grant. Detroit: Gale, 1989. 117–35.

Katz, Joseph, ed. *Stephen Crane in the West and Mexico*. Kent, OH: Kent State University, 1970.

Wolford, Chester L. *Stephen Crane: A Study of the Short Fiction*. Boston: Twayne, 1989.

THE BLUE HOTEL

—————◦<◆>◦—————

I

The Palace Hotel at Fort Romper was painted a light blue, a shade that is on the legs of a kind of heron, causing the bird to declare its position against any background. The Palace Hotel, then, was always screaming and howling in a way that made the dazzling winter landscape of Nebraska seem only a grey swampish hush. It stood alone on the prairie, and when the snow was falling the town two hundred yards away was not visible. But when the traveller alighted at the railway station he was obliged to pass the Palace Hotel before he could come upon the company of low clapboard houses which composed Fort Romper, and it was not to be thought that any traveller could pass the Palace Hotel without looking at it. Pat Scully, the proprietor, had proved himself a master of strategy when he chose his paints. It is true that on clear days, when the great transcontinental expresses, long lines of swaying Pullmans, swept through Fort Romper, passengers were overcome at the sight, and the cult that knows the brown-reds and the subdivisions of the dark greens of the East expressed shame, pity, horror, in a laugh. But to the citizens of this prairie town and to the people who would naturally stop there, Pat Scully had performed a feat. With this opulence and splendour, these creeds, classes, egotisms, that streamed through Romper on the rails day after day, they had no colour in common.

As if the displayed delights of such a blue hotel were not sufficiently enticing, it was Scully's habit to go every morning and evening to meet the leisurely trains that stopped at Romper and work his seductions upon any man that he might see wavering, gripsack in hand.

One morning, when a snow-crusted engine dragged its long string of freight cars and its one passenger coach to the station, Scully performed the marvel of catching three men. One was a shaky and quick-eyed Swede, with a great shining cheap valise; one was a tall bronzed cowboy, who was on his way to a ranch near the Dakota line; one was a little silent man from the East, who didn't look it, and didn't announce it. Scully practically made them prisoners. He was so nimble and merry and kindly that each probably felt it would be the height of brutality to try to escape. They trudged off over the creaking board sidewalks in the wake of the eager little Irishman. He wore a heavy fur cap squeezed tightly down on his head. It caused his two red ears to stick out stiffly, as if they were made of tin.

At last, Scully, elaborately, with boisterous hospitality, conducted them through the portals of the blue hotel. The room which they entered was small. It seemed to be merely a proper temple for an enormous stove, which, in the centre, was humming with godlike violence. At various points on its surface the iron had become luminous and glowed yellow from the heat. Beside the stove Scully's son Johnnie was playing High-Five with an old farmer who had whiskers both grey and sandy. They were quarrelling. Frequently the old farmer turned his face toward a box of sawdust—coloured brown from tobacco juice—that was behind the stove, and spat with an air of great impatience and irritation. With a loud flourish of words Scully destroyed the game of cards, and bustled his son upstairs with part of the baggage of the new guests. He himself conducted them to three basins of the coldest water in the world. The cowboy and the Easterner burnished themselves fiery red with this water, until it seemed to be some kind of metal-polish. The Swede, however, merely dipped his fingers gingerly and with trepidation. It was notable that throughout this series of small ceremonies the three travellers were made to feel that Scully was very benevolent. He was conferring great favours upon them. He handed the towel from one to another with an air of philanthropic impulse.

Afterward they went to the first room, and, sitting about the stove, listened to Scully's officious clamour at his daughters, who were preparing the midday meal. They reflected in the silence of experienced men who tread carefully amid new people. Nevertheless, the old farmer, stationary, invincible in his chair near the warmest part of the stove, turned his face from the sawdust-box frequently and addressed a glowing commonplace to the strangers. Usually he was answered in short but adequate sentences by either the cowboy or the Easterner. The Swede said nothing. He seemed to be occupied in making furtive estimates of each man in the room. One might have thought that he had the sense of silly suspicion which comes to guilt. He resembled a badly frightened man.

Later, at dinner, he spoke a little, addressing his conversation entirely to Scully. He volunteered that he had come from New York, where for ten years he had worked as a tailor. These facts seemed to strike Scully as fascinating, and afterward he volunteered that he had lived at Romper for fourteen years. The Swede asked about the crops and the price of labour. He seemed barely to listen to Scully's extended replies. His eyes continued to rove from man to man.

Finally, with a laugh and a wink, he said that some of these Western communities were very dangerous; and after his statement he straightened his legs under the table, tilted his head, and laughed again, loudly. It was plain that the demonstration had no meaning to the others. They looked at him wondering and in silence.

II

As the men trooped heavily back into the front room, the two little windows presented views of a turmoiling sea of snow. The huge arms of the wind were making attempts—mighty, circular, futile—to embrace the flakes as they sped. A gatepost like a still man with a blanched face stood aghast amid this profligate fury. In a hearty voice Scully announced the presence of a blizzard. The guests of the blue hotel, lighting their pipes, assented with grunts of lazy masculine contentment. No island of the sea could be exempt in the degree of this little room with its humming stove. Johnnie, son of Scully, in a tone which defined his opinion of his ability as a card-player, challenged the old farmer of both grey and sandy whiskers to a game of High-Five. The farmer agreed with a contemptuous and bitter scoff. They sat close to the stove, and squared their knees under a wide board. The cowboy and the Easterner watched the game with interest. The Swede remained near the window, aloof, but with a countenance that showed signs of an inexplicable excitement.

The play of Johnnie and the grey-beard was suddenly ended by another quarrel. The old man arose while casting a look of heated scorn at his adversary. He slowly buttoned his coat, and then stalked with fabulous dignity from the room. In the discreet silence of all the other men the Swede laughed. His laughter rang somehow childish. Men by this time had begun to look at him askance, as if they wished to inquire what ailed him.

A new game was formed jocosely. The cowboy volunteered to become the partner of Johnnie, and they all then turned to ask the Swede to throw in his lot with the little Easterner. He asked some questions about the game, and, learning that it wore many names, and that he had played it when it was under an alias, he accepted the invitation. He strode toward the men nervously, as if he expected to be assaulted. Finally, seated, he gazed from face to face and laughed shrilly. This laugh was so strange that the Easterner looked up quickly, the cowboy sat intent and with his mouth open, and Johnnie paused, holding the cards with still fingers.

Afterward there was a short silence. Then Johnnie said, "Well, let's get at it. Come on now!" They pulled their chairs forward until their knees were bunched under the board. They began to play, and their interest in the game caused the others to forget the manner of the Swede.

The cowboy was a board-whacker. Each time that he held superior cards he whanged them, one by one, with exceeding force, down upon the improvised table, and took the tricks with a glowing air of prowess and pride that sent thrills of indignation into the hearts of his opponents. A game with a board-whacker in it is sure to become intense. The countenances of the Easterner and the Swede were miserable whenever the cowboy thundered down his aces and kings, while Johnnie, his eyes gleaming with joy, chuckled and chuckled.

Because of the absorbing play none considered the strange ways of the Swede. They paid strict heed to the game. Finally, during a lull caused by a new deal, the Swede suddenly addressed Johnnie: "I suppose there have been a good many men killed in this room." The jaws of the others dropped and they looked at him.

"What in hell are you talking about?" said Johnnie.

The Swede laughed again his blatant laugh, full of a kind of false courage and defiance. "Oh, you know what I mean all right," he answered.

"I'm a liar if I do!" Johnnie protested. The card was halted, and the men stared at the Swede. Johnnie evidently felt that as the son of the proprietor he should make a direct inquiry. "Now, what might you be drivin' at, mister?" he asked. The Swede winked at him. It was a wink full of cunning. His fingers shook on the edge of the board. "Oh, maybe you think I have been to nowheres. Maybe you think I'm a tenderfoot?"

"I don't know nothin' about you," answered Johnnie, "and I don't give a damn where you've been. All I got to say is that I don't know what you're driving at. There hain't never been nobody killed in this room."

The cowboy, who had been steadily gazing at the Swede, then spoke: "What's wrong with you, mister?"

Apparently it seemed to the Swede that he was formidably menaced. He shivered and turned white near the corners of his mouth. He sent an appealing glance in the direction of the little Easterner. During these moments he did not forget to wear his air of advanced pot-valour. "They say they don't know what I mean," he remarked mockingly to the Easterner.

The latter answered after prolonged and cautious reflection. "I don't understand you," he said, impassively.

The Swede made a movement then which announced that he thought he had encountered treachery from the only quarter where he had expected sympathy, if not help. "Oh, I see you are all against me. I see—"

The cowboy was in a state of deep stupefaction. "Say," he cried, as he tumbled the deck violently down upon the board, "say, what are you gittin' at, hey?"

The Swede sprang up with the celerity of a man escaping from a snake on the floor. "I don't want to fight!" he shouted. "I don't want to fight!"

The cowboy stretched his long legs indolently and deliberately. His hands were in his pockets. He spat into the sawdust-box. "Well, who the hell thought you did?" he inquired.

The Swede backed rapidly toward a corner of the room. His hands were out protectingly in front of his chest, but he was making an obvious struggle to control his fright. "Gentlemen," he quavered, "I suppose I am going to be killed before I can leave this house! I suppose I am going to be killed before I can leave this house!" In his eyes was the dying-swan look. Through the windows could be seen the snow turning blue in the shadow of dusk. The wind tore at the house, and some loose thing beat regularly against the clapboards like a spirit tapping.

A door opened, and Scully himself entered. He paused in surprise as he noted the tragic attitude of the Swede. Then he said, "What's the matter here?"

The Swede answered him swiftly and eagerly: "These men are going to kill me."

"Kill you!" ejaculated Scully. "Kill you! What are you talkin'?"

The Swede made the gesture of a martyr.

Scully wheeled sternly upon his son. "What is this, Johnnie?"

The lad had grown sullen. "Damned if I know," he answered. "I can't make no sense to it." He began to shuffle the cards, fluttering them together with an angry snap. "He says a good many men have been killed in this room, or something like that. And he says he's going to be killed here too. I don't know what ails him. He's crazy, I shouldn't wonder."

Scully then looked for explanation to the cowboy, but the cowboy simply shrugged his shoulders.

"Kill you?" said Scully again to the Swede. "Kill you? Man, you're off your nut."

"Oh, I know," burst out the Swede. "I know what will happen. Yes, I'm crazy—yes. Yes, of course, I'm crazy—yes. But I know one thing—" There was a sort of sweat of misery and terror upon his face. "I know I won't get out of here alive."

The cowboy drew a deep breath, as if his mind was passing into the last stages of dissolution. "Well, I'm doggoned," he whispered to himself.

Scully wheeled suddenly and faced his son. "You've been troublin' this man!"

Johnnie's voice was loud with its burden of grievance. "Why, good Gawd, I ain't done nothin' to 'im."

The Swede broke in. "Gentlemen, do not disturb yourselves. I will leave this house. I will go away, because"—he accused them dramatically with his glance—"because I do not want to be killed."

Scully was furious with his son. "Will you tell me what is the matter, you young divil? What's the matter, anyhow? Speak out!"

"Blame it!" cried Johnnie in despair, "don't I tell you I don't know? He—he says we want to kill him, and that's all I know. I can't tell what ails him."

The Swede continued to repeat: "Never mind, Mr. Scully; never mind. I will leave this house. I will go away, because I do not wish to be killed. Yes, of course, I am crazy—yes. But I know one thing! I will go away. I will leave this house. Never mind, Mr. Scully; never mind. I will go away."

"You will not go 'way," said Scully. "You will not go 'way until I hear the reason of this business. If anybody has troubled you I will take care of him. This is my house. You are under my roof, and I will not allow any peaceable man to be troubled here." He cast a terrible eye upon Johnnie, the cowboy, and the Easterner.

"Never mind, Mr. Scully; never mind. I will go away. I do not wish to be killed." The Swede moved toward the door which opened upon the stairs. It was evidently his intention to go at once for his baggage.

"No, no," shouted Scully peremptorily; but the white-faced man slid by him and disappeared. "Now," said Scully severely, "what does this mane?"

Johnnie and the cowboy cried together: "Why, we didn't do nothin' to 'im!"

Scully's eyes were cold. "No," he said, "you didn't?"

Johnnie swore a deep oath. "Why, this is the wildest loon I ever see. We didn't do nothin' at all. We were jest sittin' here playin' cards, and he—"

The father suddenly spoke to the Easterner. "Mr. Blanc," he asked, "what has these boys been doin'?"

The Easterner reflected again. "I didn't see anything wrong at all," he said at last, slowly.

Scully began to howl. "But what does it mane?" He stared ferociously at his son. "I have a mind to lather you for this, me boy."

Johnnie was frantic. "Well, what have I done?" he bawled at his father.

III

"I think you are tongue-tied," said Scully finally to his son, the cowboy, and the Easterner; and at the end of this scornful sentence he left the room.

Upstairs the Swede was swiftly fastening the straps of his great valise. Once his back happened to be half turned toward the door, and, hearing a noise there, he wheeled and sprang up, uttering a loud cry. Scully's wrinkled visage showed grimly in the light of the small lamp he carried. This yellow effulgence, streaming upward, coloured only his prominent features, and left his eyes, for instance, in mysterious shadow. He resembled a murderer.

"Man! man!" he exclaimed, "have you gone daffy?"

"Oh, no! Oh, no!" rejoined the other. "There are people in this world who know pretty nearly as much as you do—understand?"

For a moment they stood gazing at each other. Upon the Swede's deathly pale cheeks were two spots brightly crimson and sharply edged, as if they had been carefully painted. Scully placed the light on the table and sat himself on the edge of the bed. He spoke ruminatively. "By cracky, I never heard of such a thing in my life. It's a complete muddle. I can't, for the soul of me, think how you ever got this idea into your head." Presently he lifted his eyes and asked: "And did you sure think they were going to kill you?"

The Swede scanned the old man as if he wished to see into his mind. "I did," he said at last. He obviously suspected that this answer might precipitate an outbreak. As he pulled on a strap his whole arm shook, the elbow wavering like a bit of paper.

Scully banged his hand impressively on the footboard of the bed. "Why, man, we're goin' to have a line of ilictric street-cars in this town next spring."

"'A line of electric street-cars,'" repeated the Swede, stupidly.

"And," said Scully, "there's a new railroad goin' to be built down from Broken Arm to here. Not to mintion the four churches and the smashin' big brick school-house. Then there's the big factory, too. Why, in two years Romper'll be a met-tro-*pol*-is."

Having finished the preparation of his baggage, the Swede straightened himself. "Mr. Scully," he said, with sudden hardihood, "how much do I owe you?"

"You don't owe me anythin'," said the old man, angrily.

"Yes, I do," retorted the Swede. He took seventy-five cents from his pocket and tendered it to Scully; but the latter snapped his fingers in disdainful refusal. However, it happened that they both stood gazing in a strange fashion at three silver pieces on the Swede's open palm.

"I'll not take your money," said Scully at last. "Not after what's been goin' on here." Then a plan seemed to strike him. "Here," he cried, picking up his lamp and moving toward the door. "Here! Come with me a minute."

"No," said the Swede, in overwhelming alarm.

"Yes," urged the old man. "Come on! I want you to come and see a picter—just across the hall—in my room."

The Swede must have concluded that his hour was come. His jaw dropped and his teeth showed like a dead man's. He ultimately followed Scully across the corridor, but he had the step of one hung in chains.

Scully flashed the light high on the wall of his own chamber. There was revealed a ridiculous photograph of a little girl. She was leaning against a balustrade of gorgeous decoration, and the formidable bang to her hair was prominent. The figure was as graceful as an upright sled-stake, and, withal, it was of the hue of lead. "There," said Scully, tenderly, "that's the picter of my little girl that died. Her name was Carrie. She had the purtiest hair you ever saw! I was that fond of her, she—"

Turning then, he saw that the Swede was not contemplating the picture at all, but, instead, was keeping keen watch on the gloom in the rear.

"Look, man!" cried Scully, heartily. "That's the picter of my little gal that died. Her name was Carrie. And then here's the picter of my oldest boy, Michael. He's a lawyer in Lincoln, an' doin' well. I gave that boy a grand eddication, and I'm glad for it now. He's a fine boy. Look at 'im now. Ain't he bold as blazes, him there in Lincoln, an honoured an' respicted gintleman! An honoured and respicted gintleman," concluded Scully with a flourish. And, so saying, he smote the Swede jovially on the back.

The Swede faintly smiled.

"Now," said the old man, "there's only one more thing." He dropped suddenly to the floor and thrust his head beneath the bed. The Swede could hear his muffled voice. "I'd keep it under me piller if it wasn't for that boy Johnnie. Then there's the old woman—Where is it now? I never put it twice in the same place. Ah, now come out with you!"

Presently he backed clumsily from under the bed, dragging with him an old coat rolled into a bundle. "I've fetched him," he muttered. Kneeling on the floor, he unrolled the coat and extracted from its heart a large yellow-brown whisky-bottle.

His first manoeuvre was to hold the bottle up to the light. Reassured, apparently, that nobody had been tampering with it, he thrust it with a generous movement toward the Swede.

The weak-kneed Swede was about to eagerly clutch this element of strength, but he suddenly jerked his hand away and cast a look of horror upon Scully.

"Drink," said the old man affectionately. He had risen to his feet, and now stood facing the Swede.

There was a silence. Then again Scully said: "Drink!"

The Swede laughed wildly. He grabbed the bottle, put it to his mouth; and as his lips curled absurdly around the opening and his throat worked, he kept his glance, burning with hatred, upon the old man's face.

IV

After the departure of Scully the three men, with the card-board still upon their knees, preserved for a long time an astounded silence. Then Johnnie said: "That's the doddangedest Swede I ever see."

"He ain't no Swede," said the cowboy, scornfully.

"Well, what is he then?" cried Johnnie. "What is he then?"

"It's my opinion," replied the cowboy deliberately, "he's some kind of a Dutchman." It was a venerable custom of the country to entitle as Swedes all light-haired men who spoke with a heavy tongue. In consequence the idea of the cowboy was not without its daring. "Yes, sir," he repeated. "It's my opinion this feller is some kind of a Dutchman."

"Well, he says he's a Swede, anyhow," muttered Johnnie, sulkily. He turned to the Easterner: "What do you think, Mr. Blanc?"

"Oh, I don't know," replied the Easterner.

"Well, what do you think makes him act that way?" asked the cowboy.

"Why, he's frightened." The Easterner knocked his pipe against a rim of the stove. "He's clear frightened out of his boots."

"What at?" cried Johnnie and the cowboy together.

The Easterner reflected over his answer.

"What at?" cried the others again.

"Oh, I don't know, but it seems to me this man has been reading dime novels, and he thinks he's right out in the middle of it—the shootin' and stabbin' and all."

"But," said the cowboy, deeply scandalized, "this ain't Wyoming, ner none of them places. This is Nebrasker."

"Yes," added Johnnie, "an' why don't he wait till he gits *out West?*"

The travelled Easterner laughed. "It isn't different there even—not in these days. But he thinks he's right in the middle of hell."

Johnnie and the cowboy mused long.

"It's awful funny," remarked Johnnie at last.

"Yes," said the cowboy. "This is a queer game. I hope we don't git snowed in, because then we'd have to stand this here man bein' around with us all the time. That wouldn't be no good."

"I wish pop would throw him out," said Johnnie.

Presently they heard a loud stamping on the stairs, accompanied by ringing jokes in the voice of old Scully, and laughter, evidently from the Swede. The men around the stove stared vacantly at each other. "Gosh!" said the cowboy. The door flew open, and old Scully, flushed and anecdotal, came into the room. He was jabbering at the Swede, who followed him, laughing bravely. It was the entry of two roisterers from a banquet hall.

"Come now," said Scully sharply to the three seated men, "move up and give us a chance at the stove." The cowboy and the Easterner obediently sidled their chairs to make room for the newcomers. Johnnie, however, simply arranged himself in a more indolent attitude, and then remained motionless.

"Come! Git over, there," said Scully.

"Plenty of room on the other side of the stove," said Johnnie.

"Do you think we want to sit in the draught?" roared the father.

But the Swede here interposed with a grandeur of confidence. "No, no. Let the boy sit where he likes," he cried in a bullying voice to the father.

"All right! All right!" said Scully, deferentially. The cowboy and the Easterner exchanged glances of wonder.

The five chairs were formed in a crescent about one side of the stove. The Swede began to talk; he talked arrogantly, profanely, angrily. Johnnie, the cowboy, and the Easterner maintained a morose silence, while old Scully appeared to be receptive and eager, breaking in constantly with sympathetic ejaculations.

Finally the Swede announced that he was thirsty. He moved in his chair, and said that he would go for a drink of water.

"I'll git it for you," cried Scully at once.

"No," said the Swede, contemptuously. "I'll get it for myself." He arose and stalked with the air of an owner off into the executive parts of the hotel.

As soon as the Swede was out of hearing Scully sprang to his feet and whispered intensely to the others: "Upstairs he thought I was tryin' to poison 'im."

"Say," said Johnnie, "this makes me sick. Why don't you throw 'im out in the snow?"

"Why, he's all right now," declared Scully. "It was only that he was from the East, and he thought this was a tough place. That's all. He's all right now."

The cowboy looked with admiration upon the Easterner. "You were straight," he said. "You were on to that there Dutchman."

"Well," said Johnnie to his father, "he may be all right now, but I don't see it. Other time he was scared, but now he's too fresh."

Scully's speech was always a combination of Irish brogue and idiom, Western twang and idiom, and scraps of curiously formal diction taken from the story-books and newspapers. He now hurled a strange mass of language at the head of his son. "What do I keep? What do I keep? What do I keep?" he demanded, in a voice of thunder. He slapped his knee impressively, to indicate that he himself was going to make reply, and that all should heed. "I keep a hotel," he shouted. "A hotel, do you mind? A guest under my roof has sacred privileges. He is to be intimidated by none. Not one word shall he hear that would prijudice him in favour of goin' away. I'll not have it. There's no place in this here town where they can say they iver took in a guest of mine because he was afraid to stay here." He wheeled suddenly upon the cowboy and the Easterner. "Am I right?"

"Yes, Mr. Scully," said the cowboy, "I think you're right."

"Yes, Mr. Scully," said the Easterner, "I think you're right."

V

At six-o'clock supper, the Swede fizzed like a fire-wheel. He sometimes seemed on the point of bursting into riotous song, and in all his madness he was encouraged by old Scully. The Easterner was encased in reserve; the cowboy sat in wide-mouthed amazement, forgetting to eat, while Johnnie wrathily demolished great plates of food. The daughters of the house, when they were obliged to replenish the biscuits, approached as warily as Indians, and, having succeeded in their purpose, fled with ill-concealed trepidation. The Swede domineered the whole feast, and he gave it the appearance of a cruel bacchanal. He seemed to have grown suddenly taller; he gazed, brutally disdainful, into every face. His voice rang through the room. Once when he jabbed out harpoon-fashion with his fork to pinion a biscuit, the weapon nearly impaled the hand of the Easterner, which had been stretched quietly out for the same biscuit.

After supper, as the men filed toward the other room, the Swede smote Scully ruthlessly on the shoulder. "Well, old boy, that was a good, square meal." Johnnie looked hopefully at his father; he knew that shoulder was tender from an old fall; and, indeed, it appeared for a moment as if Scully was going to flame out over the matter, but in the end he smiled a sickly smile and remained silent. The others understood from his manner that he was admitting his responsibility for the Swede's new view point.

Johnnie, however, addressed his parent in an aside. "Why don't you license somebody to kick you downstairs?" Scully scowled darkly by way of reply.

When they were gathered about the stove, the Swede insisted on another game of High-Five. Scully gently deprecated the plan at first, but the Swede turned a wolfish glare upon him. The old man subsided, and the Swede canvassed the others. In his tone there was always a great threat. The cowboy and the Easterner both remarked indifferently that they would play. Scully said that he would presently have to go to meet the 6.58 train, and so the Swede turned menacingly upon Johnnie. For a moment their glances crossed like blades, and then Johnnie smiled and said, "Yes, I'll play."

They formed a square, with the little board on their knees. The Easterner and the Swede were again partners. As the play went on, it was noticeable that the cowboy was not board-whacking as usual. Meanwhile, Scully, near the lamp, had put on his spectacles and, with an appearance curiously like an old priest, was reading a newspaper. In time he went out to meet the 6.58 train, and, despite his precautions, a gust of polar wind whirled into the room as he opened the door. Besides scattering the cards, it chilled the players to the marrow. The Swede cursed frightfully. When Scully returned, his entrance disturbed a cosy and friendly scene. The Swede again cursed. But presently they were once more intent, their heads bent forward and their hands moving swiftly. The Swede had adopted the fashion of board-whacking.

Scully took up his paper and for a long time remained immersed in matters which were extraordinarily remote from him. The lamp burned badly, and once he stopped to adjust the wick. The newspaper, as he turned from page to page, rustled with a slow and comfortable sound. Then suddenly he heard three terrible words: "You are cheatin'!"

Such scenes often prove that there can be little of dramatic import in environment. Any room can present a tragic front; any room can be comic. This little den was now hideous as a torture-chamber. The new faces of the men themselves had changed it upon the instant. The Swede held a huge fist in front of Johnnie's face, while the latter looked steadily over it into the blazing orbs of his accuser. The Easterner had grown pallid; the cowboy's jaw had dropped in that expression of bovine amazement which was one of his important mannerisms. After the three words, the first sound in the room was made by Scully's paper as it floated forgotten to his feet. His spectacles had also fallen from his nose, but by a clutch he had saved them in air. His hand, grasping the spectacles, now remained poised awkwardly and near his shoulder. He stared at the card-players.

Probably the silence was while a second elapsed. Then, if the floor had been suddenly twitched out from under the men they could not have moved quicker. The five had projected themselves head-long toward a common point. It happened that Johnnie, in rising to hurl himself upon the Swede, had stumbled slightly because of his curiously instinctive care for the cards and the board. The loss of the moment allowed time for the arrival of Scully, and also allowed the cowboy time to give the Swede a great push which sent him staggering back. The men found tongue together, and hoarse shouts of rage, appeal, or fear burst from every throat. The cowboy pushed and jostled feverishly at the Swede, and the Easterner and Scully clung wildly to Johnnie; but through the smoky air, above the swaying bodies of the peace-compellers, the eyes of the two warriors ever sought each other in glances of challenge that were at once hot and steely.

Of course the board had been overturned, and now the whole company of cards was scattered over the floor, where the boots of the men trampled the fat and painted kings and queens as they gazed with their silly eyes at the war that was waging above them.

Scully's voice was dominating the yells. "Stop now! Stop, I say! Stop, now—"

Johnnie, as he struggled to burst through the rank formed by Scully and the Easterner, was crying, "Well, he says I cheated! He says I cheated! I won't allow no man to say I cheated! If he says I cheated, he's a—!"

The cowboy was telling the Swede, "Quit, now! Quit, d'ye hear—"

The screams of the Swede never ceased: "He did cheat! I saw him! I saw him—"

As for the Easterner, he was importuning in a voice that was not heeded: "Wait a moment, can't you? Oh, wait a moment. What's the good of a fight over a game of cards? Wait a moment—"

In this tumult no complete sentences were clear. "Cheat"—"Quit"—"He says"—these fragments pierced the uproar and rang out sharply. It was remarkable that, whereas Scully undoubtedly made the most noise, he was the least heard of any of the riotous band.

Then suddenly there was a great cessation. It was as if each man had paused for breath; and although the room was still lighted with the anger of men, it could be seen that there was no danger of immediate conflict, and at once Johnnie, shouldering his way forward, almost succeeded in confronting the Swede. "What did you say I cheated for? What did you say I cheated for? I don't cheat, and I won't let no man say I do!"

The Swede said, "I saw you! I saw you!"

"Well," cried Johnnie, "I'll fight any man what says I cheat!"

"No, you won't," said the cowboy. "Not here."

"Ah, be still, can't you?" said Scully, coming between them.

The quiet was sufficient to allow the Easterner's voice to be heard. He was repeating, "Oh, wait a moment, can't you? What's the good of a fight over a game of cards? Wait a moment!"

Johnnie, his red face appearing above his father's shoulder, hailed the Swede again. "Did you say I cheated?"

The Swede showed his teeth. "Yes."

"Then," said Johnnie, "we must fight."

"Yes, fight," roared the Swede. He was like a demoniac. "Yes, fight! I'll show you what kind of a man I am! I'll show you who you want to fight! Maybe you think I can't fight! Maybe you think I can't! I'll show you, you skin, you card-sharp! Yes, you cheated! You cheated! You cheated!"

"Well, let's go at it, then, mister," said Johnnie, coolly. The cowboy's brow was beaded with sweat from his efforts in intercepting all sorts of raids. He turned in despair to Scully. "What are you goin' to do now?"

A change had come over the Celtic visage of the old man. He now seemed all eagerness; his eyes glowed.

"We'll let them fight," he answered, stalwartly. "I can't put up with it any longer. I've stood this damned Swede till I'm sick. We'll let them fight."

VI

The men prepared to go out of doors. The Easterner was so nervous that he had great difficulty in getting his arms into the sleeves of his new leather coat. As the cowboy drew his fur cap down over his ears his hands trembled. In fact, Johnnie and old Scully were the only ones who displayed no agitation. These preliminaries were conducted without words.

Scully threw open the door. "Well, come on," he said. Instantly a terrific wind caused the flame of the lamp to struggle at its wick, while a puff of black smoke sprang from the chimney-top. The stove was in mid-current of the blast, and its voice swelled to equal the roar of the storm. Some of the scarred and bedabbled cards were caught up from the floor and dashed helplessly against the farther wall. The men lowered their heads and plunged into the tempest as into a sea.

No snow was falling, but great whirls and clouds of flakes, swept up from the ground by the frantic winds, were streaming southward with the speed of bullets. The covered land was blue with the sheen of an unearthly satin, and there was no other hue save where, at the low, black railway station—which seemed incredibly distant—one light gleamed like a tiny jewel.

As the men floundered into a thigh-deep drift, it was known that the Swede was bawling out something. Scully went to him, put a hand on his shoulder, and projected an ear. "What's that you say?" he shouted.

"I say," bawled the Swede again, "I won't stand much show against this gang. I know you'll all pitch on me."

Scully smote him reproachfully on the arm. "Tut, man!" he yelled. The wind tore the words from Scully's lips and scattered them far alee.

"You are all a gang of—" boomed the Swede, but the storm also seized the remainder of this sentence.

Immediately turning their backs upon the wind, the men had swung around a corner to the sheltered side of the hotel. It was the function of the little house to preserve here, amid this great devastation of snow, an irregular V-shape of heavily encrusted grass, which crackled beneath the feet. One could imagine the great drifts piled against the windward side. When the party reached the comparative peace of this spot it was found that the Swede was still bellowing.

"Oh, I know what kind of a thing this is! I know you'll all pitch on me. I can't lick you all!"

Scully turned upon him panther-fashion. "You'll not have to whip all of us. You'll have to whip my son Johnnie. An' the man what troubles you durin' that time will have me to dale with."

The arrangements were swiftly made. The two men faced each other, obedient to the harsh commands of Scully, whose face, in the subtly luminous gloom, could be seen set in the austere impersonal lines that are pictured on the countenances of the Roman veterans. The Easterner's teeth were chattering, and he was hopping up and down like a mechanical toy. The cowboy stood rock-like.

The contestants had not stripped off any clothing. Each was in his ordinary attire. Their fists were up, and they eyed each other in a calm that had the elements of leonine cruelty in it.

During this pause, the Easterner's mind, like a film, took lasting impressions of three men—the iron-nerved master of the ceremony; the Swede, pale, motionless, terrible; and Johnnie, serene yet ferocious, brutish yet heroic. The entire prelude had in it a tragedy greater than the tragedy of action, and this aspect was accentuated by the long, mellow cry of the blizzard, as it sped the tumbling and wailing flakes into the black abyss of the south.

"Now!" said Scully.

The two combatants leaped forward and crashed together like bullocks. There was heard the cushioned sound of blows, and of a curse squeezing out from between the tight teeth of one.

As for the spectators, the Easterner's pent-up breath exploded from him with a pop of relief, absolute relief from the tension of the preliminaries.

The cowboy bounded into the air with a yowl. Scully was immovable as from supreme amazement and fear at the fury of the fight which he himself had permitted and arranged.

For a time the encounter in the darkness was such a perplexity of flying arms that it presented no more detail than would a swiftly revolving wheel. Occasionally a face, as if illumined by a flash of light, would shine out, ghastly and marked with pink spots. A moment later, the men might have been known as shadows, if it were not for the involuntary utterance of oaths that came from them in whispers.

Suddenly a holocaust of warlike desire caught the cowboy, and he bolted forward with the speed of a broncho. "Go it, Johnnie! go it! Kill him! Kill him!"

Scully confronted him. "Kape back," he said; and by his glance the cowboy could tell that this man was Johnnie's father.

To the Easterner there was a monotony of unchangeable fighting that was an abomination. This confused mingling was eternal to his sense, which was concentrated in a longing for the end, the priceless end. Once the fighters lurched near him, and as he scrambled hastily backward he heard them breathe like men on the rack.

"Kill him, Johnnie! Kill him! Kill him! Kill him!" The cowboy's face was contorted like one of those agony masks in museums.

"Keep still," said Scully, icily.

Then there was a sudden loud grunt, incomplete, cut short, and Johnnie's body swung away from the Swede and fell with sickening heaviness to the grass. The cowboy was barely in time to prevent the mad Swede from flinging himself upon his prone adversary. "No, you don't," said the cowboy, interposing an arm. "Wait a second."

Scully was at his son's side. "Johnnie! Johnnie, me boy!" His voice had a quality of melancholy tenderness. "Johnnie! Can you go on with it?" He looked anxiously down into the bloody, pulpy face of his son.

There was a moment of silence, and then Johnnie answered in his ordinary voice, "Yes, I—it—yes."

Assisted by his father he struggled to his feet. "Wait a bit now till you git your wind," said the old man.

A few paces away the cowboy was lecturing the Swede. "No, you don't! Wait a second!"

The Easterner was plucking at Scully's sleeve. "Oh, this is enough," he pleaded. "This is enough! Let it go as it stands. This is enough!"

"Bill," said Scully, "git out of the road." The cowboy stepped aside. "Now." The combatants were actuated by a new caution as they advanced toward collision. They glared at each other, and then the Swede aimed a lightning blow that carried with it his entire weight. Johnnie was evidently half-stupid from weakness, but he miraculously dodged, and his fist sent the overbalanced Swede sprawling.

The cowboy, Scully, and the Easterner burst into a cheer that was like a chorus of triumphant soldiery, but before its conclusion the Swede had scuffled agilely to his feet and come in berserk abandon at his foe. There was another perplexity of flying arms, and Johnnie's body again swung away and fell, even as a bundle might fall from a roof. The Swede instantly staggered to a little wind-waved tree and leaned upon it, breathing like an engine, while his savage and flame-lit eyes roamed from face to face as the men bent over Johnnie. There was a splendour of isolation in his situation at this time which the Easterner felt once when, lifting his eyes from the man on the ground, he beheld that mysterious and lonely figure, waiting.

"Are you any good yet, Johnnie?" asked Scully in a broken voice.

The son gasped and opened his eyes languidly. After a moment he answered, "No I ain't—any good—any—more." Then, from shame and bodily ill, he began to weep, the tears furrowing down through the bloodstains on his face. "He was too—too—too heavy for me."

Scully straightened and addressed the waiting figure. "Stranger," he said, evenly, "it's all up with our side." Then his voice changed into that vibrant huskiness which is commonly the tone of the most simple and deadly announcements. "Johnnie is whipped."

Without replying, the victor moved off on the route to the front door of the hotel.

The cowboy was formulating new and unspellable blasphemies. The Easterner was startled to find that they were out in a wind that seemed to come direct from the shadowed arctic floes. He heard again the wail of the snow as it was flung to its grave in the south. He knew now that all this time the cold had been sinking into him deeper and deeper, and he wondered that he had not perished. He felt indifferent to the condition of the vanquished man.

"Johnnie, can you walk?" asked Scully.

"Did I hurt—hurt him any?" asked the son.

"Can you walk, boy? Can you walk?"

Johnnie's voice was suddenly strong. There was a robust impatience in it. "I asked you whether I hurt him any!"

"Yes, yes, Johnnie," answered the cowboy, consolingly; "he's hurt a good deal."

They raised him from the ground, and as soon as he was on his feet he went tottering off, rebuffing all attempts at assistance. When the party rounded the corner they were fairly blinded by the pelting of the snow. It burned their faces like fire. The cowboy carried Johnnie through the drift to the door. As they entered, some cards again rose from the floor and beat against the wall.

The Easterner rushed to the stove. He was so profoundly chilled that he almost dared to embrace the glowing iron. The Swede was not in the room. Johnnie sank into a chair and, folding his arms on his knees, buried his face in them. Scully, warming one foot and then the other at a rim of the stove, muttered to himself with Celtic mournfulness. The cowboy had removed his fur cap, and with a dazed and rueful air he was running one hand through his tousled locks. From overhead they could hear the creaking of boards, as the Swede tramped here and there in his room.

The sad quiet was broken by the sudden flinging open of a door that led toward the kitchen. It was instantly followed by an inrush of women. They precipitated themselves upon Johnnie amid a chorus of lamentation. Before they carried their prey off to the kitchen, there to be bathed and harangued with that mixture of sympathy and abuse which is a feat of their sex, the mother straightened herself and fixed old Scully with an eye of stern reproach. "Shame be upon you, Patrick Scully!" she cried. "Your own son, too. Shame be upon you!"

"There, now! Be quiet, now!" said the old man, weakly.

"Shame be upon you, Patrick Scully!" The girls, rallying to this slogan, sniffed disdainfully in the direction of those trembling accomplices, the cowboy and the Easterner. Presently they bore Johnnie away, and left the three men to dismal reflection.

VII

"I'd like to fight this here Dutchman myself," said the cowboy, breaking a long silence.

Scully wagged his head sadly. "No, that wouldn't do. It wouldn't be right. It wouldn't be right."

"Well, why wouldn't it?" argued the cowboy. "I don't see no harm in it."

"No," answered Scully, with mournful heroism. "It wouldn't be right. It was Johnnie's fight, and now we mustn't whip the man just because he whipped Johnnie."

"Yes, that's true enough," said the cowboy; "but—he better not get fresh with me, because I couldn't stand no more of it."

"You'll not say a word to him," commanded Scully, and even then they heard the tread of the Swede on the stairs. His entrance was made theatric. He swept the door back with a bang and swaggered to the middle of the room. No one looked at him. "Well," he cried, insolently, at Scully, "I s'pose you'll tell me now how much I owe you?"

The old man remained stolid. "You don't owe me nothin'."

"Huh!" said the Swede, "huh! Don't owe 'im nothin'."

The cowboy addressed the Swede. "Stranger, I don't see how you come to be so gay around here."

Old Scully was instantly alert. "Stop!" he shouted, holding his hand forth, fingers upward. "Bill, you shut up!"

The cowboy spat carelessly into the sawdust-box. "I didn't say a word, did I?" he asked.

"Mr. Scully," called the Swede, "how much do I owe you?" It was seen that he was attired for departure, and that he had his valise in his hand.

"You don't owe me nothin'," repeated Scully in the same imperturbable way.

"Huh!" said the Swede. "I guess you're right. I guess if it was any way at all, you'd owe me somethin'. That's what I guess." He turned to the cowboy. "'Kill him! Kill him! Kill him!'" he mimicked, and then guffawed victoriously. "'Kill him!'" He was convulsed with ironical humour.

But he might have been jeering the dead. The three men were immovable and silent, staring with glassy eyes at the stove.

The Swede opened the door and passed into the storm, giving one derisive glance backward at the still group.

As soon as the door was dosed, Scully and the cowboy leaped to their feet and began to curse. They trampled to and fro, waving their arms and smashing into the air with their fists. "Oh, but that was a hard minute!" wailed Scully. "That was a hard minute! Him there leerin' and scoffin'! One bang at his nose was worth forty dollars to me that minute! How did you stand it, Bill?"

"How did I stand it?" cried the cowboy in a quivering voice. "How did I stand it? Oh!"

The old man burst into sudden brogue. "I'd loike to take that Swade," he wailed, "and hould 'im down on a shtone flure and bate 'im to a jelly wid a shtick!"

The cowboy groaned in sympathy. "I'd like to git him by the neck and ha-ammer him"—he brought his hand down on a chair with a noise like a pistol-shot—"hammer that there Dutchman until he couldn't tell himself from a dead coyote!"

"I'd bate 'im until he—"

"I'd show *him* some things—"

And then together they raised a yearning, fanatic cry—"Oh-o-oh! if we only could—"

"Yes!"

"Yes!"

"And then I'd—"

"O-o-oh!"

VIII

The Swede, tightly gripping his valise, tacked across the face of the storm as if he carried sails. He was following a line of little naked, grasping trees which, he knew, must mark the way of the road. His face, fresh from the pounding of Johnnie's fists, felt more pleasure than pain in the wind and the driving snow. A number of square shapes loomed upon him finally, and he knew them as the houses of the main body of the town. He found a street and made travel along it, leaning heavily upon the wind whenever, at a corner, a terrific blast caught him.

He might have been in a deserted village. We picture the world as thick with conquering and elate humanity, but here, with the bugles of the tempest pealing, it was hard to imagine a peopled earth. One viewed the existence of man then as a marvel, and conceded a glamour of wonder to these lice which were caused to cling to a whirling, fire-smitten, ice-locked, disease-stricken, space-lost bulb. The conceit of man was explained by this storm to be the very engine of life. One was a coxcomb not to die in it. However, the Swede found a saloon.

In front of it an indomitable red light was burning, and the snowflakes were made blood-colour as they flew through the circumscribed territory of the lamp's shining. The Swede pushed open the door of the saloon and entered. A sanded expanse was before him, and at the end of it four men sat about a table drinking. Down one side of the room extended a radiant bar, and its guardian was leaning upon his elbows listening to the talk of the men at the table. The Swede dropped his valise upon the floor, and smiling fraternally upon the barkeeper, said, "Gimme some whisky, will you?" The man placed a bottle, a whisky-glass, and a glass of ice-thick water upon the bar. The Swede poured himself an abnormal portion of whisky and drank it in three gulps. "Pretty bad night," remarked the bartender, indifferently. He was making the pretension of blindness which is usually a distinction of his class; but it could have been seen that he was furtively studying the half-erased blood-stains on the face of the Swede. "Bad night," he said again.

"Oh, it's good enough for me," replied the Swede, hardily, as he poured himself some more whisky. The barkeeper took his coin and manoeuvred it through its reception by the highly nickelled cash-machine. A bell rang; a card labelled "20 cts." had appeared.

"No," continued the Swede, "this isn't too bad weather. It's good enough for me."

"So?" murmured the barkeeper languidly.

The copious drams made the Swede's eyes swim, and he breathed a trifle heavier. "Yes, I like this weather. I like it. It suits me." It was apparently his design to impart a deep significance to these words.

"So?" murmured the bartender again. He turned to gaze dreamily at the scroll-like birds and bird-like scrolls which had been drawn with soap upon the mirrors in back of the bar.

"Well, I guess I'll take another drink," said the Swede, presently. "Have something?"

"No, thanks; I'm not drinkin'," answered the bartender. Afterward he asked, "How did you hurt your face?"

The Swede immediately began to boast loudly. "Why, in a fight. I thumped the soul out of a man down here at Scully's hotel."

The interest of the four men at the table was at last aroused.

"Who was it?" said one.

"Johnnie Scully," blustered the Swede. "Son of the man what runs it. He will be pretty near dead for some weeks, I can tell you. I made a nice thing of him, I did. He couldn't get up. They carried him in the house. Have a drink?"

Instantly the men in some subtle way encased themselves in reserve. "No, thanks," said one. The group was of curious formation. Two were prominent local business men; one was the district attorney; and one was a professional gambler of the kind known as "square": But a scrutiny of the group would not have enabled an observer to pick the gambler from the men of more reputable pursuits. He was, in fact, a man so delicate in manner, when among people of fair class, and so judicious in his choice of victims, that in the strictly masculine part of the town's life he had come to be explicitly trusted and admired. People called him a thoroughbred. The fear and contempt with which his craft was regarded were undoubtedly the reason why his quiet dignity shone conspicuous above the quiet dignity of men who might be merely hatters, billiard-markers, or grocery clerks. Beyond an occasional unwary traveller who came by rail, this gambler was supposed to prey solely upon reckless and senile farmers, who, when flush with good crops, drove into town in all the pride and confidence of an absolutely invulnerable stupidity. Hearing at times in circuitous fashion of the despoilment of such a farmer, the important men of Romper invariably laughed in contempt of the victim, and if they thought of the wolf at all, it was with a kind of pride at the knowledge that he would never dare think of attacking their wisdom and courage. Besides, it was popular that this gambler had a real wife and two real children in a neat cottage in a suburb, where he led an exemplary home life; and when any one even suggested a discrepancy in his character, the crowd immediately vociferated descriptions of this virtuous family circle. Then men who led exemplary home lives, and men who did not lead exemplary home lives, all subsided in a bunch, remarking that there was nothing more to be said.

However, when a restriction was placed upon him—as, for instance, when a strong clique of members of the new Pollywog Club refused to per-

mit him, even as a spectator, to appear in the rooms of the organization—
the candour and gentleness with which he accepted the judgement disarmed
many of his foes and made his friends more desperately partisan. He invariably distinguished between himself and a respectable Romper man so
quickly and frankly that his manner actually appeared to be a continual
broadcast compliment.

And one must not forget to declare the fundamental fact of his entire
position in Romper. It is irrefutable that in all affairs outside his business,
in all matters that occur eternally and commonly between man and man,
this thieving card-player was so generous, so just, so moral, that, in a contest, he could have put to flight the consciences of nine-tenths of the citizens of Romper.

And so it happened that he was seated in this saloon with the two
prominent local merchants and the district attorney.

The Swede continued to drink raw whisky, meanwhile babbling at the
barkeeper and trying to induce him to indulge in potations. "Come on. Have
a drink. Come on. What—no? Well, have a little one, then. By gawd, I've
whipped a man tonight, and I want to celebrate. I whipped him good, too.
Gentlemen," the Swede cried to the men at the table, "have a drink?"

"Ssh!" said the barkeeper.

The group at the table, although furtively attentive, had been pretending to be deep in talk, but now a man lifted his eyes toward the Swede and
said, shortly, "Thanks. We don't want any more."

At this reply the Swede ruffled out his chest like a rooster. "Well," he
exploded, "it seems I can't get anybody to drink with me in this town. Seems
so, don't it? Well!"

"Ssh!" said the barkeeper.

"Say," snarled the Swede, "don't you try to shut me up. I won't have it. I'm
a gentleman, and I want people to drink with me. And I want 'em to drink
with me now. Now do you understand?" He rapped the bar with his knuckles.

Years of experience had calloused the bartender. He merely grew sulky.
"I hear you," he answered.

"Well," cried the Swede, "listen hard then. See those men over there? Well,
they're going to drink with me, and don't you forget it. Now you watch."

"Hi!" yelled the barkeeper, "this won't do!"

"Why won't it?" demanded the Swede. He stalked over to the table, and
by chance laid his hand upon the shoulder of the gambler. "How about
this?" he asked wrathfully. "I asked you to drink with me."

The gambler simply twisted his head and spoke over his shoulder. "My
friend, I don't know you."

"Oh, hell!" answered the Swede, "come and have a drink."

"Now, my boy," advised the gambler, kindly, "take your hand off my shoulder and go 'way and mind your own business." He was a little, slim man, and it seemed strange to hear him use this tone of heroic patronage to the burly Swede. The other men at the table said nothing.

"What! You won't drink with me, you little dude? I'll make you, then! I'll make you!" The Swede had grasped the gambler frenziedly at the throat, and was dragging him from his chair. The other men sprang up. The barkeeper dashed around the corner of his bar. There was a great tumult, and then was seen a long blade in the hand of the gambler. It shot forward, and a human body, this citadel of virtue, wisdom, power, was pierced as easily as if it had been a melon. The Swede fell with a cry of supreme astonishment.

The prominent merchants and the district attorney must have at once tumbled out of the place backward. The bartender found himself hanging limply to the arm of a chair and gazing into the eyes of a murderer.

"Henry," said the latter, as he wiped his knife on one of the towels that hung beneath the bar rail, "you tell 'em where to find me. I'll be home, waiting for 'em." Then he vanished. A moment afterward the barkeeper was in the street dinning through the storm for help and, moreover, companionship.

The corpse of the Swede, alone in the saloon, had its eyes fixed upon a dreadful legend that dwelt atop of the cash-machine: "This registers the amount of your purchase."

IX

Months later, the cowboy was frying pork over the stove of a little ranch near the Dakota line, when there was a quick thud of hoofs outside, and presently the Easterner entered with the letters and the papers.

"Well," said the Easterner at once, "the chap that killed the Swede has got three years. Wasn't much, was it?"

"He has? Three years?" The cowboy poised his pan of pork, while he ruminated upon the news. "Three years. That ain't much."

"No. It was a light sentence," replied the Easterner as he unbuckled his spurs. "Seems there was a good deal of sympathy for him in Romper."

"If the bartender had been any good," observed the cowboy, thoughtfully, "he would have gone in and cracked that there Dutchman on the head with a bottle in the beginnin' of it and stopped all this here murderin'."

"Yes, a thousand things might have happened," said the Easterner, tartly.

The cowboy returned his pan of pork to the fire, but his philosophy continued. "It's funny, ain't it? If he hadn't said Johnnie was cheatin' he'd be alive this minute. He was an awful fool. Game played for fun, too. Not for money. I believe he was crazy."

"I feel sorry for that gambler," said the Easterner.

"Oh, so do I," said the cowboy. "He don't deserve none of it for killin' who he did."

"The Swede might not have been killed if everything had been square."

"Might not have been killed?" exclaimed the cowboy. "Everythin' square? Why, when he said that Johnnie was cheatin' and acted like such a jackass? And then in the saloon he fairly walked up to git hurt?" With these arguments the cowboy browbeat the Easterner and reduced him to rage.

"You're a fool!" cried the Easterner, viciously. "You're a bigger jackass than the Swede by a million majority. Now let me tell you one thing. Let me tell you something. Listen! Johnnie *was* cheating!"

"Johnnie," said the cowboy, blankly. There was a minute of silence, and then he said, robustly, "Why, no. The game was only for fun."

"Fun or not," said the Easterner, "Johnnie was cheating. I saw him. I know it. I saw him. And I refused to stand up and be a man. I let the Swede fight it out alone. And you—you were simply puffing around the place and wanting to fight. And then old Scully himself! We are all in it! This poor gambler isn't even a noun. He is a kind of an adverb. Every sin is the result of a collaboration. We, five of us, have collaborated in the murder of this Swede. Usually there are from a dozen to forty women really involved in every murder, but in this case it seems to be only five men—you, I, Johnnie, old Scully; and that fool of an unfortunate gambler came merely as a culmination, the apex of a human movement, and gets all the punishment."

The cowboy, injured and rebellious, cried out blindly into this fog of mysterious theory: "Well, I didn't do anythin', did I?"

Discussion Questions

1. Describe the misperceptions about the West that seem to motivate the Swede, as well as other characters. Then, explain the tragic perspective the story takes on these misperceptions.
2. To what extent do you believe the Swede is "heroic"? Likewise, to what extent do you find him a fool suffering from limited awareness?
3. Explain the role of the Easterner in the conclusion and Crane's choice of this character to assume this role.
4. Reread the passage beginning "We picture the world. . . ," in which the narrator comments on the blizzard when the Swede leaves the hotel (page 250). Explain how this passage suggests a theme for the story.

one, but we can go where it is."
ual Samaritan, and with one

he inquired.
lips, "shoot me."
horse around. By twisting
lp the anguished stranger
oy Bert Barricune hated
e let Foster lie where he
full of water.
up. After the third fail-
u after all?"
to do first."
'Well, I should think
returned with bed-

e and said, "Not yet,
nd set up camp—
ched on his heels
in, got his clothes
ricune observed,
th a quirt.
has a right to

shake them.

's over that
you leave.

lanced at
who was
he one-
til Bar-
n stop
ether,

an

d

DOROTHY JOHNSON
(1905–1984)

Born in Iowa, Johnson soon moved when her father's health forced him to give up farming and venture west to Montana, where the family settled in Whitefish, a railroad town near the Canadian border. Her parents' backgrounds as teachers shaped her interest in reading, which she did constantly in her youth. While still in high school she wrote occasionally for the local paper, *The Kalispell Inter Lake*, but later dismissed her journalistic ability because she was too timid to interview strangers. Though she began college as a pre-med major at Montana State, her natural aptitudes soon convinced her to transfer to the University at Missoula, where she took up English and writing. She began publishing poetry and short stories in the college literary magazine (Alter 5–8).

In 1928, she moved to Okanogan, Washington, to work as a stenographer and continued to work on her fiction. After two years, Johnson relocated to Wisconsin, where her mother had remarried, and soon wrote her first published story, "Bonnie George Campbell," which earned $400 from *The Saturday Evening Post*. A self-assured author at 24, Johnson nonetheless waited eleven years to see another story in print. In the meantime, she wrote advertising copy for five years and then moved to New York to work for Gregg Publishing. There, she found it difficult to make personal contacts and spent much of her spare time writing. In 1940, visiting Wisconsin again, she began a successful series of stories about the West that were first bought by *The Post* and later collected as *Beulah Bunny Tells All* (1942). In the 1940s, Johnson began visiting the New York libraries and museums in order to learn about Western topics, such as the Plains Indians (Alter 8–12). In fact, her reading of Robert Lowrie's *The Crow Indians* gave her the cultural understanding that later helped her create "A Man Called Horse" (22).

Finally, her love for the West and discomfort with city people led to her return to Montana in 1950, where she began working as a journalist and photographer for *The Whitefish Pilot*. In 1953, Johnson began a fourteen-year tenure as secretary and manager of the Montana Press Association, while also teaching journalism at the University in Missoula. That year also saw Ballantine's publication of her Western story collection, titled initially *Indian Country* and subsequently *A Man Called Horse*, after its final story was made into a popular film starring Richard Harris (Cinema Center, 1970). Many of these stories concern a clash between cultures—Anglo and Native American, or Eastern and Western. Many also create an awareness of and sympathy toward the Native perspective.

After ten years of work, she finally saw *The Hanging Tree* (1957) published as a novella along with nine other stories under the same covers. The novella was Johnson's first work to become a movie, starring Gary Cooper (Warner, 1959). The second was "The Man Who Shot Liberty Valance," which became a respected John Ford film starring John Wayne, Vera Miles, and James Stewart (Paramount, 1962).

In the late 1950s, she shifted her focus from the short-story market, which she felt was doomed by television, to the juvenile market, in which she earned success with nine titles through the 1960s and 1970s. But she never lost her interest in Indian peoples, portraying in *Buffalo Woman* (1977) and *All the Buffalo Returning* (1979) stories of cultural dissolution and spiritual regeneration among the Lakota (Alter 12–15). The former novel even won recognition as the National Cowboy Hall of Fame's Western Heritage Outstanding Novel for 1978.

Johnson's Western stories may be appreciated for their economi style, even their lack of description. Her narratives are advanced emotion and action, while the meaning is highlighted by ironic hum She seems most concerned by how strength of character is develop in response to a harsh environment. Furthermore, the best of her ries create a reversal in perspective that avoids conventional exp tions. With an accurate rendering of frontier reality, Johnson as readers to relive the past not as they might expect it, but as the front the psychological reality of its conflicts.

"The Man Who Shot Liberty Valance" was first published *mopolitan* in 1949. The following text is from the reprint i *Country* (New York: Ballantine Books, 1953), pages 180–97.

Alter, Judy. *Dorothy Johnson*. Boise, ID: Boise State University, 19

THE MAN WHO SHOT LIBERTY V

———◆———

Bert Barricune died in 1910. Not more than a dozen p for his funeral. Among them was an earnest young reporte for a human-interest story; there were legends that the old ma

"The boss was a big man with black hair, dark eyes, and two gold teeth in front. The other two—"

"I know. Liberty Valance and a couple of his boys. Just what's your complaint, now?" Foster began to understand that no help was going to come from the marshal.

"They rob you?" the marshal asked.

"They didn't search me."

"Take your gun?"

"I didn't have one."

"Steal your horse?"

"Gave him a crack with a quirt, and he left."

"Saddle on him?"

"No. I left it out there."

The marshal shook his head. "Can't see you got any legal complaint," he said with relief. "Where was this?"

"On a road in the woods, by a creek. Two days' walk from here."

The marshal got to his feet. "You don't even know what jurisdiction it was in. They knocked you around; well, that could happen. Man gets in a fight—could happen to anybody."

Foster said dryly, "Thanks a lot."

The marshal stopped him as he reached the door. "There's a reward for Liberty Valance."

"I still haven't got a gun," Foster said. "Does he come here often?"

"Nope. Nothing he'd want in Twotrees. Hard man to find." The marshal looked Foster up and down. "He won't come after you here." It was as if he had added, *Sonny!* "Beat you up once, he won't come again for that."

And I, Foster realized, am not man enough to go after him.

"Fact is," the marshal added, "I can't think of any bait that would bring him in. Pretty quiet here. Yes sir." He put his thumbs in his galluses and looked out the window, taking credit for the quietness.

Bait, Foster thought. He went out thinking about it. For the first time in a couple of years he had an ambition—not a laudable one, but something to aim at. He was going to be the bait for Liberty Valance and, as far as he could be, the trap as well.

At the Elite Cafe he stood meekly in the doorway, hat in hand, like a man who expects and deserves to be refused anything he might ask for. Clearing his throat, he asked, "Could I work for a meal?"

The girl who was filling sugar bowls looked up and pitied him. "Why, I should think so. Mr. Anderson!" She was the girl who had walked away with Barricune, scolding him.

The proprietor came from the kitchen, and Ranse Foster repeated his question, cringing, but with a suggestion of a sneer.

"Go around back and split some wood," Anderson answered, turning back to the kitchen.

"He could just as well eat first," the waitress suggested. "I'll dish up some stew to begin with."

Ranse ate fast, as if he expected the plate to be snatched away. He knew the girl glanced at him several times, and he hated her for it. He had not counted on anyone's pitying him in his new role of sneering humility, but he knew he might as well get used to it.

When she brought his pie, she said, "If you was looking for a job . . ."

He forced himself to look at her suspiciously. "Yes?"

"You could try the Prairie Belle. I heard they needed a swamper."

Bert Barricune, riding out to the river camp for his bedroll, hardly knew the man he met there. Ranse Foster was haughty, condescending, and cringing all at once. He spoke with a faint sneer, and stood as if he expected to be kicked.

"I assumed you'd be back for your belongings," he said. "I realized that you would change your mind."

Barricune, strapping up his bedroll, looked blank. "Never changed it," he disagreed. "Doing just what I planned, I never give you my bedroll."

"Of course not, of course not," the new Ranse Foster agreed with sneering humility. "It's yours. You have every right to reclaim it."

Barricune looked at him narrowly and hoisted the bedroll to sling it up behind his saddle. "I should have left you for the buzzards," he remarked.

Foster agreed, with a smile that should have got him a fist in the teeth. "Thank you, my friend," he said with no gratitude. "Thank you for all your kindness, which I have done nothing to deserve and shall do nothing to repay."

Barricune rode off, scowling, with the memory of his good deed irritating him like lice. The new Foster followed, far behind, on foot.

Sometimes in later life Ranse Foster thought of the several men he had been through the years. He did not admire any of them very much. He was by no means ashamed of the man he finally became, except that he owed too much to other people. One man he had been when he was young, a serious student, gullible and quick-tempered. Another man had been reckless and without an aim; he went West, with two thousand dollars of his own, after a quarrel with the executor of his father's estate. That man did not last long. Liberty Valance had whipped him with a quirt and kicked him into unconsciousness, for no reason except that Liberty, meeting him and knowing him for a tenderfoot, was able to do so. That man died on the prairie. After that, there was the man who set out to be the bait that would bring Liberty Valance into Twotrees.

Ranse Foster had never hated anyone before he met Liberty Valance, but Liberty was not the last man he learned to hate. He hated the man he himself had been while he waited to meet Liberty again.

The swamper's job at the Prairie Belle was not disgraceful until Ranse Foster made it so. When he swept floors, he was so obviously contemptuous of the work and of himself for doing it that other men saw him as contemptible. He watched the customers with a curled lip as if they were beneath him. But when a poker player threw a white chip on the floor, the swamper looked at him with half-veiled hatred—and picked up the chip. They talked about him at the Prairie Belle, because he could not be ignored.

At the end of the first month, he bought a Colt .45 from a drunken cowboy who needed money worse than he needed two guns. After that, Ranse went without part of his sleep in order to walk out, seven mornings a week, to where his first camp had been and practice target shooting. And the second time he overslept from exhaustion, Joe Mosten of the Prairie Belle fired him.

"Here's your pay," Joe growled, and dropped the money on the floor.

A week passed before he got another job. He ate his meals frugally in the Elite Cafe and let himself be seen stealing scraps off plates that other diners had left. Lillian, the older of the two waitresses, yelled her disgust, but Hallie, who was young, pitied him.

"Come to the back door when it's dark," she murmured, "and I'll give you a bite. There's plenty to spare."

The second evening he went to the back door, Bert Barricune was there ahead of him. He said gently, "Hallie is my girl."

"No offense intended," Foster answered. "The young lady offered me food, and I have come to get it."

"A dog eats where it can," young Barricune drawled.

Ranse's muscles tensed and rage mounted in his throat, but he caught himself in time and shrugged. Bert said something then that scared him: "If you wanted to get talked about, it's working fine. They're talking clean over in Dunbar."

"What they do or say in Dunbar," Foster answered, "is nothing to me."

"It's where Liberty Valance hangs out," the other man said casually. "In case you care."

Ranse almost confided then, but instead said stiffly, "I do not quite appreciate your strange interest in my affairs."

Barricune pushed back his hat and scratched his head. "I don't understand it myself. But leave my girl alone."

"As charming as Miss Hallie may be," Ranse told him, "I am interested only in keeping my stomach filled."

"Then why don't you work for a living? The clerk at Dowitts' quit this afternoon."

Jake Dowitt hired him as a clerk because nobody else wanted the job.

"Read and write, do you?" Dowitt asked. "Work with figures?"

Foster drew himself up. "Sir, whatever may be said against me, I believe I may lay claim to being a scholar. That much I claim, if nothing more. I have read law."

"Maybe the job ain't good enough for you," Dowitt suggested.

Foster became humble again. "Any job is good enough for me. I will also sweep the floor."

"You will also keep up the fire in the stove," Dowitt told him. "Seven in the morning till nine at night. Got a place to live?"

"I sleep in the livery stable in return for keeping it shoveled out."

Dowitt had intended to house his clerk in a small room over the store, but he changed his mind. "Got a shed out back you can bunk in," he offered, "You'll have to clean it out first. Used to keep chickens there."

"There is one thing," Foster said. "I want two half-days off a week."

Dowitt looked over the top of his spectacles. "Now what would you do with time off? Never mind. You can have it—for less pay. I give you a discount on what you buy in the store."

The only purchase Foster made consisted of four boxes of cartridges a week.

In the store, he weighed salt pork as if it were low stuff but himself still lower, humbly measured lengths of dress goods for the women customers. He added vanity to his other unpleasantnesses and let customers discover him combing his hair admiringly before a small mirror. He let himself be seen reading a small black book, which aroused curiosity.

It was while he worked at the store that he started Twotrees' first school. Hallie was responsible for that. Handing him a plate heaped higher than other customers got at the cafe, she said gently, "You're a learned man, they say, Mr. Foster."

With Hallie he could no longer sneer or pretend humility, for Hallie was herself humble, as well as gentle and kind. He protected himself from her by not speaking unless he had to.

He answered, "I have had advantages, Miss Hallie, before fate brought me here."

"That book you read," she asked wistfully, "what's it about?"

"It was written by a man named Plato," Ranse told her stiffly. "It was written in Greek."

She brought him a cup of coffee, hesitated for a moment, and then asked, "You can read and write American, too, can't you?"

"English, Miss Hallie," he corrected. "English is our mother tongue. I am quite familiar with English."

She put her red hands on the cafe counter. "Mr. Foster," she whispered, "will you teach me to read?"

He was too startled to think of an answer she could not defeat.

"Bert wouldn't like it," he said. "You're a grown woman besides. It wouldn't look right for you to be learning to read now."

She shook her head. "I can't learn any younger." She sighed. "I always wanted to know how to read and write." She walked away toward the kitchen, and Ranse Foster was struck with an emotion he knew he could not afford. He was swept with pity. He called her back.

"Miss Hallie. Not you alone—people would talk about you. But if you brought Bert—"

"Bert can already read some. He don't care about it. But there's some kids in town." Her face was so lighted that Ranse looked away.

He still tried to escape. "Won't you be ashamed, learning with children?"

"Why, I'll be proud to learn any way at all," she said. He had three little girls, two restless little boys, and Hallie in Twotrees' first school sessions—one hour each afternoon, in Dowitt's storeroom. Dowitt did not dock his pay for the time spent, but he puzzled a great deal. So did the children's parents. The children themselves were puzzled at some of the things he read aloud, but they were patient. After all, lessons lasted only an hour.

"When you are older, you will understand this," he promised, not looking at Hallie, and then he read Shakespeare's sonnet that begins:

No longer mourn for me when I am dead
Than you shall hear the surly sullen bell

and ends:

Do not so much as my poor name rehearse,
But let your love even with my life decay,
Lest the wise world should look into your moan
And mock you with me after I am gone.

Hallie understood the warning, he knew. He read another sonnet, too:

When in disgrace with Fortune and men's eyes,
I all alone beweep my outcast state,

and carefully did not look up at her as he finished it:

For thy sweet love rememb'red such wealth brings
That then I scorn to change my state with kings.

Her earnestness in learning was distasteful to him—the anxious way she grasped a pencil and formed letters, the little gasp with which she always began to read aloud. Twice he made her cry, but she never missed a lesson.

He wished he had a teacher for his own learning, but he could not trust anyone, and so he did his lessons alone. Bert Barricune caught him at it on one of those free afternoons when Foster, on a horse from the livery stable, had ridden miles out of town to a secluded spot.

Ranse Foster had an empty gun in his hand when Barricune stepped out from behind a sandstone column and remarked, "I've seen better."

Foster whirled, and Barricune added, "I could have been somebody else—and your gun's empty."

"When I see somebody else, it won't be," Foster promised.

"If you'd asked me," Barricune mused, "I could've helped you. But you didn't want no helping. A man shouldn't be ashamed to ask somebody that knows better than him." His gun was suddenly in his hand, and five shots cracked their echoes around the skull-white sandstone pillars. Half an inch above each of five cards that Ranse had tacked to a dead tree, at the level of a man's waist, a splintered hole appeared in the wood. "Didn't want to spoil your targets," Barricune explained.

"I'm not ashamed to ask you," Foster told him angrily, "since you know so much. I shoot straight but slow. I'm asking you now."

Barricune, reloading his gun, shook his head. "It's kind of late for that. I come out to tell you that Liberty Valance is in town. He's interested in the dude that anybody can kick around—this here tenderfoot that boasts how he can read Greek."

"Well," said Foster softly. "Well, so the time has come."

"Don't figure you're riding into town with me," Bert warned. "You're coming all by yourself."

Ranse rode into town with his gun belt buckled on. Always before, he had carried it wrapped in a slicker. In town, he allowed himself the luxury of one last vanity. He went to the barbershop, neither sneering nor cringing, and said sharply, "Cut my hair. Short."

The barber was nervous, but he worked understandably fast.

"Thought you was partial to that long wavy hair of yourn," he remarked.

"I don't know why you thought so," Foster said coldly.

Out in the street again, he realized that he did not know how to go about the job. He did not know where Liberty Valance was, and he was determined not to be caught like a rat. He intended to look for Liberty.

Joe Mosten's right-hand man was lounging at the door of the Prairie Belle. He moved over to bar the way.

"Not in there, Foster," he said gently. It was the first time in months that Ranse Foster had heard another man address him respectfully. His presence was recognized—as a menace to the fixtures of the Prairie Belle.

When I die, sometime today, he thought, they won't say I was a coward. They may say I was a damn fool, but I won't care by that time.

"Where is he?" Ranse asked.

"I couldn't tell you that," the man said apologetically. "I'm young and healthy, and where he is is none of my business. Joe'd be obliged if you stay out of the bar, that's all."

Ranse looked across toward Dowitt's store. The padlock was on the door. He glanced north, toward the marshal's office.

"That's closed, too," the saloon man told him courteously. "Marshal was called out of town an hour ago."

Ranse threw back his head and laughed. The sound echoed back from the false-fronted buildings across the street. There was nobody walking in the street; there were not even any horses tied to the hitching racks.

"Send Liberty word," he ordered in the tone of one who has a right to command. "Tell him the tenderfoot wants to see him again."

The saloon man cleared his throat. "Guess it won't be necessary. That's him coming down at the end of the street, wouldn't you say?"

Ranse looked, knowing the saloon man was watching him curiously.

"I'd say it is," he agreed. "Yes, I'd say that was Liberty Valance."

"I'll be going inside now," the other man remarked apologetically. "Well, take care of yourself." He was gone without a sound.

This is the classic situation, Ranse realized. Two enemies walking to meet each other along the dusty, waiting street of a western town. What reasons other men have had, I will never know. There are so many things I have never learned! And now there is no time left.

He was an actor who knew the end of the scene but had forgotten the lines and never knew the cue for them. One of us ought to say something, he realized. I should have planned this all out in advance. But all I ever saw was the end of it.

Liberty Valance, burly and broad-shouldered, walked stiff-legged, with his elbows bent.

When he is close enough for me to see whether he is smiling, Ranse Foster thought, somebody's got to speak.

He looked into his own mind and realized, This man is afraid, this Ransome Foster. But nobody else knows it. He walks and is afraid, but he is no coward. Let them remember that. Let Hattie remember that.

Liberty Valance gave the cue. "Looking for me?" he called between his teeth. He was grinning.

Ranse was almost grateful to him; it was as if Liberty had said, The time is now!

"I owe you something," Ranse answered. "I want to pay my debt."

Liberty's hand flashed with his own. The gun in Foster's hand exploded, and so did the whole world.

Two shots to my one, he thought—his last thought for a while.

He looked up at a strange, unsteady ceiling and a face that wavered like a reflection in water. The bed beneath him swung even after he closed his eyes. Far away someone said, "Shove some more cloth in the wound. It slows the bleeding."

He knew with certain agony where the wound was—in his right shoulder. When they touched it, he heard himself cry out.

The face that wavered above him was a new one. Bert Barricune's.

"He's dead," Barricune said.

Foster answered from far away, "I am not."

Barricune said, "I didn't mean you."

Ranse turned his head away from the pain, and the face that had shivered above him before was Hallie's, white and big-eyed. She put a hesitant hand on his, and he was annoyed to see that hers was trembling.

"Are you shaking," he asked, "because there's blood on my hands?"

"No," she answered. "It's because they might have been getting cold."

He was aware then that other people were in the room; they stirred and moved aside as the doctor entered.

"Maybe you're gonna keep that arm," the doctor told him at last. "But it's never gonna be much use to you."

The trial was held three weeks after the shooting, in the hotel room where Ranse lay in bed. The charge was disturbing the peace; he pleaded guilty and was fined ten dollars.

When the others had gone, he told Bert Barricune, "There was a reward, I heard. That would pay the doctor and the hotel."

"You ain't going to collect it," Bert informed him. "It'd make you too big for your britches." Barricune sat looking at him for a moment and then remarked, "You didn't kill Liberty."

Foster frowned. "They buried him."

"Liberty fired once. You fired once and missed. I fired once, and I don't generally miss. I ain't going to collect the reward, neither. Hallie don't hold with violence."

Foster said thoughtfully, "That was all I had to be proud of."

"You faced him," Barricune said. "You went to meet him. If you got to be proud of something you can remember that. It's a fact you ain't got much else."

Ranse looked at him with narrowed eyes. "Bert, are you a friend of mine?"

Bert smiled without humor. "You know I ain't. I picked you up off the prairie, but I'd do that for the lowest scum that crawls. I wisht I hadn't."

"Then why—"

Bert looked at the toe of his boot. "Hallie likes you. I'm a friend of Hallie's. That's all I ever will be long as you're around."

Ranse said, "Then I shot Liberty Valance." That was the nearest he ever dared come to saying "Thank you." And that was when Bert Barricune started being his conscience, his Nemesis, his lifelong enemy and the man who made him great.

"Would she be happy living back East?" Foster asked. "There's money waiting for me there if I go back."

Bert answered, "What do you think?" He stood up and stretched. "You got quite a problem, ain't you? You could solve it easy by just going back alone. There ain't much a man can do here with a crippled arm."

He went out and shut the door behind him.

There is always a way out, Foster thought, if a man wants to take it. Bert had been his way out when he met Liberty on the street of Twotrees. To go home was the way out of this.

I learned to live without pride, he told himself. I could learn to forget about Hallie.

When she came, between the dinner dishes and setting the tables for supper at the cafe, he told her.

She did not cry. Sitting in the chair beside his bed, she winced and jerked one hand in protest when he said, "As soon as I can travel, I'll be going back where I came from."

She did not argue. She said only, "I wish you good luck, Ransome. Bert and me, we'll look after you long as you stay. And remember you after you're gone."

"How will you remember me?" he demanded harshly.

As his student she had been humble, but as a woman she had her pride. "Don't ask that," she said, and got up from the chair.

"Hallie, Hallie," he pleaded, "how can I stay? How can I earn a living?"

She said indignantly, as if someone else had insulted him, "Ranse Foster, I just guess you could do anything you wanted to."

"Hallie," he said gently, "sit down."

He never really wanted to be outstanding. He had two aims in life: to make Hallie happy and to keep Bert Barricune out of trouble. He defended Bert on charges ranging from drunkenness to stealing cattle, and Bert served time twice.

Ranse Foster did not want to run for judge, but Bert remarked, "I think Hallie would kind of like it if you was His Honor." Hallie was pleased but not surprised when he was elected. Ranse was surprised but not pleased.

He was not eager to run for the legislature—that was after the territory became a state—but there was Bert Barricune in the background, never urging, never advising, but watching with half-closed, bloodshot eyes. Barricune, who never amounted to anything, but never intruded, was a living, silent reminder of three debts: a hat full of water under the cottonwoods, gunfire in a dusty street, and Hallie, quietly sewing beside a lamp in the parlor. And the Fosters had four sons.

All the things the opposition said about Ranse Foster when he ran for the state legislature were true, except one. He had been a lowly swamper in a frontier saloon; he had been a dead beat, accepting handouts at the alley entrance of a cafe; he had been despicable and despised. But the accusation that lost him the election was false. He had not killed Liberty Valance. He never served in the state legislature.

When there was talk of his running for governor, he refused. Handy Strong, who knew politics, tried to persuade him.

"That shooting, we'll get around that. 'The Honorable Ransome Foster walked down a street in broad daylight to meet an enemy of society. He shot him down in a fair fight, of necessity, the way you'd shoot a mad dog—but Liberty Valance could shoot back, and he did. Ranse Foster carries the mark of that encounter today in a crippled right arm. He is still paying the price for protecting law-abiding citizens. And he was the first teacher west of Rosy Buttes. He served without pay.' You've come a long way, Ranse, and you're going further."

"A long way," Foster agreed, "for a man who never wanted to go anywhere. I don't want to be governor."

When Handy had gone, Bert Barricune sagged in, unwashed, unshaven. He sat down stiffly. At the age of fifty, he was an old man, an unwanted relic of the frontier that was gone, a legacy to more civilized times that had no place for him. He filled his pipe deliberately. After a while he remarked, "The other side is gonna say you ain't fitten to be governor. Because your wife ain't fancy enough. They're gonna say Hallie didn't even learn to read till she was growed up."

Ranse was on his feet, white with fury. "Then I'm going to win this election if it kills me."

"I don't reckon it'll kill you," Bert drawled. "Liberty Valance couldn't."

"I could have got rid of the weight of that affair long ago," Ranse reminded him, "by telling the truth."

"You could yet," Bert answered. "Why don't you?"

Ranse said bitterly, "Because I owe you too much. . . . I don't think Hallie wants to be the governor's lady. She's shy."

"Hallie don't never want nothing for herself. She wants things for you. The way I feel, I wouldn't mourn at your funeral. But what Hallie wants, I'm gonna try to see she gets."

"So am I," Ranse promised grimly.

"Then I don't mind telling you," Bert admitted, "that it was me reminded the opposition to dig up that matter of how she couldn't read."

As the Senator and his wife rode out to the airport after old Bert Barricune's barren funeral, Hallie sighed. "Bert never had much of anything. I guess he never wanted much."

He wanted you to be happy, Ranse Foster thought, and he did the best he knew how.

"I wonder where those prickly-pear blossoms came from," he mused.

Hallie glanced up at him, smiling. "From me," she said.

Discussion Questions

1. After identifying the myths and Western story conventions that Johnson contradicts in this story, speculate about her purpose in doing so.
2. Compare and contrast the characters of Bert Barricune and Ransome Foster, including the roles they represent among Western "types."
3. Explain the role of Hallie in helping to "settle" the West. Why does she choose Ransome over Bert?

Fig. 5.3 James Earle Fraser, *The End of the Trail* (1915). Donald C. and Elizabeth M. Dickinson Research Center, National Cowboy and Western Heritage Museum, Oklahoma City, OK.

THE WESTERN

—<♦>—

BY THOMAS SCHATZ
(1948–)

"This is the West, sir.
When the legend becomes fact, print the legend."
—Newspaper editor in *The Man Who Shot Liberty Valance*

WESTERN AS GENRE

The Western is without question the richest and most enduring genre of Hollywood's repertoire. Its concise heroic story and elemental visual appeal render it the most flexible of narrative formulas, and its life span has been as long and varied as Hollywood's own. In fact, the Western genre and the American cinema evolved concurrently, generating the basic framework for Hollywood's studio production system. We might look to Edwin S. Porter's *The Great Train Robbery* in 1903 as the birth not only of the movie Western but of the commercial narrative film in America; and to Thomas Ince's mass production of William S. Hart horse operas during the teens as the prototype for the studio system.

The origins of the Western formula predated the cinema, of course. Its genealogy encompassed colonial folk music, Indian captivity tales, James Fenimore Cooper's *Leather-Stocking Tales,* nineteenth-century pulp romances, and a variety of other cultural forms. These earlier forms began to develop the story of the American West as popular mythology, sacrificing historical accuracy for the opportunity to examine the values, attitudes, and ideals associated with westward expansion and the taming and civilizing of the West. Not until its immortalization on film, however, did the Western genre certify its mythic credentials. The significance and impact of the Western as America's foundation ritual have been articulated most clearly and effectively in the cinema—the medium of twentieth-century technology and urbanization. And it was also in the cinema that the Western could reach a mass audience which actively participated in the gradual refinement and evolution of its narrative formula.

THE EARLY FILMS

As America's first popular and industrial mass art form, the commercial cinema assumed a privileged but paradoxical function in its development of the Western myth. As a narrative mass medium, the cinema provided an ideal vehicle for disseminating the Western formula to the culture at large; as a commercial industry, it embodied those very socioeconomic and technological values which the Western anticipated in tracing the steady progression of American civilization. The height of the Western's popularity—from the late 1930s through the '50s—spanned an era when the American West and its traditional values were being threatened and displaced by the Modern Age. Twentieth-century technology and industry, the Depression with its Dust Bowl and flight to the cities, the ensuing World War and the birth of atomic power, the Cold War and the Korean conflict—these and other historical factors overwhelmed America's "Old West" and at the same time enhanced its mythic status. In constructing and gradually formalizing the actions and attitudes from the past on a wide screen, the Western genre created a mythical reality more significant and pervasive—and perhaps in some ways more "real"—than the historical West itself.

As cultural and historical documents, the earlier silent Westerns differ from the later Westerns. In fact, these earlier films have a unique and somewhat paradoxical position: Although they were made on the virtual threshold of the Modern Age, they also came at a time when westward expansion was winding down. Certain early cowboy heroes like "Bronco Billy" Anderson and William S. Hart did lay the groundwork for the heroic and stylized mythology of movie Westerns. But many other films, like *The Covered Wagon* (1923) and *The Iron Horse* (1924), were really historical dramas, depicting as accurately as possible the actuality of westward expansion. (In fact, *The Great Train Robbery* related events that had occurred only a few years previously and as such was something of a turn-of-the-century gangster film.) But eventually, the cumulative effects of Western storytelling in the face of contemporary civilization's steady encroachment served to subordinate the genre's historical function to its mythical one. In other words, efforts to document the historical West on film steadily gave way to the impulse to exploit the past as a means of examining the values and attitudes of contemporary America.

It's important to note in this context that during the Depression, as Hollywood moved into the sound era, the historical epics, which had dominated mainstream Western film production in the teens and '20s, faded from the screen, and the genre survived primarily in the form of low-budget "B" productions. These films rounded out the newly introduced double features and also served to provide John Wayne, who made dozens of these "B" Westerns, with considerable acting experience. Occasional Westerns like *The Virginian* (1929), *Cimarron* (1930), and *The Plainsman* (1936) attracted the attention of mass audiences, but both the technical restrictions of early "talkies" and Hollywood's preoccupation during the '30s with contemporary urban themes effectively pushed the Western out of mainstream production.

The Western returned to widespread popularity in the late 1930s. The growing historical distance from the actual West along with developments in film technology—especially a quieter, more mobile camera and more sophisticated sound recording techniques—gave the genre new life. The tendency today is to laud John Ford's *Stagecoach* in 1939 for regenerating the Western movie formula, although Ford's film was only one of several popular mainstream Westerns produced in 1939 and 1940, among them *Jesse James, Dodge City, Destry Rides Again, Union Pacific, Frontier Marshal* (all 1939), *Sante Fe Trail, Virginia City, The Westerner, The Return of Frank James, Arizona,* and *When the Daltons Rode* (1940). The following war years proved to be a watershed period for the genre and for Hollywood filmmaking in general—but by then the Western's basic structural design was well established and its gradual refinement already begun.

THE LANDSCAPE OF THE WEST

When we step back to get a broader picture, we notice that the Western depicts a world of precarious balance in which the forces of civilization and savagery are locked in a struggle for supremacy. As America's foundation ritual, the Western projects a formalized vision of the nation's infinite possibilities and limitless vistas, thus serving to "naturalize" the policies of westward expansion and Manifest Destiny. It is interesting in this regard that we as a culture have found the story of the settlement of the "New World" beyond the Alleghenies and the Mississippi even more compelling than the development of the colonies or the Revolutionary War itself. Ironically, the single most evocative location for Western filmmaking and perhaps the genre's most familiar icon (after the image of John Wayne) is Arizona's Monument Valley, where awesome stone formations reach up to the gods but the desolate soil around them is scarcely suitable for the rural–agricultural bounty which provided America's socioeconomic foundation. The fact is, of course, that Hollywood's version of the Old West has as little to do with agriculture—although it has much to do with rural values—as it does with history. The landscape with its broad expanses and isolated communities was transformed on celluloid into a familiar iconographic arena where civilized met savage in an interminable mythic contest.

The Western's essential conflict between civilization and savagery is expressed in a variety of oppositions: East versus West, garden versus desert, America versus Europe, social order versus anarchy, individual versus community, town versus wilderness, cowboy versus Indian, schoolmarm versus dancehall girl, and so on. Its historical period of reference is the years following the Civil War and reaching into the early twentieth century, when the western United States, that precivilized locale, was establishing codes of law and order as a basis for contemporary social conditions. The opening of virtually any Western "cues" us in to these oppositions: cowboys pausing on a hillside during a cattle drive to gaze at the isolated community in the distance (*My Darling Clementine*, 1946); a lone cowboy, who after riding into a pastoral valley, is accused by an anxious homesteader of gunslinging for land-hungry local ranchers (*Shane*, 1953); a rider on a mountainside watching railroad workers blast a tunnel above him and outlaws rob a stagecoach below (*Johnny Guitar*, 1954); the distant cry of a locomotive whistle and a shot of a black, serpentine machine winding toward us through the open plains as the steam from its engine fills the screen (*The Man Who Shot Liberty Valance*, 1962).

JOHN FORD'S *STAGECOACH*

Even as early as Ford's 1939 film, *Stagecoach*, these oppositions are presented concisely and effectively. Ford's film marks the debut of Monument Valley in the Western genre, a fitting arena for the most engaging and thematically complex of all prewar Westerns.

The film opens with a shot of Monument Valley, framed typically beneath a sky which takes up most of the screen. Eventually we hear two riders approaching from across the desert and then see them coming toward us. As the riders near the camera, Ford cuts from this vast, panoramic scene to the exterior of a cavalry camp, and the horizon is suddenly cluttered with tents, flagstaffs, and soldiers. The riders gallop into the camp, dismount, and rush into the post. In the next shot, a group of uniformed men huddle around a telegraph machine. Just before the lines go dead, the telegraph emits a single coded word: "Geronimo."

This sequence not only sets the thematic and visual tone for Ford's film with economy of action and in striking visual terms, but also reflects the basic cultural and physical conflicts which traditionally have characterized the Western form. In Hollywood's version the West is a vast wilderness dotted with occasional oases—frontier towns, cavalry posts, isolated campsites, and so forth—which are linked with one another and with the civilized East by the railroad, the stagecoach, the telegraph: society's tentacles of progress. Each oasis is a virtual society in microcosm, plagued by conflicts both with the external, threatening wilderness and also with the anarchic or socially corrupt members of its own community. Ford's stagecoach, for example, is journeying to Lordsburg (what better name for an oasis of order in a vast wasteland?) through hostile Indian country. Its passengers must contend not only with Indian attacks but also with the conflicts which divide the group itself. The stagecoach carries a righteous sheriff, a cowardly driver, an alcoholic doctor, an embezzling bank executive, a whiskey drummer, a gold-hearted prostitute, a genteel gambler, an Eastern-bred lady, and the hero, an escaped convict bent upon avenging his brother's murder and, simultaneously, his own wrongful imprisonment.

In this film, as in the Western generally, the conflicts within the community reflect and intensify those between the community and its savage surroundings. The dramatic intensity in *Stagecoach* only marginally relates to the disposition of the hero, whose antisocial status (as a convict) is not basic to his character but results from society's lack of effective order and justice. Wayne portrays the Ringo Kid as a naïve, moral man of the earth who takes upon himself the task of righting that social and moral imbalance. He is also a living manifestation of the Western's basic conflicts. Like the sheriff who bends the law to suit the situation, the banker who steals from his own bank, the kindly whore, or the timid moralizer who sells whiskey, Ringo must find his own way through an environment of contrary and ambiguous demands.

Ford's orchestration of the community's complex, contradictory values renders *Stagecoach* a truly distinctive film, setting it apart both dramatically and thematically from earlier Westerns. Within a simplistic cavalry-to-the-rescue and shoot-out-on-Main-Street formula, Ford's constellation of social outcasts represents a range of social issues from alcoholism to white-collar crime to individual self-reliance. Through these characters Ford fleshes out values and contradictions basic to contemporary human existence.

The appeal of the stagecoach's passengers derives from their ambiguous social status. Often they are on the periphery of the community and some-how at odds with its value system. Perhaps the most significant conflict in the Western is the community's demand for order through cooperation and compromise versus the physical environment's demand for rugged individ-ualism coupled with a survival-of-the-fittest mentality. In *Stagecoach*, each of the three central figures—Ringo, Doc Boone (Thomas Mitchell), and Dallas (Claire Trevor)—is an outcast who has violated society's precepts in order to survive: Ringo is an accused murderer and escaped convict sworn to take the law into his own hands, while Doc Boone has turned to alcohol and Dallas to prostitution to survive on the frontier.

We are introduced to Dallas and Doc Boone as they are being driven out of town by the Ladies' Law and Order League, a group of puritanical, civic-minded women dedicated to upholding community standards. This scene is played for both comic and dramatic effect, but it does establish conformity and Victorian moralizing as elements of a well-ordered society. This initial view of the community's repressive and depersonalizing demands eventu-ally is qualified by the film's resolution, however. Ringo and Dallas finally are allowed by the sheriff to flee to Ringo's ranch across the border. As the two ride away to begin a new life together, the camera lingers on Doc Boone, ever the philosopher, who muses, "Well, they're saved from the blessings of civilization." Beneath his veneer of cynicism, however, is an optimistic vision: the uncivilized outlaw-hero and a woman practicing society's oldest profession have been united and go off to seek the promise of the American West's new world.

THE CHANGING VISION OF THE WEST

The gradual fading of this optimistic vision, more than anything else, char-acterizes the evolution of the Western genre. As the formula was refined through repetition, both the frontier community and its moralistic standard-bearers are depicted in increasingly complex, ambiguous, and unflattering terms. The Western hero, in his physical allegiance to the environment and his moral commitment to civilization, embodies this ambiguity. As such he tends to generate conflict through his very existence. He is a man of action and of few words, with an unspoken code of honor that commits him to the vulnerable Western community and at the same time motivates him to remain distinctly apart from it. As the genre develops, the Westerner's role as promoter of civilization seems to become almost coincidental. Eventually, his moral code emerges as an end in itself.

The stability of the Westerner's character—his "style," as it were—doesn't really evolve with the genre. Instead, it is gradually redefined by the community he protects. Both the hero and the community establish their values and world view through their relationship with the savage milieu, but as the community becomes more civilized and thus more institutionalized, capitalistic, and corrupt, it gradually loses touch with the natural world from which it sprang. Because the Westerner exists on the periphery of both the community and the wilderness, he never loses touch with either world. His mediating function between them becomes increasingly complex and demanding as the society becomes more insulated and self-serving.

Actually, the image of the classic Westerner who mediates the natural and cultural environments while remaining distinct from each does not emerge as a mainstream convention until the mid-'40s. In earlier films, the narrative conflicts were usually resolved with the suggestion that the Westerner might settle down within the community which his inclination toward violence and gunplay has enabled him to protect. The promise of marriage between Ringo and Dallas is indicative of this tendency, although their shared outlaw status and their eventual flight to Mexico undercut any simplistic reading of the film's prosocial resolution. A typical example of this tendency is William Wyler's 1940 film, *The Westerner*. In this film, the hero, Cole Hardin (Gary Cooper), mediates a violent confrontation between anarchic cattlemen and defenseless, idealistic homesteaders. These distinct communities are depicted in two narrative movements. The first shows Hardin's arrival and near lynching in a lawless cattle town run by the outrageous Judge Roy Bean (Walter Brennan), the self-appointed "law west of the Pecos." The second follows the hero's gradual assimilation into the community of homesteaders and his courtship of the farmer's daughter, Jane Ellen (Doris Davenport).

Bean's and Jane Ellen's worlds are locked in the familiar cattleman-homesteader struggle for control of the land, and Hardin is the only character who can function effectively in both worlds. Thus Wyler's film (from Jo Swerling's script) develops the classic configuration of the anarchic world of Male Savagery pitted against the civilized world of Woman and Home. The heroic Westerner, again, is poised between the two. Throughout the first half of the film, in which the competing ideologies are established, this configuration remains in perfect balance. Eventually, however, Hardin is won over by the woman-domesticator and turns against Bean, throwing off the film's narrative equilibrium. After Hardin prevails against Bean in a climactic gunfight, the Westerner is able to settle down with Jane Ellen in "the promised land."

Nothing could be more damaging to the hero's image, of course. He has compromised his self-styled, renegade world view by acquiescing to civilization's emasculating and depersonalizing demands. The earlier silent Westerns and their later low-budget counterparts had understood the logic of sending the Westerner "into the sunset" after the requisite showdown, thereby sustaining the genre's prosocial function while reaffirming the hero's essential individuality. Perhaps it was John Ford's experience with silent Westerns that motivated him to temper the marital and communal values of *Stagecoach*'s resolution, or perhaps it was his intuitive understanding of what made the Western genre work. But certainly the ambiguous ending of Ford's film renders it decidedly more effective than most of the Westerns of its day. It was not actually until World War II and the ensuing post-war productions, though, that the Western hero and his particular role within the Western milieu would be radically reconsidered along the lines previously established in *Stagecoach*.

*   *   *

SHANE: THE INITIATE-HERO AND THE INTEGRATION OF OPPOSITES

This motif is used most effectively, perhaps, in *Shane*. The story is filtered through the consciousness of a young boy (Brandon De Wilde as Joey Starrett), and much of the film's clarity of vision and idealized simplicity derives from his naïve perspective. The actions of the principal characters, the setting of a lush green valley, even the distant Rocky Mountains, attain a dreamlike quality under George Stevens' direction and Loyal Grigg's cinematography.

The film opens with Shane (Alan Ladd) riding into the pastoral valley where ranchers and homesteaders are feuding. (As in *The Westerner*, "open range" and fenced-in farmland manifest the genre's nature/culture opposition.) Shane is a man with a mysterious past who hangs up his guns to become a farm laborer for Joe Starrett (Van Heflin), the spokesman for the homesteaders in their conflict with the villainous Ryker brothers.

The film is a virtual ballet of oppositions, all perceived from Joey's viewpoint. These oppositions become a series of options for him—and us—that he must negotiate in order to attain social maturity. The following diagram summarizes these oppositions.

SHANE

Joe Starrett	Wilson
Family	Ryker brothers
Homesteaders	Ranchers
Domestication	Male isolation
Woman's world	Man's world
Fence	Open range
Crops, sheep	Cattle
Farm tools	Guns
Social law	Primitive law
Equality	Survival of the fittest
Future	Past

Not only does this diagram indicate the elaborate *doubling* in the narrative, but it also points up the hero's mediation of both the rancher-homesteader conflict and the boy's confused notions of his ideal father figure. Although Starrett is the bravest and most capable of the homesteaders—and the only one respected and feared by the ranchers—he is basically a farmer of rural sensibilities and simple values. Starrett is clearly no match for Shane in either Joey's or his wife's (Jean Arthur) eyes, although the family proves strong enough to withstand the interloper's influence. By the end of the film, Marion's attraction to Shane complements her son's, although her family and her role as mother-domesticator remain her first concerns. In accord with her son's (and the genre's) sexual naiveté, the thought of Shane's and Marion's romantic entanglement is only a frustrating impossibility. Among Joey's parting cries to Shane as he rides away at the film's end is, "Mother wants you."

This sexual-familial conflict is, however, tangential to the film's central opposition between fenced land and open range. Nevertheless, it does reaffirm Shane's commitment to the values of home and family rather than those of power and capital. During the course of the film, Shane offers his services to the other farmers, but he is never really accepted because of his past and his stoic, detached manner. The cattlemen, who are generally seen drinking in the local saloon or else out harassing "sodbusters," show more respect for Shane than do the farmers, and attempt to recruit him at higher pay. Shane refuses, so the Rykers bring in Wilson (Jack Palance), a *doppelganger* from Shane's gunfighting past. Here, as in many genre films involving a violent, nomadic hero, the only real difference between the protagonist (Shane) and his antagonistic double (Wilson) has to do with their respective attitudes about social order and the value of human life.

The film ends with Shane knocking Starrett out with his pistol after a fierce fist-fight. He knows he must face Wilson and the Rykers alone. Joey follows Shane to town to watch the confrontation in the deserted saloon. Shane prevails against the men but is wounded, and he rides off into the mountains as Joey's calls echo after him. Those mountains, which like Shane's mysterious, violent past had remained in the background throughout the film, emerge now as his Olympus, as the Westerner's mythic realm beyond the reality of dirt farms and ramshackle towns.

But while Shane's heroic stature is affirmed, there is still a shade of ambiguity which tempers that stature. Just before the gunfight in the darkened saloon, Shane suggests to Ryker that "his days are numbered." "What about you, gunfighter?" asks Ryker. "The difference is, I know it," replies Shane, who then turns to the black-clad Wilson. The two simply stare at one another before the exchange of ritual dialogue that will initiate the gunfight. As in an earlier scene when the two had met and silently circled each other, a mutual understanding and respect is implicit in the look they exchange in addition to the promise of a violent, uncompromising confrontation. After the gunfight Shane tells Joey that "There's no living with the killing," but it's clear enough from the relationship established between Shane and Wilson that there's no living without it either. . . . These men know their fate all too well. They purposefully end their days in a fashion that they could control and that we in the audience come to expect.

As these various examples indicate, the Westerner is motivated to further the cause of civilization by his own personal code of honor, which seems to be existentially derived. Often this code leads him to an act of vengeance. The vengeful hero is different from the classic Westerner in that his past—either his entire past or an isolated incident—is of immediate concern and provides him with a clear sense of mission. But he does share with the classic hero his characteristic function: he is an isolated, psychologically static man of personal integrity who acts because society is too weak to do so. And it is these actions that finally enforce social order but necessitate his departure from the community he has saved. In *Stagecoach*, *Winchester 73* (1950), *The Searchers* (1956), *One-Eyed Jacks* (1961), *Nevada Smith* (1966), and countless other revenge Westerns, the hero rids society of a menace, but in so doing, he reaffirms his own basic incompatibility with the community's values.

Occasionally the hero will accept a job as lawman to carry out his vengeance, as in *Dodge City* and *My Darling Clementine*, but once he has satisfied his personal drives, he leaves the community to fend for itself. In those films, it is assumed that the hero's elimination of the power-hungry town boss and his henchmen has purified the community and given it lasting social order. The destruction of the Clantons at the O.K. Corral by the Earp brothers and Doc Holliday in *My Darling Clementine* serves both to avenge the murder of James Earp and also to project an image of an orderly Tombstone into the indefinite future. As Wyatt Earp and his brother (Henry Fonda and Ward Bond) ride off across Monument Valley after their gunfight, the new schoolmarm from the East waves to them, framed in long-shot against the infinite expanse of desert and sky. With this image Ford captures and freezes forever—like the English poet John Keats' ageless figures on a Grecian urn—the Western's principal characters and their contradictory yet complementary ideals.

THE CHANGING HERO: THE "PSYCHOLOGICAL" AND "PROFESSIONAL" WESTERNS

As an element of our national mythology, the Western represents American culture, explaining its present in terms of its past and virtually redefining the past to accommodate the present. The image of the Western community in Hollywood movies tends to reflect our own beliefs and preoccupations, and the Western's evolution as a genre results both from the continual reworking of its own rules of construction and expression and also from the changing beliefs and attitudes of contemporary American society.

As American audiences after World War II became saturated with the classic Western formula and also more hardbitten about sociopolitical realities, the image of the Western community changed accordingly, redefining the hero's motivation and his sense of mission. Hence the "psychological" Westerns of the late 1940s and the 1950s that traced the Westerner's neuroses (and eventual psychoses) stemming from his growing incompatibility with civilization as well as the cumulative weight of society's unreasonable expectations.

One of the more notable examples of this development is Fred Zinneman's *High Noon*, in which a local lawman (Gary Cooper) awaits the arrival of outlaws bent on avenging his having sent their leader to prison. The wait for the arrival of the outlaws provides the dramatic tension in the film, which is heightened by the fact that the townspeople ignore or evade Cooper's appeals for assistance. After he and his Quaker wife (Grace Kelly), a woman committed to nonviolence for religious reasons, finally confront and dispose of the outlaws, Cooper throws his badge into the dirt and leaves the community to fend for itself.

Howard Hawks' *Rio Bravo* (1958), supposedly a belated answer to Zinneman's "knee-jerk liberalism," describes a similar situation in an even more claustrophobic and helpless community. From Hawks' typically machismo perspective, however, the local lawman (John Wayne, with deputies Dean Martin, Walter Brennan, and Ricky Nelson) continually rejects offers of aid from the frightened citizenry, insisting, "This is no job for amateurs." Wayne and his cohorts prevail, and thus both the heroes and the community emerge with integrity intact. While *High Noon* and *Rio Bravo* each project substantially different views of the community and its redeemer-hero, both underscore the hero's incompatibility with that community. Ultimately, it is the hero's professional integrity and sense of responsibility to his job as lawman which induce him to act as an agent of social order.

The "professional" Western was, in fact, Hollywood's own answer to the psychological Western, much as Hawks' film had answered Zinneman's. In general, the psychological Western poses the question: how can the morally upright, socially autonomous Westerner continue to defend a repressive, institutionalized, cowardly, and thankless community without going crazy? The professional Western answers this question in one of two ways. The Westerner either works for pay and sells his special talents to the community that must evaluate his work on its own terms or else he becomes an outlaw.

The prospect of the classic, morally upright Westerner turning from his self-styled code of honor is closely related to the changing view of society in the Western. As the community's notion of law and order progressively squeezes out those rugged individualists who made such order possible, the Westerners turn to each other and to the outlaws they had previously opposed. At this point, the "honor among thieves" that the Westerner can find with other lawless types is preferable to buckling under to the community's emasculating demands.

Consequently, many recent Westerns incorporate a group that is led by an aging but still charismatic hero figure and whose demand of payment, either as professional killers or as outlaws, undercuts the classic Westerner's moral code. Thus the professional Westerns of the past two decades, most notably *Rio Bravo, The Magnificent Seven, The Professionals, El Dorado, The Wild Bunch, True Grit, Butch Cassidy and the Sundance Kid, The Cowboys, The Great Northfield Minnesota Raid, The Culpepper Cattle Company,* and *The Missouri Breaks.*

Gone in these films is the isolated, heroic cowboy with no visible means of support whose moral vision and spiritual values set him apart from—and essentially above—the community he defends. Now he is cynical, self-conscious, and even "incorporated"; these traits render him increasingly unheroic, more like one of us. Still, despite his gradual descent from heroic demigod (superior in many ways to nature as well as to other men) in early Westerns to a psychologically more complex and generally more sympathetic character, the Westerner does maintain distinct traces of his isolated sense of honor. He strikes a romantic pose even in the face of extinction.

Sam Peckinpah's *The Wild Bunch* (1969), for example, describes the exploits of an outlaw collective (William Holden, Ernest Borgnine, Warren Oates, Edmund O'Brien, Ben Johnson, et al.) in their sustained rampage through the American Southwest and in Mexico just before the outbreak of World War I. Whereas the outlaw collective violates with equal disregard the laws of God, man, and nature, the real villain of the piece is progress. Big business, typified by the banks and the railroad, force the Bunch out of the United States and into a confrontation with a corrupt Mexican bandit army. When one of their own group is captured and tortured by the Mexican bandits (whose leader has given up his horse for an automobile and is doing business with German warmongers), the Bunch undertakes a final, suicidal act of heroism—something that is very much in America's "national interest." In one of the most spectacular showdowns ever filmed, the Wild Bunch and the bandit army destroy each other in a quick-cut, slow-motion dream of blood and death.

This paradoxical resolution is in much the same vein as those in *The Magnificent Seven* and *Butch Cassidy*. In both of these films, although outlaw collectives are forced by time and civilization to practice their trade outside the United States, they retain a certain allegiance to their heroic code with its basis in American ideology. And in all three films, the outlaw collective regenerates the sense of group mission—one similar to that which had been subdued by advancing civilization on the American frontier. This sense of mission still determines the behavior and attitude of the collective, and as such it almost becomes an end in itself: the heroic mediator's social function emerges as a self-indulgent, formalized ritual.

Sam Peckinpah has understood and articulated, perhaps better than any Western filmmaker since John Ford, the concept of the Westerner who has outlived his role and his milieu. Particularly in *Ride the High Country* (1962), *Major Dundee* (1964), *The Wild Bunch* (1969), and *The Ballad of Cable Hogue* (1970), Peckinpah evokes a strong sense of irony and nostalgia in his presentation of a cast of aging heroic misfits. His men are hopelessly—and even tragically—at odds with the inexorable flow of history. The most evocative of these films is *Ride the High Country,* made in the same year as Ford's *The Man Who Shot Liberty Valance.* (Both films express regret over the passing of the Old West and its values.) The film stars Randolph Scott and Joel McCrae, two familiar cowboys from countless '40s and '50s

Westerns, who are now reduced to tending bar and sharpshooting in a Wild West show. The opening sequence in *Ride the High Country* immediately establishes the hero's displacement in the new West and shows what he must do to contend with it. McCrae (as Steven Judd) arrives in town having given up his bartending job to guard a mine shipment, happy to return to the type of work which had sustained him through his more productive years. The town itself is modern, with automobiles, policemen, and even a Wild West show, where Judd finds his former deputy, Gil Westrum (Randolph Scott), reduced to a sideshow attraction. This opening sequence not only pits the old West against the new, but it also sets up an opposition between McCrae/Judd and Scott/Westrum. The former has retained his idealistic desire to continue as an agent of social order; the latter manifests a pragmatic willingness to make a profit off his former lawman status. Judd recruits Westrum to help him with the mine shipment, although Westrum agrees only because he assumes he'll eventually grab it for himself. Judd's reactionary idealism and Westrum's self-serving adaptability provide the central conflict throughout the film. This split is intensified by the presence of an initiate-hero (Ron Starr as Heck Longtree) who must decide between the two opposing world views. The initiate ultimately rejects Westrum's scheme to rob the shipment, and Westrum himself finally elects to join Judd and Longtree in a climactic showdown with another band of outlaws. The flexible, practical Westrum and the initiate Longtree survive the gunfight, but Judd falls, mortally wounded.

The film's closing shot is an over-the-shoulder, point-of-view shot from ground level, where we gaze with the dying Judd at the "high country" in the distance. As in the closing sequence in *Shane* (although this film is much bleaker in its outlook), the Westerner's status is reaffirmed in mythic proportions. However, instead of riding into the mountains as Shane had done, into that timeless terrain beyond the reach of civilization, Judd must be satisfied with only a dying glimpse of them.

But not even Peckinpah's jaded vision can match that of Robert Altman's remarkable 1972 Western, *McCabe and Mrs. Miller*. In Altman's film, the reluctant hero miraculously prevails against three killers only to freeze to death as he lies wounded and drifting snow covers him. Actually, the plot in Altman's film is somewhat similar to that in *Shane*. A charismatic figure with a violent but shadowy past makes his presence felt in a community and finally confronts single-handedly those power-hungry forces seeking control of the town.

The two films have little in common otherwise. Whereas *Shane* rode into a lush, pastoral valley wearing fringed buckskins and a six-gun, McCabe (Warren Beatty) rides into the dismal, rain-drenched town of Presbyterian Church in a suit and a derby and carrying a concealed derringer. Rather than working the land, McCabe provides the mining community with its first whorehouse. In *McCabe*, it is not the land which must be protected, but rather the business which has become the lifeblood of that particular community: McCabe's brothel. Marion Starrett's pure woman-domesticator is countered here by Constance Miller (Julie Christie), an experienced madam and prostitute (sex is simply a commodity of exchange), who expands McCabe's meager enterprise into the realm of big business.

The final showdown is precipitated when McCabe refuses to sell out his share of the "house" to an unseen corporation. As McCabe conducts an elaborate, cat-and-mouse gun battle through the streets with three hired killers sent by the corporation, the other townspeople are busy fighting a fire in the community's half-built church. In an ironic counterpoint to the sunlit communal celebration on the church foundation in Ford's *My Darling Clementine* (1946), here the townsfolk work together to save a church which few of them would ever consider attending. In reality, the church in *McCabe* is just an empty shell, a façade as hollow as the values and the future of the community itself. McCabe's genuine act of heroism goes unnoticed as the townspeople work futilely to rescue a formal edifice without spiritual substance. Against his own better judgment, and against his beloved Mrs. Miller's protestations, McCabe finally joins those countless other Western heroes, reaffirming his own individual identity, protecting his own homestead and reinforcing the Western's essential theme that "a man's gotta do what he's gotta do."

* * *

JOHN FORD AND THE EVOLUTION OF THE WESTERN

. . . . With each successive Western after *Stagecoach*, Ford's attitude toward the classic Western formula became increasingly self-conscious, both stylistically and thematically. Gradually, he shifted his cinematic and narrative emphasis from the "subject matter" of the genre to its narrative form and cultural function. The question of influence is always difficult, even when considering so inventive a filmmaker working within so conventional a form. When we examine Ford's contributions to the genre, however, it seems fairly simple to determine that he was among the most (if not the most) influential of Western film directors. Further, the evolution of Ford's treatment of the genre is indicative of its overall historical development. In order to examine this development in some detail, we will compare and contrast four Ford Westerns produced in consecutive decades, all of which were widely popular when they were released and are now considered among Hollywood's greatest Westerns: *Stagecoach* (1939), *My Darling Clementine* (1946), *The Searchers* (1956), and *The Man Who Shot Liberty Valance* (1962).

STAGECOACH AS AN ADVANCE IN THE GENRE

As I have already discussed, *Stagecoach* involves a straightforward narrative of classic Western concerns: the legendary, psychologically uncomplicated and stable hero (John Wayne as the Ringo Kid) helps protect the occupants of a stage from an Indian attack so that he can reach Lordsburg and avenge his brother's murder. After single-handedly ridding the town of the menacing Plummer brothers, Ringo leaves with Dallas to ride into the sunset and the promise of a new life beyond the limitless horizon.

Stagecoach, often criticized as being cliched or conventional, actually represented a considerable advance in imagery and thematic complexity over previous and then-current Westerns—despite its essentially one-dimensional characters, its cavalry-to-the-rescue climax, and its "escape hatch" solution to Ringo's outlaw status. The film is visually unprecedented, both in its depiction of Monument Valley as the archetypal Western milieu and also in Ford's sensitive, controlled camerawork. Ford neatly balances the vast expanse of the valley against the enclosed, socially defined space of the stagecoach, the way stations, and other interior locations. He establishes a visual opposition that intensifies the hero's divided self (uncivilized renegade versus agent of social order) and the genre's essential nature/culture opposition.

Stagecoach also anticipates Ford's narrative and visual concern for community ritual, which became more pronounced in his later Westerns. As Ford well understood, these rituals—dances, weddings, funerals, and in this case, a childbirth—are virtually punctuation marks of the genre itself. They formally articulate and define the community and its collective values.

Ford establishes both his characters and his dominant themes by tracing the travelers' reactions to a variety of familiar events that emphasize many of society's values: the "democratic" balloting to decide whether to press on in the face of Indian attacks; a group meal in which seating arrangements and body language indicate the social status and attitudes of the participants; the unexpected birth of a baby to one of the travelers. The childbirth sequence is especially significant, complicating the journey's progress but also positing the savage wilderness as a potential utopia for future generations. It is during this crisis that Ringo's fellow renegades, Doc Boone and Dallas, verify their heroic credentials. They add a moral and humanistic dimension to the stagecoach's world in microcosm. The other passengers may represent more traditional roles of a civilized society, but these two transcend such a civilization characterized by its concern for social status and material wealth.

After Boone sobers up and successfully delivers the baby, Dallas cares for the mother and child through the night. As she shows the newborn child to the group, she and Ringo form a silent union (in a telling exchange of close-ups) that is realized in their later embrace. With this silent exchange, Ford isolates Ringo, Dallas, and the child as a veritable Holy Family of the frontier, and the motif is strengthened by the couple's final flight into the desert at film's end. It is thus the family, the nuclear social unit, that brings together Westerner and Woman and offers the promise of an ideal frontier community.

CLEMENTINE: A UTOPIAN WESTERN

My Darling Clementine (1946), like *Stagecoach,* closes with a figurative embrace between Westerner and Woman, but in that later film the redeemer-hero rides off alone. There is only a vague suggestion that he will return to Clementine (Cathy Downs) and the community. In fact, *Clementine* is much less naïve than *Stagecoach* in its recognition of the hero's basic inability to reconcile his individual and social roles. Still, it might well be considered more naïve in its idealized portrayal of Wyatt Earp (Henry Fonda) as the stoic, self-reliant redeemer.

Ringo's character was essentially one-dimensional and static, but Ringo's outlaw status (although unjustified) gave an ambiguous edge to his prosocial, redemptive actions. *Clementine's* hero and community, on the other hand, are depicted in the most positive light the Arizona sun could produce, and in that sense it is the more overtly mythic, classical Western of the two. The elements Ford had introduced in *Stagecoach*—sound, iconography (Monument Valley and John Wayne), and the orchestration of themes, values, and characters—solidify in *Clementine* into an unyielding and unqualified ritual form, celebrating the promise of the epic-heroic figure and the utopian community.

Like Ringo (and later Ethan Edwards in *The Searchers*), Earp is motivated by vengeance: after the Clantons kill his younger brother and steal his cattle, Earp accepts the job as Tombstone's marshal (which he had rejected earlier) and vows over his brother's grave to avenge his death. As Earp says over his brother's grave early in the film, "Maybe when we leave this country, kids like you will be able to grow up and live safe." Although his primary motives involve blood lust, Earp's legal status renders him beyond reproach. Only one aspect of *Clementine* offsets Earp's spit-and-polish demeanor and provides an ambiguous edge to the narrative—the presence of Doc Holliday (Victor Mature) as Tombstone's resident saloon keeper and charismatic authority figure.

The device of using another central character who shares the hero's prosocial allegiance but not his motivation or world view appears frequently in Westerns. This "double" generally points up both the primitive and the cultivated characteristics of the hero and his milieu. Earp and Holliday emerge as oppositional figures on various levels: Earp is the archetypal Westerner, Holliday is a well-educated, Eastern-bred doctor; Earp is a stoic, laconic militarist who uses force only when necessary, Holliday is cultured and articulate but also prone to violent outbursts; both run the town with self-assured authority, but Earp disdains Holliday's penchant for gunplay; Earp is a natural man who operates on instinct and savvy, Holliday is a cultivated man seeking refuge in the West from a failed romance and a demanding career.

Holliday is an interesting and somewhat unusual character within the Ford constellation. Like Doc Boone and later Dutton Peabody in *Liberty Valance*, he is cultured enough to quote Shakespeare but cannot live with himself or the savage environment without alcohol. Unlike the drunken philosophers in these films, however, his age and physical abilities are roughly on a par with the hero's, so he counters Earp on considerably more than just an attitudinal level.

The sharpest distinction between Earp and Holliday, of course, involves the film's namesake, Clementine Carter. Clementine has followed Holliday from Boston, virtually stepping over the dead gunfighters the temperamental doctor has left in his wake. Once she catches up with Holliday in Tombstone, Clementine must confront her own "primitive" double—the character of Chihuahua (Linda Darnell), a saloon girl of questionable breeding. Complementing the film's dominant law-and-order opposition, then, which pits the Earps and Holliday against the Clantons, are the foursome of Wyatt, Doc, Clementine, and Chihuahua, who form a fascinating network of interrelationships.

It is finally (and predictably) Clementine who tempers Earp's character. She gives a touch of humanity to his rigid attitude and takes the edge off his mythic stature. Apparently, as long as the Eastern figure is either a woman or an aging, philosophical alcoholic (this is invariably the case in Ford's Westerns), then he or she conceivably has something to contribute to the settling of the wilderness. Holliday's character is doomed from the start, however, and only time will tell whether a faster gunman or his diseased lungs will finish him. Through Earp and his mission, Holliday is able to die heroically in the climactic gunfight. Thus he joins Chihuahua, his female counterpart, who had died earlier under his own apparently misguided scalpel.

Like *Stagecoach*, *Clementine* was filmed on location in Monument Valley and on black-and-white film stock. The visual style in *Clementine* is considerably more lyrical and expressive than in the earlier film, however, especially in those daylight sequences where Ford frames the desert and monuments beyond the town in elaborate compositions. There is little sense of the horizon beyond the community in this film. This is partially because of the preponderance of night sequences, most of which focus either upon Doc's alcoholic rages or the Clantons' maniacal carrying-on. In the daylight sequences, we generally are only able to glimpse the horizon through man-made structures like fenceposts, boardwalks, and so on.

In the oft-cited church sequence, one of those rare moments when it seems as if the entire narrative is concentrated into a single image, Ford orchestrates an array of visual opposition. We see the contrast of earth and sky, of rugged terrain against horizon, of Monument Valley's vast panorama framed by the rafters and flagstaffs of the half-built church, of man and nature. In an eloquent ritual sequence, the townspeople hold a Sunday square dance, an interesting juxtaposition to the anarchic behavior of Tombstone's nighttime revelers. Earp approaches with Clementine, and the preacher orders the townspeople to stand aside "for the new marshal and his lady fair." As the two dance, framed against the sky, the genre's array of prosocial values and ideals coalesces into an extremely simple yet eternally evocative image.

Those ideals are affirmed as the Earps clean up Tombstone—just as Ringo had cleaned up Lordsburg—in a violent, climactic gun battle. But whereas the gunfight in *Stagecoach* occurs offscreen (Ford shows us Ringo from low-angle falling and firing his rifle, then the camera pulls in on the anxious Dallas), in *Clementine* it is an elaborate, murderous ballet. Ford contends that he choreographed the O.K. Corral sequence after the "real" Wyatt Earp's own description of the legendary battle; the conflict does seem like a military operation. Despite its ties with history, though—and there are few in this mythic tale—the gunfight is not staged in a naturalistic manner. Rather, it seems to be a dream of voices, gunshots, and dust.

The gunfight is initiated when a stagecoach passes the corral, raising clouds of dust. The six participants move in and out of the frame and the dust, firing at one another until only Wyatt and his brother Morgan (Ward Bond) remain standing. This ritualistic dance of death serves both to contrast and complement the earlier dance in the half-built church: social integration is viable only if community order is maintained. With that order ensured, Wyatt promises Clementine, who is now the new schoolmarm, that one day he will return. He and his brother then leave the community and ride westward across Monument Valley.

*　*　*

FORD'S MASTERPIECE: *THE SEARCHERS*

The Searchers is the story of an obsessive, nomadic hero (Wayne as Ethan Edwards) who arrives home after a three-year disappearance. Edwards had fought in the Civil War and then had vanished, apparently somewhere in Mexico. The day after he turns up, a band of renegade Indians massacre his family. We learn that Ethan's former sweetheart, Martha (Dorothy Jordan), now his brother's wife, had been sexually violated before she was killed, and that her two daughters were kidnapped by the Indians. The massacre sets Ethan and a young initiate-hero, Martin Pawley (Jeffrey Hunter), off on an epic, decade-long journey throughout the West (Monument Valley).

The object of their pursuit is the leader of the renegade Indian band, Scar (Henry Brandon), who has taken the sole living captive from the massacre as his squaw. Pawley, himself a one-eighth Cherokee who had been found in his infancy by Ethan and had been raised by the Edwards family during Ethan's prolonged absence, is intent upon returning his foster sister to civilization. Ethan's intentions are a good deal less altruistic. He is bent upon killing Scar to avenge his brother's wife's death, and he also plans to kill the captive squaw whom he considers unfit to return to the world of the White Man.

Throughout Ethan and Martin's search, the linear, chronological aspects of the complex narrative are subordinate to its oppositional structure, which centers on Ethan's character. The search itself does provide a temporal framework for the story, but the events depicted do not really fit into a cause-and-effect pattern. Instead, they progressively reveal and qualify the Westerner's contradictory, multi-faceted personality. The entire film, in fact, might be read as a procession of characters with whom Ethan is doubled.

Upon his initial return, Ethan is set in opposition with his brother Aaron, a simple man of the earth who had remained in Texas and had wed Ethan's sweetheart, raised a family, and cultivated the wilderness in the name of civilization. This nomad-homesteader opposition is accentuated on the morning after Ethan's return when the Reverend-Captain Samuel Johnson Clayton (Ward Bond) thunders into the Edwards' household to enlist Aaron and Martin's aid in his pursuit of Scar's renegade band. Clayton is also a composite of contradictions, although he seems sufficiently comfortable with his dual institutional role of lawman and clergyman. His prosocial beliefs and functions offset Ethan's nomadic, antisocial nature both spiritually and socially. Even though they once were officers for the Confederacy, the men now sit on opposite sides of an ideological fence. Unlike Clayton, Ethan did not attend the Confederate surrender and he still relishes his status as rebel. "I figure a man's only good for one oath at a time," he tells Clayton. "I still got my saber . . . Didn't turn it into no plowshare, neither." This attitude sets Ethan against both Aaron, the man who allowed himself to be domesticated by a woman and the land, and also Clayton, the warrior who now fights for both the laws of man and God.

Ethan's only law is his own, fashioned from his long-standing rapport with the wilderness. His character is shown throughout as being ignorant and unsympathetic to civilization and its ways, but his understanding of the desert expanse and his natural environment far surpasses that of any other white man in the film. He is in touch with his surroundings but out of touch with his people, and he clearly likes it that way.

Ethan's only connection with civilization is his feeling for Martha. For him, she transcends the distinction between the civilized and the savage. From the opening shot of the film when Martha glimpses Ethan approaching across the desert and welcomes him back into the familial fold, Ford subtly indicates that she is his reason for returning. After the massacre when Ethan comes back to the burnt-out homestead, she is the only family member to whom he calls out. Once he finds her body, Ethan's deepest fears and anxieties are animated and his obsessive search is set in motion.

The thematic core of *The Searchers* revolves around a series of male/female relationships involving sexual union, sexual taboo, and sexual violation: Ethan and Martha, Aaron and Martha, Scar and Martha, and by extension Scar and Martha's daughter Lucy (whom he rapes and kills after the massacre) and also daughter Debbie (whom he eventually takes for his squaw). Scar's sexual violation of Martha and her daughters, and Ethan's maniacal desire to avenge the deed by killing the Indian as well as his own niece, draw the two men into an intense and perverse rapport.

The relationship between Westerner and Woman had been a significant but generally subordinate motif in earlier films, but here it emerges as a dominant, motivating factor in the narrative. In a classical Western like *My Darling Clementine*, the hero's repression of his sexual and domestic inclinations was a positive character trait: as high priest of order in the West he was committed to an unspoken code of chastity and self-enforced solitude. In *The Searchers*, the hero's sexual repression—based in his guilt-ridden feelings about Martha and her daughters' violation—assumes psychotic proportions and finds release only when Ethan finally scalps Scar. That task completed, and his obsessions restored to their proper subliminal realm, Ethan turns his back on both the white and Indian cultures and wanders across the desert into oblivion.

While Scar and his renegade band appear to be a rather traditional threat to the civilized homesteaders, Ford's depiction of Indian culture and of the Scar-Ethan relationship appears to radically transform the Western's traditional portrayal of inhuman "Redskins." Unlike *Stagecoach*, where the Indians were simply natural hazards and had no individual or cultural identity, here they are the creators of an autonomous civilization which virtually mirrors the whites'. (In discussing *The Searchers*, Ford once stated: "The audience likes

FROM "THE WESTERN" 291

to see Indians get killed. They don't consider them as human beings—with a great culture of their own—quite different from our own. If you analyzed the thing carefully, however, you'd find that their religion is very similar to ours.")

Because of this sympathetic portrayal of Indian culture, Scar and Ethan are cast in a curiously similar social status. Both are renegades from their own civilizations who violently avenge their respective families. Scar's two sons had been killed by whites years earlier, and his slaughter of Ethan's family is simply one in a series of retributions. Like Ethan, Scar knows the language and the cultural codes of his enemy, and like Ethan he has cultivated a hatred for that enemy so intense that it ultimately seems to transcend the original motivating desire for vengeance.

Scar and Ethan's relationship as brothers under the skin is enhanced by Ford's casting a blue-eyed (but well-tanned) Anglo, Henry Brandon, as Scar. Ford prided himself on casting of real Native Americans in his Westerns, but authenticity in this case was less vital than rhetorical and symbolic expression. Scar's physical characteristics distinguish him from his own people and accentuate his rapport with the Westerner. Their physical and motivational similarities are intensified when Ethan and Scar finally meet late in the film. In a bristling confrontation in Scar's camp, Ford mirrors not only their dialogue ("You speak good English"/"You speak good Comanche"), but he also mirrors our own perceptions of the two men. By filming the confrontation in a rare exchange of over-the-shoulder shots, he encourages the audience to assume Scar's as well as Ethan's viewpoint.

Ultimately, the similarities between Ethan and Scar, between protagonist and antagonist, underscore Ford's evolving conception of the conflicts and threats within the Western milieu. No longer does the Westerner have to deal with faceless "Injuns" who throw the defenseless community into chaos; now the threat involves that very same nomadic, self-reliant individuality which society cannot tolerate and which is shared by both the hero and the Indian. Ironically, this incompatibility between Ford's hero and society grows to a point where the hero's very presence generates disorder. The coincidence of Ethan's and later, Scar's unannounced arrivals into the precariously balanced community, coupled with their similar moral codes and renegade reputations, finally make it rather difficult to distinguish between Demon Indian and Redeemer Westerner.

Ethan's absolute, uncompromising, and obsessive character is continually juxtaposed with the initiate-hero, Martin Pawley. Martin embodies the opposites which Ethan cannot tolerate—he, like the captive Debbie, is both Family and Indian, both civilized and savage, both loved and hated. Martin accepts his dualities, however, and his capacity for reason and compromise repeatedly undercuts Ethan's manic quest for revenge. When Ethan tries to stir up Martin's blood lust by telling him that one of the scalps on Scar's lodgepole belongs to Martin's mother, Martin replies, "It don't make no difference." Martin learns the ways of the desert and the land from Ethan, but his ultimate goal is to return Debbie to her people and to settle a homestead with his childhood sweetheart, Laurie (Vera Miles). Martin is the one who finally kills Scar, not aggressively but in an act of self-defense, and this enables him to return to Laurie in Texas and to commit himself to rural and domestic values which Ethan had been unable (or unwilling) to do years earlier with Martha.

Significantly, though, once Martin honors that commitment, his role as initiate-hero evaporates, and he all but disappears from the narrative. The film's final moments focus not upon Martin's integration into the community but upon Ethan's inability to do so. Although finally able to embrace Debbie and return her to civilization, reaffirming his fundamental belief in Woman and Family, Ethan cannot commit his own life to those values. In the film's closing shot, Ethan stares through the doorway at the family's reunion celebration (and beyond it to the audience), then turns and slowly walks off across Monument Valley as the door closes and leaves the screen in darkness. This image reprises the film's opening shot, wherein Martha had opened a door to reveal Ethan approaching from the distance. This visual motif reaffirms our own perspective from inside the secure, if somewhat repressive, confines of society. It also demonstrates the hero's basic inability to pass through that doorway and enjoy civilized existence. Like the dead Indian whose eyes Ethan had shot out early in the search, Ethan is doomed to wander forever between the winds, endlessly traversing the mythic expanse of Monument Valley.

FORD'S FAREWELL TO THE WESTERNER

If we were to look to a small ranch outside the community of Shinbone some six years later, we might be able to hazard a guess about Ethan's fate after the close of *The Searchers*. Made between *Two Rode Together* (1961) and *How the West Was Won* (1963, in which Ford directed the Civil War episode), *The Man Who Shot Liberty Valance* is Ford's nostalgic and bittersweet farewell to the Westerner and his vanishing ideals.

The story is deceptively simple: Ransom Stoddard (Jimmy Stewart), an aging United States senator, has returned to the prosperous and progressive town of Shinbone where he had begun his career as a lawyer. Accompanied by his wife, Hallie (Vera Miles), Stoddard comes to town to attend the funeral of Tom Doniphon, a forgotten cowboy. The funeral must be financed by the county because Doniphon died without money, home, or even a handgun. At the inducement of an aggressive newspaper editor, Stoddard explains his presence and the significance of Doniphon through an extended flashback that takes up most of the film.

The flashback traces Stoddard's journey West fresh out of law school, his confrontation during the trip with a brutal, psychopathic outlaw (Lee Marvin as Liberty Valance), and his befriending of a charismatic but essentially aloof local rancher, Doniphon, played, of course, by John Wayne—here regenerating the epic Westerner. Stoddard promotes statehood for the community, while Valance is hired by ranchers "north of the Picket Wire" to prevent it, and the conflict between Stoddard and Valance intensifies until they meet in a traditional gunfight. Valance is killed, and Stoddard goes on to build a career as "the man who shot Liberty Valance."

We later learn (in a flashback within a flashback, a narrative device we hardly expect within the Western's usually straightforward story construction) that Doniphon, not Stoddard, was responsible for killing Valance. In this act of heroic self-destruction, Doniphon bequeaths to Stoddard the leadership of the community and, even more significantly, the hand of his "gal" Hallie.

After Stoddard completes the flashback story, the newspaper editor tears up his notes and throws them into the fire, delivering the film's—and Ford's—definitive self-critical statement: "This is the West, sir. When the legend becomes fact, print the legend." *Liberty Valance* is, in effect, Ford's effort to print both the fact and the legend, both history and myth, and to suggest how the two interpenetrate one another. Ford is no longer primarily concerned with the vision of contemporary America drawn from stories about its past; instead, he concentrates on the very process whereby our present demands for a favorable vision distort and manipulate the past. Whereas *Stagecoach* and *My Darling Clementine* overtly celebrated the culture's idealized self-image, *Liberty Valance* deconstructs and critiques that image, finally acknowledging the necessary role of myth and legend in the development of history and civilization.

To examine the Western's amalgam of fact and fiction, Ford creates a world of formal artifice, a timeless theatrical realm in which the allegory is enacted. Abandoning the wide expanse of Monument Valley and the filmic "realism" of wide-screen color and location shooting, Ford shot *Liberty Valance* in black and white, and almost all of the flashback episode was performed on a sound stage. The opening and closing sequences of the film establish Shinbone roughly at the turn of the century, and are shot in exteriors under natural light. When Stoddard begins his flashback, however, Ford depicts the stagecoach amid the artificial trappings of a Western studio set under artificial studio lighting. In case we missed the point, a masked figure (who turns out to be Valance) comes from behind a *papier-mâché* boulder, dressed in a white, floor-length overcoat, and shouts, "Stand and deliver." He proceeds to rob the stage and terrorize its occupants, tearing apart Stoddard's law books after giving him a brutal lesson in "Western law."

With this initial flashback, Ford establishes conflict dramatically (Stoddard versus Valance) and thematically (Eastern versus Western law), as well as chronologically ("new" versus "old" Shinbone) and filmically (the actual Shinbone versus the stylized realm of the flashback).

Thus, Ford's distinction between fact and legend involves not only character, story, and thematics, but also the structuring of space (exterior versus studio, nature versus artifice) and time (present versus past). Whereas all Westerns address two time frames—the old West and the immediate present—*Liberty Valance* addresses three. Placing the *act of telling* (i.e., Stoddard's flashback "confession" to the reporter in turn-of-the-century Shinbone) between past and present reinforces Ford's concern with the *process* of myth-making. The film's narrative framework, the stark stylization of the flashback story, and Ford's treatment of the principal figures all give the flashback a remarkable dreamlike quality. It is shown as the aging Stoddard might have imagined it. Stoddard himself looks much the same in the flashback as in the opening despite the quarter-century lapse—only his whitened hair indicates the advancing years. We never actually see Doniphon in the new Shinbone sequences, although his presence is felt even before the flashback when Stoddard opens the casket and orders the mortician to put Doniphon's boots and spurs on him. Doniphon, like Valance, has no business in the new Shinbone, with its telephones, paved sidewalks, and irrigation projects. Stoddard's "social man" has outlived the legendary Shinbone of his own imagination to survive in the modern world, but Doniphon and Valance, two self-consciously mythic figures, are consigned to the realm of memory and legend.

There are three mediating characters in *Liberty Valance*. First, the newspaper editor in the new Shinbone—vastly different from Dutton Peabody (Edmund O'Brien), the *Shinbone Star's* founding editor (as witnessed in the flashback) and another of Ford's philosophical drunks—who functions much like Ford the filmmaker, mediating legend and fact, myth and history, past and present. Then there is Tom Doniphon, who mediates Valance's primitive savagery and Stoddard's naive idealism. Finally, we have Hallie, who like the editor—and the audience—must decide between Stoddard and Doniphon, between the promise of "a garden of real roses" and the cactus rose. Before Stoddard begins his flashback, Hallie rides off to Doniphon's deserted, burnt-out home to pick a cactus rose, and she eventually leaves it on his casket. The rose represents the torn allegiance felt by Hallie, Ford, and the audience between garden and desert, between nature and civilization.

Although Stoddard is the narrative focus and the guiding sensibility of the film—it is, after all, his story—the cactus rose is the film's emotional and thematic core, its symbol of a lost age when civilization and wilderness coexisted in a precarious but less compromising balance. (Tom often brought Hallie cactus roses when he came courting.) Ford does not mean, however, to condemn Hallie's choice of Stoddard any more than he means to indict the Western genre itself. Hallie's choice ultimately is as inevitable as ours: We were destined to follow a certain historical path in order to reach our present cultural condition, and we keep rewriting history to convince ourselves that we have taken the "right" path, that our destiny represents the fulfillment of promises made and kept.

As Stoddard's train winds back East to Washington in the film's closing sequence, he and Hallie agree to return eventually to Shinbone to live out their lives. What draws them back West, it seems, is a sense of loss and the ghost of Tom Doniphon—who was, as Ford said, "the central character, the motivation for the whole thing." Ringo, Wyatt Earp, and Ethan Edwards never lost sight of the horizon, and each was able to escape an enclosing, repressive society, avoiding what Doc Boone had termed "the blessings of civilization." No such option was available to Tom Doniphon, however. His killing of Valance, which he himself describes as "cold-blooded murder," is finally an act of self-destruction. As surely as he eliminates Valance and saves Stoddard, he is committing himself to a life of isolated uselessness.

The ideal union of Westerner and Woman in the family, the one social institution revered by all of Ford's essentially antisocial heroes, has regressed from a reality (Ringo and Dallas) to a promise (Wyatt and Clementine) to an untenable situation (Ethan and Martha) to an outright impossibility (Tom and Hallie). With the steady enclosure of the genre's visual and thematic horizons, the hero's options are reduced to one single, inexorable reality: Doniphon does not ride off into the sunset or across Monument Valley, but into the Valley of Death.

With Tom Doniphon's death, Ford bids farewell to the Westerner and his heroic code. *The Man Who Shot Liberty Valance* is a fitting epitaph. It traces the death of that code and the basis for its mythic legacy. Some critics have noted the similarities in story and character between this film and *My Darling Clementine*, but the evolution of Ford's perspective and the genre's changing thematic emphases render the differences of those films more significant than their similarities. Time has turned Ford's—and the genre's—initial optimism into a mixture of cynicism and regret. Stoddard's glad-handing politician and Hallie's overwhelming nostalgia are the only elements remaining of the genre's faded utopian vision.

No filmmaker understood or articulated that vision with the style, sensitivity, and consistent quality of John Ford, and although the Western genre survives him it will be forever in his debt. Not only was Ford the best of Hollywood's Western storytellers, but he brought to that story a depth and complexity that place his Westerns among the most significant films of the American cinema.

◆ ◆ ◆

FOCUS ON FILM:
ROBERT ALTMAN'S
McCABE AND MRS. MILLER (1971)

1. Compare and contrast the characters of the two major roles in the film. Cite examples of specific scenes or actions to support your generalizations about each character.
2. Compare and contrast the characters of the Cowboy and the Kid. Explain how each character is juxtaposed to the other to help reveal his true nature.
3. If you have not already done so, read the Appendix, "How to Watch a Film." Then, analyze the pacing of the film. Try to explain the important messages developed in the first half hour, even though the "action" seems somewhat slow and disconnected. Or, if you think these scenes fail to keep your interest as a viewer, explain why. Likewise, explain the pacing and cross-cutting of the final shots of the film, depicting the showdown and the fire.
4. Explain your judgment of Mrs. Miller's actions toward the end of the film. Do you blame her for her attitude toward McCabe? Do you find her irresponsible or escapist in some ways? Explain her motivations.
5. Explain three or more Western myths that director Robert Altman is challenging in his film. To what extent do you find this film more "realisitic" than a traditional Western film, such as *Stagecoach*, *Red River*, *Shane*, or *High Noon*?

TOPICS FOR RESEARCH AND WRITING

1. Analyze the religious and fire imagery in "The Blue Hotel." Consider its purpose and its contribution to a central theme of the story.
2. Analyze the two main characters in *McCabe and Mrs. Miller*. Consider to what extent their relationship is portrayed as a matter of business, pleasure, power, or sincere respect and affection.

3. Review the Appendix, "How to Watch a Film." Then, explain the meanings of violence in *McCabe and Mrs. Miller*. First, consider the significance within the narrative. Is it associated with heroic deeds, as in traditional Westerns? Is it given a motivation, such as revenge or a pathological personality? What does it mean to the film's characters? Why and when does it occur? Second, consider the significance to the viewer. Is violence used to shock or to manipulate the viewer's emotions, to add drama to a scene, to overtly express a character's persona, to make a symbolic statement? How do you as a viewer become involved in the film's scenes of violence? Use these two questions—about narrative and cinematic technique—to formulate your thesis.

4. Compare and contrast Harte's characterization of the gambler in "The Outcasts of Poker Flat" with Crane's characterization of the gambler in "The Blue Hotel." To what extent does Crane's characterization of the gambler follow Western story conventions, and to what extent does it create a realistic portrait of human motivation?

5. Compare and contrast Crane's characterization of Mr. Blanc, the Easterner, with that of Bill, the cowboy, in "The Blue Hotel." Try to generalize these characters as "types" of the Eastern and the Western personalities.

6. Define the elements of the popular Western as represented by Grey's "The Ranger" in Chapter 3. Then, compare and contrast these elements with Twain's "literary" narrative about the West. Explain how Twain's *Roughing It* both reinforces and undercuts some of the expectations of the Western genre and speculate on his purpose in doing so.

7. Reread Schatz's definition of the "professional" Western movie (pages 281–84) and view the film *The Missouri Breaks*. Then, evaluate Schatz's definition against your own interpretation of the film, arguing what his notion of a "professional" Western explains well or fails to explain.

8. Read Stephen Crane's "The Bride Comes to Yellow Sky" in *The Open Boat and Other Tales* (New York: Knopf, 1926), pages 87–102. Then, compare and contrast to "The Blue Hotel." Describe to what extent both stories present similar misperceptions about the West. Then, explain how "Bride" creates a comic perspective while "Hotel" creates a tragic perspective on these same misperceptions.

9. Read Stephen Tatum, "Dime Novels," in *The BFI Companion to the Western*, ed. Edward Buscombe (New York: Atheneum, 1988), pages 109–11. After summarizing the narrative pattern, the use of landscape, and the hero of the traditional Western story, contrast how *McCabe and Mrs. Miller* departs from that tradition. Explain the purpose of this film in challenging the tradition. In other words, what kind of story can it tell by abandoning the expectations of the Western genre?

10. View either *The Oxbow Incident* or *The Missouri Breaks*. Explain the theme of justice and vigilantism in the film. Then, identify and analyze specific Western myths that the film seems to undercut, criticize, or debunk.

11. Review the Appendix, "How to Watch a Film." Then, view the John Ford film based on Dorothy Johnson's "The Man Who Shot Liberty Valance." After rereading the story, compare and contrast the film version. Consider elements that you believe are treated more effectively in the film version. That is, consider what the film adds to the story narrative and analyze the effectiveness of these changes as realized in the film.

12. Read David Lusted, "Social Class and the Western as Male Melodrama," in *The Book of Westerns*, ed. Ian Cameron and Douglas Pye (New York: Continuum, 1996), pages 63–74. Then, apply this analysis to the male protagonist in *McCabe and Mrs. Miller*. How does McCabe's struggle to assert his masculine identity help to explain his motivations toward Mrs. Miller, as well as his "heroic" struggle against the mining company?

CHAPTER

6

WOMEN IN THE WEST

INTRODUCTION

American history has long slighted the stories of women in the West, and to do so perpetuates a kind of unreality that also characterizes much of canonical Western American literature and images from popular culture. According to Patricia Limerick, when history first became an academic discipline specializing in written records, it lost access to evidence from oral traditions and cultural practices. These materials became the purview of anthropology. Fortunately, over the last thirty years, revisionist, feminist, and multidisciplinary research in American culture has begun to recover some of the women's stories that were concealed in obscure government documents, published only in limited editions, or never written down. By reading such primary materials as women's diaries of the Overland Trail from 1840 to 1870, "we begin to see history as the stuff of daily struggle" (Schlissel 16), rather than a story of great men, a single momentum of expansion and progress, or a series of heroic adventures. Limerick's example of Christian missionary Narcissa Whitman "provides little support for the images of life in the West as free, adventurous, and romantic. Most of the time, she worked" (38). Thus, through the eyes of female pioneers, we can recognize the realistic human meanings of their struggle, which are often glossed over in most autobiographies and fiction written by men. According to Lillian Schlissel,

Women did not greet the idea of going West with enthusiasm, but rather . . . worked out a painful negotiation with historical imperatives and personal necessity. . . . Women were neither brave adventurers nor sunbonneted weepers. They were vigorous and given to realism and stoicism. The West to them meant the challenge of rearing a family and maintaining domestic order against the disordered life on the frontier. Once embarked on the journey, they were determined and energetic in their efforts to make the move a success. (155)

Women's viewpoints also provide specific data that serve to "correct the historical record." For instance, their pioneer journals record the extent to which Native Americans assisted the travelers, often trading for food, rather than attacking them. Instead, the enemies of the journey are portrayed as accidents and disease, especially dysentery, which caused death by dehydration and exhaustion, and cholera, which killed thousands on the road during the epidemics of the mid-nineteenth century. In addition, the women's records reveal that "in the patriarchal values of rural communities there were interfaces where women were more independent—and independent in more ways—than has been commonly assumed" (Schlissel 15). For instance, if a husband died along the trail, his widow assumed full responsibility for taking the family wagon West and filing her land claim alone. In fact, homesteading was an attractive proposition for both widows with children and young single women as well. By 1910, women comprised 10 percent of all homesteaders (Luchetti and Olwell 35). "Women's work" came to range beyond traditional domestic chores, including "herding cattle, checking trap lines, or seeding the rows with corn" (31). Women were also free to engage in lucrative businesses, such as restaurants, hotels, and laundries, although their ceaseless labor was exhausting.

Revisionist histories of the American West have sought out the "gritty, recognizably physical reality" (Limerick 51) of gender relations, revealing that "the creature known as 'the pioneer woman' is a generic concept imposed on a diverse reality" (50). Moreover, the stereotypical Western woman—the prostitute—in no way represents frontier females in reality, as historians have discovered by investigating prostitution as a social practice. Just as female homesteaders were racially mixed, so too were the ranks of prostitutes composed of white, black, Hispanic, Native American, and Asian women. Although a few rose from the ranks to become wealthy madams, whose influence never forestalled regular pay-offs to the local sheriff, many impoverished frontier women were driven by desperation to sell their bodies, and Chinese prostitutes were in slavery to their pimps. While women

attempted to avoid conceiving, many bore children, and daughters often followed their mothers into a profession where suicide was the most common
means of retirement. Oddly enough, despite the sentimental stereotype of
the "whore with a heart of gold" and despite their wild and exotic appeals to
lonely miners, prostitutes actually had a conservative effect in glorifying the
safety of marriage to a female population eager to realize expectations for
greater social freedoms in the West. Likewise, prostitution provided an outlet for male sexuality, thereby encouraging the belief that morally correct
wives and daughters should be physically pure and modest in their desires.
The practice of prostitution was thus compatible with a Christian society
because "the elevation of respectable women rested on the downgrading of
the disreputable" (Limerick 50). Finally, the study of Western prostitution
reveals a social dynamic in the mining country that mirrored the male
laborers who were also treated like objects by their corporate employers.
This parallel form of exploitation and oppression again challenges the myth
of Manifest Destiny, portrayed in traditional Western histories as a mono-
lithic sweep of Euro-Americans victimizing the Indians (51). In fact, the
frontier was multidimensional, with individuals from differing races, eth-
nicities, classes, and genders often fighting one other for a home and a
future. The social dynamics were complex, including "struggles to control
resources, social adaptation and cultural change, and relationships of power
and dependency" (Jameson and Armitage 4).

This concern for the political and economic parameters of the frontier—which are easily masked by the mythic and moral conflicts in classic
Western stories—becomes more readily apparent through a feminist analysis of the shifting meanings of gender. Through the perspective of gender,
we can understand the degree to which various groups of "new Americans"
negotiated between assimilation to Western culture and preservation of
their cultural heritage, and between victimization and self-determination.
"Gender is fundamentally a concept of relationship. . . . It involves different
systems of family and kinship and how men and women operate within
these structures; it defines acceptable sexual behavior, appropriate work
roles, and differential access to authority and power for women and men"
(Jameson and Armitage 8). Moreover, in the energetic and transformative
environment of the West, the concept of gender changed as "various women
and men redefined manhood and womanhood" (13). By considering the
forgotten West, particularly in "the histories of racial ethnic women. . . , we
begin to see just how many different ways people interpreted what it meant
to be female or male, how many malleable and variable customs knit gender
in work, kinship, sexuality, and family, in relationships of power and privi-
lege" (13). In the autobiography and fiction of this chapter, readers should

try to apply this concept of gender to women's stories, paying particular attention to interpersonal relationships of intimacy and/or power, and trying to read through melodramatic conventions.

Thus, an inclusive history and literature of Western women opens the door to revealing a multitude of "others"—the cultural and racial "minorities" that are often neglected in traditional histories and literatures of the American West. In contrast to the East, which was largely inhabited by Euro-Americans, by 1900 significant populations of Japanese, Chinese, Native-American, and even black women were living west of the Mississippi (Luchetti and Olwell). In any case, a realistic assessment of the nineteenth-century West reveals "the most culturally diverse section of the country. From 1860 to 1900 between a third and a fourth of all people living in the West had been born in another country. When this immigrant population is added to second-generation immigrant children, and to native-born Indians and Mexican-Americans, native-born Euro-Americans become a distinct minority" (Jameson and Armitage 4). Yet, this minority has, in most cases, left the records in history and literature that we read today. Once we begin to acknowledge the outsiders in the traditional narratives of the West, we begin to realize their presence, and often their silence, throughout that terrain. Thus, an inclusive history must recover or reconstruct the stories of such groups as the Basques, Irish, Cornish, Welsh, Norwegians, Swedes, Russian and Polish and German Jews, Finns, Italians, Serbs, Croats, and Hungarians; in doing so, we "confront the immense ethnic diversity packed into the racial category 'white'" (Jameson and Armitage 4, 10). Likewise, we must recover the stories of not only the eastward pioneers—the Chinese, Japanese, Filipinos, and Koreans; but also the "interior immigrants"—the Indians and Hispanics, who have inhabited the West for centuries, but have crossed the many borders of culture to trade, to worship, to intermarry, and to share their indigenous perspectives. Finally, though stories of the Western cavalry have included the contributions of the "Buffalo Soldiers," we must also recover the stories of ex-slaves who came West to become ranchers, farmers, miners, and business owners.

As one example among racial minorities, free blacks sought the apparent opportunities of the West, which proved greater than in the South or the East, although social acceptance by white communities was always unlikely. By 1830, ex-slaves in the Territories numbered 13,000. After the Civil War, even more emigrants escaped the South; there were 44,903 ex-slaves in the Territories by 1870. Many were drawn to California, where gold-mines and boom towns demanded labor of all kinds and where the society was more open since it was changing so fast. However, black women found less opportunity than the men, partly because of sexist occupational bias. In addition, to work as a seamstress, laundress, or domestic servant, black women often had to compete with the Chinese, who generally worked for lower wages. There were also no legal protections for blacks; if they were jailed and tried, even for debt, they could not testify on their own behalf and could depend for help only on the patronage of a wealthy white friend, if they were lucky (Luchetti and Olwell 43–45). In many new Western states, such as Oregon, black homesteaders were made entirely unwelcome. Though the 1857 state constitution outlawed slavery, it also excluded free blacks (Limerick 278). Nonetheless, despite racial and gender discrimination, many black women did get ahead. Biddy Mason traveled by oxcart from Georgia to Los Angeles in 1851, began working as a confinement nurse for $2.50 a week, invested her meager savings in real estate, and gradually built up a fortune. Aunt Clara Brown, starting penniless in Central City, Colorado, saved $10,000 from doing laundry and invested the money in a wagon train company that hired and transported freed slaves from the South. Mammy Pleasant, sent North by her master to be educated, instead married a black Bostonian who died and left her $50,000. With this capital, she relocated to San Francisco and started a boarding house. Due to her wealth, she was also able to challenge the discrimination of the trolley company, which allowed a lighter-skinned black to ride and refused her passage; she hired an attorney and successfully sued for damages (Luchetti and Olwell 46–47).

Actually, this incident indicates a pattern about the tolerance of any racial ethnic woman in the West. Not only lighter-skinned blacks who might "pass" for white, but also any minority member who abandoned her ethnic dress, home language, religion, and cultural behaviors in order to conform to white, middle-class values and manners was more socially accepted. One source of social pressure to conform were the women humanitarian reformers, who organized "settlement houses," as well as missions and schools. For example, after General John Bidwell stole the land and exploited the labor of the Maidu and Bahapki Indians in Chico, California, his wife Annie tried to change their religion, child-rearing practices, and family relationships (Jameson and Armitage 230). In general, middle-class white women tried "to gain social authority by exercising deeply held moral commitments to help other women who did not necessarily share their values and assumptions" (145). In fact, the women's attempts at social "reform" were motivated by "the desirability of 'more civilized' Christian values and Euro-American gender roles" (145). Their programs, no matter how well-intentioned, were ethnocentric and class-biased, representing another form of colonizing conquered peoples.

Such pressures of assimilation were great, but most racial ethnic women resisted conforming to some extent. In fact, they "were selective about what practices they adopted, and drew from their own communities and cultures competing symbols of selfhood and empowerment" (Jameson and Armitage 459). For example, "when Mexican American women assembled home altars, Issei [first-generation Japanese-American] women wrote poetry, or Jewish women lit Sabbath candles, they affirmed sources of identity that remained meaningful in new circumstances" (459). To make these choices, women had to resist contemporary images from popular culture, which in most cases were degrading racist and sexist stereotypes, such as the "mammies," "hot tamales," and "China dolls" portrayed in twentieth-century films. Still, second-generation daughters were affected by such stereotypes and created new identities, in opposition to tradition, by adopting behaviors from "borrowed cultural forms, like advice columns, fashion magazines, and the images they saw on the silver screen" (Jameson and Armitage 459).

In such processes of identity formation, it is important to recognize the concept of agency. In previous histories, racial ethnic women have been represented as "supporting players in a Euro-American story" (Jameson and Armitage 11). Instead, our new histories must abandon the privileging of white experience and recognize that Western women's stories are more than a record of victimization. That is, we must seek to understand the ways in which women resisted mainstream cultural values, "with the power to make their own life choices and self-definitions. Such an approach in no way denies the possibility that racial ethnic women may be forced to interact with oppressors on unfavorable terms or may make choices that seem to be contrary to their own self interest" (Jameson and Armitage 19). Rather, recognizing their agency in their own lives ensures a historical perspective that is insistently political, forever aware that past actions have shaped the Western landscape to the benefit of some and the detriment of others, creating injustices and prejudices that live on today.

Recognizing the realities of agency and the multiplicity of cultural exchange among American peoples, this anthology includes a selection of nonmainstream viewpoints from women and racial ethnic groups in this and the following two chapters. Of course, we must acknowledge that such inclusions are partial; that many worthy voices remain unheard; that the task of reassessing our history, literatures, and cultures will never arrive at a comprehensive story of the West. Nor should it. Still, as you read these selections, it will be helpful to review this chapter introduction in order to reconsider and apply the concepts of "minority" perspective, gender, assimilation, and cultural resistance.

Jameson, Elizabeth, and Susan Armitage, eds. *Writing the Range: Race, Class, and Culture in the Women's West*. Norman, OK: University of Oklahoma, 1997.

Limerick, Patricia Nelson. *The Legacy of Conquest: The Unbroken Past of the American West.* New York: Norton, 1987.

Luchetti, Cathy, and Carol Olwell, eds. *Women of the West.* New York: Orion, 1982.

Schlissel, Lillian. *Women's Diaries of the Westward Journey.* New York: Schocken, 1982.

ANGELINE MITCHELL BROWN
(1854–1909)

As a baby, this pioneer of the Southwest traveled with her parents from Massachusetts to the Kansas frontier with a group of abolitionist settlers trying to ensure that the territory became a free or non-slaveholding state (Moynihan, Armitage, and Dichamp 268). As a young woman, she attended Kansas State Agricultural College in Manhattan for two years, studying Latin, German, English literature, rhetoric, geometry, trigonometry, philosophy, physical geography, geology, American history, instrumental music, and drawing. However, in March 1871 she left Kansas State to assist her mother through a serious illness and did not return. The following winter, she enrolled in the University of Kansas at Lawrence and completed her education in June 1873 (Mitchell).

Two years later, she moved with her family once more to Prescott, in Arizona territory, where her father surveyed for the government and served as justice of the peace (Moynihan et al. 268). Mitchell began teaching school in town, but wanted to live and work on the frontier, so she found a position in the remote district of Tonto, though both her parents and her fiancé objected to the remoteness and crudeness of the settlement. However, one educational advantage of the district was that Mitchell was able to take her students exploring at ancient Pueblo Indian ruins. After the school year partially recorded below, Mitchell married George Brown, a territorial legislator and Prescott sheriff.

The manuscript of "Diary of a School Teacher on the Arizona Frontier, September 5, 1880–February 10, 1881," is used by permission of the Angie M. Brown Collection, Sharlot Hall Museum, Prescott, Arizona. The text for the following excerpts is from the collection of pioneer women narratives in *So Much to Be Done* (cited below), pages 269–78, 281–83, and 286–88.

Mitchell, Angeline. "Diary of a College Student in Kansas, 1869–1873" [manuscript]. Angie M. Brown Collection, Sharlot Hall Museum, Prescott, Arizona. Microform Readex Number MISC0053.

Moynihan, Ruth B., Susan Armitage, and Christiane Fisher Dichamp, ed. *So Much to Be Done: Women Settlers on the Mining and Ranching Frontiers*. Lincoln, NE, and London: University of Nebraska, 1990.

FROM "DIARY OF A SCHOOL TEACHER ON THE ARIZONA FRONTIER"

———‹◆›———

SEPT. 5TH SUNDAY

I wrote Hancock [to accept the Tonto School] and Geo. [her fiancé] went down about 10 & found out from Dan O'Leary and St. James . . . . concerning the Tonto road—then came back at 12 and "said things" about my *craziness* in wanting to go to such an out of the way place & I merely reminded him that I promised him I'd go to the most "barbarous" country I could if he ran for anything on the ticket & he promised not to and I abandoned my intention of going to St. Johns-Apache Co.—that he broke his share of the agreement and I thought *Tonto* would answer my purpose *nearly* as well as *St Johns* (which latter school was now engaged) and therefore I should go to Tonto. That I hoped he'd be willing to take me there but if he wasn't I'd go to Phoenix by Stage & get some way of going to Tonto Basin from there. He looked disgusted—but the whole thing is a little amusing & we both laughed & he said he'd assuredly take me if I was going anyhow, & that settled it. . . .

SEPT. 6TH

Washed my duds, then sorted trunks & boxes for Tonto. Can only take a little trunk & it is hard to decide what I can do without. Geo. went home at 1. Josie & Mrs. K. came out & they said more "things". Mother will go with us, & she is merely *resigned* not *jubilant*. Really one would think I was going to the Feejee Isles.

*   *   *

SEPT. 17

Ma sick with crampcolic part of the night. All right today, also had a bad pain in her lungs so I did her up in mustard, rubbed her in liniment & dosed her with hot wiskey & she got better. Started at 7 without breakfast as water was non est. Went to a grove of fine pines & there got breakfast. Drove to Strawberry & then to Pine Cr. & camped at the Mormon's ranch. This man has 2 or else 3 wives & we saw 16 children sitting on some logs, that seemed to be nerly the same age & size & looked exactly alike, about as wild as quail. There are also an assorted variety of dogs. . . . Tonight after the cows were milked the 16 *twins* & about as many older ones each with a bowl of bread & milk, scattered around the yard and eat their suppers. Geo. says he counted them & there were 73—but he exaggerates a trifle tho'. There really are 22 or 23 of the kids but I don't suppose they belong to one family. . . .

SEPT. 23

Geo. & Ma started for Green Valley & today for the first time in my life I know what it is to feel utterly cast away & homesick. This is desolation itself here, high frowning hills, long stretch of dusty road, no fields, no trees except a few near what is, part of the year a creek, no shade near the house, no porch around it, no furniture in it, except a broken cook stove, two shaky tables, a rough board bedstead, 3 or 4 home made camp stools, an almanac & 3 or 4 papers a month old, and a law book & book of forms—1/2 a dozen plates, 3 saucers, 2 cups, & 3 or 4 tin plates, steel knives & forks—a tin can lid for salt & lard buckets to cook in & a wooden box or two—a gourd dipper, an old tin water pail & ditto milk pail & a nice new style churn, 2 battered tubs, a broom, & a rough bench & dozen good milk pans, a piece of tin with holes punched for a skimmer & a lot of iron & tin spoons, ass't sizes & all ages constitute the house hold goods of this family. I'm not sherring them, I'm simply filled with amazement that people sensible, nice people can live in such a way! Oh yes—there's a block with 3 nails in it for one candle stick & a bottle for another! The beds are ticks filled with hay the pillows about the same hard anyway & there's only one: Heavens! will my boarding place be a duplicate?

* * *

SEPT. 26

Andy & Jane B. & I went to Vinyards at Adams. . . . We reached John Vinyard's about 5. Mrs. V——— is a sister of Mrs. Blake's. Mr. Harrer father of the girls was there also, & their younger sister Alice. The V's have 5 children, Will, John, Green, Ezra, & baby Agnes. The house consists of 1 room 16 x 16, dirt floor, pole house, thatched flat roof, no windows but open spaces (small) in the sides: It has a rough fireplace & in this house live V & his wife & 5 children and Alice & I are to stay temporarily: Great Stars! It is located in a lovely place: trees & fine views on all sides & nothing bleak or dreary about it. As to the furniture, 2 rough double bunks for bedsteads & hay filled ticks (but 4 pillows & that's *luck*) clean, abundant, home made quilts, a long home made dining table, uncertain on one leg, two or three boxes, used as trunks pushed under the "bunks", 6 or 7 home made stools; a rough kitchen table; a fair cook stove, & a fair collection of heavy white crockery & quite a lot of tins. Calico curtains round one "bunk", & a cracker box cradle, a small lamp & some more block or bottle candle sticks, a bible, almanac & one or two stock books & a few old papers &—, that's about all! Everything is clean & tidy tho' and the family are very kind & pleasant spoken. V. is over six ft. & built in proportion while Mrs. V——— is not much over 4 & weighs, I guess almost 90 lbs!

* * *

OCT. 6 WEDNESDAY

Last night I was wakened from sleep sometime after midnight by a tremendous purring noise and while wondering what it could be I partly raised in bed and looked through a chink some 3 inches wide—at the side of the bed where a pole was taken out from the wall for ventilation & was teribly frightened by having the mouth & nose of some animal thrust just opposite my face—in an attempt to reach me—&, as I darted back with a scream, to see a big, furry paw stick through the crack evidently trying to catch hold of me. I nearly fell out of bed over Alice in my anxiety to get out of the vicinity of that paw & roused the family with my shrieks which were echoed from outside by a long, peculiar wail like a woman or child crying. Then I knew what it was for I've heard that wail many a time before—it was a "cougar"—or "mountain lion" or "California lion". Vinyard had hung a small piece of beef up in the house close to the roof & on this same side—near a "chink or two"—not as wide as the "window" over the bed. The lion had scented it & was trying to reach it when my moving about attracted his attention & I presume angered him. The sound that awakened me was his purring, which I had never before happened to hear one of them do. Peering cautiously out of a smaller crack we, Alice and I—could see in the clear moonlight three of them prowling around—1 a cub—& probably the others were its parents. After watching awhile & being certain that no amount of clawing, even if he tried it again—would admit—of the lion reaching me while I lay down—I fell asleep again & the last sound I heard was one of the big "cats" climbing up the side of the house to the roof—probably thinking to reach that much desired beef from there. . . .

*   *   *

OCT 18TH MONDAY

This morning we rose about our usual time. Alice, Clara, Abbie, Mrs. H. and I. Clara went to Vinyards for milk and the other four of us and oh yes, I forgot Janie & the baby—well, the other 5 of us (baby don't count) were eating breakfast when a great hullabaloo arose at the creek crossing just below our house, shouting and splashing of water. Alice remarked, "That's Bal, crossing his band of cattle, I guess," when up to the house with a horrible whoop rode a band of Indians. The chief rode his horse into the house but when he found he could not sit erect on the animal after he got inside & could barely turn around on him he dismounted, turned (walking him all over Mr. H's bed which was still on the floor) and led him out. Then returned followed by Indians till they quite filled the small room. We counted 14 & 1 half grown boy. The bucks were in war paint & each had on a cartridge belt well filled pistol in holster, a fine Gov't rifle in his hands and all but one or two had big wicked looking knives. The boy had a knife & bow & arrows. We sat as if petrified thinking our time had come when Mrs. Harer (who is as brave a frontier woman as ever lived & is quite accustomed to the Indians as she has long lived near the San Carlos Reservation) arose put on a brave face and stepping to the Chief held out her hand with the customary, "How." The Chief only gave a savage grunt and put his hand behind him. Janie's baby on our bed in the corner cried & she trying to profit by her mothers example rose & during the second while every Indian watched her movements Alice close to the middle door, slid thro it like a flash, seized Abbie (who on the chief's first appearance had hid in the corner of the back room & whom the Indians had not seen) and squeezing thro' a narrow space near the kitchen chimney fled, as I was certain, to Jon. V to warn them & get help if she could. Baffled in her first overtures to the chief Mrs. H. demanded their passes but the chief said they had none as they were not from San Carlos. Mrs. H asked where they were from (the conversation was principally in Mexican which all the Indians of this country speak) & he said they were "Papagoes,"—that was an awful lie for there's very little similarity between the Apache & Papago tribes. Janie was trying to hush her baby & the chief glanced her way as if anxious to see the child, now usually the greatest mark of friendship one can show these savages is to exhibit their tiny white & pink babies to them & usually the Indians consider it an honor, so Janie plucking up courage moved a little nearer & unrolled the shawl & showed the chief what a tiny morsel he was but he only frowned the fiercer & made a motion as if to seize the child & fling him down but Janie clasped him closer & carried him to the farthest corner & deposited him & then resumed her seat at the table near me, close by her baby & between the Indians & it. The Chief and his band surveyed us in ominous silence, three lone defenceless women, one old, small & gray, one a slender girl, & the third, weak from recent confinement & now pale as death; then after a few guttural sentences to each other, they seemed to decide on a plan. Grasping Mrs. H firmly the chief held her hands behind her while one of the others tied them tightly with a buckskin thong. Then she was led to the opposite corner from us placed in a chair & tied to the chair while a handkerchief lying handy was bound over her mouth. She struggled desperately but uselessly. During this performance Jane & I sat motionless—I could not have moved an eyelash—if by doing so I could have escaped what I believed to be the awful & certain death that awaited, for I was actually paralyzed by fright—& I believe Janie was in a similar condition. I sat with my head a trifle drooping & my hands folded—pushed just a little back from the end of the table—one of the ugliest & most hideously painted of the Indians came & stood as nearly in front of me as my position permitted. Of course I did not look up at him, I *couldn't,* but putting his hand under my chin he jerked my head back with a force that nearly broke my neck. I looked at him then straight, & unflinchingly in his cruel gleaming eyes & I know I wondered if Satan in all his kingdom had a more fiendish looking devil—something in my expression seemed to please him—the fear I could not hide probably, & with a wild whoop that made our nerves tingle (tho' neither Janie nor I jumped as one would suppose we would) he grabbed that great knife of his & grabbing me by my hair threw my head back & drew his knife, I thought, over my throat but he did not touch it—that's sure or I wouldn't be writing this tonight. I think he must have touched my flesh with the back of the knife for I am sure I felt the cold of the steel. I think I must have looked surprised when he dropped my head & I discovered it still rested securely on my shoulders, at any rate another pleased look came into his eyes—then he tore my sleeves open & pinched my arms & shoulders till I am blue-green & black most all over them, he slapped my cheeks pulled my ears & pinched them—& then grabbed me by my bangs & pretended to scalp me & not a sound did I utter all that time—I really believe if he had tied me to a stake & set fire to me I could not have even groaned, & I'm sure I could not have resisted. At last as if tired he paused a minute & I glanced at Jane. Poor girl—she had been submitted to the same torments only she wore earrings & the brute had torn one entirely down thro' her ear & the other nearly & the blood was running freely from them. She like myself had not made a sound & for a similar reason. At last my tormentor returned to his charge but he wheeled the chair around & caused me to face the others & I suddenly saw that one Indian had my trunk open and had turned over some ribbons & things & I knew in a minute he'd reach my bundle of photos & a lot of little keepsakes & that would be the last I'd see of them—queer notion, to think of a trifling thing like that when I was *positive* that in an hour or whenever that fellow got done amusing himself—I'd be killed—but I'm not accountable for the vagary—but the thought put life into me and I sprang from my chair so suddenly that the buck did not have time to stop me if he had wanted to, rushed to the Indian at my trunk who had just got a photo in his hand, grabbed it from him & delt him a blow in the face so unexpected that he fairly staggered, flung the picture into the trunk—& the lid down—turned the key, & snapped the catches & put the key down my neck. The Indian whom I struck made a move as if to spring upon me but the chief said a word or two & he slunk back scowling. The buck to whom apparently the others had given me, stepped forward—gave me a jerk & fling & sat me down so solidly that it took my breath, in the chair I had left. He stood & looked at me a while & I felt again as if paralyzed & not able to stir. Then he, still regarding me closely, spoke to Jane's persecutor & they talked (in Apache) a little. Then my demon spoke to the chief, he in turn, to the other Indians & to my horror they all filed out got on their horses & rode off leaving those two with us. Then the one I seemed to belong to said something to the other and walked out. I sat still for there did not seem to be anything else to do. Suddenly Jane's possessor grasped me by the arm, jerked me out of the chair & led me to the third & unoccupied corner of our brush house—stopped me about two ft. from it & dropped my arm. I stood as he had left me—head a bit forward arms by my sides, motionless; a rustle made me raise my head a bit and there within a foot of me & aimed squarely at my head was a Winchester rifle & as I gazed squarely at it I wondered that it had never before occurred to me what a *big barrel* those guns had. I heard the click of the trigger *very* clearly—then—instead of finding myself dead—I was again grasped by Jane's Indian & dropped into my chair while *my* Indian—who had had the rifle at my head came in & up to me and said, "Heap brave squaw, mucho brave—mucho. Una pocita (thats not spelled right but it sounds like it) muchacha esta much brave"—! Such a funny mixture of Spanish & English! Then they turned to Jane and called her, "mucho brave", "una bravisto mujer" & lots of such phrases, all meaning that they thought we were "brave". At first I thought they were making game of us but soon realized they were serious & really thought that it was courage that had prevented us from screaming or fainting or crying when they tormented us and that while we had been so paralyzed with fear & terror as to be utterly powerless to scream or even speak or to move hardly of our own volition. They ascribed it to pride & bravery. Well! thats good! Mrs. Harer says she thinks the manner in which I sprang on that Indian at my trunk & made him leave it went far toward causing them to think that if I wished to I could cry or scream or struggle but then Jane & I were both acting on the principle that we would not give them the satisfaction of acting as though they hurt us. She also says that it was an inspiration that seized me to do that as the Apaches are great admirers of courage in anyone particularly white women & that she believes we would have suffered much worse indignities if they had not been forced to respect our stoical courage! It looks to me like a silly piece of extreme idiocy on my part to think of trifles like that—with death by torture staring me in the face, for not till they led me to the chair away from the gun—did one gleam of hope dawn on me. . . . [The Apaches later returned and said they scared the women only as a joke.]

*   *   *

OCT. 26

Worse and more of it:—Baby grew easier about 1 & we went to sleep—Mrs. Hook slept with me & she snored & snorted so & then tossed around like a restless child that my sleep was of short duration. While I was meditating about sliding out on the floor with a quilt, there arose a great barking of coyotes & bellowing of cattle some ways up the mountain side above us. It awakened us all and in a minute we heard the hoof beats of the panic stricken cattle & their bellowing grew nearer. We sprang out of bed & rushed in a body for the door sure that the stampeding herd would rush straight thro' our frail house & probably crush us as well. Everyone grabbed the first thing they could that would aid in frightening them. Alice & I were first out & each had a sheet so we ran round to the side the cattle were coming from & faced them & indeed it was a sight. Not more than a hundred yards away, tearing along in that manner peculiar to a badly frightened herd of stampeding cattle & making straight thro' our house in their mad rush for the creek & safety—were about 100 head of stock. We took a firm hold of our sheets flapped them up & down & ran forward yelling as loud as we could while directly behind came Mrs. Harer & Mrs. Hook each beating a tin pan with a stick & yelling & behind them Clara & Belle with an old tin can & a spoon for Belle and a big white apron & an old tin horn of Abbie's (who is at Vinyard's) for Clara, each swelling the noise as well as they could & Clara wildly waving her apron in one hand. Such an awful pow-wow was too much for the cattle & they swerved passed each side of us & our house, so close they nearly grazed us and went on tearing thro the bushes & rushed across the creek—then we returned out of breath & badly scared to find poor Janie lying just outside the door in a faint with her baby wrapped in a blanket close to her. Her strength was not sufficient for the shock. We brought her to & took care of baby & built up a little fire & got hot water to make tea for Jane & at last subsided into our "peaceful beds." This morning we find that the cattle demolished our brush shade that we fixed to wash under—trampled our one tub & the wash bucket & bench & a stool we had there into a shapeless mass of sticks and battered tin. Also that a skirt of mine & some things of Alice & Clara's have been either trampled under the wreck of a clump of bushes we used as a "clothes line" or carried in fragments away on their horns. Thank Heaven the damage is no more serious—five minutes of inaction on our part & awful would have been the results.

*   *   *

DEC. 22ND

It rained most of the night but this morning is pleasant tho' the mud is absolutely without bottom. Started fairly early but only got to the neighborhod of Tempe & camped tonight near a Mexican's house—as it is the only place one can get good drinking water—every ditch etc. is so muddy. The Mexican came out to camp and talked to Mr. Harer and after he went back she, the senora, sent a message inviting the "senoras" to come up to the porch which was dry. We went & it was clean & we were muddy—but she insisted so shedding our rubbers we went up & soon she brought us a brush to brush the mud from our shoes if we wished as we most certainly did wish to. . . . She speaks a little English, I a little Spanish (Sarah doesn't know any yet) and we *pretended* to understand & got along fine. She *watched* me so closely it was uncomfortable & paid some attention to Sarah & was kind to us both. When we came out to go to camp where the men had supper ready she stepped up & kissed me Spanish style to my great surprise. Sarah & I discussed it & concluded I must resemble some dear friend—& I'm tanned enough to resemble *any* Mexican! Mrs. Hazelton was in a bad humor evidently at the woman's preference for me tho! I can't see how I was to blame. We were just eating supper when a fine looking lad appeared & addressed me in Spanish—I shook my head for I did not understand him & he spoke to Mrs. Harer who is "up" in the lingo. She told me Senora—(we disagree as to the name. *I* think it was Garcia—) has invited you to supper. "Only me?" I asked & she said "Thats all he said," "Then tell him it is impossible." She did so after telling me I had best go as it would be a novelty but I wouldn't. . . . [Senora Garcia sent another invitation.] Then he and Mrs. Harer held a conversation and Mrs. H, with fun in her eyes, translated, "She wants the young lady & when I asked which he said she wanted the one with the red lips, the eyes & the hands.". . . "he says the *tall* young lady—and she wants her to come up for a while as she will have some friends arrive soon & she thinks the young lady may enjoy it." . . . I thought a minute and Sarah urged me to go—& I decided I'd see what a Mexican evening party might be like. I *did* want Sarah to go for I'd enjoy it lots more but how could she when she was not asked! I said, "Tell him I'll be there in ten minutes." . . . The young fellow had put some boards down from the camp to the walk inside the gate (about 50 ft I guess) and I got there without getting at all muddy. He led me to his mother who kissed me twice then introduced the boys as Ramon & Manuel. She insisted on my eating some "dulcies" (delicious cookies) and drinking some coffee in spite of my assurance that I was not hungry. Then Ramon took a guitar & played and she showed me a number of curiosities from Old Mexico & from Arizona ruins & seemed delighted to find that "specimens" were something I delighted in. After that a dozen young "senors" and "senoritas" arrived and I found they were celebrating some kind of a fete day—of the Senora's, birth, wedding, or something. They seemed surprised to see me & well they might be—but she introduced me to them as kindly as if I were a long lost relative just arrived. . . . We had music, singing also & dancing & games till we were all tired & then refreshments of all sorts of "dulcies" (sweets of any kind), preserves, bread, "chicken Tomales" & goodness knows what and some sort of Mexican liquor, coffee and chocolate. At last I said I must go and they came over & bade me "good night" or "buenos noches" one by one & wished me a pleasant journey and a speedy return to Tonto—(as I had promised to stay a day on my way to the Basin, if I could) and the girls kissed me Spanish style— and the young men shook hands—then the Senora went on the porch with me & kissed me again & Ramon took me home. I certainly had a jolly time— I crawled in, after getting into my flannel gown, beside Sarah & was soon sound asleep. . . .

Discussion Questions

1. Describe the concerns that Brown emphasizes in her narrative. What details about daily life seem to interest her? Then, describe your own response to her interests or details; for instance, were you surprised by anything you read?
2. How do her concerns resemble and differ from those of the Western male narratives you have read in Chapters 2 or 3? Mention specific examples to support your viewpoint. Try to explain similarities and differences.
3. Explain any recurring themes you find in Brown's diary.

Fig. 6.1 W. H. D. Koerner, *Madonna of the Prairie* (1922). Buffalo Bill Historical Center, Cody, WY; gift of the artist's heirs, W. H. D. Koerner, III, and Ruth Koerner Oliver; 25.77.

MARY HUNTER AUSTIN
(1868–1934)

A Westerner by acclimation, Austin was born and nurtured a Midwesterner, in Carlinville, Illinois. In a conventional, Methodist, middle-class family, she was the elder daughter and most rebellious child of four (O'Grady 33). In 1884, she enrolled in her hometown's Blackburn College, where she studied science and art. The next year, she suffered a nervous breakdown and transferred to the Illinois State Normal School in Bloomington. However, after recovering she returned to Blackburn and graduated in 1888 (O'Grady 34). Then, another traumatic event was the family's move to the San Joaquin Valley near Rancho Tejon, a hundred miles north of Los Angeles, where her elder brother, George, was homesteading. Her writing developed, in part, as a means to express the alienation she felt in losing her identity and security in a homeplace (Hoyer 23).

Upon crossing the Sierra Nevada Mountains, her first response to the desert was as sudden as it was powerful. As she recorded in her somewhat fictionalized autobiography, *Earth Horizon* (1932), she felt "something brooding and aloof, charged with a dire indifference, of which she was never for an instant afraid" (qtd. in O'Grady 34). When the family homestead failed in the California drought, Austin was forced to find teaching work, taking private pupils from among her valley neighbors. However, her literary development profited from fraternizing with some of these neighbors—especially when listening to the recollections of General Edward Beale, former sidekick to Kit Carson (1809–1868), and of Jose Lopez, the General's foreman at Rancho Tejon. These tales about local history, Indians, and pioneers became raw material for her early Western works, *The Land of Little Rain* (1903) and *Lost Borders* (1909). She married Stafford Wallace Austin in 1891 and moved to Lone Pine in the Owens Valley, east of the Sierras. The following year Mary Austin published her first story, "The Mother of Felipe," in the influential San Francisco literary magazine *Overland Monthly*. Shortly after, even as she realized her marriage was failing due to incompatibility and Wallace's "emotional desertion," she gave birth to a daughter, who proved to be severely retarded. As an escape from her unsatisfying personal life, Austin spent her energy on a growing professional life (O'Grady 35–40). She succeeded in regularly publishing short stories, sketches, and poems in popular periodicals. For the fourteen years that she lived in the Owens Valley, the desert proved the greatest influence on her life; her relations with the local Paiutes and Shoshones also contributed much to both her spirituality and her writing (Hoyer 23).

In *The Land of Little Rain*, she announced three concerns that she would explore for the rest of her life: natural and human relationships with the land, interculturalism in the Southwest, and a feminism at odds not only with male-dominated society, but also with most other contemporary writers and thinkers. First, the book demonstrated how the ruggedness of the land "promotes qualities such as hardiness, adaptability, and frugality in the people, animals and the natural environment" (Hoyer 23). Moreover, the desert assumes the role of another character, essential to her vision rather than merely background (O'Grady 38–39). Second, when she celebrates the European, Hispanic, and Native American cross-cultural traditions of the Southwest, she promotes the hope that her adopted region "could provide the foundation of an emerging American culture that would be unified yet retain the individual strands of its fibers" (Hoyer 22). Third, she also captures how men and women experience the desert differently. In her autobiography, Austin tried to explain these gender-based responses: whereas men indulged in the romance of possibilities and the enchantments of distant perspectives, women realized daily limitations, "hung there suspended between hopes that refused to eventuate, life slipping away from them" (qtd. in O'Grady 37). Likewise, where others accepted a sexist social organization without question, Austin challenged the injustice of the constraints placed on women.

After the success of her first book, she did buck convention and left her husband, though they were not officially divorced until 1914. In 1905, she decided to place her daughter permanently in a state institution and to move to Carmel in order to join the artist colony there. However, when diagnosed with terminal breast cancer in 1907, she decided to visit Europe, where her symptoms mysteriously disappeared. She stayed for two years, living mostly in Rome and London, where she met such literary figures as H. G. Wells, George Bernard Shaw, Henry James, and Joseph Conrad. During this period, she completed the stories for *Lost Borders* (O'Grady 39–40).

Most of these eighteen tales and sketches were again set in "the land of little rain." However, there was more character development and drama than in the meditative pieces of her first book (Hoyer 25), and feminist themes became a major thread in the narratives. Hardly a sentimentalist about the purity of living in nature, Austin considered that the desert could provoke a skeptical questioning of the values of society or humanity: "Out there where the borders of conscience break down, where there is no convention, and behavior is of little account except as it gets you your desire, almost anything might happen" (Austin 3). One of the first Euro-American writers to consider the social meanings of living in this inhospitable landscape, she gave a feminine character to that environment in a famous passage:

> It is men who go mostly into the desert, who love it past all reasonableness, slack their ambitions, cast off old usages, neglect their families because of the pulse and beat of a life laid bare to its thews and sinews. . . . If the desert were a woman, I know well what like she would be: deep-breasted, broad in the hips, tawny, with tawny hair, great masses of it lying smooth along her perfect curves, full lipped like a sphinx, but not heavy lidded like one, eyes sane and steady as the polished jewel of her skies, such a countenance as should make men serve without desiring her, such a largeness to her mind as should make their sins of no account, passionate, but not necessitous, patient—and you could not move her, no, not if you had all the earth to give, so much as one tawny hair-breadth beyond her own desires. If you cut very deeply into any soul that has the mark of the land upon it, you find such qualities as these. (Austin 10–11)

Besides this inclination to anthropomorphize, a sophisticated technical development central to *Lost Borders* is that "Austin positions her narrator as a negotiator between conflicting stories and interpretations" (Hoyer 25). According to critic Linda Karell, in "The Walking Woman" this viewpoint presents an ambiguity in the conclusion, rather than a resolution, which allows the writer to emphasize "the tension between an essential female identity and a socially constructed one" (qtd. in Hoyer 25).

This story was first published in *Atlantic Monthly* (August 1907), but the texts for it and "The Fakir" derive from *Lost Borders* (New York: Harper, 1909), pages 195–209 and pages 111–34, respectively. As a test of reader expectations and Austin's creativity, read only the first six paragraphs of "The Fakir" and record what you think will happen between Netty Saybrick and Frank Challoner. How do you think the story will end? Then, when you finish reading the story, assess your prediction in discussion question 1 on page 334.

Austin, Mary Hunter. "The Land." *Lost Borders*. New York: Harper, 1909. 1–11.

Hoyer, Mark T. "Mary Austin." *Dictionary of Literary Biography, Volume 206: Twentieth-Century American Western Writers, 1st Series*. Ed. Richard H. Cracroft. Detroit: Gale, 1999. 20–32.

O'Grady, John P. "Mary Hunter Austin." *American Nature Writers, Volume 1*. Ed. John Elder. New York: Scribner's, 1996. 31–51.

THE FAKIR

Whenever I come up to judgment, and am hard pushed to make good on my own account (as I expect to be), I shall mention the case of Netta Saybrick, for on the face of it, and by all the traditions in which I was bred, I behaved rather handsomely. I say on the face of it, for except in the matter of keeping my mouth shut afterward, I am not so sure I had anything to do with the affair. It was one of those incidents that from some crest of sheer inexplicableness seems about to direct the imagination over vast tracts of human experience, only to fall away into a pit of its own digging, all fouled with weed and sand. But, by keeping memory and attention fixed on its pellucid instant as it mounted against the sun, I can still see the Figure shining through it as I saw it that day at Posada, with the glimmering rails of the P. and S. running out behind it, thin lines of light toward the bar of Heaven.

Up till that time Netta Saybrick had never liked me, though I never laid it to any other account than Netta's being naturally a little fool; afterward she explained to me that it was because she thought I gave myself airs. The Saybricks lived in the third house from mine, around the corner, so that our back doors overlooked each other, and up till the coming of Doctor Challoner there had never been anything in Netta's conduct that the most censorious of the villagers could remark upon. Nor afterward, for that matter. The Saybricks had been married four years, and the baby was about two. He was not an interesting child to anybody but his mother, and even Netta was sometimes thought to be not quite absorbed in him.

Saybrick was a miner, one of the best drillers in our district, and consequently away from home much of the time. Their house was rather larger than their needs, and Netta, to avoid loneliness more than for profit, let out a room or two. That was the way she happened to fall into the hands of the Fakir.

Franklin Challoner had begun by being a brilliant and promising student of medicine. I had known him when his natural gifts prophesied the unusual, but I had known him rather better than most, and I was not surprised to have him turn up five years later at Maverick as a Fakir.

It had begun in his being poor, and having to work his way through the Medical College at the cost of endless pains and mortification to himself. Like most brilliant people, Challoner was sensitive and had an enormous egotism, and, what nearly always goes with it, the faculty of being horribly fascinating to women. It was thought very creditable of him to have put himself through college at his own charge, though in reality it proved a great social waste. I have a notion that the courage, endurance, and steadfastness which should have done Frank Challoner a lifetime was squeezed out of him by the stress of those overworked, starved, mortifying years. His egotism made it important to his happiness to keep the centre of any stage, and this he could do in school by sheer brilliance of scholarship and the distinction of his struggles. But afterward, when he had to establish himself without capital among strangers, he found himself impoverished of manliness. Always there was the compelling need of his temperament to stand well with people, and almost the only means of accomplishing it his poverty allowed was the dreadful facility with which he made himself master of women. I suppose this got his real ability discredited among his professional fellows. Between that and the sharp need of money, and the incredible appetite which people have for being fooled, somewhere in the Plateau of Fatigue between promise and accomplishment, Frank Challoner lost himself. Therefore, I was not surprised when he turned up finally at Maverick, lecturing on phrenology, and from the shape of their craniums advising country people of their proper careers at three dollars a sitting. He advertised to do various things in the way of medical practice that had a dubious sound.

It was court week when he came, and the only possible lodging to be found at Netta Saybrick's. Doctor Challoner took the two front rooms as being best suited to his clients and himself, and I believe he did very well. I was not particularly pleased to see him, on account of having known him before, not wishing to prosecute the acquaintance; and about that time Indian George brought me word that a variety of *redivivus* long sought was blooming that year on a certain clayey tract over toward Waban. It was not supposed to flower oftener than once in seven years, and I was five days finding it. That was why I never knew what went on at Mrs. Saybrick's. Nobody else did, apparently, for I never heard a breath of gossip, and *that* must have been Doctor Challoner's concern, for I am sure Netta would never have known how to avoid it.

Netta was pretty, and Saybrick had been gone five months. Challoner had a thin, romantic face, and eyes—even I had to admit the compelling attraction of his eyes; and his hands were fine and white. Saybrick's hands were cracked, broken-nailed, a driller's hands, and one of them was twisted from the time he was leaded, working on the Lucky Jim. If it came to that, though, Netta's husband might have been anything he pleased, and Challoner would still have had his way with her. He always did with women, as if to make up for not having it with the world. And the life at Maverick was deadly, appallingly dull. The stark houses, the rubbishy streets, the women who went about in them in calico wrappers, the draggling speech of the men, the wide, shadowless table-lands, the hard, bright skies, and the days all of one pattern, that went so stilly by that you only knew it was afternoon when you smelled the fried cabbage Mrs. Mulligan was cooking for supper.

At this distance I cannot say that I blamed Netta, am not sure of not being glad that she had her hour of the rose-red glow—*if* she had it. You are to bear in mind that all this time I was camping out in the creosote belt on the slope of Waban, and as to what had really happened neither Netta nor Challoner ever said a word. I keep saying things like this about Netta's being pretty and all, just as if I thought they had anything to do with it; truth is, the man had just a gift of taking souls, and I, even I, judicious and disapproving—but you shall hear.

At that time the stage from Maverick was a local affair going down to Posada, where passengers from the P. and S. booked for the Mojave line, returning after a wait of hours on the same day.

It happened that the morning I came back from Waban, Doctor Challoner left Maverick. Being saddle weary, I had planned to send on the horses by Indian George, and take the stage where it crossed my trail an hour out from Posada, going home on it in the afternoon. I remember poking the botany-case under the front seat and turning round to be hit straight between the eyes, as it were, by Netta Saybrick and Doctor Challoner. The doctor was wearing his usual air of romantic mystery; wearing it a little awry—or perhaps it was only knowing the man that made me read the perturbation under it. But it was plain to see what Netta was about. Her hat was tilted by the jolting of the stage, white alkali dust lay heavy on the folds of her dress, and she never would wear hair-pins enough: but there was that in every turn and posture, in every note of her flat, childish voice, that acknowledged the man beside her. Her excitement was almost febrile. It was part of Netta's unsophistication that she seemed not to know that she gave herself away, and the witness of it was that she had brought the baby.

You would not have believed that any woman would plan to run away with a man like Frank Challoner and take that great, heavy-headed, drooling child. But that is what Netta had done. I am not sure it was maternal instinct, either; she probably did not know what else to do with him. He had pale, protruding eyes and reddish hair, and every time he clawed at the doctor's sleeve I could see the man withhold a shudder.

I suppose it was my being in a manner confounded by this extraordinary situation that made it possible for Doctor Challoner to renew his acquaintance with more warmth than the facts allowed, he fairly pitched himself into an intimacy of reminiscence, and it was partly to pay him for this, I suppose, and partly to gratify a natural curiosity, that made me so abrupt with him afterward. I remember looking around, when we got down, at the little station where I must wait two hours for the return stage, at the seven unpainted pine cabins, at the eating-house, and the store, and the two saloons, in the instant hope of refuge, and then out across the alkali flat fringed with sparse, unwholesome pickle-weed, and deciding that that would not do, and then turning round to take the situation by the throat, as it were. There was Netta, with that great child dragging on her arm and her hat still on one side, with a silly consciousness of Doctor Challoner's movements, and he still trying for the jovial note of old acquaintances met by chance. In a moment more I had him around the corner of the station-house and out with my question.

"Doctor Challoner, are you running away with Netta Saybrick?"

"Well, no," trying to carry it jauntily; "I think she is running away with me." Then, all his pretension suddenly sagging on him like an empty cayaque: "On my soul, I don't know what's got into the woman. I was as surprised as you were when she got on the stage with me"—on my continuing to look steadily at him—"she was a pretty little thing . . . and the life is devilish dull there. . . . I suppose I flirted a little"—blowing himself out, as it were, with an assumption of honesty—"on my word, there was nothing more than that."

Flirted! He called it that; but women do not take their babies and run away from home for the sake of a little flirting. The life was devilish dull—did he need to tell me that! And she was pretty—well, whatever had happened he was bound to tell me that it was nothing, and I was bound to behave as if I believed him.

"She will go back," he began to say, looking bleak and drawn in the searching light. "She must go back! She must!"

"Well, maybe you can persuade her," said I; but I relented after that enough to take care of the baby while he and Netta went for a walk.

The whole mesa and the flat crawled with heat, and the steel rails ran on either side of them like thin fires, as if the slagged track were the appointed way that Netta had chosen to walk. They went out as far as the section-house and back toward the deserted station till I could almost read their faces clear, and turned again, back and forth through the heat-fogged atmosphere like the figures in a dream. I could see this much from their postures, that Challoner was trying to hold to some consistent attitude which he had adopted, and Netta wasn't understanding it. I could see her throw out her hands in a gesture of abandonment, and then I saw her stand as if the Pit yawned under her feet. The baby slept on a station bench, and I kept the flies from him with a branch of pickle-weed. I was out of it, smitten anew with the utter inutility of all the standards which were not bred of experience, but merely came down to me with the family teaspoons. Seen by the fierce desert light they looked like the spoons, thin and worn at the edges. I should have been ashamed to offer them to Netta Saybrick. It was this sense of detached help-lessness toward the life at Maverick that Netta afterward explained she and the other women sensed but misread in me. They couldn't account for it on any grounds except that I felt myself above them. And all the time I was sick with the strained, meticulous inadequacy of my own soul. I understood well enough, then, that the sense of personal virtue comes to most women through an intervening medium of sedulous social guardianship. It is only when they love that it reaches directly to the centre of consciousness, as if it were ultimately nothing more than the instinctive movement of right love to preserve itself by a voluntary seclusion. It was not her faithlessness to Say-brick that tormented Netta out there between the burning rails; it was going back to him that was the intolerable offence. Passion had come upon her like a flame-burst, heaven-sent; she justified it on the grounds of its complete-ness, and lacked the sophistication for any other interpretation.

Challoner was a bad man, but he was not bad enough to reveal to Netta Saybrick the vulgar cheapness of his own relation to the incident. Besides, he hadn't time. In two hours the return stage for Maverick left the station, and he could never in that time get Netta Saybrick to realize the gulf between his situation and hers.

He came back to the station after a while on some pretext, and said, with his back to Netta, moving his lips with hardly any sound: "She must go back on the stage. She must!" Then with a sudden setting of his jaws, "You've got to help me." He sat down beside me, and began to devote himself to the baby and the flies.

Netta stood out for a while expecting him, and then came and sat pro-visionally on the edge of the station platform, ready at the slightest hint of an opportunity to carry him away into the glimmering heat out toward the station-house, and resume the supremacy of her poor charms.

She was resenting my presence as an interference, and I believe always cherished a thought that but for the accident of my being there the incident might have turned out differently. I could see that Challoner's attitude, whatever it was, was beginning to make itself felt. She was looking years older, and yet somehow pitifully puzzled and young, as if the self of her had had a wound which her intelligence had failed to grasp. I could see, too, that

Challoner had made up his mind to be quit of her, quietly if he could, but at any risk of a scene, still to be quit. And it was forty minutes till stage-time.

Challoner sat on the bare station bench with his arm out above the baby protectingly—it was a manner always effective—and began to talk about "goodness," of all things in the world. Don't ask me what he said. It was the sort of talk many women would have called beautiful, and though it was mostly addressed to me, it was every word of it directed to Netta Saybrick's soul. Much of it went high and wide, but I could catch the pale reflection of it in her face like a miner guessing the sort of day it is from the glimmer of it on a puddle at the bottom of a shaft. In it Netta saw a pair of heroic figures renouncing a treasure they had found for the sake of the bitter goodness by which the world is saved. They had had the courage to take it while they could, but were much too exemplary to enjoy it at the cost of pain to any other heart. He started with the assumption that she meant to go back to Maverick, and recurred to it with a skilful and hypnotic insistence, painting upon her mind by large and general inference the picture of himself, helped greatly in his career by her noble renunciation of him. As a matter of fact, Saybrick, if his wife really had gone away with Doctor Challoner, would have followed him up and shot him, I suppose, and no end of vulgar and disagreeable things might have come from the affair; but Challoner managed to keep it on so high a plane that even I never thought of them until long afterward. And right here is where the uncertainty as to the part I really played begins. I can never make up my mind whether Challoner, from long practice in such affairs, had hit upon just the right note of extrication, or whether, cornered, he fell back desperately on the eternal rightness. And what was he, to know rightness at his need?

He was terribly in earnest, holding Netta's eyes with his own; his forehead sweated, hollows showed about his eyes, and the dreadful slackness of the corner of the mouth that comes of the whole mind being drawn away upon the object of attack to the neglect of its defences. He was so bent on getting Netta fixed in the idea that she must go back to Maverick that if she had not been a good deal of a fool she must have seen that he had given away the whole situation into my hands. I believed—I hope—I did the right thing, but I am not sure I could have helped taking the cue which was pressed upon me; he was as bad as they made them, but there I was lending my whole soul to the accomplishment of his purpose, which was, briefly, to get comfortably off from an occasion in which he had behaved very badly.

All this time Challoner kept a conscious attention on the stage stables far at the other end of the shadeless street. The moment he saw the driver come out of it with the horses, the man's soul fairly creaked with the release of tension. It released, too, an accession of that power of personal fascination for which he was remarkable.

Netta sat with her back to the street, and the beautiful solicitude with which he took up the baby at that moment, smoothed its dress and tied on its little cap, had no significance for her. It was not until she heard the rattle of the stage turning into the road that she stood up suddenly, alarmed. Challoner put the baby into my arms.

Did I tell you that all this time between me and this man there ran the inexplicable sense of being bonded together; the same suggestion of a superior and exclusive intimacy which ensnared poor Netta Saybrick no doubt, the absolute call of self and sex by which a man, past all reasonableness and belief, ranges a woman on his side. He was a Fakir, a common quack, a scoundrel if you will, but there was the call. I had answered it. I was under the impression, though not remembering what he said, when he had handed me that great lump of a child, that I had received a command to hold on to it, to get into the stage with it, and not to give it up on any consideration; and without saying anything, I had promised.

I do not know if it was the look that must have passed between us at that, or the squeal of the running-gear that shattered her dream, but I perceived on the instant that Netta had had a glimpse of where she stood. She saw herself for the moment a fallen woman, forsaken, despised. There was the Pit before her which Challoner's desertion and my knowledge of it had digged. She clutched once at her bosom and at her skirts as if already she heard the hiss of crawling shame. Then it was that Challoner turned toward her with the Look.

It rose in his face and streamed to her from his eyes as though it were the one thing in the world of a completeness equal to the anguish in her breast, as though, before it rested there, it had been through all the troubled intricacies of sin, and come upon the root of a superior fineness that every soul feels piteously to lie at the back of all its own affronting vagaries, brooding over it in a large, gentle way. It was the forgiveness—nay, the obliteration of offence—and the most Challoner could have known of forgiveness was his own great need of it. Out of that Look I could see the woman's soul rising rehabilitated, astonished, and on the instant, out there beyond the man and the woman, between the thin fiery lines of the rails, leading back to the horizon, the tall, robed Figure writing in the sand.

Oh, it was a hallucination, if you like, of the hour, the place, the perturbed mind, the dazzling glimmer of the alkali flat, of the incident of a sinful woman and a common fakir, faking an absolution that he might the more easily avoid an inconvenience, and I the tool made to see incredibly by some trick of suggestion how impossible it should be that any but the chief of sinners should understand forgiveness. But the Look continued to hold the moment in solution, while the woman climbed out of the Pit. I saw her put out her hand with the instinctive gesture of the sinking, and Challoner take it with the formality of farewell; and as the dust of the arriving stage billowed up between them, the Figure turned, fading, dissolving . . . but with the Look, consoling, obliterating. . . . He too . . . !

"It was very good of you, Mrs. Saybrick, to give me so much of a good-bye . . ." Challoner was saying as he put Netta into the stage; and then to me, "You must take good care of her . . . good-bye."

"Good-bye, Frank"—I had never called Doctor Challoner by his name before. I did not like him well enough to call him by it at any time, but there was the Look; it had reached out and enwrapped me in a kind of rarefied intimacy of extenuation and understanding. He stood on the station platform staring steadily after us, and as long as we had sight of him in the thick, bitter dust, the Look held.

If this were a story merely, or a story of Franklin Challoner, it would end there. He never thought of us again, you may depend, except to thank his stars for getting so lightly off, and to go on in the security of his success to other episodes from which he returned as scatheless.

But I found out in a very few days that whether it was to take rank as an incident or an event in Netta Saybrick's life depended on whether or not I said anything about it. Nobody had taken any notice of her day's ride to Posada. Saybrick came home in about ten days, and Netta seemed uncommonly glad to see him, as if in the preoccupation of his presence she found a solace for her fears.

But from the day of our return she had evinced an extraordinary liking for my company. She would be running in and out of the house at all hours, offering to help me with my sewing or to stir up a cake, kindly offices that had to be paid in kind; and if I slipped into the neighbors' on an errand, there a moment after would come Netta. Very soon it became clear to me that she was afraid of what I might tell. So long as she had me under her immediate eye she could be sure I was not taking away her character, but when I was not, she must have suffered horribly. I might have told, too, by the woman's code; she was really not respectable, and we made a great deal of that in Maverick. I might refuse to have anything to do with her and justified myself explaining why.

But Netta was not sure how much I knew, and could not risk betrayal by a plea. She had, too, the natural reticence of the villager, and though she must have been aching for news of Doctor Challoner, touch of him, the very sound of his name, she rarely ever mentioned it, but grew strained and thinner; watching, watching.

If that incident was known, Netta would have been ostracized and Saybrick might have divorced her. And I was going dumb with amazement to discover that nothing had come of it, nothing *could* come of it so long as I kept still. It was a deadly sin, as I had been taught, as I believed—of damnable potentiality; and as long as nobody told it was as if it had never been, as if that look of Challoner's had really the power as it had the seeming of absolving her from all soil and stain.

I cannot now remember if I was ever tempted to tell on Netta Saybrick, but I know with the obsession of that look upon my soul I never did. And in the mean time, from being so much in each other's company, Netta and I became very good friends. That was why, a little more than a year afterward, she chose to have me with her when her second child was born. In Maverick we did things for one another that in more sophisticated communities go to the service of paid attendants. That was the time when the suspicion that had lain at the bottom of Netta's shallow eyes whenever she looked at me went out of them forever.

It was along about midnight and the worst yet to come. I sat holding Netta's hands, and beyond in the room where the lamp was; the doctor lifted Saybrick through his stressful hour with cribbage and toddy. I could see the gleam of the light on Saybrick's red, hairy hands, a driller's hands, and whenever a sound came from the inner room, the uneasy lift of his shoulders and the twitching of his lip; then the doctor pushed the whiskey over toward him and jovially dealt the cards anew.

Netta, tossing on her pillow, came into range with Saybrick's blunt profile outlined against the cheaply papered wall, and I suppose her husband's distress was good to her to see. She looked at him a long time quietly.

"Henry's a good man," she said at last.

"Yes," I said; and then she turned to me narrowly with the expiring spark of anxious cunning in her eyes.

"And I've been a good wife to him," said she. It was half a challenge. And I, trapped by the hour, became a fakir in my turn, called instantly on all my soul and answered—with the Look—"Everybody knows that, Netta"—held on steadily until the spark went out. However I had done it I could not tell, but I saw the trouble go out of the woman's soul as the lids drooped, and with it out of my own heart the last of the virtuous resentment of the untempted. I had really forgiven her; how then was it possible for the sin to rise up and trouble her more? Mind you, I grew up in a church that makes a great deal of the forgiveness of sins and signifies it by a tremendous particularity about behavior, and the most I had learned of the efficient exercise of forgiveness was from the worst man I had ever known.

About an hour before dawn, when a wind began to stir, and out on the mesa the coyotes howled returning from the hunt, stooping to tuck the baby in her arms, I felt Netta's lips brush against my hand.

"You've been mighty good to me," she said. Well—if I were pushed for it, I should think it worth mentioning—but I am not so sure.

THE WALKING WOMAN

———⟨◆⟩———

The first time of my hearing of her was at Temblor. We had come all one day between blunt, whitish bluffs rising from mirage water, with a thick, pale wake of dust billowing from the wheels, all the dead wall of the foot-hills sliding and shimmering with heat, to learn that the Walking Woman had passed us somewhere in the dizzying dimness, going down to the Tulares on her own feet. We heard of her again in the Carrisal, and again at Adobe Station, where she had passed a week before the shearing, and at last I had a glimpse of her at the Eighteen-Mile House as I went hurriedly northward on the Mojave stage; and afterward sheepherders at whose camps she slept, and cowboys at rodeos, told me as much of her way of life as they could understand. Like enough they told her as much of mine. That was very little. She was the Walking Woman, and no one knew her name, but because she was a sort of whom men speak respectfully, they called her to her face Mrs. Walker, and she answered to it if she was so inclined. She came and went about our western world on no discoverable errand, and whether she had some place of refuge where she lay by in the interim, or whether between her seldom, unaccountable appearances in our quarter she went on steadily walking, was never learned. She came and went, oftenest in a kind of muse of travel which the untrammelled space begets, or at rare intervals flooding wondrously with talk, never of herself, but of things she had known and seen. She must have seen some rare happenings, too—by report. She was at Maverick the time of the Big Snow, and at Tres Pinos when they brought home the body of Morena; and if anybody could have told whether De Borba killed Mariana for spite or defence, it would have been she, only she could not be found when most wanted. She was at Tunawai at the time of the cloud-burst, and if she had cared for it could have known most desirable things of the ways of trail-making, burrow-habiting small things.

All of which should have made her worth meeting, though it was not, in fact, for such things I was wishful to meet her; and as it turned out, it was not of these things we talked when at last we came together. For one thing, she was a woman, not old, who had gone about alone in a country where the number of women is as one in fifteen. She had eaten and slept at the herder's camps, and laid by for days at one-man stations whose masters had no other touch of human kind than the passing of chance prospectors, or the halting of the tri-weekly stage. She had been set on her way by teamsters who lifted her out of white, hot desertness and put her down at the crossing of unnamed ways, days distant from anywhere. And through all this she passed unarmed and unoffended. I had the best testimony to this, the witness of the men themselves. I think they talked of it because they were so much surprised at it. It was not, on the whole, what they expected of themselves.

Well I understand that nature which wastes its borders with too eager burning, beyond which rim of desolation it flares forever quick and white, and have had some inkling of the isolating calm of a desire too high to stoop to satisfaction. But you could not think of these things pertaining to the Walking Woman; and if there were ever any truth in the exemption from offence residing in a frame of behavior called ladylike, it should have been inoperative here. What this really means is that you get no affront so long as your behavior in the estimate of the particular audience invites none. In the estimate of the immediate audience—conduct which affords protection in Mayfair gets you no consideration in Maverick. And by no canon could it be considered ladylike to go about on your own feet, with a blanket and a black bag and almost no money in your purse, in and about the haunts of rude and solitary men.

There were other things that pointed the wish for a personal encounter with the Walking Woman. One of them was the contradiction of reports of her—as to whether she was comely, for example. Report said yes, and again, plain to the point of deformity. She had a twist to her face, some said; a hitch to one shoulder; they averred she limped as she walked. But by the distance she covered she should have been straight and young. As to sanity, equal incertitude. On the mere evidence of her way of life she was cracked; not quite broken, but unserviceable. Yet in her talk there was both wisdom and information, and the word she brought about trails and water-holes was as reliable as an Indian's.

By her own account she had begun by walking off an illness. There had been an invalid to be taken care of for years, leaving her at last broken in body, and with no recourse but her own feet to carry her out of that predicament. It seemed there had been, besides the death of her invalid, some other worrying affairs, upon which, and the nature of her illness, she was never quite clear, so that it might very well have been an unsoundness of mind which drove her to the open, sobered and healed at last by the large soundness of nature. It must have been about that time that she lost her name. I am convinced that she never told it because she did not know it herself. She was the Walking Woman, and the country people called her Mrs. Walker. At the time I knew her, though she wore short hair and a man's boots, and had a fine down over all her face from exposure to the weather, she was perfectly sweet and sane.

I had met her occasionally at ranch-houses and road-stations, and had got as much acquaintance as the place allowed; but for the things I wished to know there wanted a time of leisure and isolation. And when the occasion came we talked altogether of other things.

It was at Warm Spring in the Little Antelope I came upon her in the heart of a clear forenoon. The spring lies off a mile from the main trail, and has the only trees about it known in that country, first you come upon a pool of waste full of weeds of a poisonous dark green, every reed ringed about the water-level with a muddy white incrustation. Then the three oaks appear staggering on the slope, and the spring sobs and blubbers below them in ashy-colored mud. All the hills of that country have the down plunge toward the desert and back abruptly toward the Sierra. The grass is thick and brittle and bleached straw-color toward the end of the season. As I rode up the swale of the spring I saw the Walking Woman sitting where the grass was deepest, with her black bag and blanket, which she carried on a stick, beside her. It was one of those days when the genius of talk flows as smoothly as the rivers of mirage through the blue hot desert morning.

You are not to suppose that in my report of a Borderer I give you the words only, but the full meaning of the speech. Very often the words are merely the punctuation of thought; rather, the crests of the long waves of inter-communicative silences. Yet the speech of the Walking Woman was fuller than most.

The best of our talk that day began in some dropped word of hers from which I inferred that she had had a child. I was surprised at that, and then wondered why I should have been surprised, for it is the most natural of all experiences to have children. I said something of that purport, and also that it was one of the perquisites of living I should be least willing to do without. And that led to the Walking Woman saying that there were three things which if you had known you could cut out all the rest, and they were good any way you got them, but best if, as in her case, they were related to and grew each one out of the others. It was while she talked that I decided that she really did have a twist to her face, a sort of natural warp or skew into which it fell when it was worn merely as a countenance, but which disappeared the moment it became the vehicle of thought or feeling.

The first of the experiences the Walking Woman had found most worth while had come to her in a sand-storm on the south slope of Tehachapi in a dateless spring. I judged it should have been about the time she began to find herself, after the period of worry and loss in which her wandering began. She had come, in a day pricked full of intimations of a storm, to the camp of Filon Geraud, whose companion shepherd had gone a three days' *pasear* to Mojave for supplies. Geraud was of great hardihood, red-blooded, of a full laughing eye, and an indubitable spark for women. It was the season of the year when there is a soft bloom on the days, but the nights are cowering cold and the lambs tender, not yet flockwise. At such times a sandstorm works incalculable disaster. The lift of the wind is so great that the whole surface of the ground appears to travel upon it slantwise, thinning out miles high in air. In the intolerable smother the lambs are lost from the ewes; neither dogs nor man make headway against it.

The morning flared through a horizon of yellow smudge, and by mid-forenoon the flock broke.

"There were but the two of us to deal with the trouble," said the Walking Woman. "Until that time I had not known how strong I was, nor how good it is to run when running is worth while. The flock travelled down the wind, the sand bit our faces; we called, and after a time heard the words broken and beaten small by the wind. But after a little we had not to call. All the time of our running in the yellow dusk of day and the black dark of night, I knew where Filon was. A flock-length away, I knew him. Feel? What should I feel? I knew. I ran with the flock and turned it this way and that as Filon would have.

"Such was the force of the wind that when we came together we held by one another and talked a little between pantings. We snatched and ate what we could as we ran. All that day and night until the next afternoon the camp kit was not out of the cayaques. But we held the flock. We herded them under a butte when the wind fell off a little, and the lambs sucked; when the storm rose they broke, but we kept upon their track and brought them together again. At night the wind quieted, and we slept by turns; at least Filon slept. I lay on the ground when my turn was and beat with the storm. I was no more tired than the earth was. The sand filled in the creases of the blanket, and where I turned, dripped back upon the ground. But we saved the sheep. Some ewes there were that would not give down their milk because of the worry of the storm, and the lambs died. But we kept the flock together. And I was not tired."

The Walking Woman stretched out her arms and clasped herself, rocking in them as if she would have hugged the recollection to her breast.

"For you see," said she, "I worked with a man, without excusing, without any burden on me of looking or seeming. Not fiddling or fumbling as women work, and hoping it will all turn out for the best. It was not for Filon to ask, Can you, or Will you. He said, Do, and I did. And my work was good. We held the flock. And that," said the Walking Woman, the twist coming in her face again, "is one of the things that make you able to do without the others."

"Yes," I said; and then, "What others?"

"Oh," she said, as if it pricked her, "the looking and the seeming."

And I had not thought until that time that one who had the courage to be the Walking Woman would have cared! We sat and looked at the pattern of the thick crushed grass on the slope, wavering in the fierce noon like the waterings in the coat of a tranquil beast; the ache of a world-old bitterness sobbed and whispered in the spring. At last—

"It is by the looking and the seeming," said I, "that the opportunity finds you out."

"Filon found out," said the Walking Woman. She smiled; and went on from that to tell me how, when the wind went down about four o'clock and left the afternoon clear and tender, the flock began to feed, and they had out the kit from the cayaques, and cooked a meal. When it was over, and Filon had his pipe between his teeth, he came over from his side of the fire, of his own notion, and stretched himself on the ground beside her. Of his own notion. There was that in the way she said it that made it seem as if nothing of the sort had happened before to the Walking Woman, and for a moment I thought she was about to tell me one of the things I wished to know; but she went on to say what Filon had said to her of her work with the flock. Obvious, kindly things, such as any man in sheer decency would have said, so that there must have something more gone with the words to make them so treasured of the Walking Woman.

"We were very comfortable," said she, "and not so tired as we expected to be. Filon leaned up on his elbow. I had not noticed until then how broad he was in the shoulders, and how strong in the arms. And we had saved the flock together. We felt that. There was something that said together, in the slope of his shoulders toward me. It was around his mouth and on the cheek high up under the shine of his eyes. And under the shine the look—the look that said, 'We are of one sort and one mind'—his eyes that were the color of the flat water in the toulares—do you know the look?"

"I know it."

"The wind was stopped and all the earth smelled of dust, and Filon understood very well that what I had done with him I could not have done so well with another. And the look—the look in the eyes—"

"Ah-ah—!"

I have always said, I will say again, I do not know why at this point the Walking Woman touched me. If it were merely a response to my uncon-scious throb of sympathy, or the unpremeditated way of her heart to declare that this, after all, was the best of all indispensable experiences; or if in some flash of forward vision, encompassing the unimpassioned years, the stir, the movement of tenderness were for me—but no; as often as I have thought of it, I have thought of a different reason, but no conclusive one, why the Walking Woman should have put out her hand and laid it on my arm.

"To work together, to love together," said the Walking Woman, withdrawing her hand again; "there you have two of the things; the other you know."

"The mouth at the breast," said I.

"The lips and the hands," said the Walking Woman. "The little, pushing hands and the small cry." There ensued a pause of fullest understanding, while the land before us swam in the noon, and a dove in the oaks behind the spring began to call. A little red fox came out of the hills and lapped delicately at the pool.

"I stayed with Filon until the fall," said she. "All that summer in the Sierras, until it was time to turn south on the trail. It was a good time, and longer than he could be expected to have loved one like me. And besides I was no longer able to keep the trail. My baby was born in October."

Whatever more there was to say to this, the Walking Woman's hand said it, straying with remembering gesture to her breast. There are so many ways of loving and working, but only one way of the first-born. She added after an interval, that she did not know if she would have given up her walking to keep at home and tend him, or whether the thought of her son's small feet running beside her in the trails would have driven her to the open again. The baby had not stayed long enough for that. "And whenever the wind blows in the night," said the Walking Woman, "I wake and wonder if he is well covered."

She took up her black bag and her blanket; there was the ranch-house of Dos Palos to be made before night, and she went as outliers do, without a hope expressed of another meeting and no word of good-bye. She was the Walking Woman. That was it. She had walked off all sense of society-made values, and, knowing the best when the best came to her, was able to take it. Work—as I believed; love—as the Walking Woman had proved it; a child—as you subscribe to it. But look you: it was the naked thing the Walking Woman grasped, not dressed and tricked out, for instance, by prejudices in favor of certain occupations; and love, man love, taken as it came, not picked over and rejected if it carried no obligation of permanency; and a child; any way you get it, a child is good to have, say nature and the Walking Woman; to have it and not to wait upon a proper concurrence of so many decorations that the event may not come at all.

At least one of us is wrong. To work and to love and to bear children. That sounds easy enough. But the way we live establishes so many things of much more importance.

Far down the dim, hot valley I could see the Walking Woman with her blanket and black bag over her shoulder. She had a queer, sidelong gait, as if in fact she had a twist all through her. Recollecting suddenly that people called her lame, I ran down to the open place below the spring where she had passed. There in the bare, hot sand the track of her two feet bore evenly and white.

Discussion Questions

1. First, write down your prediction for the conclusion to "The Fakir." How does your idea compare to the ending that Austin wrote? Explain one point that Austin may be making in this conclusion.
2. Compare and contrast Austin's depictions of gender relations in "The Fakir" to those of Zane Grey in "The Ranger" in Chapter 3. Whose perspective do you find more romantic and why? Whose perspective do you feel is more characteristic of women and men today?
3. Explain a theme for "The Walking Woman." You may base this on (A) "the three things which if you had known you could cut out all the rest"; (B) "She had walked off all sense of society-made values"; or (C) another idea you find central to the story.
4. Analyze how the desert is depicted in "The Walking Woman" and compare to Austin's comments about the desert at the beginning of *Lost Borders* (quoted in the Austin biography page 318).

SUI SIN FAR
(1865–1914)

The author, first published under her "English" name of Edith Maude Eaton, was the eldest daughter of a British merchant and a Chinese missionary girl educated in England. Sui Sin Far's pathway to becoming a Westerner was unusual since she was born in Macclesfield, Cheshire County, a silk-producing region, and her family did not emigrate to North America until 1872. Shortly before, China had been forced to admit merchants and missionaries as the consequence of treaties made after a series of wars. Thus, European and North American businesses began exploiting China's resources, including its cheap labor (Ling and White-Parks 2). However, once guest workers arrived, there were strong feelings against them. When the family first lived in the United States, in Hudson City, New York, Sui Sin Far and her elder brother Charlie suffered verbal abuse and physical attacks from American children. The family soon settled in Montreal, but there racism was just as prevalent (Sui Sin Far, "Leaves").

In her youth she keenly felt her difference from her Canadian neighbors. In fact, not only were the citizens of European heritage prejudiced against her, but even the full-blooded Chinese were prejudiced against the "half white" ("Leaves" 223). As the eldest girl, Sui Sin Far chose not to marry and served as a second mother to thirteen siblings. The economic burdens on the family were tremendous, especially since her father had sunk from the merchant to the working class. From the age of 10, when she quit formal schooling, she helped to support her family (Ling and White-Parks 3). She was always physically frail and suffered attacks of "nervous sickness." At the age of 14, she contracted rheumatic fever, which retarded her growth and left her subject to recurrent attacks ("Sui Sin Far" 290–91).

Between 1894 and 1897, while still living at home in Montreal, she was running her own stenography and typing service, writing for the local newspapers, and gradually finding more time to devote to writing short fiction. In this period of intense anti-Chinese sentiment, her journalism expressed an obvious sympathy toward the Chinese in North America while most reporters blandly repeated racist sentiments. After the transcontinental railroads were completed, there was a backlash against Chinese workers. The U.S. Congress had passed the Chinese Exclusion Act in 1882, while three years later the Canadian Parliament had imposed a head tax of $50 on every Chinese worker coming into the country. When, in 1896, Parliament considered increasing the tax to $500 to discourage immigration, Sui Sin Far responded with "brilliantly tongue-in-cheek" arguments to support the Chinese cause (White-Parks 170–71). In "A Plea for the Chinaman," she used ironic wit to invert the delegates' own arguments that the Chinese are a corrupting influence: "It is so absurd. Surely those who are 'controlled by the higher influences of civilization' cannot succumb to those who obey 'the lower forces of barbarism'" (*Mrs. Spring* 194). Even in this clearly pro-Chinese broadside, Sui Sin Far continued to mask her personal identity and assumed the perspective of an objective outsider, signing her article only "E. E." for Edith Eaton, her professional name and English persona.

Her work schedule was a constant strain on her health. She moved West in 1898 on her doctor's advice after a bout of rheumatic fever had left her shrunken to only eighty-four pounds ("Leaves" 226). Moving to San Francisco, where she could stay with a sister, Sui Sin Far found work typing for a railway agency for $5 a month and soliciting subscriptions to the *San Francisco Bulletin* among Chinatown residents. She also worked as a stenographer and legal typist in Seattle and as a journalist on trips along the coast to Los Angeles ("Sui Sin Far" 293–94). For over a dozen years, she stayed out West, where her friends were more forward-thinking than in Eastern Canada, "more genuine, more sincere, with less of the form of religion, but more of its spirit" ("Leaves" 230).

In 1909, with the publication of a journalistic series on "The Chinese in America" and her autobiographical "Leaves from the Mental Portfolio of an Eurasian," Sui Sin Far experienced a liberating breakthrough in revealing her own identification with her fellow immigrants (White-Parks 173). This was the first writing she signed with her own name, admitting her Chinese heritage and speaking from her own personal experience of racial prejudice and persecution. By the time she moved to Boston in 1910, she was writing fiction, published in the prestigious *New England Magazine*, that criticized American Christian efforts to assimilate "immigrant cultures" and "colonized races" (White-Parks 174–75). Despite her own continual feelings of racial ambiguity, she asserted, "individuality is more than nationality" ("Leaves" 230). Despite years of racist repression, she finally succeeded in creating her own identity through her writing.

The short story "In the Land of the Free" was first published in the New York *Independent* (2 September 1909), pages 504–8. The text here is from *Mrs. Spring Fragrance and Other Writings* (cited below), pages 93–101.

Ling, Amy, and Annette White-Parks. "Introduction." In Sui Sin Far, *Mrs. Spring Fragrance and Other Writings*. Ed. Amy Ling and Annette White Parks. Urbana and Chicago: University of Illinois, 1995.

Sui Sin Far. "Leaves from the Mental Portfolio of an Eurasian" [1909]. *Mrs. Spring Fragrance and Other Writings*. Ed. Amy Ling and Annette White-Parks. Urbana and Chicago: University of Illinois, 1995. 218–30.

Sui Sin Far. "Sui Sin Far, the Half Chinese Writer, Tells of Her Career" [1912]. *Mrs. Spring Fragrance and Other Writings*. Ed. Amy Ling and Annette White-Parks. Urbana and Chicago: University of Illinois, 1995. 288–96.

White-Parks, Annette. "Introduction to Part Two: Other Works." In Sui Sin Far, *Mrs. Spring Fragrance and Other Writings*. Ed. Amy Ling and Annette White-Parks. Urbana and Chicago: University of Illinois, 1995. 169–77.

IN THE LAND OF THE FREE

I

"See, Little One—the hills in the morning sun. There is thy home for years to come. It is very beautiful and thou wilt be very happy there."

The Little One looked up into his mother's face in perfect faith. He was engaged in the pleasant occupation of sucking a sweetmeat; but that did not prevent him from gurgling responsively.

"Yes, my olive bud; there is where thy father is making a fortune for thee. Thy father! Oh, wilt thou not be glad to behold his dear face. 'Twas for thee I left him."

The Little One ducked his chin sympathetically against his mother's knee. She lifted him on to her lap. He was two years old, a round, dimple-cheeked boy with bright brown eyes and a sturdy little frame.

"Ah! Ah! Ah! Ooh! Ooh! Ooh!" puffed he, mocking a tugboat steaming by.

San Francisco's waterfront was lined with ships and steamers, while other craft, large and small, including a couple of white transports from the Philippines, lay at anchor here and there off shore. It was some time before the Eastern Queen could get docked, and even after that was accomplished, a lone Chinaman who had been waiting on the wharf for an hour was detained that much longer by men with the initials U.S.C. on their caps, before he could board the steamer and welcome his wife and child.

"This is thy son," announced the happy Lae Choo.

Hom Hing lifted the child, felt of his little body and limbs, gazed into his face with proud and joyous eyes; then turned inquiringly to a customs officer at his elbow.

"That's a fine boy you have there," said the man. "Where was he born?"

"In China," answered Hom Hing, swinging the Little One on his right shoulder, preparatory to leading his wife off the steamer.

"Ever been to America before?"

"No, not he," answered the father with a happy laugh.

The customs officer beckoned to another.

"This little fellow," said he, "is visiting America for the first time."

The other customs officer stroked his chin reflectively.

"Good day," said Hom Hing.

"Wait!" commanded one of the officers. "You cannot go just yet."

"What more now?" asked Hom Hing.

"I'm afraid," said the first customs officer, "that we cannot allow the boy to go ashore. There is nothing in the papers that you have shown us—your wife's papers and your own—having any bearing upon the child."

"There was no child when the papers were made out," returned Hom Hing. He spoke calmly; but there was apprehension in his eyes and in his tightening grip on his son.

"What is it? What is it?" quavered Lae Choo, who understood a little English.

The second customs officer regarded her pityingly.

"I don't like this part of the business," he muttered.

The first officer turned to Hom Hing and in an official tone of voice, said:

"Seeing that the boy has no certificate entitling him to admission to this country you will have to leave him with us."

"Leave my boy!" exclaimed Hom Hing.

"Yes; he will be well taken care of, and just as soon as we can hear from Washington he will be handed over to you."

"But," protested Hom Hing, "he is my son."

"We have no proof," answered the man with a shrug of his shoulders; "and even if so we cannot let him pass without orders from the Government."

"He is my son," reiterated Hom Hing, slowly and solemnly. "I am a Chinese merchant and have been in business in San Francisco for many years. When my wife told to me one morning that she dreamed of a green tree with spreading branches and one beautiful red flower growing thereon, I answered her that I wished my son to be born in our country, and for her to prepare to go to China. My wife complied with my wish. After my son was born my mother fell sick and my wife nursed and cared for her; then my father, too, fell sick, and my wife also nursed and cared for him. For twenty moons my wife care for and nurse the old people, and when they die they bless her and my son, and I send for her to return to me. I had no fear of trouble. I was a Chinese merchant and my son was my son."

"Very good, Hom Hing," replied the first officer. "Nevertheless, we take your son."

"No, you not take him; he my son too."

It was Lae Choo. Snatching the child from his father's arms she held and covered him with her own.

The officers conferred together for a few moments; then one drew Hom Hing aside and spoke in his ear.

Resignedly Hom Hing bowed his head, then approached his wife. "'Tis the law," said he, speaking in Chinese, "and 'twill be but for a little while— until tomorrow's sun arises."

"You, too," reproached Lae Choo in a voice eloquent with pain. But accustomed to obedience she yielded the boy to her husband, who in turn delivered him to the first officer. The Little One protested lustily against the transfer; but his mother covered her face with her sleeve and his father silently led her away. Thus was the law of the land complied with.

II

Day was breaking. Lae Choo, who had been awake all night, dressed herself, then awoke her husband.

"'Tis the morn," she cried. "Go, bring our son."

The man rubbed his eyes and arose upon his elbow so that he could see out of the window. A pale star was visible in the sky. The petals of a lily in a bowl on the windowsill were unfurled.

"'Tis not yet time," said he, laying his head down again.

"Not yet time. Ah, all the time that I lived before yesterday is not so much as the time that has been since my little one was taken from me."

The mother threw herself down beside the bed and covered her face.

Hom Hing turned on the light, and touching his wife's bowed head with a sympathetic hand inquired if she had slept.

"Slept!" she echoed, weepingly. "Ah, how could I close my eyes with my arms empty of the little body that has filled them every night for more than twenty moons! You do not know—man—what it is to miss the feel of the little fingers and the little toes and the soft round limbs of your little one. Even in the darkness his darling eyes used to shine up to mine, and often have I fallen into slumber with his pretty babble at my ear. And now, I see him not; I touch him not; I hear him not. My baby, my little fat one!"

"Now! Now! Now!" consoled Hom Hing, patting his wife's shoulder reassuringly; "there is no need to grieve so; he will soon gladden you again. There cannot be any law that would keep a child from its mother!"

Lae Choo dried her tears.

"You are right, my husband," she meekly murmured. She arose and stepped about the apartment, setting things to rights. The box of presents she had brought for her California friends had been opened the evening before; and silks, embroideries, carved ivories, ornamental lacquer-ware, brasses, camphorwood boxes, fans, and chinaware were scattered around in confused heaps. In the midst of unpacking the thought of her child in the hands of strangers had overpowered her, and she had left everything to crawl into bed and weep.

Having arranged her gifts in order she stepped out on to the deep balcony.

The star had faded from view and there were bright streaks in the western sky. Lae Choo looked down the street and around. Beneath the flat occupied by her and her husband were quarters for a number of bachelor Chinamen, and she could hear them from where she stood, taking their early morning breakfast. Below their dining-room was her husband's grocery store. Across the way was a large restaurant. Last night it had been resplendent with gay colored lanterns and the sound of music. The rejoicings over "the completion of the moon," by Quong Sum's firstborn, had been long and loud, and had caused her to tie a handkerchief over her ears. She, a bereaved mother, had it not in her heart to rejoice with other parents. This morning the place was more in accord with her mood. It was still and quiet. The revellers had dispersed or were asleep.

A roly-poly woman in black sateen, with long pendant earrings in her ears, looked up from the street below and waved her a smiling greeting. It was her old neighbor, Kuie Hoe, the wife of the gold embosser, Mark Sing. With her was a little boy in yellow jacket and lavender pantaloons. Lae Choo remembered him as a baby. She used to like to play with him in those days when she had no child of her own. What a long time ago that seemed! She caught her breath in a sigh, and laughed instead.

"Why are you so merry?" called her husband from within.

"Because my Little One is coming home," answered Lae Choo. "I am a happy mother—a happy mother."

She pattered into the room with a smile on her face.

* * *

The noon hour had arrived. The rice was steaming in the bowls and a fragrant dish of chicken and bamboo shoots was awaiting Hom Hing. Not for one moment had Lae Choo paused to rest during the morning hours; her activity had been ceaseless. Every now and again, however, she had raised her eyes to the gilded clock on the curiously carved mantelpiece. Once, she had exclaimed:

"Why so long, oh! why so long?" Then apostrophizing herself: "Lae Choo, be happy. The Little One is coming! The Little One is coming!" Several times she burst into tears and several times she laughed aloud.

Hom Hing entered the room; his arms hung down by his side.

"The Little One!" shrieked Lae Choo.

"They bid me call tomorrow."

With a moan the mother sank to the floor.

The noon hour passed. The dinner remained on the table.

III

The winter rains were over: the spring had come to California, flushing the hills with green and causing an ever-changing pageant of flowers to pass over them. But there was no spring in Lae Choo's heart, for the Little One remained away from her arms. He was being kept in a mission. White women were caring for him, and though for one full moon he had pined for his mother and refused to be comforted he was now apparently happy and contented. Five moons or five months had gone by since the day he had passed with Lae Choo through the Golden Gate; but the great Government at Washington still delayed sending the answer which would return him to his parents.

* * *

Hom Hing was disconsolately rolling up and down the balls in his abacus box when a keen-faced young man stepped into his store.

"What news?" asked the Chinese merchant.

"This!" The young man brought forth a typewritten letter. Hom Hing read the words:

> Re Chinese child, alleged to be the son of Hom Hing, Chinese merchant, doing business at 425 Clay street, San Francisco.
>
> Same will have attention as soon as possible.

Hom Hing returned the letter, and without a word continued his manipulation of the counting machine.

"Have you anything to say?" asked the young man.

"Nothing. They have sent the same letter fifteen times before. Have you not yourself showed it to me?"

"True!" The young man eyed the Chinese merchant furtively. He had a proposition to make and he was pondering whether or not the time was opportune.

"How is your wife?" he inquired solicitously—and diplomatically.

Hom Hing shook his head mournfully.

"She seems less every day," he replied. "Her food she takes only when I bid her and her tears fall continually. She finds no pleasure in dress or flowers and cares not to see her friends. Her eyes stare all night. I think before another moon she will pass into the land of spirits."

"No!" exclaimed the young man, genuinely startled.

"If the boy not come home I lose my wife sure," continued Hom Hing with bitter sadness.

"It's not right," cried the young man indignantly. Then he made his proposition.

The Chinese father's eyes brightened exceedingly.

"Will I like you to go to Washington and make them give you the paper to restore my son?" cried he. "How can you ask when you know my heart's desire?"

"Then," said the young fellow, "I will start next week. I am anxious to see this thing through if only for the sake of your wife's peace of mind."

"I will call her. To hear what you think to do will make her glad," said Hom Hing.

He called a message to Lae Choo upstairs through a tube in the wall. In a few moments she appeared, listless, wan, and hollow-eyed; but when her husband told her the young lawyer's suggestion she became as one electrified; her form straightened, her eyes glistened; the color flushed to her cheeks.

"Oh," she cried, turning to James Clancy, "You are a hundred man good!"

The young man felt somewhat embarrassed; his eyes shifted a little under the intense gaze of the Chinese mother.

"Well, we must get your boy for you," he responded. "Of course"—turning to Hom Hing—"it will cost a little money. You can't get fellows to hurry the Government for you without gold in your pocket."

Hom Hing stared blankly for a moment. Then: "How much do you want, Mr. Clancy?" he asked quietly.

"Well, I will need at least five hundred to start with."

Hom Hing cleared his throat.

"I think I told to you the time I last paid you for writing letters for me and seeing the Custom boss here that nearly all I had was gone!"

"Oh, well then we won't talk about it, old fellow. It won't harm the boy to stay where he is, and your wife may get over it all right."

"What that you say?" quavered Lae Choo.

James Clancy looked out of the window.

"He says," explained Hom Hing in English, "that to get our boy we have to have much money."

"Money! Oh, yes."

Lae Choo nodded her head.

"I have not got the money to give him."

For a moment Lae Choo gazed wonderingly from one face to the other; then, comprehension dawning upon her, with swift anger, pointing to the lawyer, she cried: "You not one hundred man good; you just common white man."

"Yes, ma'am," returned James Clancy, bowing and smiling ironically.

Hom Hing pushed his wife behind him and addressed the lawyer again: "I might try," said he, "to raise something; but five hundred—it is not possible."

"What about four?"

"I tell you I have next to nothing left and my friends are not rich."

"Very well!"

The lawyer moved leisurely toward the door, pausing on its threshold to light a cigarette.

"Stop, white man; white man, stop!"

Lae Choo, panting and terrified, had started forward and now stood beside him, clutching his sleeve excitedly.

"You say you can go to get paper to bring my Little One to me if Hom Hing give you five hundred dollars?"

The lawyer nodded carelessly; his eyes were intent upon the cigarette which would not take the fire from the match.

"Then you go get paper. If Hom Hing not can give you five hundred dollars—I give you perhaps what more that much."

She slipped a heavy gold bracelet from her wrist and held it out to the man. Mechanically he took it.

"I go get more!"

She scurried away, disappearing behind the door through which she had come.

"Oh, look here, I can't accept this," said James Clancy, walking back to Hom Hing and laying down the bracelet before him.

"It's all right," said Hom Hing, seriously, "pure China gold. My wife's parent give it to her when we married."

"But I can't take it anyway," protested the young man.

"It is all same as money. And you want money to go to Washington," replied Hom Hing in a matter of fact manner.

"See, my jade earrings—my gold buttons—my hairpins—my comb of pearl and my rings—one, two, three, four, five rings; very good—very good—all same much money. I give them all to you. You take and bring me paper for my Little One."

Lae Choo piled up her jewels before the lawyer.

Hom Hing laid a restraining hand upon her shoulder. "Not all, my wife," he said in Chinese. He selected a ring—his gift to Lae Choo when she dreamed of the tree with the red flower. The rest of the jewels he pushed toward the white man.

"Take them and sell them," said he. "They will pay your fare to Washington and bring you back with the paper."

For one moment James Clancy hesitated. He was not a sentimental man; but something within him arose against accepting such payment for his services.

"They are good, good," pleadingly asserted Lae Choo, seeing his hesitation.

Whereupon he seized the jewels, thrust them into his coat pocket, and walked rapidly away from the store.

IV

Lae Choo followed after the missionary woman through the mission nursery school. Her heart was beating so high with happiness that she could scarcely breathe. The paper had come at last—the precious paper which gave Hom Hing and his wife the right to the possession of their own child. It was ten months now since he had been taken from them—ten months since the sun had ceased to shine for Lae Choo.

The room was filled with children—most of them wee tots, but none so wee as her own. The mission woman talked as she walked. She told Lae Choo that little Kim, as he had been named by the school, was the pet of the place, and that his little tricks and ways amused and delighted every one. He had been rather difficult to manage at first and had cried much for his mother; "but children so soon forget, and after a month he seemed quite at home and played around as bright and happy as a bird."

"Yes," responded Lae Choo. "Oh, yes, yes!"

But she did not hear what was said to her. She was walking in a maze of anticipatory joy.

"Wait here, please," said the mission woman, placing Lae Choo in a chair. "The very youngest ones are having their breakfast."

She withdrew for a moment—it seemed like an hour to the mother— then she reappeared leading by the hand a little boy dressed in blue cotton overalls and white-soled shoes. The little boy's face was round and dimpled and his eyes were very bright.

"Little One, ah, my Little One!" cried Lae Choo.

She fell on her knees and stretched her hungry arms toward her son.

But the Little One shrunk from her and tried to hide himself in the folds of the white woman's skirt.

"Go'way, go'way!" he bade his mother.

Discussion Questions

1. Analyze the theme of "In the Land of the Free" and explain its relation to its title.
2. Explain how James Clancy, the lawyer, is portrayed in the story. Explain your own opinion of his character, but also indicate, citing a brief quotation, how the narrator withholds judgment of the lawyer.

LINDA HASSELSTROM
(1943–)

Born in Texas, the author moved to South Dakota when her mother divorced in 1947. Five years later, she was adopted by her mother's second husband, John Hasselstrom, whose own father had emigrated from Sweden to the Black Hills area at the turn of the century. Thus, she grew up on a ranch, committed from an early age to a physically demanding and passionate relationship to the land. When she was only nine years old, she began writing a novel, and this interest continued by publishing stories and poems in local magazines during high school and college. In 1965, she earned a B.A. in English and Journalism from the University of South Dakota. Four years later, she completed an M.A. in American Literature at the University of Missouri. In 1971, she returned to South Dakota with her first husband to start a literary magazine, *Sunday Clothes*, which she published through periods of financial crisis for eleven years, long after her first marriage ended in 1973. During this period, she continued to work on her father's ranch, to take on temporary editing jobs, and to teach at local colleges and at the Prairie Winds Young Writers' Conference. She also became an environmental activist focused on banning nuclear power plants, radioactive waste dumps, and uranium mining. In 1979, she married George Snell, an outdoorsman and frontier-history buff who became an active partner on the ranch (Danker 337–39).

In 1984, she published her first volume of poetry, *Caught by One Wing*, and received a National Endowment for the Arts fellowship to continue her writing. Three years later, her perseverance paid off in the simultaneous publication of three volumes: a second poetry collection, *Roadkill*; a journal, *Windbreak: A Woman Rancher on the Northern Plains*; and an essay collection, *Going Over East: Reflections of a Woman Rancher*. In 1990, the Center for Western Studies in Sioux Falls, South Dakota, honored her as the first woman to receive its Western American Writer award. The following year, she published a collection of poetry and essays, *Land Circle: Writings Collected from the Land*, but was also forced to leave the ranch when her father demanded that she quit writing in order to devote more time to the family business. Though this transition was hard and she had problems living with "the noise and pace of city life," for the first time she was able to devote her full attention to developing her craft, without the daily demands of other work (Danker 338–40).

All of her writing concerns "the duties of ranch life, the beauties and hazards of the natural world, the importance of protecting the prairie environment, and the joys, griefs, humor, and courage of those who make their living on the land" (Danker 337). In *Windbreak* (1987), she organizes her journal entries by season and emphasizes the unremitting force of weather in the northern plains. In a subsequent *Life* magazine essay, "Journal of a Woman Rancher" (1989), Hasselstrom reflects on the intimate and demanding relationship between the natural world and the enduring people who serve the land. After relating a cow's death during calving, she comments, "Spring always brings this tart mixture of life and death, and I am oddly heartened to see it again, to know I am part of the cycle. . . . Perhaps knowing deep darkness helps us to open ourselves to the joys of greening grass to feed new calves that will feed our families" (qtd. in Danker 344). In *Land Circle* (1991), she meditates on her relationship with the environment: "The lessons of the ranch can be summarized in a way that is almost absurdly simple, yet they cover the larger work of my life as a rancher and a writer, as well as my politics and religion. . . . The lessons I have learned concern birth, death, and the responsibility for the life between" (qtd. in Danker 346). In effect, her works reflect the "conviction that the goals of environmentalism and family (noncorporate) ranching are compatible" (337). In essays and poetry, she continues to insist on the compatibility of cattle and wildlife, of both loving and killing the animals that enrich human connections to the land.

The following selections are from *Dakota Bones: Collected Poems of Linda Hasselstrom* (Granite Falls, MN: Spoon River Poetry Press, 1993), pages 5, 8–9, and 34–35.

Danker, Kathleen. "Linda Hasselstrom." *American Nature Writers, Volume I.* Ed. John Elder. New York: Charles Scribner's Sons, 1996. 337–48.

SPRING

———<◆>———

Spring is here:
the first skunk lies dead
at the highway's rim,
white fur still bright,
nose stained with one drop of blood.

A calf born dead yesterday
was found by coyotes in the night:
only the head and one front foot remain.
The cat preens in a pile of meadowlark feathers.
A blue jay is eating baby robins.
The hens caught a mouse in their corn
this morning; pecked it to shrieking shreds.

It's spring:
time to kill the kittens.
Their mewing blends with the meadowlark song.
I tried drowning them once;
it was slow, painful.
Now I bash each with a wrench,
once, hard.

Each death makes a dull sound,
going deep in the ground
without
reverberations.

SEASONS IN SOUTH DAKOTA

—for Rodney, who asked

I
Dirty snow left in the gullies, pale
green spread overnight on the hills
mark spring.
　　　　　Taking corn to the hens
I hear a waterfall of redwing blackbird song.
When I open the windows to their raucous mating
I let in something else as well:
soon I'll pace the hills under the moon.

II
Watching struggling heifers birth,
greasing the tractor, I may miss
summer.
　　　　Like spring, it bursts open:
blooming hay demands the mower,
All day I ride the tractor,
isolated by roar.
it's time to turn the bulls out
to the cows, check leaning fences.
Even in summer nights' sweat
I hate to sleep alone.
When I'm too tired to care,
I still hear the larks, feel
the cold flow in each window at dawn.

III

Autumn whistles in some day when I'm
riding the gray gelding
bringing in fat calves for sale:
the air quick-chills, grass turns brown.
Last fall I found two gray hairs;
just as quick, winter came:

I was hurrying to pile fresh wood
from the one-woman crosscut saw
when the first flakes crowded the sky.

IV

Despite the feeding, pitching hay to
black cows with frost-rimmed eyes,
cutting ice on the dam under the eyes
of sky and one antelope,
there's still time to sit before the fire,
curse the dead cold outside,
the other empty chair.

HOMESTEADING IN DAKOTA

It was a typical prairie homestead:
a hundred sixty dusty acres
with not one tree.
Mr. Fisher put up a soddy for his wife, five kids,
and dug a well by hand the first month.
The kids and the woman worked the winch
after the well got below ten feet.
                              He cut logs
in the hills ten miles away for a solid barn,
log-roofed. Once they were settled he went
to the mines in Deadwood, seventy miles away,
for winter cash.
                    She stayed in the soddy,
milked the cow, dug out a little garden,
struggling with the sod laced together by buffalo grass
roots. Now and then she'd stop for breath, shade
her eyes, look at the horizon line
drawn smooth against the sun.

Mr. Fisher—she called him that—
came home when he could,
once or twice a month all summer. Neighbors
helped her catch the cow, fight fire, sit up
when the youngest child died.
                                Once
he got a late start, rode in at midnight.
Fumbling at the low door, he heard struggle inside.
The kids were all awake, pale blank faces
hanging in the dark.
                        When he pushed aside
the curtain to the double bunk
he saw the window open,
a white-legged form running in the moonlight,
his wife's screaming face.
He shot once out the window, missed;
shot her and didn't.

The neighbors said Black Douglas, on the next claim,
walked for a month like he had cactus in his feet.
The kids grew up wild as coyotes.
                        He never went to trial.
He'd done the best he could;
not his fault the dark spoiled his aim the first time.

Discussion Questions

1. In "Spring," list the images you found surprising or dramatic. What feelings or tendencies are usually associated with this season? By contrast, generalize about what characterizes this season in the poem.
2. In the final stanza, what can "Each death" refer to? Explain how "without / reverberations" suggests a theme for the poem.
3. Analyze the sounds that characterize the seasons in stanzas I, II, and III of "Seasons in South Dakota." By contrast, is winter silent? Explain.
4. In stanza I of this poem, what does "something else" refer to? Why will the speaker "pace the hills"? Quote phrases in stanzas II, III, and IV that relate to this concern. Explain one constant feature that the speaker lives with throughout the seasons. Then explain how this concern suggests a theme for the poem.
5. Quoting several words or phrases as evidence, describe the tone or feeling expressed in "Homesteading in Dakota."

6. Describe the personalities of Mr. and Mrs. Fisher as depicted in this poem. Explain the judgment against Mr. Fisher in the line "He'd done the best he could."
7. Citing images and quoting phrases from all three poems, explain one or more unifying concerns or themes in Hasselstrom's poetry.

DRAG'S A LIFE: WOMEN, GENDER, AND CROSS-DRESSING IN THE NINETEENTH-CENTURY WEST

————⟨◆⟩————

BY EVELYN A. SCHLATTER

"A woman shall not wear anything that pertains to a man, nor shall a man put on a woman's garment."

—*Deuteronomy* 22:5

What the real West most offered men was the most difficult for women to attain—independence. Even though it was legally acceptable for women to take land in their own names, most did not do so as lone, single women. For a woman, setting out alone was extremely risky, usually because of unwanted male attentions. The West, even though it claimed to offer a taste of freedom for all, was a man's world. Some women, therefore, chose to adopt male garb and "pass" as men. They crossed the boundary between male and female not so much to stretch the limits of nineteenth-century roles but rather to escape the restrictions of womanhood and to seek opportunities available to westering men. The choices these women made and the strategy they employed make sense within the context of the economic and intimate crosscurrents of gender and the ways in which clothing marked and created that context in the late nineteenth century. . . ."

The nineteenth-century West, for entirely practical and nonmystical reasons, proved an ideal destination for some female cross-dressers who wanted what a male world offered. They came west in search of personal independence, employment, or freedom from abusive male partners or family members. Some were in search of lost male lovers while others wished to live in peace with female lovers. Many came because of a combination of these factors. Whatever their individual reasons, cross-dressed women went west to find places for themselves, and they often gravitated to urban or urbanizing areas.

Certain western regions, because of their industrial and economic foundations, tended to attract a certain type of clientele. Growing urban centers and boomtowns in mining areas offered anonymity and opportunity to those who came to stay or simply passed through. Mining camps, especially, may have appealed to women cross-dressers because of the skewed sex ratios. A lone man in a mining camp or a quickly growing city was one of hundreds or even thousands. One more man among so many others garnered little scrutiny. . . .

Newspaper correspondent Albert D. Richardson toured western mining regions between 1857 and 1867. He recorded his experiences and published them after his ten-year odyssey. One of his anecdotes described meeting a man who had advertised for "a young lad to bring water, black his boots and keep the sanctum in order." The caution he added to his advertisement was that "no young woman in disguise need apply." Richardson stated that such a stipulation "was needful in a mining country," because of his own knowledge of several male impersonators he himself had met, "each telling some romantic story of her past life." He dismissed them as being of "the wretched class against which society shuts its iron doors, bidding them hasten uncared-for to destruction."[10]

Richardson's admonishments are part of a backlash against not only westering male impersonators but their predecessors. Westward women cross-dressers are part of a long romantic literary tradition in Euro-American history in which male impersonators enjoyed a bit of fame and perhaps a bit of infamy as well. Among the best-documented seventeenth- and eighteenth-century cross-dressers were soldiers and sailors who took on the guise of men in order to support themselves financially, act on patriotic impulses, escape abusive men, follow male lovers or relatives to battle or sea. Others wished to live in peace with female lovers. A few of these women who served admirably at sea or in battle prior to the nineteenth century revealed their secrets and published biographies, garnering friendly public attention. Some, even after "coming out" as women, were granted military pensions.[11] Their hard work and service to their countries as men made them novelties in the public eye, true, but heroic novelties nonetheless.

The American Revolution and the Civil War witnessed a flurry of male impersonation; a few cross-dressed women published accounts of their endeavors and scores more died on the battlefield.[12] In spite of the literary tradition, sharpened gender distinctions found expression in mid- to late-nineteenth-century commentary from people like correspondent Richardson. Western women cross-dressers increasingly suffered the burgeoning backlash.

Charlotte Arnold was one of these unfortunate women; she was arrested some twenty times for cross-dressing. Refusing to pay the fines, Arnold did jail time instead. Lillie Hitchcock Coit, who had a penchant for visiting San Francisco night spots in male attire, managed to avoid arrest, possibly because she was wealthy and city officials attributed her behavior to "eccentricity."[13] An Arizona woman, Mary Sawyer (a.k.a. Mollie Monroe), was not so fortunate and ended up in a Stockton, California, asylum in 1877. Sawyer spent Arizona's boom years mining, cross-dressing, drinking, and taking different men as sexual partners. The judge who finally sentenced her to the asylum could have done so on the basis of any of these behaviors, which were all "unwomanly" and subject to local regulation. Sawyer's alcoholism coupled with her cross-dressing and her refusal to settle down in a heterosexual monogamous union may have played most heavily in her sentence.[14]

In 1860, during Colorado's gold-rush years, a Denver woman in male attire attracted the attention of an eastern correspondent during an auction. He described her as dressed in "nicely fitting coat, vest, pants, boots, and beaver.... She frequently appears on horseback, and always astride the saddle." The letter writer further complained about what he perceived as evident moral decay. As the woman in male attire wandered the auction grounds, an immigrant man gambled with dice and the auctioneer solicited bids for the effects of a man who had died in a fire. "Is it surprising," the correspondent lamented, "that Christianity, in the midst of so much wickedness, should make but moderate progress?"[15]

Five years later, a Denver newspaper's editors reported a woman "perambulating" the city's streets in "bifurcated raiment." They suggested she had "best look out or she will be snatched."[16] The veiled warning was no idle threat for Colorado women. In 1887, Georgie Phillips, in and out of courts for ten years, served sixty days in jail. The policeman who arrested her stated that she "made a rather good looking 17 year old boy" but because of her history with the police, she could not fool him. Georgie was knock-kneed. Her crimes included charges of vagrancy and wearing men's clothes in public.[17]

Legal proscription of cross-dressing represents state and local attempts to control sexual behavior through the regulation of appearance.[18] Denver, like many American cities, included a lewd behavior statute in its ordinances. Cross-dressing in public fell under this designation. In 1875, anyone who appeared "in any public place within this city in a state of nudity, or in a dress not belonging to his or her sex, or in an indecent or lewd dress" was subject to pay "not less than ten dollars, nor more than one hundred dollars." Such acts were deemed "Offences against Good Morals and Decency."[19]

In spite of moral implications, Denver newspapers continued to print stories that involved women cross-dressers. In one 1889 issue of the *Denver Times*, several anecdotes that involved women wearing men's clothing appeared. Clearly, Denver officials were concerned about how far and for what reasons a woman pushed the bounds of propriety. If a cross-dressed woman was in the company of a man, then she seems to have avoided strict legal prosecution. Women who operated outside of heterosexual unions, on the other hand, were not so fortunate. Without male lovers or relatives to speak for them and with the presumption of sexual deviance hovering over them, cross-dressers who eschewed male companionship for whatever reasons received stricter punishment than their male-companioned counterparts.

The *Denver Times* details the following occurrences. Two men arrived in Cheyenne, Wyoming, looking for work. Both were printers. One, Jack Bennett, had a union card and soon obtained employment. His partner, "Jimmie," and he were inseparable during the week they spent in Cheyenne before deciding to go further west. The night before their scheduled departure, a saloon altercation with another group of printers resulted in the revelation of Jimmie's true identity—Jack's sister. The two departed Cheyenne hastily the next morning.[20] Jimmie may have been Jack's lover rather than sister; Jack made it a point to call her his sister, but the article's writer implies that Jack was merely claiming that she was. If Jimmie was actually Jack's lover, he may have claimed siblinghood in order to ensure that he could be a legal protector for her, especially if the two were not married.

In another incident, a Boston merchant disguised his mistress as a man, claiming she was his son, Arthur. They hobnobbed at a swanky hotel in Manitou Springs, an elegant spa near Colorado Springs. Arthur's true identity was soon discerned by private detectives the merchant's wife had hired. "Arthur" was arrested. The merchant paid the thousand-dollar bond only to be rebuffed; his mistress fled before the trial and his wife divorced him.[21]

A lighter occurrence in 1889 concerned two Denver men strolling downtown after dark. A police sergeant confronted the two, alert immediately to the fact that one was a woman. She was, in fact, her male companion's wife and had expressed an interest in seeing Denver's night life. Her husband had agreed to her request, loaned her one of his suits, and escorted her on their jaunt. The policeman, for his part, merely issued a warning and asked that the husband take his wife home.[22]

Because the cross-dresser had been in the company of her husband, and therefore within the sanctity of a heterosexual union with a proper guardian, the policeman let the two off with merely a warning. Georgie Phillips was a different matter. In 1887, the same issue of the *Times* reported, Georgie, dressed as a man, attempted to rent a room with a female companion in a Denver building. The proprietor, however, was a detective who had arrested her several times in the past, and Georgie and companion quickly left the premises before he could do so again.[23]

Women whose primary affective relationships involved other women were subject to greater public scrutiny than cross-dressers, as long as the latter had male lovers. A *Denver Times* account of two women in Colorado's Pitkin County demonstrates the growing public fear of homosexual relationships between women: "Society in this section of the county has been rent from center to circumference during the last six weeks over the sensational love affair between Miss Clara Dietrich, postmistress and general storekeeper at Emma [the town in question], and Miss Ora Chatfield . . . which culminated . . . in the elopement of the two ladies who are now supposed to be stopping at a hotel in Denver."[24]

The article then describes the two and plays upon fears of predatory women who draw younger, more innocent women into their clutches. Dietrich and Chatfield were cousins; Dietrich was the older of the two. The two lived together for a time, but Chatfield apparently succumbed to "nervous prostration" and an investigation (presumably family-initiated) revealed that she was madly in love with Dietrich. A warrant was issued for Dietrich's arrest in order to ascertain her sanity. Upon her arrest, the two women's correspondence was appropriated and turned over to the local sheriff. After an initial outcry, the two women then instigated a ruse; Dietrich left for Aspen under the auspices of marrying a man there and Chatfield claimed to be off to visit relatives. Neither did what they said; they instead fled the vicinity together, allegedly headed for Denver. One man commenting on the affair said that aside from the "unnatural affection for each other," the two women appeared to be "perfectly rational."[25]

By the late nineteenth century, scientific and public rhetoric about the dangers of homosexuality intertwined with male fears of women wresting political and economic clout from men. Women who cross-dressed—and, by extension, women who acted independently of men—were now conflated with those who expressed homosexual desires and, consequently, were construed to be "sick."[26]

Regardless of how public and legal opinion viewed them, male impersonators were as varied as the society within which they moved. Some married men or, like Mary Sawyer, had several male partners. Others maintained relationships with women. Still others may have had relationships with both men and women or with no one at all. Jeanne Bonnet, a Parisian transplant in San Jose, California, formed a gang of thieves in which her lover, Blanche Buneau, was also a member. Another San Jose gender-crosser, known as businessman Milton Matson, was engaged to Helen Fairweather, a San Francisco schoolteacher.[27]

In spite of rising public disapproval of their actions, some nineteenth-century women managed to find opportunities for better lives through cross-dressing. Male clothing offered them personal security, independence, and the chance to improve their economic positions without having to marry men. Others took to the road, wearing their new identities at first like stiff new boots, later like a favorite pair of trousers—comfortable and secretly familiar. Seeking new beginnings, some women gender-crossers headed for parts unknown where they might live as the men they projected. The West, as its mystique suggests, offered some of these cross-dressers the chance to begin anew.

In 1906, Gilbert Allen published a story he said he had heard from a Rocky Mountain prospector:

> I was a scout for the government during the early frontier days. . . . This duty often carried me over the overland trail, and on several such occasions I had particularly noticed one pony rider who, when met with in his run by night or day, was wont to flit by me like a ghost. He rode the best of horses, was trim as a dandy in his dress of top boots, corduroy pants, velvet sack coat, neglige shirt and slouch hat. He was small, graceful and handsome enough for a girl, but he had a pluck nothing yet had daunted.[28]

The rider called himself Brown. He had endured confrontations with outlaws and Indians, he said, but he never spoke in detail of his past. When the prospector-scout discovered the rider's true sex, he agreed to keep the secret. Several months later, when he returned to the station where Brown habitually started her run, he discovered that she was gone, having suddenly given up her place as rider and headed back east.

Her stint as a man, it transpired, had begun when she followed a male lover who had fled to the West, accused of a crime Brown believed he hadn't committed. She had gone west to find him. One day, while traveling with the prospector-scout, she became involved in an altercation with a group of outlaws. She shot one only to discover that he was the lover she sought. As he lay dying, he told her that he had, indeed, committed the crime of which he was accused. It was at this juncture that the prospector-scout discovered Brown's true identity.[29]

Some women cross-dressers, like Brown, became Pony Express riders. Others turned to banditry. In New Mexico, a masked desperado with a beltful of guns held up a stage between Deming and Silver City. Upon closer examination, one of the stagehands discerned that the bandit was actually a woman. She robbed all present of their cash, taking a particularly large roll from "the heaviest fellow in the bunch." She then summarily dismissed her victims and took off her mask, pointing at the heavyset fellow. "This measly hound here," she allegedly announced, "was once my husband. I got a divorce from him up at Las Vegas and for a year I never could get a cent out of him for alimony." Therefore, she finished, "I've taken the law in my own hands as a high spirited woman should." And with that, the witness stated, she "swung her hat by way of farewell and disappeared in the chaparral bushes."[30]

Oklahoma's Tom King was legendary for her outlaw deeds. She escaped from an El Reno jail but was later captured in Kansas. Involved in various illicit practices, including horse theft, she had spent years on the run from federal marshals. In one incident, she passed herself off as a wealthy Texas ranchman, wearing "high heeled boots, ponderous spurs and the regulation sombrero." Rumor had it that she was not "altogether a white woman." It was said that she had been born in the Ozark Mountains in southwest Missouri, where her father (also Tom King) operated an illegal still and peddled contraband whiskey. One or both of her parents may have been either Native American or African American; regardless, known sources on King's ethnicity are silent, exemplifying once again the difficulty involved in finding women of color who cross-dressed.[31]

Not all women cross-dressers, when found out, ended up in asylums, courts, or jails. Some managed to win public support. Stockton, California, provides a case in point. The city's favorite gender-crosser, known as Babe Bean, lived on a houseboat on nearby McLeod's Lake. Arrested in 1897 at age twenty for cross-dressing, she wrote out her story because she claimed to have lost her speech in an accident. As a man, she wrote, "I can travel freely, feel protected and find work."[32]

Though her neighbors called her "Jack," she noted that her real name was Babe Bean. She refused to discuss her family but claimed they were "one of the best in the land." Her mother, fearing for her tomboy daughter's future, had seen fit to consign her to a convent. At fifteen, Bean had married her brother's best friend in order to escape the convent and to see the world. She divorced him a few months later and wandered for four years through mountains, cities, and hobo camps. Bean often expressed regret that her "rough manner" may have offended her mother, whom she claimed to "love with all her heart."[33]

Intrigued by the young male impersonator and perhaps taking pity upon Bean because of her romantically tragic story, many Stockton residents began to treat her with affectionate curiosity. The local bachelor's club granted her an honorary membership and the *Stockton Evening Mail* hired her as a reporter, though some did not find Bean's social conduct amusing. A letter that appeared in the paper from the "Girls of Stockton" demanded to know "why Babe Bean should be allowed to dress that way, while if any of the rest of us wanted to walk out in that kind of costume for a change, we would be arrested quicker than quick. There used to be a law against females dressing like the male human being, but it seems not to apply to Babe Bean."[34]

Reasons for Bean's cross-dressing in full view of the public eye without further legal harassment remain obscure. She may simply have won local support through the force of her personality. The fact that she was mute (or claimed to be so) may have softened legislative hearts toward her. Or perhaps local governing officials saw no harm in allowing Bean to live as she chose, as long as she stayed out of real trouble. Besides, the explanation she offered—escaping from convent life—and her desire to protect her family identity may have garnered sympathy from Stockton residents.

With the outbreak of the Spanish-American War in 1898, Babe Bean disappeared both from local headlines and from Stockton, only to surface in the American forces as Lieutenant Jack Garland. After the war, Garland moved to San Francisco where she served as a male nurse during the earthquake and fire of 1906. She also provided emergency medical care for the homeless during these disasters. Garland stayed on in San Francisco for the next thirty years in various rooming houses and operated as a free lance social worker for the homeless and hungry. In 1936, "Uncle Jack" collapsed and was summarily rushed to a hospital where she died. Hospital attendants, at first treating the death as routine, discovered not only the true sex of Jack Garland but her other two identities. It seems Babe Bean had been born Elvira Virginia Mugarrieta, daughter of Jose Marcos Mugarrieta, a Mexican military commander who, while in New Orleans, had met Bean's mother, Eliza Alice Denny Garland, the daughter of Rice Garland, Louisiana congressman and later Louisiana supreme court judge.[35]

Unlike Babe Bean, who managed to beat the system, most nineteenth-century women cross-dressers were in constant danger of exposure, arrest, or incarceration in jails or insane asylums. Some came west to seek the mother lodes of opportunity offered to their biological male counterparts who sometimes colluded with them. But the West, however seductive its promise of liberation, replicated many Euro-American social expectations and restrictions that dealt with sex and gender. Nevertheless, the rewards were worth the risks. Cross-dressing kept women off the public dole, protected them from sexual harassment, and enabled escape from abusive male partners or relatives. But it required the construction of a new self at the expense of the old in a social climate intent upon maintaining a woman's "proper place."

In 1992, TriStar Pictures released Maggie Greenwald's production of *The Ballad of Little Jo*, starring actress Suzy Amis as Jo Monaghan. Little Jo had gained notoriety upon her death around the turn of the century when her neighbors first discovered that the slightly built rancher was a woman. Greenwald's telling of Josephine Monaghan's story portrays a young woman who takes to male attire in order to escape family disgrace back east and to protect herself from unwanted, often violent male advances as she wends her way west to Idaho. Jo realizes that any opportunities for economic independence are much greater for her as a man than as a woman. She manages to save enough money to purchase a small ranch where she spends the rest of her life, mostly alone, jealously guarding the secret of her identity. Amis's Monaghan is desperately unapproachable and solitary. Beneath her prickly exterior, though, the audience senses a heavy sorrow and repressed guilt: Little Jo has left her son back east with her sister, who has told him his mother is dead, even though the two women correspond throughout Monaghan's life.

The Ballad of Little Jo is not an adventurous shoot-'em-up in which the bad guy gets his comeuppance and the good-girl-dressed-as-guy finds happiness in the arms of the leading man or at least happiness in a dress. The only respite Greenwald gives Monaghan is a brief relationship with a Chinese man whom Jo has saved from a lynching. When he dies after a long illness, Jo reverts to her secluded and detached existence. And so she remains until her death, as solitary and lonely as she was most of her life.[36]

The Ballad of Little Jo is not glamorous. As a result, as Greenwald learned, it did not do well at the box office. We can understand women dressing like men, as long as they still look like women, but we can't deal with women actually changing gender identities and passing as men. To do so threatens heterosexual constructions of gender and male authority. Amis's Jo Monaghan as the cross-dressed woman eschews all "feminine" characteristics and appearances and does not marry the handsome leading man. No one rides off into the sunset. No one wears a white hat. And the ending isn't happy. This is a true-to-life "western." Idaho gives Little Jo a new beginning, spectacular views, employment, personal liberty. But the price is enormous personal sacrifice.

The real Jo Monaghan, like so many other gender-crossers, at once subverted the nineteenth-century gender system and also affirmed it. By adopting the dress and mannerisms of the opposite sex, male impersonators became men. Their actions did not necessarily pave the way for feminism, though they proved threatening for many in the West, as reflected in the press and in popular fiction. For example, though many gender-crossers voted in western territories and states that had not yet granted women the vote, their actions went unremarked because they could not reveal their secret at risk of personal safety and livelihood. Ironically, the women who were discovered may have unwittingly created a feminist dialogue—however brief it seemed—in public discourse. By fooling men and gaining access to a male power structure, these women demonstrated that gender is not immutable, not biologically ordained—something far more threatening to a bipolar gender system than the simple act of appropriating male clothing.

However we imagine the "frontier" and the liberty it promised some people, the fact remains that it was and still is as much a creation of long-standing sociocultural desires as it was and is a historical process or a specific region. New beginnings in the West were actually reconstructions of old ways, but some women managed to prove that men, like women, are *made*, not necessarily *born*, which just goes to show that clothes could and did make the man.

NOTES

[Since nine paragraphs have been omitted from the opening of this article, footnotes refer to the original numbering and begin with number 10.]

Many thanks to Sue Armitage and Betsy Jameson for their attentive and gentle editing and continued guidance. Their comments and insights have proven both immensely helpful and often soothing.

10. Albert D. Richardson, *Beyond the Mississippi: From the Great River to the Great Ocean 1857–1867* (Hartford, Conn.: American Publishing, 1867), 200.

11. Ireland's Christian Davies (1667–1739) became Christopher Welsh to follow a missing husband into the British army. She traveled extensively throughout Europe and earned a military pension after her service. See C. J. S. Thompson, *The Mysteries of Sex: Women Who Posed as Men and Men Who Impersonated Women* (New York: Causeway Books, 1974; orig. pub. 1938), and Estelle Jelinek, "Disguise Autobiographies: Women Masquerading as Men," *Women's Studies International Forum* 10, no. 1 (1987): 53–62. Regarding Davies, see Jelinek, 54–55.

One of the best-known military cross-dressers was an Englishwoman, Hannah Snell (1723–92). Snell took the guise of a man and enlisted in the army in order to pursue an unfaithful husband. It took nine years of continuous lobbying before the English government grudgingly granted Snell her pension. See Jelinek, "Disguise Autobiographies," 55, and Julie Wheelwright, *Amazons and Military Maids: Women Who Dressed as Men in the Pursuit of Life, Liberty and Happiness* (Boston: Pandora Press, 1989). See also Snell's memoirs, *The Female Soldier, or the Surprising Life and Adventures of Hannah Snell* (London: R. Walker, 1750).

12. See Richard Hall, *Patris in Disguise: Women Warriors of the Civil War* (New York: Marlowe and Company, 1993), xi, 107–32. Deborah Sampson (another spelling is "Samson") is one of the best-known male impersonators who fought in the Revolutionary War; two others are Margaret Corbin and Nancy Hart. Ibid., xi. A Cuban-born woman who successfully passed as a man in the Confederate ranks joined as Harry T. Buford. See Loreta Janeta Velazquez's autobiography, edited by C. J. Worthington, titled *The Woman in Battle: a Narrative of the Exploits, Adventures, and Travels of Madame Loreta Janeta Velazquez, Otherwise Known as Lieutenant Harry T. Buford, Confederate States Army* (Hartford, Conn.: Belknap, 1876). Sarah Emma Edmonds served for the Union as Frank Thompson. Her autobiography is *Nurse and Spy in the Union Army: Comprising the Adventures and Expe-*

riences of a Woman in Hospitals, Camps, and Battlefields (Hartford, Conn.: W. S. Williams, 1864). Charley (Charlotte) "Hatfield" also served in the Union Army for an Iowa regiment after an unsuccessful attempt to both strike it rich in the Pikes Peak gold rush and track down an errant paramour. The biographical, somewhat exaggerated tale of "Mountain Charley" is *The Adventures of Mrs. E. J. Guerin Who Was Thirteen Years in Male Attire as Mountain Charley* (Norman: University of Oklahoma Press, 1968) with introduction by Fred M. Mazzulla and William Kostka. The exploits and adventures of Charley entered western lore via an alleged confidant named George West, who began publishing excerpts from her life in 1885. See Hall, *Patriots in Disguise*, chap. 13.

13. Cited in the San Francisco Lesbian and Gay History Project (hereafter SFLGHP), "'She Even Chewed Tobacco': A Pictorial Narrative of Passing Women in America," in *Hidden from History: Reclaiming the Gay and Lesbian Past*, eds. Martin Duberman, Martha Vicinus, and George Chauncey, Jr. (New York: Meridian Books, 1989), 187.

14. Susan L. Johnson, "Sharing Bed and Board: Cohabitation and Cultural Difference in Central Arizona Mining Towns, 1863–1873," in *The Women's West*, eds. Susan Armitage and Elizabeth Jameson (Norman: University of Oklahoma Press, 1984), 84–86.

15. Libeus Barney, *Letters of the Pike's Peak Gold Rush: Early-Day Letters by Libeus Barney, Reprinted from the Bennington Banner, Vermont, 1859–1860* (San Jose, Calif.: The Talisman Press, 1959). This particular letter is dated 7 February 1860. The notation is Denver City, Jefferson Territory, Rocky Mountains.

16. *Rocky Mountain News* (Denver, Colo.), 20 September 1865.

17. *Denver Times*, 13 July 1889. The article is titled "Women Who Wear Trousers."

18. Mary Whisner, "Gender-Specific Clothing Regulation: A Study in Patriarchy," *Harvard Women's Law Journal* 5, no. 1 (Spring 1982): 97–98.

19. Section 3, Article I, *Denver City Ordinances*, Chapter VI. The same code and penalty was in effect in 1927. By 1950, the ordinance specified only men who appeared publicly in women's clothing. The presence of women in the workplace during World War II rendered the statute obsolete, since many women had to adopt trousers in order to work many wartime jobs. Cross-dressed men who appeared in public were continually arrested in Denver through the 1960s and on into the 1970s. It is my understanding that the ordinance finally went off the books in 1974.

20. *Denver Times*, 13 July 1889.

21. Ibid.

22. Ibid.

23. Ibid.

24. *Denver Times*, 6 July 1889. The headline and accompanying blurb is "Lovelorn Girls . . . Strange Infatuation of a Pair of Female Cousins. Vain Efforts to Check It . . . A Beautiful Aspen Girl Passionately in Love With Her Cousin, Who Reciprocates Her Affection With Masculine Ardor."

25. Ibid.

26. Julie Wheelwright argues that psychological redefinition of cross-dressing as deviant behavior swayed public opinion into viewing women who gender-crossed as "sick." See *Amazons and Military Maids*, 155. For primary documentation, see, for example, Richard von Krafft-Ebing, *Psychopathia Sexualis*, 1886. This book has several later editions. See also the works of Havelock Ellis, especially *The Psychology of Sex: A Manual for Students* (London: Heinemann, 1933) and *Sexual Inversion* (Philadelphia: E. A. Davis, 1915). Vern L. Bullough offers a recent survey of sexological research in *Science in the Bedroom: A History of Sex Research* (New York: Basic Books, 1994).

27. SFLGHP, "'She Even Chewed Tobacco,'" 188–89.

28. Gilbert Allen, "The Woman Express Rider," *The Frontier* 4, no. 12 (June 1906): 14. Allen alleges that a prospector he met while traveling through the Rocky Mountains told this tale.

29. Ibid., 14–15.

30. "Frontier Sketches," *Denver Field and Farm*, 1387 (31 August 1912): 8. Author unknown.

31. "Frontier Tales," *Denver Field and Farm*, 452 (1 September 1894): 6. Author unknown.

32. SFLGHP, "'She Even Chewed Tobacco,'" 187.

33. Ibid., 189–90.

34. Ibid., 190.

35. Louis Sullivan, *From Female to Male: The Life of Jack Bee Garland* (Boston: Alyson Publications, 1990), 154–56. The San Francisco Lesbian and Gay History Project lists Mugarrieta as founder of the Mexican consul[ate] in San Francisco ("'She Even Chewed Tobacco,'" 191–92). Sullivan states that Mugarrieta was actually an appointee to the consulship in 1857. Mexican General Placido Vega removed him from his post in 1863. Because of his political ties and because of subsequent political disorganization in Mexico, Mugarrieta was unable to collect his military salaries, and he ended up trying to support his family as a Spanish teacher and translator in San Francisco. Sullivan, *From Female to Male*, 156–57.

36. I found a biography of Jo Monaghan in the 13 March 1904 *Rocky Mountain News Magazine*. The *News* is a Denver newspaper and the magazine insert started to appear on Sundays and holidays during the later years of the nineteenth century. Greenwald took some poetic license with Monaghan's story; the paper mentions the Chinese man who worked for a brief time on Jo's ranch but does not discuss any intimate relationship the two may have had. According to the newspaper, Monaghan was from Buffalo, New York, and was a member of an upper-crust family. Just prior to her societal debut shortly after the Civil War, she got involved with a man of whom her parents disapproved. When she became pregnant with his child, the man refused to marry her and her parents disowned her. She sought employment commensurate with her education but found it near impossible to support herself and her son. She did maintain contact with her sister, who asked Jo to move back into the family household following the deaths of both parents. Jo refused the offer, possibly trying to save her sister further embarrassment, and instead opted to head west. Leaving her infant son with her sister, Josephine Monaghan undertook the journey as Jo Monaghan. Eventually she settled in Idaho. Both Greenwald's version and the 1904 biography concur that Little Jo was extremely private and had no friends and few visitors but that she was "liked by all. He never did anyone any harm and bore no man ill-will." *Rocky Mountain News Magazine*, 13 March 1904.

Discussion Questions

1. Describe the cultural codes and expectations that Western women contradicted when they cross-dressed and assumed male identities. To what extent are these cultural codes in effect today?

2. Compare and contrast the female cross-dresser in Schlatter's article with the character of Mary Austin's "The Walking Woman." To what extent does the latter gain respect by behaving "like a man"?

◆ ◆ ◆

FOCUS ON FILM:
KING VIDOR'S *DUEL IN THE SUN* (1946)

1. Explain the racial stereotypes the film exploits and how supposedly racially motivated behaviors figure in the plot line.
2. Analyze the opposing character traits between Señor Chavez and Senator McCanles, Pearl Chavez and Laura Bell, Lewt and Jesse.
3. Analyze the interpersonal conflicts that lead to the disintegration of the McCanles family. By comparison, explain the resolution of the political conflict in the film. To what extent are similar forces at work in the social and personal struggles?

TOPICS FOR RESEARCH AND WRITING

1. With several examples, including the climactic scene, explain the theme of violence in *Duel in the Sun*. What is its purpose and value? What are the alternatives to violence, and how are they represented as ineffective? What is the relationship between violence and sexuality?
2. Analyze the moral commentary *Duel in the Sun* makes on both race and gender.
3. Compare and contrast Angeline Brown's "Diary of a School Teacher" with Lewis Garrard's "The Village" in Chapter 2. Compare not only how men and women are portrayed in the stories, but also the topics that interest the writers.
4. Compare and contrast the treatment of the love theme in Austin's "The Fakir" and in *Duel in the Sun*. Focus on the roles of Netta and Pearl, Austin's narrator and Laura Bell, Franklin Challoner and Lewt McCanles.
5. Compare and contrast the characters of Roseta in Grey's "The Ranger" and of Austin's "The Walking Woman." Determine which differences may be explained by racial or class differences between the characters.
6. Compare and contrast the character of the narrators in Mary Austin's "The Walking Woman" and "The Fakir" with the character of "Mrs. Walker" herself. Especially consider the narrators' alliance to middle-class culture, values, and gender roles.
7. If you have read Louis L'Amour's *The Daybreakers*, analyze the roles of women in the West based on Drusilla Alvarado. If you like, compare and contrast her range of freedoms and responsibilities with those of one of the female characters in this chapter.

8. If you have read Jack Schaefer's *Shane,* respond to topic 7 in relation to Marian Starrett. If you like, read pages 311–314 of James Work's essay "Settlement Waves" in *Shane: The Critical Edition,* ed. James C. Work (Lincoln, NE: University of Nebraska, 1984). Then, use whatever you find helpful in this article to develop your own response, being careful to give credit to Work for his ideas.

9. View the film *The Ballad of Little Jo* (1992), directed by Maggie Green-wald. Beginning with a summary of Evelyn Schlatter's commentary on the film in "Drag's a Life," analyze Jo's struggle for self-determination in the "masculine" West, including not only her work, but also her attempts at personal relationships.

10. Read Jon Lewis's "Wild, Wild Women" from *The Mammoth Book of the West* (New York: Carroll and Graf, 1996), pages 328–35. Compare and contrast Lewis's account of cross-dressers and other "unconformist women" with Schlatter's essay, "Drag's a Life." What seems to be his main point in this chapter, and how is this different from Schlatter's point? Explain how his consideration of prostitutes, gamblers, and "women outlaws," along with cross-dressers, reflects on the issue of women's challenges to traditional gender roles on the frontier. Do you believe Lewis contributes to or reassesses Western myths?

11. Read Isabel Allende's chapter "El Dorado" from her novel *Daughter of Fortune* (trans. Margaret Sayers Peden, New York: HarperCollins, 1999), pages 269–86. First, compare and contrast Allende's fictional treatment of cross-dressing among the California forty-niners with Schlatter's essay, "Drag's a Life." Then, explain the positive advantages of the male role for Allende's heroine, Eliza, including its contribution to her own sense of identity and self-fulfillment.

CHAPTER

7

—⟨◆⟩—

NATIVE AMERICAN
IMAGES AND VOICES

INTRODUCTION

According to a Sioux legend related by Chief Luther Standing Bear, "it was hundreds and perhaps thousands of years since the first man sprang from the earth in the midst of the great plains." The man awoke alone, emerged and freed his body from the soil, and faced the sun to strengthen his limbs. Then, "he bounded and leaped about, a free and joyous creature. From this man sprang the Lakota nation. . . . So this land of the great plains is claimed by the Lakotas as their very own. We are of the soil and the soil is of us" (qtd. in Turner 125–26). Rather than literal history, this story reflects a spiritual truth of the Sioux tribes, who migrated to the plains from the woodlands of the Great Lakes in the seventeenth century. Nonetheless, a variety of origin myths, like this one, have been recounted in song and story from generation to generation by each of three hundred tribal communities living in the West. Such stories suggest "the seamlessness of human life" for Native Americans, who traditionally made no distinction among religion, hunting, warfare, the creation of the cosmos, the naming of a chief, or the naming of a child (Revard 134). All human activity was unified by ceremony, song, and prayer. This oral tradition and the "cultural landscape" created by the reciprocal relationship between humans and their environment was really the beginning of American Western literature (Evers and Pavich 11).

According to Mary Brave Bird, "the land is sacred. These words are set at the core of our being. The land is our mother, the rivers our blood" (qtd. in Narins and Stanley 109). This consciousness, typical of native peoples, is alien to the Euro-American tradition of "taming" the land. Therefore, Native American literature—rising as it does from ancient aboriginal traditions of ritual, myth, and prayer—has a history and character very different from the American pioneer tradition. It incorporates the notions of performance, truth-telling, and cultural transmission by initiating the young into mystery (Evers and Pavich 13). Thus, every traditional narrative has its origin in the potential for personal spiritual transformation.

A second type of oral tale is marked by formulaic beginnings and endings as "fictional"; its purposes include both entertainment and the instruction of children by their elders. Like European fables, stories of this sort involve typical characters, like Coyote; episodic adventures; and creative embellishment through variations in performance style. Though such stories are humorous, there are lessons to be drawn from them, often about moral behavior. Just as contemporary Native American authors have employed traditional techniques of allusion and open-ended narrative interpretations, they have also adapted legendary figures, such as the trickster, to create fictional stories for nontraditional goals, such as social protest (Evers and Pavich 15–16).

Beginning in the late nineteenth century, a nontraditional narrative genre was adopted by Native American "authors"—the autobiography. Sometimes, the process of recording the story involved the oral tradition when a transcriber, and sometimes a translator, worked as intermediaries to set down the story told by a Native American elder, such as John G. Neihardt's account of the Sioux visionary in *Black Elk Speaks* (1932). The "collection" and "interpretation" of such an autobiography resembles the processes used by ethnologists, linguists, and folklorists since the nineteenth century—processes that have been subject to a constant debate about the literal accuracy versus emotional meaning rendered by translation (Evers and Pavich 21–22). But even when autobiography is dictated, as was also the case with *Geronimo: His Own Story* (1906), the rendering even in English conveys the Native American sense that "cosmos, country, self, and home are inseparable" (Revard 127). Sometimes, as with Sarah Winnemucca's *Life Among the Piutes; Their Wrongs and Claims* (1883), the author has received editorial help. More recently, Indian writers have had complete control over their own life histories, as in *The Names: A Memoir* (1976), by N. Scott Momaday, whose mother raised him speaking English as his "native" language.

The themes of these three forms of narrative are strikingly consistent, including "the sense of the sacred, the sense of the beautiful, the sense of place and the sense of community" (Evers and Pavich 20). Since religion is central to

Native American life, the words in these narratives, along with ritual actions, perform invocations upon the spiritual powers that infuse the world. And since harmony between Indians and nature is also central, words help to discover and reestablish unity after disruption of both sacred and human order. Likewise, the sense of harmony is beautiful, and the linguistic forms of traditional tales—the repetition, symmetry, and balanced rhetorical contrast of ideas—convey part of the meaning in an oral narrative. Moreover, these forms convey the sense of the sacred through an emotional connection between the individual and his or her community and religion (Evers and Pavich). In contrast to the traditional Euro-American emphasis on "the control and exploitation of nature," Native American narratives often dwell on sacred spots, such as holy mountains, mythic caves, or even a place consecrated by an individual spiritual experience. Thus, the "land ethic" described in the works of Momaday "holds the promise of reinvigorating modern society by reconnecting it to the sources of vitality inherent in the natural world" (Schubnell 642). Finally, the sense of community so pervasive in native literatures subsumes relationships not only with the village or tribe, but also with other creatures—recalling mythic times when humans interacted equally with animals through a "respect and concern for all creation" (Evers and Pavich 21).

Contemporary Native American writers, especially since Momaday's Pulitzer Prize–winning novel *House Made of Dawn* (1968), have ingeniously incorporated the oral tradition into "non-linear, non-chronological, ritual" narratives that reenact the "inclusiveness" of Indian consciousness, as opposed to traditional Old World rationalist thought based on "division and separation" (Allen 1058). Such fiction has a ceremonial component because its protagonists choose to risk the paranormal experiences of spiritual journeys or visions in order to seek knowledge that will benefit the family or tribe. Of course, such fiction depicts the sociological dimension, exploring cultural conflicts between Indians and whites, and the psychological dimension, exploring the protagonist's alienation, struggles for self-knowledge and purification, and finally the realization and acceptance of the individual's responsibility to the community. But these themes are related through an accumulation of details and actions, rather than a linear causal sequence, always with "a sense of events as occurring in an extended, circular, unified field of interaction" (Allen 1059). One literary technique for emphasizing this unity is the inclusion of traditional ceremonial passages within the narrative. For instance, in *House Made of Dawn*, Momaday frames the entire story by beginning and ending with a traditional Navaho healing prayer that expresses the central symbol connecting the related stories of the novel (Allen). In relying on ritual as a unifying principle, however, the Indian author often risks losing the non-Indian audience. Therefore, contemporary Native American writers create other formal structures, compatible with the spiritual undercurrent, to convey a complex narrative. For instance, in *The Way to Rainy Mountain* (1969), Momaday relates a "pilgrimage to his homeland" through three literary structures, "combining scholarly—mainly historical—vignettes with personal narrative and traditional Kiowa tales" (Allen 1062).

Throughout their work, contemporary Native American authors cannot escape their histories of political, economic, and cultural repression and racism in this country. Embracing the "burdens of racial identities," they must often assert, at least to white audiences, that "the tribes have not accepted oblivion" (Vizenor 3–4). Even if their stories do not deal directly with white–Indian conflicts, they still must express themselves—at least in writing English—from within and simultaneously against the tradition of "mainstream" literature of the American West. Readers studying that tradition must be especially acute in perceiving not only what is revealed through unconventional literary structures or ceremonial patterns, but also what remains unstated, undifferentiated, and undefined in Native American narratives. In other words, all readers must learn to reconceptualize through holistic perception.

In the visual arts, Native American painters, potters, graphic artists, and sculptors have also attempted to reject and reform past Euro-American images of Indians promoted by both museum art and popular media. As early as the 1830s, painter George Catlin began lamenting the decline of the Plains Indians and sought to preserve their "nobility" and simplicity in his idealized portraits of them. In *Letters and Notes on the Manners, Customs, and Conditions of North American Indians* (1844), he represented them as a people blissfully "uncontaminated" by the acquisitive, mercenary commercial culture of the United States. Though sad about the demise of their culture, he accepted it as inevitable and took consolation in recording the Noble Red Man "image" for posterity (Limerick 181–83). A similar tone of nostalgic loss is struck by James Fraser's *End of the Trail* (1915), a "heroic"-sized eighteen-foot sculpture depicting an Indian slumped on a pony in exhaustion, with spear dangling toward the ground. Though the figure was apparently intended as a reverent and sympathetic memorial to a noble and valiant people, for many Native Americans it represents the defeat and subjugation of Indians a hundred years ago. Contemporary Indian artists are creating images that challenge this sentimentality and replace its focus on the past with vibrant, often comical, self-conscious, and proud representations of their people.

Allen, Paula Gunn. "American Indian Fiction, 1968–1983." *A Literary History of the American West.* Ed. Thomas J. Lyon, et al. Fort Worth, TX: Texas Christian University Press and The Western Literature Association, 1987. 1058–66.

Evers, Larry, and Paul Pavich. "Native Oral Traditions." *A Literary History of the American West*. Ed. Thomas J. Lyon, et al. Fort Worth, TX: Texas Christian University Press and The Western Literature Association, 1987. 11–28.

Limerick, Patricia Nelson. *The Legacy of Conquest: The Unbroken Past of the American West*. New York: Norton, 1987.

Narins, Brigham, and Deborah A. Stanley. "Mary Brave Bird [Mary Crow Dog]." *Contemporary Literary Criticism, Volume 93*. Detroit: Gale, 1996. 108–13.

Revard, Carter. "History, Myth, and Identity Among Osages and Other Peoples." *Nothing But the Truth: An Anthology of Native American Literature*. Ed. John L. Purdy and James Ruppert. Upper Saddle River, NJ: Prentice Hall, 2001. 126–40. First published in *Family Matters, Tribal Affairs* by Carter Revard. Tucson, AZ: University of Arizona, 1998.

Schubnell, Matthias. "N. Scott Momaday." *American Nature Writers, Volume II*. Ed. John Elder. New York: Charles Scribner's Sons, 1996. 639–49.

Turner III, Frederick W., ed. *The Portable North American Indian Reader*. New York: Viking/Penguin, 1974.

Vizenor, Gerald. *Native American Literature: A Brief Introduction and Anthology*. New York: HarperCollins, 1995.

SARAH WINNEMUCCA
(1844–1891)

Born Thocmetony (Shell Flower) in what is now northern Nevada, the author was the daughter of Old Winnemucca, a Paiute tribal leader and medicine man, and the granddaughter of Truckee, who she claimed was the chief of all the Paiute people. Educated at the Convent of Notre Dame (1858–1861) in San Jose, California, Winnemucca took on a leadership role even as a young woman. Contact with whites became a problem for the Paiutes when hordes of emigrants passed through tribal lands to reach the California goldfields. This went on for over a decade, but when the federal government began trying to pressure the tribe to relocate to southern Oregon, she openly criticized unfair policies of land acquisition and reservation management, even though her family remained committed to peaceful coexistence. In the negotiations during the Snake War of 1866, she worked as the official interpreter between the U.S. military and the Paiute and Shoshone tribes. In the mid-1870s, she served as a schoolteacher and interpreter at the Malheur Reservation in Oregon.

In the Bannock War of 1878, she became an intermediary between the U.S. cavalry and the Shoshone, Bannock, and Paiute peoples living in Oregon and Idaho. Performing a public, heroic role unusual for a Paiute woman, she showed repeated fortitude and courage in negotiating between the embattled foes, sometimes riding between hostile camps more than a hundred miles in one day. Despite previous government assurances that she had conveyed to her starving people, the tribe was forced to march through deep shows in the dead of winter from Malheur to the Yakima Reservation in Washington state. In 1879, she began a lecture tour in San Francisco to publicize unfair federal policies toward Native Americans and continued her campaign to the East Coast. There, she was invited to Washington, DC, along with her father and brother, to discuss the plight of the Paiutes with federal officials. After several months, the Secretary of the Interior agreed to let the tribe return to Malheur, but he was unwilling to grant any provisions for the relocation (Witalec 675–78).

As a public figure, arguing passionately against federal injustices and white hypocrisy, Winnemucca delivered over three hundred speeches. Appearing in a full buckskin outfit, she deliberately allowed herself to be presented as "Princess Sarah Winnemucca of the Piutes," thus playing on her audience's enthusiasm for exotic royalty. While touring the East, she was fortunate in meeting Mary Tyler Mann, widow of educator Horace Mann (1796–1859). Mann became something of a patron, garnering Winnemucca speaking invitations, editing the author's erratic spelling and punctuation, and even gathering subscriptions to pay the initial printing costs of her book (Witalec 678–82).

More than an autobiography, *Life among the Piutes* (1883) combines ethnography and a history of Paiute–white relations from Winnemucca's birth to 1883. It is true that she uses her own story to dramatize the plight of her people, so the narrative has been criticized as historically inaccurate. Granted, she does include lengthy quotations of speeches and dialogues that she must have created, rather than memorized, and these passages not only enhance her image, but also demonstrate the government's injustices toward her people from the single perspective of her own persona. Nonetheless, to judge the persuasive passages by the standards of scholarly history seems unfair. Editor Mary Mann was convinced of the book's essential veracity, as she hints in the preface: "I was always considered fanatical about Indians, but I have a wholly new conception of them now, and we civilized people may well stand abashed before their purity of life & and their truthfulness." Stylistically, the dialogues help to convey a performative dimension of the narrative that may derive from the Native American oral tradition. In most respects, especially for its time, *Life among the Piutes* is quite an experiment in argumentation and life history. Winnemucca's most effective passages are those direct oratories that convince through eloquence and emotional appeals to create sympathy in the reader. In addition, ignoring previous models of American female autobiography—captivity and slave narratives—she abandons the spiritual and confessional mode of the former genre, but also forgoes the victimized role of the latter genre. Instead, she creates an independent, courageous, vigorous persona engaged in a story of heroic struggle (Witalec).

The following excerpts from *Life among the Piutes* are from the original edition (New York: Putnam's Sons, 1883), pages 48–54, 76–78, and 86–90.

Witalec, Janet, ed. "Sarah Winnemucca." *Native North American Literature.* Detroit: Gale, 1994. 675–82.

FROM *LIFE AMONG THE PIUTES*

◆━━━◆◆◆━━━◆

FROM CHAPTER II.
DOMESTIC AND SOCIAL MORALITIES

The grandmothers have the special care of the daughters just before and after they come to womanhood. The girls are not allowed to get married until they have come to womanhood; and that period is recognized as a very sacred thing, and is the subject of a festival, and has peculiar customs. The young woman is set apart under the care of two of her friends, somewhat older, and a little wigwam, called a teepee, just big enough for the three, is made for them, to which they retire. She goes through certain labors which are thought to be strengthening, and these last twenty-five days. Every day, three times a day, she must gather, and pile up as high as she can, five stacks of wood. This makes fifteen stacks a day. At the end of every five days the attendants take her to a river to bathe. She fasts from all flesh-meat during these twenty-five days, and continues to do this for five days in every month all her life. At the end of the twenty-five days she returns to the family lodge, and gives all her clothing to her attendants in payment for their care. Sometimes the wardrobe is quite extensive.

It is thus publicly known that there is another marriageable woman, and any young man interested in her, or wishing to form an alliance, comes forward. But the courting is very different from the courting of the white people. He never speaks to her, or visits the family, but endeavors to attract her attention by showing his horsemanship, etc. As he knows that she sleeps next to her grandmother in the lodge, he enters in full dress after the family has retired for the night, and seats himself at her feet. If she is not awake, her grandmother wakes her. He does not speak to either young woman or grandmother, but when the young woman wishes him to go away, she rises and goes and lies down by the side of her mother. He then leaves as silently as he came in. This goes on sometimes for a year or longer, if the young woman has not made up her mind. She is never forced by her parents to marry against her wishes. When she knows her own mind, she makes a confidant of her grandmother, and then the young man is summoned by the father of the girl, who asks him in her presence, if he really loves his daughter, and reminds him, if he says he does, of all the duties of a husband. He then asks his daughter the same question, and sets before her minutely all her duties. And these duties are not slight. She is to dress the game, prepare the food, clean the buckskins, make his moccasins, dress his hair, bring all the wood,—in short, do all the household work. She promises to "be himself," and she fulfils her promise. Then he is invited to a feast and all his relatives with him. But after the betrothal, a teepee is erected for the presents that pour in from both sides.

At the wedding feast, all the food is prepared in baskets. The young woman sits by the young man, and hands him the basket of food prepared for him with her own hands. He does not take it with his right hand; but seizes her wrist, and takes it with the left hand. This constitutes the marriage ceremony, and the father pronounces them man and wife. They go to a wigwam of their own, where they live till the first child is born. This event also is celebrated. Both father and mother fast from all flesh, and the father goes through the labor of piling the wood for twenty-five days, and assumes all his wife's household work during that time. If he does not do his part in the care of the child, he is considered an outcast. Every five days his child's basket is changed for a new one, and the five are all carefully put away at the end of the days, the last one containing the navel-string, carefully wrapped up, and all are put up into a tree, and the child put into a new and ornamented basket. All this respect shown to the mother and child makes the parents feel their responsibility, and makes the tie between parents and children very strong. The young mothers often get together and exchange their experiences about the attentions of their husbands; and inquire of each other if the fathers did their duty to their children, and were careful of their wives' health. When they are married they give away all the clothing they have ever worn, and dress themselves anew. The poor people have the same ceremonies, but do not make a feast of it, for want of means.

Our boys are introduced to manhood by their hunting of deer and mountain-sheep. Before they are fifteen or sixteen, they hunt only small game, like rabbits, hares, fowls, etc. They never eat what they kill themselves, but only what their father or elder brothers kill. When a boy becomes strong enough to use larger bows made of sinew, and arrows that are ornamented with eagle-feathers, for the first time, he kills game that is large, a deer or an antelope, or a mountain-sheep. Then he brings home the hide, and his father cuts it into a long coil which is wound into a loop, and the boy takes his quiver and throws it on his back as if he was going on a hunt, and takes his bow and arrows in his hand. Then his father throws the loop over him, and he jumps through it. This he does five times. Now for the first time he eats the flesh of the animal he has killed, and from that time he eats whatever he kills but he has always been faithful to his parents' command not to eat what he has killed before. He can now do whatever he likes, for now he is a man, and no longer considered a boy. If there is a war he can go to it; but the Piutes, and other tribes west of the Rocky Mountains, are not fond of going to war. I never saw a war-dance but once. It is always the whites that begin the wars, for their own selfish purposes. The government does not take care to send the good men; there are a plenty who would take pains to see and understand the chiefs and learn their characters, and their good will to the whites. But the whites have not waited to find out how good the Indians were, and what ideas they had of God, just like those of Jesus, who called him Father, just as my people do, and told men to do to others as they would be done by, just as my people teach their children to do. My people teach their children never to make fun of any one, no matter how they look. If you see your brother or sister doing something wrong, look away, or go away from them. If you make fun of bad persons, you make yourself beneath them. Be kind to all, both poor and rich, and feed all that come to your wigwam, and your name can be spoken of by every one far and near. In this way you will make many friends for yourself. Be kind both to bad and good, for you don't know your own heart. This is the way my people teach their children. It was handed down from father to son for many generations. I never in my life saw our children rude as I have seen white children and grown people in the streets.

The chief's tent is the largest tent, and it is the council-tent, where everyone goes who wants advice. In the evenings the head men go there to discuss everything, for the chiefs do not rule like tyrants; they discuss everything with their people, as a father would in his family. Often they sit up all night. They discuss the doings of all, if they need to be advised. If a boy is not doing well they talk that over, and if the women are interested they can share in the talks. If there is not room enough inside, they all go out of doors, and make a great circle. The men are in the inner circle, for there would be too much smoke for the women inside. The men never talk without smoking first. The women sit behind them in another circle, and if the children wish to hear, they can be there too. The women know as much as the men do, and their advice is often asked. We have a republic as well as you. The council-tent is our Congress, and anybody can speak who has anything to say, women and all. They are always interested in what their husbands are doing and thinking about. And they take some part even in the wars. They are always near at hand when fighting is going on, ready to snatch their husbands up and carry them off if wounded or killed. One splendid woman that my brother Lee married after his first wife died, went out into the battlefield after her uncle was killed, and went into the front ranks and cheered the men on. Her uncle's horse was dressed in a splendid robe made of eagles' feathers and she snatched it off and swung it in the face of the enemy, who always carry off everything they find, as much as to say, "You can't have that—I have it safe"; and she staid and took her uncle's place, as brave as any of the men. It means something when the women promise their fathers to make their husbands *themselves.* They faithfully keep with them in all the dangers they can share. They not only take care of their children together, but they do everything together; and when they grow blind, which I am sorry to say is very common, for the smoke they live in destroys their eyes at last, they take sweet care of one another. Marriage is a sweet thing when people love each other. If women could go into your Congress I think justice would soon be done to the Indians. I can't tell about all Indians; but I know my own people are kind to everybody that does not do them harm; but they will not be imposed upon, and when people are too bad they rise up and resist them. This seems to me all right. It is different from being revengeful. There is nothing cruel about our people. They never scalped a human being. . . .

FROM CHAPTER V. RESERVATION OF PYRAMID AND MUDDY LAKES

This reservation, given in 1860, was at first sixty miles long and fifteen wide. The line is where the railroad now crosses the river, and it takes in two beau-

tiful lakes, one called Pyramid Lake, and the one on the eastern side, Muddy
Lake. No white people lived there at the time it was given us. We Piutes have
always lived on the river, because out of those two lakes we caught beautiful
mountain trout, weighing from two to twenty-five pounds each, which
would give us a good income if we had it all, as at first. Since the railroad ran
through in 1867, the white people have taken all the best part of the reservation from us, and one of the lakes also.

The first work that my people did on the reservation was to dig a ditch,
to put up a grist-mill and saw-mill. Commencing where the railroad now
crosses at Wadsworth they dug about a mile; but the saw-mill and grist-mill
were never seen or heard of by my people, though the printed report in the
United States statutes, which my husband found lately in the Boston
Athenaeum, says twenty-five thousand dollars was appropriated to build
them. Where did it go? The report says these mills were sold for the benefit
of the Indians who were to be paid in lumber for houses, but no stick of
lumber have they ever received. My people do not own any timber land now.
The white people are using the ditch which my people made to irrigate their
land. This is the way we are treated by our white brothers. Is it that the government is cheated by its own agents who make these reports?

In 1864–5 there was a governor by the name of Nye. There were no
whites living on the reservation at that time, and there was not any agent as
yet. My people were living there and fishing, as they had always done. Some
white men came down from Virginia City to fish. My people went up to Carson City to tell Governor Nye that some white men were fishing on their
reservation. He sent down some soldiers to drive them away. Mr. Nye is the
only governor who ever helped my people,—I mean that protected them
when they called on him in this way.

In 1865 we had another trouble with our white brothers. It was early
in the spring, and we were then living at Dayton, Nevada, when a company
of soldiers came through the place and stopped and spoke to some of my
people, and said, "You have been stealing cattle from the white people at
Harney Lake." They said also that they would kill everything that came in
their way, men, women, and children. The captain's name was Wells. The
place where they were going to is about three hundred miles away. The
days after they left were very sad hours, indeed. Oh, dear readers, these soldiers had gone only sixty miles away to Muddy Lake, where my people
were then living and fishing, and doing nothing to any one. The soldiers
rode up to their encampment and fired into it, and killed almost all the
people that were there. Oh, it is a fearful thing to tell, but it must be told.
Yes, it must be told by me. It was all old men, women and children that
were killed; for my father had all the young men with him, at the sink of

Carson on a hunting excursion, or they would have been killed too. After the soldiers had killed all but some little children and babies still tied up in their baskets, the soldiers took them also, and set the camp on fire and threw them into the flames to see them burn alive. I had one baby brother killed there. My sister jumped on father's best horse and ran away. As she ran, the soldiers ran after her; but, thanks be to the Good Father in the Spirit-land, my dear sister got away. This almost killed my poor papa. Yet my people kept peaceful.

That same summer another of my men was killed on the reservation. His name was Truckee John. He was an uncle of mine, and was killed by a man named Flamens, who claimed to have had a brother killed in the war of 1860, but of course that had nothing to do with my uncle. About two weeks after this, two white men were killed over at Walker Lake by some of my people, and of course soldiers were sent for from California, and a great many companies came. They went after my people all over Nevada. Reports were made everywhere throughout the whole country by the white settlers, that the red devils were killing their cattle, and by this lying of the white settlers the trail began which is marked by the blood of my people from hill to hill and from valley to valley. The soldiers followed after my people in this way for one year, and the Queen's River Piutes were brought into Fort Churchill, Nevada, and in that campaign poor General McDermit was killed. These reports were only made by those white settlers so that they could sell their grain, which they could not get rid of in any other way. The only way the cattle-men and farmers get to make money is to start an Indian war, so that the troops may come and buy their beef, cattle, horses and grain. The settlers get fat by it. . . .

Now, dear readers, this is the way all the Indian agents get rich. The first thing they do is to start a store; the next thing is to take in cattle men, and cattle men pay the agent one dollar a head. In this way they get rich very soon, so that they can have their gold-headed canes, with their names engraved on them. The one I am now speaking of is only a sub-agent. He told me the head agent was living in Carson City, and he paid him fifteen hundred dollars a year for the use of the reservation. Yet, he has fine horses and cattle and sheep, and is very rich. The sub-agent was a minister; his name was Balcom. He did not stay very long, because a man named Batemann hired some Indians to go and scare him away from the reservation, that he might take his place. The leader of these Indians was named Dave. He was interpreter at the Pyramid Lake Reservation. So Batemann got the minister away, and then he got rich in the same way.

While Batemann was agent, I was asked to act as interpreter to the Shoshones by a man called Captain Dodge, agent for the Shoshone Indians.

He was going to issue clothing to them at a place called Battle Mountain. My brother Natchez went all about to summon the people there. I told Colonel Dodge all about our agent at Pyramid Lake Reservation. He said he would go to see him, which he did. It took three days for the people to come up. Oh, such an issue! It was enough to make a doll laugh. A family numbering eight persons got two blankets, three shirts, no dress-goods. Some got a fish-hook and line; some got one and a half yards of flannel, blue and red; the largest issue was to families that camped together, numbering twenty-three persons: four blankets, three pieces of red flannel, and some of blue, three shirts, three hooks and lines, two kettles. It was the saddest affair I ever saw. There were ready-made clothes of all kinds, hats, shoes, and shawls, and farming utensils of all kinds. Bales upon bales of clothing were sent away to Salt Lake City. After the issue, the things were all to be put into one place. Holy songs were offered up to the Great Spirit Father. The things were blessed before they were to be worn, and all the young men put the blankets round them and danced. In the morning some of the men went round with only one leg dressed in flannel, which made all the white people laugh. At this issue our agent, Mr. Batemann, gave the Shoshones one ton of flour before this new agent, which made me very angry, and I talked to him before Colonel Dodge. I said, "You come up here to show off before this man. Go and bring some flour to my people on Humboldt River, who are starving, the people over whom you are agent. For shame that you who talk three times a day to the Great Father in Spirit-land should act so to my people." This man called himself a Christian, too.

Then came another agent by the name of Spencer. He was a better one than we had ever had. He issued some blankets to some old men and women and blind people and gave brother some pieces of land to work upon. He then gave my people wagons,—about ten altogether; and he had his daughter brought as a teacher, at the rate of fifty dollars a month. But he soon died, and then came our present agent. He was not married at the time, but he very soon learned that there was money to be made, so he went back and got married. Of course he put his wife in as teacher. Mr. MacMasters, for that is his name, has his own method of making my people divide the produce. If they raise five sacks of grain, they give one sack for the Big Father in Washington; if they have only three sacks, they still have to send one. Every fourth load of hay goes to the Big Father at Washington, yet he does not give my people the seed. The head-farmer, who is called Mushrush, never shows my people how to work. This is why they said, "Why does the Big Father want us to pay him when he does not give us the seed? We have to pay for the seed ourselves." Both the agent and farmer told my people they would have to pay it or the Big Father would take away their wagons. So my people talked it over and said, "We will pay it." Later they got up a paper, which the agent and the farmer wanted my people to sign. The sub-chief would not put his hand to the pen. He said to the agent,—

"I have been working for so many years, and I have never received anything as yet. You say it is supplies you are sending me and my people; but I am sick and tired of lies, and I won't sign any paper." Of course our agent, Mr. MacMasters, told him to leave the reservation. His wagon was taken from him. At this my people sent me down to San Francisco to tell the commanding officer. I did so. I gave Gen. McDowell a full account of the doings, and he reported him to the authorities. The following spring my poor brother Natchez went to the agent and asked him to help him to a plough, and to give him a set of harness. He told my brother to go away. "You and your sister," he said, "talk about me all the time. I don't want you and your sister here." At this my poor brother got angry and said to him, "This is my reservation, not yours. I am going to stay here just as long as I like. My poor father and I never got so much as an old rag from any agent that ever came here." At this our minister got angry, and telegraphed to the soldiers to come and take brother and carry him to the Acotrass [Alcatraz] Islands. He wrote a letter, saying all my people wanted him to send my brother away where they could never see him any more. After he had written it, he called up all the head men of our people, and told them he had written to their father in Washington for good clothing for them, and wished them to sign the paper. Of course, they did not know any better; they put their names to the paper, and signed their chief away! So the soldiers came and took brother to San Francisco, Cal. Brother was only there a little while when two white men whose lives he had saved went and took him out and sent him home, and wrote to our minister agent. Of course I knew not what was in the letter.

Dear reader, I must tell a little more about my poor people, and what we suffer at the hands of our white brothers. Since the war of 1860 there have been one hundred and three (103) of my people murdered, and our reservations taken from us; and yet we, who are called blood-seeking savages, are keeping our promises to the government. Oh, my dear good Christian people, how long are you going to stand by and see us suffer at your hands? Oh, dear friends, you are wrong when you say it will take two or three generations to civilize my people. No! I say it will not take that long if you will only take interest in teaching us; and, on the other hand, we shall never be civilized in the way you wish us to be if you keep on sending us such agents as have been sent to us year after year, who do nothing but fill their pockets, and the pockets of their wives and sisters, who are always put in as teachers, and paid from fifty to sixty dollars per month, and yet they do not teach. The farmer is generally his cousin, his pay is nine hundred dollars ($900) a year, and his brother is a clerk. I do not know his name. The blacksmith and carpenter have from five hundred to eleven hundred dollars per year. I got this from their own statements. I saw a discharged agent while I was on my way here, who told me all the agents had to pay so much to the Secretary of the Interior, who had to make up what he paid to the agents. This I know to be a true confession, or the Secretary of the Interior and all the government officers would see into the doings of these Christian agents. Year after year they have been told of their wrong-doings by different tribes of Indians. Yet it goes on, just the same as if they did not know it. . . .

Discussion Questions

1. Analyze the persona Winnemucca creates through these excerpts from her biography. Describe the tone of her writing, the values she seems to express, and the personality traits that you can infer from the two passages. To what extent is the persona that the author creates through her writing effective in achieving her persuasive goal?

2. In her chapter titled "Domestic and Social Moralities," Winnemucca provides ethnographic or anthropological details about her tribe of Paiute Indians. Summarize the topics she describes and define one consistent concern or theme of this chapter.

3. Compare Winnemucca's description of the Paiutes in this chapter with (A) Lewis's description of the Shoshone culture in the second passage from the *Journals* in Chapter 1 and (B) Garrard's description of the Cheyenne culture in Chapter 2. Is the Native American viewpoint in Winnemucca's description substantially different from the Euro-American viewpoints in Lewis's and Garrard's descriptions? If so, in what way? Which of the three accounts did you find the most "objective" or scientific? Why? Which of the three accounts did you find the most emotionally engaging? Why? Are there ways in which these oppositional judgments of "objective" or "emotional" are unfair to these texts or irrelevant to your experience of reading them? If so, explain.

4. In her chapter titled "Reservation of Pyramid and Muddy Lakes," Winnemucca's purpose is clearly rhetorical—to persuade white readers (in the nineteenth century) of the injustices that the federal government and its agents perpetuated on the Paiute people. Describe the evidence she relates to support her argument. To what extent did you find this evidence convincing?

Fig. 7.1 *Salish Handbag, Montana* (ca. 1915–1920). Buffalo Bill Historical Center, Cody, WY; Simplot Collection, gift of J. R. Simplot; NA.203.818.

N. SCOTT MOMADAY
(1934–)

Born in Oklahoma, the author claims Kiowa heritage on his father's side, and both Cherokee and French heritage on his mother's side. His parents worked as teachers, so Momaday gained a strong interest in language and literature from the English-language stories read to him by his mother and from the Kiowa tales recounted by his grandmother and his father. His youth was spent on Navaho reservations in the Southwest, where he experienced the Native American traditions of oral stories and religious rituals. In 1946, the family settled at Jemez Pueblo, New Mexico, which became his most memorable childhood home (Trimble). He attended the University of New Mexico, left for a year of law school, but returned to complete his bachelor's degree in political science in 1958. Then, he began teaching on the Jicarilla Apache Reservation. In 1959, he won a prestigious Wallace Stegner Creative Writing Fellowship at Stanford University and began studying with not only Stegner, but also poet Yvor Winters, who was to prove a tremendous influence on the budding writer (Velie).

An aspiring academic, Momaday earned a master's degree in 1960 and a Ph.D. in 1963, writing a dissertation under the influence of Edmund Wilson (Trimble). He went on to teach English and comparative literature—including courses in the Native American oral tradition—at the University of California at Santa Barbara and Berkeley, as well as Stanford and the University of Arizona (Coltelli). During his research to prepare for teaching American Indian studies, he gathered together a book of Kiowa tales that he privately printed as *The Journey to Tai-Mei* (1967), which he later incorporated into *The Way to Rainy Mountain* (1969). Just as important was his opportunity to view the sacred Sun Dance doll of Tai-mei, which the Kiowa tribe had stored away since 1888. For Momaday, this was an intensely religious experience which gave him an intimate connection to the past and culture of his tribe (Velie).

His first writing was poetry, which has influenced the rhythm and imagery of his fictional prose, but he has also written autobiography and essays. After achieving fame with his fiction, he became a prolific lecturer and an accomplished painter, like his father. Drawing from his Native American heritage and identity, Momaday has developed three related themes throughout his work: Indians' relationship with the earth, imaginatively experienced; the power of language; and self-knowledge (Trimble). His first novel, *House Made of Dawn* (1968), tells of a recovery of Native American identity in the anti-hero Abel, a Navaho World War II veteran who feels alienated not only from white society, but also from the Pueblo reservation where he returns to try to find himself. Momaday makes clear that Abel's "personal and cultural alienation correlates with his emotional and geographical distance from his ancestral land" (Schubnell 645). But before he can find himself in this sacred space, Abel must first wander in the spiritually arid urban landscape of Los Angeles, where he meets the Reverend Tosamah, the major figure in the excerpt below. The Reverend is a mouthpiece for Momaday's own views about the power of language, even though this character is truly no friend to the protagonist. In fact, he "detests Abel for being a 'longhair'—an unassimilated Indian who is looked down upon by whites and is therefore a discredit to his race" (Velie 163). However, Abel transcends this perspective, while expressing both the ambivalence of Indian identity and the necessity of actively determining the self within the mix of Southwestern cultures: Hispanic Catholic, Pueblo Indian, Anglo-American, and Navaho. *House Made of Dawn*, which won the Pulitzer Prize in 1969, ushered in a veritable renaissance of Native American writers.

His second book, *The Way to Rainy Mountain*, is a tribal history structured by the Kiowas' journey from their ancestral lands in the northern Rockies to the plains of Oklahoma. On this slow migration that becomes a dramatic cultural transformation, the tribe adopts the Sun Dance religion from the Crows and the horse from the whites, thereby choosing a warrior lifestyle of hunting, thievery, and fighting. One importance of this work is Momaday's preservation and celebration of the traditional Kiowa narratives that impart the tribe's essential myths. In *The Names* (1977), Momaday writes a childhood memoir that examines the relationship between language and human significance, and the nature of ethnic Indian identity (Velie). After this book, he published nothing for over a decade, working more on painting than writing. This experience provided ample background for *The Ancient Child* (1989), a novel about an unfulfilled but internationally successful painter who must discover his Kiowa roots in order to overcome a nervous breakdown and to satisfy his religious longings. The novel ends with his transformation into a bear through a ritual ceremony. Unlike modernist novelists who might use mythology as "symbolism or allegory, he is writing about a different plane of reality" (Velie 168). In effect, the author is recreating a mythic present infused by aspects of the past and the supernatural.

In many ways, Momaday has successfully combined two very different literary traditions: a postmodern sensibility toward nonsequential narrative, fragmented characters, and open-ended interpretation with a richly textured oral style that finds meaning through tribal community and a mystical experience of nature. From this perspective, "nature integrates sense perception and memory, fusing the visible with collective and personal wisdom about the universe" (Schubnell 640). For instance, just as Canyon de Chelly became a sacred place for the Southwest Indians, the personal experience of places where we feel at home is made sacred by treasuring and preserving them in imagination; as these places are shared through story and a mythologizing process, they become a community resource. This "imaginative involvement in the natural world . . . relies, in native cultures, on the racial experience that is perpetuated through the oral tradition" (641). What Momaday has achieved—through fiction, poetry, and memoir—is a literary re-creation of that tradition.

The text for the excerpt from *House Made of Dawn* is from the reprint edition (New York: Perennial, 1989), pages 89–98.

Coltelli, Laura. "N. Scott Momaday." *Winged Words: American Indian Writers Speak*. Lincoln and London: University of Nebraska, 1990. 88–100.

Schubnell, Matthias. "N. Scott Momaday." *American Nature Writers, Volume II*. Ed. John Elder. New York: Scribner's, 1996. 639–49.

Trimble, Martha S. "N. Scott Momaday." *Fifty Western Writers: A Bio-Bibliographical Sourcebook*. Ed. Fred Erisman and Richard W. Etulain. Westport, CN: Greenwood, 1982. 313–224.

Velie, Alan R. "N. Scott Momaday." *Dictionary of Literary Biography, Volume 143: American Novelists since World War II, 3rd Series*. Ed. James R. Giles and Wanda H. Giles. Detroit: Gale, 1994. 159–70.

FROM *HOUSE MADE OF DAWN*
THE PRIEST OF THE SUN

◆——◆◆——◆

The Priest of the Sun lived with his disciple Cruz on the first floor of a two-story red-brick building in Los Angeles. The upstairs was maintained as a storage facility by the A. A. Kaul Office Supply Company. The basement was a kind of church. There was a signboard on the wall above the basement steps, encased in glass. In neat, movable white block letters on a black field it read:

LOS ANGELES
HOLINESS PAN-INDIAN RESCUE MISSION
Rev. J. B. B. Tosamah, Pastor & Priest of the Sun
Saturday 8:30 P.M.
"The Gospel According to John"
Sunday 8:30 P.M.
"The Way to Rainy Mountain"
Be kind to a white man today

The basement was cold and dreary, dimly illuminated by two 40-watt bulbs which were screwed into the side walls above the dais. This platform was made out of rough planks of various woods and dimensions, thrown together without so much as a hammer and nails; it stood seven or eight inches above the floor, and it supported the tin firebox and the crescent altar. Off to one side was a kind of lectern, decorated with red and yellow symbols of the sun and moon. In back of the dais there was a screen of purple drapery, threadbare and badly faded. On either side of the aisle which led to the altar there were chairs and crates, fashioned into pews. The walls were bare and gray and streaked with water. The only windows were small, rectangular openings near the ceiling, at ground level; the panes were covered over with a thick film of coal oil and dust, and spider webs clung to the frames or floated out like smoke across the room. The air was heavy and stale; odors of old smoke and incense lingered all around. The people had filed into the pews and were waiting silently.

Cruz, a squat, oily man with blue-black hair that stood out like spines from his head, stepped forward on the platform and raised his hands as if to ask for the quiet that already was.

Everyone watched him for a moment; in the dull light his skin shone yellow with sweat. Turning slightly and extending his arm behind him, he said, "The Right Reverend John Big Bluff Tosamah."

There was a ripple in the dark screen; the drapes parted and the Priest of the Sun appeared, moving shadow-like to the lectern. He was shaggy and awful-looking in the thin, naked light: big, lithe as a cat, narrow-eyed, suggesting in the whole of his look and manner both arrogance and agony. He wore black like a cleric; he had the voice of a great dog:

"'In principio erat Verbum.' Think of Genesis. Think of how it was before the world was made. There was nothing, the Bible says. 'And the earth was without form, and void; and darkness was upon the face of the deep.' It was dark, and there was nothing. There were no mountains, no trees, no rocks, no rivers. There was nothing. But there was darkness all around, and in the darkness something happened. Something happened! There was a single sound. Far away in the darkness there was a single sound. Nothing made it, but it was there; and there was no one to hear it, but it was there. It was there, and there was nothing else. It rose up in the darkness, little and still, almost nothing in itself—like a single soft breath, like the wind arising; yes, like the whisper of the wind rising slowly and going out into the early morning. But there was no wind. There was only the sound, little and soft. It was almost nothing in itself, the smallest seed of sound—but it took hold of the darkness and there was light; it took hold of the stillness and there was motion forever; it took hold of the silence and there was sound. It was almost nothing in itself, a single sound, a word—a word broken off at the darkest center of the night and let go in the awful void, forever and forever. And it was almost nothing in itself. It scarcely was; but it was, and everything began."

Just then a remarkable thing happened. The Priest of the Sun seemed stricken; he let go of his audience and withdrew into himself, into some strange potential of himself. His voice, which had been low and resonant, suddenly became harsh and flat; his shoulders sagged and his stomach protruded, as if he had held his breath to the limit of endurance; for a moment there was a look of amazement, then utter carelessness in his face. Conviction, caricature, callousness: the remainder of his sermon was a going back and forth among these.

"Thank you so much, Brother Cruz. Good evening, blood brothers and sisters, and welcome, welcome. Gracious me, I see lots of new faces out there tonight. *Gracious me!* May the Great Spirit—can we knock off that talking in the back there?—be with you always.

"'In the beginning was the Word.' I have taken as my text this evening the almighty Word itself. Now get this: 'There was a man sent from God, whose name was John. The same came for a witness, to bear witness of the Light, that all men through him might believe.' Amen, brothers and sisters, Amen. And the riddle of the Word, 'In the beginning was the Word. . . .' Now what do you suppose old John *meant* by that? That cat was a preacher, and, well, you know how it is with preachers; he had something big on his mind. Oh my, it was big; it was the *Truth*, and it was heavy, and old John hurried to set it down. And in his hurry he said too much. 'In the beginning was the Word, and the Word was with God, and the Word was God.' It was the Truth, all right, but it was more than the Truth. The Truth was overgrown with fat, and the fat was God. The fat was *John's* God, and God stood between John and the Truth. Old John, see, he got up one morning and caught sight of the Truth. It must have been like a bolt of lightning, and the sight of it made him blind. And for a moment the vision burned on in back of his eyes, and he knew what it was. In that instant he saw something he had never seen before and would never see again. That was the instant of revelation, inspiration, Truth. And old John, he must have fallen down on his knees. Man, he must have been shaking and laughing and crying and yelling and praying—all at the same time—and he must have been drunk and delirious with the Truth. You see, he had lived all his life waiting for that one moment, and it came, and it took him by surprise, and it was gone. And he said, 'In the beginning was the Word. . . .' And, man, right then and there he should have stopped. There was nothing more to say, but he went on. He had said all there was to say, everything, but he went on. 'In the beginning was the Word. . . .' Brothers and sisters, *that* was the Truth, the whole of it, the essential and eternal Truth, the bone and blood and muscle of the Truth. But he went on, old John, because he was a preacher. The perfect vision faded from his mind, and he went on. The instant passed, and then he had nothing but a memory. He was desperate and confused, and in his confusion he stumbled and went on. 'In the beginning was the Word, and the Word was with God, and the Word was God.' He went on to talk about Jews and Jerusalem, Levites and Pharisees, Moses and Philip and Andrew and Peter. Don't you see? Old John *had* to go on. That cat had a whole lot at stake. He couldn't let the Truth alone. He couldn't see that he had come to the end of the Truth, and he went on. He tried to make it bigger and better than it was, but instead he only demeaned and encumbered it. He made it soft and big with fat. He was a preacher, and he made a complex sentence of the Truth, two sentences, three, a paragraph. He made a sermon and theology of the Truth. He imposed his idea of God upon the everlasting Truth. 'In the beginning was the Word. . . .' And that is all there was, and it was enough.

"Now, brothers and sisters, old John was a white man, and the white man has his ways. Oh gracious me, he has his ways. He talks about the Word. He talks through it and around it. He builds upon it with syllables, with pre-fixes and suffixes and hyphens and accents. He adds and divides and multi-plies the Word. And in all of this he subtracts the Truth. And, brothers and sisters, you have come here to live in the white man's world. Now the white man deals in words, and he deals easily, with grace and sleight of hand. And in his presence, here on his own ground, you are as children, mere babes in the woods. You must not mind, for in this you have a certain advantage. A child can listen and learn. The Word is sacred to a child.

"My grandmother was a storyteller; she knew her way around words. She never learned to read and write, but somehow she knew the good of reading and writing; she had learned how to listen and delight. She had learned that in words and in language, and there only, she could have whole and con-summate being. She told me stories, and she taught me how to listen. I was a child and I listened. She could neither read nor write, you see, but she taught me how to live among her words, how to listen and delight. 'Storytelling; to utter and to hear. . . .' And the simple act of listening is crucial to the concept of language, more crucial even than reading and writing, and language in turn is crucial to human society. There is proof of that, I think, in all the his-tories and prehistories of human experience. When that old Kiowa woman told me stories, I listened with only one ear. I was a child, and I took the words for granted. I did not know what all of them meant, but somehow I held on to them; I remembered them, and I remember them now. The sto-ries were old and dear; they meant a great deal to my grandmother. It was not until she died that I knew how *much* they meant to her. I began to think about it, and then I knew. When she told me those old stories, something strange and good and powerful was going on. I was a child, and that old woman was asking me to come directly into the presence of her mind and spirit; she was taking hold of my imagination, giving me to share in the great fortune of her wonder and delight. She was asking me to go with her to the confrontation of something that was sacred and eternal. It was a timeless, *timeless* thing; nothing of her old age or of my childhood came between us.

"Children have a greater sense of the power and beauty of words than have the rest of us in general. And if that is so, it is because there occurs— or reoccurs—in the mind of every child something like a reflection of all human experience. I have heard that the human fetus corresponds in its development, stage by stage, to the scale of evolution. Surely it is no less reasonable to suppose that the waking mind of a child corresponds in the same way to the whole evolution of human thought and perception.

"In the white man's world, language, too—and the way in which the white man thinks of it—has undergone a process of change. The white man takes such things as words and literatures for granted, as indeed he must, for nothing in his world is so commonplace. On every side of him there are words by the millions, an unending succession of pamphlets and papers, letters and books, bills and bulletins, commentaries and conversations. He has diluted and multiplied the Word, and words have begun to close in upon him. He is sated and insensitive; his regard for language—for the Word itself—as an instrument of creation has diminished nearly to the point of no return. It may be that he will perish by the Word.

"But it was not always so with him, and it is not so with you. Consider for a moment that old Kiowa woman, my grandmother, whose use of language was confined to speech. And be assured that her regard for words was always keen in proportion as she depended upon them. You see, for her words were medicine; they were magic and invisible. They came from nothing into sound and meaning. They were beyond price; they could neither be bought nor sold. And she never threw words away.

"My grandmother used to tell me the story of Tai-me, of how Tai-me came to the Kiowas. The Kiowas were a sun dance culture, and Tai-me was their sun dance doll, their most sacred fetish; no medicine was ever more powerful. There is a story about the coming of Tai-me. This is what my grandmother told me:

> Long ago there were bad times. The Kiowas were hungry and there was no food. There was a man who heard his children cry from hunger, and he began to search for food. He walked four days and became very weak. On the fourth day he came to a great canyon. Suddenly there was thunder and lightning. A Voice spoke to him and said, "Why are you following me? What do you want?" The man was afraid. The thing standing before him had the feet of a deer, and its body was covered with feathers. The man answered that the Kiowas were hungry. "Take

me with you," the Voice said, "and I will give you whatever you want." From that day Tai-me has belonged to the Kiowas.

"Do you see? There, far off in the darkness, something happened. Do you see? Far, far away in the nothingness something happened. There was a voice, a sound, a word—and everything began. The story of the coming of Tai-me has existed for hundreds of years by word of mouth. It represents the oldest and best idea that man has of himself. It represents a very rich literature, which, because it was never written down, was always but one generation from extinction. But for the same reason it was cherished and revered. I could see that reverence in my grandmother's eyes, and I could hear it in her voice. It was that, I think, that old Saint John had in mind when he said, 'In the beginning was the Word. . . .' But he went on. He went on to lay a scheme about the Word. He could find no satisfaction in the simple fact that the Word was; he had to account for it, not in terms of that sudden and profound insight, which must have devastated him at once, but in terms of the moment afterward, which was irrelevant and remote; not in terms of his imagination, but only in terms of his prejudice.

"Say this: 'In the beginning was the Word. . . .' There was nothing. There was *nothing!* Darkness. There was darkness, and there was no end to it. You look up sometimes in the night and there are stars; you can see all the way to the stars. And you begin to know the universe, how awful and great it is. The stars lie out against the sky and do not fill it. A single star, flickering out in the universe, is enough to fill the mind, but it is nothing in the night sky. The darkness looms around it. The darkness flows among the stars, and beyond them forever. In the beginning flat is how it was, but there were no stars. There was only the dark infinity in which nothing was. And something happened. At the distance of a star something happened, and everything began. The Word did not come into being, but *it was.* It did not break upon the silence, but *it was older than the silence and the silence was made of it.*

"Old John caught sight of something terrible. The thing standing before him said, 'Why are you following me? What do you want?' And from that day the Word has belonged to us, who have heard it for what it is, who have lived in fear and awe of it. In the Word was the beginning; '*In the beginning was the Word. . . .*'"

The Priest of the Sun appeared to have spent himself. He stepped back from the lectern and hung his head, smiling. In his mind the earth was spinning and the stars rattled around in the heavens. The sun shone, and the moon. Smiling in a kind of transport, the Priest of the Sun stood silent for a time while the congregation waited to be dismissed.

"Good night," he said, at last, "and get yours". . . .

Discussion Questions

1. Explain Reverend Tosamah's description of white people's relationship to language. By contrast, how does Tosamah characterize Indians' relationship to language?
2. Explain the connection Tosamah makes between the Gospel of John and Kiowa mythology. Why is it important that this character connect "white" Christianity with Indian religion for his audience at the Pan-Indian Rescue Mission? Speculate about Momaday's message in developing the character of this preacher.

RAY A. YOUNG BEAR
(BIRTHDATE UNKNOWN)

Born of Mesquakie heritage on the Tama Indian Reservation in Iowa, the author has never strayed far from this location or his concerns for his people. He is cofounder, with his wife, of the Woodland Song Dance Troupe of Arts Midwest, which has celebrated and perpetuated tribal traditions of song and dance for many years. Like this "performative" activity, Young Bear's poetry recreates "the old story world" of oral tradition. According to James Ruppert, the poet "tries to have us experience that world—the powers, the perceptions and amazing occurrences germane to it" (qtd. in Witalec 684). Like Momaday, Young Bear uses language not merely as metaphor, but to recreate magical events. Thus, if his poetry uses the means of dreams or visions to transform the world, then the poet also questions the stability of identity—for himself, as well as for his readers, who also experience these transformations in the nature of things (Witalec).

After the 1980 publication of his first volume of poetry, *Winter of the Salamander*, Young Bear received critical praise and national attention, including numerous invitations to teach at universities in the Southwest and Far West. In his home state, at the University of Iowa, he has taught a course in American Indian Literature as part of the American Studies program. His second book of verse, *The Invisible Musician* (1990), was equally successful, though again some poems concern the anxieties of modern America, especially the confusion, anger, loss, and despair in Native American lives. Young Bear's reputation for storytelling was further enhanced by his fictionalized autobiography, *Black Eagle Child: The Facepaint Narratives* (1992), which weaves spirituality, tribal memory, Mesquakie vocabulary, poetry, and picaresque humor in an exploration of the identity and the redemption he has found through writing (Witalec). Even so, as James Ruppert suggests, that exploration hardly makes for conventional narrative: "Young Bear feels free to juxtapose memories, speculations, history, myth, social comment, and the images of popular culture" (qtd. in Witalec 689). Moreover, there are impenetrable mysteries in the book because the author feels the need to "document his heritage without betraying tribal secrets" (Witalec 683). As in his poetry, there are some symbols that we cannot penetrate, some events that are contradictory and irresolvable, some transformations that we cannot follow. And yet the perceptions we can gain are worth the difficulties.

The text of "morning talking mother" is from *Winter of the Salamander: The Keeper of Importance* (New York: Harper & Row, 1980), pages 40–41. The text of "The Language of Weather" is from *The Invisible Musician* (Duluth, MN: Holy Cow! Press, 1990), pages 6–7.

Witalec, Janet, ed. "Ray A. Young Bear." *Native North American Literature.* Detroit: Gale, 1994. 683–91.

morning talking mother

———<◆>———

tonight, i encircle myself to a star
and my love for the earth shimmers
like schools of small rainbow-colored fish,
lighting the drowned walnut trees inside
the brown flooded rivers
swelling birth along the woods.
i think of each passing day when time expands,
bringing the land against my chest
and the birds keep walking as they

sing wildly over our house:
be in this daylight with me.
push yourself from the walls.
let me see you walk beneath me.
let me see your head sway.
let me see you breathe.
everyone has been up into the daylight.

i walk over her head and remember
of being told that no knives
or sharp objects must pierce
inside her hair.
this is her hair.
another grandmother whose hair
i am combing.
there are paths winding over her face
and every step is the same:
the feeling of one who is well known,
one who knows the warmth rising
as morning talking mother.

in her hands she prepares snow for the visitor.
she sprinkles the snow into the bare hills
and valleys where in the spring
after the plants have grown
people with medicine eyes come
to lift the plants from her head
taking them home to the sick.

i remember as i was looking out
from my eyes that my eyes were like windows
smeared and bent out of proportion,
that the earth was curved from where
i was sitting, cars came and disappeared.
it was summer and i sat on a blanket.
i watched my grandmother as she came to me,
holding a skillet, she set it down beside me
and she fanned the smoke which came from medicine
crackling over the hot coals
towards me.

THE LANGUAGE OF WEATHER

The summer rain isn't here yet,
but I hear and see the approaching
shadow of its initial messenger:
Thunder.
The earth's bright horizon
sends a final sunbeam directly
toward me, skimming across the tops
of clouds and hilly woodland.
All in one moment, in spite
of my austerity, everything
is aligned: part-land, part-cloud,
part-sky, part-sun and part-self.
I am the only one to witness
this renascence.
Before darkness replaces the light
in my eyes, I meditate briefly
on the absence of religious
importunity; no acknowledgement
whatsoever for the Factors
which make my existence possible.
My parents, who are hurrying
to overturn the reddish-brown dirt
around the potato plants, begin to talk
above the rumbling din.
"Their mouths are opening.
See that everyone in the household
releases parts of ourselves
to our Grandfathers."
While raindrops begin to cool
my face and arms, lightning
breaks a faraway cottonwood
in half; small clouds of red
garden dust are kicked into
the frantic air by grasshoppers
in retreat.
I think of the time I stood
on this same spot years ago,

but it was under moonlight,
and I was watching this beautiful
electrical force dance above
another valley.
In the daylight distance,
a stray spirit whose guise
is a Whirlwind, spins and attempts
to communicate from its ethereal
loneliness.

Discussion Questions

1. In "morning talking mother," identify the references made by the personal pronouns. To whom or what does the "i"—the speaker of the poem—seem to refer? Does the identity seem to change in stanzas 2 and 4? Explain who "you" refers to in stanza 1. Who does "her" and "she" refer to in stanzas 2 and 3?
2. Quoting several phrases, describe the tone or attitude of this poem.
3. Describe the relationship between the speaker and his grandmother.
4. Explain the meaning of the title, "morning talking mother."
5. In four or five sentences, paraphrase "The Language of Weather."
6. After looking up the word "importunity" in a dictionary, explain the meaning of the phrase "the absence of religious / importunity" and its relation to the rest of the poem.
7. Why is it important that "everyone . . . / releases parts of ourselves / to our Grandfathers"?
8. Explain the significance of a memory from "years ago" to the present experience that the poem recounts.

Fig. 7.2 David Bradley, *American Indian Gothic* (1993), lithograph on paper. Buffalo Bill Historical Center, Cody, WY; gift of Mrs. Damaris D. W. Ethridge; 1.84.5.

LOUISE ERDRICH
(1954–)

Born in Minnesota, near the Turtle Mountain Chippewa reservation in North Dakota, the author was the eldest of seven children (Trotsky). A strong influence was her severe Catholic upbringing in Wahpeton, North Dakota, but she was also exposed to the storytelling of her German-

American father and of her maternal grandparents whom she visited on the reservation. Her parents, both teachers for the Bureau of Indian Affairs, encouraged her childhood story-writing efforts, though she never spoke a tribal language and was little aware of her Native American heritage (Witalec). That ignorance changed at Dartmouth, where she enrolled in 1972, when the college first accepted female students and initiated an innovative Native-American Studies program with anthropologist Michael Dorris as chair. In his classes, Erdrich began to explore her own Chippewa heritage, which has stimulated her writing ever since (Trotsky).

As a young adult, the author worked in a variety of jobs, including beet-weeder, lifeguard, waitress, poetry teacher to prison inmates, hospital psychiatric aide, and construction flagger. After completing her B.A. at Dartmouth, she did graduate work at Johns Hopkins, where she also taught writing for a year, earning an M.A. in 1979 (Witalec). She returned to Dartmouth as a visiting fellow and writer-in-residence. At a reading that Erdrich gave, Dorris was impressed with her poetry and became interested in collaborating with her, so they began trading drafts of stories and poems they were working on. The following year, she served as editor for *The Circle*, the newspaper of the Boston Indian Council. This experience with urban, mixed-blood Indians further validated her own confusion about her ethnic identity and stimulated her interest in writing about her Native American roots (Trotsky).

When Dorris returned to New Hampshire from a research trip, Erdrich moved back too, and the couple began writing short stories together. In fact, the collaboration was so successful that one story, "The World's Greatest Fisherman," won a $5,000 prize, and Erdrich decided to expand this work into her first novel, *Love Medicine* (1984). As they worked together, their relationship grew more personal, and they were married in 1981. Their collaboration technique was meticulous, if not exhausting. Typically, the originating author of an idea would create a first draft and then receive editing suggestions from the other. This process might be repeated through five drafts, until both would read the manuscript aloud and edit every word together (Trotsky). This process has helped to create rich narratives, dense with incident and idiosyncratic characterizations. *Love Medicine*, a complex Faulkneresque story told by seven narrative voices, won the 1985 National Book Critics Circle Award for best fiction.

In subsequent novels—*The Beet Queen* (1986) and *Tracks* (1988)—Erdrich has developed many of the same characters and settings as in the first book, and these works have also become national best-sellers. In the series, the author "explores universal family life-cycles while also communicating a sense of the changes and loss involved in the twentieth-century

Native American experience" (Trotsky 126). Erdrich's major theme in these works is the breakdown of families and the sustaining continuity of reservation culture even amid the traumatic dislocation and marginalization of Indian life. Among many families in these novels, mothers abandon their children, while fathers are either abusive or absent, emotionally and physically. However, Erdrich is most concerned with the tribal members who share the mothering role toward the cast-off children. According to Hertha D. Wong, "mothering is not merely an activity but an orientation to the world—a recognition of a responsibility to the interrelatedness of all beings" (qtd. in Witalec 278). But this sustaining relationship is available only on the reservation, so those who leave—both children and parents—suffer alienation from their immediate family and their tribal community. Thus, a related theme in Erdrich's work is that of homecoming, which is especially acute among the mixed-bloods, whose ethnicity and personal identity are often in doubt (Witalec).

These themes of cultural conflict and continuity are also treated in Erdrich's poetry, but developed in a less narrative style. Rather, her poems are generally brief and lyrical, expressing poignant situations and strong emotional turns. She is especially effective at "infusing the commonplace and mundane with the richness of myth" (Witalec 277).

The text of "Indian Boarding School: The Runaways" is from *Jacklight* (New York: Henry Holt, 1984), page 11.

Trotsky, Susan M., ed. "Louise Erdrich." *Contemporary Authors, New Revision Series, Volume 41*. Detroit: Gale, 1994. 124–28.

Witalec, Janet, ed. "Louise Erdrich." *Native North American Literature*. Detroit: Gale, 1994. 276–89.

INDIAN BOARDING SCHOOL: THE RUNAWAYS

Home's the place we head for in our sleep.
Boxcars stumbling north in dreams
don't wait for us. We catch them on the run.
The rails, old lacerations that we love,
shoot parallel across the face and break
just under Turtle Mountains. Riding scars
you can't get lost. Home is the place they cross.

The lame guard strikes a match and makes the dark
less tolerant. We watch through cracks in boards
as the land starts rolling, rolling till it hurts
to be here, cold in regulation clothes.
We know the sheriff's waiting at midrun
to take us back. His car is dumb and warm.
The highway doesn't rock, it only hums
like a wing of long insults. The worn-down welts
of ancient punishments lead back and forth.

All runaways wear dresses, long green ones,
the color you would think shame was. We scrub
the sidewalks down because it's shameful work.
Our brushes cut the stone in watered arcs
and in the soak frail outlines shiver clear
a moment, things us kids pressed on the dark
face before it hardened, pale, remembering
delicate old injuries, the spines of names and leaves.

Discussion Questions

1. This poem teases the reader with an account that seems to be a dream. If so, why do the runaways get caught?
2. In the first stanza, why are rail lines compared to "lacerations" and "scars"? Point out other words or phrases in the poem that repeat this imagery and explain their meaning.
3. Interpret the images in the final five lines of the poem and the commentary these lines make on the previous lines and stanzas.

MARY BRAVE BIRD
(1953–)

After an eventful early life, the author has written two autobiographies, with some assistance from Richard Erdoes, in her middle years. She was born on the Rosebud Reservation in South Dakota, but was raised with little awareness of her Sioux heritage. In fact, her mother refused to speak the native language with Brave Bird because she believed that knowledge of Indian culture would inhibit her daughter's assimilation into mainstream white society. In any case, Brave Bird was raised mostly by her grandparents and sent, at an early age, to the St. Francis Catholic boarding school, where she was physically and emotionally abused—the topic of the excerpt below. As a teenager, she rebelled from this rigid discipline, abandoned formal education, led an unstable existence, living both on and off the reservation, and suffered from alcohol abuse. During this time, she also developed an interest in her native heritage and, in 1971, joined the American Indian Movement (AIM). The following year, she participated in a protest march and occupation of the headquarters for the Bureau of Indian Affairs in Washington, DC (Narins and Stanley; Rooney).

The turning point in Brave Bird's life came in 1973 during the occupation of the church, museum, and trading post at Wounded Knee, South Dakota, the 1890 site of the last major "battle" between the U.S. cavalry and Native Americans, in which 29 soldiers died and 200 Indians—many of them unarmed women and children—were massacred. During the 71-day "siege" by FBI agents and Pine Ridge Reservation police, Brave Bird went into labor and delivered her first of five children. During this protest, she also became acquainted with Leonard Crow Dog, a Sioux medicine man and Indian rights activist who revived the Ghost Dance and whom she later married. Much of her first book, *Lakota Woman* (1990), details the difficulties she shared in living with the intensely idealistic AIM leader, the challenges of sexism in relationships as well as in the movement, and her initial exposure to native spiritual rituals, such as the Sun Dance ceremony, through which she gained a sense of wholeness and survival. Brave Bird's feminism is clear in comparing the contemporary record of beatings and rapes to the traditional tribal power of women, as manifested in the continued performance of puberty ceremonies and the myth of White Buffalo Woman. Thus, Brave Bird's narrative is structured by cyclical patterns that connect contemporary and personal events to Indian history and heritage (Narins and Stanley; Rooney). Praising both the sympathetic humor and the painful realism of *Lakota Woman*, Indian activist Mahtowin remarks, "Nowhere in American popular culture will you find the strong, resourceful, hilarious and human Native women. . . . Things are better at least in the realm of literature" (qtd. in Narins and Stanley 111). This first autobiography won the American Book Award in 1991.

Brave Bird then wrote *Ohitika Woman* (1993), which depicts the author's life between 1977 and 1992. This tale includes depressing details of repeated alcohol and drug abuse, beatings by lovers, crushing poverty, homeless shelters, and a near-fatal drunken-driving accident. However, the author also tells promising stories of her involvement with the rituals of sweat lodges and spirit communication in the

Native American Church, with her children, and with her second husband, Rudi, a tattoo artist. In this autobiography, Brave Bird also criticizes federal oppression of native peoples and the faddish exploitation of Indian spirituality by "plastic medicine men" and women who market New Age seminars to "whites seeking for something that they hope will give meaning to their empty lives" (qtd. in Narins and Stanley 111). While lacking the historical impact of the first volume, this second work at least shows the values of endurance and commitment: Brave Bird has survived violence and alienation to reach a new understanding with her mother, to care for her children, to find stability in a new relationship, and to share the wisdom of her experience (Narins and Stanley).

The text of the excerpt below is from Mary [Brave Bird] Crow Dog and Richard Erdoes, *Lakota Woman* (New York: Grove Press, 1990), pages 28–41.

Narins, Brigham, and Deborah A. Stanley. "Mary Brave Bird [Mary Crow Dog]." *Contemporary Literary Criticism, Volume 93*. Detroit: Gale, 1996. 108–13.

Rooney, Terrie M., ed. "Crow Dog, Mary (Mary Brave Bird)." *Contemporary Authors, Volume 154*. Detroit: Gale, 1997. 95–96.

FROM *LAKOTA WOMAN*

CIVILIZE THEM WITH A STICK

—◆—

... Gathered from the cabin, the wickiup, and the tepee,
partly by cajolery and partly by threats;
partly by bribery and partly by force,
they are induced to leave their kindred
to enter these schools and take upon themselves
the outward appearance of civilized life.
                    —*Annual Report of the Department of Interior, 1901*

It is almost impossible to explain to a sympathetic white person what a typical old Indian boarding school was like; how it affected the Indian child suddenly dumped into it like a small creature from another world, helpless, defenseless, bewildered, trying desperately and instinctively to survive and sometimes not surviving at all. I think such children were like the victims of Nazi concentration camps trying to tell average, middle-class Americans what their experience had been like. Even now, when these schools are much improved, when the buildings are new, all gleaming steel and glass, the food tolerable, the teachers well trained and well-intentioned, even trained in child psychology—unfortunately the psychology of white children, which is different from ours—the shock to the child upon arrival is still tremendous. Some just seem to shrivel up, don't speak for days on end, and have an empty look in their eyes. I know of an eleven-year-old on another reservation who hanged herself, and in our school, while I was there, a girl jumped out of the window, trying to kill herself to escape an unbearable situation. That first shock is always there.

Although the old tiyospaye [the extended family group] has been destroyed, in the traditional Sioux families, especially in those where there is no drinking, the child is never left alone. It is always surrounded by relatives, carried around, enveloped in warmth. It is treated with the respect due to any human being, even a small one. It is seldom forced to do anything against its will, seldom screamed at, and never beaten. That much, at least, is left of the old family group among full-bloods. And then suddenly a bus or car arrives, full of strangers, usually white strangers, who yank the child out of the arms of those who love it, taking it screaming to the boarding school. The only word I can think of for what is done to these children is kidnapping.

Even now, in a good school, there is impersonality instead of close human contact; a sterile, cold atmosphere, an unfamiliar routine, language problems, and above all the *maza-skan-skan*, that damn clock—white man's time as opposed to Indian time, which is natural time. Like eating when you are hungry and sleeping when you are tired, not when that damn clock says you must. But I was not taken to one of the better, modern schools. I was taken to the old-fashioned mission school at St. Francis, run by the nuns and Catholic fathers, built sometime around the turn of the century and not improved a bit when I arrived, not improved as far as the buildings, the food, the teachers, or their methods were concerned.

In the old days, nature was our people's only school and they needed no other. Girls had their toy tipis and dolls, boys their toy bows and arrows. Both rode and swam and played the rough Indian games together. Kids watched their peers and elders and naturally grew from children into adults. Life in the tipi circle was harmonious—until the whiskey peddlers arrived with their wagons and barrels of "Injun whiskey." I often wished I could have grown up in the old, before-whiskey days.

Oddly enough, we owed our unspeakable boarding schools to the do-gooders, the white Indian-lovers. The schools were intended as an alternative to the outright extermination seriously advocated by generals Sherman and Sheridan, as well as by most settlers and prospectors overrunning our land. "You don't have to kill those poor benighted heathen," the do-gooders said, "in order to solve the Indian Problem. Just give us a chance to turn them into useful farmhands, laborers, and chambermaids who will break their backs for you at low wages." In that way the boarding schools were born. The kids were taken away from their villages and pueblos, in their blankets and moccasins, kept completely isolated from their families—sometimes for as long as ten years—suddenly coming back, their short hair slick with pomade, their necks raw from stiff, high collars, their thick jackets always short in the sleeves and pinching under the arms, their tight patent leather shoes giving them corns, the girls in starched white blouses and clumsy, high-buttoned boots—caricatures of white people. When they found out—and they found out quickly—that they were neither wanted by whites nor by Indians, they got good and drunk, many of them staying drunk for the rest of their lives. I still have a poster I found among my grandfather's stuff, given to him by the missionaries to tack up on his wall. It reads:

1. Let Jesus save you.
2. Come out of your blanket, cut your hair, and dress like a white man.
3. Have a Christian family with one wife for life only.
4. Live in a house like your white brother. Work hard and wash often.
5. Learn the value of a hard-earned dollar. Do not waste your money on giveaways. Be punctual.
6. Believe that property and wealth are signs of divine approval.
7. Keep away from saloons and strong spirits.
8. Speak the language of your white brother. Send your children to school to do likewise.
9. Go to church often and regularly.
10. Do not go to Indian dances or to the medicine men.

The people who were stuck upon "solving the Indian Problem" by making us into whites retreated from this position only step by step in the wake of Indian protests.

The mission school at St. Francis was a curse for our family for generations. My grandmother went there, then my mother, then my sisters and I. At one time or other every one of us tried to run away. Grandma told me once about the bad times she had experienced at St. Francis. In those days they let students go home only for one week every year. Two days were used up for transportation, which meant spending just five days out of three hundred and sixty-five with her family. And that was an improvement. Before grandma's time, on many reservations they did not let the students go home at all until they had finished school. Anybody who disobeyed the nuns was severely punished. The building in which my grandmother stayed had three floors, for girls only. Way up in the attic were little cells, about five by five by ten feet. One time she was in church and instead of praying she was playing jacks. As punishment they took her to one of those little cubicles where she stayed in darkness because the windows had been boarded up. They left her there for a whole week with only bread and water for nourishment. After she came out she promptly ran away, together with three other girls. They were found and brought back. The nuns stripped them naked and whipped them. They used a horse buggy whip on my grandmother. Then she was put back into the attic—for two weeks.

My mother had much the same experiences but never wanted to talk about them, and then there I was, in the same place. The school is now run by the BIA—the Bureau of Indian Affairs—but only since about fifteen years ago. When I was there, during the 1960s, it was still run by the Church. The Jesuit fathers ran the boys' wing and the Sisters of the Sacred Heart ran us—with the help of the strap. Nothing had changed since my grandmother's days. I have been told recently that even in the '70s they were still beating children at that school. All I got out of school was being taught how to pray. I learned quickly that I would be beaten if I failed in my devotions or, God forbid, prayed the wrong way, especially prayed in Indian to Wakan Tanka, the Indian Creator.

The girls' wing was built like an F and was run like a penal institution. Every morning at five o'clock the sisters would come into our large dormitory to wake us up, and immediately we had to kneel down at the sides of our beds and recite the prayers. At six o'clock we were herded into the church for more of the same. I did not take kindly to the discipline and to marching by the clock, left-right, left-right. I was never one to like being forced to do something. I do something because I feel like doing it. I felt this way always, as far as I can remember, and my sister Barbara felt the same way. An old medicine man once told me: "Us Lakotas are not like dogs who can be trained, who can be beaten and keep on wagging their tails, licking the hand that whipped them. We are like cats, little cats, big cats, wildcats, bobcats, mountain lions. It doesn't matter what kind, but cats who can't be tamed, who scratch if you step on their tails." But I was only a kitten and my claws were still small.

Barbara was still in the school when I arrived and during my first year or two she could still protect me a little bit. When Barb was a seventh-grader she ran away together with five other girls, early in the morning before sunrise. They brought them back in the evening. The girls had to wait for two hours in front of the mother superior's office. They were hungry and cold, frozen through. It was wintertime and they had been running the whole day without food, trying to make good their escape. The mother superior asked each girl, "Would you do this again?" She told them that as punishment they would not be allowed to visit home for a month and that she'd keep them busy on work details until the skin on their knees and elbows had worn off. At the end of her speech she told each girl, "Get up from this chair and lean over it." She then lifted the girls' skirts and pulled down their underpants. Not little girls either, but teenagers. She had a leather strap about a foot long and four inches wide fastened to a stick, and beat the girls, one after another, until they cried. Barb did not give her that satisfaction but just clenched her teeth. There was one girl, Barb told me, the nun kept on beating and beating until her arm got tired.

I did not escape my share of the strap. Once, when I was thirteen years old, I refused to go to Mass. I did not want to go to church because I did not feel well. A nun grabbed me by the hair, dragged me upstairs, made me stoop over, pulled my dress up (we were not allowed at the time to wear jeans), pulled my panties down, and gave me what they called "swats"— twenty-five swats with a board around which Scotch tape had been wound. She hurt me badly.

My classroom was right next to the principal's office and almost every day I could hear him swatting the boys. Beating was the common punishment for not doing one's homework, or for being late to school. It had such a bad effect upon me that I hated and mistrusted every white person on sight, because I met only one kind. It was not until much later that I met sincere white people I could relate to and be friends with. Racism breeds racism in reverse.

The routine at St. Francis was dreary. Six A.M., kneeling in church for an hour or so; seven o'clock, breakfast; eight o'clock, scrub the floor, peel spuds, make classes. We had to mop the dining room twice every day and scrub the tables. If you were caught taking a rest, doodling on the bench with a fingernail or knife, or just rapping, the nun would come up with a dish towel and just slap it across your face, saying, "You're not supposed to be talking, you're supposed to be working!" Monday mornings we had cornmeal mush, Tuesday oatmeal, Wednesday rice and raisins, Thursday cornflakes, and Friday all the leftovers mixed together or sometimes fish. Frequently the food had bugs or rocks in it. We were eating hot dogs that were weeks old, while the nuns were dining on ham, whipped potatoes, sweet peas, and cranberry sauce. In winter our dorm was icy cold while the nuns' rooms were always warm.

I have seen little girls arrive at the school, first-graders, just fresh from home and totally unprepared for what awaited them, little girls with pretty braids, and the first thing the nuns did was chop their hair off and tie up what was left behind their ears. Next they would dump the children into tubs of alcohol, a sort of rubbing alcohol, "to get the germs off." Many of the nuns were German immigrants, some from Bavaria, so that we sometimes speculated whether Bavaria was some sort of Dracula country inhabited by monsters. For the sake of objectivity I ought to mention that two of the German fathers were great linguists and that the only Lakota-English dictionaries and grammars which are worth anything were put together by them.

At night some of the girls would huddle in bed together for comfort and reassurance. Then the nun in charge of the dorm would come in and say, "What are the two of you doing in bed together? I smell evil in this room. You girls are evil incarnate. You are sinning. You are going to hell and burn forever. You can act that way in the devil's frying pan." She would get them out of bed in the middle of the night, making them kneel and pray until morning. We had not the slightest idea what it was all about. At home we slept two and three in a bed for animal warmth and a feeling of security.

The nuns and the girls in the two top grades were constantly battling it out physically with fists, nails, and hair-pulling. I myself was growing from a kitten into an undersized cat. My claws were getting bigger and were itching for action. About 1969 or 1970 a strange young white girl appeared on the reservation. She looked about eighteen or twenty years old. She was pretty and had long, blond hair down to her waist, patched jeans, boots, and a backpack. She was different from any other white person we had met before. I think her name was Wise. I do not know how she managed to overcome our reluctance and distrust, getting us into a corner, making us listen to her, asking us how we were treated. She told us that she was from New York. She was the first real hippie or Yippie we had come across. She told us of people called the Black Panthers, Young Lords, and Weathermen. She said, "Black people are getting it on. Indians are getting it on in St. Paul and California. How about you?" She also said, "Why don't you put out an underground paper, mimeograph it. It's easy. Tell it like it is. Let it all hang out." She spoke a strange lingo but we caught on fast.

Charlene Left Hand Bull and Gina One Star were two full-blood girls I used to hang out with. We did everything together. They were willing to join me in a Sioux uprising. We put together a newspaper which we called the *Red Panther*. In it we wrote how bad the school was, what kind of slop we had to eat—slimy, rotten, blackened potatoes for two weeks—the way we were beaten. I think I was the one who wrote the worst article about our principal of the moment, Father Keeler. I put all my anger and venom into it. I called him a goddam wasičun son of a bitch. I wrote that he knew nothing about Indians and should go back to where he came from, teaching white children whom he could relate to. I wrote that we knew which priests slept with which nuns and that all they ever could think about was filling their bellies and buying a new car. It was the kind of writing which foamed at the mouth, but which also lifted a great deal of weight from one's soul.

On Saint Patrick's Day, when everybody was at the big pow-wow, we distributed our newspapers. We put them on windshields and bulletin boards, in desks and pews, in dorms and toilets. But someone saw us and snitched on us. The shit hit the fan. The three of us were taken before a board meeting. Our parents, in my case my mother, had to come. They were told that ours was a most serious matter, the worst thing that had ever happened in the school's long history: One of the nuns told my mother, "Your daughter really needs to be talked to." "What's wrong with my daughter?" my mother asked. She was given one of our *Red Panther* newspapers. The nun pointed out its name to her and then my piece, waiting for mom's reaction. After a while she asked, "Well, what have you got to say to this? What do you think?"

My mother said, "Well, when I went to school here, some years back, I was treated a lot worse than these kids are. I really can't see how they can have any complaints, because we was treated a lot stricter. We could not even wear skirts halfway up our knees. These girls have it made. But you should forgive them because they are young. And it's supposed to be a free country, free speech and all that. I don't believe what they done is wrong." So all I got out of it was scrubbing six flights of stairs on my hands and knees, every day. And no boy-side privileges.

The boys and girls were still pretty much separated. The only time one could meet a member of the opposite sex was during free time, between four and five-thirty, in the study hall or on benches or the volleyball court outside, and that was strictly supervised. One day Charlene and I went over to the boys' side. We were on the ball team and they had to let us practice. We played three extra minutes, only three minutes more than we were supposed to. Here was the nuns' opportunity for revenge. We got twenty-five swats. I told Charlene, "We are getting too old to have our bare asses whipped that way. We are old enough to have babies. Enough of this shit. Next time we fight back." Charlene only said, "Hoka-hay!"

We had to take showers every evening. One little girl did not want to take her panties off and one of the nuns told her, "You take those underpants off— or else!" But the child was ashamed to do it. The nun was getting her swat to threaten the girl. I went up to the sister, pushed her veil off, and knocked her down. I told her that if she wanted to hit a little girl she should pick on me, pick one her own size. She got herself transferred out of the dorm a week later.

In a school like this there is always a lot of favoritism. At St. Francis it was strongly tinged with racism. Girls who were near-white, who came from what the nuns called "nice families," got preferential treatment. They waited on the faculty and got to eat ham or eggs and bacon in the morning. They got the easy jobs while the skins, who did not have the right kind of background—myself among them—always wound up in the laundry room sorting out ten bushel baskets of dirty boys' socks every day. Or we wound up scrubbing the floors and doing all the dishes. The school therefore fostered fights and antagonism between whites and breeds, and between breeds and skins. At one time Charlene and I had to iron all the robes and vestments the priests wore when saying Mass. We had to fold them up and put them into a chest in the back of the church. In a corner, looking over our shoulders, was a statue of the crucified Savior, all bloody and beaten up. Charlene looked up and said, "Look at that poor Indian. The pigs sure worked him over." That was the closest I ever came to seeing Jesus.

I was held up as a bad example and didn't mind. I was old enough to have a boyfriend and promptly got one. At the school we had an hour and a half for ourselves. Between the boys' and the girls' wings were some benches where one could sit. My boyfriend and I used to go there just to hold hands and talk. The nuns were very uptight about any boy-girl stuff. They had an exaggerated fear of anything having even the faintest connection with sex. One day in religion class, an all-girl class, Sister Bernard singled me out for some remarks, pointing me out as a bad example, an example that should be shown. She said that I was too free with my body. That I was holding hands which meant that I was not a good example to follow. She also said that I wore unchaste dresses, skirts which were too short, too suggestive, shorter than regulations permitted, and for that I would be punished. She dressed me down before the whole class, carrying on and on about my unchastity.

I stood up and told her, "You shouldn't say any of those things, miss. You people are a lot worse than us Indians. I know all about you, because my grandmother and my aunt told me about you. Maybe twelve, thirteen years ago you had a water stoppage here in St. Francis. No water could get through the pipes. There are water lines right under the mission, underground tunnels and passages where in my grandmother's time only the nuns and priests could go, which were off-limits to everybody else. When the water backed up they had to go through all the water lines and clean them out. And in those huge pipes they found the bodies of newborn babies. And they were white babies. They weren't Indian babies. At least when our girls have babies, they don't do away with them that way, like flushing them down the toilet, almost.

"And that priest they sent here from Holy Rosary in Pine Ridge because he molested a little girl. You couldn't think of anything better than dump him on us. All he does is watch young women and girls with that funny smile on his face. Why don't you point him out for an example?"

Charlene and I worked on the school newspaper. After all we had some practice. Every day we went down to Publications. One of the priests acted as the photographer, doing the enlarging and developing. He smelled of chemicals which had stained his hands yellow. One day he invited Charlene into the darkroom. He was going to teach her developing. She was developed already. She was a big girl compared to him, taller too. Charlene was nicely built, not fat, just rounded. No sharp edges anywhere. All of a sudden she rushed out of the darkroom, yelling to me, "Let's get out of here! He's trying to feel me up. That priest is nasty." So there was this too to contend with—sexual harassment. We complained to the student body. The nuns said we just had a dirty mind.

We got a new priest in English. During one of his first classes he asked one of the boys a certain question. The boy was shy. He spoke poor English, but he had the right answer. The priest told him, "You did not say it right. Correct yourself. Say it over again." The boy got flustered and stammered. He could hardly get out a word. But the priest kept after him: "Didn't you hear? I told you to do the whole thing over. Get it right this time." He kept on and on.

I stood up and said, "Father, don't be doing that. If you go into an Indian's home and try to talk Indian, they might laugh at you and say, 'Do it over correctly. Get it right this time!'"

He shouted at me, "Mary, you stay after class. Sit down right now!"

I stayed after class, until after the bell. He told me, "Get over here!" He grabbed me by the arm, pushing me against the blackboard, shouting, "Why are you always mocking us? You have no reason to do this."

I said, "Sure I do. You were making fun of him. You embarrassed him. He needs strengthening, not weakening. You hurt him. I did not hurt you."

He twisted my arm and pushed real hard. I turned around and hit him in the face, giving him a bloody nose. After that I ran out of the room, slamming the door behind me. He and I went to Sister Bernard's office. I told her, "Today I quit school. I'm not taking any more of this, none of this shit anymore. None of this treatment. Better give me my diploma. I can't waste any more time on you people."

Sister Bernard looked at me for a long, long time. She said, "All right, Mary Ellen, go home today. Come back in a few days and get your diploma." And that was that. Oddly enough, that priest turned out okay. He taught a class in grammar, orthography, composition, things like that. I think he wanted more respect in class. He was still young and unsure of himself. But I was in there too long. I didn't feel like hearing it. Later he became a good friend of the Indians, a personal friend of myself and my husband. He stood up for us during Wounded Knee and after. He stood up to his superiors, stuck his neck way out, became a real people's priest. He even learned our language. He died prematurely of cancer. It is not only the good Indians who die young, but the good whites, too. It is the timid ones who know how to take care of themselves who grow old. I am still grateful to that priest for what he did for us later and for the quarrel he picked with me—or did I pick it with him?—because it ended a situation which had become unendurable for me. The day of my fight with him was my last day in school.

Discussion Questions

1. Compare/contrast Brave Bird's chapter with the second excerpt from Winnemucca's *Life Among the Piutes*, which considers reservation life. Describe the problems in Indian–white relations that are common to both works. Describe the differences between the ways Winnemucca dealt with these problems in the nineteenth century and the ways Brave Bird dealt with them in 1970.

2. The prologue to the chapter refers to a routine practice, popular from the late nineteenth century through the mid-twentieth century, of sending Native American children away from their families and cultures on the reservations to all-Indian boarding schools. Quoting a couple of striking phrases from the passage, comment on your response to reading it. Then, explain the prologue's purpose in relation to Brave Bird's personal narrative about the mission school at St. Francis.

3. Brave Bird mentions very little about her classroom lessons. What does she actually learn in school?

4. Compare/contrast this excerpt from Brave Bird's autobiography and Erdrich's poem, "Indian Boarding School: The Runaways."

DIANE GLANCY
(1941–)

Born in Kansas City, Missouri, the author was influenced strongly by her Native American heritage, even though her mother's ancestors were English and German and her father was only one-quarter Cherokee. In *Claiming Breath* (1992), she wrote about her difficult reconciliation between her father's "Arkansas back-hill culture" and Indian background and the "will and order and persistence of the Anglo culture" that characterized her mother (qtd. in Witalec 302). Her identity as a mixed blood is a major theme of this journal of a year spent traveling across Arkansas and Oklahoma as an itinerant artist-in-residence. As she explores the Cherokee inspiration to her imagination and creativity, she weaves in "memories of childhood, a failed marriage, and her struggle with career and poetic vocation" (Witalec 302). In striving to resolve a divided self, she is able to question the "practice of participation in and exclusion from more than one culture" (303), and thus reveal the border-life of a Native American writer.

Glancy published her first of eight poetry books in 1982 and earned an M.A. in creative writing from Oklahoma's Central State University in 1983. After serving as poet laureate for the Five Civilized Tribes from 1984 to 1986, she attended the Writers' Workshop at the University of Iowa, earning her M.F.A. in 1988. Through the 1980s, she worked as a professor of English at various universities, also writing three prize-winning plays. Since 1988, she has taught at Macalester College in St. Paul, Minnesota.

Her works have been praised for "her realistic depictions of the effects of assimilation, her thoughtful examination of cultural differences, and her emphasis on renewal and survival" (Witalec 298). Her first fiction collection, *Trigger Dance* (1990), explores the problem of Native American identity, given a heritage whose cultural roots have been destroyed. Glancy depicts bleak scenes of "abandonment, illiteracy and abuse . . . , discrimination, familial crisis and blatant Government neglect" (Ferber qtd. in Witalec 300), but does so with arresting passion and eloquence. Likewise, her stories in *Firesticks* (1993) convey humor amid the tragedy of Indian lives, integrity amid the echoes of defeat, and transcendence through integrating the "spirit world" into the everyday.

About her own work, Glancy has said, "I want to represent life with respect. . . . I want to write about the dignity of the common man and the uniqueness of the ordinary moment. I want to have the courage to face the wilderness within. It provides tension. And I want to have a sense of self as whole even though fragmented. It gives voice" (qtd. in Witalec 301). Moreover, she makes special claims for the moral value of her verse: "Indian poetry, especially, should promote stability, precision, hope. It should be a salve for the broken race. . . . If our poetry is a vent for anger, it should also transcend" (298).

The text for the following poem is reprinted from *Offering: Poetry and Prose* (Duluth, MN: Holy Cow! Press, 1988), pages 59–60.

Witalec, Janet, ed. "Diane Glancy." *Native North American Literature*. Detroit: Gale, 1994. 298–303.

BLACK KETTLE NATIONAL GRASSLANDS, WESTERN OKLAHOMA

We feel them for some time now,
a residue as though from a dream,
watching from the crawling hills
and lines of trees in the draw:
Chief Black Kettle and his tribe,
frozen white as clouds in the sun.

Gullies gouge the red soil like war-
paint but there was not time for that
when Custer waited the night in a
blizzard and rode at dawn from the
ridge into the Cheyenne winter camp.

In the museum: stirrup, bit, rifle-
shells, pouch, arrowheads from the
battle ground; and from the hills,
a pack-mule feed-bag and a soldier's
mess kettle, dented as old maps
of attack plans.

Like dreams, it all takes place
in an instant. From the moment
I hear the sound until I wake,
you say is only seconds. Between
the cats fighting outside the
window this morning is my long dream.

And here, in glass cases, relics of
the Seventh Cavalry and a tribe
of Indians. A chief who wanted peace.
A general who fought for westward
expansion.

Down the road, under a circular
break in the clouds, an irrigation-

pipe on crude tractor-wheels
washes their battlefield.

An early morning dream returns:
a werewolf with black hair on its face,
tied up, held captive with others
in beds. I walk past them
and someone sprays vinegar-water.
I brush it away with irritation,
and the snarling cats wake me.
I cannot sleep again to find what happens.

Black Kettle had his own dream of a
wolf with blood on its face and knew
they would die, like all of us,
but not when.

Now I stand on the road where Custer
waited. Some of the artifacts
from two races still buried in the ground.
A strange time warp hidden
like the end of a dream.

I look at the Washita Creek where
Black Kettle fell, and his wife with him,
a few yards away. The tribe still
running in all ways.

Before they could bury him, his flesh
was torn by wolves
as though he once dreamed he would die,
knowing at last, it would be then.

In the draw, the Indian tribe thaws.
They speak with sign language like trees.
The sudden smell of wet buffalo robes,
and a small howl from the soft lining
of the throat.

We listen to winds over the grasslands:
once through this country is enough.

Discussion Questions

1. Explain how the poet contrasts the past and the present. Analyze the images that represent each time period.
2. Describe the functions of the several uses of the word "dream."
3. Explain the images of the wolf in stanzas 7, 8, 11, and 12. How are they connected? How does the meaning change through these stanzas?
4. Interpret the final line of the poem.

Fig. 7.3 Bennie Buffalo, *Cheyenne in the Moon* (1991), lithograph on paper. Donald C. and Elizabeth M. Dickinson Research Center, National Cowboy and Western Heritage Museum, Oklahoma City, OK; 96.27.0308.

SHERMAN ALEXIE
(1966–)

Born upon the Spokane Indian Reservation in Wellpinit, Washington, the author still makes his home there, and it is a major setting for his works. His father, an alcoholic, was absent for much of his youth, but his mother worked at the Wellpinit Trading Post to support the family. He read voraciously as a child and decided to attend the public school in Reardan, some thirty miles from home, in order to gain the college preparatory skills that would ensure his acceptance to an academically rigorous college (Witalec). After attending Spokane's Gonzaga University for two years, he transferred in 1987 to Washington State University in Pullman, where he began writing poetry and short stories. When he left in 1991, he was still three credits short of graduating. Nonetheless, in 1995 the school granted him a B.A. in American studies, along with an Alumni Achievement Award (Brill).

He began writing for journals and popular magazines and published his first chapbook of poetry, *I Would Steal Horses*, in 1992. This was but the beginning of a prolific five-year period in which he churned out nine more books of poetry and fiction, including two novels. His works cover a wide range of topics and themes about contemporary Native Americans: "pain and humor, hunger and survival, love and anger, broken treaties, Manifest Destiny, basketball, car wrecks, commodity food, U.S. Department of Housing and Urban Development houses, smallpox blankets, and promises and dreams" (Brill 4). Through all his depictions of the physical and mental cruelty that Indians suffer, including "their own self-hatred and sense of powerlessness," there is still "a sense of respect and compassion for characters that are in seemingly hopeless situations" (Witalec 119).

Possibly his most popular work, *The Lone Ranger and Tonto Fistfight in Heaven* (1993) uses ironic humor as social criticism, while presenting bizarre and desperate responses to a chaotic world as sincere acts of dignity and self-assertion. Alexie's style is very much a part of his urgent message, composed as "a collage of dreams, journal entries, quotes from other native writers, archival letters, fictional Kafkaesque court transcripts, tribal newspaper reports, drug trips, and basketball games" (Witalec 123). Even though the disjunction of the narrative is very contemporary, he also enacts the oral tradition through demanding that his reader/listener participate in creating the story. Sometimes he achieves this through disconcerting shifts in person, from the distancing voice of third person to the personal address of second person, involving the reader directly in a dialog; and even to the intimate first person, identifying speaker and listener together. Another means of approximating the oral style is providing the reader with an explanation or coda at the end of a puzzling story or poem. Although the images of the world he shares are harsh, Alexie affirms that Indians can and do survive through their relationships and through mythmaking. In a sense, becoming a writer and wielding the power of language is a means of salvation (Brill).

The text for the following poem is from *The Summer of Black Widows* (Brooklyn: Hanging Loose Press, 1996), pages 94–95.

Brill, Susan B. "Sherman Alexie." *Dictionary of Literary Biography, Volume 175: Native American Writers of the United States.* Ed. Kenneth M. Roemer. Detroit: Gale, 1997. 3–10.

Witalec, Janet, ed. "Sherman Alexie." *Native North American Literature.* Detroit: Gale, 1994. 119–24.

HOW TO WRITE THE
GREAT AMERICAN INDIAN NOVEL

All of the Indians must have tragic features: tragic noses, eyes, and arms.
Their hands and fingers must be tragic when they reach for tragic food.

The hero must be a half-breed, half white and half Indian, preferably
from a horse culture. He should often weep alone. That is mandatory.

If the hero is an Indian woman, she is beautiful. She must be slender
and in love with a white man. But if she loves an Indian man

then he must be a half-breed, preferably from a horse culture.
If the Indian woman loves a white man, then he has to be so white

that we can see the blue veins running through his skin like rivers.
When the Indian woman steps out of her dress, the white man gasps

at the endless beauty of her brown skin. She should be compared to
nature:
brown hills, mountains, fertile valleys, dewy grass, wind, and clear
water.

If she is compared to murky water, however, then she must have a
    secret.
Indians always have secrets, which are carefully and slowly revealed.

Yet Indian secrets can be disclosed suddenly, like a storm.
Indian men, of course, are storms. They should destroy the lives

of any white women who choose to love them. All white women
    love
Indian men. That is always the case. White women feign disgust

at the savage in blue jeans and T-shirt, but secretly lust after him.
White women dream about half-breed Indian men from horse cultures.

Indian men are horses, smelling wild and gamey. When the Indian man
unbuttons his pants, the white woman should think of topsoil.

There must be one murder, one suicide, one attempted rape.
Alcohol should be consumed. Cars must be driven at high speeds.

Indians must see visions. White people can have the same visions
if they are in love with Indians. If a white person loves an Indian

then the white person is Indian by proximity. White people must
    carry
an Indian deep inside themselves. Those interior Indians are half-breed

and obviously from horse cultures. If the interior Indian is male
then he must be a warrior, especially if he is inside a white man.

If the interior Indian is female, then she must be a healer, especially if
    she is inside
a white woman. Sometimes there are complications.

An Indian man can be hidden inside a white woman. An Indian
    woman
can be hidden inside a white man. In these rare instances,

everybody is a half-breed struggling to learn more about his or her
    horse culture.
There must be redemption, of course, and sins must be forgiven.

For this, we need children. A white child and an Indian child, gender
not important, should express deep affection in a childlike way.

In the Great American Indian novel, when it is finally written,
all of the white people will be Indians and all of the Indians will be
    ghosts.

Discussion Questions

1. Describe the tone or feeling that the poem conveys. What is the effect of
   such words and statements as "mandatory" (stanza 2), "That is always the
   case" (stanza 9), "of course" (stanzas 8 and 18), and "obviously" (stanza 15)?
2. List the major components of "the Great American Indian novel."
   Explain the stereotypes that the author is mocking in his formula.
3. Describe how the author represents interracial sexuality and explain the
   comparisons (metaphors and similes) associated with Indian women
   and Indian men.
4. Explain the role of violence in the novel formula. What is the speaker's
   attitude toward this component?
5. Interpret the final stanza. How does it comment on the previous lines?

◆ ◆ ◆

FOCUS ON FILM:
CHRIS EYRE'S *SMOKE SIGNALS* (1998)

1. The film is very self-conscious in making fun of popular conceptions
   about Native Americans and Indian culture. Describe several examples
   of this awareness and explain what you believe to be its purpose. Who
   do you think is the audience for these jokes? Why?
2. Compare and contrast the characters of Victor and Thomas, including
   their attitude toward whites.
3. Explain the meaning of Victor's quest to bring his father home.
4. Thomas voices the theme of "forgiveness" in the final moments of the film.
   Analyze the larger theme about being an Indian in contemporary America.

TOPICS FOR RESEARCH AND WRITING

1. In "The Priest of the Sun," Tosamah says that he learned from his story-
   telling grandmother "the simple act of listening is crucial to the concept

of language. . . , and language in turn is crucial to human society." He also says that the oral tradition "represents a very rich literature, which, because it was never written down, was always but one generation from extinction. But for the same reason it was cherished and revered." Explain the concepts of listening and the special value of the oral tradition in this excerpt from Momaday's work.

2. Selecting two or three of the poems by different authors in this chapter, formulate your thesis defining a common concern or theme. Compare and contrast the imagery in each poem that suggests this common theme.

3. Selecting two or more poems, compare and contrast the work(s) of Young Bear in this chapter with the work(s) of Hasselstrom in Chapter 6. Consider such poetic dimensions as tone, word choice, imagery, metaphor, simile, and theme.

4. Find three or four samples of magazine advertisements depicting Indians. Contemporary ads for commemorative plates, Southwestern vacations, pueblo pottery, and turquoise jewelry often depict images of Native Americans, but you can find a wider variety of examples from library collections of old *Life, Horizons, National Geographic,* or *Nature* magazines. Analyzing both the words and the images, develop your own interpretation of how Indians are represented in these ads.

5. Read Harmut Lutz, "Indians/Native Americans," in *The BFI Companion to the Western,* ed. Edward Buscombe (New York: Atheneum, 1988), pages 155–59. Compare the traditional representations of Indians in conventional Western films with the representations by Chris Eyre (director) and Sherman Alexie (screenwriter) in *Smoke Signals.* In what way does the Native American film respond to those former cinematic portraits? To what extent do you believe the film transcends the tradition to create believable, human characters in its Indian protagonists? To what extent does the film rely on stereotypes?

6. Follow the directions for writing about visual images in Chapter 4, topic 3, pages 208–9. Select three or four of the contemporary Indian paintings collected in *Powerful Images: Portrayals of Native America* by Sarah E. Boehme et al. (Seattle and London: Museums West and the University of Washington, 1998) and focus your essay on interpreting these paintings. To help you interpret the images, you can also read and refer to Mike Leslie, "Native American Artists: Expressing Their Own Identity" in the same collection, pages 111–33.

7. Follow the directions for writing about visual images in Chapter 4, topic 3, pages 208–9. To view some of the photographs of Edward S. Curtis, open *www.library.yale.edu/beinecke/brblcoll/htm.* Click on Digital Images and select Edward S. Curtis. To help you interpret the pho-

tographs, you can also read and refer to William N. Goetzmann, "The Arcadian Landscapes of Edward S. Curtis," in *Perpetual Mirage: Photographic Narratives of the Desert West*, ed. May Castleberry (New York: Whitney Museum of American Art, 1996), pages 82–91.

8. Compare/contrast two autobiographical works.

   A. Consider the excerpts from Winnemucca and Brave Bird in this chapter. In what ways are Indian struggles in the nineteenth century different from those in the twentieth century? In what ways are they the same? What common themes arise for both authors?

   B. Read Chapter 19, "Across the Big Water," and Chapter 24, "The Butchering at Wounded Knee," in Black Elk, *Black Elk Speaks*, as told to John Neihardt (New York: William Morrow, 1932). Compare and contrast these samples from an "oral autobiography" with the selection from Winnemucca in this chapter. What do the two excerpts set in the nineteenth century share? In what ways are their struggles different? What common themes arise for both authors?

9. If you have read Leslie Silko's *Storyteller*, select one of these topics.

   A. Explain a major theme: the importance of family; Indian vs. white education; racial conflict; Native American ethics; the reader as "greenhorn" to the Indian culture; or the importance of place.

   B. Explain the use of photographs in the novel. How are they used to reinforce details from the text, and how are they used to make other statements that the words do not or cannot make? Try to reach an overall generalization about the photographs' function. Would something be lost if the pictures were omitted from the book? What?

   C. Choosing two or three myths, explain how these traditional stories help the reader to understand the daily lives of the Indians who live by these myths. You might compare events and characters in the myths to events and characters in the stories that Silko tells about friends and relatives.

   D. Apply Momaday's concept of the oral tradition (topic 1) to Silko's work, quoting and interpreting passages from *Storyteller*.

10. Read Philip Burnham, "The Return of the Native: The Politics of Identity in American Indian Fiction of the West," in *Reading the West: New Essays on the Literature of the American West*, ed. Michael Kowalewski (Cambridge, UK: Cambridge University, 1996), pages 199–212. After summarizing Burnham's main points, apply his argument to *Smoke Signals*. To what extent does his interpretation of the "politics of identity" explain the central conflict and the quest in the film?

CHAPTER

8

———◆‹◆›◆———

THE NEW WEST

INTRODUCTION

In *American Places* (1981), novelist, conservationist, and historian Wallace Stegner reflects on the contemporary Western landscape, lamenting the decline of traditional family ranches and the trends toward urbanization and exploitative tourism:

> This is obviously country where people and the land get on well together, where the prevailing economy not only doesn't harm the land, but with good management may sometimes improve it. The life here is rich, strenuous, and satisfying. Can that condition hold? Does the family ranch get absorbed into the corporate ranch owned by a bank or by a limited partnership whose primary goal is tax writeoffs? And will the corporate ranch stick to cattle, or will it turn to more profitable uses for the land—dudes, summer cottages, subdivisions, vacation condominiums? Can country like this remain a difficult and satisfying workground that enlists body, brain, and heart, or is it inevitably going to get turned into a playground, with every deterioration that becoming a playground connotes? (Stegner and Stegner 112)

These words seem nostalgic and despairing, though later in the book he is more optimistic: "There are signs of a change in American expectations, an alteration of the free land and unregulated individualism myths. . . . It seems that ordinary citizens have become less commonly raiders and more commonly conservers and stewards" (188).

Stegner voices a central Western tension between "progress" and exploitation of resources, between social values and private greed. This conflict is ever more compelling in a time and place we can call the New West. Even as early as the 1950s, historian Walter Prescott Webb observed, "One of the paradoxes of the West is that, with its excess of land and dearth of people, it is already an urban society" because its population has concentrated around limited natural and artificial water resources, forming "an oasis civilization" (28). By the 1980s, Western population growth assumed a somewhat different pattern. Particularly in the Mountain West, "the nonurban counties increased faster than the nation as a whole, and more quickly than regional metropolitan areas" (Knight 185). For instance, between 1969 and 1987, 19 percent of agricultural lands were converted to ranchette subdivisions in Park County, Wyoming, while the losses were 16 percent in Teton County, Idaho, and 23 percent in Gallatin County, Montana (Knight 185).

These figures not only suggest that Stegner's concerns are well founded, but may also indicate the insidious Euro-American irresponsibility toward the land and our misapprehension that nature is separate from the human world. In fact, William Cronon argues that contemporary American idealism toward federally managed "wilderness"—an artificially protected pseudo-natural environment—allows us to evade responsibility for the modern, urban-industrial civilization we truly inhabit, with "little hope of discovering what an ethical, sustainable, honorable human place in nature might actually look like" (81). Still, American history has forced Western writers to reconsider John Muir's "spiritual landscape" and to reenvision the meaning of "wide open spaces."

To a large extent, social and environmental changes in the twentieth-century West reflect widespread consequences of rapid industrialization, urbanization, and population migration that began during World War II and has continued in periodic surges ever since. According to Carl Abbott, even during the first four decades of the twentieth century, the federal government had shaped the West by developing and controlling its natural resources: settling public lands; creating national parks; encouraging timber harvest; and building massive dams, irrigation systems, and hydroelectric projects. During the Depression, an expanded federal bureaucracy supported wheat prices; built trails and campsites in national forests; and erected public buildings, water-treatment plants, and bridges. Western state economies have continued to receive significant federal contributions because most Western states consist of nearly 50 percent federal lands, including national forest or grazing land, Indian reservations, military bases, and national parks (Abbott).

According to Richard White, between 1941 and 1945 the government dramatically accelerated growth by spending about $70 billion on factories, military installations, and infrastructure in the West, especially in the coastal states of California, Oregon, and Washington. The federal Defense Plant Corporation financed and owned 58 percent of new aluminum plants and 71 percent of airplane factories in the West. Likewise, western shipyards produced over half of the wartime Navy fleet. By 1943, West Coast shipyards employed 500,000 workers; by 1944, Boeing's Puget Sound aircraft factories had boosted their workforce from 4,000 to 50,000. The traditional Western economic base of farming, ranching, and mining also prospered: for instance, the Great Plains wheat crop doubled between 1939 and 1947; Wyoming farming income more than doubled during the war years; and Montana farming income nearly tripled between 1940 and 1948 (White 496–502).

The federal government also funded Western universities during the war years, granting them $99 million for research—more money than had ever been spent by all the institutions combined. Many university research centers—especially those studying nuclear and rocket science, such as Berkeley's Lawrence Livermore facility and Cal Tech's Jet Propulsion Laboratory—began a dependence on military funding that carried through the Cold War and continues today. The Department of Defense also brought together billions of dollars and thousands of scientists and technicians to develop the atomic bomb at Los Alamos, New Mexico, and Hanford, Washington, thus inaugurating the nuclear West (White 502–3).

All these wartime increases in defense spending, productive capacity, and labor demands were accompanied by massive population shifts as workers moved West to new economic opportunities. Richard White reports that, between 1940 and 1950, nearly 8 million workers migrated from both rural and urban areas to Western cities and towns—half of these to the Pacific Coast states. Between 1940 and 1943 alone, population in these states and in the Southwest grew by about 40 percent. Migration to the cities created a labor shortage in agriculture. Under the bracero program beginning in 1942, the feds contracted 200,000 Mexican seasonal farm laborers, but the relatively attractive wages encouraged even more Mexicans to work illegally across the border. About 340,000 blacks from Texas and Louisiana migrated to California, settling primarily in Los Angeles or the San Francisco Bay Area, to share in the wartime boom and to escape entrenched racial discrimination. Native Americans also left their reservations in record numbers: 25,000 to serve in the military and 40,000 to work in West-Coast defense industries or agriculture. About two months after Pearl Harbor, the forced relocation of 120,000 Japanese-American families to concentration camps established another pattern of "migration" in the West. By 1942, farm labor shortages encouraged daily work-release programs that put about 10,000 of these "prisoners" in the fields (White 503–11).

When the war was over, many westerners braced for the slowdown in the "boom-and-bust" cycle that was so much a part of their heritage. However, declines in production were only temporary as the economy readjusted. According to White, construction businesses boomed as many ex-soldiers, discharged on the West Coast, settled there and used their guaranteed V.A. loans to buy houses. Factories retooled to build consumer goods, federal funds poured into building a superhighway system, and West-Coast aircraft plants transformed themselves into the aerospace industry, heavily dependent on continued military spending. By 1962, Pacific Coast factories shared nearly 50 percent of all research-and-development contracts for the Defense Department (White 513–15). Likewise, federal contracts supported "the development and utilization of new electronic and information technologies in the newly high-tech cities of the West" (Abbott 491). In agriculture, the growth of large-scale farming, dependent on machinery and chemicals, continued the wartime decline of small farms, thus sending more people to the cities for wage-labor. Through all these dramatic economic changes during and after World War II, Western communities were united by a continuing dependence on the federal government and by "a dual labor system based on race" (White 539). In this system, Hispanic, black, Asian, and Native American "minorities" worked mostly in unskilled, wearisome farm labor, while whites took on the skilled tasks and managerial positions.

This system was effectively challenged by the civil rights movement in the 1960s, which brought dramatic changes in not only racist employment practices, but also in racial attitudes among a wide spectrum of Americans. Likewise, federal immigration policies contributed to sweeping shifts in the ethnic diversity of the West. According to Richard White, the Immigration Act of 1965 rejected the previous policy of favoritism toward northern Europe and implemented a "uniform preference system" that considers not only economic skills and education as criteria, but also refugee status and family connections among U.S. citizens (White 597). However, Congress could not anticipate the consequences of American military involvements in Vietnam and Central America, nor the demise of the Mexican economy and the subsequent massive illegal immigration. As Deutsch, Sanchez, and Okihiro have noted, Asian and Latino refugees flooded into the country, especially into the West, in the 1970s and 1980s, especially altering the urban population profile. Between 1965 and 1990, one-quarter of all legal immigrants settled in California. The national Asian-American population increased from 1 million to 5 million between 1965 and 1985, and this group included not the "traditional" minority of Japanese-Americans but a new variety of Chinese, Filipino, Vietnamese, "Asian Indian," Laotian, and Cambodian peoples. Likewise, the Hispanic population, which grew to 15 million by 1985, consisted of not only Mexicans, but also immigrants from Cuba, El Salvador, Guatemala, Nicaragua, Dominican Republic, and Columbia. In the context of this largest-growing minority in the United States, whose population lived mostly in the West, it is important to note the influence of César Chávez's United Farm Workers, the first widely successful labor organization to unionize agricultural workers and to launch an effective consumer boycott (Deutsch et al. 646–51). When this union of mostly Filipino- and Mexican-Americans settled their five-year strike against grape growers in 1970, it was also a victory for "Chicano" consciousness and a growing Latino cultural awareness.

These changes in the economics and social fabric of twentieth-century America have had a direct influence on the literatures of the West. As ethnic minorities in America have gained more awareness of and control over their own histories and material destinies, their literatures have flourished. Especially since World War II, black, Asian-American, Chicano, and Native-American writers have contributed, from the wealth of their differing heritages, works about the West that force a reassessment of its literary tradition. Readers today cannot escape a curiosity about the silences reinforced by the earlier traditional literature of the mythic West. Thus, scholars and editors have recovered manuscripts or out-of-print works to discover the lost stories and neglected voices from the Western past—mostly those of women and non-Euro-Americans. Moreover, scholars now examine the full significance of these early Western works through the interests of recent critical theory: "a complex crossing of all kinds of boundaries (linguistic, cultural, geographical); a sense of subjectivities as contingent, multiple, contested, and culturally produced; an acute awareness of the importance of history" (Campbell 8–9). Of course, contemporary critics of Western literature cannot eliminate their own investment in ideology or myth, but they do attempt to bring an awareness of their perspectives into their interpretations.

Likewise, steeped in the tradition of mythic Western literature but unwilling to repeat it, post-war writers have attempted to reevaluate the previous imaginings about the West against the blunt reality of their own perceptions—the grit, the spit, the killing-blizzard, the sun-in-the-eyes genuine article. The Western writers who matured in the 1940s and 1950s—including Wallace Stegner, Walter Van Tilburg Clark, Bernard de Voto, A. B. Guthrie, Jr., Dorothy Johnson, and Frank Waters—"had to confront the myths head on . . . by re-creating a historical West that was a palpable, believable place" (Martin and Barasch xi). The following generation of writers that matured in the "New West" of the 1970s and 1980s—including Edward Abbey, Ivan Doig, Louise Erdrich, Richard Ford, William Kittredge, Larry McMurtry, John Nichols, Leslie Silko, and James Welch—began to express our culture's "tensions, anxieties, and frustrations about contemporary life," and to offer warnings about "the spiritually devastating advance of civilization's urbanization and industrialization" (Siegel 1182). In other words, these contemporary writers are willing to tell stories of local struggles, of family history and relationships, but not in isolation from national currents of social change and political conflict. The new Western writers are not willing to saddle up their ponies and "light out for the territory" at the sign of trouble, even persistent trouble. Rather, their writing insists "that amid the chaos of change and conflict there is something important to be gained by somehow sitting out the storms huddled together" (Martin and Barasch xvii). Their stories tell of staying put, making do, and sometimes even finding satisfaction amid the difficulties.

Thus, the writers of the New West oppose the tradition in a number of ways. First, most deny the nostalgic frontier mythology by recovering and creating new parables that incorporate the moral and political complexities of Western history. Second, while affirming the mythic potential of human relationships with the land, contemporary writers reject the simplistic moral image of a garden in the desert. In fact, much of current Western writing records a tragic destruction, involving urban landscapes as well as natural environments. As if to balance John Muir's unbridled enthusiasm with Rachel Carson's warnings of environmental apocalypse, much of contemporary "nature" writing combines scientific research with poetic interpretations and personal reflections, often admitting the limits to any single mode of perception. Third, according to Gregory Morris, the writers of the New West are often overtly political, realizing that regional struggles for land, water, and natural environment have national motivations, with corporate and government influences, and international consequences. Fourth, these writers express themselves in a variety of genres, not only in fiction and poetry but often in essays that explore the complex relations among self, place, and literature (Morris).

The challenging landscape continues to force Western writers to confront their relationships to nature, never allowing an escape from "the strange tyranny of distance or the quiet crush of isolation" (Martin and Barasch xii). According to Marilynne Robinson, "the true, abiding myth of the West is that there is an intense, continuous, and typically wordless conversation between attentive people and the landscape they inhabit, and that this can be the major business of a very rich life" (150). In spite of sometimes expressing the bitter realities of "cramped towns, cramped families, and cramped possibilities" in the West, these writers continue to celebrate "awesome spaces and desires" (White 629). William Kittredge eloquently expresses the frustrations of this complex contradiction: "Our societies in the American West . . . seem to share some sense that an expansive, generous life is possible in this open space. You can be anything you can manage—that's the message we get. But of course, that message is not necessarily true" (xix). But if nagging doubt is a natural outcome of repeated disappointments— dying stock, failing farms, depleted mines, a boom-and-bust economy, the ravages of tourism and ranchette subdivisions—then Kittredge offers in response a modest heroism illustrated by the Plains Indian narratives: "stories about embracing the munificence which is as much a part of life as our isolations, stories about making as much of what we have as is possible" (xxi).

At the heart of writing in the New West is a sincere re-interpretation of history that questions how Western myths continue to shape the present. Robinson states a fully articulated definition of this relationship: "I believe myths to be complex narratives in which human cultures stabilize and encode their deepest ambivalences. They give a form to contradiction that has the appearance of resolution. . . . The West was an event in the life of the whole country, an astonishingly apt metaphor for a historic doubt as to the compatibility of freedom and civilization" (136–37). As you read the following selections in this chapter, try to apply Robinson's notion of myth and her interpretation of the West to the various ways in which writers express new beliefs about their region and its peoples.

Abbott, Carl. "The Federal Presence." *The Oxford History of the American West.* Ed. Clyde A. Milner II, Carol A. O'Connor, and Martha A. Sandweiss. New York: Oxford University, 1994. 468–99.

Campbell, SueEllen. "'Connecting the Countrey': What's New in Western Lit Crit." *Updating the Literary West.* Ed. Thomas J. Lyon, et al. Fort Worth, TX: Texas Christian University Press and The Western Literature Association, 1997. 3–16.

Cronon, William. "The Trouble with Wilderness; or, Getting Back to the Wrong Nature." *Uncommon Ground: Toward Reinventing Nature.* Ed. William Cronon. New York: Norton, 1995. 69–90.

Deutsch, Sarah, George J. Sanchez, and Gary Okihiro. "Contemporary Peoples/Contested Places." *The Oxford History of the American West.* Ed. Clyde A. Milner II, Carol A. O'Connor, and Martha A. Sandweiss. New York: Oxford University, 1994. 639–69.

Kittredge, William, ed. *The Portable Western Reader.* New York: Penguin, 1997.

Knight, Richard L. "Field Report from the New American West." *Wallace Stegner and the Continental Vision: Essays on Literature, History, and Landscape.* Ed. Curt Meine. Washington, DC, and Covelo, CA: Island Press, 1997. 181–200.

Martin, Russell, and Marc Barasch, ed. *Writers of the Purple Sage: An Anthology of Recent American Western Writing.* New York: Penguin, 1984.

Morris, Gregory L. "Introduction." *Talking Up a Storm: Voices of the New West.* Lincoln and London: University of Nebraska, 1994. xi–xix.

Robinson, Marilynne. "Hearing Silence: Western Myth Reconsidered." *The True Subject: Writers on Life and Craft.* Ed. Kurt Brown. Saint Paul, MN: Graywolf Press, 1993. 135–51.

Siegel, Mark. "Contemporary Trends in Western American Fiction." *A Literary History of the American West.* Ed. Thomas J. Lyon, et al. Fort Worth, TX: Texas Christian University Press and The Western Literature Association, 1987. 1182–1201.

Stegner, Wallace, and Page Stegner. *American Places.* New York: Dutton, 1981.

Webb, Walter Prescott. "The American West: Perpetual Mirage." *Harper's,* May 1957, 25–31.

White, Richard. *"It's Your Misfortune and None of My Own": A History of the American West.* Norman, OK: University of Oklahoma, 1991.

WAKAKO YAMAUCHI
(1924–)

Born in Westmorland, California, the author has illuminated "the stoic and shamed emotional world" of the Issei, the first-generation Japanese immigrants like her parents, who "constantly looked back to Japan for its traditions, values, and rewards" (Hongo 1–3). The middle child of five, Yamauchi often employs the narrative perspective of the Nisei, the second-generation Japanese-Americans, who were less inhibited by the pull of tradition and more concerned with negotiating the new culture and finding some success in the new land. Growing up "in the enclave community of Japanese-American farmers in southern California's Imperial Valley," the author shuttled between this segregated world to the rural public schools (Hongo 3). Since by law Japanese immigrants could not buy property, her father worked as a tenant farmer and the family moved often, following whatever labor opportunities presented themselves. They finally settled down to run a hotel for migrant Japanese farm laborers, and by 1942 Yamauchi was about to graduate from high school in Oceanside when the family was ordered to the Poston Relocation Center in Arizona (Hongo 3).

There, she found the opportunity to work as a layout artist with the camp newspaper, alongside the writer Hisaye Yamamoto, who had published articles and stories in Japanese-American periodicals before the war and began writing a column on Nisei life at the camp. The women became fast friends and colleagues. After signing a "loyalty oath" in 1944, Yamauchi worked in Chicago, but returned to camp in 1945 for her father's funeral and was among the last internees to be released. She moved to San Diego with her family, but in 1946 she left for Los Angeles to study drawing, painting, and layout. After a year, she met Chester Yamauchi, who had befriended her older brother at the Tule Lake internment camp, which isolated Japanese-Americans who refused to sign the "loyalty oath." By 1948, she had quit art school and married Chester, supporting him through various jobs while he attended UCLA. For ten years she performed the chores of wife and mother. In 1958, she began writing again, at home, feeling "emotionally restless and questioning" (Hongo 3–4).

The following year she was offered a graphic artist position on the bilingual newspaper *Los Angeles Rafu Shimpo*, but struck a deal with the editor to publish her writing occasionally. In 1974, her story "And the Soul Shall Dance" was reprinted in the influential Asian-American literature anthology, *Aiiieeee!*, and suddenly the demand for "minority" literature blossomed. In the introduction, editor Frank Chin criticized popular American culture for its stereotypical representations of Asian-Americans and its exclusion of valid role models in educational materials; he also provoked fellow artists to fill this gap and to shape their own identities by publishing their own literature (Hongo 4–5).

Suddenly, Yamauchi's literary career took off. She divorced in 1975 and began writing full-time. She revised her *Aiiieeee!* story into a play, which was then produced to rave reviews in Los Angeles and reproduced for PBS broadcast in 1977. Through the early nineties, Yamauchi wrote six full-length dramas performed across the country, including productions at Joseph Papp's New York Public Theater, the Yale Repertory Theater, and UCLA. During this period, she also produced a string of stories, essays, and memoirs (Hongo 5–6).

According to the author herself, "repression, yearning, and inner life are at the heart of my stories" (qtd. in Hongo 6). But according to critic Amy Ling, Yamauchi's fiction presents "not depressing stories of 'victimization'. . . , but moving testaments to human endurance, survival, and strength" (qtd. in Hongo 6). The work actually seems quiet and restrained because the "emotional intensity" of her characters is controlled by a limited narrative viewpoint. For instance, in "And the Soul Shall Dance," the daughter of the Murata family only hints at her own mother's unhappy marriage and her own father's mental cruelty. Rather, the young girl is more concerned with the open violence and rebellion in the Oka family. And she is captivated by the romantic longings and sensuality of Mrs. Oka, who, despite her strangeness and instability, "insists on a measure of imaginative and emotional freedom" (Hongo 8). Likewise, the naïve narrator only hints at conflicts with the mainstream American culture through allusions to the movies, which represent an alien white society of "liberty and self-possession, of physical sensuousness and emotional freedom" (Hongo 8). While Yamauchi depicts Japanese-American experience, her themes are universal: "she writes of regret and from an acute knowledge of the limits of passion and imagination to transform bleak and circumscribed lives" (16).

"And the Soul Shall Dance" was originally published in the *Los Angeles Rafu Shimpo Holiday Supplement* in December, 1966. The text is from the collection *Songs My Mother Taught Me* (cited below), pages 19–24.

Hongo, Garrett. "Introduction." *Songs My Mother Taught Me: Stories, Plays, and Memoir.* By Wakako Yamauchi. New York: The Feminist Press at The City University of New York, 1994. 1–16.

AND THE SOUL SHALL DANCE

———<◆>———

It's all right to talk about it now. Most of the principals are dead, except, of course, me and my younger brother, and possibly Kiyoko Oka, who might be near forty-five now because, yes, I'm sure of it, she was fourteen then. I was nine, and my brother about four, so he hardly counts. Kiyoko's mother is dead, my father is dead, my mother is dead, and her father could not have lasted all these years with his tremendous appetite for alcohol and pickled chiles—those little yellow ones, so hot they could make your mouth hurt—he'd eat them like peanuts and tears would surge from his bulging thyroid eyes in waves and stream down the coarse terrain of his face.

My father farmed then in the desert basin resolutely named Imperial Valley, in the township called Westmorland, twenty acres of tomatoes, ten of summer squash, or vice versa, and the Okas lived maybe a mile, mile and a half, across an alkaline road, a stretch of greasewood, tumbleweed, and white sand, to the south of us. We didn't hobnob much with them because, you see, they were a childless couple and we were a family: father, mother, daughter, and son and we went to the Buddhist church on Sundays, where my mother taught Japanese, and the Okas kept pretty much to themselves. I don't mean they were unfriendly—Mr. Oka would sometimes walk over (he rarely drove) on rainy days, all dripping wet, short and squat under a soggy newspaper, pretending to need a plow blade or a file, and he would spend the afternoon in our kitchen drinking sake and eating chiles with my father. As he got drunk, his large mouth would draw down, and with the stream of tears, he looked like a kindly weeping bullfrog.

Not only were they childless, impractical in an area where large families were looked upon as labor potentials, but there was a certain strangeness about them. I became aware of it the summer our bathhouse burned down and my father didn't get right down to building another, and a Japanese without a bathhouse . . . well, Mr. Oka offered us the use of his. So every night that summer we drove to the Okas for our bath, and we came in frequent contact with Mrs. Oka, and this is where I found the strangeness.

Mrs. Oka was small and spare. Her clothes hung on her like loose skin, and when she walked, the skirt about her legs gave her a sort of webbed look. She was pretty in spite of the boniness and the dull calico and the barren look. I know now she couldn't have been over thirty. Her eyes were large and a little vacant, although once I saw them fill with tears—the time I insisted we take the old Victrola over and we played our Japanese records for her. Some of the songs were sad, and I imagined the nostalgia she felt, but my mother said the tears were probably from yawning or from the smoke of her cigarettes. I thought my mother resented her for not being more hospitable; indeed, never a cup of tea appeared before us, and between them the conversation of women was totally absent: the rise and fall of gentle voices, the arched eyebrows, the croon of polite surprise. But more than this, Mrs. Oka was different.

Obviously she was shy, but some nights she disappeared altogether. She would see us drive into her yard and then lurch from sight. She was gone all evening. Where could she have hidden in that two-room house—where in that silent desert? Some nights she would wait out our visit with enormous forbearance, quietly pushing wisps of stray hair behind her ears and waving gnats away from her great moist eyes, and some nights she moved about with nervous agitation, her khaki canvas shoes slapping loudly as she walked. And sometimes there appeared to be welts and bruises on her usually smooth brown face, and she would sit solemnly, hands on her lap, eyes large and intent on us. My mother hurried us home then: "Masako, no need to wash well. Hurry."

You see, being so poky, I was always last to bathe. I think the Okas bathed after we left because my mother often reminded me to keep the water clean. The routine was to lather outside the tub (there were buckets and pans and a small wooden stool), rinse off the soil and soap, and then soak in the tub of hot water and contemplate. Rivulets of perspiration would run down the scalp.

When my mother pushed me like this, I dispensed with ritual, rushed a bar of soap around me, and splashed about a pan of water. So hastily toweled, my wet skin trapped the clothes to me, impeding my already clumsy progress. Outside, my mother would be murmuring her many apologies and my father, I knew, would be carrying my brother whose feet were already sandy. We would hurry home.

I thought Mrs. Oka might be insane and I asked my mother about it, but she shook her head and smiled with her mouth drawn down and said that Mrs. Oka loved to drink. This was unusual, yes, but there were other unusual women we knew. Mrs. Naka was bought by her husband from a geisha house; Mrs. Tani was a militant Christian Scientist; Mrs. Abe, the midwife, was occult. My mother's statement explained much: sometimes Mrs. Oka was drunk and sometimes not. Her taste for liquor and cigarettes was a step into the realm of men; unusual for a Japanese wife, but at that time, in that place, and to me, Mrs. Oka loved her sake in the way my father and Mr. Oka loved theirs, the way I loved my candy. That her psychology may have demanded this anesthetic, that she lived with something unendurable, did not occur to me. Nor did I perceive the violence of the purple welts—or the masochism that permitted her to display these wounds to us.

In spite of her masculine habits, Mrs. Oka was never less than a woman. She was no lady in the area of social amenities, but the feminine in her was innate and never left her. Even in her disgrace she was a small broken sparrow, slightly floppy, too slowly enunciating her few words, too carefully rolling her Bull Durham, cocking her small head and moistening the ocher tissue. Her aberration was a protest of the life assigned her; it was obstinate but unobserved, alas, unattended. "Strange" was the only concession we granted her.

Toward the end of summer, my mother said we could not continue bathing at the Okas'; when winter set in we'd all catch our death from the commuting, and she'd always felt dreadful about our imposition on Mrs. Oka. So my father took the corrugated tin sheets he'd found on the highway and had been saving for some other use and built our bathhouse again. Mr. Oka came to help.

While they raised the quivering tin walls, Mr. Oka began to talk. His voice was sharp above the low thunder of the metal sheets.

He told my father he had been married previously in Japan to the present Mrs. Oka's older sister. He had a child by the marriage, Kiyoko, a girl. He had left the two to come to America, intending to send for them soon, but shortly after his departure, his wife passed away from an obscure stomach ailment. At the time, the present Mrs. Oka was young and had foolishly become involved with a man of poor reputation. The family was anxious to part the lovers and conveniently arranged a marriage by proxy and sent him his dead wife's sister. Well, that was all right, after all, they were kin and it would be good for the child when she came to join them. But things didn't work out that way—year after year he postponed calling for his daughter, couldn't get the price of the fare together, and the wife . . . ahhh, the wife . . . Mr. Oka's groan was lost in the rumble of his hammering.

He cleared his throat. The girl was now fourteen and begging to come to America to be with her own real family. The relatives had forgotten the favor he'd done in accepting a slightly used bride, and now they tormented his daughter for being forsaken. True, he'd not sent much money, but if they knew, if they only knew how it was here.

"Well," he sighed, "who could be blamed? It's only right she be with me anyway."

"That's right," my father said.

"Well, I sold the horse and some other things and managed to buy a third-class ticket on the Taiyo-Maru. Kiyoko will get here the first week of September." Mr. Oka glanced toward my father, but my father was peering into a bag of nails. "I'd be much obliged to you if your wife and little girl," he rolled his eyes toward me, "would take kindly to her. She'll be lonely."

Kiyoko-san came in September. I was surprised to see so very nearly a woman—short, robust, buxom—the female counterpart of her father: thyroid eyes and protruding teeth, straight black hair banded impudently into two bristly shucks, Cuban heels and white socks. Mr. Oka proudly brought her to us.

For the first time to my recollection, he touched me; he put his fat hand on the top of my head. "Little Masako here is very smart in school. She will help you with your schoolwork, Kiyoko," he said.

I had so looked forward to Kiyoko-san's arrival. She would be my soul mate; in my mind I had conjured a girl of my own proportions: thin and tall but with the refinement and beauty I didn't yet possess that would surely someday come to the fore. My disappointment was keen and apparent. Kiyoko-san stepped forward shyly, then retreated with a short bow and small giggle, her fingers pressed to her mouth.

My mother took her away. They talked for a long time—about Japan, about enrollment in American school, the clothes Kiyoko-san would need, and where to look for the best values. As I watched them, it occurred to me that I had been deceived. This was not a child, this was a woman. The smile pressed behind her fingers, the way of her nod, so brief, like my mother when father scolded her. The face was inscrutable, but something shrank visibly, like a piece of silk in water. I was disappointed. Kiyoko-san's soul was barricaded in her unenchanting appearance and the smile she fenced behind her fingers.

She started school from third grade, one below me, and as it turned out, she quickly passed me by. There wasn't much I could help her with except to drill her on pronunciation—the *L* and *R* sounds. Every morning walking to our rural school: land, leg, library, loan, lot. Every afternoon returning home: ran, rabbit, rim, rinse, roll. That was the extent of our communica-tion—friendly but not close.

One particularly cold November night—the wind outside was icy—I was sitting on my bed, my brother's and mine, oiling the cracks on my chapped hands by lamplight—someone rapped urgently at our door. It was Kiyoko-san; she was hysterical, she wore no wrap, her teeth were chattering, and except for the thin straw zori, her feet were bare. My mother led her to the kitchen, started a pot of tea, and gestured to my brother and me to retire. I lay very still but, because of my brother's restless tossing and my father's snoring, was unable to hear much. I was aware, though, that drunken and savage brawling had brought Kiyoko-san to us. Presently they came to the bedroom. I feigned sleep. My mother gave Kiyoko-san a gown and pushed me over to make room for her. My mother spoke firmly: "Tomorrow you will return to them; you must not leave them again. They are your people." I could almost feel Kiyoko-san's short nod.

All night long I lay cramped and still, afraid to intrude into her hulking back. Two or three times her icy feet jabbed into mine and quickly retreated. In the morning I found my mother's gown neatly folded on the spare pillow. Kiyoko-san's place in bed was cold.

She never came to weep at our house again, but I know she cried. Her eyes were often swollen and red. She stopped much of her giggling and rou-tinely pressed her fingers to her mouth. Our daily pronunciation drill petered off from lack of interest. She walked silently with her shoulders hunched, grasping her books with both arms, and when I spoke to her in my halting Japanese, she absently corrected my prepositions.

Spring comes early in the valley; in February the skies are clear though the air is still cold. By March, winds are vigorous and warm and wildflowers dot the desert floor, cockleburs are green and not yet tenacious, the sand is crusty underfoot, everywhere there is the smell of things growing, and the first tomatoes are showing green and bald.

As the weather changed, Kiyoko-san became noticeably more cheerful. Mr. Oka, who hated so to drive, could often be seen steering his dusty old Ford over the road that passes our house, and Kiyoko-san, sitting in front, would sometimes wave gaily to us. Mrs. Oka was never with them. I thought of these trips as the westernizing of Kiyoko-san: with a permanent wave, her straight black hair became tangles of frantic curls, between her textbooks she carried copies of Modern Screen and Photoplay, her clothes were gay with print and piping, and she bought a pair of brown suede shoes with alligator trim. I can see her now, picking her way gingerly over the white peaks of alkaline crust.

At first my mother watched their coming and going with vicarious pleasure: "Probably off to a picture show; the stores are all closed at this hour," she might say. Later her eyes would get distant and she would muse, "They've left her home again; Mrs. Oka is alone again."

Now when Kiyoko-san passed by or came in with me on her way home, my mother would ask about Mrs. Oka—how is she, how does she occupy herself these rainy days, or these windy or warm or cool days. Often the answers were polite: "Thank you, we are fine." But sometimes Kiyoko-san's upper lip would pull over her teeth, and her voice would become soft and she would say, "Always drinking and fighting." At those times my mother would invariably say, "Endure; soon you will be marrying and going away."

Once a young truck driver delivered crates at the Oka farm, and he dropped back to our place to tell my father that Mrs. Oka had lurched behind his truck while he was backing up and very nearly let him kill her. Only the daughter pulling her away saved her, he said. Thoroughly unnerved, he stopped by to rest himself and talk about it. Never, never, had he seen a drunken Japanese woman. My father nodded gravely. "Yes, it's unusual," he said and drummed his knee with his fingers.

Evenings were longer now, and when my mother's migraines drove me from the house in unbearable self-pity, I would take walks in the desert. One night with the warm wind against me, the primrose and yellow poppies closed and fluttering, the greasewood swaying in languid orbit, I lay on the white sand beneath a shrub and tried to disappear.

A voice clear and sweet cut through the half-dark of the evening:

Akai kuchibiru	Red lips
Kappu ni yosete	Press against a glass
Aoi sake nomya	Drink the green wine
Kokoro ga odoru	And the soul shall dance

Mrs. Oka appeared to be gathering flowers. Bending, plucking, standing, searching, she added to a small bouquet she clasped. She held them away, looked at them slyly, lids lowered, demure; then in a sudden and sinuous movement, she broke into a stately dance. She stopped, gathered more flowers, and breathed deeply into them. Tossing her head, she laughed softly from her dark throat. The picture of her imagined grandeur was lost to me, but the delusion that transformed a bouquet of tattered petals and sandy leaves, and the loneliness of a desert twilight into a fantasy that brought such joy and abandon made me stir with discomfort. The sound broke Mrs. Oka's dance. Her eyes grew large and her neck tense—like a cat on prowl. She spied me in the bushes. A peculiar chill ran through me. Then abruptly and with childlike delight, she scattered the flowers around her and walked away singing:

Falling, falling, petals on a wind . . .

That was the last time I saw Mrs. Oka. She died before the spring harvest. It was pneumonia. I didn't attend the funeral, but my mother said it was sad. Mrs. Oka looked peaceful, and the minister expressed the irony of the long separation of mother and child and the short-lived reunion. Hardly a year together, he said. We went to help Kiyoko-san address and stamp those black-bordered acknowledgments.

When harvest was over, Mr. Oka and Kiyoko-san moved out of the valley. We never heard from them or saw them again. I suppose in a large city, Mr. Oka found some sort of work, perhaps as a janitor or a dishwasher, and Kiyoko-san grew up and found someone to marry.

Discussion Questions

1. The narrator characterizes Mrs. Oka's smoking and drinking as "masculine habits," but then qualifies: "Her aberration was a protest of the life assigned her." Describe the features of her life that she protests against. To what extent does she protest against America itself?

2. By contrast, Kiyoko-san is "westernized." Analyze the significance of her particular transformations. In what ways does she adopt American culture? What is her motivation for assimilation?

3. Explain the significance of the story's title and a theme that the title suggests.

4. Compare/contrast "And the Soul Shall Dance" with the story by Sui Sin Far in Chapter 6. To what extent do both authors examine the "Americanization" of immigrants? Describe the "Western" themes or concerns both authors consider in their Asian-American stories.

RAYMOND BARRIO
(1921–1996)

Born in New Jersey, of Spanish immigrants who came to the United States in 1920, the author was raised with mixed Hispanic and Anglo-American influences. Barrio's father died in a factory accident when he was only four, so he and his brother were raised in foster homes while their mother persisted in her career as a Spanish dancer. After moving to California in 1936, he made his home there except for his military duty in Europe from 1943 to 1946. After studying at Yale and the University of Southern California, he attended the University of California at Berkeley and received a bachelor's degree in 1947. He continued his training at the Art Center College of Los Angeles, where he earned a Bachelor's of Fine Arts in 1952. He worked continually as an artist, although he earned his livelihood by teaching art, Chicano literature, and creative writing for years at several California community colleges and universities (Akers).

His first publications were art studies and textbooks, but his reputation depends entirely upon his social protest novel, *The Plum Plum Pickers* (1969). This story was first considered by publishers to be too regional and limited in topic to gain a wide readership. Only after he published the work himself and sold 10,000 copies in two years was he able to interest a mainstream publisher, Harper and Row, to buy the rights. But he continued to operate Ventura Press, the publishing house he started. "Primarily a study of exploitation of migrant laborers by Northern California agribusiness," the novel was written just as César Chávez and his United Farm Workers were starting to get national press attention, so Barrio's topic was certainly timely (Akers 49). He got the idea for the story from his personal friendship with a migrant family in the Santa Clara Valley, but he portrays a realistically mixed group of Mexican, Anglo, and Chicano fruit pickers, along with the Chicano and Anglo overseers and owners that abuse their workers for maximum profit (Akers).

The plot line is simple enough; however, the structure is deliberately fragmented and nonlinear. In a loose narrative design of thirty-five episodes, Barrio brings the world of the picker into the foreground of the reader's consciousness:

> Fragments of dialogue, interior monologue, narration, and intermittent description are effectively supplemented with

graffiti, verses of popular songs in both Spanish and English,
radio broadcasts, bulletin-board announcements for the
pickers, newspaper articles, and even picking instructions
from a government pamphlet. (Akers 50)

He employs a technique that recalls both John Steinbeck's "camera
eye" in *The Grapes of Wrath* and John Dos Passos's biographical
sketches in *The U.S.A. Trilogy*; his pseudo-documentary devices historically frame and enrich the farmworkers' struggles in the Santa Clara
Valley. At heart, "Barrio's sense of a great cause" electrifies a story that
also "exposes injustice, deception, disillusionment, self-destruction,
and resistance" (Akers 50).

The text for the following selection from *The Plum Plum Pickers* is
Chapter 10 of the second edition (Tempe: Bilingual Press at Arizona
State University, 1986), pages 84–94.

Akers, John C. "Raymond Barrio." *Dictionary of Literary Biography, Volume 82:
Chicano Writers, First Series*. Ed. Francisco A. Lomeli and Carl R. Shirley.
Detroit: Gale, 1989. 48–51.

FROM *THE PLUM PLUM PICKERS*

THE CAMPESINOS

D awn.
Outside, the coolest night.
Outside, the soft, plush, lingering sheen of nightlight.
Within his breezy air-conditioned shack Manuel lay half asleep in the
middle of the biggest apricot orchard in the world, nothing but apricot trees
all around, in one of a long double row of splintered boards nailed together
and called a shack. A migrant's shack. He struggled to come awake. Everything seemed to be plugged up. A distant roar closed in steadily. He awoke
in a cold sweat. He sat up abruptly in the cold darkness.
The roar grew louder and louder. He leaned forward, hunched in his
worn, torn covers, and peered through the grimy window. A huge black
monster was butting through trees, moving and pitching about, its head-
lights piercing the armor of night, then swinging away again as the roaring

lessened. Manuel smiled. The roar of a tractor. He rubbed the sleep from his eyes. He stretched his aching arms and shoulders. He thought of Lupe and the kids back in Drawbridge.

On the very brink of the full onslaught of summer's punishing heat, with the plums and pears and apricots fattening madly on every vine, branch, bush, and limb in every section of every county in the country, pickers were needed right now immediately on every farm and orchard everywhere and all at once. The frantic demand for pickers increased rapidly as the hot days mounted. That sure looked good out there. What a cool job that was. Driving a tractor at night. Maybe he could get Ramiro to teach him to drive one.

Manuel well knew what his physical energy was.

His physical energy was his total worldly wealth.

No matter how anxious he was to work, he did have his limit. He had to rest his body. The finger joint he'd injured still hurt. He missed Lupe's chatter. He'd signed up with that shrewd contractor, Roberto Morales, that shrewd, fat, energetic *contratista*, manipulator of migrating farmworkers, that smiling middleman who promised to deliver so many hands to the moon at such and such a time at such and such an orchard at such and such a price, for such a small commission. A tiny percentage. Such a little slice. Silvery slavery—modernized.

Roberto Morales, an organization man, was a built-in toll gate. A parasite. A collector of drops of human sweat. An efficiency expert. Had he not been Mexican, he would have made a fantastic capitalist, like Turner. He was Turner upside down. Sucking blood from his own people. With the help and convenient connivance of Turner's insatiable greed.

The agricultural combine's imperative need to have its capital personally plucked when ripe so as to materialize its honest return on its critical investment in order to keep its executives relaxed in blue splendor in far-off desert pools was coupled to the migrant workers' inexorable and uncompromising need to earn pennies to fend off stark starvation.

Good money.

Good dough.

Good hard work.

Pick fast.

Penny a bucket.

Check off.

Get the count right.

Cotsplumsprunespeachesbeanspeas.

Pods.

The seed of life.

And:—don't complain . . .

Manuel lay back in the blackness. As the darkness receded and the light of day started creeping imperiously across its own land, he thought that these powerful orchard land owners were awfully generous to give him such a beautiful hostel to stop in overnight. The skylight hotel. There the land stood. A heaving, sleeping mother earth. A marvelous land. Ripening her fruit once again. Once more. Ripening it fatly and pregnantly for the thousandth time. It must be plucked said the wise man. For it cannot hang around on limbs a minute extra. At no man's convenience. As soon as the baby's ready. Lush and full of plump juices. Hugging its new seed around its own ripeness. The plum and the cot and the peach and the pear must plummet again to earth. Carrying the seed of its own delicate rebirth and redestruction back home to earth again. A clever mother earth who in her all-but-unbelievable generosity was capable of giving man fivefold, tenfold the quantity of fruit he could himself eat, five times fifty, and yet the pickers were never paid enough to satisfy their hunger beyond their actual working hours. And yet it was called a moral world. An ethical world. A good world. A happy world. A world full of golden opportunities. Manuel simply couldn't figure it out.

What was wrong with the figures?

Why was mother earth so generous? And men so greedy?

You got twenty-five cents a basket for tomatoes. A dollar a crate for some fruit. You had to work fast. That was the whole thing. A frantic lunatic to make your barely living wage. If you had no rent to pay, it was OK. You were ahead, amigo. Pay rent, however, stay in one place, and you couldn't migrate after other easy pickings. The joy of working was looking over your dreams locked to hunger.

Manuel studied the whorls in the woodwork whirling slowly, revealed in the faint crepuscular light penetrating his shack. His cot was a slab of half-inch plywood board twenty-two inches wide and eight feet long, the width of the shack, supported by two two-by-four beams butted up against the wall at both ends beneath the side window. The shack itself was eight by twelve by seven feet high. Its roof had a slight pitch. The rain stains in the ceiling planks revealed the ease with which the rain penetrated. Except for two small panes of glass exposed near the top, most of the window at the opposite end was boarded up. A single, old, paint-encrusted door was the only entry. No curtains. No interior paneling. Just a shack. A shack of misery. He found he was able to admire and appreciate the simplicity and the strength of the construction. He counted the upright studs, level, two feet apart, the double joists across the top supporting the roof. Cracks and knotholes aplenty, in the wall siding, let in bright chinks of light during the day and welcome wisps of clear fresh air at night. The rough planking of the siding was stained dark.

The floor was only partly covered with odd sections of plywood. Some of the rough planking below was exposed, revealing cracks leading down to the cool black earth beneath. A small thick table was firmly studded to a portion of the wall opposite the door. A few small pieces of clear lumber stood bunched together, unsung, unused, unhurried, in the far corner. An overhead shelf, supported from the ceiling by a small extending perpendicular arm, containing some boxes of left-over chemicals and fertilizers, completed the furnishings in his temporary abode.

It was habitable.

He could raise his family in it.

If they were rabbits.

The first rays of a brute new day clinked in through the small rectangle of panes. The ray hovered, then peaked, then rested on the covers pushed up by his knees. He recalled his mountain trips with his uncle to the great forbidding *barrancas* near Durango in Central Mexico, and stopping to rest in the middle of the wild woods, and coming unexpectedly upon a crumbling, splintered hulk of a shack that was all falling apart. It barely gave them shelter from the sudden pelting storm they were trying to escape, he as a young frightened boy, but shelter it was—and how beautiful that experience was, then, for they were free, daring, adventurers, out there in that wilderness, alone and daring, with nothing between them and God's own over-powering nature, alone. They belonged to nothing. To no one. But themselves. They were dignity purified. No one forced them to go or stay there. They were delighted and grateful to the shack. For the protection it afforded them. Though it was hardly more than a ratty pile of splinters. Far worse than this one he was now occupying . . . but also somehow far more beautiful in his memory.

And now. Here he was. Shut up in this miserable shack. So sturdily built. Thinking how it sickened him inside because it was more a jail cell than a shelter. He didn't care how comfortable and convenient the growers made the shacks for him. They were huts of slavery. What he wanted was an outlet for his pride. A sudden fierce wave of anger made him want to cross the shack with his fists. There had to be some way to cross the ungulfable bridge. Why was necessity always the bride of hunger? To be free . . . ah, and also to be able to eat all one wanted. My heart, *mi corazon*, why did work always have to blend with such misery? The welcome warmth of the sun's early rays, penetrating more, warmed his frame. But it was a false, false hope. He knew it. The work that lay ahead of him that day would drain and stupify and fatigue him once again to the point of senseless torpor, ready to fall over long before the work day was done. And that fatigue wasn't nearly so bad to bear as the deadly repetitious monotony of never changing, never resting, doing the same plucking over and over and over again. But he had to do it.

He had no choice. It was all he could do. It had to be done if he wanted the money. And he had to have the money, if he wanted to feed his family. The brain in his arms was his only capital. Not very much, true, but it was the only sacrifice he could offer the money gods, the only heart he could offer on the pyramid of gold.

His life. *La gran vida.*

Wide awake now, fully refreshed, his whole body lithe and toned, Manuel was ashamed to find himself eager to start in work, knowing that he would do well, but ashamed because he could think of nothing he would rather do more. The final step.

The final the final the final the final the final the final step.

To want to work oneself to death. *A la muerte.* It wasn't the work itself that bothered him. It was the total immersion, the endless, ceaseless, total use of all his energies and spirit and mind and being that tore him apart within. He didn't know what else he was good for or could do with his life. But there had to be something else. He had to be something more than a miserable plucking animal. Pluck pluck pluck. Feed feed feed. Glug glug glug. Dressing quickly, rolling up his blanket roll and stuffing it into a corner to use again that night, Manuel stepped coolly out into the morning sweetness and breathed the honeyscented humidity rinsing air rising from the honied soil, and joined the thickening throng of his fellow pluckers milling about the large open barn serving as a cookout. Feeding all the pickers was another of the fat man's unholy prerogatives, for he cheated and over-priced on meals too. Roberto Morales, the fat man, the shrewd *contratista*, was a bully man, busily darting his blob about, exhorting his priceless pickers to hurry, answering questions, giving advice, in the cool half-light, impatiently, pushing, giving orders. Manuel, in order to avoid having to greet him, scowled at his toes when Roberto came trouncing by, saying, "*Apurense, companeros,* hurry, hurry, hurry, amigos." Sure. Amigos. Si. Si. Frens. They all gulped their food down hurriedly, standing. Just like home. Paper plates, plastic cups. Wooden spoons. And bits of garbage flying into large canisters. Then in the still cool nightlike morning air, like a flood of disturbed birds, they all picked up their pails and filed into the orchard.

The apricots were plump.

Smooth.

A golden syrupy orange.

Manuel popped two into his mouth, enjoying their cool natural sweetness after the bitter coffee. He knew he could not eat too many. His stomach muscles would cramp. Other pickers started pulling rapidly away from him. Let them. Calmly he calculated the struggle. Start the press sure, slow, and keep it going steady. Piecework. Fill the bucket, fill another, and still another.

The competition was among a set of savages, as savage for money as himself, savages with machetes, hacking their way through the thickets of modern civilization back to the good old Aztec days, waiting to see who'd be first in line to wrench his heart out. Savage beasts, eager to fill as many buckets as possible in as short a time as possible, cleaning out an entire orchard, picking everything in sight clean, tons of fruit, delivering every bit of ripe fruit to the accountants in their cool air-conditioned orifices.

The competition was not between pickers and growers.

It was between pickers—Jorge and Guillermo.

Between the poor and the hungry, the desperate, and the hunted, the slave and the slave, slob against slob, the depraved and himself. You were your own terrible boss. That was the cleverest part of the whole thing. The picker his own bone picker, his own willing built-in slave driver. God, that was good! That was where they reached into your scrotum and screwed you royally and drained your brain and directed your sinews and nerves and muscles with invisible fingers. To fatten their coffers. And drive you to your coffin. That sure was smart. Meant to be smart. Bookkeepers aren't dumb. You worked hard because you wanted to do that hard work above everything else. Pick fast pick hard pick furious pick pick pick. They didn't need straw bosses studying your neck to see if you kept bobbing up and down to keep your picking pace up. Like the barn-stupid chicken, you drove yourself to do it. You were your own money monkey foreman, monkey on top of your own back.

You over-charged yourself.

With your own frenzy.

Neat.

You pushed your gut and your tired aching arms and your twitching legs pumping adrenalin until your tongue tasted like coarse sandpaper.

You didn't even stop to take a drink, let alone a piss, for fear you'd get fined, fired, or bawled out.

And then, after all that effort, you got your miserable pay.

Would the bobbing boss's sons stoop to that?

His fingers were loose and dexterous now. The plump orange balls plopped pitter patter like heavy drops of golden rain into his swaying, sweaty canvas bucket. His earnings depended entirely on how quickly he worked and how well he kept the pressure up. The morning sun was high. The sweet shade was fragrant and refreshing and comfortable under the leafy branches. The soil too was still cool and humid. It was going to be another hot one.

There.

Another row ended.

He swung around the end of the row and for a moment he was all alone, all by himself. He looked out far across the neighboring alfalfa field, dark green and rich and ripe. Then he looked at the long low Diablo Range close by, rising up into the misty pale blue air kept cool by the unseen bay nearby. This was all his. For a flowing, deceptive minute, all this rich, enormous terrain was all his. All this warm balmy baby air. All this healthful sunny breeze. All those hills, this rich fertile valley, these orchards, these tiled *huertas*, these magnificent farms, all, all his . . . for his eyes to feast upon. It was a moment he wished he could capture forever and etch permanently on his memory, making it a part of living life for his heart to feast joyously on, forever. Why couldn't he stop? Why? Why couldn't he just put the bucket down and open his arms and walk into the hills and merge himself with the hills and just wander invisibly in the blue?

What Manuel couldn't really know was that he was completing yet another arc in the unending circle that had been started by one of his Mexican forebears exactly two hundred years before—for even the memory of history was also robbed from him—when Gaspar de Portola, hugging the coastline, nearing present-day San Francisco, climbed what is now Sweeney Ridge, and looked down upon San Francisco's magnificent landlocked Bay, overlooking what is now the International Airport.

Both don Gaspar and don Manuel were landlords and landless at precisely the same instant of viewing all this heady beauty. And both were equally dispossessed. Both were also possessed of a keen sense of pride and natural absorption with the ritual and mystery of all life. The living that looked mighty good in a flash to Manuel lasted a good deal longer for don Gaspar whose stumbling accident swept him into the honored and indelible pages of glorious history.

Manuel was now a mere straw among the enormous sludge of humanity flowing past, a creature of limb and his own driving appetites, a creature of heed and need. Swinging around another end run he placed his ladder on the next heavy limb of the next pregnant tree. He reached up. He plucked bunches of small golden fruit with both hands. He worked like a frenzied windmill in slow motion. He cleared away an arc as far as the circumference of his plucking fingers permitted. A living model for da Vinci's outstretched man. Adam heeding God's moving finger. He moved higher. He repeated another circle. Then down and around again to another side of the tree, until he cleared it, cleared it of all visible, viable, delectable, succulent fruit. It was sweet work. The biggest difference between him and the honey-gathering ant was that the ant had a home.

Several pickers were halfway down the next row, well in advance of him. He was satisfied he was pacing himself well. Most of the band was still behind him. The moving sun, vaulting the sky dome's crackling earth parting with its bronzing rays, pounded its fierce heat into every dead and living crevice. Perspiration poured down his sideburns, down his forehead, down his cheek, down his neck, into his ears, off his chin. He tasted its saltiness with the tip of his dry tongue. He wished he'd brought some salt tablets. Roberto Morales wasn't about to worry about the pickers, and Manuel wasn't worried either. Despite the heat, he felt some protection from the ocean and bay. It had been much, much worse in Texas, and much hotter in Delano in the San Joaquin valley and worst of all in Satan's own land, the Imperial Valley.

No matter which way he turned, he was trapped in an endless maze of apricot trees, as though forever, neat rows of them, neatly planted, row after row, just like the blackest bars on the jails of hell. There had to be an end. There had to be. There—trapped. There had to be a way out. Locked. There had to be a respite. Animal. The buckets and the crates kept piling up higher. Brute. He felt alone. Though surrounded by other pickers. Beast. Though he was perspiring heavily, his shirt was powder dry. Savage. The hot dry air. The hot dry air sucking every drop of living moisture from his brute body. Wreck. He stopped and walked to the farthest end of the first row for some water, raised the dented dipper from the brute tank, drank the holy water in great brute gulps so he wouldn't have to savor its tastelessness, letting it spill down his torn shirt to cool his exhausted body, to replenish his brute cells and animal pores and stinking follicles and pig gristle, a truly refined wreck of an animal, pleased to meetcha. Predator.

Lunch.

Almost too exhausted to eat, he munched his cheese with tortillas, smoked on ashes, then lay back on the cool ground for half an hour. That short rest in the hot shade replenished some of his humor and resolve. He felt his spirit swell out again like a thirsty sponge in water. Then up again. The trees. The branches again. The briarly branches. The scratching leaves. The twigs tearing at his shirt sleeves. The ladder. The rough bark. The endlessly unending piling up of bucket upon box upon crate upon stack upon rack upon mound upon mountain. He picked a mountain of cots automatically. An automator. A beast. A ray of enemy sun penetrated the tree that was hiding him and split his forehead open. His mind whirred. He blacked out. Luckily he'd been leaning against a heavy branch. His feet hooked to the ladder's rung. His half-filled bucket slipped from his grasp and fell in slow motion, splattering the fruit he'd so laboriously picked. To the ground. Robert happened by and shook his head. "Whatsamatter, can't you see straight, *pendejo*." Manuel was too tired even to curse. He should have had some salt pills.

Midafternoon.

The summer's fierce zenith passed overhead. It passed. Then dropped. It started to light the ocean behind him, back of the hills. Sandy dreams. Cool nights. Cold drinks. Soft guitar music with Lupe sitting beside him. All wafting through his feverish moments. Tiredness drained his spirit of will. Exhaustion drained his mind. His fingers burned. His arms flailed the innocent trees. He was slowing down. He could hardly fill his last bucket. Suddenly the whistle blew. The day's work was at last ended.

Ended!

The *contratista* Roberto Morales stood there.

His feet straddled. Mexican style. A real robber. A Mexican general. A gentlemanly, friendly, polite, grinning, vicious, thieving brute. The worst kind. To his own people. Despite his being a fellow Mexican, despite his torn, old clothing, everyone knew what kind of clever criminal he was. Despite his crude, ignorant manner, showing that he was one of them, that he'd started with them, that he grew up with them, that he'd suffered all the sordid deprivations with them, he was actually the shrewdest, smartest, richest cannibal in forty counties around. They sure couldn't blame the *gueros* for this miscarriage. He was a crew chief. How could anyone know what he did to his own people? And what did the *gueros* care? So the anglo growers and *guero* executives, smiling in their cool filtered offices, puffing their elegant thin cigars, washed their clean blond bloodless dirtless hands of the whole matter. All they did was hire Roberto Morales. Firm, fair, and square. For an agreed-upon price. Good. How he got his people down to the pickings was no concern of theirs. They were honest, those *gueros*. They could sleep at night. They fulfilled their end of the bargain, and cheated no one. Their only crime, their only soul grime indeed was that they just didn't give a shit how that migratory scum lived. It was no concern of theirs. Their religion said it was no concern of theirs. Their wives said it was no concern of theirs. Their aldermen said it was no concern of theirs. Their—

Whenever Roberto Morales spoke, Manuel had to force himself not to answer. He had to keep his temper from flaring.

"Now," announced Morales at last, in his friendliest tone. "Now. I must take two cents from every bucket. I am sorry. There was a miscalculation. Everybody understands. Everybody?" He slid his eyes around, smiling, palms up.

The tired, exhausted pickers gasped as one.

Yes. Everyone understood. Freezing in place. After all that hard work.

"Any questions, men?"

Still grinning, knowing, everyone realizing that he had the upper hand, that that would mean a loss of two or three dollars out of each picker's pay that day, a huge windfall for Morales. "You promised to take nothing!" Manuel heard himself saying. Everyone turned in astonishment to stare at Manuel.

"I said two cents, hombre. You got a problem or what?"

"You promised."

The two men, centered in a huge ring of red-ringed eyes, glared at each other. Reaching for each other's jugular. The other exhausted animals studied the tableau through widening eyes. It was so unequal. Morales remained calm, confident, studying Manuel. As though memorizing his features. He had the whole advantage. Then, with his last remaining energy, Manuel lifted his foot and clumsily tipped over his own last bucket of cots. They rolled away in all directions around everyone's feet.

Roberto Morales' eyes blazed. His fists clenched. "You pick them up, Gutierrez."

So. He knew his name. After all. For answer, Manuel kicked over another bucket, and again the fruit rolled away in all directions.

Then an astonishing thing happened.

All the other pickers moved toward their own buckets still standing beside them on the ground awaiting the truck gatherer, and took an ominous position over them, straddling their feet over them. Without looking around, without taking his eyes off Manuel, Roberto Morales said sharply, "All right. All right, men. I shall take nothing this time."

Manuel felt a thrill of power course through his nerves.

He had never won anything before. He would have to pay for this, for his defiance, somehow, again, later. But he had shown defiance. He had salvaged his money savagely and he had earned respect from his fellow slaves. The gringo *hijos de la chingada* would never know of this little incident, and would probably be surprised, and perhaps even a little mortified, for a few minutes. But they wouldn't give a damn. It was bread, pan y tortillas out of his children's mouths. But they still wouldn't give a single damn. Manuel had wrenched Morales' greedy fingers away and removed a fat slug of a purse from his sticky grasp. And in his slow way, in his stupid, accidental, dangerous way, Manuel had made an extravagant discovery, as don Gaspar had also made two centuries before, in almost exactly the same spot. And that was—that a man counted for something. For men, Manuel dimly suspected, are built for something more important and less trifling than the mere gathering of prunes and apricots, hour upon hour, decade upon decade, insensibly, mechanically, antlike. Men are built to experience a certain sense of honor and pride.

Or else they are dead before they die.

Discussion Questions

1. Explain to what extent Manuel "possesses" the land and to what extent it "possesses" him. Copy two short quotations that illustrate his contradictory relationship with the land.
2. Explain the motivations for Manuel's actions in the conclusion of "The Campesinos."

RICHARD HUGO
(1923–1982)

Born in Seattle, the poet grew up there and attended public schools. Beginning in 1943, he served during World War II as a bombadier in the U.S. Army Airs Corps. His later poems concerning that experience combine toughness with reflection. Returning to Seattle, he began writing poetry, earned his B.A. at the University of Washington by 1948, and continued for graduate school. In 1951, he began working for Boeing, but completed his M.A. the following year. He stayed on at Boeing, working at various jobs for another eleven years. In 1961, he published his first book of poems, *A Run of Jacks*, and began teaching at the University of Montana, Missoula, as a visiting lecturer in 1964. He went on to become Professor of English and director of the creative writing program there, taking some time off to establish the creative writing program at the University of Colorado (Group).

His poetry concerns nature, but not in the Romantic vein. Rather, Hugo creates symbolic images through dense description of Western environments, trying to "arouse emotional response through the description itself" (Group 370). The conflict in his work is often between humans and their environment so that the speaker in the poem "is wrestling with the brute realities of his world; each perception is another lunge or twist and demands another effort of will and muscle" (Skelton xix). In his fourth collection, *The Lady in Kicking Horse Reservoir* (1973), he demonstrates—in a self-confident and personal style—his own viewpoint that "an act of imagination is an act of self-acceptance" (qtd. in Group 371). In essence, "Hugo's poetry is tough, violent, tragic. His world is largely a ruined one, but it contains men who have the courage to face that ruin, and, as a consequence, even the most bitter poems are positive rather than negative, and their energy is triumphant" (Skelton xx).

The following poem appeared in *The Lady in Kicking Horse Reservoir*, but the text is from *Making Certain It Goes On: The Collected Poems of Richard Hugo* (Norton, 1984), pages 216–17.

Group, Bob. "Richard Hugo." *American Poets since World War II, Part 1: A–K.* Ed. Donald J. Greiner. Detroit: Gale, 1980. 369–74.

Skelton, Robin, ed. "Introduction." *Five Poets of the Pacific Northwest.* Seattle: University of Washington, 1964. xv–xxv.

DEGREES OF GRAY IN PHILIPSBURG

You might come here Sunday on a whim.
Say your life broke down. The last good kiss
you had was years ago. You walk these streets
laid out by the insane, past hotels
that didn't last, bars that did, the tortured try
of local drivers to accelerate their lives.
Only churches are kept up. The jail
turned 70 this year. The only prisoner
is always in, not knowing what he's done.

The principal supporting business now
is rage. Hatred of the various grays
the mountain sends, hatred of the mill,
The Silver Bill repeal, the best liked girls
who leave each year for Butte. One good
restaurant and bars can't wipe the boredom out.
The 1907 boom, eight going silver mines,
a dance floor built on springs—
all memory resolves itself in gaze,
in panoramic green you know the cattle eat
or two stacks high above the town,
two dead kilns, the huge mill in collapse
for fifty years that won't fall finally down.

Isn't this your life? That ancient kiss
still burning out your eyes? Isn't this defeat
so accurate, the church bell simply seems
a pure announcement: ring and no one comes?
Don't empty houses ring? Are magnesium
and scorn sufficient to support a town,
not just Philipsburg, but towns
of towering blondes, good jazz and booze
the world will never let you have
until the town you came from dies inside?

Say no to yourself. The old man, twenty
when the jail was built, still laughs
although his lips collapse. Someday soon,
he says, I'll go to sleep and not wake up.
You tell him no. You're talking to yourself.
The car that brought you here still runs.
The money you buy lunch with,
no matter where it's mined, is silver
and the girl who serves your food
is slender and her red hair lights the wall.

Discussion Questions

1. With several examples of words, phrases, and/or images, describe the tone or feeling of the poem.
2. Identify whom the speaker addresses in stanzas 1, 3, and 4. Who is the "you" who seems to be visiting Philipsburg? What does this person learn about the town?
3. Analyze the meanings of the different colors in the poem.
4. Explain what is particularly "Western" in the topics, imagery, and themes of the poem.

WILLIAM KITTREDGE
(1932–)

"Few active writers from the West compare with Kittredge for his intimate, extensive, and profound knowledge and understanding of the region" (McFarland 171). Indeed, he is unusual in having been raised as a Western cattleman and then—in the great tradition of the land of promises—reinventing himself as a Western writer. Born in Portland, Oregon, the author can trace his American heritage to a relative who arrived in the colonies in 1660. His own grandfather created a farming and ranching dynasty in southeastern Oregon before his death in 1958. However, his ruthlessness harmed the land with poisons just as it alienated his family. Kittredge's own father resented the pressure he felt to become a rancher instead of pursuing his ambition to study law. He drank excessively in frustration, which contributed to the dissolution of his marriage, so Kittredge's own upbringing was far from an achievement of the American dream (McFarland 165).

His youth began with riding horses and helping with chores on the farm. Not so unusual for his generation, he attended college at Oregon State, studied agriculture, and played football; less usual were his decisions to quit college sports after a year because he lacked speed and toughness and to study creative writing with Bernard Malamud, who influenced Kittredge to become a writer. He married his first wife in 1951 and graduated in 1953, after which he spent four years in photographic intelligence for the Air Force—two of these overseas, in Guam. By 1958, his hitch was up and he returned to the family ranch with every intention of taking over management. Looking back on this decision later, Kittredge has said it was "a mistake that cost me a decade" (qtd. in McFarland 166). The early 1960s were not happy times at home. He suffered a mental breakdown in 1961, had several affairs and a heavy drinking habit, and divorced in 1967 when his family sold their Eastern Oregon property.

He married his second wife, immediately and unwisely, and moved to Iowa to join the Writers' Workshop, where he studied with Robert Coover. By 1969 he had already started publishing stories in small journals, earned his M.F.A., and moved to Missoula to take a job teaching English at the University of Montana. He eventually directed the creative writing program there and became close friends with poet Richard Hugo, who also inspired his writing. By 1973, his second marriage had ended, in part due to his overwhelming ambition. Becoming more intent on succeeding as a writer, he spent the school year 1973–1974 on a Wallace Stegner Fellowship at Stanford University, but it was really at a Western film conference at Sun Valley, Idaho, where he found "his central theme: the delusive nature of the popular Western myth" (McFarland 166).

Likewise, in response to the Western history of imperialist conquest and the exploitive values his ranching family had lived by, he began a search for compassion and intimacy. It is through his nonfiction—the essays in *Owning It All* (1987) and *Who Owns the West?* (1996) and his memoir, *Hole in the Sky* (1992)—that he explores the possibilities for a new Western myth. The memoir, especially, serves as a kind of confession and penitence, not only for his own reckless disregard for others' feelings, but also for "what he and his family did to both the physical and social landscape" (McFarland 169). In a 1989 interview, Kittredge remarked that his memoir "ends up being an ecology book; it's a story about taking care of ourselves and taking care of the world and how to conduct ourselves in what I conceive to be proper ways" (qtd. in Morris 173). His two story collections, *The Van Gogh Field and Other Stories* (1978) and *We Are Not in this Together* (1984), seem more bitter, portraying a modern Montana landscape of violence and death.

Together, these five books of fiction and nonfiction would establish any writer's reputation. But Kittredge has become a rather prolific man of letters in several capacities. From 1982 through 1986, with Steven Krauzner he coauthored nine formula Westerns in the *Cord* series for Ballantine Books under the pseudonym Owen Rountree. They created a couple of heroic bank robbers—Cord, the man of action, and Chi, an attractive Mexican female partner—and then churned out a string of adventure conflicts with evil villains and realistic historical situations set in Western locales. Apparently, the pulp novels required only two or three weeks to write and netted each author a flat $3,000 fee (McFarland 168). Besides this lucrative creative activity, Kittredge has also edited or written introductions for over a dozen books. Chief among his editing achievements have been *The Last Best Place: A Montana Anthology* (1988), which he did with his partner Annick Smith; and *The Portable Western Reader* (1997), a knowledgeable selection of Indian tales, traditional stories and poems, and multicultural literature of the contemporary West. Perhaps one reason he includes so many Native American stories in this collection is that they express his own central theme. They are about coming home, "staying put and making peace with what you've got" (qtd. in Morris 178).

The text of "Redneck Secrets" is from the collection *Owning It All* (Saint Paul, MN: Graywolf Press, 1987), pages 80–90.

McFarland, Ron. "William Kittredge." *Dictionary of Literary Biography: Volume 212: Twentieth-Century American Western Writers, Second Series*. Ed. Richard H. Cracroft. Detroit: Gale, 1999. 164–71.

Morris, Gregory L. "William Kittredge." *Talking Up a Storm: Voices of the New West*. Lincoln and London: University of Nebraska, 1994. 167–84.

REDNECK SECRETS

—◆—<◆>—◆—

B ack in my more scattered days there was a time when I decided the solution to all life's miseries would begin with marrying a nurse. Cool hands and commiseration. She would be a second-generation Swedish girl who left the family farm in North Dakota to live a new life in Denver, her hair would be long and silvery blonde, and she would smile every time she saw me and always be after me to get out of the house and go have a glass of beer with my buckaroo cronies.

Our faithfulness to one another would be legendary. We would live near Lolo, Montana, on the banks of the Bitterroot River where Lewis and Clark camped to rest on their way West, "Traveler's Rest," land which floods a little in the spring of the year, a small price to pay for such connection with mythology. Our garden would be intricately perfect on the sunny uphill side of our 26 acres, with little wooden flume boxes to turn the irrigation water down one ditch or another.

We would own three horses, one a blue roan Appaloosa, and haul them around in our trailer to jackpot roping events on summer weekends. I wouldn't be much good on horseback, never was, but nobody would care. The saddle shed would be tacked to the side of our doublewide expando New Moon mobile home, and there would be a neat little lawn with a white picket fence about as high as your knee, and a boxer dog called Aces and Eights, with a great studded collar. There would be a .357 magnum pistol in the drawer of the bedside table, and on Friday night we would dance to the music of old-time fiddlers at some country tavern and in the fall we would go into the mountains for firewood and kill two or three elk for the freezer. There would be wild asparagus along the irrigation ditches and morels down under the cottonwoods by the river, and we would always be good.

And I would keep a journal, like Lewis and Clark, and spell bad, because in my heart I would want to be a mountain man—"We luved aft the movee in the bak seet agin tonite."

We must not gainsay such Western dreams. They are not automatically idiot. There are, after all, good Rednecks and bad Rednecks. Those are categories.

So many people in the American West are hurt, and hurting. Bad Rednecks originate out of hurt and a sense of having been discarded and ignored by the Great World, which these days exists mostly on television, distant and most times dizzily out of focus out here in Redneck country.

Bad Rednecks lose faith and ride away into foolishness, striking back. The spastic utility of violence. The other night in a barroom, I saw one man turn to another, who had been pestering him with drunken nonsense. "Son," he said, "you better calm yourself, because if you don't, things are going to get real Western here for a minute."

Real Western. Back in the late '40's when I was getting close to graduating from high school, they used to stage Saturday night prizefights down in the Veterans Auditorium. Not boxing matches but prizefights, a name which rings in the ear something like *cockfight*. One night the two main-event fighters, always heavyweights, were some hulking Indian and a white farmer from a little dairy-farm community.

The Indian, I recall, had the word "Mother" carved on his hairless chest. Not tattooed, but carved in the flesh with a blade, so the scar tissue spelled out the word in livid welts. The white farmer looked soft and his body was alabaster, pure white, except for his wrists and neck, which were dark, burned-in-the-fields red, burnished red. While they hammered at each other we hooted from the stands like gibbons, rooting for our favorites on strictly territorial and racial grounds, and in the end were all disappointed. The white farmer went down like thunder about three times, blood snorting from his nose in a delicate spray and decorating his whiteness like in, say, the movies. The Indian simply retreated to his corner and refused to go on. It didn't make any sense.

We screeched and stomped, but the Indian just stood there looking at the bleeding white man, and the white man cleared his head and looked at the Indian, and then they both shook their heads at one another, as if acknowledging some private news they had just then learned to share. They both climbed out of the ring and together made their way up the aisle. Walked away.

Real Western. Of course, in that short-lived partnership of the downtrodden, the Indian was probably doomed to a lifetime on the lower end of the seesaw. No dairy farms in a pastoral valley, nor morning milking and school boards for him. But that is not the essential point in this equation. There is a real spiritual equivalency between Redmen and Rednecks. How sad and ironic that they tend to hit at each other for lack of a real target, acting out some tired old scenario. Both, with some justice, feel used and cheated and disenfranchised. Both want to strike back, which may be just walking away, or the bad answer, bloody noses.

Nobody is claiming certain Rednecks are gorgeous about their ways of resolving the pain of their frustrations. Some of them will indeed get drunk in honkytonks and raise hell and harass young men with long hair and golden earrings. These are the bad Rednecks.

Why bad? Because they are betraying themselves. Out-of-power groups keep fighting each other instead of what they really resent: power itself. A Redneck pounding a hippie in a dark barroom is embarrassing because we see the cowardice. What he wants to hit is a banker in broad daylight.

But things are looking up. Rednecks take drugs; hippies take jobs. And the hippie carpenters and the 250-pound, pigtailed lumberjacks preserve their essence. They are still isolated, outrageous, lonely, proud and mean. Any one of them might yearn for a nurse, a doublewide, a blue roan Appaloosa, and a sense of place in a country that left him behind.

Like the Indian and the buffalo on the old nickel, there are two sides to American faith. But in terms of Redneck currency, they conflict. On the one side there is individualism, which in its most radical mountain-man form becomes isolation and loneliness: the standard country-and-western lament. It will lead to dying alone in your motel room: whether gored, boozed or smacked makes little difference. On the other side there are family and community, that pastoral society of good people inhabiting the good place on earth that William Bradford and Thomas Jefferson so loved to think about.

Last winter after the snowmobile races in Seeley Lake, I had come home to stand alongside my favorite bar rail and listen to my favorite skinny Redneck barmaid turn down propositions. Did I say *home*? Anyway, standing there and feeling at home, I realized that good Redneck bars are like good hippy bars: they are community centers, like churches and pubs in the old days, and drastically unlike our singles bars where every person is so radically on his or her own.

My skinny barmaid friend looked up at one lumberjack fellow, who was clomping around in his White logger boots and smiling his most winsome. She said, "You're just one of those boys with a sink full of dishes. You ain't looking for nothing but someone dumb enough to come and wash your dishes. You go home and play your radio."

A sink full of dirty dishes. And laundry. There are aspects of living alone that can be defined as going out to the J.C. Penney store and buying $33 worth of new shorts and socks and t-shirts because everything you own is stacked up raunchy and stinking on the far side of the bed. And going out and buying paper plates at K-mart because you're tired of eating your meals crouched over the kitchen sink. You finally learn about dirty dishes. They stay dirty. And those girls, like my skinny friend, have learned a thing or two. There are genuine offers of solace and companionship, and there are dirty dishes and nursing. And then a trailer house, and three babies in three years, diapers, and he's gone to Alaska for the big money. So back to barmaiding, this time with kids to support, babysitters.

Go home and play your radio.

There is, of course, another Montana. Consider these remarks from the journals of James and Granville Stewart, 1862:

> JANUARY 1, 1862. Snowed in the forenoon. Very cold in the afternoon. Raw east wind. Everybody went to grand ball given by John Grant at Grantsville and a severe blizzard blew up and raged all night. We danced all night, no outside storm could dampen the festivities.
>
> JANUARY 2. Still blowing a gale this morning. Forty below zero and the air is filled with driving, drifting snow. After breakfast we laid down on the floor of the several rooms, on buffalo robes that Johnny furnished, all dressed as we were and slept until about two-o'clock in the afternoon, when we arose, ate a fine dinner, then resumed dancing which we kept up with unabated pleasure . . . danced until sunrise.
>
> JANUARY 3. The blizzard ceased about daylight, but it was very cold with about fourteen inches of snow badly drifted in places and the ground bare in spots. We estimated the cold at about thirty-five below, but fortunately there was but little wind. After breakfast all the visitors left for home, men, women, and children, all on horse-back. Everyone got home without frost bites.

Sounds pretty good. But Granville Stewart got his. In the great and deadly winter of 1886–1887, before they learned the need of stacking hay for winter, when more than one million head of cattle ran the Montana ranges, he lost two-thirds of his cow herd. Carcasses piled in the coulees and fence corners come springtime, flowers growing up between the ribs of dead long-horn cattle, and the mild breezes reeking with decay. A one-time partner of Stewart's, Conrad Kohrs, salvaged 3,000 head out of 35,000. Reports vary, but you get the sense of it.

Over across the Continental Divide to where the plains begin on the east side of the Crazy Mountains, in the Two Dot country, on bright mornings you can gaze across the enormous swale of the Musselshell, north and east to the Snowy Mountains, 50 miles distant and distinct and clear in the air as the one mountain bluebell you picked when you came out from breakfast.

But we are not talking spring, we are talking winter and haystacks. A man we know, let's call him Davis Patten, is feeding cattle. It's February, and the snow is drifting three feet deep along the fence lines, and the wind is carrying the chill factor down to about 30 below. Davis Patten is pulling his feed sled with a team of yellow Belgian geldings. For this job, it's either horses or a track-layer, like a Caterpillar D-6. The Belgians are cheaper and easier to start.

Davis kicks the last remnant of meadow hay, still greenish and smelling of dry summer, off the sled to the trailing cattle. It's three o'clock in the afternoon and already the day is settling toward dark. Sled runners creak on the frozen snow. The gray light is murky in the wind, as though inhabited, but no birds are flying anywhere. Davis Patten is sweating under his insulated coveralls, but his beard is frozen around his mouth. He heads the team toward the barns, over under the cottonwood by the creek. Light from the kitchen windows shows through the bare limbs. After he has fed the team a bait of oats, then Davis and his wife Loretta will drink coffee laced with bourbon.

Later they watch television, people laughing and joking in bright Sony color. In his bones Davis recognizes, as most of us do, that the principal supporting business of television is lies, truths that are twisted about a quarter turn. Truths that were never truths. Davis drifts off to sleep in his Barca-Lounger. He will wake to the white noise from a gray screen.

It is important to have a sense of all this. There are many other lives, this is just one, but none are the lives we imagine when we think of running away to Territory.

Tomorrow Davis Patten will begin his day chopping ice along the creek with a splitting maul. Stock water, a daily chore. Another day with ice in his beard, sustained by memories of making slow love to Loretta under down comforters in their cold bedroom. Love, and then quickfooting it to the bathroom on the cold floors, a steaming shower. Memories of a bed that reeks a little of child making.

The rewards of the life, it is said, are spiritual, and often they are. Just standing on land you own, where you can dig any sort of hole you like, can be considered a spiritual reward, a reason for not selling out and hitting the Bahamas. But on his winter afternoons Davis Patten remembers another life. For ten years, after he broke away from Montana to the Marines, Davis hung out at the dragster tracks in the San Joaquin Valley, rebuilding engines for great, roaring, ass-busting machines. These days he sees their stripped red-and-white dragchutes flowering only on Sunday afternoons. The "Wide World of Sports." Lost horizons. The intricate precision of cam shaft adjustments.

In the meantime, another load of hay.

Up in towns along the highline, Browning and Harlem and Malta, people are continually dying from another kind of possibility. Another shot of Beam on the rocks and Annie Greensprings out back after the bars are closed. In Montana they used to erect little crosses along the highways wherever a fatality occurred. A while back, outside Browning, they got a dandy. Eleven deaths in a single car accident. Guinness Book of World Records. Verities. The highway department has given up the practice of erecting crosses: too many of them are dedicated to the disenfranchised.

Out south of Billings the great coal fields are being strip-mined. Possibilities. The history of Montana and the West, from the fur trade to tomorrow, is a history of colonialism, both material and cultural. Is it any wonder we are so deeply xenophobic, and regard anything east of us as suspect? The money and the power always came from the East, took what it wanted, and left us, white or Indian, with our traditions dismantled and our territory filled with holes in the ground. Ever been to Butte? About half the old town was sucked into a vast open-pit mine.

Verities. The lasting thing we have learned here, if we ever learn, is to resist the beguilements of power and money. Hang on to your land. There won't be any more. Be superstitious as a Borneo tribesman. Do not let them photograph our shy, bare-breasted beauties as they wash clothes along the stream bank. Do not let them steal your soul away in pictures, because they will if they get a chance, just as Beadle's Nickel-Dime Library westerns and Gene Autry B-movies gnawed at the soul of this country where we live. Verities have to be earned, and they take time in the earning—time spent gazing out over your personal wind-glazed fields of snow. Once earned, they inhabit you in complex ways you cannot name, and they cannot be given away. They can only be transmogrified—transformed into something surreal or fantastic, unreal. And ours have been, and always for the same reason: primarily the titillation of those who used to be Easterners, who are everywhere now.

These are common sentiments here in the mountain West. In 1923 Charlie Russell agreed to speak before the Great Falls Booster Club. After listening to six or seven booster speeches, he tore up his own talk and spoke. This is what he said:

> In my book a pioneer is a man who turned all the grass upside down, strung bob-wire over the dust that was left, poisoned the water and cut down the trees, killed the Indian who owned the land, and called it progress. If I had my way, the land here would be like God made it, and none of you sons of bitches would be here at all.

So what are we left with? There was a great dream about a just and stable society, which was to be America. And there was another great dream about wilderness individuals, mountain men we have called them, who would be the natural defenders of that society. But our society is hugely corrupt, rich and impossibly complex, and our great simple individuals can define nothing to defend, nothing to reap but the isolation implicit in their stance, nothing to gain for their strength but loneliness. The vast, sad, recurrent story which is so centrally American. Western Rednecks cherish secret remnants of those dreams, and still try to live within them. No doubt a foolish enterprise.

But that's why, full of anger and a kind of releasing joy, they plunge their Snowcats around frozen lakes at 90 miles an hour, coming in for a whiskey stop with eyes glittering and icicles bright in their whiskers, and why on any summer day you can look into the sky over Missoula and see the hang-gliding daredevils circling higher than the mountains. That's why you see grown men climbing frozen waterfalls with pretty colored ropes.

And then there seems to be a shooting a week in the doublewide village. Spastic violence. You know, the husband wakes up from his drunk, lying on the kitchen floor with the light still burning, gets himself an Alka-Seltzer, stumbles into the living room, and there is Mother on the couch with half her side blown away. The 2-gauge is carefully placed back where it belongs on the rack over the breakfront. Can't tell what happened. Must have been an intruder.

Yeah, the crazy man inside us. Our friends wear Caterpillar D-9 caps when they've never pulled a friction in their lives, and Buck knives in little leather holsters on their belts, as if they might be called upon to pelt out a beaver at any moment. Or maybe just stab an empty beer can. Ah, wilderness, and suicidal nostalgia.

Which gets us to another kind of pioneer we see these days, people who come to the country with what seems to be an idea that connection with simplicities will save their lives. Which simplicities are those? The condescension implicit in the program is staggering. If you want to feel you are being taken lightly, try sitting around while someone tells you how he envies the simplicity of your life. What about Davis Patten? He says he is staying in Montana, and calling it home. So am I.

Despite the old Huckleberry Finn–mountain man notion of striking out for the territory, I am going to hang on here, best I can, and nourish my own self. I know a lovely woman who lives up the road in a log house, on what is left of a hard-earned farmstead. I'm going to call and see if she's home. Maybe she'll smile and come have a glass of beer with me and my cronies.

Discussion Questions

1. Explain what we learn about the author in the first four paragraphs, describing his "Western dream."
2. According to Kittredge, "Bad Rednecks lose faith." What faith do you believe he refers to here—faith in what?

3. Kittredge claims "there is a real spiritual equivalency between Redmen and Rednecks." Describe the comparisons between these groups that he makes throughout the essay. Do you believe these are fair comparisons? Why or why not?
4. Kittredge describes Rednecks as "isolated, outrageous, lonely, proud and mean." Which of these traits does he find admirable, or at least justifiable?
5. Explain one purpose for including the stories about Granville Stewart in the essay.
6. Kittredge claims that "Beadle's Nickel-Dime Library westerns and Gene Autry B-movies gnawed at the soul of this country where we live." Explain his meaning and give examples to show how this is true or false.

LINDA HOGAN
(1947–)

Born of a Chickasaw father and a white mother in Denver, the author grew up moving between Colorado and Oklahoma as her father was transferred in his Army career. She experienced the oral tradition by listening to stories told by her father, uncle, and grandmother, but was also steeped in the Anglo–American literary tradition through her college studies. However, in her youth she identified with working-class writers. Her first jobs were low-wage work as a nursing home aide or file clerk, and she earned her B.A. at the University of Colorado at Colorado Springs as a commuter student, always doubting the relevance of her education (Shanley). After she married and lived in Washington, DC, in her late twenties, she worked as a learning assistant for "physically challenged students" and began writing poetry to help her resolve inner conflicts over her dual heritage. However, feeling alienated in an Eastern city, she returned to Colorado for graduate school (Wong).

In 1977, she began a two-year teaching stint at Colorado Women's College in Colorado Springs. During this period, she also earned her M.A. in creative writing at the University of Colorado at Boulder and published her first volume of poetry, *Calling Myself Home*, both in 1978. She then taught for a year at the Rocky Mountain Women's Institute at the University of Denver and served, from 1980 to 1984, as poet-in-residence for the Colorado and Oklahoma Arts Councils (Shanley). From 1984 to 1989, she taught at the University of Minnesota—Twin Cities in the American and American Indian Studies program, but then returned to Boulder as a professor of English at the University of Colorado. In addition, over the years, she has volunteered at wildlife rehabilitation centers, practicing her belief in "the sacredness and interconnectedness of all life" (Wong 378).

Her writings have consistently focused on the powers of nature, especially on "regenerative female forces that shape the world" (Shanley 123). She draws on her Chickasaw heritage "to offer ancient wisdom about nature in mythological yet contemporary terms" (123–24). According to Arnold Krupnat, an unusual goal of her poetry is to integrate "spiritual consciousness and material political action" (qtd. in Shanley 126), so she can critique the racism of even "liberal" culture, while also emphasizing the continued value of native ritual. In a 1990 interview, Hogan analyzed the need for the mainstream feminist movement first to become liberated from the social constraints of the caretaker role, but then to embrace it in a more holistic, spiritual perspective: "I see a direct relationship between how we care for the animal-people and the plants and insects and land and water, and how we care for ourselves. Part of our work here is to care for life" (qtd. in Shanley 128).

Her first novel, *Mean Spirit* (1990), is overtly political in criticizing the oppression and exploitation of Native Americans and their resources during the Osage oil boom of the 1920s. And she depicts Oklahoma "not as a land of opportunity but as a land of the American Dream gone dreadfully and shamefully wrong" (Shanley 127). Moreover, she emphasizes that the treacheries of this particular incident were consistent with racist federal decisions, "with spiritual intrusion on the part of the government, in its assimilation policies and its encouragement of missionaries among the Indians" (128). In her book of seventeen essays, *Dwellings: A Spiritual History of the Living World* (1995), Hogan emphasizes "spiritual consciousness" over political critique. Like Thoreau's work, her essays dwell on "close observation of the natural world, express a desire for return to a simpler life, and call the reader to awaken to the wonder and beauty of nature" (Wong 385). However, she goes beyond the nature-writing tradition by rejecting the notions of human superiority over nature and scientific division among living things, insisting we are a part of an organic rhythm. Instead, she embraces an environmentalist perspective that incorporates the ancient wisdom of indigenous peoples, "that understands, values, and respects dream, vision, and intuition—not only rational analysis—as valid modes of knowing the world" (Wong 385).

The text of the following essay is from *Dwellings* (New York: Norton, 1995), pages 47–49, 51–62.

Shanley, Kathryn W. "Linda Hogan." *Dictionary of Literary Biography, Volume 175: Native American Writers of the U.S.* Ed. Kenneth M. Roemer. Detroit: Gale, 1997. 123–30.

Wong, Hertha D. "Linda Hogan." *American Nature Writers, Volume I.* Ed. John Elder. New York: Scribner's, 1996. 377–88.

FROM A DIFFERENT YIELD

—<◆>—

"Hosanna! The corn reached total zenith in crested and entire August. The space of summer arched earth to autumnal fruit. Out of cold and ancient sod the split of protein, the primal thunder. In the Mayan face of the tiny kernel look out the deeps of time, space, and genes. In the golden pollen, more ancient and fixed than the pyramids, is the scream of fleeing Indians, germinal mirror of endurance, reflections of mothers of different yield."

—Meridel Le Sueur

A woman once described a friend of hers as being such a keen listener that even the trees leaned toward her, as if they were speaking their innermost secrets into her listening ears. Over the years I've envisioned that woman's silence, a hearing full and open enough that the world told her its stories. The green leaves turned toward her, whispering tales of soft breezes and the murmurs of leaf against leaf.

When I was a girl, I listened to the sounds of the corn plants. A breeze would begin in a remote corner of the field and move slowly toward the closest edge, whispering. After corn harvest at my uncle's farm, the pigs would be set loose in the cornfield to feed on what corn was left behind, kernels too dry for picking, too small for sale, or cobs that were simply missed by human hands. Without a moment's hesitation, the pigs would make straight for any plant that still held an ear of corn, bypassing the others. They would listen, it seemed, to the denser song of corn where it still lived inside its dress of husk.

When I first heard of Barbara McClintock, it confirmed what I thought to be true about the language of corn. McClintock is a biologist who received a Nobel Prize for her work on gene transposition in corn plants. Her method was to listen to what corn had to say, to translate what the plants spoke into a human tongue.

In *A Feeling for the Organism*, Evelyn Fox Keller writes that McClintock came to know each plant intimately. She watched the daily green journeys of their growth from earth toward sky and sun. She knew her plants in the way a healer would know them, from inside, from the inner voices of corn and woman. Her approach to her science was alive, intuitive, and humane. It was a whole approach, one that bridged the worlds of woman and plant, and crossed over the boundary lines between species. Her respect for life allowed for a vision expanded enough, and sharp enough, to see more deeply into the mysteries of matter than did other geneticists who were at work on the same problems. Her revelation of method astonished the scientific community. She saw an alive world, a fire of life inside plants, even plants other than the corn: "In the summertime, when you walk down the road, you'll see that the tulip leaves, if it's a little warm, turn themselves around so their backs are toward the sun. Within the restricted areas in which they live, they move around a great deal. These organisms are fantastically beyond our wildest expectations."

In her book, *Adam's Task*, Vickie Hearne writes about the same kind of approach, only with animals, that McClintock used. She says there are things to be gained by respecting the intelligence of animals: "With horses, respect usually means respecting their nervousness, as in tales of retreating armies on horseback traversing mine fields, in which the only riders who survive are the ones who gave their horses their heads, or tales of police horses who snort anxiously when a car in a traffic jam turns out to be carrying the thieves who escaped capture six months earlier."

These last years, it seems that much contemporary scientific exploration has been thrown full tilt into the center of one of those minefields, and is in search of a new vision, and of renewed intuitive processes of discovery that go beyond our previous assumptions about knowledge. This new requirement of thought turns out to be one that can only be called a leap of faith. "Over and over again," Keller says of McClintock, "she tells us one must have the time to look, the patience to 'hear what the material has to say to you. One must have a feeling for the organism. . . .'"

In recent times, the term "myth" has come to signify falsehood, but when we examine myths, we find that they are a high form of truth. They are the deepest, innermost cultural stories of our human journeys toward spiritual and psychological growth. An essential part of myth is that it allows for our return to the creation, to a mythic time. It allows us to hear the world new again. Octavio Paz has written that in older oral traditions an object and its name were not separated. One equalled the other. To speak of corn, for instance, was to place the corn before a person's very eyes and ears. It was in mythic time that there was no abyss between the word and the thing it named, but he adds that "as soon as man acquired consciousness of himself, he broke away from the natural world and made himself another world inside himself."

This broken connection appears not only in language and myth but it also appears in our philosophies of life. There is a separation that has taken place between us and nature. Something has broken deep in the core of ourselves. And yet, there is another world created inside the person. In some way the balance between inner and outer worlds struggles to maintain itself in other and more complex ways than in the past. Psychologist C. A. Meier notes that as the wilderness has disappeared outside of us, it has gone to live inside the human mind. Because we are losing vast tracts of the wilderness, we are not only losing a part of ourselves, he says, but the threat to life which once existed in the world around us has now moved within. "The whole of western society," he says, "is approaching a physical and mental breaking point." The result is a spiritual fragmentation that has accompanied our ecological destruction.

In a time of such destruction, our lives depend on this listening. It may be that the earth speaks its symptoms to us. With the nuclear reactor accident in Chernobyl, Russia, it was not the authorities who told us that the accident had taken place. It was the wind. The wind told the story. It carried a tale of splitting, of atomic fission, to other countries and revealed the truth of the situation. The wind is a prophet, a scientist, a talker.

These voices of the world infuse our every act, as much as does our own ancestral DNA. They give us back ourselves, point a direction for salvation. Sometimes they even shake us down to the bedrock of our own human lives. This is what I think happened in the 1970s language experiments in which chimpanzees were taught Ameslan, American Sign Language. In *Silent Partners*, Eugene Linden discusses the results of experiments with American Sign Language and chimpanzees. Probably the best known chimp is Washoe, a wild-caught chimpanzee who learned to use 132 signs, was able to ask questions and to use the negative. The book is extremely significant to our times, not because of what it tells us about apes and their ability to communicate in signs, so much as what it reveals about human beings and our relationships with other creatures.

The heated debates about the experiments came to revolve around whether or not it was actual language the chimps used. The arguments centered on definitions of language and intelligence, obscuring the real issue, that of how we treat other living beings. A reader comes to wonder how solid we are in the security of both ourselves and our knowledge when an issue of such significant scientific and spiritual importance sparks such a great division of minds, but if we are forced to accept that animals have intelligence, language, and sensitivity to pain, including psychological trauma, this acceptance has tremendous consequences for our own species and for our future actions.

While Linden says that "it is a little unsettling to be confronted with an animal who does not automatically acknowledge your paramountcy in the natural hierarchy," he also says that the experiments were disquieting not only because of the tragic consequences they created for the animals involved but because they also revealed the very fragile underpinnings of science. At the very least, the questions raised throughout this project were primarily questions about ourselves, our own morality, our way of being in the world, and our responsibility for the caretaking of the earth. . . .

We have arrived despairingly at a time when compassion and care are qualities that do not lend themselves to the world of intellectual thought. Jimmie Durham, a Cherokee writer who was a prime mover in the development of an International Treaty Organization, wrote a poem called "The Teachings of My Grandmother," excerpted here:

> In a magazine too expensive to buy I read about
> How, with scientific devices of great complexity,
> U.S. scientists have discovered that if a rat
> Is placed in a cage in which it has previously
> Been given an electrical shock, it starts crying.
> I told my grandmother about that and she said,
> "We probably knew that would be true."

It might be that Linden comes close to the center of the dilemma about whether or not apes have language and intelligence when he says, "Perhaps it would be better to stick to figuring out the nature of stars and matter, and not to concern ourselves with creatures who threaten to paralyze us by shedding light on the true nature and origins of our abilities. Dismaying as this may sound, it is quite possible that we cannot afford to know who we are."

Not only have our actions revealed us to ourselves, and sometimes had dire results, but among many peoples educated in many European philosophical traditions, there is also an intense reaction to the bad news that cruelty is cruelty. There is a backlash effect that resists peacemaking. In 1986, I heard Betty Williams, a 1977 Nobel Peace Prize laureate from Northern Ireland, lecture in South Dakota. One afternoon Williams had witnessed the bombing death of Irish children. A little girl died in Williams's arms. The girl's legs had been severed in the explosion and had been thrown across the street from where the woman held the bleeding child. Williams went home in shock and despair. Later that night, when the shock wore off, the full impact of what she'd seen jolted her. She stepped outside her door, screaming out in the middle of the night. She knocked on doors that might easily have opened with weapons pointed at her face, and she cried out, "What kind of people have we become that we would allow children to be killed on our streets?" Within four hours the city was awake and there were sixteen thousand names on petitions for peace.

Williams's talk was interrupted at this point by a man who called out, "You're sick." Undisturbed by the heckler, Williams went on to tell how, touring the world as a peacemaker, she had left the starving people in Ethiopia for an audience with the pope. He told her, "I feel so worried about the hungry people," to which Williams responded, "Don't worry about them. Sell the Michelangelo and feed them."

Such a simple thing, to feed people. Such a common thing, to work for peace. Such a very clear thing, to know that if we injure an animal, ravage the land, that we have caused damage. And yet, we have rampant hunger and do not know, can hardly even imagine, peace. And even when animals learn to speak a language, and to communicate their misery, we still deny them the right to an existence free from suffering and pain.

I want to make two points here. One is about language and its power. While we can't say what language is much beyond saying that it is a set of signs and symbols that communicates meaning, we know it is the most highly regarded human ability. Language usage, in fact, often determines social and class order in our societal systems. Without language, we humans have no way of knowing what lies beneath the surface of one another. And yet there are communications that take place on a level that goes deeper than our somewhat limited human spoken languages. We read one another via gesture, stance, facial expression, scent. And sometimes this communication is more honest, more comprehensible, than the words we utter. . . .

Another point that needs to be made is that when issues become obscured by distorted values or abstract concepts, we lose a clarity that allows us to act even in our own best behalf, for survival not just of ourselves but of the homeland which is our life and our sustenance. These responses stand in the way of freedom from pain. They obstruct the potentials we have for a better world. It is a different yield that we desire.

It must have been obvious at the inception of the language experiments that the work's very design was to determine whether or not a speaking ape might have a consciousness similar to that of a human. However, the results were distressing and the fate of the signing chimpanzees has been disastrous, some of them having been sold to research labs for other kinds of experimentation, including AIDS research.

We might ask what is to be gained by bridging the species gap? If it is, indeed, to determine intelligence levels, it seems that the talley on the side of the chimpanzees adds up to more points than ours, since the chimps are now bilingual. But, whatever the impetus, Linden says that the loser in the conflict concerning human and animal community is science. And while the chimps are the primary victims of this ongoing struggle, we also are "victims of a skewed view of our relationship with the rest of the natural order."

What we really are searching for is a language that heals this relationship, one that takes the side of the amazing and fragile life on our life-giving earth. A language that knows the corn, and the one that corn knows, a language that takes hold of the mystery of what's around us and offers it back to us, full of awe and wonder. It is a language of creation, of divine fire, a language that goes beyond the strict borders of scientific inquiry and right into the heart of the mystery itself. LeSueur writes: "Something enters the corn at the moment of fusion of the male and female that is unknown to scientists. From some star, a cosmic quickening, some light, movement-fast chemical that engenders illuminates quickens the conception, lights the fuse." Life itself, though we live it, is unknown to us. It is an alchemical process, a creative movement and exploration with the same magic in mind as the researchers had when they originated their search for meaning and relationship within the world.

We are looking for a tongue that speaks with reverence for life, searching for an ecology of mind. Without it, we have no home, have no place of our own within the creation. It is not only the vocabulary of science we desire. We want a language of that different yield. A yield rich as the harvests of earth, a yield that returns us to our own sacredness, to a self-love and respect that will carry out to others.

In most southwestern Indian cultures, the pollen of corn is sacred pollen. It is the life-giving seed of creation and fertility. Anthropologist Ruth Underhill wrote that Papago planters of corn would speak to the life-sustaining plants. "Night after night," she says, "the planter walks around his field, singing up the corn":

The corn comes up;
It comes up green;
Here upon our fields
White tassels unfold.

Blue evening falls;
Blue evening falls;
Near by, in every direction,
It sets the corn tassels trembling.

I know that corn. I know that blue evening. Those words open a door to a house we have always lived in.

Once, I ground corn with a smooth, round stone on an ancient and sloping metate. Leaning over, kneeling on the ground, grinding the blue corn, seeing how the broken dry kernels turned soft, to fine meal, I saw a history in that yield, a deep knowing of where our lives come from, all the way back to the starch and sugar of corn.

She, the corn, is called our grandmother. She's the woman who rubbed her palms against her body and the seeds fell out of her skin. That is, they fell from her body until her sons discovered her secrets. Before she left the world, she told them how to plant. She said, plant the beans and corn together, plant their little sister, squash, between them. This, from an oral tradition, came to be rediscovered hundreds of years later, almost too late, by agriculturalists in their research on how to maintain the richness of farm soil.

Cherokee writer Carroll Arnett once gave me a bracelet of corn. There were forty-nine kernels, representing the number of clans, stitched round in a circle of life. I said, If I wear it when I die and am buried, won't it be wonderful to know that my life will grow up, out from beneath the earth? My life inside the green blades of corn, the stalks and tassels and flying pollen? That red corn, that corn will be this woman.

Imagine a woman, a scientist, listening to those rustling stalks, knowing their growth so intimately that "She could write the autobiography of every plant she worked with." What a harvest. What a different yield. In it is the pull of earth and life. The fields are beautiful.

Cornmeal and pollen are offered to the sun at dawn. The ears of the corn are listening and waiting. They want peace. The stalks of the corn want clean water, sun that is in its full clean shining. The leaves of the corn want good earth. The earth wants peace. The birds who eat the corn do not want poison. Nothing wants to suffer. The wind does not want to carry the stories of death.

At night, in the cornfields, when there is no more mask of daylight, you hear the plants talking among themselves. The wind passes through. It's all there, the languages, the voices of wind, dove, corn, stones. The language of life won't be silenced.

In Chaco Canyon, in the center, my sister Donna told me, there is a kiva, a ceremonial room in the earth. This place has been uninhabited for what seems like forever. It has been without water so long that there are theories that the ancient people disappeared as they journeyed after water. Donna said that there was a corn plant growing out of the center of the kiva. It was alone, a single plant. It had been there since the ancient ones, the old ones who came before us all, those people who wove dog hair into belts, who witnessed the painting of flute players on the seeping canyon walls, who knew the stories of corn. There was one corn plant growing out of the holy place. It planted itself yearly. It was its own mother. With no water, no person to care for it, no turning over of the soil, this corn plant rises up. Earth yields. We probably knew that would be true.

Do you remember the friend that the leaves talked to? We need to be that friend. Listen. The ears of the corn are singing. They are telling their stories and singing their songs. We knew that would be true.

Discussion Questions

1. Hogan uses the phrase "a different yield" as a kind of refrain throughout her essay. Analyze the different meanings in the different contexts of its uses. Then explain how this phrase, with its reference to corn and sacred pollen, makes an appropriate title for the essay and the major concerns that it discusses.

2. Explain how recent research and discoveries with plants, horses, and chimpanzees have challenged previous assumptions about science and knowledge.

3. Hogan defines the essential truth of "myths" as "the deepest, innermost cultural stories of our human journeys toward spiritual and psychological growth." Compare/contrast this definition with Robinson's notion of "myth" in the chapter introduction. To what extent are both writers defining the same phenomenon? To what extent are their definitions of myth incompatible?

4. In the excerpt from his poem, Cherokee writer Jimmie Durham dramatizes the words of his grandmother: "We probably knew that would be true." Explain the meaning and context for these words and show how Hogan transfers the meaning to other contexts in the essay.

◆ ◆ ◆

FOCUS ON FILM:
JOHN HUSTON'S *THE MISFITS* (1961)

1. Describe the "cowboy" values of Gay Langland.
2. What values does Guido represent?
3. Compare/contrast the scene in which Roslyn "performs" in the bar and the performance in the rodeo scene.
4. Explain what Gay gives up when he abandons the mustang round-up.
5. Explain the values Roslyn represents in this final scene.

TOPICS FOR RESEARCH AND WRITING

1. Considering the title of Huston's contemporary "Western," explain which of the principal characters are "misfits." Considering the conclusion of the film, explain how each character changes or fails to change that status. Relate your analysis to a central theme in the film.

2. Analyze the feelings about the land expressed in Barrio's "The Campesinos." Define the relationship between humans and nature in this excerpt from his novel.

3. Based on the excerpts from John Muir's *My First Summer in the Sierra* in Chapter 4, briefly define his relationship to nature. Then compare and contrast with Hogan's viewpoint in "A Different Yield."

4. Compare and contrast the essays by Kittredge and Hogan, analyzing how each writer develops his or her *ethos* or *persona* by examining the resources cited, the emotions revealed, and the ways in which you, the reader, becomes involved in the writer's experience.

5. Compare and contrast the power-of-language theme in Hogan's essay and in Momaday's "The Priest of the Sun" from Chapter 7. Speculate why this theme might have special importance to Native American writers.

6. Read "The Cowboy's Dream" from John and Alan Lomax's *Cowboy Songs and Other Frontier Ballads* (New York: Collier, 1986), pages 45–47. Also, select two other lengthy songs (more than one page) that appeal to you and photocopy the texts for all the songs you select. Analyze these songs as poetry, explaining the use of imagery, similes, metaphors, slang, and word-sounds (onomatopoeia), if relevant. Then generalize about your individual analyses and reach an overall conclusion about the language and common themes of the cowboy songs you have studied. Please attach your copies of the songs with your essay.

7. Read Phil Hardy, "Music," in *The BFI Companion to the Western*, ed. Edward Buscombe (New York: Atheneum, 1988), pages 193–95. Drawing on concepts from this article, analyze three or more country-western songs from a particular artist. You can comment on the style and instrumentation of the music, but you must quote particular lyrics from the songs to support your interpretation of the feelings, attitudes, or "messages" in the words. Try to explain what is particularly "Western" about the artist's concerns or themes.

8. Read Baxter Black's poem "The Oyster" from his book *Croutons on a Cow Pie* (Denver: Coyote Cowboy and Record Stockman, 1988), page 28. Also, select two other poems of several stanzas that appeal to you and photocopy the texts for all the poems you select. Making your notes on the copies, analyze the poetry, explaining the use of imagery, similes,

metaphors, cowboy slang, and word-sounds (onomatopoeia), if relevant. Then generalize about your individual analyses and reach a comprehensive conclusion about the language and concerns of the poems you have studied. Please attach your copies of the poems with your essay.

9. Read Helena Maria Viramontes's "The Jumping Bean" from *Pieces of the Heart: New Chicano Fiction*, ed. Gary Soto (San Francisco: Chronicle Books, 1993), pages 122–32. Select one of the following topics.

    A. Compare and contrast the character of "Papa" with that of Manuel in Barrio's *The Plum Plum Picker*. Although the scenes of their work differ, to what extent do their conflicts—inner and outer—arise from similar causes? Likewise, to what extent are their goals similar?

    B. Compare and contrast the narrative viewpoint of "the young girl" in Viramontes's story with the narrative viewpoint of Masako in Yamauchi's "And the Soul Shall Dance." Analyze how filtering the story through a child's perspective contributes to a central theme for each story and then compare these themes.

APPENDIX

—◆—

HOW TO WATCH A FILM

The horizon before you is bright with the desert sun. That dusty line shimmers in heat waves. And as you watch, there is movement, a change in the open landscape. Slowly, an image forms. A long ways off a figure appears out of the heat, out of the intense light of the sun, a man on horseback riding toward you. His gait is steady, but not slow. He seems the only living, moving thing in a wide expanse of empty sand and sky. And the rider approaches, inevitably, to command this space.

This scene is the opening of Clint Eastwood's *Pale Rider* (1985), a classically styled Western about an avenging "Preacher" who joins the common people, the small miners in this case, in their struggle against a monopolistic banker and his paid lackey, a corrupt lawman. As an introduction to this ghostly character, who recalls the figure of Death among the four horsemen of the Apocalypse, this scene sets a tone. The rider seems insubstantial, rising out of the sunlight, indistinct but menacing. According to film critic Roger Ebert, throughout the film "the Eastwood character himself is almost always backlit, so we have to strain to see him, and this strategy makes him more mysterious and fascinating than any dialogue could have" (446). Thus, the use of light and dark in the film helps to emphasize the pale rider as a shadow character, someone not quite like other mortal men.

In the cinema, meaning derives not only from plot, setting, and character—which it shares with fiction—but also from an array of presentational techniques that can affect the viewer psychologically or emotionally. We have all watched hundreds of films at the theater and on television, but often we are a passive audience manipulated by the images, unaware of being coproducers of the film experience. In part, this passivity is encouraged by the techniques of classic Hollywood films that obliterate the artifice of film-making—that bring us visually into a scene as if it were enfolding naturally before us.

The purpose of this brief overview is to develop your visual literacy and your awareness of film techniques, just as the discussion questions in the text help you develop analytical skills to apply to your readings of the anthology selections. The following cinema terms and definitions will provide you the tools to examine audience responses closely and to write critically about how our experience of a film is created. To understand film language in the context of the director's or cinematographer's or editor's choices, these terms are organized by film-making processes: *mise en scène, shot, camera angle and movement, lens, lighting, editing, color,* and *sound.* For additional details, see Louis Giannetti, *Understanding Movies,* especially Chapter 1; and Timothy Corrigan, *A Short Guide to Writing about Film,* especially Chapter 3 (both cited below). Finally, two basic critical concepts, *narrative* and *genre,* are considered in their application to the Western. Keep in mind that these are all descriptive terms that help you analyze just a few scenes while developing your interpretation of a film; in a single essay you would probably select fewer than a dozen techniques to comment on.

MISE EN SCÈNE

Originally a French term from the live theater, *mise en scène* refers to what is placed in the scene or on the stage, including the set, props, costumes, and lighting, as well as the dynamic interactions of the actors. Thus, the term "refers to all those properties of a cinematic image that exist independently from camera position, camera movement, and editing" (Corrigan 45). For traditional theater directors, decisions of "blocking" or stage movement must ensure that the audience beyond the proscenium can observe the actors, who generally should not "upstage" one another for very long. But, more importantly, the movements and gestures of the actors—no less than the tone and volume of their speech—convey emotions and suggest the remoteness or intimacy of interaction with one another and with the audience. For the film director, decisions about *mise en scène* are more complex since the "stage" can vary from interiors to expansive exteriors, such as Western landscapes, and even to imaginary spaces, as in dream sequences.

Actually, since cinema is very much a collaborative enterprise, these decisions are also shared by the cinematographer and the production designer. But in creating the world that the audience views in a film, the collaborators control the space so that viewers will read specific indicators about the dominant figure or line in the image, the edge or periphery of the scene, the spatial composition of actors in relation to one another and the setting, and even the power relationships among the actors. For instance, in the final scene of *Red River* (1948), the Tess Millay character is in a dominant position over the sprawling, fighting figures of Tom Dunson and Matthew Garth because she stands over them and shoots warning shots at them with a pistol—a reversal of the "normal" male dominance over women in the rest of the film.

At the most basic level, the film viewer's perception is controlled by the *frame*, the dividing lines between the edges of the screen image and the surrounding darkness of the theater. In many crime films, shots are often dense with images and *tightly framed* to emphasize the confinement or entrapment of the characters. By contrast, Western movies often use *loosely framed* shots with lots of space to emphasize freedom or possibility. Likewise, in exterior shots, Western scenes are often composed by two or more planes of depth, like a Bierstadt painting, so that the visual information of background, midground, and foreground often comment on one another. A related compositional feature that guides our perception is the *aspect ratio* of an image— the ratio of the frame's horizontal and vertical dimensions. Early films, until the 1950s, were shot in 1.33:1 aspect ratio, which means the image is a third wider than it is tall; this ratio is about the same as today's television image, which simplified transferring theater movies into video format. The standard aspect ratio of most contemporary films is 1.85:1. By contrast, *widescreen* films are projected in a 2.35:1 aspect ratio. The advantages of this broader image for the Western is its ability to represent epic scenes like a land rush with wagons and horses careening across the screen, or a cattle stampede, or the action of a shoot-out with multiple combatants. According to Giannetti, the widescreen image contributes to greater authenticity, by reproducing a sense of peripheral vision; and to greater objectivity, by representing a more natural spatial continuity than the standard format (169–70).

SHOT

This term refers to the image produced in a single interval between turning on the camera and turning it off. Thus, a shot can last from seconds to, usually, no more than minutes. The effect of the sequence of action is achieved through splicing or editing separate shots together.

For the purpose of analysis, shots may classified by how much the human figure is included in the frame. An *extreme long shot*—as in the example above from *Pale Rider*—is almost always an exterior view showing a locale. If the locale includes people, they appear very small. One variation is the *deep focus shot*, in which both close-up and far-off objects and people are in focus. A *long shot* is a rather imprecise term that suggests roughly the distance between the audience and the stage in live theater. A *full shot* includes the entire human figure from head to foot, good for pantomime or action scenes while capturing at least larger facial expressions. A *medium shot* shows the human body from the knees or waist up, useful for conveying movement and dialogue. Variations include the *two shot* and the *three shot*, which show two or three figures, respectively; and the *over-the-shoulder shot*, which is useful for focusing on one character who faces the camera, while including a second character whose back is toward the camera. A *close-up* shows the human face or another small object, often for special emphasis. An *extreme close-up* shows only eyes or mouth, or part of an object, for a symbolic purpose (definitions adapted from Giannetti).

Actor body position within the frame is also an aspect of how the shot is composed. *Full front* denotes directly facing the camera, thus inviting the intimacy and complicity of the viewer. *Quarter turn* denotes facing the camera at an angle, revealing the face but not as emotionally involving as the full front shot. A *profile* shot shows the actor looking off frame to the left or right. This position indicates remoteness in an actor who seems unaware of being observed. *Three-quarter turn*, with the actor looking away from the camera, with very little of the face exposed, may indicate anonymity or an antisocial quality. *Back to camera* expresses no emotion or connection to the viewer and can suggest mystery or alienation.

CAMERA ANGLE AND MOVEMENT

A *bird's-eye view* (also *crane shot* or *aerial shot*) is the seldom-experienced perspective of looking down from directly overhead, some distance from the ground. This disorienting viewpoint makes human figures appear insignificant and may emphasize the role of fate in controlling people's lives. A *high-angle* shot, a view from a distance above an object or figure, but with some angle, may be used to suggest tedious action, emphasize environment or setting, and reduce human importance. For instance, in *High Noon* (1952), this shot is used to show the Gary Cooper character, wandering alone through the empty streets of his town, fruitlessly seeking help from his neighbors to meet an impending outlaw showdown. The *eye-level shot* is the most natural viewpoint, which neither manipulates the viewer nor implies any judgment about the subject. A *low-angle shot* shows a viewpoint from below eye-level, with the camera shooting up toward figures, making them taller and more important, while the viewer is made to feel insecure and dominated. This shot is used repeatedly in *Shane* (1953) to indicate the awe young Joey Starrett feels when regarding the menacing but moral hero. This shot can also be used to create a sense of confusion or of accelerated motion, especially in scenes of violence. An *oblique angle* uses a tilted-camera viewpoint, with the usually stable horizon appearing to slant diagonally, so figures seem off-balance and the world upset. This shot, often conveying tension or anxiety, is sometimes used for *point-of-view shots*, which show exactly what a character would see from his or her eyes, especially if confused, drunk, or mentally unstable (definitions adapted from Giannetti).

In addition to manipulating the angle of a shot, the cinematographer can shape our experience of a scene through moving the camera in relation to the setting and characters. In a *tracking shot*, the camera body moves forward, backward, or laterally along a straight line (often mounted to a dolly along a track), creating on the movie screen a mobile framing that enters the scene or follows the action. These shots are often used in a long continuous take. A *pan* moves the camera body left or right on a stationary tripod, creating on the movie screen a mobile framing that scans a scene horizontally. In a *tilt*, the camera body swivels up or down on a stationary support, creating on the movie screen a mobile framing that scans the scene vertically.

In a *handheld shot*, the camera is usually mounted on the operator's shoulder, allowing great flexibility in positioning, but the frame seems jumpy and irregular, which can create a realistic or documentary effect. Conveying the viewpoint directly from a character's eyes, the *subjective camera* uses sustained handheld shooting to create an identification with the character.

LENS

The camera lens can convey a natural perspective or manipulate the visual information in an artificial way. The *normal* lens shows objects without exaggerating or reducing them in the field of vision. In 35-mm film, the normal lens is 35 to 50 mm long. A *wide-angle* lens affects perspective by distorting facial features near the camera, bending straight lines near the edges of the frame, and exaggerating the distance between the foreground and background. However, this lens achieves a *deep focus*, so that images are sharp on all distance planes, and permits the composition of the entire image from foreground to background. In 35-mm film, a wide-angle lens is 30 mm or shorter. The *telephoto* lens is a long lens that flattens images and affects a scene's perspective by enlarging distant planes, making them seem close to the foreground. In 35-mm film, a telephoto is 75 mm or longer. A technique called *racking focus* is shifting the area of sharp focus from one plane to another for effect; this is most easily achieved with a telephoto lens.

Finally, a *zoom* lens can change its focal length during a shot. Shifting toward the telephoto range enlarges the image and gives the impression of moving into the scene's space; shifting toward the wide-angle range reduces the image and gives the impression of withdrawing from the scene's space or viewing it from a larger perspective.

LIGHTING

The lighting of a scene influences the mood and our sense of literal or psychological realism. *High key* lighting is bright, even illumination with few pronounced shadows and little contrast The *fill* is a secondary light source or less bright illumination balancing the key light and reducing the shadows. *Low-key* illumination creates strong contrast between dark and light areas of the shot, with deep shadows and little fill light. *Backlighting* is an illumination behind the subject, creating a kind of silhouetting or "halo" effect around a head, used to suggest a soft, otherworldly glow. To use *available lighting* is shooting with little apparent artificial lighting set-up, using natural light (sun or moon) or an obvious light source dictated by the scene—for exterior shots, street or car lights; for interior shots a window or a lamp. This technique is often used for realistic or documentary effect, with a hard-edged quality (definitions adapted from Giannetti).

EDITING

Classic Hollywood film-making has used *continuity editing*, a system of splicing the film between different shots to maintain clear and continuous narrative action by matching screen direction (right-left relationships in a scene), movement of characters, and time relations. By contrast, *montage* is an editing method emphasizing dynamic, often discontinuous relationships between shots so that juxtaposition of images creates an association of ideas, rather than literal connections in time and space. To describe how one shot relates to another in a sequence, the *establishing shot* usually involves a distant framing, or extreme long shot, that shows spatial relations among the important characters, objects, and setting in a scene. To shift the viewer's perspective to that of a character, the *point of view (POV) shot* uses the camera as if looking from the character's eyes; this shot is usually cut in before or after a shot of the character looking at a scene. *Shot/reverse shot* editing shows alternating characters, as in a dialogue. *Over-the-shoulder shots* are a common perspective used in this style of editing. A *reaction shot* cuts away from the central action to show a character's response to it. *Crosscutting* is an editing technique that alternates shots of two or more sequences of *parallel action* occurring simultaneously in different places. The *jump cut* abruptly interrupts two shots, which disorients the viewer because of a mismatch in space or time. A *wipe* is an abrupt transition between shots or scenes created by an apparent line moving vertically, horizontally, or diagonally across the screen. Another transition between shots is the *fade*, in which a dark screen gradually brightens as a shot appears (fade-in); or the screen gradually darkens to black, or even brightens to white or a single color (fade-out). A *dissolve* is a transition between two shots during which the first image gradually disappears while the second gradually appears; sometimes, the two images can be superimposed.

COLOR

While standard today, color films were popularized primarily by the industry's initial competition with black-and-white television in the fifties. According to film historian David Cook, from 1947 to 1954 to 1970, the percentage of American feature films made in color rose from 12 percent to over 50 percent to 94 percent, respectively. By the latter date, the film industry also chose color production in order to sell to the secondary market of television, which had converted to color broadcasting by 1970 (Cook 462). Thus, when analyzing movies, students should consider whether the director's choice of black-and-white or color film is merely conventional or deliberate, and to what extent that choice enhances the viewing experience in specific ways. For instance, black-and-white film looks more harsh than color and can be shot with higher contrast for dramatic visual effects and stylization, as in *Johnny Guitar* (1954). On the other hand, as Stephen Prince points out, color creates a "more lush and vital" appearance in the Western landscape, while color design can also be used metaphorically to underscore a film's theme. For example, in *Ride the High Country* (1962), "the flaring colors of leaves in the autumn woods, high in the mountains where the story is set, visualize the film's concerns with aging and death in the autumn of life" (Prince 46).

SOUND

One critical term useful when considering sound production in cinema is *voice-over*, a narrative technique used with flashback to convey an individual perspective on events that have already occurred, often with irony and a tone of fatality. Conventionally, the musical soundtrack for a film is known as the *score*, which can be analyzed for thematic connections to the movie, whether it includes lyrics or repeats a suggestive melody. As William Phillips suggests, you can also analyze how sound effects contribute to the effectiveness and meaning of specific scenes by considering such features as the density of the sound mix, achieved through multiple sources; the selective use of silence; the interaction of sounds and images; the dominance of rhythm or melody; the repetition or variation of a musical tune over several scenes; the volume and style of the music; and the setting and mood created by music while the opening credits roll (Phillips 166–95).

NARRATIVE AND GENRE

Critical approaches to writing about film include applications of realist, auteurist, psychoanalytic, ideological, feminist, cognitive, formalist, structuralist, semiological, and historical theories (Corrigan 78–105, Giannetti 391–465, Prince 341–73). This short guide is not the place to elaborate such approaches. However, it is useful for students to recognize that a film can tell a story in dramatically different ways than can fiction or autobiography. The *narrative* is often created much more from images than from words. Thus, critics of the Western film often point to the use of landscape itself to help tell the story. For example, in *Stagecoach* (1939), several shots track the movement of a relatively tiny stage rolling through a vast expanse of Southwestern desert marked by rugged, rocky spires and mesas, as if human desires and purposes were petty in comparison to this alien space. Likewise, this forbidding landscape is often associated with the dangers of attack by the Apaches, sometimes appearing as menacing silhouettes on faraway horizons—representing almost a force of nature in the "untamed" land.

To examine other ways in which a film can tell a story, consider the following questions. What is the mix of scenes by which the sequence of the narrative is developed: panoramic vistas, representations of nature or wildlife, the characters' interaction with landscape, dialogue, intimate and public scenes, fights and other action sequences, and the characters' movement through space? To what extent are conflicts represented by individual characters, or large collectives, or perhaps nature itself? How are the rhythms of foreshadowing, suspense, crisis, and revelation created visually? How are the resolutions to conflicts represented in images? How do lighting, sound, acting style, and dialogue interact to suggest character development, and to what extent does motivation rely on stereotypical responses or more realistic ambiguity? What meaning is suggested by symbolic scenes where the composition and style of the image call attention to the artistic process itself? How does the film turn against your expectations, as an experienced viewer of Western narrative?

This last question hinges on the dimension of film *genres*, which are characterized by "a set of similar themes, characters, narrative structures, and camera techniques" (Corrigan 83). Schatz's essay in Chapter 5 goes a long way toward defining the Western genre, but some typical elements that can be briefly identified here include the theme of bringing civilization to the wild; the mythic cowboy hero, who represents an interface between law and ruthless force; a story shaped by a journey to claim land and found a town; and the brightly lit shots of an expansive camera eye, which suggests an openness to the bounty of nature. According to Giannetti, "filmmakers are attracted to genres because they automatically synthesize a vast amount of cultural information" (345–46). Part of that information includes not only social myths, such as the inevitable rewards of individual effort, but also an attitude toward reconstructing history from a rather limited Euro-American viewpoint. However, what is most interesting about generic conventions is when a particular film, using the genre self-consciously, varies the formula, challenges our expectations, or even subverts the traditional values of Western mythologies. As you watch various Western films, then, closely examine the variations. And be aware that, in some cases, analyzing a film as a blend of genres may be a useful critical approach. For instance, *Outland* (1981)—combining an outer-space setting with the struggles of an intrepid lawman—may be considered a sci-fi Western (Phillips 228). Likewise, *Oklahoma* (1955) incorporates the musical genre, *Lone Star* (1996) employs elements of *film noir*, and both *Cat Ballou* (1965) and *Blazing Saddles* (1974) are comic parodies or spoofs of the horse-opera Western.

WORKS CITED

Cook, David A. *A History of Narrative Film.* 3rd ed. New York: Norton, 1996.

Corrigan, Timothy. *A Short Guide to Writing About Film.* 3rd ed. New York: Longman Publishers, 1998.

Ebert, Roger. *Roger Ebert's Movie Home Companion, 1992 Edition.* Kansas City, MO: Andrews and McMeel, 1991.

Giannetti, Louis. *Understanding Movies.* 7th ed. Englewood Cliffs, NJ: Prentice Hall, 1996.

Phillips, William H. *Film: An Introduction.* Boston: Bedford/St. Martin's, 1999.

Prince, Stephen. *Movies and Meaning: An Introduction to Film.* Needham Heights, MA: Allyn & Bacon, 1997.

CREDITS

—◀◆▶—

Alexie, Sherman. "How to Write the Great American Indian Novel" from *The Summer of Black Widows*. Copyright © 1996 by Sherman Alexie. Reprinted by permission of Hanging Loose Press.

Barrio, Raymond. "Chapter 10" from *The Plum Plum Pickers*, second edition (1986). Copyright © 1968 by Raymond Barrio. Reprinted by permission of Bilingual Press/Editorial Bilingue, Arizona State University, Tempe, Arizona.

Brown, Angeline Mitchell. "Diary of a School Teacher on the Arizona Frontier (1880–1881)." Courtesy of Sharlot Hall Museum, Prescott, Arizona.

Crow Dog [Brave Bird], Mary, with Richard Erdoes. "Civilize Them with a Stick" from *Lakota Woman*. Copyright © 1990 by Mary Crow Dog and Richard Erdoes. Used by permission of Grove/Atlantic, Inc.

Erdrich, Louise. "Indian Boarding School: The Runaways" from *Jacklight* by Louise Erdrich, © 1984 by Louise Erdrich. Reprinted by permission of Henry Holt and Company, LLC.

Glancy, Diane. "Black Kettle National Grasslands, Western Oklahoma" from *Offering: Poetry and Prose*. Copyright © 1988 by Diane Glancy. Reprinted by permission of the author.

Grey, Zane. "The Ranger" from *Ladies Home Journal*. Copyright © 1929 by Zane Grey. Reprinted by permission of Zane Grey, Inc.

Guthrie, A. B., Jr. "Mountain Medicine" from *The Big It and Other Stories*. Copyright © 1960 by A. B. Guthrie, Jr. Reprinted by permission of Houghton Mifflin.

INDEX

Only singular forms are recorded here, whether the reference is in the singular, plural, or both. Likewise, uppercase spellings are included among lowercase entries. For convenience, film adaptations and original fiction titles are listed together.